Lovejoy's
CONCISE
COLLEGE GUIDE

by
Charles T. Straughn, II and
Barbarasue Lovejoy Straughn

MONARCH PRESS
New York

MONARCH PRESS and colophon are registered trademarks
of Simon & Schuster, Inc.
LOVEJOY'S is a registered trademark of Lovejoy's
College Guide, Inc.
Designed by Irving Perkins Associates
Manufactured in the United States of America
10 9 8 7 6 5
Library of Congress Catalog Card Number: 84-61189

ISBN: 0-671-52780-0

Acknowledged With Thanks

We wish to thank our assistants, Mrs. Gayle Thompson August and Mrs. Wendy Monnier Witterschein, for their help in the preparation of this book.

Contents

Section One
PREPARING FOR COLLEGE

Introduction and Purpose of the Book

THIS is the first edition of *Lovejoy's Concise College Guide*. The book gives the reader up-to-date information on 370 four-year colleges. All of the colleges listed are accredited by the regional accrediting body for that particular area of the country, the highest accreditation attainable. All of the colleges offer bachelor's degrees; many of them offer the associate degree as well.

Each school entry includes information on enrollment, tuition, room and board, degrees offered, mean SAT scores, mean ACT scores, student-faculty ratio, and calendar system. There is a brief description of the setting of the institution and detailed information on academic character, financial data, admissions requirements, and student life.

The criteria used for the selection of the 370 institutions are varied to include the most diverse selection of schools for you to choose from. We have included public colleges and universities, private institutions, liberal arts colleges, specialized institutions, men's colleges, women's colleges, Black institutions, military colleges. We have included the five federal academies which provide qualified, selected students with a free education. Some schools included are quite large, some are quite small.

There are colleges that have a large percentage of out-of-state enrollment. There are colleges that have free tuition. There are some 136 colleges where the total cost (tuition, room, board, and fees) is under $8,000 per year, many under $7,000, some even less than that. There are a few institutions listed where the total cost per year is in the $4,000 to $6,000 range. There are another 110 or so colleges where the total cost per year ranges from $8,000 to $11,000, and there is a third group of some 75 where the total cost exceeds $11,000 per year. There are a few colleges that offer guaranteed tuition and room and board, which means that the total cost will remain the same the entire time the student is enrolled at that college.

The colleges in this book are arranged alphabetically by state. The symbol following the name of the college indicates the price range of that institution (one *$* is tuition, room and board for under $8,000, two *$* denotes $8,000 to $11,000 and three *$* is $11,001 and above). For convenience, in the back of the book is an alphabetical index by school name.

Because of the growing number of students with varying degrees of learning disabilities, we have included a list of the colleges in this book which accept students with L.D. For further and more complete information on this subject, consult our forthcoming book, *Lovejoy's Four-Year College Guide for Learning Disabled Students.*

It was a very difficult task to decide which entries to include in this new Concise Guide. Inclusion does not in any way suggest that the colleges listed are the only important ones in the country, nor does it connote that those omitted are inferior institutions. Rather, we have attempted to give a wide variety of colleges and universities and thus provide the reader with a wide choice of selections to investigate.

NOTE TO THE READERS OF THIS GUIDE:

For complete information on all colleges in the United States, consult the 16th edition of *Lovejoy's College Guide.* In the 16th edition you will also find the very helpful Career Curricula Section and the Sports/Scholarship Index.

The College Selection Process— Which College Is for Me?

College selection is one of the most important decisions that students and their parents will make. If the wrong college is selected, the outcome could result in loss of time, poor grades, and little return on a large investment of money.

The process takes time and a great deal of consideration and evaluation on the part of both parent and student. The preferred way to engage in this expensive experience is to begin in the junior year of high school. This gives enough lead time to investigate the various colleges of interest, to visit some campuses, and have a chance to sort out a group of colleges that will meet the student's academic needs as well as meeting the colleges' academic criteria.

Often times the lack of prior planning brings poor results. Unfortunately, it is no secret that colleges are chosen on a whim at the last minute or on hearsay from a peer or parent's friend or relative. Some students wait until the middle of their senior year and then find that they have not taken the right subjects to meet the college's requirements, such as lacking one year of a foreign language or a math course, etc. Ideally, it is during the junior year, after colleges have been researched, that the student will know what is required. If he or she is lacking a course then it can be incorporated in his or her senior year course schedule. It is the obligation of the parents and student to communicate with the appropriate guidance counselor so that they will be aware of the student's college choices and be able to help.

The time spent in the junior search year is also the time to look for financial aid in its various forms, to find out what financial aid packages are available—what local and sports scholarships might be available at various colleges. Financial aid will be discussed in more detail later. For further information on sports scholarships, consult the 16th edition of *Lovejoy's College Guide* which has a section on intercollegiate sports and which colleges offer scholarships in these various sports.

Now, what about the student who is in his senior year and hasn't had time to do the research and planning? Depending on the student's academic strengths, college selection could be limited. However, one might consider those institutions which have a Rolling Admissions procedure, that is, one with no definite deadline for the application to be submitted, with the student receiving notification as soon as the file is completed. Colleges that use Rolling Admissions realize that in the day of multiple applications, they stand to enroll competitive students who might have been turned down by other institutions with a deadline. By the way, those institutions subscribing to the Rolling Admissions process are by no means second-rate colleges.

College selection depends on many variables. Location is one parents consider: How far are we willing to drive to visit? Do we have enough money to fly our child home for the holidays? Therefore, geographic location is important.

Assuming that you have narrowed down the possibilities, let's look at the variety of colleges within the range of, say, a five-hour ride. There will always be both state institutions and private colleges to choose from. Use this Guide for this selection process. It is recommended that you correspond with at least 10 to 15 schools requesting catalogs and application forms. After carefully reading over the material, narrow down your choice to five or seven colleges. You know your basic academic profile and you know from the Guide what test scores and brief particulars the colleges offer. Out of the seven colleges selected, it is advisable to visit at least one, more if time and money permits. After the college visits, set aside some time to meet with your guidance counselor and discuss the prospects of applying to these colleges and prepare to perform the chore of filing applications and writing brief essays that some applications require. Make sure to have good recommendations from some teachers, if required, and whatever else might be required from the colleges.

The application process differs from high school to high school. In some cases, the student brings in completed application papers and gives them to the guidance counselor to file along with the correct postage. In other cases, the student files the papers himself and the counselor sends in the transcript and other required materials. If the latter is true in your case, do yourself a favor and mail out all of the applications at the same time. We have seen cases where families mail in one application at a time and wait until they hear from that college before mailing in a second one, etc. This is an ineffective method. Although you may initially think you will save money on application fees, you will only lose out by waiting as the other colleges will have filled up during this waiting period.

THE INTERVIEW

What about the student who cannot make it to the college campus for the important interview? Have your colleges in mind, then set up an appointment with your guidance counselor and see if these particular colleges have admissions representatives coming to your school, or see if your school has a College Night and go and seek out the college representative at that time. Another option to increase awareness is College Fairs that are held throughout the country by the National Association of College Admissions Counselors. These fairs are widely represented by most of the colleges in the country. It is here that a student who has done research on colleges of interest can receive current information along with catalogs, view books, and other materials and, at the same time, have an opportunity to discuss college plans with admissions personnel. He or she can find out about financial aid and up-to-date curricula and programs. These fairs are very well received by parents and are well attended. They are worth your time and effort to visit them.

Are Interviews Important?

This question is almost always asked by parents and students. Or, put it in perspective they ask, how important are interviews? If it is at all possible to have an interview, then it is very important. I have known cases where the interview has been a plus to the student and, in given situations, has meant the difference between acceptance and rejection. An interview is an exchange between the admissions officer and the student. It is a two-way street. It gives the student a chance to find out pertinent information about the college, questions he or she may have after reading over the catalog, and questions about what is expected of him or her from the college. It gives the admissions officer an opportunity to find out what the student is like, to ask questions about the type of high school he comes from, what he has done other than his required course work, what his goals are and perhaps an idea of how he will fit in at the college. In some cases, an admissions officer may tell the student that the program in which he or she is interested might not be offered in enough depth to suit the student and the representative will recommend a college that has a stronger program in that area of study.

After the interview, there is usually a campus tour which provides an environmental insight to the parents and the student. Since it will be home for the next four years, it is important to see the campus. You wouldn't want to buy a house you hadn't seen, would you? Ask yourself some questions: Is this college going to serve my educational needs? Are the facilities adequate? Is this a college that I will be happy with socially? Does everyone go home on weekends? Does it have a friendly atmosphere? Are the students I have seen on campus happy or do they all have long faces and appear to be under tremendous academic pressure? Are they bored because the college lacks cultural activities, student government, and social life?

Each college has a personality all its own and not every college is for you. You must be objective in looking at colleges bearing in mind your own likes and dislikes, your strengths and weaknesses.

PARENTS, THIS IS FOR YOU!

You, the parents, do, indeed, have an important role in the college selection process, but it should not be a dominating one. I have seen many cases where the student went to a college and was unhappy because of parental pressure. If a student is unhappy, he or she will not do his or her best. The role the parent should play is one of guiding. To quote Charles R. Miller, former Dean of Admissions at Elmira College, who spent his whole life dealing with parents and students: "The goal of a parent is not to select the college to be considered . . . not necessarily even to suggest colleges to be considered. I believe the role of the parent is to assist in considering what kind of college or university should be explored. A parent can make a positive contribution by assisting in this phase of the process. Knowing their children better than anyone else, parents can guide them in evaluating how they 'fit' into each of several areas that should be considered." These areas are the ones we have previously discussed. In conclusion, Miller says "So, parents, get involved. You'll soon realize how much your assistance is really appreciated by your children. There is no reason why parents should not become involved in the college admissions process."

FINANCIAL AID

The question of financial aid always comes up when colleges are being selected. This is where research pays off to both the student and the parent.

While on campus, take a visit to the financial aid office and find out about your particular financial questions. The question always comes up as to whether a request for financial aid will hamper one's chances for admission. The answer is no. The admissions office and the financial aid office function as two separate areas.

There is one person in this country who is regarded by the news media and educators alike as a national expert in the field of financial aid. His name is Robert Leider. He has a financial aid service and publishes books on this subject. He can be reached at: Octameron Associates, PO Box 3437, Alexandria, Virginia 22302. The phone number is (703) 863-1019.

In order to know the players on the team you need a score card, and the same holds true in the area of financial aid; you need to know the terms:

- **Need Analysis**—An outline of the amount of money a family can contribute toward college expenses.
- **Grants**—Awards that do not require repayment.
- **Loans**—Monies that students receive which must be repaid with a slight amount of interest. In many cases, the money does not have to be repaid until after the student graduates.

- **Guaranteed Tuition**—Tuition that remains constant as long as the student is enrolled at the college.
- **National Merit Scholarship Program**—America's largest scholarship program, whereby a student who takes the PSAT/NMSQT and qualifies may get half or all of his education paid for four years.
- **CSS Financial Aid Form**—Participating colleges and universities in the College Scholarship Service require parents of applicants for financial aid to file a Financial Aid Form. This contains data about income and expenses of both father and mother, number and ages of children, whether or not they are dependents, and in school or college; data about other dependents and their relationship; data about parents' federal income tax; real estate, including present sale value of home and unpaid mortgage; and data about unusual family circumstances such as divorce, illnesses, special housing problems, etc. The CSS emphasizes that the amounts of aid awarded should be determined according to financial need.
- **Pell Grant and SEOG Grant**—These monies range up to $2,000 for the SEOG and up to $1,750 for the PELL Grant per year for four years.
- **College Work Study Program**—This gives the student the opportunity to pay off part or all of his or her educational expenses by working at a part-time job at the college itself or with a public or private nonprofit agency working in cooperation with the college. Students may work up to 40 hours per week depending on the determination of the college financial aid officer. Salary paid is at least equal to the current minimum wage but frequently is higher.
- **Guaranteed Student Loan Program**—Eligible students may borrow money directly from the bank, credit union, savings and loan association or other participating lender. The loan is guaranteed by a state or private nonprofit guarantee agency or insured by the federal government. A student may borrow up to the maximum of $2,500 per year.
- **No Need Scholarships**—These are sometimes called Presidential Scholarships and are awarded to students who achieve high grades throughout high school. They are given as an academic reward. The awards are given by the colleges and require no financial aid forms. Many colleges refer to them as merit scholarships, but they should not be confused with the National Merit Scholarships.

There are various kinds of tuition payment plans whereby the tuition is paid on a semester basis and the parents make payments monthly with interest rates added on, the way one would make car payments. Some colleges give a discount on the tuition if all four years are paid for up front in the beginning of the freshman year. There are colleges which will give a family a tuition break if more than one student is attending the same college simultaneously.

If you, the parent, are familiar with accounting practices, keep up with the latest goings on in Congress, and have sound knowledge of the latest tax laws, then you should be prepared to handle any particular financial aid situation. But if you are like the average man or woman, it would be in your best interest to seek out an accountant and have him help you with your financial aid problems. I would further advise you to be smart and do it by using Mr. Leider's publications or his financial aid consultations.

Here are a few of Mr. Leider's tips: If your family has a good income and credit history, it can tap up to 70% of the cash locked up in home equity through special credit lines offered by organizations such as Merrill Lynch Equity Access Accounts. There is a small opening fee in this. After that, you may borrow money when you need it, in the amount needed, simply by writing checks or using a special VISA card against the credit line. Interest rates usually float at the prime rate plus two percentage points. You have from five to ten years to repay the loan. Home equity loans are an extremely easy and flexible way to obtain cash flow assistance on relatively favorable terms. But care must be taken that the ease of monetary access provided by these instruments does not cause you to get into deep financial problems and lose your home.

You can borrow against your pension plan. If you work for a company with a pension or profit-sharing plan, see if you can borrow against the equity that you have built up in the plan. Or, if you are a self-employed professional with a retirement plan or if you have a Keogh Plan, you might consider giving yourself a college loan. There are three advantages to such loans: they will help with cash flow; they will reduce your asset position; and, with self-employment loans, you can set an interest rate that may help you obtain an added tax advantage.

There are some important points to be made about financial aid forms. You must have a social security card to apply for financial aid. Financial aid forms cannot be dated or submitted before January 1. Be sure you know when the colleges want you to submit the forms. If you plan on applying to six colleges and each has a different date, make a list of the dates and submit the form by the earliest of the dates on your list. The form, incidentally, will be sent to the colleges by the need analysis processor, not by you. If the earliest date falls before your income tax is completed, you can estimate the income tax information required by the form. Remember, apply early for financial assistance. College can often only meet the needs of the first applicants. Meet with the financial aid officer and tell him or her about your particular situation and he can help you and clear up any confusion about the proper steps to take in order to apply for aid.

Charles T. Straughn II, Educational Consultant and Co-Author, Lovejoy's Educational Counseling Service.

Charles T. Straughn has been counseling students and parents for college and prep school for twenty years. He has visited hundreds of colleges and schools and holds membership in numerous educational associations.

Section Two

THE COLLEGES

SYMBOLS, ABBREVIATIONS, AND GLOSSARY
OF TERMS USED IN THIS BOOK

($)—Price range of the college

The Regional Accrediting Bodies:

MSACS—Middle States Assn. of Colleges and Secondary Schools
NEASC—New England Assn. of Schools and Colleges
NCACS—North Central Assn. of Colleges and Secondary Schools
NASC—Northwest Assn. of Secondary and Higher Schools
SACS—Southern Assn. of Colleges and Secondary Schools
WASC—Western Assn. of Schools and Colleges

ADMISSIONS AND FINANCIAL AID ABBREVIATIONS:

ACH—Achievement Test (CEEB)
ACT—American College Testing Program (E-English, M-Math)
AP—Advanced Placement
CEEB—College Entrance Examination Board
CGP—Comparative Guidance and Placement Test
CLEP—College Level Examination Program
CSS—Signifies participating institution in College Scholarship Service in which parents of candidates for scholarships and financial aid agree to file confidential statements before specified winter and early spring dates. Some of the CSS participants are not members of the College Entrance Examination Board (CEEB) which organized it.
CUNY—City University of New York
CWS or CWSP—College Work-Study Program
EOG—Educational Opportunity Grants Program
FAF—Financial Aid Form
FFS—Family Financial Statement of the American College Testing Program
FISL—Federally Insured Student Loan
GED—General Equivalency Diploma
GSL or GSLP—Guaranteed Student Loan Program
GRE—Graduate Record Examinations
NDEA—National Defense Education Act
NDSL or NDSLP—National Direct Student Loan Program
NMSQT—National Merit Scholarship Qualifying Test
PELL—Basic Educational Opportunity Grant
PSAT—Preliminary Scholastic Aptitude Test
ROTC—Reserve Officers Training Corps
SAT—Scholastic Aptitude Test (M-Math, V-Verbal)
SCAT—School and College Ability Test
SEEK—Search for Education, Elevation, and Knowledge
SEOG—Supplemental Educational Opportunity Grant

SUNY—State University of New York
TAP—Tuition Assistance Plan
TOEFL—Test of English as a Foreign Language

CALENDAR SYSTEMS:

QUARTER—four 12-week quarters

TRIMESTER—three 17-week trimesters

4-1-4—three terms comprised of a 4-month term, a one month term or interim, and another 4-month term

4-4-1—two 4-month terms followed by a one-month term

4-1-5—four courses in first semester, interterm of one course, five courses in second semester

5-4-1—five courses in fall term, winter term of four courses, short term of one course

4-0-4—four courses in first semester, interterm of three-week period when students pursue academic or cultural experiences without credit or may opt to stay home, four courses in second semester

3-3—three 10-week terms, three courses per term

12-12-6—first and second semesters of 12 weeks each followed by a third term of six weeks

BIMESTER 2-2-2-2-1—four terms of two courses per term followed by a three-week intersession of one course

ADMISSIONS TERMS:

EARLY DECISION—Students with outstanding scores on eleventh grade CEEB SAT's and high class rank and grades are assured college admission as early as December of their twelfth grade if they apply by October 1 to only one institution.

EARLY ADMISSIONS—Exceptionally bright students are enrolled in college after the tenth or eleventh grade without having received their high school diploma.

ROLLING ADMISSIONS—Students apply any time after six semesters of high school work. Candidates are notified as soon as their file has been completed and they have fulfilled the college's entrance requirements.

ADVANCED PLACEMENT—Students may bypass some of the early work in college by taking freshman level courses in the latter part of their secondary schooling and receiving credit for them in college.

COLLEGE LEVEL EXAMINATION PROGRAM—Allows college credit for non-traditional college level education including independent study, correspondence, work, and on-the-job and military training.

ADMISSIONS DEFERRAL—Students are accepted but elect to wait a year before entering college.

DEGREE ABBREVIATIONS

AA—Associate in Arts
AAA—Associate in Applied Arts
AAAS—Associate in Applied Arts and Sciences
AAS—Associate in Applied Science

AB—Bachelor of Arts
ABA—Associate in Business Administration
ABEd—Bachelor of Arts in Education
AE—Agricultural Engineer or Aeronautical Engineer
AFA—Associate in Fine Arts
AGE—Associate in General Education
AGS—Associate in General Studies
ALA—Associate in Liberal Arts
AM—Master of Arts
AME—Advanced Master of Education
MAT—Master of Arts in Teaching
AgE—Agricultural Engineer
AOS—Associate in Occupational Studies
AS—Associate in Science
ASB—Associate in Specialized Business
ASN—Associate of Science in Nursing
AST—Associate in Specialized Technology
ATE—Associate in Technical Education
AVE—Associate in Vocational Education
BA—Bachelor of Arts
BAEd—Bachelor of Arts in Education
BAGE—Bachelor of Arts in General Education
BAMus—Bachelor of Arts in Music
BArch—Bachelor of Arts in Architecture
BBA—Bachelor of Business Administration
BBS—Bachelor of Business Science
BCS—Bachelor of Continuing Studies
BD—Bachelor of Divinity
BES—Bachelor of Elective Studies
BFA—Bachelor of Fine Arts
BGS—Bachelor of General Studies
BHL—Bachelor of Hebrew Literature (or Letters)
BID—Bachelor of Industrial Design
BIM—Bachelor of Industrial Management
BIS—Bachelor of Independent Studies
BLS—Bachelor of Library Science or Liberal Studies
BMus—Bachelor of Music
BMus Ed—Bachelor of Music Education
BPA—Bachelor of Professional Arts
BRE—Bachelor of Religious Education
BS—Bachelor of Science
BSAA—Bachelor of Science in Applied Arts
BSBA—Bachelor of Science in Business Administration
BSCE—Bachelor of Science in Civil Engineering
BSE—Bachelor of Science in Engineering
BSEd—Bachelor of Science in Education
BSEE—Bachelor of Science in Electrical Engineering
BSM—Bachelor in Sacred Music

BSME—Bachelor of Science in Mechanical Engineering
BSN—Bachelor of Science in Nursing
BSPA—Bachelor of Science in Public Administration
BSPh—Bachelor of Science in Pharmacy
BSS—Bachelor of Secretarial Science
BSW—Bachelor of Social Work
BT—Bachelor of Technology
BTh—Bachelor of Theology
CAS—Bachelor of Administrative Specialist, or Certificate in Advanced Studies
CE—Civil Engineer
ChE—Chemical Engineer
DB—Bachelor of Divinity
DC—Doctor of Chiropractic
DCL—Doctor of Civil Law
DD—Doctor of Divinity
DDS—Doctor of Dental Surgery
DHL—Doctor of Hebrew Literature
DLS—Doctor of Library Science
DML—Doctor of Modern Languages
DPH—Doctor of Public Health
DSW—Doctor of Social Work
DVM—Doctor of Veterinary Medicine
EE—Electrical Engineer
EM—Mining Engineer
EdB—Bachelor of Education
EdD—Doctor of Education
EdM—Master of Education
ExM—Master of Extension (Agriculture)
JD—Doctor of Jurisprudence
JSD—Doctor of Juridical Science
MA—Master of Arts
MAEd—Master of Arts in Education
MALL—Master of Arts in Liberal Learning
MALS—Master of Arts in Liberal Studies
MAR—Master of Arts in Religion
MAT—Master of Arts in Teaching
MBA—Master of Business Administration
MC—Master in Counseling
MCL—Master of Comparative Law, or Master of Civil Law
MCP—Master in Civil Planning
MDS—Master in Dental Surgery
MDiv—Master of Divinity
MFA—Master in Fine Arts
MI—Master in Instruction
MLS—Master in Library Science
MMEd—Master in Music Education
MMP—Master in Marine Policy
MPA—Master of Public Administration, or Master of Public Affairs

MPH—Master of Public Health
MPL—Master of Parliamentary Law
MRE—Master in Religious Education
MS—Master of Science
MSHE—Master of Science in Home Economics
MST—Master of Science in Teaching
MSW—Master of Social Work
MTh—Master of Theology
MURP—Master in Urban and Regional Planning
NE—Nuclear Engineer
OD—Doctor of Optometry
PhB—Bachelor of Philosophy
PhC—Pharmaceutical Chemistry, or Philosopher of Chiropractic
PhD—Doctor of Philosophy
PhM—Master of Philosophy
SJD—Doctor of Juridical Science
ScD—Doctor of Science
SEd—Specialist in Education
STD—Doctor of Sacred Theology
STL—Licentiate in Sacred Theology
STM—Master of Sacred Theology
ThB—Bachelor of Theology
ThM—Master of Theology

Alabama

ALABAMA, UNIVERSITY OF $

University 35486, (205) 348-5666
Dean of Admissions: Dr. Lawrence Durham

- **Undergraduates:** 6,314m, 5,602w
- **Tuition (1984–1985):** $1,148 (in-state), $2,464 (out-of-state)
- **Room and Board (1984–1985):** $1,880
- **Degrees offered:** BA, BS, BFA, BMus, BSN, BSW, BSEd, BSBA, BSE
- **Mean SAT:** Composite: 880,   **Mean ACT:** 21
- **Student-faculty ratio:** 17 to 1
- **Calendar system:** Semester

A public university established in 1831. 520-acre small city main campus 56 miles southwest of Birmingham. Served by air, rail, and bus.

Academic Character SACS and professional accreditation. Semester system, 3-week May interim, 2 5-week summer terms. 48 majors offered by the College of Arts & Sciences, 16 by the College of Commerce & Business Administration, 15 by the College of Education, 11 by the College of Engineering, 8 by the School of Communication, 13 by the School of Home Economics, 1 by the School of Nursing, and 3 by the School of Social Work. New College offers flexible, independent programs for highly motivated students leading to a BA or BS. Special and double majors. Minor sometimes required. Minors offered in most major fields and many additional areas. Distributive requirements. Graduate and professional degrees granted. Independent study, honors program, Phi Beta Kappa, cooperative work/study, pass/fail, internships. Preprofessional programs in dentistry, law, medicine, optometry, physical therapy, social work, and speech-language pathology. 2-year preprofessional transfer programs in dental hygiene, medical record administration, occupational therapy, pharmacy, physical therapy. 3-1 programs in dentistry and medicine. 5-year BA/MBA or BS/MBA program. Study abroad. Early childhood, elementary, secondary, and special education certification. AFROTC, ROTC. Computer center, observatory. 1,300,000-volume library.

Financial ACT FAS. University scholarships, grants, loans; PELL, SEOG, NDSL, GSL, NSL, CWS. Priority application deadline March 15.

Admissions High school graduation with 12 units required. GED accepted. ACT or SAT required. $15 application fee. Rolling admissions; deadline August 1. *Early Admission* Program. SEARCH program for concurrent enrollment. Transfers accepted. Credit possible for CEEB AP and CLEP exams. Summer Trial Admission Program.

Student Life Student government. Newspaper, magazines, yearbook, radio & TV stations. Music, debate, and drama groups. Afro-American Association. Numerous academic, honorary, political, professional, recreational, religious, service, and special interest organizations. 29 fraternities and 20 sororities, all with houses. 35% of men and 22% of women join. No coed dorms. Married-student housing. 33% of students live on campus. Liquor prohibited on campus. 9 intercollegiate sports for men, 8 for women; several intramurals. NCAA, Southeastern Conference. Student body composition: 10% Black, 89% White, 1% Other. 25% from out of state.

AUBURN UNIVERSITY $

Auburn 36849, (205) 826-4000
Director of Admissions: Charles E. Reeder

- **Undergraduates:** 9,821m, 6,905w
- **Tuition (1984–1985):** $1,080 (in-state), $2,490 (out-of-state)
- **Room and Board (1984–1985):** $2,100
- **Degrees offered:** BA, BS, BSBA, BSN, BArch, BAv Mgt, BFA, Blnd Des, Blnt Des, BLArch, BMus, BSEd, BSPharm, BText and BE
- **Mean SAT:** 484v, 552m, **Mean ACT:** 22.8
- **Student-faculty ratio:** 17 to 1
- **Calendar system:** Quarter

A public land-grant university founded in 1856. 1,871-acre small town campus 59 miles east of Montgomery and 116 miles southwest of Atlanta. Air and bus service.

Academic Character SACS and professional accreditation. Quarter system, 11-week summer term. 147 majors offered by the schools of Arts & Sciences, Education, Agriculture, Architecture & Fine Arts, Engineering, Home Economics, Business, Nursing, Pharmacy, and Veterinary Medicine. Distributive requirements. Graduate and professional degrees granted. Independent study, honors program, cooperative work/study, pass/fail, internships. Program in environmental health. Preprofessional program in hospital administration. Preprofessional and 3-1 programs in law, medicine, dentistry, optometry, and veterinary medicine. 3-2 programs in many areas including agriculture, business, engineering. Study abroad. Elementary, secondary, and special education certification. AFROTC, NROTC, ROTC. Computer center. 1,100,000-volume library with microfcrm resources.

Financial ACT FAS. University scholarships, loans; PELL, SEOG, NDSL, GSL, CWS. Priority application deadline for scholarships & loans March 15. Loan deadline 8 weeks before beginning of quarter.

Admissions High school graduation with 16 units required. Equivalency exams may be accepted. ACT or SAT required (must be ACT for AL residents). 'C' average and 18 composite ACT or similar SAT required for admission. $15 application fee. Rolling admissions; suggest applying by January of 12th year. Deadline 3 weeks before beginning of term. *Early Entrance* and *Concurrent Enrollment* programs. Admission deferral possible. Transfers accepted. Credit possible for CEEB AP and CLEP exams; departments have own placement exams.

Student Life Student government. Debate, community service. Radio and TV stations, several music, dance, and drama groups. Many athletic, academic, political, religious, honorary, and special interest organizations. 30 fraternities and 17 sororities. No coed dorms. Married-student apartments. 30% of students live on campus. Liquor prohibited. Numerous intercollegiate and intramural sports for men and women. Southeastern Conference. Student body composition: 0.5% Asian, 2.3% Black, 0.3% Hispanic, 0.1% Native American, 95.6% White, 1.2% Other. 35% from out of state.

BIRMINGHAM—SOUTHERN COLLEGE $

800 Eighth Ave. W., Birmingham 35254, (205) 328-5250
Vice President for Admissions: Robert Dortch

- **Undergraduates:** 698m, 889w
- **Tuition (1984–1985):** $5,120
- **Room and Board (1984–1985):** $2,370;   **Fees:** $200
- **Degrees offered:** BA, BS, BMus, BSME, BFA, BSN
- **Mean SAT:** 510v, 540m,   **Mean ACT:** 24
- **Student-faculty ratio:** 14 to 1
- **Calendar system:** 4–1–4

A private college founded in 1856, associated with the United Methodist Church. 200-acre wooded campus 3 miles west of Birmingham business district. Air, rail, and bus service.

Academic Character SACS and professional accreditation. 4-1-4 calendar, 9-week summer term. Majors offered in the areas of accounting, art, business administration, computer science, dance, drama & speech, education, health/phys ed/athletics, mathematics, languages & literatures, music (8), music education, music merchandising, nursing, philosophy, psychology, religion, sciences, and social sciences. Interdisciplinary and self-designed majors. Distributive requirements. Honors program, Phi Beta Kappa, pass/fail, internships. Preprofessional programs in business, law, dentistry, medicine, medical technology, optometry, and pharmacy. 3-2 engineering program with Auburn. Exchange program with U Alabama (Birmingham). Member Marine Environmental Sciences Consortium, Southern College and University Union. Washington Semester. Study abroad. Early childhood, elementary, and secondary education certification. AFROTC at Samford; ROTC at UAB. Planetarium, computer center, language lab. 132,000-volume library.

Financial CEEB CSS. College scholarships, grants, loans, tuition reduction for children of ministers and for those preparing for Christian service, deferred payment; PELL, SEOG, AL state grants, NDSL, FISL, CWS. Application deadlines March 15 (scholarships), April 15 (loans).

Admissions High school graduation with 15 units required. GED accepted. Music majors must audition. ACT or SAT required. $10 application fee. Rolling admissions; suggest applying before February 15 of 12th year. $25 deposit required on acceptance of admissions offer. *Early Admission* and *Concurrent Enrollment* programs. Admission deferral possible. Transfers accepted. Credit possible for CEEB AP and CLEP exams.

Student Life Student government. Newspaper, literary magazine, yearbook. Many music, dance, and drama groups. Black Student Union. Academic, honorary, and special interest organizations. 5 fraternities and 6 sororities, some with houses. 41% of men and women join. Unmarried students under 21 must live at home or on campus. No coed dorms. Married-student apartments. 80% of students live on campus. Liquor prohibited. Honor Code. 4 intercollegiate sports for men, 1 for women; several intramurals. NAIA, Southern States Conference. Student body composition: 0.5% Asian, 12% Black, 0.2% Hispanic, 87.3% White. 20% from out of state.

TUSKEGEE INSTITUTE $

Tuskegee 36088, (205) 727-8500
Director of Admissions: Herbet Carter

- **Undergraduates:** 1,690m, 1,710w
- **Tuition (1984–1985):** $3,500
- **Room and Board (1984–1985):** $1,900

- **Degrees offered:** BS, BA
- **Mean SAT:** 300v, 350m, **Mean ACT:** 15
- **Student-faculty ratio:** 11 to 1
- **Calendar system:** Semester

A private institute founded in 1881 by Booker T. Washington. 5,000-acre rural campus 40 miles east of Montgomery. Air, rail, and bus in Montgomery.

Academic Character SACS accreditation. Semester system, 8-week summer term. 12 majors offered by the College of Arts & Sciences, 16 by the School of Applied Sciences, 13 by the School of Education, 3 by the School of Engineering, and 1 by the School of Nursing. Courses offered in 7 additional areas. Distributive requirements. GRE required for graduation. Graduate and professional degrees granted. Independent study, honors program, pass/fail, cooperative work/study. 3-2 programs in dentistry and medicine. 2-year pre-forestry and veterinary medicine programs. Elementary, secondary, and special education certification. AFROTC, ROTC. 155,000-volume library.

Financial CEEB CSS. Institute scholarships, loans, nursing scholarships; PELL, SEOG,, NDSL, CWS. Application deadlines March 1 (scholarships), April 15 (loans).

Admissions High school graduation with 15 units required. SAT or ACT required. No application fee. Rolling admissions; suggest applying in January or February of 12th year. Deadline April 15. $15 acceptance fee and $100 room deposit required on acceptance of offer of admission. *Early Entrance* and *Early Decision* programs. Transfers accepted. Credit possible for CEEB AP and CLEP exams.

Student Life Student government, newspaper, yearbook, several music groups. Theater group, professional, honorary, and special interest organizations. 6 fraternities and 3 sororities, none with houses. 20% of men and 15% of women join. Students not living at home must live on campus. Men's and women's dorms. Married-student apartments. 75% of students live on campus. Liquor and firearms prohibited on campus. Class attendance expected. 2 semesters of phys ed required in first year. 6 intercollegiate sports; intramurals. Southern Intercollegiate Athletic Conference. Student body composition: 95% Black, 1% Hispanic, 0.7% Native American, 3% White, 0.3% Other. 65% from out of state.

Alaska

ALASKA, UNIVERSITY OF $

Fairbanks 99701, (907) 479-7821
Director of Admissions: Ann Tremarello

- **Undergraduates:** 2,417m, 2,531w
- **Tuition (1984–1985):** $600 (in-state), $1,560 (out-of-state)
- **Room and Board (1984–1985):** $2,300; **Fees:** $220
- **Degrees offered:** BA, BS, BBA, BEd, BMus, BT, AA, AAS
- **Mean ACT:** 19
- **Student-faculty ratio:** 14 to 1
- **Calendar system:** Semester

A public university established in 1915. 2,400-acre suburban campus 5 miles from Fairbanks, which has air, rail, bus service.

Academic Character NASC and professional accreditation. Semester system, 3 3-week summer terms, 1 to 6-week summer workshops. 54 majors offered by the colleges of Arts & Sciences, Environmental Sciences, and the schools of Agriculture & Land Resources Management, Education, Engineering, Management, and Mineral Industry. Minors offered in most major fields. Courses in natural and social sciences, humanities. Distributive requirements. Graduate and professional degrees granted. Preprofessional programs in dentistry, medicine, nursing, veterinary medicine. Exchange program in Japan. Elementary and secondary education certification. ROTC. Language labs. 750,000-volume library.

Financial CEEB CSS. University scholarships, grants, loans. 1st-semester non-state residents not eligible for scholarships or grants. PELL, SEOG, NDSL, CWS. Application deadlines March 1 (scholarships, grants) and August 1 (loans).

Admissions High school graduation with 16 units required. ACT required. $10 application fee. Rolling admissions; deadline August 1. $50 housing deposit required on acceptance of offer of admission. Transfers accepted. Credit possible for CEEB AP and CLEP exams; university administers departmental exams. Older residents with no formal high school education but with acceptable test scores may be accepted provisionally.

Student Life Student government, campus union. Newspaper, yearbook, radio station. Musical, athletic, honorary, religious, service, and special interest groups. Single freshmen under 21 must live at home or on campus. Coed and single-sex dorms; some married-student housing. 41% of students live on campus. Class attendance expected. 5 intercollegiate sports for men, 5 for women; intramurals. Student body composition: 1.8% Asian, 2.3% Black, 0.5% Hispanic, 12.2% Native American, 82.6% White, 0.6% Other. 19% from out of state.

Arizona

ARIZONA, UNIVERSITY OF $

Tucson 85721, (602) 626-0111
Dean of Admissions: David L. Windsor

- **Undergraduates:** 13,080m, 11,991w
- **Tuition (1984–1985):** $850 (in-state), $3,515 (out-of-state)
- **Room and Board (1984–1985):** $2,355
- **Degrees offered:** BArch, BA, BFA, BLA, BMus, BS
- **Mean SAT:** 466v, 518m,   **Mean ACT:** 21.6
- **Student-faculty ratio:** 17 to 1
- **Calendar system:** Semester

A public land-grant university established in 1885. 319-acre urban campus located in residential Tucson, which is served by air, rail, and bus.
Academic Character NCACS and professional accreditation. Semester system, 2 summer terms. 127 majors offered by the Colleges of Agriculture, Architecture, Business & Public Administration, Earth Sciences, Education, Engineering, Fine Arts, Liberal Arts, Mines, Nursing, Pharmacy, and the Schools of Health Related Professions and Home Economics. Minors in most major areas and in American Indian, Black, and women's studies. Graduate and professional degrees granted. Independent study, honors program. Phi Beta Kappa. Cooperative work/study, pass/fail, internships. Preprofessional preparation in dental hygiene, dentistry, foreign service, law, medicine, occupational therapy, optometry, osteopathy, pharmacy, physical therapy, podiatry. Study abroad in Mexico, Europe, Brazil, Egypt, Far East. Elementary, secondary, and special education certification. AFROTC, ROTC. 4,574,445-volume library.
Financial University scholarships, grants, loans. PELL, SEOG, NSS, NDSL, GSL, NSL, CWS. Priority application deadline is May 1.
Admissions High school graduation with 16 units required. ACT or SAT required. $10 application fee for out-of-state students, none for in-state. Rolling admissions; deadline July 1. $50 room deposit required on acceptance of offer of admission. Credit possible for CEEB AP and CLEP exams; university has own placement exams.
Student Life Student government, newspaper, magazines. About 200 campus organizations. 18 fraternities and 12 sororities with houses. Coed and single-sex dorms, women's cooperative dorm. Some married-student housing. 34% of students live on campus. 9 intercollegiate sports for men, 11 for women; intramurals. NCAA, Pacific-10, Western Collegiate Athletic Association. Student body composition: 1.2% Asian, 1.2% Black, 5.1% Hispanic, 0.8% Native American, 51.4% White, 40.3% Other. 21% from out of state.

ARIZONA STATE UNIVERSITY $

Tempe 85287, (602) 965-7788
Director of Admissions: Christine A. Wilkinson

- **Undergraduates:** 15,751m, 14,504w
- **Tuition (1984–1985):** $850 (in-state), $3,600 (out-of-state)

- **Room and Board (1984–1985):** $2,500
- **Degrees offered:** BA, BS, BAEd, BM, BFA, BSE, BSN, BSW
- **Mean SAT:** 454V, 508m,   **Mean ACT:** 21.2
- **Student-faculty ratio:** 18 to 1
- **Calendar system:** Semester

A public university established in 1885. 566-acre suburban campus just east of Phoenix, plus 320-acre University farm. Air, bus, and rail service.

Academic Character NCACS and professional accreditation. Semester system, 2 5-week and 1 8-week summer terms. 88 majors offered by the Colleges of Architecture, Business Administration, Education, Engineering & Applied Sciences, Fine Arts, Law, Liberal Arts, Nursing, Public Programs, and by the School of Social Work. Interdisciplinary majors possible in American, Asian, energy & environmental, film, liberal arts, Latin American, religious, and women's studies, and in gerontology. Distributive requirements. Graduate degrees granted. Independent study. Honors program. Phi Beta Kappa. Cooperative work/study, internships. Pass/fail, credit by exam. Preprofessional programs in bilingual secretarial, dentistry, foreign service, law, medicine, ministry, occupational therapy, optometry, osteopathy, pharmacy, physical therapy, podiatry. 5-year BS/MS in engineering. Study abroad. Elementary, secondary, and special education certification. AFROTC, ROTC. Language lab. 1,650,000-volume library with microform resources.

Financial CEEB CSS and ACT FAS. University scholarships, grants, and loans; PELL, SEOG, NDSL, FISL, CWS. Apply by April 15.

Admissions High school graduation required with 16 units recommended. GED accepted. Audition required for music majors. ACT or SAT required. $10 application fee for out-of-state students, none for in-state. Apply by July 31. $50 room reservation deposit suggested for boarders. *Concurrent Enrollment Program.* Transfers accepted. Credit possible for CEEB AP, CLEP, and university proficiency exams.

Student Life Student government. Newspaper, TV station. Music, drama, political, environmental, athletic, academic, religious, service, and special interest groups. 21 fraternities, 13 sororities. No coed dorms. 15% of undergraduates live on campus. 12 intercollegiate sports for men, 9 for women; intramurals. AIAW, NCAA, PAC-10, Western Collegiate Athletic Association. Student body composition: 2% Asian, 3% Black, 4% Hispanic, 2% Native American, 89% White. 25% from out of state.

Arkansas

ARKANSAS, UNIVERSITY OF $

Fayetteville 72701, (501) 575-5346
Director of Admissions: Larry F. Matthews

- **Undergraduates:** 6,595m, 4,867w
- **Tuition (1984–1985):** $900 (in-state), $2,160 (out-of-state)
- **Room and Board (1984–1985):** $1,876
- **Degrees offered:** BA, BS, BArch, BSBA, BSE, BFA, BSAgE, BSCh.E, BSA, BSHE, BLA, BMus, BSCE, BSEE, BSIE, BSME, BSIM, AA, AS
- **Mean ACT:** 19.4
- **Student-faculty ratio:** 18 to 1
- **Calendar system:** Semester

A public university established in 1871. 329-acre urban campus located in small city of Fayetteville, 2½ hours from Tulsa, 4 hours from Little Rock. Served by air and bus.

Academic Character NCACS and professional accreditation. Semester system, 9 summer terms of 3 to 12 weeks. 32 majors offered by the College of Agriculture & Home Economics, 35 by the College of Arts & Sciences, 15 by the College of Business Administration, 17 by the College of Education, 8 by the College of Engineering, and 2 by the School of Architecture. Self-designed majors. Associate degrees offered by Business Administration, Engineering, and the School of Nursing. Distributive requirements. Graduate and professional degrees granted. Independent study. Honors program. Phi Beta Kappa. Pass/fail. Preprofessional programs in chiropractic medicine, dental hygiene, dentistry, medical technology, medicine, nursing, optometry, pharmacy, physical therapy, theology. Study abroad in Japan. Elementary, secondary, and special education certification. ROTC, AFROTC. 981,000-volume library.

Financial CEEB CSS and ACT FAS. University scholarships, grants, athletic scholarships, loans; state residents receive priority consideration. PELL, NSS, NDSL, CWS. Application deadline April 1.

Admissions High school graduation with 15 units required. GED accepted. ACT with composite score of 18 required; lower scores may be accepted conditionally. $15 application fee. Rolling admissions. $60 room deposit required on acceptance of offer of admission. *Early Admission* Program. Transfers accepted. Credit possible for CEEB AP and CLEP exams.

Student Life Student government. Publications. Music and drama groups. Debate team. Religious, service, political, honorary, and special interest groups. 19 fraternities and 12 sororities. Single freshmen under 21 must live at home or on campus. Dorms for men and women. Married-student housing. 55% of students live on campus. 8 intercollegiate sports for men, 5 for women; over 100 intramural and club sports. AIAW, Southwest Conference. Student body composition: 2% Asian, 5% Black, 1% Hispanic, 1% Native American, 91% White. 18% from out of state.

HARDING UNIVERSITY $

Searcy 72143, (501) 268-6161
Director of Admissions: Durward McGaha

- **Undergraduates:** 1,418m, 1,466w
- **Tuition (1984–1985):** $2,895
- **Room and Board (1984–1985):** $2,126;   **Fees:** $192
- **Degrees offered:** BA, BBA, BS, BSN, BSW, BFA, BMus, AA
- **Mean ACT:** 19.7
- **Student-faculty ratio:** 22 to 1
- **Calendar system:** Semester

A private university affiliated with the Church of Christ, established in 1919. 200-acre rural campus located in the small city of Searcy, 45 miles from Little Rock. Served by bus; air in Little Rock.

Academic Character NCACS and professional accreditation. Semester system, 2 5-week summer terms, May intersession. 51 majors offered by the College of Arts & Sciences and the schools of Business, Education, and Nursing. Self-designed majors. American Studies program. Minor required. Minors offered in all major fields and in Greek. Courses in geography, German, Hebrew. Distributive requirements may be waived by exam. 4 Bible courses required. Masters degrees granted. Independent study. Honors program. Cooperative work/study, pass/fail, internships. Preprofessional programs in agriculture, architecture, optometry, pharmacy. 3-2 programs in engineering, dentistry, law, medical technology, medicine, nursing. 4-2 program in engineering. Study abroad. Elementary, secondary, and special education certification. Computer center. Over 200,000-volume library with microfilm resources.

Financial ACT FAS. University scholarships, loans, deferred payment; PELL, SEOG, NDSL, FISL, CWS. Application deadlines May 1 (scholarships), April 1 (loans).

Admissions High school graduation with 15 units required. ACT required. $15 application fee, $25 housing reservation due with application. Rolling admissions; suggest applying between November and February. *Early Admission* Program. Transfers accepted. Credit possible for CEEB AP and CLEP exams.

Student Life Student government. Newspaper, yearbook, radio station. Music, drama, debate groups. Intercollegiate business games. Religious, political, honorary, academic, and special interest organizations. 20 men's and 23 women's social clubs; none have houses. Single students under 23 must live on campus. No coed dorms. Married-student apartments. 80% of students live on campus. Liquor, gambling, hazing, smoking, obscene literature, profanity prohibited on campus. Students who falsify marital status dismissed. Class attendance and daily chapel required. 4 semester hours of phys ed required, except for veterans. 8 intercollegiate sports for men, 3 for women; intramurals. NAIA and Arkansas Intercollegiate Conference. Student body composition: 3% Black, 96% White, 1% Other. 72% from out of state.

OUACHITA BAPTIST UNIVERSITY $

Arkadelphia 71923, (501) 246-4531
Director of Admissions Counseling: Harold Johnson

- **Undergraduates:** 750m, 755w
- **Tuition (1984–1985):** $2,900
- **Room and Board (1984–1985):** $1,750;   **Fees:** $50
- **Degrees offered:** BA, BS, BSE, BMus, BME, BAMus
- **Mean ACT:** 19

- **Student-faculty ratio:** 17 to 1
- **Calendar system:** Semester

A private university established in 1886, affiliated with the Southern Baptist Church. 200-acre small-city campus, 70 miles from Little Rock. Served by bus and rail. Air 35 miles away in Hot Springs, and in Little Rock.

Academic Character NCACS and professional accreditation. Semester system, 2 5-week summer terms. 32 majors offered in the areas of business & economics, education, humanities, natural science, religion & philosophy, social science, and music. Distributive requirements. 2 semesters of religion required. Masters degrees granted. Independent study. Honors program. Pass/fail. Internships. Preprofessional programs in architecture, dental hygiene, dentistry, dietetics, engineering, landscape architecture, medical technology, medicine, nursing, pharmacy, physical therapy. 3-2 programs in dentistry, engineering, medicine, pharmacy. Cross-registration with Henderson State. Exchange programs with schools in Japan and Nigeria. Elementary, secondary, and special education certification. ROTC. Computer center, language lab, museum, TV studio. 104,000-volume library with microform resources.

Financial ACT FAS. University scholarships, grants, loans, ministerial scholarships; PELL, SEOG, NDSL, GSL, CWS, university has own work program. Application deadline May 1.

Admissions High school graduation with 15 units required. GED accepted. ACT required. $25 application fee. Rolling admissions; suggest applying by May 1. $100 deposit required on acceptance of offer of admission. *Early Admission* and *Concurrent Enrollment* programs. Transfers accepted. Credit possible for CEEB AP, CLEP, and ACT PEP exams; university has own advanced placement program. Academic Skills Development Program.

Student Life Student government. Newspaper, yearbook, magazine. Music and drama groups. Ethnic and women's organizations. Religious, political, academic, service, and special interest groups. 4 fraternities and 4 sororities. 10% of men and women join. All students must live at home or on campus. No coed dorms. Married-student housing. 82% of students live on campus. Liquor, drugs, gambling prohibited on campus. Class attendance required for freshmen and sophomores. Weekly chapel attendance required. 4 semesters of phys ed required. 9 intercollegiate sports for men, 3 for women; several intramural and club sports. AWISA, NAIA. Student body composition: 6% Black, 1% Hispanic, 92% White, 1% Other. 25% from out of state.

California

CALIFORNIA, UNIVERSITY OF, BERKELEY $/$$

Berkeley 94720, (415) 642-0200
Director of Admissions & Records: Robert L. Bailey

- **Undergraduates:** 11,645m, 9,622w
- **Tuition and Fees (1984–1985):** $1,346.50 (in-state), $4,910.50 (out-of-state)
- **Room and Board (1984–1985):** $3,327
- **Degrees offered:** AB, BS, OD
- **Mean SAT:** 526v, 608m
- **Student-faculty ratio:** 16 to 1
- **Calendar system:** Semester

A public university established in 1868. 1,200-acre urban campus on eastern shore of San Francisco Bay. Bus and rapid transit to San Francisco; air, rail, and bus in San Francisco.

Academic Character WASC and professional accreditation. Semester system, 8-week summer term. Over 100 majors offered in the areas of area studies, anthropolgy, architecture, arts, astronomy, biological sciences, business administration, chemistry, computer science, economics, engineering, environmental studies, film, forestry, geology, health, humanities, classical & modern languages & literatures, mass communications, mathematics, music, nutrition, philosophy & religion, physical education, physics, psychology, rhetoric, social sciences, social welfare, and zoology. Graduate and professional degrees granted. Honors program, Phi Beta Kappa. Cooperative work/study. Preprofessional programs in city & regional planning, education, law, library science, medicine, social welfare. Exchanges and transfers with other universities in the California system, and with professional schools in business administration, forestry, journalism, optometry, and veterinary science. Numerous study abroad programs. AFROTC, NROTC, ROTC. Space Sciences Lab, computer facilities, several research institutes, labs, museums. Law School. 6,000,000-volume library.

Financial CEEB CSS. University scholarships, grants, loans; PELL, SEOG, NDSL, CWS, university work program. Application deadlines November 30 (scholarships), January 15 (loans).

Admissions High school graduation with 15 units required. SAT or ACT, and 3 ACH required. Minimum GPAs and test scores. $25 application fee. Rolling admissions; deadline November 30. $50 deposit required on acceptance of offer of admission. *Early Decision* and informal *Early Entrance* programs. Transfers accepted. Credit possible for CEEB AP exams. Educational Opportunity Program.

Student Life Student government. Men's and Women's Boards. Several student publications. Debate, Radio-TV Theatre, music, dance, and drama groups. Community Project Committee, CalPIRG, Cal Camp. Many other academic, honorary, professional, and special interest organizations. 36 fraternities and 14 sororities, most with houses. 11% of students join. Coed, single-sex, special interest, cooperative, and married-student housing. 28% of students live on campus (including fraternities and sororities). 19 intercollegiate sports for men, 9 for women; intramurals. 5% of students from out of state.

CALIFORNIA, UNIVERSITY OF, DAVIS $

Davis 95616, (916) 752-2971
Registrar & Admissions Officer: Maynard C. Skinner

- **Undergraduates:** 6,565m, 7,265w
- **Tuition and Fees (1984–1985):** $1,287 (in-state), $4,851 (out-of-state)
- **Room and Board (1984–1985):** $2,775
- **Degrees offered:** BA, BS
- **Mean SAT:** 496v, 559m
- **Student-faculty ratio:** 19 to 1
- **Calendar system:** Trimester

A public university established in 1922. 3,700-acre rural campus 13 miles west of Sacramento. Served by air, rail, and bus.

Academic Character WASC and professional accreditation. Trimester system, 2 6-week summer terms. 49 majors offered by the College of Letters & Science, 40 by the College of Agricultural & Environmental Sciences, and 7 by the College of Engineering. Self-designed, dual, and multiple majors. Minors. Distributive requirements. Graduate and professional degrees granted. Independent study, honors program, Phi Beta Kappa, pass/fail, credit by exam, internships. Planned Education Leave and Work-Learn programs. Preprofessional programs in forestry and veterinary science. 2- and 3-year transfer programs with professional schools and other universities in California system. Study abroad in 19 centers. Elementary, secondary, and special education certification. ROTC. Language lab, computer center, art galleries, several research institutes. Law and medical schools. 1,755,000-volume library.

Financial CEEB CSS. University scholarships, grants, loans, Cal grants, deferred payment; PELL, SEOG, NDSL, GSL, CWS. Application deadlines January 15 (institutional scholarships), February 12 (priority: grants, loans, California Student Aid Commission).

Admissions High school graduation with 15 units required. SAT or ACT, and 3 ACH required. Minimum GPAs and test scores. $30 application fee. Rolling admissions; suggest applying after November 1 of 12th year. Deadline November 30. $50 deposit required on acceptance of admissions offer. Admission deferral possible. Transfers accepted. Credit possible for CEEB AP exams. Educational Opportunity Program.

Student Life Associated Students. Newspaper, yearbook, radio station. Several music, dance, film, and drama groups. Many athletic, academic, ethnic, honorary, political, religious, service, and special interest organizations. 19 fraternities and 12 sororities. Coed, special interest, and married-student housing. 35% of students live on campus. 10 intercollegiate sports for men, 7 for women; numerous intramural sports. Student body composition: 9% Asian, 3% Black, 3% Hispanic, 1% Native American, 71% White, 13% Other. 10% from out of state.

CALIFORNIA, UNIVERSITY OF, LOS ANGELES $

405 Hilgard Ave., Los Angeles 90024, (213) 825-3101
Director, Undergraduate Admissions: Rae Lee Siporin

- **Undergraduates:** 11,397m, 13,700w
- **Tuition (1984–1985):** $1,290 (in-state), $4,854 (out-of-state)
- **Room and Board (1984–1985):** $2,340–$2,990

- **Degrees offered:** BA, BS
- **Student-faculty ratio:** 17 to 1
- **Calendar system:** Quarter

A public university established in Los Angeles in 1919. 411-acre urban campus in the Westwood section of L.A. Air, rail, and bus service.

Academic Character WASC and professional accreditation. Quarter system, 2 6-week summer terms. 14 majors offered by the College of Fine Arts, 66 by the College of Letters & Science, 19 by the School of Engineering & Applied Science, and 1 each by the schools of Nursing and Public Health. Self-designed majors. Numerous special programs. Distributive requirements. Graduate and professional degrees granted. Independent study, honors program, Phi Beta Kappa, cooperative work/study. Preprofessional programs in architecture, dentistry, journalism, medicine. 2-2 programs with various schools in criminology, dental hygiene, nursing, optometry, pharmacy, physical therapy, public health. Study abroad. AFROTC, NROTC, ROTC. Computer. 4,346,526-volume library.

Financial University scholarships, grants, loans; PELL, SEOG, NDSL, NSL, FISL, CWS. Application deadline February 1.

Admissions High school graduation with 15 units required. SAT or ACT, and 3 ACH required. Minimum GPAs and test scores. $30 application fee. Rolling admissions. Apply as soon as possible beginning November 1. *Early Entrance* Program. Transfers accepted. Credit possible for CEEB AP exams.

Student Life Associated Students. Newspaper, yearbook. Several music, drama, film, TV, and radio groups. Debate. Many other student organizations. 27 fraternities and 18 sororities, most with houses. 22% of students join. Coed and cooperative dorms. Married-student apartments. 20% of students live on campus. 15 intercollegiate sports for men, 11 for women; several intramurals. AIAW, Pacific-10. Student body composition: 14.4% Asian, 5.3% Black, 1.5% Filipino, 6.7% Hispanic, 0.4% Native American, 70.2% White, 1.5% Other. 14% from out of state.

CALIFORNIA INSTITUTE OF TECHNOLOGY $$$

1201 E. California Blvd., Pasadena 91125, (213) 356-6341
Director of Admissions: Stirling L. Huntley

- **Undergraduates:** 690m, 139w
- **Tuition (1984–1985):** $9,300
- **Room and Board (1984–1985):** $3,500; **Fees:** $84
- **Degrees offered:** BS
- **Mean SAT:** 640v, 760m
- **Student-faculty ratio:** 3 to 1
- **Calendar system:** Quarter

A private institute known as Caltech, established in 1891, became coed in 1970. 82-acre central campus in residential area of Pasadena, ½ mile from downtown. Located 25 miles from Pacific Ocean, ½ hour from Los Angeles.

Academic Character WACS and professional accreditation. Quarter system. Majors offered in applied mathematics, applied physics, astronomy, biology, chemical engineering, chemistry, economics, electrical engineering, engineering & applied science, geochemistry, geology, geophysics, history, independent studies, literature, mathematics, physics, planetary science, and social science. Self-designed majors. Courses in 5 areas of engineering and 13 additional areas. Distributive requirements in 1st year; all graded pass/fail.

Graduate and professional degrees granted. Independent study & research encouraged in all majors. Honors programs. Humanities/Social Science Tutorial program. 5-year BA/BSEng program with 9 colleges including Bryn Mawr. Exchanges with Occidental, Scripps Colleges, and Art Center College of Design. AFROTC & NROTC at USC. Aeronautical, seismological, jet propulsion, marine, and environmental quality labs. Industrial Relations Center. 4 observatories. Computer center. 388,000-volume library.

Financial CEEB CSS. Institute scholarships, grants, loans, Cal grants; PELL, SEOG, NDSL, CWS. Application deadline February 1.

Admissions High school graduation with 15 units required. SAT and 3 ACH required. $25 application fee. Application deadline January 15. $10 fee required on acceptance of offer of admission. *Early Decision* and *Early Entrance* programs. Admission deferral possible. Transfers accepted. Institute has own advanced placement program.

Student Life Student government. Newspaper, literary magazine, yearbook. Drama, art, radio, photography, and several music groups. Elementary & secondary school tutoring. YMCA. Society of Women Engineers. Athletic, academic, political, professional, religious, honorary, and special interest groups. Freshmen urged to live in dorms. Coed, women's, and coop dorms. No married-student housing. 65% of students live on campus. 3 terms of phys ed required. 12 intercollegiate sports for men, 6 for women; men's teams (except for football & wrestling) open to women. Intramurals. SCIAC. Student body composition: 15% Asian, 2% Black, 4% Hispanic, 71% White, 8% Other (Foreign). 63% from out of state.

CALIFORNIA STATE POLYTECHNIC UNIVERSITY $

3801 W. Temple Ave., Pomona 91768, (714) 598-4592
Director of Admissions: Richard G. York

- **Undergraduates:** 9,919m, 6,782w
- **Tuition (1984–1985):** $233 (in-state), $233 + $72 per unit (out-of-state)
- **Room and Board (1984–1985):** $2,820
- **Degrees offered:** BA, BS
- **Mean SAT:** 425v, 499m
- **Student-faculty ratio:** 20 to 1
- **Calendar system:** Quarter

A public university established in 1938, became coed in 1961. 813-acre suburban campus 30 miles from Los Angeles. Air, rail, and bus service.

Academic Character WASC and professional accreditation. Quarter system, summer term. 13 majors offered by the School of Agriculture, 18 by the School of Arts, 6 by the School of Business Administration, 7 by the School of Engineering, 3 by the School of Environmental Design, and 10 by the School of Science. Distributive requirements. GRE required for graduation. Masters degrees granted. Internships, cooperative work/study. Preprofessional programs in dentistry, medicine, veterinary medicine. Southern California Ocean & Desert Studies Consortium. Numerous study abroad programs. Elementary, secondary, and special education certification. ROTC on campus & at Claremont Colleges; AFROTC at UCLA & USC. Extensive agricultural facilities. Computer. 342,000-volume library with microform resources.

Financial CEEB CSS. University scholarships, grants, loans, Cal grants; PELL, SEOG, NDSL, CWS. Application deadline April 15.

Admissions High school graduation with college prep program required. Interview & portfolio required for architecture applicants. SAT or ACT required. Minimum grades and test scores. $30 application fee. Rolling admissions; suggest applying in November. *Early Entrance* Program. Transfers accepted. Credit possible for CEEB AP exams, and for previous military experience. Educational Opportunity Program.

Student Life Student government. Newspaper, literary magazine, yearbook. Several music groups. Arabian horse shows. Drama, debate, religious, and special interest clubs. Fraternities and sororities. Coed and single-sex dorms. No married-student housing. 7% of students live on campus. 8 intercollegiate sports for men, 5 for women; numerous intramurals. AIAW, NCAA, CCAA. Student body composition: 8.1% Asian, 2.7% Black, 8.5% Hispanic, 0.9% Native American, 76.8% White, 3% Other. 1.3% from out of state.

CALIFORNIA STATE UNIVERSITY, CHICO $

1st & Normal Streets, Chico 95929, (916) 895-6116
Director of Admissions: Ken Edson

* **Undergraduates:** 6,342m, 6,328w
* **Tuition and Fees (1984–1985):** $726 (in-state), $3,750 (out-of-state)
* **Room and Board (1984–1985):** $3,060
* **Degrees offered:** BA, BS
* **Mean SAT:** 425v, 470m,   **Mean ACT:** 19.1
* **Student-faculty ratio:** 18 to 1
* **Calendar system:** Semester

A public university founded in 1887. Small city campus and farm located in the Sierra foothills 90 miles north of Sacramento. Air and bus nearby.

Academic Character WASC and professional accreditation. Semester system, winter intersession, 2 5½- and 1 11-week summer terms. Over 70 majors offered in the areas of agriculture, area studies, arts & humanities, biological sciences, business administration, child development, community services, computer science, engineering, home economics, industrial arts & technologies, languages & literatures, mathematics, nursing, physical education, physical sciences, psychology, public administration, social sciences, speech, and vocational education. Self-designed and special majors. Distributive requirements. MA, MS, MBA, MPA granted. Independent study, honors program, cooperative work/study, pass/fail, credit by exam, internships. Preprofessional programs in dentistry, forestry, law, library science, medicine, optometry, pharmacy, physical therapy, theology, veterinary medicine. Exchanges with U of New Hampshire, Center for Intercultural Studies, Eagle Lake Field Station. Study abroad. Elementary, secondary, and special education certification with graduate work. ROTC at UCal, Davis. Computer. Language lab. Media center. 556,277-volume library.

Financial CEEB CSS and ACT FAS. University scholarships, loans, Cal grants; PELL, SEOG, NSS, GSL, NDSL, NSL, CWS. Application deadline March 1.

Admissions High school graduation with college prep program recommended. Furthur requirements for nursing applicants. SAT or ACT required. Minimum grades and test scores. $30 application fee. Rolling admissions; suggest applying soon after November 1. *Early Entrance* Program. Admission deferral possible. Transfers accepted. Credit possible for CEEB AP and CLEP exams. Educational Opportunity Program. Alternative admissions for creative arts applicants.

Student Life Student Association. Newspapers, magazines, radio & TV stations. Drama, debate, several music groups. Community service projects.

Athletic, academic, honorary, religious, and special interest clubs. 12 fraternities, 9 with houses, and 7 sororities, 5 with houses. 5% join. Coed & single-sex dorms, foreign-language houses. No married-student housing. 8% of students live on campus. 11 intercollegiate sports for men, 12 for women; several intramurals. AIAW, NCAA, Far Western Athletic Conference. Student body composition: 2.1% Asian, 2.3% Black, 4% Hispanic, 0.7% Native American, 88.4% White, 2.5% Other. 1% from out of state.

CALIFORNIA STATE UNIVERSITY, LONG BEACH　　　$

1250 Bellflower Blvd., Long Beach 90840, (213) 498-4111
Dean of Admissions & Records: Leonard Kreutner

- **Undergraduates:** 14,707m, 15,492w
- **Tuition (1984–1985):** $693 (in-state), $4,203 (out-of-state)
- **Room and Board (1984–1985):** $3,200
- **Degrees offered:** BA, BS, BMus, BFA, BVEd
- **Student-faculty ratio:** 18 to 1
- **Calendar system:** Semester

A public university established in 1949. 322-acre suburban campus south of Los Angeles. Air, rail, and bus in LA.

Academic Character WASC and professional accreditation. Semester system, 3 summer terms. 68 majors offered in the areas of arts, business & management, communications, education, engineering, health sciences, home economics, humanities, industrial arts, modern languages & literatures, music, recreation, sciences, and social sciences. Minors in religious studies, women's studies. Certificates in over 15 interdisciplinary areas. Distributive requirements. Masters degrees granted. Independent study, honors program, Phi Beta Kappa, pass/fail, cooperative work/study, credit by exam. Preprofessional programs in dentistry, education, law, medicine. Educational Participation in the Community program. Several study abroad programs. AFROTC. ROTC. Over 773,610-volume library.

Financial PELL, SEOG, NDSL, FISL, NSL, CWS. Application deadline March 15.

Admissions High school graduation with college prep program recommended. SAT or ACT required. Minimum grades and test scores. $30 application fee. Rolling admissions; suggest applying soon after November 1, and before November 30. *Concurrent Enrollment* Program. Transfers accepted. Credit possible for CEEB AP exams. Educational Opportunity Program.

Student Life Student government. Newspaper, literary magazine, yearbook, radio station. Music, dance, & drama groups. Academic, athletic, service, honorary, political, religious, and special interest clubs. 12 fraternities and 7 sororities. Single students under 18 urged to live on campus. Coed and single-sex dorms. 3% of students live on campus. 12 intercollegiate sports for men, 8 for women, and coed archery, badminton, fencing; several intramurals. AIAW, NCAA, Pacific Coast Athletic Conference. Student body composition: 12% Asian, 8% Black, 7% Hispanic, 1% Native American, 56% White, 16% Other. 3% from out of state.

CALIFORNIA STATE UNIVERSITY, NORTHRIDGE　　　$

18111 Nordhoff St., Northridge 91330, (213) 885-1200
Director of Admissions & Records: Ned Reynolds

- **Undergraduates:** 24,568m, 29,644w
- **Tuition (1984–1985):** $708 (in-state), $3,240 (out-of-state)
- **Room and Board (1984–1985):** $3,960
- **Degrees offered:** BA, BS
- **Student-faculty ratio:** 34 to 1
- **Calendar system:** Semester

A public university established in 1958. 350-acre suburban campus in the San Fernando Valley, 30 miles from downtown Los Angeles. Air, rail, and bus in LA. **Academic Character** WASC and professional accreditation. Semester system, 2 6-week summer terms. 43 majors offered in the fields of arts, business administration, child development, communications, communicative disorders, computer science, engineering, health science, home economics, humanities, languages & literatures, music, psychology, recreation, sciences, social sciences. Interdisciplinary majors and minors. Distributive requirements. MA, MS, MBA, MPA, MPH granted. Independent study, pass/fail, credit by exam, internships. Preprofessional programs in dentistry, law, medicine, optometry, physical therapy. Concurrent enrollment with other state schools. Study abroad in Brazil, Canada, China, Europe, Israel, Mexico, New Zealand, Peru. Elementary, secondary, and special education certification. AFROTC at Loyola-Marymount, USC, UCLA; NROTC, ROTC at UCLA. Art gallery. Computer center. Over 800,000-volume library. **Financial** CEEB CSS. University scholarships, loans, Cal grants; PELL, SEOG, NDSL, FISL, GSL, CWS. Priority application deadline March 1. **Admissions** High school graduation with college prep program recommended. SAT or ACT required. Minimum grades and test scores. Some programs closed to non-residents. $30 application fee. Rolling admissions; suggest applying soon after November 1, and before November 30. *Early Decision, Early Admission, Concurrent Enrollment* programs. Transfers accepted. Credit possible for CEEB AP and CLEP exams. University has own advanced placement exams. Educational Opportunity Program. **Student Life** Student government. Newspaper, literary magazine, radio station. Music groups. Intercollegiate debate. Academic, athletic, service, outing, honorary, religious, and special interest clubs. 11 fraternities and 7 sororities, all with houses. 1% of men and women join. Campus apartments. 1% of students live on campus. Liquor prohibited on campus. 10 intercollegiate sports for men, 9 for women; intramural and club sports. AIAW, NCAA, California Collegiate Athletic Association. Student body composition: 7.2% Asian, 5.1% Black, 7.2% Hispanic, 0.7% Native American, 61.4% White, 18.4% Other. 3% from out of state.

HARVEY MUDD COLLEGE $$$

Claremont 91711, (714) 621-8000, ext. 3843
Dean of Admission & Financial Aid: Duncan C. Murdoch

- **Undergraduates:** 440m, 80w
- **Tuition (1984–1985):** $8,500
- **Room and Board (1984–1985):** $3,650; **Fees:** $360
- **Degrees offered:** BS
- **Mean SAT:** 610v, 720m
- **Student-faculty ratio:** 8 to 1
- **Calendar system:** Semester

A private college established in 1955. 18-acre suburban campus at the foot of the San Gabriel Mountains, 35 miles east of Los Angeles. Bus service. Rail 4 miles away. Airport 10 miles away.

Academic Character WASC and professional accreditation. Semester system. Majors offered in chemistry, engineering, mathematics, physics. Self-designed majors, interdisciplinary programs. Courses in composition, drama, economics, English & American literature, government, history, philosophy, psychology. Courses available at other Claremont colleges. Distributive requirements. Independent study/original lab research in 3rd & 4th years. Pass/fail. 5-year MEng program. Program leading to FAA Private Pilot License. ROTC; AFROTC with USC. Engineering Clinic. Black Studies and Chicano Studies Centers. Over 1,500,000-volume combined libraries.

Financial CEEB CSS. College scholarships, grants, loans, deferred payment; PELL, SEOG, NDSL, FISL, GSL, CWS. File FAF (for scholarships) by February 1.

Admissions High school graduation with 16 units required. Interview encouraged. SAT and 3 ACH required. $25 application fee. Suggest applying between October 1 and February 15. $50 deposit required on acceptance of admissions offer. *Early Decision,* limited *Early Entrance* programs. Admission deferral possible. Few transfers accepted. Credit possible for CEEB AP exams.

Student Life Student government. Newspaper, yearbook. Music and drama groups. Debate. Political, athletic, service, and special interest organizations. Freshmen must live on campus. Coed dorms. Some women live at Scripps. 95% of students live on campus. Firearms, fireworks, and public possession of liquor prohibited. 3 semesters of phys ed required. 13 intercollegiate sports for men (with Claremont McKenna), 6 for women (with Scripps and Claremont McKenna); intramurals. AIAW, NCAA, SCIAC. Student body composition: 23% Asian, 1% Black, 2% Hispanic, 1% Native American, 73% White. 40% from out of state.

HUMBOLDT STATE UNIVERSITY $

Arcata 95521, (707) 826-3421
Dean of Admissions & Records: Robert L. Hannigan

- **Undergraduates:** 2,414m, 2,217w
- **Tuition (1984–1985):** 0 (in-state), $3,510 (out-of-state)
- **Room and Board (1984–1985):** $2,948;   **Fees:** $663
- **Degrees offered:** BA, BS
- **Mean SAT:** 467v, 496m,   **Mean ACT:** 20.4
- **Student-faculty ratio:** 17 to 1
- **Calendar system:** Quarter

A public university established in 1913. 142-acre rural campus overlooking a small seacoast town 275 miles north of San Francisco. Air and bus service.

Academic Character WASC and professional accreditation. Quarter system, summer terms. Over 70 majors offered in the areas of arts, business administration, environmental & natural resources, home economics, humanities, industrial arts, journalism, languages & literatures, nursing, oceanography, physical education, sciences, social sciences, social welfare, speech, and wildlife management. Special & self-designed majors. Distributive requirements. MA, MS, MBA, MFA granted. Independent study, honors program, pass/fail, cooperative work/study, internships. Preprofessional programs in dentistry, law, medicine, veterinary medicine.

Indian Teacher Education Project, Native American Education Program in Natural Resources. National Student Exchange program. Study abroad in 24 locations. Elementary, secondary, services, and special education certification. Forest & marine science labs. Computer center, language lab. 280,000-volume library.

Financial CEEB CSS. University scholarships, BIA & Cal grants; PELL, SEOG, NSS, NDSL, GSL, NSL, CWS. Priority application deadline March 1. **Admissions** High school graduation with college prep program recommended. SAT or ACT required. Minimum grades and test scores. $25 application fee. Rolling admissions; suggest applying soon after November 1, and before November 30. *Early Decision* and *Concurrent Enrollment* programs. Transfers accepted. Credit possible for CEEB AP and CLEP exams. Educational Opportunity Program. Special programs for Native Americans. **Student Life** Student government. Newspaper, magazines, radio station. Music & theatre groups. Intercollegiate debate. Academic, athletic, ethnic, honorary, religious, social, and special interest clubs. Coed and single-sex dorms. No married-student housing. 15% of students live on campus. 6 intercollegiate sports for men, 6 for women; intramurals. NCAA, Northern California Athletic Conference. Student body composition: 2% Asian, 0.5% Black, 2.5% Hispanic, 1.5% Native American, 93.5% White. 2% from out of state.

MILLS COLLEGE $$$

Oakland 94613, (415) 430-2135
Director of Admissions: Gail Berson Weaver

- **Undergraduates:** 715w
- **Tuition (1984–1985):** $7,700
- **Room and Board (1984–1985):** $3,800;   **Fees:** $245
- **Degrees offered:** BA
- **Mean SAT:** 520v, 520m
- **Student-faculty ratio:** 10 to 1
- **Calendar system:** Semester

A private women's college founded in 1852. Graduate programs coed. 127-acre urban campus 18 miles east of San Francisco and 8 miles south of Berkeley. Air, rail, and bus service.

Academic Character WASC accreditation. Semester system. Majors offered in administration & legal processes, American civilization, art, biochemistry, biology, chemistry, child development, communication, computer science, dance, dramatic arts, economics, English, ethnic studies, fine arts, French, French studies, general studies, German studies, government, Hispanic studies, history, international relations, mathematics, music, philosophy, physical science, psychology, sociology, western literature, and women's studies. Interdisciplinary & self-designed majors. MA, MFA granted. Independent study, honors program, Phi Beta Kappa, pass/fail, internships. Preprofessional programs in medicine, health sciences, law. 3-2 engineering programs with UCal (Berkeley), Stanford, Boston U, Washington U (St. Louis). 5-yr BA/MS in statistics or computer science with Stanford. Cross-registration with Berkeley, California College of Arts & Crafts, California State U (Hayward), College of Alameda, Graduate Theological Union, and Holy Names, Merritt, and St. Mary's Colleges. Exchanges with Fisk and Howard Universities, and Agnes Scott, Barnard, Hollins, Manhattanville,

Mt. Holyoke, Simmons, Skidmore, Spelman, Swarthmore, Wellesley, and Wheaton Colleges. Washington Semester. Several study abroad programs. Early childhood, elementary, and secondary education certification. AFROTC, NROTC, ROTC at Berkeley. Art gallery, language lab. 185,000-volume library.

Financial CEEB CSS. College scholarships, grants, music & middle-income awards, loans, deferred payment; PELL, SEOG, Cal grants, NDL, FISL, CWS. Application deadline February 1.

Admissions High school graduation with 16 units required. Interview encouraged. SAT or ACT required. 3 ACH recommended. $25 application fee. Suggest applying early in 12th year; deadline February 1. $200 deposit required on acceptance of admissions offer. *Early Decision* and *Early Admission* programs. Admission deferral possible. Transfers accepted. Credit possible for CEEB AP exams. Probationary admission possible for underqualified students.

Student Life Student government. Newspaper, literary magazine, yearbook. Music, dance, and drama groups. Academic, ethnic, political, professional, religious, women's, and special interest groups. Single students under 21 must live at home or on campus. Dorms & apartments. Some married-student housing. 80% of students live on campus. Honor system. 6 intercollegiate sports for women; intramurals. AIAW, Redwood Conference. Student body composition: 13.5% Asian, 11.5% Black, 4% Hispanic, 1% Native American, 68.5% White, 1.5% Other. 35% from out of state.

NORTHROP UNIVERSITY $$/$$$

5800 West Arbor Vitae St., Inglewood 90306, (213) 641-3470
Director of Admissions: Judson W. Staples

- **Undergraduates:** 1,333m, 83w
- **Tuition (1984–1985):** $6,075
- **Room and Board (1984–1985):** $3,850–$5,030
- **Degrees offered:** BSAE, BSEE, BSETAM, BSCS
- **Mean SAT:** 450v, 525m
- **Student-faculty ratio:** 17 to 1
- **Calendar system:** Quarter

A private engineering university founded in 1943. 18-acre urban campus 10 miles southwest of Los Angeles. Air, rail, and bus in LA.

Academic Character WASC and professional accreditation. Quarter system, 11-week summer term. Majors offered in aerospace engineering, aircraft/avionics, aircraft maintenance, business administration, computer science, electronic engineering, engineering technology/manufacturing management, mechanical/civil engineering, mechanical/electrical engineering, mechanical/energy systems engineering, and mechanical engineering. Associate degrees in aircraft/avionics technology, aircraft maintenance technology, computer science technology. Technical certificate programs. Distributive requirements. Masters degrees granted. Honors program, cooperative work/study. Programs with NASA and others. AFROTC at Loyola Marymount, USC; NROTC, ROTC at UCLA. Several labs, workshops, computers. 63,802-volume library.

Financial CEEB CSS and ACT FAS. University scholarships, grants, loans, Cal grants; PELL, SEOG, NDSL, FISL, CWS. Priority application deadline April 30.

Admissions High school graduation required. GED accepted for certificate programs. SAT or ACT required. $25 application fee. Rolling admissions; suggest applying by June. Deadline in August. $75 deposit required on acceptance of admissions offer. *Early Decision* and *Early Entrance* programs. Transfers accepted. Credit possible for CEEB CLEP exams.

Student Life Student government. Newspaper, literary magazine. Flying, karate clubs. Professional, honorary, ethnic, international, religious, and special interest groups. 2 fraternities, 1 with house. 1% of men join. Coed, single-sex, and special interest housing. No married-student housing. 20% of students live on campus. Class attendance required. Intramurals. Student body composition: 17% Asian, 8% Black, 41% Foreign, 8% Hispanic, 1% Native American, 25% White. 80% from out of state.

PEPPERDINE UNIVERSITY $$$

24255 Pacific Coast Highway, Malibu 90265, (213) 456-4392
Dean of Admissions: Robert L. Fraley

- **Undergraduates:** 1,213m, 1,303w
- **Tuition (1984–1985):** $8,416
- **Room and Board (1984–1985):** $3,650; **Fees:** $15
- **Degrees offered:** BA, BS, BSM
- **Mean SAT:** 494v, 523m, **Mean ACT:** 23
- **Student-faculty ratio:** 14 to 1
- **Calendar system:** Trimester

A private university founded in 1937, affiliated with the Church of Christ. 819-acre rural Malibu campus, established in 1972, houses Seaver College and the School of Law in the mountains overlooking Malibu Beach. Graduate School of Education & Psychology and School of Business & Management located at Los Angeles campus. Air, rail, and bus 30 miles away in LA.

Academic Character WASC and professional accreditation. Trimester system, with optional 2-part spring term ending August 5. 2 majors offered by the business division, 10 by communication, 10 by humanities & fine arts, 8 by natural sciences, 1 by religion, and 8 by social science/teacher education. Distributives and 2 religion courses required. Undergraduate Assessment Exam required for seniors in their major field. Graduate and professional degrees granted. Independent study, credit by exam. Washington trimester. Year-in-Europe program. Elementary and secondary education certification. ROTC at UCLA; AFROTC at USC. Computer center. 403,657-volume libraries.

Financial CEEB CSS and ACT FAS. University scholarhips, loans, Cal grants, deferred payment; PELL, SEOG, NDSL, FISL, GSL, CWS. Application deadlines February 12 (Cal grants), April 1 (other aid).

Admissions High school graduation with 15 units required. Interview encouraged. SAT or ACT required. $25 application fee. Rolling admissions; deadline April 5. $250 deposit required on acceptance of admissions offer (May 1). *Early Decision* Program. Transfers accepted. Credit possible for CEEB AP, CLEP, and university exams.

Student Life Student government. Newspaper, magazines, yearbook, radio & TV stations. Debate, drama, music groups. Academic, service, and special interest clubs. 1st & 2nd-year students under 21 must live at home or on campus. No coed dorms. Apartments for upperclassmen. 60% of students live on campus. Liquor, drugs, firearms, gambling, profanity prohibited on campus. Weekly chapel attendance required. 4 trimesters of phys ed required.

6 intercollegiate sports for men, 3 for women; many intramurals. AIAW, NCAA, WCAC. Student body composition: 6% Asian, 11% Black, 5% Hispanic, 0.5% Native American, 76.5% White, 1% Other. 33% from out of state.

POMONA COLLEGE $$$

Claremont 91711, (714) 621-8134
Dean of Admissions: R. Fred Zuker

- **Undergraduates:** 660m, 681w
- **Tuition (1984–1985):** $8,550
- **Room and Board (1984–1985):** $3,600;   **Fees:** $242
- **Degrees offered:** BA
- **Mean SAT:** 600v, 630m,   **Mean ACT:** 29
- **Student-faculty ratio:** 10 to 1
- **Calendar system:** Semester

A private liberal arts college founded in 1887. 160-acre suburban campus 35 minutes from Los Angeles. Bus service. Rail 4 miles away. Airport 10 miles away.

Academic Character WASC accreditation. Semester system, limited summer term. Majors offered in American studies, anthropology, art, Asian studies, biology, chemistry, classics, economics, English, film studies, geology, government, history, international relations, linguistics, mathematics, modern languages & literature, music, philosophy, physics, psychology, religion, sociology, theater. Self-designed majors. Courses in astronomy, Black studies, Chicano studies, computer science, dance, education, military science, public policy, women's studies. Interdisciplinary courses. Distributive requirements. Senior project, thesis, or comprehensive exam required in major field. Independent study, Phi Beta Kappa, pass/fail, internships. Preprofessional programs in allied health fields, business, education, engineering, law, medicine, public affairs, social work, and theology. 3-2 engineering programs with Caltech and Washington U (St. Louis). Exchanges with Caltech, Colby (Maine), Smith, Swarthmore, and Fisk U (Tenn). Washington Semester. Several study abroad programs. Elementary and secondary education certification with Claremont Graduate School. ROTC. Research institutes, botanic garden, language lab, computer. Over 1,500,000-volume combined libraries.

Financial CEEB CSS. College scholarships, grants, loans, Cal grants, deferred payment; PELL, SEOG, NDSL, GSL, FISL, CWS. Application deadline February 1.

Admissions High school graduation with college prep program expected. Interview encouraged. SAT or ACT required. 3 ACH recommended. $25 application fee. Suggest applying early in 12th year; deadline February 1. $100 deposit required on acceptance of admissions offer. *Early Entrance* and *Early Decision* programs. Admission deferral possible. Transfers accepted. Credit possible for CEEB AP and CLEP exams.

Student Life Student government. Several publications. Radio station. Music, dance, drama groups. Political, honorary, religious, academic, service, and special interest organizations. 7 fraternities (3 coed) without houses. 25% of students join. Freshmen must live at home or on campus. Coed and single-sex dorms. Language clusters. No married-student housing. 90% of students live on campus. 1 semester of phys ed required. 11 intercollegiate sports for men, 6 for women; several club and intramural sports. AIAW, NAIA, NCAA,

SCIAC. Student body composition: 12% Asian, 3% Black, 4% Hispanic, 81% White. 44% from out of state.

SANTA CLARA, UNIVERSITY OF $$

Santa Clara 95053, (408) 984-4288
Director of Admissions: Daniel J. Saracino

- **Undergraduates:** 1,911m, 1,695w
- **Tuition (1984–1985):** $6,111
- **Room and Board (1984–1985):** $3,303
- **Degrees offered:** BA, BS
- **Mean SAT:** 500v, 572m
- **Student-faculty ratio:** 18 to 1
- **Calendar system:** Trimester

A private Jesuit university established in 1851, became coed in 1961. 67-acre suburban campus 46 miles south of San Francisco. Air, rail, and bus service.
Academic Character WASC and professional accreditation. Trimester system, 6-week summer term. The College of Arts & Sciences offers 14 majors for a BA and 11 majors for a BS, including a BSChem. The School of Business offers a BSCommerce in accounting, economics, finance, management, marketing, and quantitative methods. The School of Engineering offers a BS in civil engineering, computer science, engineering, electrical engineering, and mechanical engineering. Interdisciplinary and self-designed majors. Ethnic and women's studies programs. Distributives and 3 religion courses required. Thesis may be required. Masters, JD, PhD granted. 1-year paralegal certificate program. Independent study, honors program, Phi Beta Kappa, pass/fail, credit by exam. Preprofessional programs in dentistry, law, business, and medicine. Washington and UN Semesters. Study abroad in Europe and Asia. 5-year programs for elementary, secondary, and special education certification. ROTC. Language lab, computer, TV studio. 655,000-volume library.
Financial CEEB CSS. University scholarships, grants, loans, ROTC scholarships, Cal grants; PELL, SEOG, NDSL, GSL, FISL, CWS. Application deadline March 1.
Admissions High school graduation with 16 units required. Interview encouraged. SAT required. $25 application fee. Rolling admissions; deadline March 1. $100 deposit required on acceptance of admissions offer. Transfers accepted. Credit possible for CEEB AP exams.
Student Life Student government. Newspaper, literary magazine, yearbook, radio station. Dance, drama, several music groups. Intercollegiate debate. Academic, honorary, religious, service, and special interest clubs. 1 fraternity and 2 sororities. Coed and single-sex dorms, apartments. No married-student housing. 54% of students live on campus. Hazing prohibited. 12 intercollegiate sports for men, 7 for women; several intramurals. AIAW, NCAA, WCAC. Student body composition: 10% Asian, 2% Black, 6% Foreign, 5% Hispanic, 1% Native American, 76% White. 23% from out of state.

SOUTHERN CALIFORNIA, UNIVERSITY OF $$$

University Park, Los Angeles 90007, (213) 743-2311
Dean of Admissions: Jay Berger

- **Undergraduates:** 7,966m, 5,312w
- **Tuition (1984–1985):** $7,770
- **Room and Board (1984–1985):** $3,450;   **Fees:** $158
- **Degrees offered:** AB, BS, BArch, BFA, BMus, BSN, BSDental Hygiene
- **Mean SAT:** 473v, 540m,   **Mean ACT:** 25
- **Student-faculty ratio:** 14 to 1
- **Calendar system:** Semester

A private university established in 1880. 150-acre urban campus. Air, rail, and bus service.

Academic Character WASC and professional accreditation. Semester system, summer terms. Over 70 majors offered in the areas of anthropology, architecture, area studies, arts, broadcasting, business administration, cinema, communication arts & sciences, computer science, dental hygiene, engineering, humanities, languages & literatures, mathematics, music, nursing, occupational therapy, physical education, psychology, public administration, sciences, social sciences, and sports information. Individual & interdepartmental majors. Courses in other areas including Arabic & Hebrew. Distributive requirements. Graduate & professional degrees granted. Independent study, honors programs, Phi Beta Kappa, pass/fail, internships. Theatre & cinema workshops. 3-2 AB/BS engineering program. Admission to School of Pharmacy after 2 undergraduate years. Concurrent enrollment with Hebrew Union College. Washington and other semester programs. Study abroad in Costa Rica, England, Israel, Japan, Spain. 5-year programs for elementary, secondary, and special education certification. AFROTC, NROTC, ROTC. Language labs. 2,105,389-volume library.

Financial CEEB CSS. University & ROTC scholarships, handicapped student scholarship, Cal grants, deferred payment; PELL, SEOG, NDSL, GSL, CWS, university work program. Priority application deadline January 1.

Admissions High school graduation with 12 units required. Auditions required for music & drama majors. SAT or ACT required. $35 application fee. Rolling admissions; priority application deadline December 31. Deadline May 1. $50 deposit required on acceptance of admissions offer (May 1). *Early Entrance* Program. Transfers accepted. Credit possible for CEEB AP and CLEP exams. Special program for promising students with low GPA/test scores.

Student Life Student Senate. Newspaper, magazines, yearbook, radio station. Numerous music groups. Debate & drama groups. Women's center. Academic, professional, service, and special interest clubs. 25 fraternities, 23 with houses, and 13 sororities with houses. 22% of students join. Coed, single-sex, special interest, and married-student housing. 33% of students live on campus. No liquor on campus. 17 intercollegiate sports; many intramurals. NCAA, WCAA. Student body composition: 5.8% Black, 5.4% Hispanic, 0.4% Native American, 65.1% White, 23.3% Other. 30% from out of state.

STANFORD UNIVERSITY $$$

Stanford 94305, (415) 497-2091
Dean of Admissions: Fred A. Hargadon

- **Undergraduates:** 3,736m, 2,818w
- **Tuition (1984–1985):** $9,705
- **Room and Board (1984–1985):** $4,146
- **Degrees offered:** AB, BS, BAS

- **Student-faculty ratio:** 10 to 1
- **Calendar system:** Quarter

A private university established in 1891. 3,800-acre campus in the small city of Palo Alto, 30 miles south of San Francisco. Rail and bus service; airport 18 miles away.

Academic Character WASC and professional accreditation. Quarter system, 8-week summer term. Majors offered in African & Afro-American studies, American studies, anthropology, applied earth sciences (3), art (2), biological sciences, chemistry, Chinese, classics, communication, comparative literature, drama, East Asian studies, economics, engineering (8), English, French, geology, geophysics, German studies, history, human biology, humanities, international relations, Italian, Japanese, Latin American studies, linguistics, mathematical sciences, mathematics, medical microbiology, medieval studies, music, philosophy, physics, political science, psychology, religious studies, Slavic languages & literatures, sociology, Spanish, statistics, and science, technology & society. Self-designed, combined, interdisciplinary majors. Courses in astronomy, British studies, computer science, feminist studies, modern thought & literature, Portuguese, social thought & institutions, urban studies. Distributive requirements. Graduate and professional degrees granted. Independent study, honors programs, Phi Beta Kappa, pass/fail, internships. Dual degree and 3-2 programs. Exchange with Howard U. Numerous study abroad programs. Elementary, secondary, and special education certification. AFROTC at San Jose State; NROTC at UCal (Berkeley); ROTC at Santa Clara. Food Research Institute, computer center. 4,700,000-volume library.

Financial CEEB CSS. University scholarships, grants, loans, deferred payment; PELL, SEOG, NDSL, FISL, CWS. Scholarship application deadline February 1.

Admissions Strong high school preparation recommended. SAT required; ACT may be accepted. ACH strongly recommended. $30 application fee. Suggest applying as early as possible. Deadline January 1. $125 deposit required on acceptance of admissions offer. Admission deferral possible. Transfers accepted. Credit possible for CEEB AP exams.

Student Life Student government. Newspaper, literary magazine, yearbook, radio station. Drama, debate, several music groups. Academic, honorary, political, and special interest groups. 13 fraternities with houses and 6 sororities without houses. 15% of men and 10% of women join. Freshmen must live on campus. Single-sex, coed, special-interest, cooperative housing. Married-student apartments. 80% of students live on campus. 14 intercollegiate sports for men, 9 for women; intramurals. AIAW, NCAA, Athletic Association of Western Universities. Student body composition: 6% Asian, 7% Black, 7% Hispanic, 1% Native American, 79% White. 55% from out of state.

Colorado

COLORADO, UNIVERSITY OF, BOULDER $/$$

Boulder 80309, (303) 492-6301
Director of Admissions: Millard Storey

- Undergraduates: 9,670m, 8,315w
- Tuition (1984–1985): $1,214 (in-state), $5,296 (out-of-state)
- Room and Board (1984–1985): $2,606;   Fees: $260
- Degrees offered: BS, BA
- Mean SAT: 491v, 571w,   Mean ACT: 24
- Student-faculty ratio: 20 to 1
- Calendar system: Semester

A public university established in 1876. 600-acre campus in a small city environment 25 miles northwest of Denver. Bus to Denver.

Academic Character NCACS and professional accreditation. Semester system, 10-week summer term. 51 majors offered by the College of Arts and Sciences, 13 by the College of Business Administration, 3 by the School of Education, 11 by the College of Engineering and Applied Science, 3 by the School of Journalism, 15 by the College of Music, 1 by the College of Environmental Design, and 1 by the School of Pharmacy. Self-designed majors. Graduate & professional degrees granted. Independent study, honors program, Phi Beta Kappa, cooperative work/study, pass/fail. Preprofessional programs in child health, dentistry, journalism, medical technology, medicine, nursing, pharmacy, and physical therapy. Dual degree programs, including 5-year engineering/business BS. Study abroad. Elementary and secondary education certification. AFROTC, NROTC, ROTC. Computer center. Language lab. Planetarium. 1,880,000-volume library with microform resources.

Financial ACT FAS. University scholarships, grants, loans, state grants, deferred payment; PELL, SEOG, NDSL, GSL, CWS, university work-study program. Preferred application deadline March 1.

Admissions High school graduation with 15-16 units required. GED accepted. Audition required for College of Music. SAT or ACT required. $20 application fee. Rolling admissions. Apply between October 1 and May 1; non-resident quote usually filled by March. Confirmation deposit required. *Early Entrance* Program. Transfers accepted. Credit possible for CEEB AP and CLEP exams. EOP for minority students.

Student Life Student Union. Daily newspaper, yearbook, literary magazine. Several music, dance, and drama groups. Debate. Religious, service, academic, and special interest clubs. 18 fraternities and 11 sororities, all with houses. 10% of men and 15% of women join. Freshmen under 20 must live at home or on campus. 21 coed and single-sex dorms, some with language floors. 900 married-student apartments. 25% of students live on campus. One year of phys ed required. Large intercollegiate, club, and intramural sports programs. AIAW, NCAA, Big 8 Conference. Student body composition: 2% Asian, 2% Black, 3% Hispanic, 1% Native American, 85% White, 7% Other. 33% from out of state.

COLORADO COLLEGE $$

Colorado Springs 80903, (303) 473-2233
Director of Admissions: Richard E. Wood

- **Undergraduates:** 925m, 925w
- **Tuition (1984–1985):** $7,000
- **Room and Board (1984–1985):** $2,400
- **Degrees offered:** BA
- **Mean SAT:** 550v, 585m,   **Mean ACT:** 25
- **Student-faculty ratio:** 14 to 1
- **Calendar system:** Blocks (one course at a time)

A private college founded in 1874. 79-acre urban campus 70 miles south of Denver. Air and bus service.

Academic Character NCACS and professional accreditation. Modular calendar (4 blocks first semester, 5 second), 8-week summer term. Majors offered in anthropology, art, biology, business economics, chemistry, classics, economics, English, French, fine arts (drama), geology, German, history, liberal arts & sciences, mathematics, music, philosophy, physics, political economy, political science, psychology, religion, sociology, and Spanish. 3-1 medical technology major. Self-designed and double majors. Interdisciplinary programs. Courses in 6 additional areas. Distributive requirements. Exam and/or GRE required in some majors. MAT granted. Independent study, seminars, research stressed. Phi Beta Kappa, cooperative work/study, pass/no credit, internships. 3-2 program in forestry with Duke. 2-2 medical technology and nursing programs with Rush U. 5-yr engineering programs with 4 other colleges. 6-yr BA/JD program with Columbia U. Numerous cooperative programs with schools throughout the country. Study abroad. Elementary and secondary education certification. ROTC at U of Southern Colorado. Computer services. Language lab. 300,000-volume library.

Financial CEEB CSS and ACT FAS. College scholarships, grants, loans, deferred payment; PELL, SEOG, NDSL, GSL, CWS. Application deadline February 15.

Admissions High school graduation with minimum 15 units expected. ACT or SAT required. $20 application fee. Application deadline February 15. $100 tuition and $50 room deposits required on acceptance of admissions offer. *Early Action* decisions made on an individual basis. Admission deferral possible. Transfers accepted. Credit possible for CEEB AP exams.

Student Life Campus government. Newspaper, yearbook, literary magazine, radio station. Music and drama groups. Debate. Mountain Club. Women's Commission. Ethnic, honorary, academic, professional, political, and religious groups. 5 fraternities with houses; 4 sororities without houses. 33% of students join. Seniors, veterans, and married students may live off campus. Coed and single-sex dorms. Language houses. 70% of students live on campus. 3.2% beer allowed on campus. 14 intercollegiate sports for men, 9 for women; extensive intramural program. AIAW, NAIA, NCAA, WCHA. Student body composition: 2% Asian, 3% Black, 4% Hispanic, 1% Native American, 90% White. 63% from out of state.

COLORADO SCHOOL OF MINES $/$$

Golden 80401, (303) 279-0300
Director of Admissions: A. William Young

- **Undergraduates:** 1,840m, 460w
- **Tuition (1984–1985):** $2,310 (in-state), $6,318 (out-of-state)
- **Room and Board (1984–1985):** $2,900; **Fees:** $310
- **Degrees offered:** BS in engineering specializations
- **Mean SAT:** 535v, 640m, **Mean ACT:** 26
- **Student-faculty ratio:** 16 to 1
- **Calendar system:** Semester

A public college established in 1874. 207-acre campus in the small town of Golden, 13 miles west of Denver. Air, rail, and bus in Denver.
Academic Character NCACS and professional accreditation. Semester system, 6-week field summer term, 8-week academic summer term. Majors offered in chemical & petroleum-refining engineering, geological engineering, geophysical engineering, metallurgical engineering, mineral engineering (civil, electrical, mechanical), mineral engineering chemistry, mineral engineering mathematics, mineral engineering physics, mining engineering, and petroleum engineering. Minors offered in some major fields and in environmental science and mineral economics. Courses in area studies, economics, English, German, history, philosophy, psychology, Russian, sociology, Spanish. 30 hours in 300 and 400 series technical courses required. MS, ME, PhD granted. Honors program. Cooperative work/study. Geophysics field camp 90 miles away in Fairplay. Petroleum field camp 280 miles away in Rangeley. Experimental mine 25 miles away in Idaho Springs. Colorado Energy Research and other institutes. ROTC; AFROTC & NROTC at UCol, Boulder. Computer center. 215,000-volume library.
Financial ACT FAS. College scholarships, grants, loans; PELL, SEOG, NDSL, CWS, state work program. Preferred application deadline March 5.
Admissions High school graduation with 15½ units required. GED accepted. SAT or ACT required. $10 application fee for out-of-state students. Rolling admissions; suggest applying by April 1. Application deadline is 21 days before registration. $50 room deposit required on acceptance of admissions offer ($25 refundable until August 1). *Early Entrance* Program. Transfers accepted. Credit possible for CEEB AP and CLEP exams. Summer Intensive English program for foreign students.
Student Life Student government. Newspaper, yearbook, press club, radio club. Band and chorus. Ski club. Engineering societies. Religious, service, academic, and special interest groups. 6 fraternities, all with houses; 35% of men join. 2 sororities without houses. Coed and single-sex dorms. Married-student apartments. 25% of students live on campus. Class attendance required. 4 semesters of phys ed required. 14 intercollegiate sports for men, 2 for women; intramurals. AIAW, NAIA, NCAA, Rocky Mountain Athletic Conference. Student body composition: 2% Asian, 1% Black, 2% Hispanic, 95% White. 30% from out of state.

COLORADO STATE UNIVERSITY $

Fort Collins 80523, (303) 491-7201
Director of Admissions: John F. Kennedy

- **Undergraduates:** 7,641m, 7,610w
- **Tuition (1984–1985):** $1,159 (in-state), $4,411 (out-of-state)
- **Room and Board (1984–1985):** $2,500; **Fees:** $287
- **Degrees offered:** BS, BA, BAEd, BFA, BMus
- **Mean SAT:** 466v, 524m, **Mean ACT:** 22.7

- **Student-faculty ratio:** 18 to 1
- **Calendar system:** Semester

A public land-grant university established in 1870. 400-acre campus in the small city of Fort Collins, 65 miles north of Denver. Rail and bus service.
Academic Character NCACS and professional accreditation. Semester system, 4-, 8-, and 12-week summer terms, interim. 91 majors offered by the colleges of Arts, Humanities & Social Science, Natural Science, Agriculture, Business, Engineering, Forestry & Natural Resources, Home Economics, Veterinary Medicine & Biomedical Sciences, and Professional Studies. Minors. Interdisciplinary programs in 8 areas. Distributive requirements. Graduate and professional degrees granted. Independent study, honors program, Phi Beta Kappa, cooperative work/study, pass/fail, internships. Preprofessional program in veterinary science. Study abroad. Elementary, secondary, art, music, and physical education certification. ROTC, AFROTC. Language lab. Computer center. Agricultural Experiment Station research done on campus with 8 off-campus stations in Colorado. 1,200,000-volume library.
Financial ACT FAS. University scholarships, grants, loans, state grants; PELL, SEOG, NDSL, GSL, CWS. Preferred application deadline April 1.
Admissions High school graduation with 15 units required. Additional requirements for some programs. GED accepted. SAT or ACT required. $15 application fee. Rolling admissions; suggest applying early in 12th year. *Early Admission* Program. Transfers accepted. Credit possible for CEEB AP and CLEP exams. Project GO for disadvantaged and minority students. Summer program for underprepared students.
Student Life Associated students. Newspaper, yearbook, radio station. Special events board. Over 200 campus groups in academic, political, recreational, religious, service, and special interest areas. 12 fraternities and 9 sororities, all with houses. 10% of men and women join. Freshmen under 21 must live at home or on campus. Coed dorms. Honors residence, special-interest corridors. Married-student apartments. 33% of students live on campus. 2 semesters of phys ed required. Many intercollegiate and intramural athletics for men and women. AIAW, NCAA, Western Athletic Conference. Student body composition: 1% Asian, 1% Black, 3% Hispanic, 1% Native American, 91% White, 3% Other. 25% from out of state.

DENVER, UNIVERSITY OF $$

2301 South Gaylord, Denver 80208, (303) 753-2036
Director of Admissions: N. Kip Howard

- **Undergraduates:** 1,921m, 1,925w
- **Tuition (1984–1985):** $6,696
- **Room and Board (1984–1985):** $2,805–$2,955
- **Degrees offered:** BA, BS, BFA, BMus, BMus Ed, BSAT, BSBA, BSAcc, BSCHE, BSN
- **Mean SAT:** 486v, 528m,   **Mean ACT:** 24
- **Student-faculty ratio:** 13 to 1
- **Calendar system:** Trimester

A private university founded in 1864, affiliated with the Methodist Church. University acquired Colorado Women's College in 1982. Suburban main campus in a residential section of Denver, College of Law in the business district. Air, rail, and bus service.

Academic Character NCACS and professional accreditation. Trimester system, 9-week summer term, December interterm. 56 majors offered in the areas of accounting, animal technology, arts, area studies, business administration, computer science, education, engineering, hotel & restaurant, languages & literatures, music, philosophy/religion, physical education, real estate & construction, sciences, social sciences, speech/communications. Major in nursing for students who are RNs. Distributive requirements. Graduate and professional degrees granted. Independent study, honors program, Phi Beta Kappa, internships. Preprofessional programs in dentistry, engineering, law, librarianship, medicine, theology. 3-2 program in liberal arts/business. Clinical education for audiologists, speech & hearing therapists, psychologists, and special education teachers. Study abroad. Elementary, secondary, and special education certification. AFROTC, ROTC at University of Colorado. Language lab, computer center, A-V services, observatory. 1,300,000-volume library.

Financial CEEB CSS and ACT FAS. College scholarships, grants, loans, state grants, deferred payment; PELL, SEOG, NDSL, GSL, CWS. Preferred application deadline April 1.

Admissions High school graduation or 15 units required. Nursing applicants must be RNs. Interview encouraged. ACT or SAT required. $15 application fee. Rolling admissions; suggest applying by April 1. Deadline July 1. $100 tuition and $100 room deposits required on acceptance of admissions offer (both refundable until May 1). *Early Decision* and *Early Admission* programs. Admission deferral possible. Transfers accepted. Credit possible for CEEB AP and CLEP exams.

Student Life Student Senate. Newspaper, yearbook, radio station. Music groups. 5 major drama productions annually. Debate. Religious, academic, professional, and special interest groups. 10 fraternities and 6 sororities, all with houses. 17% of men and 13% of women join. Coed, special-interest dorms. Cooperative apartments for single and married students. 85% of freshmen live on campus. 3 quarters of phys ed required. 7 intercollegiate sports for men, 7 for women; extensive intramural program. AIAW, NAIA. Student body composition: 1.4% Asian, 1.9% Black, 2.1% Hispanic, 0.5% Native American, 87.4% White, 6.7% Other. 57% from out of state.

REGIS COLLEGE $$

3539 West 50th Avenue, Denver 80221 (303) 458-4900
Director of Admissions: Domenic N. Teti

- **Undergraduates:** 570m, 540w
- **Tuition (1984–1985):** $5,830
- **Room and Board (1984–1985):** $3,500;   **Fees:** $100
- **Degrees offered:** BA, BS
- **Mean SAT:** 420v, 460m,   **Mean ACT:** 20
- **Student-faculty ratio:** 15 to 1
- **Calendar system:** Semester

A private Roman Catholic college established in 1877 under the auspices of the Society of Jesus. Became coed in 1968. 90-acre suburban campus. Air, rail, and bus service.

Academic Character NCACS and professional accreditation. Semester system, 10-week summer term, summer workshops. Majors offered in accounting, biology, business administration, chemistry, ecology, economics, education, English, environmental studies/human ecology, French, history, mathematics, media studies, medical record administration, medical technology, philosophy, political science, psychology, religious studies, sociology, Spanish, theatre/English, and theater studies. Self-designed and interdivisonal majors. Courses offered in 15 additional areas. Distributives and 9 religious studies credits required. Independent study, honors program, pass/fail, extensive internships. Preprofessional programs in dentistry, law, medicine. 3-2 engineering program with Marquette and Washington Universities. Study abroad in Europe & Japan. Elementary and secondary education certification. AFROTC at University of Colorado. Seismic observatory. Language lab. 65,000-volume library.

Financial CEEB CSS and ACT FAS. College scholarships, loans; continuing education, state, and teacher grants; deferred payment; PELL, SEOG, NDSL, GSL, CWS. Application deadline April 1.

Admissions High school graduation with 15 units required. GED accepted. Interview encouraged. SAT or ACT required. $10 application fee. Rolling admissions; suggest applying by January. $100 ($50 for day student) deposit required on acceptance admissions offer. Credit possible for CEEB AP, CLEP, ACT PEP exams; college has own advanced placement program.

Student Life Student Senate. Newspaper, yearbook, radio station. Glee club. Debate. Theater Guild. Ski club. Academic, religious, service, and special interest groups. Academic and social fraternities and sororities without houses. Single freshmen and sophomores under 21 must live at home or on campus. Coed dorms. No married-student housing. 50% of students live on campus. 8 intercollegiate sports for men, 2 for women; intramurals. AIAW, NAIA, NCAA, Rocky Mountain Athletic Conference. 55% of students from out of state.

UNITED STATES AIR FORCE ACADEMY $

USAFA 80840, (303) 472-2640
Director of Admissions: Colonel Warren L. Simmons

- **Undergraduates:** 3,772m, 506w
- **Degrees offered:** BS
- **Mean SAT:** 553v, 648m
- **Student-faculty ratio:** 13 to 1
- **Calendar system:** Semester

A United States Service Academy established in 1954 to train officers for the Air Force. Every cadet is commissioned as a 2nd lieutenant on graduation, and must serve 5 years in the Air Force. Became coed in 1976. 18,000-acre rural campus 8 miles north of Colorado Springs. Air and bus service.

Academic Character NCACS and professional accreditation. Semester system, 3 3-week summer terms for upperclass students, 6-week basic training for new students in June. Majors offered in aeronautical engineering, astronautical engineering, aviation sciences, basic sciences, behavioral sciences, biological sciences, chemistry, civil engineering, computer science, economics, electrical engineering, engineering, engineering mechanics, engineering sciences, geography, history, humanities, international affairs, management, mathematical sciences, operations research, physics, and social sciences. Program emphasizes leadership, academic, military, and athletic training. Distributive requirements. GRE required for graduation. Independent study, honors program, some pass/fail. Exchange programs with French Air Force Academy, other US service academies. Visits with Argentinian, British, and Canadian academies. Aeronautics, instrumentation, radio frequency, research, language labs. Computer center, observatory, planetarium. 2 3,500-foot parallel airstrip runways. 405,000-volume library with microform resources.

Financial Full 4-year government scholarships for all students including tuition, room, board, and medical care. $350 monthly pay for personal needs. $500 uniform deposit required of all first-year students.

Admissions High school graduation required; 15 units recommended. GED accepted. Applicants must be 17-21 years of age on admission, unmarried, US citizens. Interview required. Medical exam and candidate fitness test required. ACT or SAT required. Suggest filing Precandidate Questionnaire in spring of 11th year; deadline December of 12th year. Apply to Member of Congress for nomination by spring of 11th year. Candidate must accept offer by May 1. $500 uniform deposit due upon arrival. *Early Decision* Program. Transfers accepted as freshmen. Credit possible for CEEB AP exams; academy has own advanced placement program.

Student Life Air Force Cadet Wing. Newspaper, literary magazine, yearbook. Choir, drum & bugle corps. Debate. Drama group. Over 70 competitive, recreational, and professional activities; religious, support, and special interest groups. All cadets must live on campus. Coed dorms. Juniors and seniors may have cars. Liquor prohibited on campus. Class attendance required. Cadets may not marry. Honor code, military rules, uniforms required. 8 semesters of phys ed and intercollegiate/intramural sports participation required. 17 intercollegiate and 13 intramural sports. Western Athletic Conference. Student body composition: 3% Asian, 7% Black, 4% Hispanic, 1% Native American, 85% White. Students appointed from all states.

Connecticut

BRIDGEPORT, UNIVERSITY OF $$

Bridgeport 06602, (203) 576-4552
Director of Admissions: Richard D. Huss

- **Undergraduates:** 2,202m, 1,994w
- **Tuition (1984–1985):** $6,260
- **Room and Board (1984–1985):** $3,326;   **Fees:** $183
- **Degrees offered:** BA, BS, BFA, BES, BMus, AA, AS
- **Mean SAT:** 427v, 466m
- **Student-faculty ratio:** 13 to 1
- **Calendar system:** Semester

A private university established in 1927. 90-acre urban campus overlooking Long Island Sound, 55 miles from New York City. Served by bus, rail, air.
Academic Character NEASC and professional accreditation. Semester system, 2 5-week summer terms. 24 majors offered by the College of Arts & Humanities, 8 by the College of Business & Public Management, 11 by the College of Health Sciences, and 8 by the College of Science Engineering. Self-designed majors. Distributive requirements. MA, MS, JD granted. Independent study. Honors program. Cooperative work/study, pass/fail, internships. Dual degree programs. Elementary, secondary, and early childhood education certification. ROTC. Continuing Education Program. Computer center, language lab. 325,000-volume library.
Financial CEEB CSS. University scholarships, loans, deferred payment; PELL, SEOG, NSS, NDSL, NSL, CWS, work program at Conn. State. Application deadline April 1.
Admissions High school graduation with 16 units required. GED and State High School Equivalency certificates accepted. Audition required for music, art, theatre majors; recommended for cinema majors. SAT or ACT required. ACH recommended. $25 application fee. Rolling admissions; application deadline August 1. $200 tuition and $200 room deposits required on acceptance of admissions offer. *Early Decision* and *Early Admission* programs. Admission deferral possible. Transfers accepted. Credit possible for CEEB AP and CLEP exams; university exams used for placement. Basic Studies Program for underprepared students.
Student Life Student government. Newspaper, yearbook, magazine, radio station. Music and drama groups. Cultural activities. Service, academic, and special interest organizations. 4 fraternities and 3 sororities without houses. 3% of men and women join. Single freshmen and sophomores under 21, except veterans, must live at home or on campus. Coed and single-sex dorms. Married-student housing off campus. 50% of students live on campus. 8 intercollegiate sports for men, 7 for women; 9 intramurals. AIAW, EAIAW, ECAC, NCAA, New England College Athletic Conference. Student body composition: 1% Asian, 2% Black, 1% Hispanic, 1% Native American, 85% White, 10% Other. 39% from out of state.

CONNECTICUT, UNIVERSITY OF $

Storrs 06268, (203) 486-3137
Director of Admissions: John W. Vlandis

- **Undergraduates:** 7,723m, 8,476w
- **Tuition (1984–1985):** $1,665 (in-state), $4,656 (out-of-state)
- **Room and Board (1984–1985):** $2,400
- **Degrees offered:** BA, BS, BFA, BMus
- **Mean SAT:** 502v, 555m
- **Student-faculty ratio:** 15 to 1
- **Calendar system:** Semester

A public university established in 1881. 2,800-acre rural campus, 30 miles from Hartford. Served by bus. Air and rail in Hartford.

Academic Character NEASC and professional accreditation. Semester system, 2 6-week summer terms. 9 majors offered by the College of Agriculture & Natural Resources, 30 by the College of Liberal Arts & Sciences, 3 by the School of Allied Health Professions, 11 by the School of Business Administration, 12 by the School of Education, 7 by the School of Engineering, 17 by the School of Fine Arts, and 3 by the School of Home Economics & Family Studies; also majors in nursing and pharmacy. MA, MS, MD, DMD, JD, PhD granted. Phi Beta Kappa. 3-2 program in pharmacy. 2-2 program in nursing. Cooperative program with other New England state schools. Study abroad. Elementary, secondary, and early childhood education certification. ROTC, AFROTC. Research Institutes. Branch campuses throughout the state offer first 2 years of most programs. Computer center, language lab. 3,000,000-volume library with microform resources.

Financial CEEB CSS and ACT FAS. University scholarships, grants, loans; PELL, SEOG, NDSL, GSL, NSL, CWS. Scholarship application deadline February 15.

Admissions High school graduation with 16 units required. 10% quota on students from out of state. SAT required. $20 application fee. Rolling admissions; preferred deadlines March 1 (in-state), February 15 (out-of-state). $60 deposit required by May 1. *Early Admission* and *Early Decision* programs. Admission deferral possible. Transfers accepted in some programs. Credit possible for CEEB AP exams; university has own advanced placement program.

Student Life Student government. Newspaper, magazine, yearbook, radio & TV stations. Music, drama, debate groups. Many religious, academic, honorary, professional, service, and special interest groups. Freshmen under 21 must live at home or on campus. No married-student housing. 75% of students live on campus. Resident freshmen and sophomores may not have cars on campus. Many intercollegiate and intramural sports for men and women. AIAW, ECAC, NCAA, Yankee and Big East Conferences. Student body composition: 0.7% Asian, 3.5% Black, 1.1% Hispanic, 0.1% Native American, 94.6% White.

CONNECTICUT COLLEGE $$$

New London 06320, (203) 447-7511
Dean of Admissions: Jeanette B. Hersey

- **Undergraduates:** 700m, 1100w
- **Tuition (1984–1985):** $9,500
- **Room and Board (1984–1985):** $2,750
- **Degrees offered:** BA
- **Mean SAT:** 540v, 580m
- **Student-faculty ratio:** 12 to 1
- **Calendar system:** Semester

A private college established in 1911, became coed in 1969. 680-acre campus overlooking Long Island Sound, 2 miles from downtown New London, midway between Boston & New York. Served by air, rail, and bus.

Academic Character NEASC accreditation. Semester system, 6-week summer term. 34 majors offered in the arts & sciences, classics, languages, mathematics, humanities, social sciences, and religion, plus 9 interdisciplinary majors. Self-designed majors. Courses in education. Distributive requirements. MA, MAT, MFA in Dance granted. Independent study. Honors program. Phi Beta Kappa. Pass/fail. Internships. Cross-registration with Trinity, Coast Guard Academy, Wesleyan. Programs with Institute for Architecture & Urban Studies (New York City), National Theatre Institute, and Mystic Seaport. 12-College Exchange. Washington Semester. Study abroad in 10 countries. Elementary, secondary, and special education certification. Computer center, botanic garden, 415-acre arboretum, observatory, language lab, children's school. 352,000-volume library.

Financial CEEB CSS. University scholarships, grants, loans, deferred payment; PELL, SEOG, GSL, NDSL, CWS. File FAF and application by February 15.

Admissions High school graduation with 16 units required. Interview encouraged. SAT or ACT, and 3 ACH required. $30 application fee. Application deadline February 1. $100 deposit required on acceptance of offer of admission. *Early Admission* and *Early Decision* programs. Admission deferral possible. Transfers accepted. Credit possible for CEEB AP exams; college has own advanced placement program.

Student Life Student government. Newspapers, magazine, Journal of Arts & Sciences, yearbook, radio station. Music, dance, drama groups. Religious, service, academic, and special interest groups. Students with parental consent may live off campus. 20 coed dorms including language, special interest, and cooperative housing. 96% of students live on campus. 8 intercollegiate sports for men, 9 for women; intramurals. New England Small College Athletic Conference. 72% from out of state.

FAIRFIELD UNIVERSITY $$

Fairfield 06430, (203) 255-5411
Dean of Admissions: David M. Flynn

- **Undergraduates:** 1,430m, 1,457w
- **Tuition (1984–1985):** $6,100
- **Room and Board (1984–1985):** $3,400; **Fees:** $140
- **Degrees offered:** BA, BS
- **Mean SAT:** 522v, 564m, **Mean ACT:** 25
- **Student-faculty ratio:** 16 to 1
- **Calendar system:** Semester

A private Jesuit university established in 1942, became coed in 1970. 200-acre suburban campus 5 miles from Bridgeport, 50 miles from New York City. Served by bus and rail; air in Bridgeport.

Academic Character NEASC and professional accreditation. Semester system, 6-week summer term. Majors offered in American studies, economics, English, fine arts, history, biology, chemistry, mathematics, accounting, finance, management, marketing, modern languages, philosophy, politics, religious studies, sociology, nursing, physics, and psychology. Minors offered in all major fields and in several additional areas, including Latin American and

Caribbean studies. Distributive requirements. MA, MS granted. Independent study. Honors program. Internships. Preprofessional programs in accounting, business, dentistry, law, and medicine. 3-2 program in engineering with UConn. Cross-registration with Sacred Heart and University of Bridgeport. Study abroad. Washington Semester. Secondary education, supervisory, administrative, and counseling certification. Computer center, language lab, TV studio. 300,000-volume library with microform resources.

Financial CEEB CSS. University scholarships, grants, loans, deferred payment; PELL, SEOG, NSL, NDSL, FISL, CWS, campus employment. Scholarship application deadline February 1.

Admissions High school graduation with 15 units required. SAT or ACT, and 3 ACH required. $25 application fee. Application deadline March 1. $100 tuition and $100 room deposits required on acceptance of offer of admission. *Early Decision* and *Early Admission* programs. Admission deferral possible. Transfers accepted. Credit possible for CEEB AP and CLEP exams.

Student Life Student government. Newspapers, magazine, yearbook, radio station. Music, debate, drama groups. Religious, political, service, honorary, academic, and special interest groups. Students live off campus when housing is unavailable. Some coed dorms. No married-student housing. 60% of students live on campus. Freshmen may not have cars on campus. Class attendance required for freshmen. 8 intercollegiate sports for men, 4 for women; 15 intramural and club sports. AIAW, NCAA. Student body composition: 2% Black, 1% Hispanic, 97% White. 53% from out of state.

HARTFORD, UNIVERSITY OF $$$

West Hartford 06117, (203) 243-4296
Director of Admissions: Walter M. Bortz, III

- **Undergraduates:** 2,199m, 1,745w
- **Tuition (1984–1985):** $7,100
- **Room and Board (1984–1985):** $3,975; **Fees:** $460
- **Degrees offered:** BA, BS, BFA, BMus, BMus Ed, BSE, AA, AS
- **Mean SAT:** 445V, 491m
- **Student-faculty ratio:** 16 to 1
- **Calendar system:** Semester

A private non-sectarian university established in 1877. 200-acre suburban campus in residential section of West Hartford, 4 miles from downtown. Served by air, rail, bus.

Academic Character NEASC and professional accreditation. Semester system, 2 6-week summer terms. 64 majors offered by the colleges of Arts & Sciences, Basic Studies, Business & Public Administration, Education & Allied Services, Engineering, Fine Arts, Music, and Technology. Self-designed majors. AA and AS offered in basic studies, communication, humanities, social sciences, biological sciences, physical sciences. Distributive requirements. Graduate and professional degrees granted. Independent study. Honors program. Cooperative work/study, pass/fail, internships. Preprofessional programs in dentistry, law, medicine, optometry, osteopathy, podiatry. 3-1 program in medical technology. 5-year programs for a BA/MBA, BS/MBA, BMus/MBA, BA/MPA, or BS/MPA. Cooperative program with 6 area schools. Study abroad. Early childhood, elementary, secondary, and special education certification. ROTC at UConn. Computer center, language lab, A-V center, environmental center. 280,000-volume library with microform resources.

Financial CEEB CSS. University scholarships, grants, athletic scholarships, loans, 2nd-family-member discount; PELL, SEOG, NDSL, CWS. Suggest applying as early as possible.

Admissions High school graduation with 16 units required. Portfolio review required for art majors; audition, music theory, and music aptitude tests for music majors. SAT or ACT required. $25 application fee. Rolling admissions; suggest applying early in 12th year, and by February 1 for housing and/or finanical aid. Application deadline June 1. $100 tuition and $100 room deposits required on acceptance of offer of admission. *Early Admission* and *Concurrent Enrollment* programs. Early notification. Admission deferral possible. Transfers accepted. Credit possible for CEEB AP and CLEP exams. College of Basic Studies for underprepared students.

Student Life Student associations. Newspaper, magazines, yearbook, radio station. Music and drama groups. Film series. Over 90 religious, academic, honorary, professional, and special interest groups. 1 fraternity and 3 sororities. 1% of men and women join. Freshmen must live at home or on campus. Coed and single-sex dorms, special interest housing. 47% of students live on campus. 6 intercollegiate sports for men, 6 for women; several intramural and club sports. AIAW, EAIAW, ECAC, NCAA, New England College Athletic Conference. Student body composition: 3% Asian, 5% Black, 2% Hispanic, 1% Native American, 89% White. 63% from out of state.

TRINITY COLLEGE $$$

Hartford 06106, (203) 527-3151
Director of Admissions: Donald Dietrich

- **Undergraduates:** 868m, 779w
- **Tuition (1984–1985):** $8,620
- **Room and Board (1984–1985):** $3,200;   **Fees:** $380
- **Degrees offered:** BA
- **Mean SAT:** 560v, 590m
- **Student-faculty ratio:** 12 to 1
- **Calendar system:** Semester

A private college established in 1823, became coed in 1969. 90-acre rural campus on hilltop away from Hartford's business center. Served by air, rail, and bus.

Academic Character NEASC accreditation. Semester system, 2 5-week summer terms. 32 majors offered in the areas of American studies, arts, classics, comparative literature, computer, economics, engineering, English, history, intercultural studies, languages, mathematics, music, philosophy, political science, psychology, religion, sociology, sciences, theatre, and urban/environmental studies. Interdisciplinary majors. MA, MLA, MS granted. Independent study. Phi Beta Kappa. Pass/fail. Internships. 3-2 BS/MS in engineering with Hartford Graduate Center. 12-College Exchange. Chinese literature & language at Central Conn State. Williams-Mystic Program in Maritime Studies. Cooperative program in elementary education with St. Joseph's. Washington Semester. Off-campus study in the US. Study abroad. Language lab. 625,000-volume library.

Financial CEEB CSS. College scholarships, grants, scholarships for students preparing for the ministry, loans, deferred payment; PELL, SEOG, NSS, NDSL, CWS, college has own work program. Application deadline February 1.

Admissions High school graduation with 11 units required. SAT or ACT, and English ACH required. $30 application fee. Application deadline January 1. *Early Decision* and *Early Admission* programs. Admission deferral possible. Transfers accepted. Credit possible for CEEB AP exams.

Student Life Student government. Newspaper, magazine, yearbook, radio station. Music, drama, film, political groups. Religious, service, academic, and special interest groups. 6 coed fraternities with houses, and 2 sororities without houses. Coed dorms. Some married-student housing. 90% of students live on campus. 14 intercollegiate sports for men, 10 for women; intramurals. ECAC, NCAA. Student body composition: 3% Black, 1% Hispanic, 94% White, 2% Other. 75% from out of state.

U.S. COAST GUARD ACADEMY $

New London 06320, (203) 444-8503
Director of Admissions: Capt. R. T. Getman

- **Undergraduates:** 700m, 100w
- **Degrees Offered:** BS
- **Mean SAT:** 559v, 643m, **Mean ACT:** 24e, 29m
- **Student-faculty ratio:** 8 to 1
- **Calendar system:** Semester

A public academy established in 1876 to train officers for the Coast Guard. Every cadet must serve 5 years as a commissioned officer following graduation. Became coed in 1976. 100-acre small-city campus on the banks of the Thames River, 50 miles from Hartford. Served by air, rail, and bus.

Academic Character NEASC and professional accreditation. Semester system, 6-week required summer term. Majors offered in civil engineering, electrical engineering, government, management, marine engineering, marine science, mathematical sciences, ocean engineering, and physical science. Courses in 11 additional areas. Independent study. Honors program. Academy Scholars Program. Summer training cruises. Summer programs in aviation orientation, and training in seamanship, navigation, damage control, and fire fighting. 124,000-volume library.

Financial Full 4-year government scholarship for all students. Monthly basic pay of $461. $300 uniform deposit.

Admissions High school graduation with 15 units required. Applicants must be 17-21 years of age on admission, unmarried, US citizens, without parental obligations. Appointments made on basis of nationwide competition. SAT or ACT required. Application deadline December 15. *Early Decision* Program. Transfers not accepted. Placement possible for CEEB AP exams.

Student Life Magazine, yearbook. Music, debate, drama, radio groups. Religious and special interest groups. Coed dorms. All cadets must live on campus. Only first class cadets (seniors) may have cars on campus. 8 semesters of phys ed required. 14 intercollegiate sports for men, 6 for women; women may participate in men's intercollegiates. Intramural and club sports. Intercollegiate or intramural participation required. ECAC, NCAA, NEIAA. Student body composition: 3% Asian, 2% Black, 2% Hispanic, 1% Native American, 92% White. 93% from out of state.

WESLEYAN UNIVERSITY $$$

Middletown 06457, (203) 347-9411
Director of Admissions: Karl M. Furstenberg

- **Undergraduates:** 1,350m, 1,250w
- **Tuition (1984–1985):** $9,250
- **Room and Board (1984–1985):** $3,600; **Fees:** $455
- **Degrees offered:** BA
- **Mean SAT:** 619v, 635m
- **Student-faculty ratio:** 11 to 1
- **Calendar system:** Semester

A private, non-sectarian university established in 1831, became coed in 1969. 100-acre small-city campus on the Connecticut River, 17 miles south of Hartford, 20 miles from New Haven. Served by air, rail, and bus.

Academic Character NEASC accreditation. Semester system. 37 majors offered in the areas of English language & composition, ancient & modern languages & literatures, philosophy & religion, arts, history & social sciences, mathematics, and natural sciences, including African, Russian, and East Asian studies and interdepartmental majors. Self-designed majors. Courses in urban and women's studies. Distributive expectations. MA, MALS, PhD granted. Independent study. Honors program. Phi Beta Kappa. Pass/fail. Apprentice program. Internships. Intensive Language Program. 3-2 programs in engineering with Caltech and Columbia. Concurrent BA/MA program. 12-College Exchange. Study abroad. Elementary, secondary, and special education certification. Computer, language lab, observatory. Center for Afro-American Studies. 900,000-volume library.

Financial CEEB CSS. University scholarships, grants, loans; PELL, SEOG, NDSL, FISL, CWS. Application deadline February 1.

Admissions High school graduation required. SAT or ACT, and 3 ACH required. $30 application fee. Application deadline January 15. $100 deposit required on acceptance of offer of admission. *Early Admission, Early Decision,* and *Concurrent Enrollment* programs. Admission deferral possible. Some transfers accepted. Credit possible for CEEB AP exams.

Student Life Newspapers, magazine, yearbook, radio stations. Music, drama, debate groups. Religious, political, social action, service, academic, and special interest groups. 9 fraternities with houses. 10% of men join. Freshmen must live on campus. Coed, single-sex, special interest, and coop housing. 95% of students live on campus. Scholarship students may not have cars on campus. 14 intercollegiate sports for men, 11 for women; extensive intramural program. AIAW, ECAC, NCAA, New England Small College Athletic Conference. Student body composition: 5% Asian, 8% Black, 3% Hispanic, 84% White. 83% from out of state.

YALE UNIVERSITY $$$

1502A Yale Station, New Haven 06520, (203) 436-0300
Dean of Admissions: Worth David

- **Undergraduates:** 2,875m, 2,231w
- **Tuition (1984–1985):** $9,750
- **Room and Board (1984–1985):** $4,200
- **Degrees offered:** BA, BS
- **Mean SAT:** 660v, 680m
- **Student-faculty ratio:** 7 to 1
- **Calendar system:** Semester

A private university established in 1701, became coed in 1969. 175-acre urban campus in center of New Haven. Served by air, bus, and rail.

Academic Character NEASC and professional accreditation. Semester system. 59 majors offered in the areas of languages & literatures, humanities, social sciences, and natural sciences, engineering, and mathematics. Self-designed majors. Courses in 31 additional areas. Senior general exam required in some fields. Graduate and professional degrees granted. Independent study. Phi Beta Kappa. Pass/fail. Accelerated degree, early concentration program. 5-year BA with junior year in underdeveloped country. Summer Language Institute. Study abroad. Computer center, observatory, accelerators, museums. Art gallery. Over 7.5 million-volume library.

Financial CEEB CSS. University scholarships, loans, Parent Loan Plan, Yale Bursary Program; PELL, SEOG, NDSL, FISL, CWS. Application deadline January 15.

Admissions High school graduation with 16 units recommended. SAT and 3 ACH required. $35 application fee. Application deadline January 2. *Early Action* and *Early Admission* programs. Admission deferral possible. Credit possible for CEEB AP exams.

Student Life Newspaper, magazines, yearbook, radio station. Music, debate, drama, film groups. Religious, service, language, academic, political, and special interest groups. 3 fraternities (2 coed) without houses; less than 5% join. Sophomores and juniors may live off campus with parental consent. Assigned housing in 12 residential colleges which provide dining, social, and athletic facilities. Married-student apartments. 89% of students live on campus. Many intercollegiate, intramural, and club sports for men and women. Ivy League. Student body composition: 6% Asian, 6% Black, 3% Hispanic, 79% White, 6% Other. 90% from out of state.

Delaware

DELAWARE, UNIVERSITY OF $

Newark 19711, (302) 738-8123
Dean of Admissions: Douglas McConkey

- **Undergraduates:** 5,262m, 6,939w
- **Tuition (1984–1985):** $1,590 (in-state), $4,200 (out-of-state)
- **Room and Board (1984–1985):** $2,340 (in-state), $2,440 (out-of-state);
  Fees: $81
- **Degrees offered:** BS, BA
- **Mean SAT:** 487v, 539m
- **Student-faculty ratio:** 17 to 1
- **Calendar system:** Semester with voluntary 5-week winter session

A public university established in 1743. 1,500-acre suburban campus in the town of Newark, 14 miles from Wilmington. Rail and bus in Wilmington.
Academic Character MSACS and professional accreditation. 4-1-4 system, summer terms. 9 majors offered by the College of Agricultural Sciences, 49 by the College of Arts & Sciences, 3 by the College of Business & Economics, 2 by the College of Education, 4 by the College of Engineering, 12 by the College of Human Resources, 1 by the College of Nursing, 3 by the College of Life & Health Sciences, and 2 by the College of Physical Education, Athletics, & Recreation. Associate, graduate, and professional degress granted. Honors program, Phi Beta Kappa. Preprofessional programs in dentistry, law, marine studies, medicine, theology, and veterinary science. 5-year liberal arts/engineering program. Elementary and secondary education certification. ROTC, AFROTC. Agricultural & experimental farm adjoining campus, experimental substation in Georgetown. Marine studies field station in Lewes. Language lab. 1,750,000-volume library.
Financial CEEB CSS. University scholarships, grants, loans; PELL, SEOG, NDSL, CWS. Application deadline May 1.
Admissions High school graduation with 11-16 units recommended. Specific course requirements for some programs. SAT required. ACH recommended. $25 application fee. Rolling admissions; application deadline March 1. Limited *Early Admission* Program. Admission deferral possible. Transfers accepted. Credit possible for CEEB AP; university has advanced placement program.
Student Life Student government. Newspaper, yearbook, radio station. Music & drama groups. Debate. Athletic, academic, ethnic, honorary, political, religious, service, and special interest groups. 16 fraternities with houses; 6 sororities without houses. 6% of men live in fraternities. Coed dorms. Apartments for single & married students. Special interest & language housing. 57% of students live on campus. Cars usually prohibited for boarders. 11 intercollegiate sports for men, 9 for women; intramurals. Student body composition: 0.4% Asian, 5% Black, 0.4% Hispanic, 0.1% Native American, 94.1% White. 44% from out of state.

District of Columbia

AMERICAN UNIVERSITY, THE $$$

Washington 20016, (202) 686-2211
Dean of Admissions & Financial Aid: Rebecca R. Dixon

- **Undergraduates:** 1,778m, 2,261w
- **Tuition and fees (1984–1985):** $7,670
- **Room and Board (1984–1985):** $3,656
- **Degrees offered:** BA, BS
- **Mean SAT:** 511v, 529m
- **Student-faculty ratio:** 13 to 1
- **Calendar system:** Semester

A private university affiliated with the Methodist Church, established in 1893. 74-acre campus located in a residential section of urban Washington, which is served by air, rail, and bus.

Academic Character MSACS and professional accreditation. Semester system, 5 summer terms. 71 majors offered by the Colleges of Arts & Sciences, Public Affairs, and the Schools of Business Administration and Nursing. Self-designed majors. University also contains the Schools of Education, Government & Public Administration, International Service, Law, Justice, and the Wesley Theological Seminary, Center for Technology & Administration, and Division of Continuing Education. Distributive requirements. Graduate and professional degrees granted. Honors programs. Cooperative work/study, pass/fail, internships. Preprofessional programs in dentistry, law, medicine, secondary education, social work, theology. 3-2 engineering programs. Host for 140-member Washington Semester Program. Elementary, secondary, and special education certification. ROTC, AFROTC. Research centers. Language lab, computer center, radio & TV facilities. 400,000-volume library with microform resources.

Financial CEEB CSS. University scholarships, grants, loans, deferred payment; PELL, SEOG, NDSL, CWS. Application deadline March 1.

Admissions High school graduation with 16 units required. Equivalency diplomas accepted. SAT or ACT required; SAT preferred. English ACH required for placement. $20 application fee. Rolling admissions; deadline February 1. $100 deposit required on acceptance of offer of admission. University early decision and *Early Entrance* programs. Admission deferral possible. Transfers accepted. Credit possible for CEEB AP and CLEP exams. Special admission program for local and adult applicants.

Student Life Student government. Newspapers, literary magazine, yearbook, radio station. Music, drama, debate clubs. Service, professional, academic, religious organizations. 4 fraternities, 3 with houses, and 6 sororities without houses. 5% of undergraduates join. No married-student housing. Living-learning centers. 43% of students live on campus. Many intercollegiate and intramural sports for men and women. AIAW, ECC, EIAC, NAIA. Student body composition: 2% Asian, 10.1% Black, 2.4% Hispanic, 0.1% Native American, 72.8% White, 12.6% Other. 92% from outside the District.

CATHOLIC UNIVERSITY OF AMERICA $$

4th Street & Michigan Avenue, N.E., Washington 20064, (202) 635-5305
Director of Admissions & Financial Aid: Robert J. Talbot

- **Undergraduates:** 1,256m, 1,295w
- **Tuition (1984–1985):** $6,650
- **Room and Board (1984–1985):** $3,500;   **Fees:** $120
- **Degrees offered:** BA, BS, BFA
- **Mean SAT:** 510v, 530m
- **Student-faculty ratio:** 13 to1
- **Calendar system:** Semester

A private university established in 1887, affiliated with the Roman Catholic Church. Urban residential campus. Served by air, bus, and rail.

Academic Character MSACS and professional accreditation. Semester system, summer terms. 30 majors offered by the School of Arts & Sciences, 9 by the School of Engineering & Architecture, 6 by the School of Music, and 1 by the School of Nursing. Joint major programs. Distributives and 3-4 religion courses required for graduation. Graduate and professional degrees granted. Independent and accelerated study, honors program, Phi Beta Kappa. Cooperative work/study, pass/fail, internships. Preprofessional programs in business, dentistry, foreign service, law, medicine. Joint degree programs include BA/MA, BA/JD, BA/MSW, BS/MSLS, BSArch/BCE. Study abroad. Elementary, secondary, and special education certification. ROTC at Howard U; AFROTC at Georgetown. 1,000,000-volume library.

Financial CEEB CSS. University scholarships, grants, loans; Catholic scholarships, tuition discounts for simultaneously enrolled siblings. College Aid Plan, PELL, SEOG, NDSL, NSL, GSL, CWS. Application deadline February 1.

Admissions High school graduation with 15 units recommended. Audition required for music majors. SAT or ACT required; SAT preferred. $20 application fee. Rolling admissions; no deadline. $100 deposit required on acceptance of admissions offer (May 1). *Early Entrance* and University early decision programs. Admission deferral possible. Transfers accepted. Credit possible for CEEB AP, CLEP, and ACH exams. University has own advanced placement program.

Student Life Student government. Newspaper, yearbook, radio station. Music groups. Debate. Academic, honorary, professional, special interest organizations. Partnership Program for minority students. 3 fraternities and 3 sororities without houses. 20% of men and 15% of women join. Coed, single-sex, and quiet dorms. 60% of students live on campus. 9 intercollegiate sports for men, 5 for women; intramurals. Student body composition: 1.3% Asian, 5.5% Black, 1.7% Hispanic, 0.2% Native American, 82.9% White, 8.4% Other. 70% of students from outside the District.

GALLAUDET COLLEGE $

Washington 20002, (202) 651-5000
Director of Admissions & Records: Jerald M. Jordan

- **Undergraduates:** 526m, 732w
- **Tuition (1984–1985):** $1,684
- **Room and Board (1984–1985):** $2,846;   **Fees:** $120
- **Degrees offered:** BA, BS
- **Student-faculty ratio:** 6 to 1
- **Calendar system:** Semester

A private college established in 1864, it is the only liberal arts college in the world exclusively for the deaf. 92-acre urban campus. Air, rail, and bus service.

Academic Character MSACS and professional accreditation. Semester system, 2 3-week summer terms. Majors offered in American studies, art, biology, business administration, chemistry, computer mathematics, economics, education, English, general science, German, government, history, home economics, mathematics, philosophy, physical education, physics, psychology, romance languages, social work, and theatre arts. Associate degree in interpreting for the deaf. Distributive requirements. MA, MS, MBA, PhD granted. Independent study. Honors program. Pass/fail. Cooperative work/study, internships. Associate member of the 9-institution Consortium of Universities of the Washington Metropolitan Area. Exchange programs with Oberlin and Western Maryland Colleges. Study abroad. International Center on Deafness. Elementary, secondary, and special education certification. Demonstration elementary school and model secondary school for the deaf. TV studio. Computer center. Library of 397,000 print and non-print materials, and an extensive collection of materials on deafness.
Financial CEEB CSS. College scholarships, grants, grants-in-aid, loans; PELL, GSL, NDSL, CWS. Application deadlines April 1 (scholarships & grants) and May 1 (loans).
Admissions High school graduation required; college prep program with algebra recommended. GED accepted. Gallaudet entrance exam and proof of hearing impairment required. SAT or ACT accepted but not required. Application deadline January 1. $50 deposit required with acceptance of admissions offer (May 1). *Early Entrance* and *Early Decision* programs. Admission deferral possible. Transfers accepted. Credit possible for CEEB CLEP subject exams. Preparatory year and tutorial help for students accepted with academic deficiencies.
Student Life Student government. Newspaper, literary magazine, yearbook. Religious, athletic, ethnic, drama, and special interest groups. 3 fraternities and 3 sororities. 20% of men and 15% of women join. No single-sex dorms or married-student housing. 90% of students live on campus. Preparatory (pre-freshman) year students may not have cars. 4 semesters of phys ed required. 11 intercollegiate sports for men, 8 for women; intramurals. AIAW, NCAA. Student body composition: 1% Asian, 10% Black, 3% Hispanic, 1% Native American, 70% White, 15% Other. 96% from outside the District.

GEORGE WASHINGTON UNIVERSITY $$/$$$

Washington 20052, (202) 676-6040
Director of Admissions: Joseph Y. Ruth

- Undergraduates: 2,979m, 2,822w
- Tuition (1984–1985): $6,710–$7,370
- Room and Board (1984–1985): $3,990; Fees: $200
- Degrees offered: BA, BMus, BS, BBA, AA, AS
- Mean SAT: 530v, 560m, Mean ACT: 25.4
- Student-faculty ratio: 14 to 1
- Calendar system: Semester

A private university established in 1821 by an Act of Congress. 30-acre campus located in the federal section of Washington, close to the White House and Kennedy Center. Air, bus, and rail service.
Academic Character MSACS and professional accreditation. Semester system, 3 summer terms. Over 100 majors offered by the undergraduate divisions: Columbian College of Arts & Sciences, and the schools of Allied

Health Science, Education & Human Development, Engineering & Applied Science, Government & Business Administration, and Public & International Affairs. Double, self-designed, and interdisciplinary majors. Distributive requirements. Graduate and professional degrees granted. Independent study, honors program. Phi Beta Kappa. Cooperative work/study in engineering. Internships. Preprofessional programs in law and medicine. 3-2 engineering programs. Member of 9-institution Consortium of Universities of the Washington Metropolitan Area; cross-registration possible. Study abroad. Exchange with American College (Paris). Elementary, secondary, and special education certification. AFROTC, ROTC. Computer center, language lab. 1,126,064-volume library.

Financial CEEB CSS. University scholarships, grants, loans, deferred payment; PELL, SEOG, NDSL, CWS. Application deadline February 1.

Admissions High school graduation with 15 units required. SAT or ACT required; SAT preferred. $20 application fee. Rolling admissions; deadline March 1. $200 tuition and $100 room deposits required on acceptance of offer of admission (May 1). *Early Entrance* Program. Transfers accepted. Credit possible for CEEB AP and CLEP exams, and for University's proficiency exams.

Student Life Student government. Newspaper, literary magazine, yearbook, radio station. Music, drama, dance, debate, and other special interest groups. 11 fraternities with houses, 4 sororities with club rooms. 5% of men and 3% of women join. Some university-owned apartments. 35% of students live in dorms. School of Education has phys ed requirements. 9 intercollegiate sports for men, 9 for women; intramurals. Student body composition: 3.5% Asian, 6.4% Black, 2.5% Hispanic, 0.3% Native American, 76.5% White, 9.8% Other. 95% from outside the District.

GEORGETOWN UNIVERSITY $$$

Washington 20057, (202) 625-3051
Director of Admissions: Charles A. Deacon

- **Undergraduates:** 2,643m, 2,735w
- **Tuition (1984–1985):** $8,500
- **Room and Board (1984–1985):** $3,400
- **Degrees offered:** BA, BS
- **Mean SAT:** 608v, 623m, **Mean ACT:** 29 composite
- **Student-faculty ratio:** 14 to 1
- **Calendar system:** Semester

A private Roman Catholic university conducted by Jesuits, established in 1789, became coed in 1968. 110-acre campus in residential area of northwest Washington, overlooking the Potomac River and Virginia. Air, bus, and rail service.

Academic Character MSACS and professional accreditation. Semester system, 2 5-week summer terms. 40 majors offered by the College of Arts & Sciences and the schools of Business Administration, Foreign Service, and Languages & Linguistics. Distributives and 2 theology courses required. Graduate and professional degrees granted. Pre-Honors English and liberal arts seminar for selected freshmen. Independent study, honors program. Phi Beta Kappa. Internships. Pass/fail. Preprofessional programs in dentistry, law, medicine. 3-2 physics/engineering program with Catholic U. Member of 9-institution Consortium of Universities of the Washington Metropolitan Area; cross-registration possible. Junior year and summer school abroad. ROTC;

AFROTC at Howard U. Seismological observatory, computer center, language lab. 1,500,000-volume libraries plus access to 240 libraries in the area.

Financial CEEB CSS. University scholarships, grants, deferred payment; PELL, SEOG, NSS, NDSL, FISL, NSL, GSL, CWS. Application deadlines January 31 (scholarships & grants), January 15 (loans).

Admissions High school graduation with 16 units required. Interview strongly recommended. SAT or ACT required, 3 ACH recommended. $30 application fee. Application deadline January 15. $300 deposit required on acceptance of offer of admission (May 1). *Early Decision* and *Early Admission* programs. Admission deferral possible. Transfers accepted. Credit possible for CEEB AP exams.

Student Life Student government. Newspapers, literary magazines, yearbook. Music, drama, debate groups. Honorary, religious, political, special interest, community service organizations. Freshmen must live at home or on campus. Coed dorms. University-owned apartments, special interest housing. 60% of students live on campus. Class attendance required. 13 intercollegiate sports for men, 9 for women; intramurals. Student body compositon: 8% Black, 87% White, 5% Other. 90% from outside the District.

HOWARD UNIVERSITY $

2400 Sixth Street, N.W., Washington 20059, (202) 636-6200
Dean of Admissions & Records: William H. Sherrill

- **Undergraduates:** 3,684m, 4,607w
- **Tuition (1984–1985):** $2,700
- **Room and Board (1984–1985):** $2,780;   **Fees:** $345
- **Degrees offered:** BA, BS
- **Mean SAT:** 405v, 426m
- **Student-faculty ratio:** 7 to 1
- **Calendar system:** Semester

A private university established in 1867. 4 campuses: 89-acre main, 22-acre west, 108-acre Beltsville, and Divinity School Campus, in urban Washington. Air, rail, and bus service.

Academic Character MSACS and professional accreditation. Semester system, 2 summer terms. Over 90 majors offered by the Colleges of Allied Health Sciences, Fine Arts, Liberal Arts, Nursing, Pharmacy & Pharmacal Sciences, and the Schools of Architecture & Planning, Business & Public Administration, Communications, Education, Engineering, Human Ecology, Social Work. Minors. Over 65 graduate and professional degrees granted. Independent study, honors program. Phi Beta Kappa. Cooperative work/study, internships. University Without Walls. 3-3 bachelor's/JD and MBA/JD program with School of Law. Coordinated attendance program: courses available at American, Catholic, George Washington, and Georgetown Universities. Domestic exchange program, International Student Exchange Program. Elementary and secondary education certification. AFROTC, ROTC. Language labs, art gallery. 1,242,553-volume library.

Financial CEEB CSS. University scholarships, loans, grants, deferred payment; PELL, SEOG, SSIG, NSS, GSL, NSL, FISL, NDSL, HEAL, CWS. University has own work program. Application deadline April 1.

Admissions High school graduation required. Music majors must audition or submit tape; art majors must submit portfolio. SAT and 3 ACH required. $25 application fee. Rolling admissions; deadline April 1. $75 deposit required on acceptance of offer of admission. College of Liberal Arts has *Early Entrance* Program and may give credit for CEEB AP exams and college-level high school work. Transfers accepted. Center for Academic Reinforcement.

Student Life Student Council. Newspaper, magazines, yearbook, radio station. Music, drama, dance groups. Debate. Service fraternity, honor societies, International Club, special interest organizations. 4 fraternities, 4 sororities; 15% of Liberal Arts students join. University housing limited. 30% of students live on campus. Liquor, hazing prohibited. 4 semesters of phys ed required. 11 intercollegiate sports for men, 3 for women; intramurals. NCAA, Mid-Eastern Athletic Conference. Student body composition: 1% Asian, 79.6% Black, 16.5% Foreign, 0.4% Hispanic, 0.1% Native American, 2.4% White. 66% from outside District.

Florida

ECKERD COLLEGE $$

PO Box 12560, St. Petersburg 33733, (813) 867-1166
Director of Admissions and Records: Richard R. Hallin, PhD

- **Undergraduates:** 518m, 540w
- **Tuition (1984–1985):** $6,575
- **Room and Board (1984–1985):** $2,700;   **Fees:** $100
- **Degrees offered:** BA, BS
- **Mean SAT:** 480v, 505m,   **Mean ACT:** 22
- **Student-faculty ratio:** 14 to 1
- **Calendar system:** 4–1–4

A private college affiliated with the Presbyterian Church, established in 1958.
281-acre subtropical suburban campus on Boca Ciega Bay. Air, rail, and bus in
St. Petersburg.

Academic Character SACS accreditation. 4-1-4 calendar, 2 4-week
summer modules. 31 majors offered in humanities, science, business,
education. College organized by interdisciplinary subject
groupings (collegia): Behavioral Science, Comparative Cultures, Creative
Arts, Letters, Natural Sciences. 3-week freshman autumn term and first year
make up Foundation Collegium, studying Western Heritage. 4 courses
required of sophomores and juniors in areas of aesthetic, cross-cultural,
environmental, and social relations perspective. Judeo-Christian Perspective
course required of seniors plus senior seminar, thesis or comprehensive
exam. Self-designed majors. Independent and accelerated study. Credit/no
credit, internships. Women's Studies program. Preprofessional programs in
many fields. 3-2 engineering program with Washington University, Auburn,
Columbia, Georgia Tech. Extensive study abroad. Elementary, secondary,
and early childhood education certification. ROTC. Primate lab. Language
lab. 170,000-volume library.

Financial CEEB CSS. College scholarships, grants, loans; PELL, SEOG,
GSL, NDSL, state grants and vouchers, installment and deferred payment
plans. Application deadline April 1 for scholarships, none for loans.

Admissions High school graduation with 13 units recommended. GED
accepted. Interview highly recommended. SAT or ACT required. $15
application fee. Rolling admissions; suggest applying by December. $100
deposit required on acceptance of admission. *Early Admission* and *Early
Decision* programs. Transfers accepted. One-year admission deferral
possible. Credit possible for CEEB AP and CLEP exams.

Student Life Association of Students. Newspaper, literary magazine,
yearbook, radio station. Music and drama groups. Afro-American Society.
Waterfront program: over 50 boats. Honorary and special interest groups.
Students under 23 must live at home or on campus. Self-governing residential
houses for 34-36 students. Coed and single-sex dorms. 85% of students live on
campus. 8 intercollegiate sports for men, 8 for women; extensive intramural
program. AIAW, NCAA, Sunshine State Conference. Student body
composition: 1% Asian, 5% Black, 3% Hispanic, 84% White, 7% Other. 65%
from out of state.

EMBRY-RIDDLE AERONAUTICAL UNIVERSITY $

Star Route, Box 540, Bunnell 32010, (904) 673-3180
Dean of Admissions: Peter Brooker

- **Undergraduates:** 5,339m, 457w
- **Tuition (1984–1985):** $3,450
- **Room and Board (1984–1985):** $1,150;   **Fees:** $15 + labs
- **Degrees offered:** AS, BS
- **Student-faculty ratio:** 18 to 1
- **Calendar system:** Trimester

A private university established in 1926. 86-acre campus located at Daytona Beach Regional Airport; (see also Embry-Riddle, Prescott, AR). International campus: centers near airports in 80 U.S. and European areas.

Academic Character SACS and professional accreditation. Trimester system, 2 8-week summer terms. 11 majors offered in aeronautical engineering, science, studies; general and professional aeronautics; aviation administration, computer science, maintenance management, management, and technology. Areas of Concentration in all major fields and in 11 additional areas. Courses in humanities, social & physical sciences. Distributive requirements; Basic Skills Test required. MAS, MAM, MBA/A granted. Independent study. Cooperative work/study, internships. Non-degree programs. FAA exam preparation. Two degrees possible. 80 campuses at military bases abroad. Cross-registration with Barry. SOC. ROTC, AFROTC; NROTC at Pensacola, PLCP Marine Corps at Quantico. Late model, fully-equipped aircraft, "Gemini Flight" concept, training simulators. Computer center. 52,000-volume library.

Financial CSS FAF. University scholarships, grants, loans, tuition waivers; PELL, SEOG, NDSL, GSL, CWS; university has own work program. Early application recommended.

Admissions Open admissions. GED accepted. Interview required of handicapped students. E-RAU Medical Report, FAA Medical Certificate (Class I or II) required. SAT or ACT required. $25 application fee. Rolling admissions; apply at least 60 days before enrollment date. $150 tuition deposit and $95 room deposit required on acceptance of offer of admission, refundable 60 days before enrollment date. *Early Admission* Program. Transfers accepted. Credit possible for CEEB AP and CLEP exams, and for military, aeronautical, and professional experience.

Student Life Student government. Student representation on University Board of Trustees. Newspaper, yearbook. Professional, honorary, athletic, religious, and special interest groups. Several fraternities without houses. On-campus housing limited. Some coed dorms. 25% of students live on campus. Class attendance expected. Dorm regulations enforced. 8 intramural sports. Student body composition: 1.2% Asian, 3.2% Black, 1.1% Hispanic, 0.4% Native American, 89.4% White.

FLAGLER COLLEGE $

St. Augustine 32084, (904) 829–6481
Director of Admissions: William T. Abare, Jr.

- **Undergraduates:** 420m, 589w
- **Tuition (1984–1985):** $3,050
- **Room and Board (1984–1985):** $1,930

- **Degrees offered:** BA
- **Mean SAT:** 430v, 440m, **Mean ACT:** 18
- **Student-faculty ratio:** 22 to 1
- **Calendar system:** Semester

A private college established in 1968, became coed in 1971. 29-acre campus located in historic town. Served by bus; airport and train 30 miles away in Jacksonville.

Academic Character SACS accreditation. Semester system, 1 3-week, 2 5-week summer terms. Majors offered in art, business administration, education, humanities, social sciences, physical education. Self-designed majors. Minors offered in most major fields and in 9 additional areas. Distributive requirements. Independent study. Internships. Preprofessional programs in business, education, human services, journalism, law, youth ministries. Study in Mexico. Elementary, secondary, and special education certification. ROTC. 61,000-volume library.

Financial CEEB CSS and ACT FAS. College scholarships, grants, loans, deferred payment plan. PELL, SEOG, NDSL, FISL, CWS. Application deadline April 1.

Admissions High school graduation with 16 units required. GED accepted. Interview recommended. SAT or ACT required. $15 application fee. Rolling admissions; suggest applying by April 1. $100 tuition and $100 room deposits required on acceptance of offer of admission. *Early Admission* Program. Transfers accepted. Admission deferral possible. Credit possible for CEEB AP and CLEP exams.

Student Life Student government. Newspaper, literary magazine, yearbook. Extensive drama program. Academic, honorary, and service groups. Freshmen must live on campus. Limited dorm space; students urged to submit forms and payment before April 1. Single-sex dorms. No married-student housing. 56% of students live on campus. Liquor prohibited on campus. No interdorm visitation. Attendance in class regulated. 6 intercollegiate sports for men, 4 for women; 8 intramural sports. AIAW, NAIA. Student body composition: 4% Black, 93% White, 3% Other. 58% from out of state.

FLORIDA, UNIVERSITY OF $

Gainesville 32611, (904) 392-1365
Director of Admissions: James B. Parrish

- **Undergraduates:** 15,842m, 12,330w
- **Tuition (1984–1985):** $790 (in-state), $2,250 (out-of-state)
- **Room and Board (1984–1985):** $2,875; **Fees:** $54
- **Degrees offered:** BA, BS
- **Mean SAT:** 513v, 574m
- **Student-faculty ratio:** 12 to 1
- **Calendar system:** Semester

A public university established in 1853. 1,800-acre suburban campus, served by air, rail, and bus.

Academic Character SACS and professional accreditation. Semester system, 2 5-week summer terms. 15 majors offered by the College of Agriculture, 3 by the College of Architecture, 7 by the College of Business Administration, 19 by the College of Education, 15 by the College of Engineering, 13 by the College of Fine Arts, 4 by the School of Forest Resources & Conservation, 5 by the College of Health Related Professions, 5 by the College of Journalism & Communications, 31 by the College of Liberal Arts & Sciences, 3 by the College of Physical Education, and 1 each by the School of Accounting, Center for Latin American Studies, College of Medicine, College of Nursing, and College of Pharmacy. Self-designed majors. Distributive requirements. Graduate degrees granted. Accelerated study. Honors programs. Phi Beta Kappa. Cooperative work/study, pass/fail, internships. Several preprofessional programs. Study abroad. Elementary, secondary, and special education certification. ROTC, AFROTC, NROTC. Computer center, language labs. Art gallery, museum. Broadcast facility. 2,600,000-volume library with microform resources.

Financial CEEB CSS. University scholarships, grants, loans; NSL, PELL, NDSL, GSL, deferred payment plan, CWS. Application deadline March 1.

Admissions High school graduation with 12-14 units required. SAT or ACT required. $15 application fee. Rolling admissions. Room deposit due when accept admissions offer. *Early Decision, Early Admission* programs. Transfers accepted. Credit possible for CEEB AP and CLEP exams.

Student Life Student government. Newspaper, radio and TV stations. Music, theatre, debate groups. Over 150 organizations. 30 fraternities, 20 sororities, most with houses; 20% join. Married-student housing. 27% of students live on campus. 8 intercollegiate sports for men, 7 for women; extensive intramurals. NCAA, SAC, AIAW. Student body composition: 0.8% Asian, 5.6% Black, 4.1% Hispanic, 0.1% Native American, 89.4% White. 10% from out of state.

FLORIDA INSTITUTE OF TECHNOLOGY $

150 West University, Melbourne 32901, (305) 723-3701
Director of Admissions: Robert S. Heidinger

- **Undergraduates:** 2,752m, 1,196w
- **Tuition (1984-1985):** $4,740
- **Room and Board (1984-1985):** $2,610; **Fees:** $210
- **Degrees offered:** AS, BS
- **Mean SAT:** 470v, 555m, **Mean ACT:** 25
- **Student-faculty ratio:** 18 to 1
- **Calendar system:** Quarter

A private university established in 1958. 16-acre campus in beach community; branch campus 85 miles south at Jensen Beach. Served by air and bus.

Academic Character SACS and professional accreditation. Quarter system, summer term. 25 majors offered by School of Science & Engineering, 3 by School of Aeronautics, and 7 at Jensen Beach Campus. Distributive requirements. Graduate degrees granted. Some independent study. Phi Beta Kappa. Cooperative work/study. AS programs at Jensen Beach in oceangraphic, electronics, environmental, marine, medical, photographic, underwater, and petroleum technologies. 2-year program at Cape Kennedy Regional Airport for pilots and in air commerce. English training for foreign students. Exchange program with High Point College. Study abroad. Secondary science education certification. ROTC. 120,000-volume library.

Financial CEEB CSS. University scholarships, grants, loans; PELL, SEOG, NDSL, FISL, CWS, deferred payment plan. Application deadline March 15.

Admissions High school graduation with 11 or more units required with more units in sciences expected. GED accepted. SAT or ACT required. $15 application fee. Rolling admissions; application deadline is June 30. $50 tuition and $100 room deposits required on acceptance of offer of admission.

Early Admission Program. Transfers accepted. Admission deferral possible. Credit possible for CEEB AP and CLEP exams; university has own advanced placement program.

Student Life Student government. Newspaper, radio station. Stage band. Drama club. Volunteer ambulance. Athletic, departmental, honorary, religious, tutoring, service, and special interest groups. 10 fraternities and 1 sorority. Single students with less than 45 credit hours must live on campus. Coed and single-sex dorms. 60% of students live on campus. Class attendance is required. 10 intercollegiate sports for men, 6 for women; intramural and club sports. Student body composition: 0.7% Asian, 2.6% Black, 2.6% Hispanic, 80.3% White, 13.71% Other. 75% from out of state.

FLORIDA STATE UNIVERSITY $

Tallahassee 32306, (904) 644-6200
Director of Admissions: Peter F. Metarko

- **Undergraduates:** 7,401m, 8,626w
- **Tuition (1984–1985):** $850 (in-state), $2,178 (out-of-state)
- **Room and Board (1984–1985):** $2,120
- **Degrees offered:** BS, BA, BFA
- **Mean SAT:** 488v, 529m,   **Mean ACT:** 23
- **Student-faculty ratio:** 19 to 1
- **Calendar system:** Semester

A public university established in 1851. 343-acre urban campus. Served by air and bus.

Academic Character SACS and professional accreditation. Semester system. 28 majors offered by the College of Arts & Sciences, 10 by the College of Business, 2 by the College of Communication, 16 by the College of Education, 4 by the College of Social Science, 5 by the School of Home Economics, 6 by the School of Music, 3 by the School of Visual Arts, and 1 each by the Schools of Dance, Criminology, Nursing, Social Work, and Theatre. Interdisciplinary majors. Distributive requirements. Graduate degrees granted. Independent and accelerated study. Honors program. Cooperative work/study, limited pass/fail, credit by exam, internships. Cross-registration with area schools. Study abroad. Elementary, secondary, and special education certification. ROTC, AFROTC; NROTC at Florida A&M. Oceanographic Institute. Art gallery. Museum. Computer center. 1,393,156-volume library with microform resources.

Financial CEEB CSS and ACT FAS. University scholarships, grants, loans, out-of-state tuition waivers, PELL, SEOG, NDSL, CWS. Application deadline March 1.

Admissions High school graduation with 7 units, 2.5 GPA, and SAT 950 composite or ACT 21 composite (3.0 GPA and SAT 1000 composite or ACT 23 composite for out-of-state applicants) required. Audition required for music and dance. $15 application fee. Rolling admissions. *Early Admission* and *Concurrent Enrollment* programs. Transfers accepted. Credit possible for CEEB AP and CLEP exams. Horizons Unlimited Program for disadvantaged.

Student Life Student government. Newspaper, magazines, yearbook, radio and TV stations. Music, dance, and drama groups. Debates. Circus. Departmental, honorary, religious, and service groups. 20 fraternities and 20 sororities, all with houses. 25% of students join. Freshmen encouraged to live on campus. Married-student housing. Cooperative houses for academically talented. 25% live on campus. Liquor prohibited. Honor code. Attendance in class expected. 8 intercollegiate sports for men, 8 for women; extensive intramural and club sports program. 10% from out of state.

MIAMI, UNIVERSITY OF $$

Coral Gables 33124, (305) 284-4323
Director of Admissions: George F. Giampetro

- **Undergraduates:** 4,400m, 3,300w
- **Tuition (1984–1985):** $6,950
- **Room and Board (1984–1985):** $3,000;   **Fees:** $220
- **Degrees offered:** BA, BS, BFA, BBA, BSEd, BSN, BMus, BArch, BSSysAnal, BGS, BSE
- **Mean SAT:** 490v, 540m,   **Mean ACT:** 23
- **Student-faculty ratio:** 17 to 1
- **Calendar system:** Semester

A private university established in 1925. 260-acre suburban campus on southern side of small city, 15 minutes from downtown Miami. Served by air, bus, and rail.
Academic Character SACS and professional accreditation. Semester system, 2 6-week summer terms. 33 majors offered in the College of Arts & Sciences, 11 in the School of Business Administration, 7 in the School of Education & Allied Professions, 7 in the School of Engineering & Architecture, 8 in the School of Music; Nursing. Non-major program in Afro-American studies. Honors and Privileged Studies programs. Preprofessional programs in dentistry, law, medicine. Credit-only option; credit by examination. Study abroad. ROTC, AFROTC. Computer center. 1,132,000-volume library.
Financial CEEB CSS. University scholarships, grants, and loans; PELL, SEOG, NDSL, NSL, FISL, CWS . Application deadline March 1.
Admissions High school graduation with 16 units required. $25 application fee. Rolling admissions; application deadline July 15. *Early Admission* Program. Transfers accepted. Credit possible for CEEB AP and CLEP exams.
Student Life Student government. Newspaper, magazine, 7 professional magazines, yearbook, radio station. Rathskeller. Drama. Over 200 honorary, professional, religious, special interest, and service groups. 12 fraternities, 7 with houses; 9 sororities, no houses. 8%-10% of men and 8% of women join. Freshmen live on campus. Limited housing for upperclass and married students. 42% live on campus. 6 intercollegiate sports for men, 6 for women; extensive intramural sports. AIAW. Student body composition: 2.3% Asian, 7.2% Black, 18.8% Hispanic, 0.4% Native American, 71.2% White.32% from out of state.

NEW COLLEGE OF THE UNIVERSITY OF SOUTH FLORIDA $

5700 North Tamiami Trail, Sarasota 33580. (813) 355-7671, Ext. 201
Director of Admissions: Roberto Noya

- **Undergraduates:** 175m, 175w
- **Tuition (1984–1985):** $947 (in-state), $2,426 (out-of-state)
- **Room and Board (1984–1985):** $2,475
- **Degrees offered:** BA
- **Mean SAT:** 613v, 618m,   **Mean Act:** 27.5
- **Student-faculty ratio:** 8 to 1
- **Calendar system:** 4–1–4

A public college established in 1964. Became a separate college of the University of South Florida in 1975. 100-acre suburban campus adjacent to the Ringling Museum of Art, and between the towns of Bradenton and Sarasota. Served by air, rail, and bus.

Academic Character SACS accreditation. 4-1-4 system. 22 majors offered in the humanities, natural sciences, and social sciences. Self-designed majors. 7 contracts, 3 independent study projects, thesis, and baccalaureate exam required. Independent study. Tutorials. No letter grades. Internships, field work. Classes at USF. Study abroad. Computer center. Electron microscope. 150,000-volume library with microform resources.

Financial College scholarships, grants, loans, merit awards, out-of-state tuition waivers, NDSL, FISL. Suggested application deadline is February 1.

Admissions High school graduation with college preparatory program recommended. Interview required for local residents. SAT or ACT required; SAT preferred. $15 application fee. Rolling admissions. *Early Decision* and *Early Admission* programs. Admission deferral possible.

Student Life Student government. Newspaper, literary magazine, yearbook. Music, dance, drama groups. Athletic, academic, special interest groups. Freshmen must live at school. Athletic activities. 50% of students from out of state.

ROLLINS COLLEGE $$

Winter Park 32789, (305) 646-2161
Director of Admissions: Julia H. Ingraham

- **Undergraduates:** 675m, 675w
- **Tuition (1984–1985):** $6,985
- **Room and Board (1984–1985):** $2,765; **Fees:** $226
- **Degrees offered:** BA
- **Mean SAT:** 470v, 510m
- **Student-faculty ratio:** 13 to 1
- **Calendar system:** 4–1–4

A private college established in 1885. 65-acre suburban campus in small city, 5 miles from Orlando and 120 miles from Jacksonville. Air, rail, and bus in Orlando.

Academic Character SACS and professional accreditation. 4-1-4 system. Majors offered in the arts, education, languages, theatre, natural sciences, social studies, music. Minors offered in business administration, computer science, religion, Russian, speech. Area studies majors available. Independent study. Honors program. Preprofessional programs in business, dentistry, law, medicine, ministry. 4-1 program in business administration offered at Rollins' Crummer School of Finance and Business Administration. 3-2 engineering programs with Auburn, Columbia, Georgia Tech, Washington U. 3-2 forestry program with Duke and U of Florida. Study abroad. Elementary and secondary education certification. AFROTC at U of Central Florida. Merrill-Palmer Program. Computer and language labs. 223,721-volume library with microform resources.

Financial CEEB CSS. College scholarships, grants, loans; PELL, SEOG, NDSL, CWS, Tuition Plan, Inc. Application deadline March 1.

Admissions High school graduation with 15 units recommended. Interview recommended. Audition or tape required for music majors. SAT or ACT required; 3 ACH recommended. $20 application fee. Application deadline March 1. $100 tuition and $150 room deposits required on acceptance of offer of admission. *Early Admission* and *Early Decision* programs. Transfers accepted. Admission deferral possible. Credit possible for CEEB AP and CLEP exams.

Student Life Student government. Newspaper, literary magazine, yearbook, radio station. Music and drama groups. "Real World" program. Student pub. Honorary and special interest groups. 6 fraternities and 6 sororities; all have houses. 40% of students join. Most freshmen live on campus. 24-hour visitation. Coed dorms. No married-student housing. 75% of students live on campus. Narcotics prohibited on campus. 2 years phys ed required. 8 intercollegiate sports for men, 8 for women; intramurals. AIAW, NCAA, Sunshine State Conference. Student body composition: 0.3% Asian, 2.5% Black, 3% Hispanic, 94.2% White. 55% from out of state.

SAINT LEO COLLEGE $

Saint Leo 33574, (904) 588-8283
Director of Admissions: Reverend J. Dennis Murphy, OSB

- **Undergraduates:** 600m, 500w
- **Tuition (1984–1985):** $4,095
- **Room and Board (1984–1985):** $1,500;   **Fees:** $305
- **Degrees offered:** BA, BS, BSW
- **Mean SAT:** 450v, 450m,   **Mean ACT:** 18
- **Student-faculty ratio:** 17 to 1
- **Calendar system:** Semester

A private college affiliated with the Order of Saint Benedict. 50-acre rural campus 30 miles northeast of Tampa. College bus to Tampa on opening, closing, and vacation days.

Academic Character SACS accreditation. Semester system, 6-week summer term. Majors offered in accounting, art, art management, biology, business administration, business education, criminology, dance-theatre, early childhood education, elementary education, English, history, human resources administration, management, marketing, medical technology (3-1), music, physical education, political science, psychology, real estate, religious education, religious study, restaurant management, secondary education, social work, sociology, special education, theatre-dance, secretarial science. Associate degrees in criminal justice, real estate, liberal arts, and secretarial science. Distributive requirements; 3 courses in philosophy/theology required. Independent study. Research options. Internships. Preprofessional programs in dentistry, law, medicine, nursing, osteopathy, pharmacy, veterinary medicine. Study abroad. Early childhood, elementary, secondary, and special education certification. ROTC. Language lab. 90,000-volume library with microform resources.

Financial CEEB CSS and ACT FAS. College scholarships, grants, loans, tuition reduction for 2nd family member. PELL, SEOG, NDSL, GSL, CWS, Florida Tuition Voucher Program, Insured Tuition Payment Plan, Academic Management Services, Inc. Preferred application deadline April 15.

Admissions High school graduation with 16 units required. GED accepted. Interview recommended. SAT or ACT required. $15 application fee. Rolling admissions; suggest applying early in 12th year. $100 tuition deposit required on acceptance of offer of admission. *Early Admission* Program. Transfers accepted. Admission deferral possible. Credit possible for CEEB AP and CLEP exams.

Student Life Student government. Yearbook. Music and theatre groups. Dance. Honor Society. Academic, service, and special interest groups. Fraternities and sororities. Single freshmen and sophomores (except veterans) live at home or on campus. 85% live on campus. 4 hours of phys ed required. 7 intercollegiate sports for men, 5 for women; extensive intramural programs. AIAW, NCAA. Student body composition: 11% Black, 5% Hispanic, 70.1% White. 53% from out of state.

STETSON UNIVERSITY $

DeLand 32720, (904) 7344121
Director of Admissions: Gary A. Meadows

- **Undergraduates:** 900m, 1,100w
- **Tuition (1984–1985):** $4,990
- **Room and Board (1984–1985):** $2,220; **Fees:** $200
- **Degrees offered:** BA, BS, BBA, BM, BSME
- **Mean SAT:** 514v, 551m, **Mean ACT:** 24
- **Student-faculty ratio:** 18 to 1
- **Calendar system:** Semester

A private university affiliated with the Baptist Church, established in 1883. 100-acre campus located in small city 20 miles west of Daytona Beach and 100 miles south of Jacksonville. Served by air, rail, and bus.
Academic Character SACS and professional accreditation. Semester system, 8-week summer term. 24 majors offered in the College of Liberal Arts, 5 in the School of Business Administration, 8 in the School of Music. Biblical studies and church leadership majors through Extension Division of Christian Education. Interdepartmental majors in social science and urban studies. Self-designed majors. Minors offered. Distributive requirements. 2 religion courses required. Independent and accelerated study. Honors programs. "Music Only" program for faculty-approved musicians. Phi Beta Kappa. Some pass/fail options, internships. Preprofessional programs in dentistry, law, medical technology, medicine, ministry, nursing, veterinary medicine. 3-2 program in engineering with U of Florida, U of Central Florida, and Washington U (MO); in forestry with Duke. 3-1 program in medical technology. Cross-registration with 4 area colleges. Study abroad. Elementary, secondary, and special education certification. ROTC. United Nations Semester. Language lab. 300,000-volume library with microform resources.
Financial CEEB CSS. University scholarships, grants, loans; pre-ministerial, academic, athletic, music scholarships. PELL, SEOG, NDSL, FISL, CWS, Tuition Plan, Inc. Suggested application deadline March 1.
Admissions High school graduation with 14 units of a college-preparatory program required. Audition required for music majors. ACT or SAT required. 2 ACH recommended. $20 application fee. Rolling admissions; suggest applying by March 15. $100 deposit required on acceptance of offer of admission. *Early Admission* and *Early Decision* programs. Transfers accepted. Admission deferral possible. Credit possible for CEEB AP and CLEP exams. Credit also possible for summer *Advanced Study* Program.
Student Life Student government. Newspaper, literary magazine, yearbook. Music and drama groups. Debates. Departmental and special interest groups. 7 fraternities with houses; 7 sororities without houses. 42% of men and 36% of women join. Single freshmen and sophomores under 21 and all single financial aid recipients must live on campus or at home. No coed dorms. No married-student housing. 80% of students live on campus. Students must

inform Dean before marriage. 3 semesters of phys ed required of liberal arts students under 30. 4 intercollegiate sports for men, 4 for women; extensive intramurals. AIAW, NCAA, Florida Intercollegiate Athletic Conference. Student body composition: 0.8% Asian, 2.6% Black, 1.2% Hispanic, 0.2% Native American, 95% White. 30% from out of state.

TAMPA, UNIVERSITY OF $$

Tampa 33606, (813) 253-8861
Director of Admissions: Walter Turner

- **Undergraduates:** 805m, 742w
- **Tuition (1984–1985):** $6,000)
- **Room and Board (1984–1985):** $2,700;   **Fees:** $300
- **Degrees offered:** BA, BS, BFA, BM
- **Mean SAT:** 474v, 509m,   **Mean ACT:** 21
- **Student-faculty ratio:** 16 to 1
- **Calendar system:** Bimester(2–2–2–2–1)

A private university established in 1931. Campus in business area of large city. Served by air, rail, and bus.
Academic Character SACS accreditation and professional accreditation. 2-2-2-2-1 system, 2 5-week summer terms. Majors offered in English, French, history, philosophy, political science, sociology, Spanish, urban affairs, accounting, biology, business management, chemistry, criminology, economics, elementary education, finance, marine science, math, medical technology, physical education, social work, psychology, social sciences, writing, art, music. Minors in some majors and in 3 other areas. Distributive requirements. Independent and accelerated study. Limited pass/fail, internships. Medical technology students work 15 months in approved lab. Honors program. Preprofessional programs in dentistry, engineering, law, medicine, and veterinary science. Study abroad. Elementary, secondary, and speech education certification. ROTC; AFROTC through U of South Florida. Language lab. 208,000-volume library.
Financial CEEB CSS. University scholarships, grants, loans, state grants and tuition vouchers. PELL, SEOG, NDSL, GSL, CWS, College Aid Plan, Tuition Plan, Inc. Scholarship and grant application deadline March 1; loan deadline March 15.
Admissions High school graduation with 15 units required. GED accepted. SAT or ACT required. $30 application fee. Rolling admissions; suggest applying early in 12th year. $150 deposit required on acceptance of offer of admission. *Early Admission* Program. Transfers accepted. Admission deferral possible. Credit possible for CEEB AP and CLEP exams; entrance with sophomore standing possible.
Student Life Student Congress. Newspaper, literary magazine, poetry review, yearbook. Public service programs on radio and TV. Music groups and participation in Sun State Opera. Theatre. Film society. Honorary, religious, and special interest groups. 8 fraternities, 4 with houses; 3 sororities without houses. 10% of students join. Coed and single-sex dorms. No married-student housing. 71% of students live on campus. Firearms, fireworks prohibited. Attendance in class required. 9 intercollegiate sports for men, 8 for women; extensive intramurals. FIC, NCAA. Student body composition: 1% Asian, 4% Black, 10% Hispanic, 1% Native American, 84% White. 54% from out of state.

Georgia

AGNES SCOTT COLLEGE $$

Decatur 30030, (404) 373-2571
Director of Admissions: Judith Maguire Tindel

- **Undergraduates:** 543w
- **Tuition (1984–1985):** $6,500
- **Room and Board (1984–1985):** $2,700;   **Fees:** $90
- **Degrees offered:** BA
- **Mean SAT:** 544v, 543m;   **Mean ACT:** 23
- **Student-faculty ratio:** 8 to 1
- **Calendar system:** Quarter

A private college established in 1889. 100-acre suburban campus 1 mile from Atlanta. Air, rail, and bus service in Atlanta.
Academic Character SACS accreditation. Quarter system, 6-week holiday Thanksgiving - New Year. 28 majors offered in the areas of art, Bible & religion, classics, economics, English, history, international relations, languages, mathematics, music, philosophy, political science, psychology, sciences, social sciences, and theatre. Interdisciplinary and self-designed majors. Distributives and 5 quarter hours of Biblical literature required. Independent study. Phi Beta Kappa. Pass/fail. Internships. Preprofessional programs in dentistry, law, and medicine. 3-2 program with Georgia Tech in engineering, information & computer science, industrial management & management science. Washington Semester. Exchange program with Mills College. Study abroad. Elementary and secondary education certification. AFROTC & NROTC at Georgia Tech. Observatory, language lab. 165,500-volume library with microform resources.
Financial CEEB CSS and ACT FAS. College scholarships, grants, loans, deferred payment; PELL, GSL, ALAS. Priority application deadline February 15.
Admissions High school graduation with 16 units recommended. SAT or ACT required; SAT preferred. 3 ACH required. $25 application fee. Rolling admissions. $250 deposit required on acceptance of offer of admission. *Early Admission* and *Concurrent Enrollment* programs. Admission deferral possible. Transfers accepted. Credit possible for CEEB AP exams.
Student Life Student government. Newspaper, magazine, yearbook. Music, drama, dance groups. Students for Black Awareness. Religious, academic, service, and special interest groups. Students must live at home or on campus. Language halls. Married-student housing. 93% of students live on campus. Midnight curfew, class attendance requirement for fall-quarter freshmen. Attendance at 7 convocations required. 6 quarters of phys ed required. 3 intercollegiate sports; intramurals. AIAW. Student body composition: 0.9% Asian, 3.8% Black, 1.5% Hispanic, 0.4% Native American, 93.4% White. 53% from out of state.

BERRY COLLEGE $

Mount Berry 30149, (404) 235-4494
Dean of Admissions: Thomas C. Glover

- **Undergraduates:** 521m, 686w
- **Tuition (1984–1985):** $4,125
- **Room and Board (1984–1985):** $1,920–$2,385
- **Degrees offered:** BS, BA, BM, AS
- **Mean SAT:** 496v, 538m,   **Mean ACT:** 24.5
- **Student-faculty ratio:** 14 to 1
- **Calendar system:** Quarter

A private college established in 1902. 28,000-acre suburban campus bordering the small city of Rome, 65 miles from Atlanta. Served by bus.

Academic Character SACS and professional accreditation. Quarter system; December mini-term, summer quarter. 35 majors offered in the areas of business, agriculture, art, social sciences, science, education, English, foreign language, history, home economics, mathematics, music, physical education, religion & philosophy, speech & drama. Self-designed majors. Minor or double major required. Minors offered in most major fields and in 6 additional areas. Distributive requirements. 1 religion or philosophy course required. MEd, MBA granted. Independent study. Cooperative work/study, pass/fail, internships. Credit by exam. Preprofessional programs in allied health, dentistry, engineering, forestry, law, medicine, optometry, pharmacy, theology, veterinary medicine. 3-2 engineering program with Georgia Tech. Study abroad. Summer study at Gulf Coast Research Lab in Mississippi. Elementary and secondary education certification. ROTC. Language lab. 120,000-volume library with microform resources.

Financial CEEB CSS. College scholarships, grants, loans; PELL, SEOG, NDSL, Tuition Plan, Education Funds, CWS, Scholarship-Work-Loan Plan. Scholarship application deadline February 1.

Admissions High school graduation with 16 units required. SAT or ACT required. $15 application fee. Rolling admissions; suggest applying by February 1. $75 tuition and $50 room deposits required on acceptance of offer of admission. *Early Admission* and *Concurrent Enrollment* programs. Transfers accepted. Admission deferral possible. Credit possible for CEEB AP and CLEP exams.

Student Life Student government; all students join. Newspaper, magazine, yearbook. Music, debate, and drama groups. International Relations Club. Religious, service, academic, and special interest groups. Freshmen and sophomores must live at home or on campus. No coed dorms or married-student housing. 74% of students live on campus. Liquor prohibited on campus. 4 quarters of phys ed and 1 of first aid required. 5 intercollegiate sports for men, 5 for women; intramurals. AIAW, NAIA. Student body composition: 0.4% Asian, 2.7% Black, 0.7% Hispanic, 95.5% White. 26% from out of state.

EMORY UNIVERSITY $$

Atlanta 30322, (404) 329-6036
Director of Admissions: Linda S. Davis

- **Undergraduates:** 2,031m, 2,208w
- **Tuition (1984–1985):** $7,550
- **Room and Board (1984–1985):** $3,100;   **Fees:** $80
- **Degrees offered:** BA, BBA, BSN, AA
- **Mean SAT:** 550v, 600m,   **Mean ACT:** 27

- **Student-faculty ratio:** 11 to 1
- **Calendar system:** Semester

A private university affiliated with the Methodist Church, established in 1836; became coed in 1953. 600-acre suburban campus just outside Atlanta. Served by air, rail and bus.

Academic Character SACS and professional accreditation. Semester system. 5-, 6-, and 9-week summer terms. 34 majors offered by Emory College in the areas of Afro-American studies, art history, social & political sciences, science, classics, economics, education, English, foreign languages, history, international studies, mathematics, medieval & Renaissance studies, music, philosophy, religion. Other majors offered by the Schools of Business Administration and Nursing. Self-designed and joint majors. Dual degree programs in chemistry, English, history, math, math/computer science, philosophy, physics, psychology, political science, sociology. Distributive requirements. Graduate and professional degrees granted. Independent study. Honors program. Phi Beta Kappa. Pass/fail. Internships. Exchange program with 4 area schools. Washington Semester. Study abroad. Elementary and secondary education certification. ROTC at Georgia State; NROTC at Georgia Tech. Computer center, language lab. 1.8 million-volume library with microform resources.

Financial CEEB CSS. University scholarships, grants, courtesy scholarships, Methodist scholarships, loans; PELL, SEOG, NDSL, FISL, CWS. Application deadlines April 1 (scholarships), April 15 (loans).

Admissions High school graduation with 16 units required. SAT or ACT required; SAT preferred. $25 application fee. Application deadline February 15. $250 deposit required on acceptance of offer of admission. *Early Decision* and *Early Admission* programs. Transfers accepted. Admission deferral possible. Credit possible for CEEB AP and CLEP exams.

Student Life Student government. Newspaper, magazine, yearbook. Music, drama, debate groups. Black Student and Women's Liberation groups. Academic, religious, honorary, service, political, and special interest groups. 14 fraternities and 10 sororities; all have houses. 50% of students join. Freshmen must live at home or on campus. Coed and single-sex dorms. Married-student housing. 70% of students live on campus. Dormitory freshmen may not have cars on campus during weekday. 2 years of phys ed required. 5 intercollegiate sports for men, 4 for women; intramurals. AIAW, NCAA. Student body composition: 4% Asian, 6% Black, 2% Hispanic, 83% White, 5% Other. 80% from out of state.

GEORGIA, UNIVERSITY OF $

Athens 30602, (404) 453-5187
Director of Admissions: M. Overton Phelps

- **Undergraduates:** 9,000m, 10,000w
- **Tuition, Room and Board (1984–1985):** $4,200 (in-state), $6,150 (out-of-state)
- **Degrees offered:** AB, BS, BFA, BMus, BBA, BLA, ABJ
- **Mean SAT:** 483v, 533m
- **Student-faculty ratio:** 29 to 1
- **Calendar system:** Quarter

A public university established in 1785. 3,500-acre campus in Athens, 80 miles from Atlanta. Served by air, rail, and bus.

Academic Character SACS and professional accreditation. Quarter system, summer term. 24 majors offered by the College of Agriculture, 49 by the Franklin College of Arts & Sciences, 15 by the College of Business Administration, 24 by the College of Education, 16 by the College of Home Economics, 1 by the School of Environmental Design, 5 by the School of Forest Resources, 8 by the Henry Grady School of Journalism, 1 by the School of Pharmacy, and 1 by the School of Social Work. Self-designed majors. Graduate and professional degrees granted. Independent study. Honors program. Phi Beta Kappa. Pass/fail. Internships. Preprofessional programs in allied health, dentistry, forest resources, medicine, optometry, veterinary medicine, and for all professional schools and colleges in the University. 3-2 program in engineering with Georgia Tech. 3-1 programs in medicine, dentistry, veterinary medicine. Study abroad. Elementary, secondary, and special education certification. ROTC, AFROTC. Language lab, gerontology center, museum. 2,062,499-volume library with microform resources.

Financial CEEB CSS. University scholarships and loans, health professions loans; PELL, SEOG, NDSL, GSL, CWS. Scholarship application deadline April 15.

Admissions High school graduation with 16 units required. SAT required. $15 application fee. Rolling admissions; suggest applying by end of 1st semester. $50 room deposit required on acceptance of offer of admission. *Early Admission* and *Early Decision* programs. Transfers accepted. Credit possible for CEEB AP and CLEP exams; University has own advanced placement program.

Student Life Student government. Newspaper, yearbook, other publications. Music, debate, drama groups. 370 registered religious, honorary, academic, and special interest groups. 30 fraternities and 19 sororities, all with houses. 21% of men and 26% of women join. Coed and single-sex dorms; married-student apartments. 30% of students live on campus. Phys ed required for freshmen and sophomores. Many intercollegiate and intramural sports. Southeastern Conference. Student body composition: 0.4% Asian, 4.5% Black, 0.5% Hispanic, 0.1% Native American, 90.1% White, 4.4% Other. 17% from out of state.

GEORGIA INSTITUTE OF TECHNOLOGY $

Atlanta 30332, (404) 894-4154
Director of Admissions: Jerry L. Hitt

- **Undergraduates:** 6,887m, 1,888w
- **Tuition (1984–1985):** $1,132 (in-state), $5,076 (out-of-state)
- **Room and Board (1984–1985):** $2,550; **Fees:** $241.50
- **Degrees offered:** BS, BSE
- **Mean SAT:** 524v, 632m
- **Student-faculty ratio:** 18 to 1
- **Calendar system:** Quarter

A public institute established in 1885, became coed in 1952. 300-acre urban campus in downtown Atlanta. Served by air, rail, and bus.

Academic Character SACS and professional accreditation. Quarter system, 11-week summer term. BS offered in applied biology, applied mathematics, applied physics, applied psychology, architecture, building construction, chemistry, economics, health physics, health systems, industrial design, industrial management, information & computer science, management science, physics, textile chemistry, and textiles; BE offered in aerospace, ceramic, chemical, civil, electrical, industrial, mechanical, nuclear, and textile engineering, and in engineering science and mechanics. Self-designed majors. Dual degree programs. Courses offered in languages and social sciences. Distributive, English proficiency, and major area exam requirements. MS, PhD granted. Honors program. Cooperative work/study, internships. Pass/fail. 3-2 program in engineering with 100 institutions. Study abroad. ROTC, NROTC, AFROTC. Secondary education certification. Computer center. Experimental centers for engineering, health systems, water resources, nuclear research, environmental resources, bioengineering, radiological protection. 1,300,000-volume library with microform resources.

Financial CEEB CSS. Institute scholarships, grants, loans, deferred payment; PELL, SEOG, NDSL, FISL, CWS; institute has own work program. Application deadline February 15.

Admissions High school graduation with 10-11 units required. SAT required. $15 application fee. Rolling admissions; application deadlines April 1 (in-state), January 1 (out-of-state). $100 tuition and $75 room deposits required on acceptance of offer of admission. *Early Decision* and *Early Admission* programs. Admission deferral possible. Transfers accepted. Credit possible for CEEB AP exams.

Student Life Student government. Newspaper, technical publication, yearbook, radio station. Music, debate, drama groups. Religious, political, and special interest groups. 29 fraternities and 4 sororities, all with houses. 35% of men and 25% of women join. Single freshmen must live at home or on campus. N coed dorms. Cooperative dorms. Married-student housing. 45% of students live on campus. Liquor at student functions, gambling, drugs, hazing prohibited on campus. 3 hours of phys ed, including swimming, required. Several intercollegiate sports for men, 5 for women; intramurals for men. ACC. Student body composition: 4% Asian, 6% Black, 3% Hispanic, 1% Native American, 86% White. 47% from out of state.

MOREHOUSE COLLEGE $

Atlanta 30314, (404) 681-2800
Director of Admissions: Robert E. Miller

- **Undergraduates:** 2,001m
- **Tuition (1984–1985):** $3,480
- **Room and Board (1984–1985):** $2,560; **Fees:** $380
- **Degrees offered:** BA, BS
- **Mean SAT:** 380v, 420m
- **Student-faculty ratio:** 18 to 1
- **Calendar system:** Semester

A private college established in 1867. 40-acre urban campus in Atlanta. Served by air, bus, and rail.

Academic Character SACS accreditation. Semester system, 8-week summer term. 33 majors offered by the departments of English, Foreign Languages, Philosophy & Religion, Music, Art, Drama, Biology, Chemistry, Mathematics, Physics, Psychology, Engineering, Economics & Business Administration, Computer Science, History, Political Science, Sociology, Teacher Education, and Health & Physical Education. Minors offered in African studies, Afro-American studies, Caribbean studies, and library science. Courses in non-Western studies, Russian, Swahili. Distributive requirements. 1 religion course and senior comprehensive exam required. Phi

Beta Kappa. Internships. Preprofessional programs in dentistry, medicine, pharmacy. Cooperative programs with Interdenominational Theological Center, Clark, Morris Brown, Spelman. 3-2 program in engineering with Georgia Tech. Early childhood, elementary, and secondary education certification. ROTC, AFROTC, NROTC at Georgia Tech. 300,000-volume library serves all members of Atlanta U. Center.

Financial CEEB CSS. College scholarships, Georgia incentive grants, loans; PELL, SEOG, GSL, NDSL, CWS. Member United Negro College Fund. Application deadline April 15 (scholarships, loans), June 1 (Georgia incentive grants). $80 acceptance fee required within 20 days of award.

Admissions High school graduation with 12 units required. GED accepted. SAT required. $15 application fee. Rolling admissions; application deadline April 15. $80 deposit required on acceptance of offer of admission. *Early Admission* Program. Transfers accepted.

Student Life Newspaper, yearbook. Music, debate, drama groups. Honorary, academic, and special interest groups. 4 fraternities; all have houses. 16% join. Freshmen must live on campus. 50% of students live on campus. Liquor and weapons prohibited on campus. Attendance in class and at weekly chapel required. Phys ed required for freshmen. 5 intercollegiate sports; intramurals. NCAA, SIAC. Student body composition: 100% Black. 70% from out of state.

SPELMAN COLLEGE $

Atlanta 30314, (404) 681-3643, ext. 300
Director of Admissions: Juanita Wallace Dillard

- **Undergraduates:** 1,642w
- **Tuition (1984–1985):** $3,350
- **Room and Board (1984–1985):** $2,730;   **Fees:** $465
- **Degrees offered:** BA, BS
- **Mean SAT:** 400v, 400m,   **Mean ACT:** 17
- **Student-faculty ratio:** 18 to 1
- **Calendar system:** Semester

A private college established in 1881. 32-acre urban campus in Atlanta. Served by air and bus.

Academic Character SACS accreditation. Semester system, 8-week summer term with Atlanta U. Majors offered in art, biochemistry, biology, chemistry, child development, computer sciences, drama, economics, English, French, German, health/physical education, history, mathematics, music, natural sciences, philosophy, physics, political science, psychology, sociology, and Spanish. Distributive requirements. Independent study. Honors program. Phi Beta Kappa. Pass/fail. Internships. Member Atlanta U. Center. 3-2 program in engineering with Georgia Tech or Boston U. 3-1 program in medicine. Preprofessional program in medicine. Exchange with Mount Holyoke, Simmons, Smith, and Wellesley Colleges. Study abroad. ROTC, AFROTC; NROTC through Morehouse College. Elementary, secondary, and special education teacher training. Nursery-Kindergarten school, language lab. 553,197-volume library; 250,000-volume library with microform resources available through Atlanta U. Center.

Financial CEEB CSS. College scholarships and loans; PELL, SEOG, NDSL, deferred payment plan, CWS. Application deadline April 1.

Admissions High school graduation with 15 units required. SAT or ACT required. Interview may be required. $20 application fee. Application deadline January 15. Notification by March 1. $100 deposit required on acceptance of offer of admission. *Early Decision* and *Early Admission* programs. Transfers accepted. Admission deferral possible. Credit possible for CEEB AP and CLEP exams.

Student Life Student government. Newspaper, magazine, yearbook. Music, drama, dance groups. Academic, political, religious, service, and special interest groups. Students may live off campus. Honors dorm. No married-student housing. 58% of students live on campus. Juniors and seniors may have cars on campus. Liquor and illegal drugs prohibited on campus; cigarette smoking allowed in some areas. Limited class absences. Attendance at biweekly convocations required. 4 semesters of phys ed required. 2 intercollegiate and 6 intramural sports. Student body composition: 100% Black. 66% from out of state.

Hawaii

CHAMINADE UNIVERSITY OF HONOLULU $

3140 Waialae Avenue, Honolulu 96816, (808) 735-4735
Director of Admissions: William F. Murray, Jr.

- **Undergraduates:** 524m, 440w
- **Tuition (1984–1985):** $3,480
- **Room and Board (1984–1985):** $2,818; **Fees:** $90
- **Degrees offered:** BA, BS, BBA, BFA, BGS, AA, AGS
- **Mean SAT:** 377v, 453m, **Mean ACT:** 19
- **Student-faculty ratio:** 16 to 1
- **Calendar system:** Semester

A private university founded in 1955 by the Roman Catholic Marianist order. 67-acre campus in residential St. Louis Heights area of Honolulu, overlooking Diamond Head and Waikiki.
Academic Character WASC accreditation. Semester system, 2 6-week summer terms; accelerated semester system in evening and off-campus programs. Majors in accounting, American studies, applied math, art, behavioral sciences, biology, business administration, chemistry, computer science, criminal justice, education, English, general business, general psychology, history, humanities, international studies, management science, marketing science, philosophy, political science, psychology, religious studies, social studies, sociology, and studio art. Special majors. Minors in most major areas and in anthropology, drama, physics, speech communications. Associate degrees in business management, history, leadership management, criminal justice, social studies. Distributives and 6 semester hours of religious studies required. MBA granted. Directed independent reading and research. Internships. Credit/no credit option, credit by exam. Preprofessional programs in biomedical sciences and law. Concurrent enrollment possible with UHawaii at Manoa, Brigham Young U in Hawaii, Hawaii Loa, Hawaii Pacific. Semester at Sea. Provisional early childhood (Montessori), elementary, and secondary education certification; 5th-Year Certificate Program. ROTC and AFROTC through UHawaii at Manoa. 55,000-volume library.
Financial CEEB CSS. University scholarships and grants, state grants & loans; PELL, SEOG, NDSL, GSL, CWS. Application deadline March 15.
Admissions High school graduation with 15 units required. Interview recommended. SAT or ACT required. $25 application fee. Rolling admissions; deadline August 1. $25 tuition and $50 room deposits required on acceptance of offer of admission. *Early Decision, Early Entrance, Concurrent Enrollment* programs. Admission deferral possible. Transfers accepted. Credit possible for CEEB AP and CLEP exams, and for life/work experience. College prep program in reading, English, and math.
Student Life Student government. Newspaper, literary magazine, yearbook. Drama groups. Honor societies. Special interest clubs. Coed, single-sex, and special interest housing. Apartments. 25% of students live on campus. Class attendance expected. 4 intercollegiate sports for men and women; intramurals. NAIA, NCAA. Student body composition: 54% Asian, 3% Black, 1% Hispanic, 1% Native American, 41% White. 43% of students from out of state.

HAWAII, UNIVERSITY OF, AT HILO $

1400 Kapiolani Street, Hilo 96720, (808) 961-9311
Admissions Coordinator: Peggy Yorita

- **Undergraduates:** 1,656m, 1,901w
- **Tuition (1984–1985):** $760 (in-state), $2,870 (out-of-state)
- **Room and Board (1984–1985):** $2,228;   **Fees:** $30
- **Degrees offered:** BA, BBA, BS, AA, AS
- **Mean SAT:** 393v, 465m
- **Student-faculty ratio:** 17 to 1
- **Calendar system:** Semester

A public university organized in 1970 and including Hawaii Community College, Center for Continuing Education, College of Agriculture, and College of Arts & Sciences. 2 campuses comprising 80 acres in Hilo on Hawaii, 200 air miles from Honolulu. Airport, bus station.

Academic Character WASC and professional accreditation. Semester system, 6-week summer term. Majors in animal husbandry, general agriculture, tropical crop production (BS); anthropology, biology, business administration, chemistry, economics, English, geography, Hawaiian studies, history, liberal studies, linguistics, math, music, philosophy, physics, political science, psychology, social science, sociology, speech (BA, BBA); AA, AS, and certificates in 18 vocational-technical areas. Individual programs possible. Distributive requirements. Inter-college registration possible. 2-year transfer programs in engineering, nursing; 1-year transfer program in home economics. Biomedical research program, Marine Option Program. Study abroad. Provisional elementary and secondary education certification. Farm laboratory. Computer center. 160,000-volume library with microform resources.

Financial CEEB CSS. University scholarships and loans, state scholarships and loans; PELL, SEOG, NSS, NDSL, GSL, NSL, PLUS, CWS. Application deadline March 1.

Admissions High school graduation with 15 units required for 4-year programs; age of 18 required for 2-year programs. GED accepted. SAT or ACT required. $10 application fee for out-of-state applicants. Rolling admissions; deadline July 15. *Early Admission* Program. Transfers accepted. Credit possible for CEEB AP and CLEP exams, and for university language placement tests.

Student Life Student government. Newspaper. Music and drama organizations. Academic, honorary, religious, political, and special interest groups. Limited on-campus housing. Married-student housing. Coed dorms. 13% of students live on campus. Limited parking on campus. Permission required for liquor at campus activities. No lethal weapons allowed in or around dorms. 5 intercollegiate sports for men, 3 for women; intramurals. AIAW, NAIA, NCAA. Student body composition: 56% Asian/Pacific, 7% Foreign, 6% Hispanic, 22% White, 9% Other. 12% from out of state.

Idaho

IDAHO, COLLEGE OF $

2112 Cleveland, Caldwell 83605, (208) 459-5011
Dean of Admissions & External Affairs: Brett S. Harrell

- **Undergraduates:** 326m, 305w
- **Tuition (1984–1985):** $5,072
- **Room and Board (1984–1985):** $2,556; **Fees:** $175
- **Degrees offered:** BA, BS, BBA
- **Mean SAT:** 480v, 510m, **Mean ACT:** 22.2
- **Student-faculty ratio:** 13 to 1
- **Calendar system:** 4–1–4

A private college affiliated with the United Presbyterian Church, and founded in 1891. Campus in the small town of Caldwell, 25 miles west of Boise. Bus and train stations in Caldwell, airport in Boise.

Academic Character NASC accreditation. 4-1-4 system, 6-week summer term. Majors offered in American studies, art, biology, business administration, chemistry, elementary education, English literature, English teaching, history, human ecology, human services, math, math/computer science, math teaching, music, philosophy, phys ed, political science, psychology, religion, social studies teaching, sociology, zoology. J.A. Albertson School of Business offers a BBA in accounting, business administration, computer information systems. Minors possible in most major areas. Distributives and 1 Biblical literature course required. MAEd, MEd granted; Planned Fifth-Year Program offers advanced (non-Master's) education certification. Interdisciplinary study. Independent study. Honors programs. Pass/fail, credit by exam. Internships. Preprofessional programs in dentistry, medicine, optometry, physical therapy, seminary studies, veterinary medicine. 3-2 engineering program with Columbia, U of Idaho, Washington U (MO), Stanford. Study abroad. Elementary and secondary education certification. Computer system. 155,000-volume library.

Financial CEEB CSS (preferred) and ACT FAS. College scholarships, grants, loans; Presbyterian scholarships, grants, and loans; Native American Education Grants; PELL, SEOG, SSIG, PLUS, FISL, GSL, NDSL, CWS, college part-time employment. Budgeted tuition payment plan. File application with application for admission.

Admissions High school graduation required with 12 units recommended. GED accepted. Interview suggested. ACT or SAT required. $15 application fee. Rolling admissions. Apply any time after beginning of 11th year. $45 deposit required on acceptance of offer of admission. Non-degree-credit *Concurrent Enrollment* Program. Transfers accepted. Credit possible for CEEB AP and CLEP exams. Probational, provisional, and conditional admission possible.

Student Life Student government. Newspaper, yearbook. Literary, drama, music, religious, and political groups. Special academic societies. Honorary service societies. 3 fraternities and 4 sororities without houses. Single freshmen & sophomores under 21 must live at home or on campus. Dorms for men and women. Dining hall. Class attendance expected. 3 phys ed courses required. 2 intercollegiate sports for men, 2 for women; intramural and club sports.

IDAHO, UNIVERSITY OF $

Moscow 83843, (208) 885-6326
Director of Admissions & Registrar: Matt Telin

- **Undergraduates:** 4,232m, 2,648w
- **Tuition (1984–1985):** 0 (in-state), $2,000 (out-of-state)
- **Room and Board (1984–1985):** $2,000;   **Fees:** $816
- **Degrees offered:** BA, BS
- **Mean SAT:** 445v, 488m,   **Mean ACT:** 21.2
- **Student-faculty ratio:** 18 to 1
- **Calendar system:** Semester

A public university established in 1889. 1,450-acre campus and college farm in the small city of Moscow, 85 miles from Spokane, WA and 310 miles from Boise, ID.

Academic Character NASC and professional accreditation. Semester system, 8-week summer term. 132 majors offered by the Colleges of Agriculture, Art & Architecture, Business & Economics, Education, Engineering, Letters & Sciences, Mines & Earth Resources, and Forestry, Wildlife, & Range Sciences. Combined programs possible. 1- and 2-year pre-nursing programs. Distributive requirements. Graduate & professional degrees granted. Honors program; Phi Beta Kappa. Pass/fail. Study abroad. Elementary, secondary, and special education certification. ROTC, NROTC; AFROTC at Washington State. Language labs. 975,000-volume library.

Financial CEEB CSS. University and merit scholarships, deferred payment; PELL, SEOG, SSIG, NDSL, FISL, GSL, CWS. Application deadline March 1.

Admissions High school graduation with 15 units required. Out-of-state applicant must graduate in top 50% of class. SAT or ACT required. $10 application fee. Rolling admissions; deadline August 1. $25 deposit required on acceptance of offer of admission. *Early Decision* and *Early Entrance* programs. Admission deferral possible. Transfers accepted. Credit possible for CEEB AP and CLEP exams. Students with academic deficiencies may be considered for admission.

Student Life Student government. Newspaper, yearbook, radio & TV stations. Music and debate groups. Dance and drama productions. Young Democrats, Young Republicans. Many academic, athletic, honorary, service, and special interest groups. 18 fraternities and 9 sororities; all with houses. 16% of men and 22% of women join. Married-student housing. Men's and women's co-op dorms. 45% of students live on campus. Class attendance expected. 2 semesters of phys ed required; freshman women must complete one course in healthful living. 8 intercollegiate sports for men, 8 for women; intramurals. AIAW, NCAA, Big Sky, Northwest College Women's Sports Association. Student body composition: 1% Asian, 0.5% Black, 0.6% Hispanic, 0.6% Native American, 94.6% White, 2.7% Other. 20% from out of state.

IDAHO STATE UNIVERSITY $

Pocatello 83209, (208) 236-0211
Director of Admissions: Tim Hayhurst

- **Undergraduates:** 1,819m, 1,621w
- **Tuition and Fees (1984–1985):** $811 (in-state), $2,711 (out-of-state)
- **Room and Board (1984–1985):** $1,660–$1,840

- **Degrees offered:** BA, BS, BMus, BVTE, BUS, BBA, AA, AS
- **Mean ACT:** 18.1
- **Student-faculty ratio:** 15 to 1
- **Calendar system:** Semester

A public university established in 1901, and located in the eastern residential section of Pocatello. Air and bus services in Pocatello.

Academic Character NASC and professional accreditation. Semester system, 8-week summer term. 6 majors offered by College of Business, 7 by College of Education, 6 by College of Health-Related Professions, 32 by College of Liberal Arts, 21 by School of Vocational-Technical Education. Other divisions are College of Pharmacy, School of Engineering, School of Graduate Studies. Distributive requirements. Graduate degrees granted. Noncredit independent study. Honors program. Pass/fail option. Preprofessional programs in dental hygiene, dentistry, law, optometry, osteopathy, medicine, pharmacy, veterinary medicine. 3-2 engineering, 2-2 agriculture and forestry, and 3-1 medical technology programs. Cooperative program in dentistry with Creighton U. Radiation protection "training-study" program. Elementary and secondary education certification. ROTC. 1,000,000-volume library.

Financial CEEB CSS. University scholarships, grants, loans; state scholarships, health professional loans, non-resident fee waivers; PELL, SSIG, SEOG, GSL, NDSL, NSL, CWS. Application deadlines in April (scholarships, grants) and May 1 (loans).

Admissions Open admission to high school graduates who specify ISU as a choice on their ACT form. ACT required for placement and counseling. No application fee. Application deadline August 1. $35 housing reservation deposit required. *Early Entrance* Program. Transfers accepted (minimum out-of-state GPA of 2.0 required). Credit possible for CEEB AP exams.

Student Life Student government. Newspaper, yearbook. University Bank. Music groups. Honorary drama group. Young Democrats, Young Republicans. Crafts workshop. Honorary, professional, religious, special interest groups. 5 fraternities, 4 with houses, and 3 sororities with a shared dorm. 10% of men and women join. Dorms for men & women. Some married-student apartments. 20% of students live on campus. Liquor not allowed on campus. Class attendance expected. 10 intercollegiate sports for men; intramurals. NCAA, Big Sky. Student body composition: 1.3% Asian, 0.7% Black, 1% Hispanic, 0.5% Native American, 96.5% White. 8% from out of state.

Illinois

AUGUSTANA COLLEGE $$

639 38th Street, Rock Island 61201, (309) 794-7341
Vice-President for Admissions & Financial Aid: Ralph Starenko

- **Undergraduates:** 1,081m, 1,120w
- **Tuition (1984–1985):** $5,613
- **Room and Board (1984–1985):** $2,520; **Fees:** $42
- **Degrees offered:** BA, BMus, BMus Ed
- **Mean Sat:** 500v, 500m, **Mean ACT:** 24
- **Student-faculty ratio:** 17 to 1
- **Calendar system:** Quarter

A private college established in 1860, affiliated with the Lutheran Church. 110-acre urban campus in a small city overlooking the Mississippi River, 165 miles from Chicago. Served by air, rail, and bus.

Academic Character NCACS and professional accreditation. Quarter system, 7 3- to 9-week summer terms. Over 40 majors offered in the areas of liberal arts, sciences, education, engineering, computer science, medical technology, medicine, music, physical education, public administration, religion, urban studies, Scandinavian, Spanish, and speech. Distributives and 12 credits in religion required. Masters degrees granted. Interdisciplinary studies and special sequences. Journalism concentration. Independent study. Honors program. Phi Beta Kappa. Pass/fail, internships. Preprofessional programs in law, ministry, pharmacy, physiotherapy, veterinary medicine. 3-2 engineering program with U of Illinois, Northwestern, Purdue. 3-2 forestry and environmental management programs with Duke. Washington Semester. Study abroad. Elementary and secondary education certification. Speech and Hearing Center. Computer center. Language lab. Planetarium. 230,000-volume library.

Financial CEEB CSS and ACT FAS. College scholarships, grants, loans, state grants, pre-ministerial loans, tuition reduction for 2nd family member, deferred payment. PELL, SEOG, NDSL, CWS.

Admissions High school graduation with 16 units recommended. GED accepted. Interview encouraged. SAT or ACT required. $15 application fee. Rolling admissions; suggest applying early in 12th year. $100 deposit required on acceptance of offer of admission. *Early Decision* Program. Transfers accepted. Credit possible for CEEB AP exams; college has own advanced placement program.

Student Life Student Union. Newspaper, literary magazines, yearbook, radio station. Music and drama groups. Handel Oratorio Society. Debate. Black Student Union. Cheerleaders. Feminist forum. Athletic, academic, honorary, political, religious, service, and social groups. 6 fraternities and 6 sororities without houses. 40% of men and 35% of women join. Students must live at home or on campus. Single-sex dorms. No married-student housing. 65% live on campus. Liquor and gambling prohibited. 4 activity courses required. 9 intercollegiate sports for men, 7 for women; extensive intramural program. AIAW, College Conference of Illinois and Wisconsin. Student body composition: 0.2% Asian, 7% Black, 0.5% Hispanic, 92.3% White. 16% from out of state.

BRADLEY UNIVERSITY $$

Peoria 61625, (309) 676-7611
Director of Admissions: Robert G. Voss

- **Undergraduates:** 2,635m, 1,944w
- **Tuition (1984–1985):** $5,750
- **Room and Board (1984–1985):** $2,800;   **Fees:** $10
- **Degrees offered:** BA, BS, BFA, BMus, BMus Ed, BSCE, BSEE, BSIE, BSME, BSCon
- **Mean SAT:** 480v, 550m,   **Mean ACT:** 24
- **Student-faculty ratio:** 16 to 1
- **Calendar system:** Semester

A private university established in 1897. 65-acre urban residential campus halfway between St. Louis and Chicago.

Academic Character NCACS and professional accreditation. Semester system, 2 5-week summer terms, 3-week interim term. 7 majors offered by the College of Business Administration, 26 by Communications & Fine Arts, 10 by Education, 10 by Engineering & Technology, 2 by Health Sciences, 26 by Liberal Arts & Sciences, and 2 by the Institute of International Studies. Minors offered. Academic Exploration Program. Black studies program. Masters degrees granted. Phi Beta Kappa. Cooperative work/study, pass/fail, internships, credit by exam. Preprofessional programs in allied health, law. 3-1 program in medical technology. 5-year liberal arts & MBA program. Washington semester. Study abroad. Elementary, secondary, and special education certification. ROTC. Urban Studies Institute. College of Continuing Education. Computer center. Language labs. Over 350,000-volume library with microform resources.

Financial CEEB CSS. University scholarships, grants, loans, deferred and monthly payment plans; PELL, SEOG, NSS, NDSL, CWS. Priority to early applicants; notification starts January 15.

Admissions High school graduation with 9 units required. GED accepted. Interview highly recommended. Requirements vary for individual majors. Audition required for music majors. SAT or ACT required. $20 application fee. Rolling admissions; apply between August 1 and June 1. $100 tuition deposit required on acceptance of offer of admission; $50 room deposit due on registration. *Early Admission* Program. Bradley Preference Plan. Admission deferral possible. Transfers accepted. Credit possible for CEEB AP and CLEP exams.

Student Life Student Senate and Supreme Court. AWS. Newspaper, yearbook, radio and TV stations. Many music groups. Debate, discussion, oratory. Theatre. Athletic, honorary, professional, religious, and special interest groups. 17 fraternities, 10 sororities; all with houses. 30% of men and 26% of women join. Juniors and seniors may live off campus. Single-sex and coed dorms. Student apartments. 90% of students live on campus. 3 hours of phys ed required of all education students. 7 intercollegiate sports for men, 5 for women; several club and intramural sports. AIAW, NCAA, Missouri Valley Athletic Conference. Student body composition: 8% Black, 2% Hispanic, 90% White. 21% from out of state.

CHICAGO, THE UNIVERSITY OF $$$

Chicago 60637, (312) 753-1234
Dean of Admissions & Financial Aid: Dan Hall

- **Undergraduates:** 1,758m, 1,172w
- **Tuition** (1984–1985): $8,685
- **Room and Board** (1984–1985): $4,100;   **Fees:** $267
- **Degrees offered:** BA, BS
- **Median SAT:** 620v, 645m,   **Median ACT:** 29
- **Student-faculty ratio:** 6 to 1
- **Calendar system:** Quarter

A private university established in 1890. 171-acre urban campus. Served by air, rail, and bus.

Academic Character NCACS and professional accreditation. Quarter system, 10-week summer term. 13 majors offered by the division of Biological Sciences, 19 by Humanities, 6 by Physical Sciences, and 12 by Social Sciences. New Collegiate Division offers interdisciplinary programs in arts and sciences. Common core program required of all freshmen. Graduate and professional degrees granted. Independent study. Honors program. Phi Beta Kappa. Pass/fail. Preprofessional programs in business, law, library science, social work. BA/MA, BS/MS programs in several areas. Study abroad. Many research labs and institutes. Language lab. 3,500,000-volume library with microform resources.

Financial CEEB CSS. University scholarships, grants, loans, monthly payment plans; PELL, SEOG, NDSL, FISL, CWS. Scholarship application deadline January 15.

Admissions High school graduation required. Interview strongly recommended. SAT or ACT required. $20 application fee. Application deadline January 15. $50 class and $50 room deposits due on acceptance of admissions offer (May 1). *Early Notification* and *Early Admission* programs. Admission deferral possible. Transfers accepted. Credit possible for CEEB AP and university placement tests.

Student Life Student Government. Newspaper, magazines, yearbook, radio station. Music and drama groups. Debate. Over 100 student organizations. 5 fraternities. 10% of men join. Freshmen must live at home or on campus. Married-student housing. 65% of students live on campus. 1 year of phys ed required. Extensive intercollegiate and intramural sports. AIAW. Student body composition: 7.4% Asian, 5.3% Black, 3.2% Hispanic, 0.1% Native American, 84% White. 67% from out of state.

DePAUL UNIVERSITY $

25 East Jackson Blvd., Chicago 60604 (312) 321-7600
Dean of Undergraduate Assessment & Admissions: Dr. L. Edward Allemand

- **Undergraduates:** 3,508m, 4,186w
- **Tuition** (1984–1985): $4,920
- **Room and Board** (1984–1985): $2,900;   **Fees:** $30
- **Degrees offered:** BA, BS, BFA
- **Mean SAT:** 500v, 520m,   **Mean ACT:** 22
- **Student-faculty ratio:** 18 to 1
- **Calendar system:** Quarter

A private, Roman Catholic university controlled by the Vincentian Fathers. Established in 1898, became coed in 1911. 30-acre urban Lincoln Park Campus located 15 minutes from the Loop; 3-building Lewis Center at Jackson and Wabash Avenues. Served by air, rail, and bus.

Academic Character NCACS and professional accreditation. Quarter system, 2 day and 2 evening summer terms. 6 majors offered by the College of Commerce, 28 by the College of Liberal Arts & Sciences, 6 by the Goodman School of Drama, 8 by the School of Education, and 11 by the School of Music. Minors offered in some major fields. Distributives, and religion & philosophy courses required. Graduate and professional degrees granted. Independent study. Honors program. Some pass/fail, internships, credit by exam. Preprofessional program in law. 3-2 program in engineering with Urbana, Notre Dame, USC; 3-2 or 2-3 programs with Detroit, U of Illinois (Chicago), Northwestern, Iowa State, Ohio State. Early admission to graduate schools possible. Study abroad. Elementary and secondary education certification. ROTC. Language lab. 446,410-volume library.

Financial CEEB CSS. University scholarships, grants, loans, state grants, deferred payment; PELL, SEOG, NSS, NDSL, GSL, NSL, CWS. Recommended application deadline May 1.

Admissions High school graduation with 16 units recommended. Interview recommended. Audition required for music and drama majors. SAT or ACT required. $20 application fee. Rolling admissions; suggest applying early in 12th year. Deadline July 1. *Early Admission, Early Decision, Concurrent Enrollment* programs. Transfers accepted. Credit possible for CEEB AP, CLEP, and University exams.

Student Life Student government. Programming Board. Newspaper, literary magazine, radio station. Music and drama groups. College Democrats. Academic, honorary, religious, and special interest groups. 8 fraternities and 4 sororities without houses. Coed dorms. Married-student housing. 5% of students live on campus. Liquor and gambling prohibited. 6 intercollegiate sports for men, 4 for women; intramurals. AIAW, NCAA. Student body composition: 2.8% Asian, 10.4% Black, 3.7% Hispanic, 0.1% Native American, 81.9% White, 1.1% Other. 5.4% from out of state.

ILLINOIS, UNIVERSITY OF, URBANA—CHAMPAIGN CAMPUS $

Urbana 61801, (217) 333-1000
Director of Admissions: Gary R. Engelgau

- **Undergraduates:** 14,223m, 11,766w
- **Tuition (1984–1985):** $1,248 (lower division in-state), $3,744 (lower division out-of-state), $1,486 (upper division in-state), $4,458 (upper division out-of state)
- **Room and Board (1984–1985):** $2,910 **Fees:** $474
- **Degrees offered:** BA, BS
- **Mean SAT:** 524v, 585m, **Mean ACT:** 26.3
- **Student-faculty ratio:** 11 to 1
- **Calendar system:** Semester

A public university established in 1867. 703-acre campus, 130 miles south of Chicago. Served by air, rail, and bus.

Academic Character NCACS and professional accreditation. Semester system, 8-week summer term. 20 majors offered by the College of Agriculture, 3 by Applied Life Studies, 3 by Commerce & Business Administration, 3 by Communications, 7 by Education, 16 by Engineering, 23 by Fine & Applied Arts, 46 by Liberal Arts & Sciences. Self-designed majors. Minors in some fields. Distributive requirements. Graduate and professional degrees granted. Independent study. Honors program. Phi Beta Kappa. Cooperative work/study in industrial education and engineering. Pass/fail, internships. Many preprofessional programs. 5-year engineering/agricultural science, engineering/liberal arts & sciences programs. 5-year BS/MS in accountancy program. 2-year programs in aviation. Medical Center in Chicago. Study abroad & exchange programs in Colombia, England, Europe, Japan, Mexico, Puerto Rico, Russia. Elementary, secondary, and special education certification. ROTC, NROTC, AFROTC. 9,599,336-volume library with microform resources.

Financial CEEB CSS and ACT FAS. University scholarships, grants, loans; PELL, SEOG, NDSL, GSL, CWS. Priority application deadline March 14.

Admissions High school graduation with 15 units required. Interview or audition required for some majors. SAT or ACT required. $20 application fee. Priority application deadline November 15. Later applications as space is available; deadline 2 weeks before registration. *Early Admission* and *Concurrent Enrollment* programs. Admission deferral possible. Transfers accepted. Credit possible for CEEB AP and CLEP exams; university placement exams. Educational Opportunities Program.

Student Life 550 academic, political, professional, religious, social, and special interest groups. 48 fraternities and 24 sororities with houses. 16% of men and 11% of women join. Single students under 21 or with less than 60 credit hours must live off campus. Coed and single-sex dorms. French & coop houses. Beckwith Living Center for handicapped students. Married-student apartments. 52% of students live on campus. 12 intercollegiate sports for men, 8 for women; many intramural & recreational sports. AIAW, NCAA, Big Ten. Student body composition: 3% Asian, 3% Black, 1% Hispanic, 0.3% Native American, 87% White, 5.7% Other. 3% from out of state.

ILLINOIS STATE UNIVERSITY, NORMAL $

Normal 61761, (309) 438-2111
Director of Admissions: Wilbur Venerable

- **Undergraduates:** 8,233m, 9,482w
- **Tuition (1984–1985):** $1,359 (in-state), $2,908 (out-of-state)
- **Room and Board (1984–1985):** $2,190
- **Degrees offered:** BA, BS, BFA, BMus, BMusEd, BSEd
- **Mean ACT:** 20.16
- **Student-faculty ratio:** 18 to 1
- **Calendar system:** Semester

A public university established in 1857. 711-acre small-city campus, 130 miles from Chicago. Air, rail, and bus service in twin city of Bloomington.

Academic Character NCACS and professional accreditation. Semester system, 8-week summer term plus 3-week pre-term. 55 majors offered in the areas of agriculture, computer science, criminal justice, health, physical education, recreation, dance, home economics, industrial technology, social work, speech, business, education, fine arts, and liberal arts & sciences. Self-designed majors. Minors offered in all major fields and in 11 additional areas, including consumer education, ethnic studies, Latin American studies, and Russian. Graduate degrees granted. Independent study. Honors program. Cooperative work/study, pass/fail, internships. Preprofessional programs in dentistry, engineering, law, medicine, social work, veterinary medicine. 3-2 program in engineering with U of Illinois. Exchange program with other state universities. Study abroad. Elementary, secondary, and special education certification. ROTC. Language lab. 1,181,947-volume library.

Financial ACT FAS. University scholarships, grants, loans; PELL, SEOG, NDSL, GSL, CWS. Application deadline April 1.

Admissions High school graduation required. ACT required; SAT may be substituted by out-of-state applicants. Rolling admissions. *Early Admission, Concurrent Enrollment, Early Decision* programs. Transfers accepted. Credit possible for CEEB AP and CLEP exams. High Potential Student Program for disadvantaged students.

Student Life Student Association. Newspaper, literary magazine, radio & TV stations. Music and drama groups. Film society. ACLU. Gay Alliance. Friends of Old Time Music. Debate. Athletic, academic, service, political, religious, and special interest groups. 18 fraternities and 15 sororities, most with houses. 2 coed social organizations. 4-semester residency required of all freshmen. Coed and single-sex dorms. International House. Married-student housing. 39% of students live on campus. Attendance in class expected. 3 hours of phys ed required for education majors. 11 intercollegiate sports for men, 11 for women; intramurals. Golf course. AIAW, Missouri Valley Athletic Conference. Student body composition: 2% Asian, 7% Black, 0.5% Hispanic, 82.5% White, 8% Other. 2% from out of state.

KNOX COLLEGE $$

Galesburg 61401, (309) 343-0112
Director of Admissions: David C. Tilley

- **Undergraduates:** 493m, 426w
- **Tuition (1984–1985):** $7,338
- **Room and Board (1984–1985):** $2,520;   **Fees:** $102
- **Degrees offered:** BA
- **Mean SAT:** 525v, 570m,   **Mean ACT:** 25
- **Student-faculty ratio:** 11 to 1
- **Calendar system:** Trimester

A private college established in 1837. 60-acre urban campus, 200 miles north of St. Louis & 180 miles southwest of Chicago. Served by air, rail, and bus.
Academic Character NCACS and professional accreditation. Trimester system. Majors offered in American studies, art (2), biology, chemistry, classics, computer science, economics & business administration, education (2), English (2), French, geology, German, German area studies, history, international relations, mathematics, music, philosophy, physics, political science, psychology, Russian, Russian area studies, sociology & anthropology, Spanish, and theatre. Self-designed, interdepartmental, interdisciplinary majors. Distributives and 2 terms of freshman preceptorials required. Independent study. Senior honors program. Phi Beta Kappa. Limited pass/fail, internships. Preprofessional programs in dentistry, medical technology, medicine, nursing, veterinary medicine. 3-2 programs in engineering with Columbia, Stanford, Washington, Illinois, and RPI. 3-2 forestry & environmental management program with Duke. 3-3 programs in law with Chicago, Columbia. 3-2 MBA program with Washington. Physical education, medical technology, and nursing programs with Rush. Social work program with U of Chicago. Member of Associated Colleges of the Midwest. Special prorgams include the Oak Ridge Science Semester, Chicago Urban Education Semester, Rocky Mountains Geology Semester, Newberry Library Humanities Seminar, Washington Semester. Study in Europe, Costa Rica, Japan, India, and Hong Kong. Elementary and secondary education certification. ROTC. Language lab. Wilderness Research Station. 200,000-volume library with microform resources.

Financial CEEB CSS. College scholarships, grants, loans, payment plans; PELL, SEOG, NDSL, work program.

Admissions High school graduation with 15 units required. Interview recommended. SAT or ACT required. $15 application fee. Rolling admissions. $100 deposit required on acceptance of offer of admission; refundable at commencement or end of academic year. Limited *Early Admission* Program. Admission deferral possible. Transfers accepted. Credit possible for CEEB AP and CLEP exams. Special admissions program for minority students.

Student Life Student-faculty government. Newspaper, literary magazine, yearbook, radio station. Music and drama groups. Art exhibits. Academic, ethnic, political, service, and special interest groups. 5 fraternities with houses; 3 sororities with joint recreational building. 25% of students join. Most students required to live on campus. Coed and single-sex dorms. 1 cooperative and some special interest houses. 99% of students live on campus. Many intercollegiate and intramural sports. AIAW, Midwest Athletic Conference. Student body composition: 1.5% Asian, 3% Black, 1% Hispanic, 0.1% Native American, 94.4% White. 18% from out of state.

LAKE FOREST COLLEGE $$

Lake Forest 60045, (312) 234-3100
Dean of Admissions: Francis B. Gummere, Jr.

- **Undergraduates:** 532m, 546w
- **Tuition (1984–1985):** $8,180
- **Room and Board (1984–1985):** $2,390;   **Fees:** $130
- **Degrees offered:** BA
- **Mean SAT:** 500v, 530m,   **Mean ACT:** 25
- **Student-faculty ratio:** 12 to 1
- **Calendar system:** Semester

A private college affiliated with the Presbyterian Church, established in 1857. 107-acre suburban campus on the shores of Lake Michigan, 32 miles north of Chicago. Served by air, rail, and bus.

Academic Character NCACS accreditation. Flexible semester system: 15-week fall semester, spring semester of 2 7-week terms. 7-week summer term. Majors offered in art history, biology, business, chemistry, computer studies, economics, education, English, French, German, history, mathematics, music, philosophy, physics, politics, psychology, sociology/anthropology, and Spanish. Interdisciplinary majors offered in American studies, area studies, behavioral science, comparative world literature, environmental studies, health services, humanistic inquiry, international relations, local & regional studies, and scientific inquiry. Self-designed majors. Courses in 7 additional areas, including ancient Mediterranean civilizations, Black, urban, and women's studies. Freshman Interdisciplinary Seminar. Independent study. Honors program. Phi Beta Kappa. Credit/no credit, internships. Preprofessional programs in law, medicine, dentistry, and veterinary medicine. 3-2 programs in social service and in public policy with U of Chicago. 3-2 program in engineering with Washington. Cooperative medical technology and nursing programs with Rush. Cross-registration in creative arts and women's studies with Barat. Marine biology program in Florida. Study abroad. Elementary and secondary education certification. Computer center. Language lab. Member Associated Colleges of the Midwest. Institute for Local and Regional Studies. 200,000-volume library with microform resources.

Financial College scholarships, grants, loans, payment plan; PELL, SEOG,

GSL, NDSL, CWS. Application deadlines February 1 (scholarships), March 1 (loans).

Admissions High school graduation with 16 units recommended. Interview suggested. SAT or ACT required. $15 application fee. Preferred application deadline March 1. $100 deposit required on acceptance of offer of admission. *Early Admission* and *Early Decision* programs. Admission deferral possible. Transfers accepted. Credit possible for CEEB AP exams.

Student Life Student government. Newspaper, literary & foreign language magazines, yearbook, radio station. Music, film, & theatre groups. Outing club. Black Student group. Academic, religious, service, political, honorary, social, and special interest groups. 3 fraternities and 1 sorority without houses. All freshmen and most upperclassmen live at home or on campus. Coed and single-sex dorms. Special interest housing. Coop dorms. 84% of students live on campus. Liquor prohibited to students under 21. 8 intercollegiate sports for men, 6 for women; many intramural and club sports. Midwest Collegiate Athletic Conference. Student body composition: 1% Asian, 8% Black, 2% Hispanic, 88% White. 65% from out of state.

LOYOLA UNIVERSITY $/$$

820 North Michigan Avenue, Chicago 60611, (312) 670-2900
Director of Admission Counseling: John W. Christian

- **Undergraduates:** 2,777m, 3,461w
- **Tuition (1984–1985):** $5,090
- **Room and Board (1984–1985):** $2,695–$3,250; **Fees:** $30–$80
- **Degrees offered:** BA, BS, BSN, BSEd, BAClassics
- **Mean SAT:** 469v, 501m, **Mean ACT:** 22
- **Student-faculty ratio:** 15 to 1
- **Calendar system:** Semester

A private, Roman Catholic university controlled by the Society of Jesus, established in 1870. 27-acre urban main campus on the shore of Lake Michigan, 20 minutes from downtown Chicago. 3 other campuses in the area house various Schools & Colleges of the University. Served by air, rail, and bus.

Academic Character NCACS and professional accreditation. Semester system, 1 9-week and 2 5-week summer terms. 41 majors offered in the areas of arts, sciences, business, computer science, criminal justice, dental hygiene, education, nursing, public affairs, social work, theatre, theology. Programs in Afro-American, socio-legal, women's studies. Additional courses in Arabic, Chinese, Japanese, Polish, Russian language & literature. 9 hours of theology required. Graduate and professional degrees granted. Freshman tutorials. Independent study. Honors program. Limited pass/fail. Preprofessional programs in business, dentistry, industrial relations, law, medicine, social work. Study abroad in Rome. Elementary, secondary, and special education certification. ROTC. Language lab. 796,000-volume library with microform resources.

Financial CEEB CSS. University scholarships, grants, loans, payment plans; PELL, SEOG, NSS, NDSL, CWS. Application deadline June 1.

Admissions High school graduation with 15 units required. GED accepted. SAT or ACT required. $15 application fee. Rolling admissions. $50 deposit required on acceptance of offer of admission. Transfers accepted. Credit possible for CEEB AP, CLEP, and ACT PEP exams; university has own advanced placement program.

Student Life Student government, activities board. Newspaper, literary quarterly, yearbook, radio station. Theatre group. Debate. Athletic, academic, social, and special interest groups. 11 fraternities, 2 with houses; 3 sororities without houses. 14% of men and 16% of women join. Coed and single-sex dorms. 33% of students live on campus. 7 intercollegiate sports for men, 4 for women; intramural and club sports. AIAW. Student body composition: 3.5% Asian, 8.3% Black, 4.7% Hispanic, 0.1% Native American, 82.9% White, 0.5% Other. 10% from out of state.

NORTHWESTERN UNIVERSITY $$$

633 Clark Street, Evanston 60201, (312) 492-7456
Dean of Admissions: William Ihlanfeldt, PhD

- **Undergraduates:** 3,841m, 3,321w
- **Tuition (1984–1985):** $9,615
- **Room and Board (1984–1985):** $3,703
- **Degrees offered:** BA, BB, BM
- **Mean SAT:** 590v, 630m,   **Mean ACT:** 29
- **Student-faculty ratio:** 9 to 1
- **Calendar system:** Quarter

A private university established in 1851. 170-acre suburban campus on shore of Lake Michigan, 12 miles north of Chicago. Served by air, rail, and bus.
Academic Character NCACS and professional accreditation. Quarter system, 8-week summer term. 56 majors offered by the College of Arts & Sciences, 2 by the School of Education, 3 by the School of Journalism, 6 by the School of Music, 10 by the School of Speech, 13 by the Technological Institute. Self-designed majors. Special programs in American culture, comparative literature, neuroscience, urban affairs. African, Asian, and women's studies. Distributive requirements. Graduate degrees granted. Writer's workshop. Independent study; voluntary tutorials. Honors program. Phi Beta Kappa. Cooperative education in Technological Institute. Pass/no credit, internships. Preprofessional programs in law, medicine, management, and others. 3-year degree program in Arts & Sciences; 4-year master's program in 5 areas. 3-2 management program. 2-4 honors program with Northwestern Medical School. Integrated Science Program. Combined BA-professional degree program from Northwestern Dental or Medical School. Medical technology and physical therapy programs with Medical School. Thematic residential colleges in commerce & industry, community studies, and philosophy & religion. Study abroad. Education certification. NROTC. English Curriculum and Social Studies Curriculum Study Centers. Transportation Center. Traffic Institute. Archaeological Field School. 2,900,000-volume library with microform resources.
Financial CEEB CSS. University scholarships, grants, and loans, PELL, SEOG, NDSL, CWS. Application deadline February 1.
Admissions High school graduation with 16 units required. Interview encouraged. SAT or ACT, and 3 ACH required. $25 application fee. Application deadline February 15; suggest filing before January 1. $200 deposit required on acceptance of admissions offer. *Early Notification* Program. Transfers accepted. Admission deferral possible. Credit possible for CEEB AP and ACH exams, and for university placement exams.
Student Life Student government. Newspaper, literary magazine, yearbook, radio station. Debates. Music and drama groups. NOVA (mental-health volunteers). Students for a Better Environment. 29 fraternities and 17

sororities; all have houses. 30% of students join. Freshmen must live on campus. Thematic dorms. 80% of students live on campus. Freshmen not permitted cars. Extensive intercollegiate and intramural sports programs. AIAW, Western Big Ten Conference. Student body composition: 2% Asian, 8.7% Black, 1.2% Hispanic, 0.1% Native American, 85.7% White. 67% from out of state.

PARKS COLLEGE OF SAINT LOUIS UNIVERSITY $

Cahokia 62206, (618) 337-7500
Director of Admissions: John Wilbur

- **Undergraduates:** 1,000m, 100w
- **Tuition (1984–1985):** $3,470
- **Room and Board (1984–1985):** $2,260;   **Fees:** $200
- **Degrees offered:** BS, AS
- **Mean SAT:** 480v, 510m,   **Mean ACT:** 21.3
- **Student-faculty ratio:** 20 to 1
- **Calendar system:** Semester

A private college established in 1927, one of the eleven colleges of St. Louis University, controlled by the Jesuits. 113-acre campus 5 miles from St. Louis. Served by air, rail, and bus in St. Louis.
Academic Character NCACS and professional accreditation. Semester system. Majors offered in aeronautical administration, aerospace engineering, aircraft maintenance engineering, aircraft maintenance engineering technology, aircraft maintenance management, aircraft maintenance management technology, aviation flight technology, aviation management, aviation science/professional pilot, meterology, and transportation, travel, & tourism. Airframe and Powerplant Technician certificate. FAA-approved flight programs. Some pass/fail. AFROTC. Aerodynamics, meterology, and other labs. Computer center. College-owned single-engine and twin-engine planes. 35,076-volume library.
Financial CEEB CSS. College scholarships, grants, and loans, state grants, PELL, SEOG, NDSL, GSL, Tuition Plan, deferred payment plans, CWS. Application deadline April 1.
Admissions High school graduation with 15 units recommended. GED accepted. Interview recommended. SAT or ACT required. $25 application fee. Rolling admissions. $400 deposit required on acceptance of admissions offer. *Concurrent Enrollment* Program. Transfers accepted. Admission deferral possible. Credit possible for CEEB AP and CLEP exams, and for college placement exams.
Student Life Student government. Newspaper, radio station. Black Student Alliance. Athletic, honorary, professional, religious, service, and special interest groups. 5 fraternities and 1 sorority, none with houses. Students must live at home or on campus. Single-sex dorms. 60% live on campus. Liquor prohibited. 4 intercollegiate sports; intramurals. NLCAA, St. Louis Area College Athletic Association. Student body composition: 1% Asian, 6% Black, 1% Hispanic, 92% White. 65% from out of state.

PRINCIPIA COLLEGE $$

Elsah 62028, (618) 374-2131
Director of Admissions: Martha Green Quirk

- **Undergraduates:** 329m, 415w
- **Tuition (1984–1985):** $6,919
- **Room and Board (1984–1985):** $3,468;   **Fees:** $75
- **Degrees offered:** BA, BS
- **Mean SAT:** 485v, 520m,   **Mean ACT:** 21
- **Student-faculty ratio:** 13 to 1
- **Calendar system:** Quarter

A private college for Christian Scientists, established in 1910. 2,800-acre campus overlooking the Mississippi River, 10 miles from Alton. Public transportation to St. Louis, 40 miles away.
Academic Character NCACS accreditation. Quarter system, 3-week December term. 22 majors in liberal arts & sciences, business, education, religion, and special studies. Self-designed majors. 1-2 religion courses required. Courses in 8 additional areas. Independent and accelerated study. Honors program in some departments. Internships. 2-year pre-engineering program. Special studies off-campus; study abroad. Elementary and secondary education certification. Language lab. 135,000-volume library.
Financial CEEB CSS. College scholarships and loans, PELL, International scholarships, Tuition Plan, deferred payment plans.
Admissions High school graduation with 16 units recommended. Interview recommended. SAT or ACT required; foreign language ACH required for placement. $25 application fee. Rolling admissions. $100 deposit required on acceptance of offer of admission. Transfers accepted. Admission deferral possible. Credit possible for CEEB AP, International Baccalaureate, and CLEP exams.
Student Life Student government. Newspaper, yearbook, radio station. Music and drama groups. Academic, honorary, service, and special interest groups. 98% of students live on campus. No married-student housing. 6 quarters of phys ed required. Liquor, drugs, and tobacco prohibited. 10 intercollegiate sports for men, 8 for women; extensive intramurals. AIAW, NCAA. Student body composition: 1% Black, 99% White. 95% from out of state.

WHEATON COLLEGE $$

Wheaton 60187, (312) 682-5000
Director of Admissions: Stuart O. Michael

- **Undergraduates:** 1,084m, 1,118w
- **Tuition (1984–1985):** $5,800
- **Room and Board (1984–1985):** $2,660
- **Degrees offered:** AB, BS, BMus, BMus Ed
- **Mean SAT:** 536v, 557m,   **Mean ACT:** 25.8
- **Student-faculty ratio:** 15 to 1
- **Calendar system:** Semester

A private college established in 1860. 70-acre suburban campus 25 miles west of Chicago.
Academic Character NCACS and professional accreditation. Semester system; special summer programs. 32 majors offered in ancient languages, archeology, art, Biblical studies, biology, chemistry, Christian education, economics, education, ethnomusicology, French, geology, German, history, liberal arts/engineering, literature, math, medical technology, music, nursing,

philosophy, physical education, physics, political science, psychology, religious studies, social science, sociology, Spanish, speech. Conservatory of Music. Distributive requirement. 5 Bible and apologetics courses required. Internships. Accelerated study. Some pass/fail. Preprofessional programs in business, education, engineering, government service, law, medicine, ministry, nursing, and science. Christian College Consortium. Study abroad. Several specialized summer programs off-campus. Washington Semester. ROTC. Computer. Observatory. Language lab. 155,000-volume library.

Financial CEEB CSS. College scholarships, grants, and loans, payment plans; PELL, SEOG, NDSL. Application deadline February 10.

Admissions High school graduation with 16 units required. Interview required. SAT or ACT required; accepted applicant must take ACH. Conservatory of Music has additional requirements. $20 application fee. Application deadline January 15. $100 deposit required on acceptance of admissions offer. Transfers accepted. Credit possible for CEEB AP and CLEP exams. Special programs for disadvantaged and minority students.

Student Life Student government. Newspaper, literary magazine, yearbook, radio station. Music groups. Intercollegiate debate. Inner-city tutorials. Gospel teams. Academic, professional, and special interest activities. Freshmen must live on campus. No coed dorms. College-owned residence halls, apartments, and houses. Some married-student housing. 85% of students live on campus. 6 trimesters of phys ed required. Students must agree to abstain from alcohol, tobacco, gambling, occult practices, and social dancing, and to use discretion in use of folk and interpretive dance, movies, radio, television, and theatre. Class attendance regulations. 13 intercollegiate sports for men, 7 for women; extensive intramurals. AIAW, NCAA, College Conference of Illinois and Wisconsin. Student body compositon: 2.6% Asian, 0.5% Black, 0.6% Hispanic, 0.2% Native American, 95% White, 1.5% Other. 70% from out of state.

Indiana

ANDERSON COLLEGE $

Anderson 46012, (317) 649-9071
Director of Admissions: George Nalywaiko

- **Undergraduates:** 772m, 961w
- **Tuition (1984–1985):** $4,490
- **Room and Board (1984–1985):** $1,790
- **Degrees offered:** BA, AA, AS
- **Student-faculty ratio:** 16 to 1
- **Calendar system:** Semester

A private college affiliated with the Church of God, established in 1917. 77-acre campus in a small city 40 miles from Indianapolis. Served by air and bus.

Academic Character NCACS and professional accreditation. Semester system, 3 summer terms totaling 15 weeks. 51 majors offered in the areas of art, American studies, business, religion, languages, computer science, criminal justice, science, education, political & social sciences, environmental science, history, mathematics, music, philosophy, physical education, and speech. Self-designed majors. Minor required. Distributives and 9 hours of religion/Bible required. MDiv, MRE, MARel granted. Independent study. Honors program. Pass/fail. Internships. Preprofessional programs in allied health, dentistry, law, medicine, ministry, public service. Transfer program in engineering. 2-2 BS program in nursing with Ball State. 3-1 program in medical technology with St. John's Medical Center. Study abroad. Elementary, secondary, and special education certification. Computer center, language lab, Center for Public Service. 150,000-volume library.

Financial CEEB CSS. College scholarships, grants, and loans, payment plan; PELL, SEOG, NDSL, CWS. Priority application deadline March 15 (scholarships); recommended deadline April 1 (loans).

Admissions High school graduation with 16 units recommended. SAT or ACT required. $10 application fee. Rolling admissions; suggest applying in fall. $100 deposit required on acceptance of offer of admission. Transfers accepted. Credit possible for CEEB AP and CLEP exams.

Student Life Student government. Newspaper, magazine, yearbook. Music, drama, debate organizations. Religious, honorary, political, social, and special interest groups. 5 social clubs for men and 5 for women, none with houses. 21% of men and 23% of women join. Students under 24 must live at home or on campus. No coed dorms. Married-student housing. 80% of students live on campus. Cheating, gambling, liquor, drugs prohibited. Smoking, dancing prohibited on campus. Attendance at bi-weekly convocation required. 3-4 hours of phys ed required. 8 intercollegiate sports for men, 6 for women; intramural and club sports. NAIA, NCCAA, ICAC, Hoosier-Buckeye College Conference. Student body compositon: 0.2% Asian, 5.3% Black, 0.3% Hispanic, 0.4% Native American, 92.5% White. 55% from out of state.

BUTLER UNIVERSITY $$

46th at Sunset Avenue, Indianapolis 46028, (317) 283-9255
Dean of Admissions: Stephen Bushouse

- **Undergraduates:** 857m, 1,141w
- **Tuition (1984–1985):** $5,640
- **Room and Board (1984–1985):** $2,658; **Fees:** $50
- **Degrees offered:** BA, BS, BFA, BMus, AA, AS
- **Mean SAT:** 500v, 530m
- **Student-faculty ratio:** 16 to 1
- **Calendar system:** Semester

A private university established in 1855. 300-acre campus 5 miles from downtown Indianapolis. Served by air, rail, and bus.

Academic Character NCACS and professional accreditation. Semester system, 7- and 3-week summer terms. 5 majors offered by the College of Business Administration, 19 by the College of Education, 30 by the College of Liberal Arts & Sciences, 1 by the College of Pharmacy, and 11 by the Jordan College of Fine Arts. Distributive requirements. Graduate and professional degrees granted. Honors program. Cooperative work/study, internships. Pass/fail. Preprofessional programs in dentistry, medicine, medical technology, nursing, engineering, forestry, law, ministry, dietetics. Member Consortium for Urban Education. Elementary, secondary, and special education certification. AFROTC at Indiana U-Purdue U (Indianapolis), and Indiana U (Bloomington). Observatory/planetarium. 350,000-volume library.

Financial CEEB CSS. University and state scholarships, grants, and loans; PELL, SEOG, NDSL, GSL, USAF, deferred payment plan.

Admissions High school graduation with 15 units required. Audition required for music, dance, radio/TV, and theatre majors. SAT or ACT required. $15 application fee. Rolling admissions; suggest applying during 1st semester. $150 deposit required on acceptance of offer of admission. *Early Admission* and *Concurrent Enrollment* programs. Admission deferral possible. Transfers accepted. Credit possible for CEEB AP exams.

Student Life Student government. Newspaper, magazine, special interest publications, yearbook, radio station. Many music groups. Debate, ballet, drama groups. Honorary, academic, service, religious, and special interest organizations. 7 fraternities and 7 sororities with houses. 34% of men and 35% of women join. Coed and single-sex dorms. 77% of students live on campus. 2 semesters of phys ed, dance, or marching band required. 8 intercollegiate sports for men, 5 for women; intramurals. AIAW, NCAA, Heartland Collegiate, Midwestern City Conferences. Student body composition: 5% Black, 2% Oriental, 92% White, 1% Other. 23% from out of state.

DEPAUW UNIVERSITY $$

Greencastle 46135, (317) 658-4006
Director of Admissions: David C. Murray

- **Undergraduates:** 1,105m, 1,235w
- **Tuition (1984–1985):** $6,950
- **Room and Board (1984–1985):** $2,970; **Fees:** $150
- **Degrees offered:** BA, BS, BMus
- **Mean SAT:** 510v, 560m, **Mean ACT:** 25
- **Student-faculty ratio:** 14 to 1
- **Calendar system:** 4–1–4

A private university established in 1837. 116-acre campus in small city 45 miles from Indianapolis. Served by bus; airport in Indianapolis.

Academic Character NCACS and professional accreditation. 4-1-4 system. Majors offered in anthropology, art, botany/bacteriology, chemistry, classical languages, communication, earth sciences, elementary education, English, German, health, history, mathematics, music, nursing, philosophy/religion, physics, political science, psychology, Romance languages, Russian, sociology, and zoology. Self-designed majors. Minors offered in all major fields and computer science. Distributive requirements; writing competency requirement. MA, MAT granted. Honors program. Phi Beta Kappa. Pass/fail for juniors, seniors. Internships. Cooperative engineering programs with 6 schools. Washington, UN Semesters. Study abroad. Elementary and secondary education certification. ROTC; AFROTC at Indiana U. Computer center, observatory, language lab, anthropology museum, art center. 360,000-volume library.

Financial CEEB CSS. University scholarships, grants, and loans, deferred payment plan; PELL, SEOG, NDSL, FISL, NSL, CWS, and college work program.

Admissions High school graduation with 12 units recommended. Audition required for music majors. SAT or ACT required. $20 application fee. Application deadlines December 1, February 15. $200 tuition and $100 room deposits required on acceptance of offer of admission. *Early Admission* Program. Transfers accepted. Credit possible for CEEB AP and CLEP exams and for university placement exams.

Student Life Student government. Newspaper, magazine, yearbook, radio station, TV workshop. Several music, debate, and drama organizations. Religious, academic, and special interest groups. 13 fraternities and 9 sororities with houses. 70% of students join. Coed and single-sex dorms. No married-student housing. 95% of students live on campus. Liquor, weapons prohibited on campus. Class attendance required. ½ credit in activity required. 12 intercollegiate and 10 intramural sports for men and women. AIAW, NCAA, ICC. Student body composition: 1% Asian, 2% Black, 1% Hispanic, 1% Native American, 95% White. 58% from out of state.

EARLHAM COLLEGE $$

Richmond 47374, (317) 962-6561
Dean of Admissions: Lynette Robinson-Weening

- **Undergraduates:** 471m, 564w
- **Tuition (1984–1985):** $7,254
- **Room and Board (1984–1985):** $2,514;   **Fees:** $207
- **Degrees offered:** BA
- **Mean SAT:** 530v, 570m,   **Mean ACT:** 26
- **Student-faculty ratio:** 12 to 1
- **Calendar system:** 3 ten-week terms

A private college affiliated with the Society of Friends (Quakers), established in 1847. 800-acre campus 70 miles from Indianapolis, near Ohio line. Served by air, rail, and bus.

Academic Character NCACS accreditation. Trimester system. Majors offered in African studies, biology, chemistry, classics, economics, elementary education, English, environmental studies, fine arts, French, geology, German, history, human development/social relations, Japanese studies, Latin American studies, mathematics, music, peace and conflict studies, philosophy, physical education, physics/astronomy, political science, psychology, religion, sociology/anthropology, and Spanish. Self-designed majors. Distributives senior exams, and 2 courses in religion/philosophy required. Internships. Preprofessional programs in business, engineering, environmental education, law, medicine, ministry, nursing. 3-2 programs in engineering with 5 schools, in nursing with Case Western Reserve. Several special interest study terms. Study abroad. Observatory/planetarium, computer center, East Asian center, language labs, museum. 230,000-volume library.

Financial CEEB CSS. College scholarships, grants, loans, deferred payment; PELL, SEOG, FISL, CWS, college work program. Scholarship application deadline January 1.

Admissions High school graduation with 15 units required. SAT or ACT required, SAT preferred. $15 application fee. Application deadline March 15. $100 deposit required on acceptance of offer of admission. *Early Decision* Program. Admission deferral possible. Transfers accepted. Credit possible for CEEB AP and CLEP exams.

Student Life Student government. Newspaper, magazine, yearbook, radio station. Music, drama groups. Meditation Society. Black Leadership Action Committee. Women's Center. Service, honorary, and special interest groups. Seniors may live off campus. Coed dorms. Coop, living-learning, special interest houses. Vegetarian meals offered. Married-student housing. 90% of students live on campus. Freshmen may not have cars on campus. Liquor prohibited on campus; smoking restricted. 2 years of phys ed required. 8 intercollegiate sports for men, 7 for women, 3 coed; intramurals. AIAW, NAIA, NCAA, Hoosier Buckeye Conference, Indiana Intercollegiate Athletic Association. Student body composition: 10% minority. 80% of students from out of state.

GOSHEN COLLEGE $

Goshen 46526, (219) 533-3161
Director of Admissions: Dennis Koehn

- **Undergraduates:** 461m, 627w
- **Tuition (1984–1985):** $4,875
- **Room and Board (1984–1985):** $2,120
- **Degrees offered:** BA, BSN
- **Mean SAT:** 499v, 510m
- **Student-faculty ratio:** 13 to 1
- **Calendar system:** Trimester

A private college affiliated with the Mennonite Church, established in 1894. 135-acre campus in a small town 25 miles from South Bend, 120 miles from Chicago. Served by bus. Airport in South Bend.

Academic Character NCACS and professional accreditation. Trimester system, 3 3½-week summer terms. 32 majors offered in the areas of business, arts, religion, sciences, communication, education, economics, English, family life, nutrition, foreign languages, history, ministries, mathematics, physical education, political and social sciences. Self-designed majors. Minors. Distributives and 8 hours of religion required. Trimester of international studies or study abroad required. Independent study. Honors program. Pass/fail. Credit for church-related work. Preprofessional programs in dentistry, law, nursing, medical technology, medicine, ministry, social work. 3-2 engineering program with Purdue. 2-3 pharmacy program. Elementary and secondary education certification. Many study abroad programs. Computer center. Laboratory kindergarten for education majors. Over 105,365-volume library.

Financial CEEB CSS and ACT FAS. College scholarships, grants, and loans, payment plans; PELL, SEOG, NSS, NDSL, FISL, NSL, CWS, college work program. Application deadlines March 1 (scholarships), April 1 (loans).

Admissions High school graduation with 16 units required. GED accepted. SAT or ACT required. $10 application fee. Rolling admissions. *Early Admission* Program. Transfers accepted. Credit possible for CEEB AP and CLEP exams and for college advanced placement tests.

Student Life Student government. Newspaper, magazine, yearbook, radio station. Music, drama, speaking, debate, poetry reading groups. Peace, cross-cultural societies. Black and International student groups. Academic, honorary, religious, service, and special interest groups. Seniors and students over 21 may live off campus. Coed and single-sex dorms. Small group housing. Married-student housing. 68% of students live on campus. Liquor, smoking, dancing prohibited on campus. Attendance at biweekly chapel required. 1 term of phys ed required. 7 intercollegiate sports for men, 5 for women; intramurals. NAIA, AIAW, Mid-Central Conference. Student body compositon: 1% Asian, 2% Black, 6% Foreign, 4% Hispanic, 87% White. 68% from out of state.

INDIANA UNIVERSITY $

Bloomington 47405, (812) 335-0661
Director of Admissions: Robert S. Magee

- **Undergraduates:** 12,268m, 13,281w
- **Tuition (1984–1985):** $1,500 (in-state), $4,000 (out-of-state)
- **Room and Board (1984–1985):** $2,200
- **Degrees offered:** BA, BS, BFA, BMus, BMus Ed, AS
- **Mean SAT:** 465v, 513m
- **Student-faculty ratio:** 16 to 1
- **Calendar system:** Semester

A public university established in 1820. 3,200-acre campus 50 miles from Indianapolis. Served by air and bus.

Academic Character NCACS and professional accreditation. Semester system, 6-week, 8-week, and 5 2-week summer terms. 45 majors offered by the College of Arts & Sciences, 11 by the Division of Allied Health Services, 16 by the School of Business, 7 by the School of Education, 4 by the School of Health, Physical Education, & Recreation, 16 by the School of Music, and 13 by the School of Public & Environmental Affairs. Self-designed majors. Programs in 11 additional areas. Senior thesis and exam required. Graduate and professional degrees granted. Independent study. Honors program. Phi Beta Kappa. Cooperative work/study, internships. Pass/fail. Study abroad. Elementary, secondary, and special education certification. ROTC, AFROTC. Computer center, language lab. 3,600,000-volume library.

Financial CEEB CSS. University scholarships, grants, loans, state grants; PELL, SEOG, NDSL, GSL, CWS. Application deadline February 15.

Admissions High school graduation with 15 units required. Audition required for music, ACH required for foreign language study. SAT or ACT required. $20 application fee. Rolling admissions; deadline July 15. $5 housing application fee. *Early Decision* and *Early Admission* programs. Admission deferral possible. Transfers accepted. Credit possible for CEEP AP and CLEP exams, and for university advanced placement tests. Program for Indiana minority students.

Student Life Student government. Newspaper, magazine, yearbook, radio and TV stations. Over 40 music groups. 200 special interest organizations. 32 fraternities and 19 sororities; most have houses. 10% of men and 8% of women join. Coed and single-sex dorms; special interest housing. 50% of students live on campus. Freshmen may not have cars. Many intercollegiate and intramural sports for men and women. AIAW, Big Ten, NCAA. Student body composition: 6% Black, 1% Hispanic, 92% White, 1% Other. 30% from out of state.

NOTRE DAME, UNIVERSITY OF $$

Notre Dame 46556, (219) 239-5000
Director of Admissions: John T. Goldrick

- **Undergraduates:** 5,334m, 2,074w
- **Tuition (1984–1985):** $7,080
- **Room and Board (1984–1985):** $3,365;   **Fees:** $85
- **Degrees offered:** BA
- **Mean SAT:** 552v, 637m
- **Student-faculty ratio:** 12 to 1
- **Calendar system:** Semester

A private university affiliated with the Congregation of Holy Cross, established in 1842, became coed in 1972. 1,250-acre suburban campus just outside South Bend, 90 miles from Chicago. Served by air, rail, and bus.

Academic Character NCACS and professional accreditation. Semester system, 6-week summer term. 22 majors offered by the College of Arts & Letters, 4 by the College of Business Administration, 8 by the College of Engineering, 6 by the College of Science. Distributive requirements. 6 credits in theology required. MS, MA, MBA, JD, PhD granted. Honors program. Phi Beta Kappa. Pass/fail. Preprofessional programs in dentistry, medicine, veterinary studies combined with liberal arts studies. Dual-degree programs in arts & letters/engineering. Exchange with St. Mary's College. Study abroad. Elementary, secondary, and special education certification. ROTC, AFROTC, NROTC. Many centers, laboratories, institutes. Art museum, computer center, language lab. 1,500,000-volume library with microform resources.

Financial CEEB CSS. Scholarships, grants, loans, deferred payment; PELL, SEOG, NDSL, GSL, CWS. Application deadline March 1.

Admissions High school graduation with 16 units required. SAT and 3 ACH required. $25 application fee. Rolling admissions beginning in February; application deadline March 1. $100 deposit required on acceptance of offer of admission. Transfers accepted. Credit possible for CEEB AP exams, and for university placement tests.

Student Life Student government. Newspaper, magazines, yearbook, radio and TV stations. Music, debate, drama groups. Religious, academic, and service organizations; special interest groups. Freshmen must live on campus. No coed dorms. Married-student housing. 82% of students live on campus. Class attendance required. 2 semesters of phys ed or ROTC required. 11 intercollegiate sports for men, 6 for women; intramural and club sports. AIAW, NCAA. Student body composition: 3% Asian, 3% Black, 3% Hispanic, 0.2% Native American, 90% White, 0.8% Other. 92% from out of state.

PURDUE UNIVERSITY $

West Lafayette 47907, (317) 494-1776
Director of Admissions: James Kraynak

- **Undergraduates:** 15,668m, 11,007w
- **Tuition** (1984–1985): $1,532 (in-state), $3,024 (out-of-state)
- **Room and Board** (1984–1985): $2,500
- **Degrees offered:** BA, BS, BSE, AAS
- **Mean SAT:** 465v, 540m
- **Student-faculty ratio:** 14 to 1
- **Calendar system:** Semester

A public university established in 1869. 516-acre campus across the Wabash River from small city of Lafayette, 60 miles from Indianapolis. Served by air, rail, and bus.
Academic Character NCACS and professional accreditation. Semester system, 8-week summer term. 35 majors offered in agriculture, 13 in engineering, 11 in management, 3 in pharmacy, nursing, & health sciences, 45 in science, 19 in consumer science, 52 in humanities, social science, & education, 13 in technology, and 6 in physical education. Self-designed majors. Distributive requirements. Graduate and professional degrees granted. Independent study. Honors program. Phi Beta Kappa. Cooperative work/study, internships. Pass/fail. Preprofessional programs in dentistry, law, medicine, veterinary science. Study abroad. Elementary, secondary, and special education certification. ROTC, AFROTC, NROTC. TV unit, A-V center. 1,700,000-volume library with microform resources.
Financial CEEB CSS. University scholarships, grants, loans, payment plan; PELL, SEOG, NDSL, FISL. Scholarship application deadline February 15.
Admissions High school graduation with 15 units required. SAT or ACT required. Interview recommended. Rolling admissions; suggest applying in early fall. $50 deposit required on acceptance of offer of admission. *Early Admission* Program. Transfers accepted. Credit possible for CEEB AP, CLEP, and ACH exams.
Student Life Student government. Newspaper, magazines, yearbook, radio station. Music, debate, and theatre programs. Many special interest groups. 41 fraternities and 18 sororities. Limited housing. Coed and single-sex dorms. 52% of students live on campus. Freshmen and sophomores may not have cars on campus. No liquor allowed. Many intercollegiate and intramural sports for men and women. AIAW, NCAA, Big Ten. Student body composition: 2.5% Asian, 5% Black, 0.5% Hispanic, 92% White. 30% from out of state.

ST. MARY'S COLLEGE $$

Notre Dame 46556, (219) 284-4305
Director of Admissions: Mary Ann Rowan

- **Undergraduates:** 23m, 1,810w
- **Tuition** (1984–1985): $5,850
- **Room and Board** (1984–1985): $3,038;   **Fees:** $416
- **Degrees offered:** BA, BS, BFA, BBA, BM
- **Mean SAT:** 478v, 520m,   **Mean ACT:** 23.4
- **Student-faculty ratio:** 13 to 1
- **Calendar system:** Semester

A private Roman Catholic women's college controlled by the Sisters of the Holy Cross, established in 1844. 275-acre suburban campus near South Bend. Air and rail in South Bend.

Academic Character NCACS and professional accreditation. Semester system. 21 majors offered in the liberal arts, sciences, and education, 6 in allied health fields & sciences, 6 in music; also in business administration & studio art. Courses in 4 additional areas. 3 semester hours of theology required. Interdisciplinary urban studies program. Pass/fail. Preprofessional programs in medicine and law. Exchange program with Notre Dame. Study abroad. Elementary and secondary education certification; endorsements in kindergarten and reading. ROTC, AFROTC, NROTC at Notre Dame. Language lab. 154,000-volume library.

Financial CEEB CSS. College scholarships and grants; PELL, SEOG, NDSL, College Aid Plan, some on-campus employment. Application deadline February 1.

Admissions High school graduation with 16 units required. Interview recommended. Audition required for music majors, portfolio for art majors. SAT or ACT required. $25 application fee. Modified rolling admissions; deadline March 1. *Early Admission* Program. Admission deferral possible. Transfers accepted to sophomore, junior years. Credit possible for CEEB AP, CLEP, and ACH exams.

Student Life Student government. Newspaper, magazine, yearbook. Music, drama groups. Religious, academic, service, and special interest organizations. Students expected to live on campus. Dorms and dining hall. No married-student housing. 90% of students live on campus. 13 intercollegiate sports; intramurals. AIAW. Student body composition: 1% Asian, 0.5% Black, 2% Hispanic, 96.5% White. 84% from out of state.

TAYLOR UNIVERSITY $

Upland 46989, (317) 998-2751
Director of Admissions: Ronald L. Keller

- **Undergraduates:** 753m, 806w
- **Tuition (1984–1985):** $4,780
- **Room and Board (1984–1985):** $2,286;   **Fees:** $90
- **Degrees offered:** BA, BS, BM, AA
- **Mean SAT:** 442v, 492m,   **Mean ACT:** 21
- **Student-faculty ratio:** 14 to 1
- **Calendar system:** 4–1–4

A private interdenominational Christian university established in 1846. 240-acre rural campus in Upland, 13 miles southeast of Marion. Air and bus in Marion.

Academic Character NCACS and professional accreditation. 4-1-4 system, 5-week summer term, 4-week presession. 32 majors offered in the areas of business, liberal arts, art & music, education, religious studies, physical education, and sciences. Self-designed majors. Distributive requirements. 2 Bible courses, 1 philosophy and Christian thought course required. Senior exams. Independent study. Honors program. Pass/fail. Preprofessional programs in business, engineering, law, medical technology, medicine, natural resources, nursing, theology. 3-2 program in engineering with Purdue. 3-1 medical technology program. 2-2 program in nursing with Ball State. Elementary, secondary, early childhood, and special education certification. Research under Atomic Energy Commission. Consortium with Christian colleges. Study abroad. ROTC, AFROTC, NROTC at Ball State, Purdue. Language lab. 131,000-volume library.

Financial CEEB CSS. University scholarships, grants, loans, Methodist loans, state grants, payment plan; PELL, SEOG, NDSL, GSL, PLUS, CWS, college employment program. Preferred application deadline for scholarships April 1.

Admissions High school graduation with 15 units required. Interview may be required. SAT or ACT required. $15 application fee. Rolling admissions; suggest applying before March 1. $150 deposit required on acceptance of offer of admission. Credits-in-Escrow Program. Transfers accepted. Credit possible for CEEB AP and CLEP exams.

Student Life Student government. Newspaper, magazine, yearbook. Music, drama groups. Religious and special interest groups. Students must live at home or on campus. Single-sex dorms. Married-student housing. 95% of students live on campus. Liquor, drugs, dancing, gambling, smoking, hazing prohibited. Attendance at 3 chapel services per week, church and campus services on Sunday required. 2 courses in phys ed required. 8 intercollegiate sports for men, 6 for women; intramurals. NAIA, Hoosier-Buckeye Collegiate Conference. Student body composition: 0.7% Asian, 1.1% Black, 0.2% Hispanic, 0.1% Native American, 97.1% White, 0.8% Other. 59% from out of state.

TRI-STATE UNIVERSITY $

Angola 46703, (219) 665-3141
Director of Admissions: Kent D. Myers

- **Undergraduates:** 811m, 236w
- **Tuition (1984–1985):** $4,410
- **Room and Board (1984–1985):** $2,310; **Fees:** $202
- **Degrees offered:** BA, BS, AA, AS
- **Mean SAT:** 410v, 530m, **Mean ACT:** 22
- **Student-faculty ratio:** 13 to 1
- **Calendar system:** Quarter

A private university established in 1884. 400-acre campus in small town of Angola, 45 miles from Fort Wayne. Air, rail, and bus service in Fort Wayne.

Academic Character NCACS and professional accreditation. Quarter system, 2 5-week summer terms. Majors offered in accounting, business & arts, computer science, criminal justice, elementary education, engineering administration, English & humanities, information processing, management, marketing, mathematics, office administration, physical education, science, secondary education, social studies, technical management, transportation, and aerospace, chemical, civil, electrical, and mechanical engineering. AS offered in drafting & design, accounting, secretarial science, industrial technology, criminal justice, computer technology. Cooperative work/study. Credit by exam. Year-round operation permits completion of degree in 36 months. Elementary and secondary education certification. Computer center. 91,000-volume library.

Financial CEEB CSS and ACT FAS. University scholarships, grants, loans, payment plans; PELL, SEOG, FISL, CWS. Scholarship application deadline April 1.

Admissions High school graduation with 16 units required. GED accepted. SAT or ACT recommended. $15 application fee. Rolling admissions. $40 tuition and $50 room deposits (for boarders) required on acceptance of offer of admission. *Early Admission* Program. Admission deferral possible. Transfers accepted. Credit possible for CEEB AP and CLEP exams; university has own advanced placement program.

Student Life Student government. Newspaper, yearbook, radio station. Music and drama groups. Honorary, professional, religious, and special interest groups. 8 fraternities with houses and 2 sororities without houses. 21% of men and 11% of women join. Freshmen must live at home or on campus. Single-sex dorms. 80% of students live on campus. Class attendance required. 6 hours of phys ed required. 8 intercollegiate sports for men and women; intramurals. NAIA, NCAA. Student body composition: 1% Asian, 6% Black, 1% Hispanic, 86% White, 6% Other. 58% from out of state.

VALPARAISO UNIVERSITY $$

Valparaiso 46383, (219) 464-5000
Dean of Admissions: Warren Muller

- **Undergraduates:** 1,493m, 1,807w
- **Tuition (1984–1984):** $5,600
- **Room and Board (1984–1985):** $2,290; **Fees:** $192
- **Degrees offered:** BA, BS, BMus, BMus Ed, BSBA, BSCE, BSEE, BSME, BSFA, BSHE, BSPE, BSEd, BSN, BSW
- **Mean SAT:** 480v, 540m
- **Student-faculty ratio:** 14 to 1
- **Calendar system:** Semester

A private university affiliated with the Lutheran Church, established in 1859. 310-acre semi-rural campus in small city of Valparaiso, 44 miles southeast of Chicago. Served by air, rail, and bus.

Academic Character NCACS and professional accreditation. Semester system, 8-week summer term, 4-week intensive study term. 46 majors offered by the colleges of Arts & Sciences, Business Administration, Engineering, and Nursing, and by Christ College (honors). Minors offered in computer science, Hebrew, Russian. Interdepartmental and Black studies courses. Distributive requirements including courses in religion. Masters and professional degrees granted. Independent study. Honors program. Pass/fail. Preprofessional programs in allied health sciences, dentistry, engineering, foreign service, law, medical technology, medicine, seminary education. Deaconess Training program. Merrill-Palmer Institute. Washington, UN Semesters. Urban affairs semester. Study abroad at Cambridge on Reutlingen. Elementary and secondary education certification, and special education endorsement. Computer center. Audio-visual lab, language lab. 300,000-volume library with 75,000-volume law library and microform resources.

Financial CEEB CSS. University scholarships, grants, loans, payment plans; PELL, SEOG, NDSL, CWS.

Admissions High school graduation with 15 units required. Interview encouraged. SAT or ACT required; SAT strongly preferred. $15 application fee. Rolling admissions. *Early Admission* and *Early Decision* programs. Admission deferral possible. Transfers accepted. Credit possible for CEEB AP and CLEP exams; university has own advanced placement program.

Student Life Student government. Newspaper, magazine, yearbook, radio station. Choirs, band, debate, drama clubs. Women's tutoring group. Service, academic, honorary, and special interest organizations. 12 fraternities with houses and 8 sororities in dorm. 33% of students join. Seniors, veterans, and students over 21 may live off campus. 3 dorms for men, 6 for women; 6 cafeterias. No married-student housing. 85% of students live on campus. Liquor, firearms, explosives prohibited. Honor system. Daily chapel attendance urged. 1 year of phys ed required. 9 intercollegiate sports for men, 6 for women; intramural and club sports. ICC, IIAA, AIAW, NCAA. Student body composition: 0.4% Asian, 3% Black, 0.4% Hispanic, 0.2% Native American, 95% White. 70% from out of state.

WABASH COLLEGE $$

Crawfordsville 47933, (317) 362-1400
Director of Admissions: Paul M. Garman

- **Undergraduates:** 774m
- **Tuition (1984–1985):** $6,200
- **Room and Board (1984–1985):** $2,575;   Fees: $90
- **Degrees offered:** AB
- **Mean SAT:** 510v, 590m
- **Student-faculty ratio:** 10 to 1
- **Calendar system:** Semester

A private men's college established in 1832. 50-acre campus in small city of Crawfordsville, 45 miles northwest of Indianapolis. Served by bus and rail.
Academic Character NCACS and professional accreditation. Semester system. Majors offered in biology, chemistry, classical civilization, economics, English, French, German, Greek, history, humanities, Latin, mathematics, music, philosophy, physics, political science, psychology, religion, Russian, Spanish/French, speech, theatre. Self-designed majors. Minor required. Minors offered in most major fields and in art. Distributive requirements. Comprehensive and oral exams required. Independent study. Phi Beta Kappa. Pass/fail. Internships. Preprofessional programs in medicine, dentistry, law, optometry, veterinary science. Cooperative engineering programs with Columbia U and Washington U (St. Louis). 3-3 law program with Columbia. Member Great Lakes College Association. Oak Ridge, Washington Semesters. New York arts program. Newberry Library Humanities Program. Marine biology summer terms. Study abroad in 12 countries. ROTC at Purdue. Language lab, computer center. Over 225,000-volume library.
Financial CEEB CSS. College scholarships, grants, and loans; PELL, FISL.
Admissions High school graduation with 15 units required. SAT or ACT required. $15 application fee. Rolling admissions after 15th of each month. $100 deposit required on acceptance of offer of admission. Admission deferral possible. Transfers accepted. Credit possible for CEEB AP and CLEP exams.
Student Life Student government. Newspaper, magazine, yearbook, radio station. Music, drama groups. Speakers Bureau. Malcolm X Institute. Political, religious, service, and special interest organizations. 9 fraternities with houses. 75% of men join. Freshmen and sophomores must live on campus. Dormitories and dining facilities. 95% of students live on campus. 10 intercollegiate, several intramural and club sports. NCAA. Student body composition: 2% Asian, 4% Black, 1% Hispanic, 93% White. 20% from out of state.

Iowa

COE COLLEGE $$

Cedar Rapids 52402, (319) 399-8500, (800) 332-8404 (toll-free in Iowa)
Dean of Admissions: Peter D. Feickert

- **Undergraduates:** 600m, 600w
- **Tuition (1984–1985):** $6,100
- **Room and Board (1984–1985):** $2,300; **Fees:** $90
- **Degrees offered:** BA, BSN, BSME
- **Mean SAT:** 470v, 510m, **Mean ACT:** 23
- **Student-faculty ratio:** 13 to 1
- **Calendar system:** 4–1–4

A private college affiliated with the United Presbyterian Church, established in 1851. 26-acre campus in residential section of Cedar Rapids 8 blocks from the central business district. Airport and bus station in Cedar Rapids.
Academic Character NCACS and professional accreditation. 4-1-4 system, 2 5-week summer terms. Majors offered in accounting, Afro-American studies, American studies, art, Asian studies, biology, bio-social science, business administration, chemistry, economics, English, environmental studies, French, general science, German, history, humanities, literature, mathematics, music, nursing, philosophy, philosophy/religion, physical education, physics, political science, psychology, religion, sociology, Spanish, speech, teacher education, and theatre arts. Major in computer science in cooperation with Mount Mercy and Cornell Colleges. Self-designed majors. 3- and 5-year programs in allied health sciences. Program in computer applications. Minors optional. Community service certificate program. Two courses required. Pass/fail. Accelerated study, honors program, Phi Beta Kappa. Work/service terms, internships. Independent study, sponsored team research. Cooperative work/study. Preprofessional programs in business, church service, college teaching, dentistry, government service, law, medicine. 3-1 program in medical technology, 3-2 engineering program with Washington U, 3-1 and 3-2 social service administration programs with U of Chicago. Cross-registration with Mount Mercy. Numerous exchange programs and off-campus semesters. Study abroad. Elementary and secondary education certification. Computer center, language lab. ROTC at U of Iowa. 180,000-volume library.
Financial CEEB CSS (preferred) and ACT FAS. College scholarships and grants, state scholarships and tuition grants, merit scholarships, Presbyterian scholarships, 2nd-sibling tuition reductions, payment plans; PELL, SEOG, NDSL, FISL, GSL, CWS. March 1 deadline for state grant application.
Admissions High school graduation required with 15 units recommended. SAT or ACT required; ACH recommended. Interview recommended. $15 application fee. Rolling admissions; recommended application deadline May 1. $100 deposit required on acceptance of offer of admission. *Early Entrance* Program. Admission deferral possible. Transfers accepted. Credit possible for CEEB AP and CLEP exams.
Student Life Student government. Newspaper, literary magazines, yearbook, radio station. Music, debate, drama groups. Affiliate artist program. Varsity lettermen's group. Ethnic organizations, International Club. Many academic, honorary, special interest clubs. 5 fraternities and 3 sororities

without houses. 30% of men, 25% of women join. Most single students live on campus or at home. Single-sex and coed dorms. Married-student housing. 85% of students live on campus. 10 intercollegiate sports for men, 8 for women; intramurals. AIAW, NCAA. Student body composition: 1% Asian, 3% Black, 96% White. 45% from out of state.

CORNELL COLLEGE $$

Mount Vernon 52314, (319) 895-8811
Dean of Admissions: Frank G. Krivo

- **Undergraduates:** 516m, 446w
- **Tuition (1984—1985):** $6,100
- **Room and Board (1984—1985):** $2,300;   **Fees:** $400
- **Degrees offered:** BA, BS, BMus, BPH, BSpecial Studies
- **Mean SAT:** 490v, 520m,   **Mean ACT:** 23.2
- **Student-faculty ratio:** 13 to 1
- **Calendar system:** one-course-at-a-time

A private college established in 1853. Wooded 125-acre campus in small town of Mount Vernon, 20 minutes from Cedar Rapids and Iowa City. Bus station; airport in Cedar Rapids. Campus is a national historic district.

Academic Character NCACS and professional accreditation. One-course-at-a-time calendar of 9 3½-week terms. Majors offered in American studies, art, biology, chemistry, computer science, economics/business, elementary education, English, environmental studies, French, geology, German, German studies, Greek, health/physical education, history, math, medieval & Renaissance studies, music, origins of behavior, philosophy, physics, politics, psychology, religion, Russian, Russian studies, sociology, Spanish, theatre/speech. Double, triple, interdisciplinary, and self-designed majors. BPhilosophy curriculum has no set requirements except comprehensive exam in field; BSS includes independent study, field work, audited and credited class work. Distributive requirements. Masters degrees granted. Accelerated study, honors program, Phi Beta Kappa. Interdepartmental study. Internships. Preprofessional programs in dentistry, engineering, journalism, law, medicine, sociology, theology. 3-2 health & hospital administration and accelerated MBA programs with U of Iowa. Cooperative nursing, allied health sciences programs with Rush U. Combined degree programs in engineering (with Washington U), social service administration (U of Chicago), forestry, environmental management (Duke U), and in medical technology with 2 Cedar Rapids hospitals. Exchange program with Fisk U, U of Puerto Rico, Rust College. Numerous off-campus study opportunities. Study abroad. Kindergarten through secondary education certification. Computer center, geology center and museum. 185,000-volume library.

Financial CEEB CSS and ACT FAS. College scholarships, grants, loans; state grants and scholarships, United Methodist scholarships, 50% tuition awards for children of ordained ministers; PELL, SEOG, NDSL, GSL, PLUS, CWS.

Admissions High school graduation and SAT or ACT required. Interview recommended. $15 application fee. Rolling admissions; no deadline. $100 deposit required on acceptance of offer of admission. *Early Acceptance* and *Early Decision* programs. Admission deferral possible. Transfers accepted in all 9 terms. Credit possible for CEEB AP and CLEP exams, and for college tests.

Student Life Student government. Newspaper, literary magazine, yearbook, radio station. Music groups, various public speaking organizations. Campus theatre. Writer's Club. Students for Black People Religious, honorary, academic, and special interest groups. 7 social clubs for men, 3 for women; none have houses. 30% of men, 20% of women join. Students must live on campus. Coed and single-sex dorms that are student-managed. Married-student housing. 99% of students live on campus. One course in health and physical education sometimes required. 10 intercollegiate sports for men, 7 for women; intramurals. AIAW, NCAA, Midwest Athletic Conference. Student body composition: 5% Black, 89% White, 6% Other. 71% from out of state.

DRAKE UNIVERSITY $$

Des Moines 50311, (515) 271-3182
Toll-free from IA: (800) 362-2416; from IL, MN, MO, NE, SD, WI: (800) 247-2135
From other states: (515) 271-3181 (call collect)
Executive Director of Admissions: Everett Hadley

- **Undergraduates:** 1,597m, 1,735w
- **Tuition (1984–1985):** $6,200
- **Room and Board (1984–1985):** $2,800
- **Degrees offered:** BA, BFA, BM, BSME, BSBA, BSPh
- **Mean ACT:** 21.2
- **Student-faculty ratio:** 17 to 1
- **Calendar system:** Semester

A private university established in 1881 in Des Moines. 79-acre urban campus. Airport and bus station in Des Moines.
Academic Character NCACS and professional accreditation. Semester system, 2 5-week summer terms, many workshops and short-term courses. 10 majors offered by the College of Business Administration, 7 by the College of Education, 19 by the College of Fine Arts, 26 by the College of Liberal Arts, 8 by the School of Journalism. Graduate and professional degrees granted. Honors program. Phi Beta Kappa. Some pass/fail. Cooperative work/study. Preprofessional programs in allied health, dentistry, divinity, engineering, law, medicine, social work. 5-year program in College of Pharmacy. 4-year BA/MA program. Marine science program with Southampton College. 3-1 degree programs with Drake Law School, any approved college of medicine or dentistry, Mercy and Methodist Hospital Schools of Medical Technology. 2-2, 3-2 engineering with Cornell U, Washington U. Campus afloat. Study in Appalachia. Washington and UN semesters. Study abroad. Elementary and secondary education certification. ROTC. Language lab, media service center, computer center. 481,601-volume library.
Financial CEEB CSS (preferred) and ACT FAS. University scholarships and loans, merit scholarships, state scholarships and grants, athletic grants; PELL, SEOG, NDSL, FISL, GSL, HEAL, CWS. File FAF between January 1 and March 1 for grants and loans; by March 1 for scholarships.
Admissions High school graduation with at least 11 academic units required. GED accepted. Interview encouraged. SAT or ACT required; aptitude and ACH may be requested. $25 application fee. Rolling admissions; deadline August 15. $100 housing deposit required on acceptance of offer of admission. *Early Decision, Early Admission, Concurrent Enrollment* programs. Admission deferral possible. Transfers accepted. Advanced placement credit possible. Transitional Services Program for those not granted regular admission.

Student Life Student government. Newspaper, literary magazine. Music groups. Speech team. Theatre. Student Volunteer Programs Office. Athletic, academic, special interest, religious, honorary, and professional organizations. 9 fraternities and 6 sororities, all with houses. 19% of men and 20% of women join. Single freshmen under 19 must live at home or on campus. Coed and single-sex dorms. Married-student housing. 50% of students live on campus. Liquor limited to dorms and the University Center. 8 intercollegiate sports for men, 5 for women; intramurals. AIAW, Missouri Valley Athletic Conference. Student body composition: 1.3% Asian, 6.1% Black, 0.6% Hispanic, 0.1% Native American, 90% White. 60% from out of state.

DUBUQUE, UNIVERSITY OF $

Dubuque 52001, (319) 589-3200
Director of Student Services & Admissions: Clifford Bunting

- **Undergraduates:** 650m, 449w
- **Tuition (1984–1985):** $4,950
- **Room and Board (1984–1985):** $1,900;   **Fees:** $75
- **Degrees offered:** BA, BS, BAA, BSN, AA
- **Mean ACT:** 20
- **Student-faculty ratio:** 15 to 1
- **Calendar system:** Semester

A private university affiliated with the United Presbyterian Church, established in 1852. 50-acre campus in residential Dubuque, on the Bluffs West bank of the Mississippi River, 180 miles west of Chicago. Airport and bus station in Dubuque.

Academic Character NCACS and professional accreditation. Semester system, 3 3-week summer terms. Majors offered in accounting, aviation management, biology, business administration, chemistry, computer science, earth science, economics, education, English, environmental science, flight operations, foreign language, general science, history, marketing, math, music, music education, occupational safety & health, philosophy, physical education, physics, political science, psychology, religious studies, safety education, social work, sociology, Spanish, special administration, special education, speech. 3-1 medical technology major. Nursing major for students with an RN. Art major possible through cross-registration. Self-designed majors. Distributive requirements. Honors semester, accelerated study. Independent reading and research for upperclassmen. Credit by exam, some credit/no credit. Internships, cooperative work/study. Preprofessional courses in dentistry, engineering, law, medicine, veterinary medicine, and research. Graduate Theological Seminary in Dubuque offers combined 6-year plan for undergraduates. Member of the Tri-College Cooperative Program with Clarke and Loras; cross-registration also possible with 3 local theological schools. 2-2 nursing program. 2-2 and 3-2 engineering programs. Combined programs possible with dental, medical, law, or veterinary schools. Off-campus studies. Study abroad. Elementary, secondary, and special education certification. ROTC. Language labs. Art gallery. 131,000-volume libraries with microform resources.

Financial CEEB CSS (preferred) and ACT FAS. University scholarships, grants, loans; state scholarships and tuition grants, Presbyterian scholarships and grants-in-aid; PELL, SEOG, NDSL, FISL, GSL, PLUS, CWS, part-time University employment. Application deadline August 15.

Admissions High school graduation with 15 units required. ACT or SAT required. $15 application fee. Rolling admissions; deadline August 15. $50 deposit required on acceptance of offer of admission. *Early Admission* Program. Admission deferral possible. Transfers accepted. Credit possible for CEEB AP and CLEP subject exams.

Student Life Student government. Newspaper, yearbook, radio station. Music, drama, debate groups. Political, religious, academic, honorary, and professional groups. 5 fraternities and 4 sororities, none with houses. 20% of men and women join. First-year students must live at home, with relatives, or on campus. Dormitories, one with a coed floor. Married-student housing. 55% of students live on campus. Freshmen may not have cars on campus. Liquor prohibited on campus. 8 intercollegiate sports for men, 5 for women; intramurals. AIAW, NCAA, Iowa Intercollegiate Athletic Conference. Student body composition: 5% Asian, 2% Black, 0.5% Hispanic, 0.5% Native American, 92% White. 56% from out of state.

GRINNELL COLLEGE $$

Grinnell 50112, (515) 236-7545
Director of Admissions & Student Financial Aid: John R. Hopkins

- **Undergraduates:** 557m, 550w
- **Tuition (1984–1985):** $7,594
- **Room and Board (1984–1985):** $2,345; **Fees:** $211
- **Degrees offered:** BA
- **Mean SAT:** 580v, 610m, **Mean ACT:** 28
- **Student-faculty ratio:** 11 to 1
- **Calendar system:** Semester

A private college established in 1846 in Grinnell. 90-acre small-town campus 300 miles west of Chicago and 55 miles east of Des Moines. Bus station. Airport 60 miles away in Cedar Rapids and in Des Moines.

Academic Character NCACS and professional accreditation. Semester system. Majors offered in American studies, anthropology, art, biology, chemistry, classics, economics, English, French, general science, German, history, mathematics, music, philosophy, physics, political science, psychology, religious studies, Russian, sociology, Spanish, theatre. Self-designed, interdepartmental, and interdisciplinary majors. General literary studies. No required courses except freshman tutorial. Pass/fail. Accelerated study. Internships. Phi Beta Kappa. Preprofessional programs in business, dentistry, government service, journalism, law, medicine, nursing, social work, theology. 3-2 engineering programs with CalTech, Columbia, RPI, Washington U (St. Louis). 3-3 law program with Columbia. Cooperative programs in nursing and medicine with Rush U; in special education certification with Drake U. Member of the Associated Colleges of the Midwest. Over 40 domestic and foreign off-campus programs. Exchange programs in Georgia and in Japan. 365-acre environmental research area, language lab, computer services, and art galleries. Over 250,000-volume library.

Financial CEEB CSS. College scholarships and loans, payment plan; PELL, SEOG, NDSL, FISL, GSL, college part-time employment program. Priority application deadline January 15 for scholarships and grants.

Admissions High school graduation with 16 units required. SAT or ACT required. $20 application fee. Application deadline February 15. Notification of admission March 1. $100 deposit required on acceptance of offer of admission. *Early Decision* and *Early Admission* programs. Admission deferral possible. Transfers accepted. Credit possible for CEEB AP exams.

Student Life Student government. Newspaper, literary magazine, yearbook, radio station. Music and dance groups. PIRG. Audubon Society. Women's group, Concerned Black Students. Outdoor Recreation Program. Athletic, academic, religious, service, and special interest groups. Some off-campus living allowed. Single-sex, coed, coop, and special interest housing. 92% of students live on campus. Financial aid recipients may not have cars; cars are discouraged in general. Liquor not permitted outside Pub or residence halls. Firearms prohibited in dorms. 11 intercollegiate sports for men, 8 for women; intramurals. AIAW, NCAA, Midwest Collegiate Athletic Conference. Student body composition: 2.5% Asian, 5% Black, 1.5% Hispanic, 0.2% Native American, 86% White, 4.8% Other. 89% from out of state.

IOWA, UNIVERSITY OF $

Iowa City 52242, (319) 353-3976
Director of Admissions: John E. Moore

- **Undergraduates:** 12,191m, 11,409w
- **Tuition (1984–1985):** $1,242 (in-state), $3,450 (out-of-state)
- **Room and Board (1984–1985):** $2,100
- **Degrees offered:** BA, BS, BGS, BSE (in 7 areas), BSN, BSPh, BFA, BMus
- **Mean ACT:** 23
- **Student-faculty ratio:** 20 to 1
- **Calendar system:** Semester

A public university founded in 1847 in the small town of Iowa City. 1,375-acre campus on the Iowa River, 24 miles from Cedar Rapids. Airport, bus station.

Academic Character NCACS and professional accreditation. Semester system, 8-week summer term. 85 majors offered by the colleges of Liberal Arts, Business Administration, Dentistry, Education, Engineering, Law, Medicine, Nursing, Pharmacy. College of Liberal Arts includes the schools of Fine Arts, Journalism, Letters, Library Science, Mathematical Sciences, Religion, and Social Work. Self-designed majors. Distributive requirements. Graduate and professional degrees granted. Independent study. Honors program. Phi Beta Kappa. Pass/fail. Internships. Accelerated study. 5-year BA/BS engineering program. Cooperative program in medical technology. 3-2 physical therapy, 2-2 physician's assistant programs. Exchange with Iowa State and Northern Iowa U. Study abroad. Elementary, secondary, and special education certification. ROTC, AFROTC. Newspaper production lab, TV lab, language labs. Natural history museum. Iowa Geological Survey research facilities. Hospital School for severely handicapped children. 2,400,000-volume libraries.

Financial CEEB CSS and ACT FAS. University scholarships, grants, and loans; NSS, PELL, SEOG, NDSL, FISL, NSL, CWS, university part-time employment. Priority application deadline March 1.

Admissions High school graduation with 17 units required. ACT required. $10 application fee. Application deadlines March 1 (business, pharmacy, dental hygiene), January 15 (nursing), February 1 (physical therapy), 10 days before registration (liberal arts, engineering). Rolling admissions. Admission deferral possible. Transfers accepted. Credit possible for CEEB AP and CLEP exams, and for university departmental exams. Special admission programs for minority, disadvantaged, and non-high school graduate applicants.

Student Life Student government. Newspaper, 2 radio stations. Numerous clubs, including music, drama, debate, and religious groups. 18 fraternities and 15 sororities, all with chapter houses. 18% of men and 13% of women join. Coed and women's dorms. Married-student housing. Language houses. 26% of students live on campus. Parking on campus limited. 4 semester hours of phys ed required. Intercollegiate and intramural sports for men and women. Big Ten, AIAW. Student body composition: 1.1% Asian, 2% Black, 0.9% Hispanic, 0.3% Native American, 90.9% White, 4.8% Other. 28% from out of state.

IOWA STATE UNIVERSITY OF SCIENCE AND TECHNOLOGY $

Ames 50011, (515) 294-5836
Dean of Admissions & Records: Fred C. Schlunz

- **Undergraduates:** 12,877m, 7,808w
- **Tuition (1984–1985):** $1,242 (in-state), $3,450 (out-of-state)
- **Room and Board (1984–1985):** $1,848
- **Degrees offered:** BA, BArch, BBA, BFA, BLA, BLS, BMus, BS
- **Mean ACT:** 23.5
- **Student-faculty ratio:** 18 to 1
- **Calendar system:** Semester

A public university established in 1858. 1,000-acre campus in a small city 30 miles north of Des Moines.
Academic Character NCACS and professional accreditation. Semester system, 8-week summer term. 124 majors offered by colleges of Agriculture, Design, Education, Engineering, Home Economics, and Science & Humanities. University also contains Veterinary Medicine and Graduate Colleges, and School of Business Administration. Preprofessional studies majors. Self-designed majors. Distributed Studies major may be departmental or interdepartmental. Optional minors. Distributive requirements. Graduate and professional degrees granted. Honors program, independent study. Phi Beta Kappa. Some pass/fail. Internships, cooperative work/study. International Service Program. Exchange with Regents Universities. Study abroad. Elementary, secondary, and special education certification. AFROTC, NROTC, ROTC. Many research centers, service agencies, and institutes on campus. Computation center. 1,413,991-volume library.
Financial CEEB CSS and ACT FAS. University scholarships, grants, and loans, state scholarships; PELL, SEOG, NDSL, GSL, CWS. Priority application deadline March 1.
Admissions High school graduation required; rank in upper 50% of class recommended. ACT or SAT required. $10 application fee. Rolling admissions; no deadline. *Concurrent Enrollment* and *Early Entrance* programs. Admission deferral possible. Transfers accepted. Credit possible for CEEB AP, CLEP subject, and university placement exams.
Student Life Student government. Newspaper, magazines, yearbook, radio and TV stations. Music, debate, and drama organizations. Special interest, service, professional, and honorary groups. 32 fraternities and 16 sororities, all with houses. 14% of men and 12% of women join. Married-student housing. 50% of students live on campus. Cars discouraged. Some departments have physical education requirements. 9 intercollegiate sports for men, 8 for women; intramurals. AIAW, NCAA, Big Eight. Student body composition: 0.8% Asian, 1.9% Black, 7.1% Foreign, 0.8% Hispanic, 0.1% Native American, 89.2% White. 27% from out of state.

LUTHER COLLEGE $$

Decorah 52101, (319) 387-1287
Dean of Admissions & Financial Aid: David J. Roslien

- **Undergraduates:** 918m, 1,218w
- **Tuition and Fees (1984–1985):** $5,975
- **Room and Board (1984–1985):** $2,025
- **Degrees offered:** BA
- **Mean SAT:** 500v, 550m,   **Mean ACT:** 23
- **Student-faculty ratio:** 15 to 1
- **Calendar system:** 4–1–4

A private Lutheran Church-affiliated college established in 1861. 800-acre small-town campus in the northeast corner of Iowa 15 miles south of Minnesota. Airport and bus depot in Decorah, train station in LaCrosse, WI.
Academic Character NCACS and professional accreditation. 4-1-4 system, 2 4-week summer terms. Over 35 majors offered by the divisions of mathematics & science, social sciences, and humanities, including computer science, nursing, Black studies, Scandinavian studies, political science, classical languages, and linguistics. Interdisciplinary majors offered in health education, psychobiology, and sociology-political science. Distributive requirements. Senior research paper and 3 religion or philosophy courses required for graduation. Independent study allows credit by exam. Honors program. Pass/fail. Preprofessional programs in most fields. 3-2 program in engineering with Washington U. 3-1 program in medical technology arrangeable with 8 affiliated hospitals. 3-1 medical programs possible. 2-2 or 3-2 nursing programs. 2-3 pharmacy program. Iowa General Assembly Legislative Intern Program, Washington Semester. Study abroad. Primary and secondary education certification. Planetarium, museum. Computer center, language lab. 250,000-volume library.
Financial CEEB CSS and ACT FAS. College scholarships and grants; church scholarships, state scholarships and grants; PELL, SEOG, NDSL, FISL, GSL, CWS. Application deadline May 1.
Admissions High school graduation with 15 units required. SAT, ACT, or PSAT required. $20 application fee. Rolling admissions; no deadline. $100 deposit required on acceptance of offer of admission. *Early Admission* Program. Admission deferral possible. Transfers accepted. Credit possible for CEEB AP and CLEP subject exams. Upward Bound summer project for financially disadvantaged high school students.
Student Life Student government. Newspaper, literary magazine, yearbook. Radio station. Music, debate, drama clubs. Black Student Union, Black Cultural Center. Social and academic organizations. 11 fraternities and 4 sororities. 50% of men and 45% of women join. All students live at home or on campus. Coed and single-sex dorms. Married-student housing. 95% of students live on campus. Academic honor system. 2 phys ed courses required. 12 intercollegiate sports for men, 8 for women. AIAW, NCAA, Iowa Conference. Student body composition: 4% Black, 94% White, 2% Other. 48% from out of state.

Kansas

BENEDICTINE COLLEGE $

Atchison 66002, (913) 367-5340
Director of Admissions: Ronald W. Lehmann

- **Undergraduates:** 503m, 458w
- **Tuition (1984–1985):** $4,250
- **Room and Board (1984–1985):** $2,150;   **Fees:** $22
- **Degrees offered:** BA, BM, BSME, AA
- **Mean ACT:** 21,8
- **Student-faculty ratio:** 14 to 1
- **Calendar system:** 4–4–1

A private college controlled by the Benedictines, established in 1971 through merger of St. Benedict's College and Mount St. Scholastica College. 2 campuses of 225 acres in residential section of Atchison, 50 miles from Kansas City, MO, 60 miles from Topeka. Served by bus. Airport in Kansas City.
Academic Character NCACS and professional accreditation. 4-4-1 system, 8-week summer term. Majors offered in accounting, art, arts management, biology, business administration, chemistry, communications, costume design, day care, economics, elementary education, English, fashion merchandising, French, history, home economics/community service, Latin, liberal studies, mathematics, music, music education, music marketing, natural science, philosophy, physical education, physics, political science, psychology, religious studies, restaurant management, social science, sociology, Spanish, theatre arts, theatre arts management, and youth ministries. Special, double majors. Minors offered. Courses in 9 additional areas. Distributives and 9 hours of religious studies required. Independent study. Cooperative work/study, pass/fail, internships. Preprofessional programs in dentistry, divinity, dramatics, engineering, journalism, law, medicine, nursing, pharmacy, veterinary medicine. Member Kansas City Consortium. 3-2 program in engineering with U of Kansas, several others. 3-1 medical technology program. Study abroad. Elementary, secondary, and special education certification. ROTC at Missouri Western State College; AFROTC at U of Kansas. Language, special ed labs. 284,000-volume library.
Financial ACT FAS preferred. College scholarships, grants, loans, tuition discount for 2nd family member, payment plans; PELL, SEOG, NDSL, FISL, CWS, college work program. Priority application deadline March 1.
Admissions High school graduation with 16 units required. Interview encouraged. ACT or SAT required; ACT preferred. $10 application fee. Rolling admissions, beginning November 1; suggest applying in September. $50 deposit required on acceptance of offer of admission. *Early Decision, Early Admission, Concurrent Enrollment* programs. Admission deferral possible. Transfers accepted. Credit possible for CEEB AP and CLEP exams; college has own advanced placement program. Conditional admission program.
Student Life Student government. Newspaper, magazine, yearbook, TV station. Music groups, including participation with St. Joseph (MO) Symphony. Political, religious, service, social, and special interest groups. Single students must live at home or on campus. Single-sex dorms. Some married-student housing. 96% of students live on campus. Class attendance required. 2 courses in phys ed required. 8 intercollegiate sports for men, 5 for

women; several intramurals. AIAW, NAIA. Student body composition: 7% Black, 2% Hispanic, 90% White, 1% Other. 60% from out of state.

KANSAS, UNIVERSITY OF $

Lawrence 66043, (913) 864-3911
Toll free: (800) 332-6332 (in-state), (800) 255-6322 (out-of-state)
Dean of Admissions & Records: Gil Dyck

- **Undergraduates:** 9,296m, 8,933w
- **Tuition (1984–1985):** $1,148 (in-state), $2,828 (out-of-state)
- **Room and Board (1984–1985):** $1,974
- **Degrees offered:** BA, BGS, BS, BArch, BSArchE, BSBA, BAE, BSE, BME, BSAE, BSChe, BSCE, BSEE, BSEP, BSME, BSPE, BFA, BMus, BSJ, BSN, BSOT, BSP, BSW
- **Mean ACT:** 22
- **Student-faculty ratio:** 16 to 1
- **Calendar system:** Semester

A public university established in 1866. 930-acre urban campus in Lawrence, 40 miles from Kansas City.

Academic Character NCACS and professional accreditation. Semester system, 8-week summer term. 44 majors offered by the College of Liberal Arts & Sciences, 5 by the School of Allied Health, 2 by the School of Architecture & Urban Design, 2 by the School of Business, 10 by the School of Education, 8 by the School of Engineering, 18 by the School of Fine Arts, 7 by the School of Journalism, and in nursing, pharmacy, and social welfare. Distributive requirements. Graduate and professional degrees granted. Honors program. Phi Beta Kappa. Preprofessional programs in dentistry, journalism, law, medicine, nursing, pharmacy. Study abroad. Language Institute Programs. ROTC, AFROTC, NROTC. 2,250,000-volume library.

Financial CEEB CSS. University scholarships, grants, loans, freshman engineering grants; PELL, SEOG, NDSL, CWS. Application deadline March 1.

Admissions High school graduation with 13½ units recommended. ACT required. Rolling admissions. *Early Admission* and *Early Decision* programs. Transfers accepted. Credit possible for CEEB AP exams.

Student Life Student government. Music, debate, speech, drama groups. Academic, honorary, religious, and special interest organizations. 23 fraternities and 13 sororities with houses. 12% of men and 9% of women join. Housing in scholarship halls, rooming houses, homes, dormitories, married-student apartments. 40% of students live on campus. Intercollegiate and intramural sports for men and women. Student body composition: 0.7% Asian, 3.5% Black, 1.1% Hispanic, 0.5% Native American, 87.3% White, 6.9% Other. 25% from out of state.

KANSAS STATE UNIVERSITY $

Manhattan 66506, (913) 532-6250
Director of Admissions: Richard N. Elkins

- **Undergraduates:** 8,276m, 6,308w
- **Tuition (1984–1985):** $1,180 (in-state), $3,860 (out-of-state)
- **Room and Board (1984–1985):** $1,820
- **Degrees offered:** BA, BS, BMus, BArch, AA

- **Mean ACT:** 22
- **Student-faculty ratio:** 20 to 1
- **Calendar system:** Semester

A public land-grant university established in 1863. 325-acre campus located in the small city of Manhattan, 50 miles west of Topeka and 120 miles from Kansas City. Served by air and bus.

Academic Character NCACS and professional accreditation. Semester system, 8-week summer term. 17 majors offered by the College of Agriculture, 3 by the College of Architecture & Design, 39 by the College of Arts & Sciences, 10 by the College of Engineering, 4 by the College of Home Economics, and majors in business administration and education. Special and self-designed majors. Courses in 8 additional areas. Distributive requirements. Graduate and professional degrees granted. Independent study. Honors program. Phi Beta Kappa. Pass/fail. Cooperative work/study, internships. Preprofessional programs in law, dentistry, forestry, medical technology, medicine, nursing, optometry, pharmacy, physical therapy, social work, veterinary medicine. 5-year dual degree program in engineering. 6-year veterinary medicine program. Study abroad, exchange program with Justus Liebig University in Germany. Elementary, secondary, and special education certification. South Asian center. Computer center, language lab. 900,000-volume library.

Financial ACT FAS. University scholarships, grants, loans, athletic grants-in-aid; PELL, SEOG, NDSL, GSL, PLUS, CWS, college work program. Application deadlines January 15 (scholarships), March 15 (loans).

Admissions High school graduation required. ACT required. SAT accepted. Rolling admissions. Transfers accepted. Credit possible for CEEB AP and CLEP exams; university has own advanced placement program.

Student Life Student government. Newspaper, magazine, yearbook, radio station. Several music groups. Academic, religious, service, and special interest groups. 28 fraternities and 13 sororities, most with houses. Single students under 21 must live at home or on campus. Coed, single-sex, and coop dorms. Married-student housing includes trailer area and apartments. 40% of students live on campus. Liquor prohibited, except for 3.2 beer in dorms. 2 semesters of phys ed required. 7 intercollegiate sports for men, 7 for women; intramurals. AIAW, NCAA, Big Eight. Student body composition: 1% Asian, 5% Black, 1% Hispanic, 92% White, 1% Other. 15% from out of state.

Kentucky

BEREA COLLEGE $

Berea 40404, (606) 986-9341
Director of Admissions: John S. Cook

- **Undergraduates:** 687m, 838w
- **Tuition (1984–1985):** 0
- **Room and Board (1984–1985):** $1,692;   **Fees:** $120
- **Degrees offered:** BA, BS
- **Mean SAT:** 447v, 466m,   **Mean ACT:** 19.4
- **Student-faculty ratio:** 13 to 1
- **Calendar system:** 4–1–4

A private college established in 1855 to provide Christian education opportunities for young people of the mountain region of the South. 160-acre campus with 1,100 acres of farmland in the foothills of the Cumberland Mountains, 40 miles south of Lexington. Served by bus.

Academic Character SACS and professional accreditation. 4-1-4 system, 8-week summer term. 23 majors offered in the areas of liberal arts & sciences, 10 in agriculture, business, home economics, industrial arts, and nursing. Self-designed majors. Courses offered in 6 additional areas. Distributives and 8 hours of religious and historical perspectives required. Each student works a minimum of 10 hours per week in college labor program. Independent and accelerated study. Phi Beta Kappa. Cooperative work/study, internships. Preprofessional programs in law, medicine, veterinary science. Exchange programs with various small colleges. Language majors may take junior year abroad. Elementary and secondary teacher certification. Nursery school lab. Appalachian museum. Computer, language lab. Over 230,000-volume library.

Financial CEEB CSS, ACT FAS, and state financial aid service. College scholarships, grants, loans, payment plan; PELL, SEOG, NSS, NDSL, FISL, NSL, CWS. Each student works at least 10 hours a week in a college department or in one of the student industries (bakery, tavern hotel, broomcraft, fireside weaving, needlecraft, woodcraft). Preferred application deadline is early spring.

Admissions High school graduation. Interview encouraged. SAT or ACT required. $5 application fee. Rolling admissions. $35 confirmation deposit required on acceptance of offer of admission, refundable up to 30 days before registration. *Early Admission* and *Concurrent Enrollment* programs. Transfers accepted. Credit possible for CEEB AP and CLEP exams; college has own placement program.

Student Life Student Association. Newspaper, Black student literary magazine, yearbook, radio stations. Music, drama, and dance groups. Black Student Union. Academic, honorary, religious, and special interest groups. Students must live at home or in single-sex dorms. Limited married-student housing. 80% of students live on campus. Dormitory students may not have cars on campus. 3 terms of phys ed and 1 term of health required. Regular class attendance expected. Attendance at 10 convocations each term mandatory. Liquor and narcotics prohibited. Committee of deans must approve student marriages. 8 intercollegiate sports for men, 6 for women; many intramurals. AIAW, NAIA, KIAC. Student body composition: 1% Asian,

10% Black, 89% White. 80% of students are from the mountain counties of Kentucky, Alabama, Georgia, N. Carolina, Ohio, S. Carolina, Tennessee, Virginia, and W. Virginia. 60% from out of state.

KENTUCKY, UNIVERSITY OF $

Lexington 40506, (606) 258-9000
Director of Admissions & Registrar: Elbert W. Ockerman

- **Undergraduates:** 8,880m, 8,246w
- **Tuition (1984–1985):** 1,124 (in-state), $3,202 (out-of-state)
- **Room and Board (1984–1985):** $2,418
- **Degrees offered:** BA, BAEd, BAHID, BSW, BS, BSAgE, BSFor, BSLA, BSA, BSBE, BSE, BSDiet, BSFam, BSFS, BSHE, BSN, BSPharm, BBA, BGS, BHS, BM, BFA, BArch, BSEduc, BME
- **Mean ACT:** 19.8
- **Student-faculty ratio:** 16 to 1
- **Calendar system:** Semester

A public university established in 1865. 700-acre urban campus. Served by air, rail, and bus.

Academic Character SACS and professional accreditation. Semester system, 8-week summer term, 4-week spring intersession. 13 majors offered by the College of Agriculture, 4 by the College of Allied Health Professions, 35 by the College of Arts & Sciences, 3 by the College of Business & Economics, 4 by the College of Communications, 23 by the College of Education, 8 by the College of Engineering, 7 by the College of Fine Arts, 8 by the College of Home Economics; also Colleges of Architecture, Nursing, Pharmacy, and Social Professions. Self-designed majors. Interdepartmental majors. Courses in library science and public service. Distributive requirements. Graduate and professional degrees granted. Independent and accelerated study. Honors program. Phi Beta Kappa. Cooperative work/study, pass/fail. Preprofessional programs in dentistry, pharmacy, recreation & parks administration, veterinary medicine. 3-1 and 3-2 programs in law, medicine, dentistry, forestry, and engineering. Summer Study Abroad Program. Elementary, secondary, and special education certification. ROTC, AFROTC. University operates several community colleges. Experimental Education Program. Art gallery, museum. Language lab. Nuclear reactor. 1,800,000-volume library with microform resources.

Financial CEEB CSS. University scholarships, grants, loans; PELL, SEOG, NSS, NDSL, CWS. Preferred application deadline March 15.

Admissions High school graduation required. GED accepted. ACT required. Rolling admissions; deadline June 1. *Early Admission* and *Credit in Escrow* programs. Transfers accepted. Credit possible for CEEB AP and CLEP exams.

Student Life Student government. Newspaper, literary magazine, yearbook, radio station. Music, dance, and theatre groups. Debate. Numerous academic, honorary, religious, service, and special interest groups. 24 fraternities and 16 sororities with houses. 15% of men and 17% of women join. Coed and single-sex dorms. Apartments. Married-student housing. 25% of students live on campus. 12 intercollegiate sports for men, 10 for women; many intramurals. AIAW, NCAA, Southeastern Conference. Student body composition: 1% Asian, 3% Black, 1% Hispanic, 1% Native American, 92% White, 2% Other. 14% from out of state.

LOUISVILLE, UNIVERSITY OF $

Louisville 40292, (502) 588-6531
Director of Admissions: Ray A. Stines

- **Undergraduates:** 7,750m, 7,250w
- **Tuition (1984–1985):** $1,134 (in-state), $3,212 (out-of-state)
- **Room and Board (1984–1985):** $2,040
- **Degrees offered:** BA, BM, BS, BDPT, BHS, BSBA, BSE, BSN, AA, AAS, AHS
- **Mean ACT:** 18
- **Student-faculty ratio:** 15 to 1
- **Calendar system:** Semester

A public university established in 1798. 140-acre urban campus. Served by air, rail, and bus.

Academic Character SACS and professional accreditation. Semester system, 2 summer terms. 39 majors offered by the Arts & Sciences School, 6 by the School of Business, 3 by the School of Dentistry, 4 by the School of Education, 2 by the School of Justice Administration, 3 by the School of Medicine, 9 by the School of Music, 8 by the Speed Scientific School, and 5 by the University College. Minors offered in some major fields. Distributive requirements. Graduate and professional degrees granted. Independent study. Honors program. Phi Beta Kappa. Cooperative internship in Speed School. Limited pass/fail. Preprofessional programs in optometry, pharmacy, and veterinary medicine. Cross-registration with Bellarmine, Indiana University-Southeast, Louisville Presbyterian Theological Seminary, Southern Baptist Theological Seminary, and Spalding College. Study abroad. Elementary, secondary, and special education certification. Numerous institutes and centers. Planetarium. 905,511-volume library.

Financial CEEB CSS and ACT FAS. University scholarships, grants, loans; PELL, SEOG, FISL, CWS. Application deadline April 1.

Admissions High school graduation with 15 units recommended. Audition required for music majors. ACT required. Rolling admissions. *Early Admission* and *Concurrent Enrollment* programs. Transfers accepted. Credit possible for CEEB AP and CLEP exams.

Student Life Student government. Newspaper, literary magazine, yearbook, radio station. Numerous music groups. Debate. Theatre. Athletic, academic, religious, service, and special interest groups. 10 fraternities and 9 sororities with houses. 15% of men and women join. 3 dorms. Married-student housing. 8% of students live on campus. 2 semesters of phys ed required. Freshmen may not have cars on campus. 28 sports for men, 24 for women. NCAA, Metro Conference. Student body composition: 1.3% Asian, 8.4% Black, 0.6% Hispanic, 0.1% Native American, 88.3% White, 1.3% Other. 6% from out of state.

TRANSYLVANIA UNIVERSITY $$

Lexington 40508, (606) 233-8242
Acting Director of Admissions: Wendy S. Warner

- **Undergraduates:** 317m, 338w
- **Tuition (1984–1985):** $5,675
- **Room and Board (1984–1985):** $2,550;   **Fees:** $250
- **Degrees offered:** BA

- **Mean SAT:** 545v, 523m, **Mean ACT:** 23
- **Student-faculty ratio:** 14 to 1
- **Calendar system:** 4−4−1

A private university affiliated with the Christian Church (Disciples of Christ), established in 1780. 32-acre urban campus. Served by air and bus.

Academic Character SACS accreditation. 4-4-1 system, 2 4-week summer terms. 31 majors offered in the areas of liberal arts & sciences, business, computer science, education, fine arts, medical technology, physical education, public administration, and religion. Distributive requirements. Honors program. Internships. Preprofessional programs in engineering, medicine, and veterinary medicine. 3-2 program in engineering with U of Kentucky and Washington U. 3-1 medical technology program. Study abroad. Secondary education certification. ROTC, AFROTC at U of Kentucky. Computer center. Language lab. 110,000-volume library.

Financial CEEB CSS. University scholarships, grants, loans, payment plan; PELL, SEOG, NDSL, GSL, CWS. Recommended applying by March 15.

Admissions High school graduation with 12 units required. Interview required. SAT or ACT required. $15 application fee. Rolling admissions. $125 deposit required on acceptance of offer of admission. *Early Admission* and *Early Decision* programs. Transfers accepted. Credit possible for CEEB AP and CLEP exams.

Student Life Student government. Newspaper, literary magazine, yearbook, radio station. Music and drama groups. Athletic, academic, honorary, religious, service, and special interest groups. 4 fraternities and 4 sororities; all have dormitory chapter suites. 42% of men and 49% of women join. Single underclass students must live at home or on campus. Dorms for men and women. No married-student housing. 72% of students live on campus. 3 activity courses required. 6 intercollegiate sports for men, 6 for women; extensive intramurals. NAIA, NCAA, KWIC. Student body composition: 2% Black, 94% White, 4% Other. 40% from out of state.

Louisiana

GRAMBLING STATE UNIVERSITY $

Grambling 71242, (318) 247-6941
Director of Admissions: Irene S. A. Thomas

- **Undergraduates:** 4,014 combined
- **Tuition (1984–1985):** $890 (in-state), $1,568 (out-of-state)
- **Room and Board (1984–1985):** $1,388–$1,728
- **Degrees offered:** BA, BS
- **Student-faculty ratio:** 23 to 1
- **Calendar system:** Semester

A public university established in 1901. Campus located in rural Louisiana, 5 miles west of Ruston and 60 miles east of Shreveport. Rail service in Ruston.
Academic Character SACS and professional accreditation. Semester system, 9-week summer term. 33 majors offered by the College of Arts & Sciences, 16 by the College of Business & Applied Programs, 15 by the College of Education. MS, MA granted. Honors programs. Cooperative work/study. Credit by exam. Preprofessional programs in dentistry, law, medicine, nursing. Elementary and secondary education certification. AFROTC. Audio-visual and television center. 159,148-volume library.
Financial ACT FAS. University scholarships, grants, tuition waivers, loans; PELL, SEOG, NDSL, GSL, PLUS, CWS. Application deadline June 1.
Admissions High school graduation with 16 units recommended. ACT required. $5 application fee. Rolling admissions; application deadline 30 days prior to enrollment. $50 room deposit required on acceptance of offer of admission. *Early Admission* program. Transfers accepted.
Student Life Student government. Newspaper, magazine, yearbook. Music, drama, debate, athletic, academic, honorary, religious, service, and special interest groups. 4 fraternities and 4 sororities without houses. 5% of men and women join. Single students must live at home or on campus as long as space is available. Freshmen may not have cars on campus. Class attendance required for freshmen and sophomores. 4 hours of phys ed required. Intercollegiate and intramural sports for men and women. Southwestern Athletic Conference, AIAW. Student body composition: 99% Black, 1% Other. 20% from out of state.

LOUISIANA STATE UNIVERSITY AND AGRICULTURAL AND MECHANICAL COLLEGE $

Baton Rouge 70803, (504) 388-1686
Director of Academic Services for Admissions: Ordell Griffith

- **Undergraduates:** 13,087m, 11,617w
- **Tuition (1984–1985):** $968 (in-state), $2,468 (out-of-state)
- **Room and Board (1984–1985):** $2,160
- **Degrees offered:** BA, BS, BArch, BEng Tech, BFA, BLArch, BMus, BMus Ed, BCJ, BID
- **Mean ACT:** 19.4
- **Student-faculty ratio:** 18 to 1
- **Calendar system:** Semester

A public university established in 1860. 300-acre urban campus in Baton Rouge. Air and bus service.

Academic Character SACS and professional accreditation. Semester system, 9-week summer term. 30 majors offered by the College of Agriculture, 31 by the College of Arts & Sciences, 16 by the College of Business Administration, 13 by the College of Chemistry & Physics, 21 by the College of Education, 8 by the College of Design, 11 by the College of Engineering, 3 by the General College, and 9 by the School of Music. Minors offered in some major fields. Distributive requirements. Graduate and professional degrees granted. Independent study. Honors program. Phi Beta Kappa. Cooperative work/study, pass/fail, internships. Preprofessional programs in dentistry, law, library science, medicine, nursing, social welfare, veterinary medicine, optometry, pharmacy, nuclear science, environmental studies, wetland resources. Junior Division for underprepared students. Organization for Tropical Studies. Oak Ridge Associated Universities. Exchange program with Southern University in Baton Rouge. Study abroad. Elementary, secondary, and special education certification. AFROTC & ROTC: NROTC at Southern University. Departmental libraries. Several research institutes and museums. Nuclear Science Center. Computer center, language lab. 1,844,656-volume library with microform resources and access to other area libraries.

Financial University scholarships, grants, loans. PELL, SEOG, SSIG, NDSL, CWS. Application deadlines March 31 (scholarships), June 1 (loans).

Admissions High school graduation required; college prep program suggested. ACT required. $20 application fee. Rolling admissions; application deadline July 1. $75 room reservation fee required with application. Informal early decision, *Early Admission,* and *Concurrent Enrollment* programs. Admission deferral possible. Transfers accepted. Credit possible for CEEB AP and CLEP exams. Special admission requirements for gifted & talented students. Advanced-standing program.

Student Life Student government. Newspaper, magazine, yearbook, radio station. Music, drama, academic, honorary, religious, political, and special interest groups. 23 fraternities, most with houses; 17 sororities, some with houses. 20% of men and 35% of women join. Single undergraduates with less than 30 semester hours live on campus or at home. Married-student housing. 32% of students live on campus. Drunkeness, disorderly conduct, gambling, dishonesty, hazing, rioting, possession of firearms, fireworks, or other explosives forbidden. Phys ed required of freshmen in some colleges. Class attendance expected. Numerous intercollegiate and intramural sports. AIAW, NCAA, Southeastern Conference. Student body composition: 0.2% Asian, 5.9% Black, 1.5% Hispanic, 86% White, 6.4% Other. 14% from out of state.

LOYOLA UNIVERSITY $

New Orleans 70118, (504) 865-3240
Director of Admissions: Dr. Rebecca Brechtel

- **Undergraduates:** 1,532m, 2,013w
- **Tuition (1984–1985):** $3,950
- **Room and Board (1984–1985):** $2,850;   **Fees:** $76
- **Degrees offered:** BA, BS
- **Mean SAT:** 464v, 493m,   **Mean ACT:** 22.4
- **Student-faculty ratio:** 15 to 1
- **Calendar system:** Semester

A private Roman Catholic university conducted by the Jesuits, established in

1912. 19-acre campus in a residential section of New Orleans. Air, rail, and bus service.

Academic Character SACS and professional accreditation. Semester system, 2 5-week summer terms. 28 majors offered by the College of Arts, 8 by the College of Business Administration, and 14 by the College of Music. City College (evening) offers 4 majors. Weekend College. Drama therapy and dance program. Associates degrees include business administration, criminal justice, dental hygiene. Six hours of religion/theology required. Graduate and professional degrees granted. Independent study. Honors programs. Pass/fail, cooperative work/study. Internships. Preprofessional programs in dentistry, engineering, law, medicine, pharmacy, veterinary medicine. 3-2 engineering program with U of Notre Dame. Cross-registration with St. Mary's Dominican, Xavier Universities. Exchange with Tulane. Study abroad. Elementary and secondary education certification. ROTC. AFROTC at U of New Orleans. NROTC at Tulane. Computer center. 305,000-volume library.

Financial CEEB CSS and ACT FAS. University scholarships, grants, 2nd-family-member discounts, payment plan; PELL, SEOG, NDSL, GSL, FISL, CWS. Priority application deadline April 1.

Admissions High school graduation required. GED accepted. Campus visit urged. SAT (minimum 770) or ACT (minimum 17) required. $15 application fee. Rolling admissions; deadline August 1. $50 room deposit required on acceptance of offer of admission. *Early Admission, Early Decision, Concurrent Enrollment* programs. Admission deferral possible. Transfers accepted. Credit possible for CEEB AP, CLEP, ACT, and university exams. Special admission and academic support for underprepared students.

Student Life Student government. Newspaper, magazine, yearbook. Music, drama, ballet groups. Black Student Union, International Student Association, Community Action Program. Honorary, professional, social, and special interest groups. 4 fraternities, 1 with house; 5 sororities without houses. Freshmen must live on campus or at home. Single-sex dorms. No married-student housing. 36% of students live on campus. Freshmen may not have cars on campus. Intramural sports for men and women. Student body composition: 0.7% Asian, 14% Black, 6.3% Hispanic, 0.4% Native American, 72.1% White, 6.1% Other. 28% from out of state.

TULANE UNIVERSITY OF LOUISIANA $$$

New Orleans 70118, (504) 865-5731
Tulane Director of Admissions, Jillinda G. Jonker
Newcomb Director of Admissions: Lois V. Conrad

- **Undergraduates:** 2,835m, 1,920w
- **Tuition & fees (1984–1985):** $8,000
- **Room and Board (1984–1985):** $3,400
- **Degrees offered:** BA, BS, BFA
- **Mean SAT:** 535–561v, 580–638m
- **Student-faculty ratio:** 13 to 1
- **Calendar system:** Semester

A private university containing the College of Liberal Arts and Sciences for men, Newcomb College for women, and coed undergraduate Schools of Architecture and Engineering. Established in 1834. 110-acre campus in a residential area 5 miles from downtown New Orleans. Airport, bus and rail stations nearby.

Academic Character SACS and professional accreditation. Semester system, 2 5½-week and one 8-week summer terms. 46 majors offered in the areas of art, humanities, math, science, social sciences, economics, engineering, management, physical education, education, and communications. Programs in Afro-American studies and international affairs. Distributive requirements. Graduate and professional degrees granted. Independent study. Honors programs. Phi Beta Kappa. Preprofessional programs in business administration, dentistry, law, medicine, social work. Washington Semester. Domestic interchange program. Study abroad. Pre-school, elementary, and secondary education certification. AFROTC, NROTC, ROTC. Newcomb Women's Center. Several research centers. Computer lab, language lab. 1,350,000-volume library with departmental libraries and microform resources.

Financial CEEB CSS. University scholarships, grants, loans, payment plan; PELL, SEOG, NDSL, CWS. Application deadline for scholarships and grants March 1.

Admissions High school graduation with 15 units required. SAT or ACT required. $25 application fee. Rolling admissions; deadline February 1. $100 deposit required on acceptance of offer of admission. *Early Decision, Early Admission, Concurrent Enrollment* programs. Admission deferral possible. Transfers accepted. Credit possible for CEEB AP and CLEP exams; university has own advanced placement programs.

Student Life Student government. Newspaper, yearbook, radio station. Music, debate, public speaking, drama groups. Community service, academic, religious, special interest groups. 18 fraternities with houses, 7 sororities with non-residential houses. 35% of men and 45% of women join. Freshmen must live on campus. Dorms for men and women. Married-student apartments. 60% of students live on campus. 2 years of phys ed required for Newcomb students; one year for Arts & Sciences students. Many intercollegiate, intramural, and club sports for men and women. Student body composition: 1% Asian, 4.2% Black, 4.7% Hispanic, 0.5% Native American, 83.4% White, 6.2% Other. 76% from out of state.

Maine

BATES COLLEGE $$$

Lewiston 04240, (207) 784-0181
Dean of Admissions· William Hiss

- **Undergraduates:** 725m, 700w
- **Tuition (1984–1985):** $9,560
- **Room and Board (1984–1985):** $2,640
- **Degrees offered:** BA, BS
- **Mean SAT:** 560v, 590m
- **Student-faculty ratio:** 13 to 1
- **Calendar system:** 4–4–1

A private college established in 1864. 125-acre campus in a suburban residential area at the edge of Lewiston, 35 miles northeast of Portland and 145 miles from Boston. 600-acre Bates-Morse Mountain Conservation Area near Bath. Airport and bus station in Lewiston.

Academic Character NEASC accreditation. 4-4-1 system. Majors offered in anthropology, art, biology, chemistry, economics, English, French, geology, German, history, math, music, philosophy, physics, political science, psychology, religion, rhetoric, sociology, Spanish, theatre arts. Self-designed, interdisciplinary, and double majors. Minors. Distributive requirements. Comprehensive exam and/or thesis required for graduation. Independent study. Honors program. Phi Beta Kappa. Internships, job placement for students taking leave of absence. 3-2 engineering programs with RPI and Columbia. Washington Semester, City Semester, Mystic Seaport Maritime Studies Semester. Study abroad. Secondary education certification. Language labs, computer center. 330,000-volume library with microform resources.

Financial CEEB CSS. College scholarships, loans; PELL, SEOG, NDSL, GSL, CWS. Application deadline March 1.

Admissions High school graduation required; 16 units recommended. SAT or ACT, and 3 ACH required. Interview suggested. $25 application fee. Application deadline February 1. Notification in mid-April. $200 deposit required on acceptance of admissions offer (May 1). *Early Decision* and *Early Admission* programs. Admission deferral possible. Transfers accepted. Credit possible for CEEB AP exams.

Student Life Student government. Newspaper, literary magazine, yearbook, radio station. Intercollegiate debate. Music, drama, and dance groups. Community activities club. Afro-American Society. Outing club. Political and special interest groups. Students must live at home or on campus. Dorms for men and women. 97% of students live on campus. Scholarship students must have permission to have cars on campus. One year of phys ed required. 11 intercollegiate sports for men, 10 for women; intramurals. CBB, ECAC, NCAA, NESCAC. Student body composition: 2% Black, 96% White, 2% Other. 88% from out of state.

BOWDOIN COLLEGE $$$

Brunswick 04011, (207) 725-8731
Director of Admissions: William R. Mason

- **Undergraduates:** 1,373 Combined
- **Tuition (1984–1985):** $9,325
- **Room and Board (1984–1985):** $3,375;   **Fees:** $75
- **Degrees offered:** AB
- **Student-faculty ratio:** 13 to 1
- **Calendar system:** Semester

A private college, established in 1794 and became coed in 1970. 110-acre campus in the small town of Brunswick, 25 miles northeast of Portland. Bus station in Brunswick, airport in Portland.

Academic Character NEASC and professional accreditation. Semester system. Majors offered in Afro-American studies, archaeology-classics, art, biology, chemistry, classics, economics, English, environmental studies, German, government & legal studies, history, math, music, philosophy, physics & astronomy, psychology, religion,Romance languages, sociology & anthropology. Self-designed, interdepartmental, joint, and double majors possible. Distributive requirements. Senior comprehensive exams in some majors. Independent study, honors programs and projects. Senior research fellowships. Phi Beta Kappa. Preprofessional programs in law, medicine. 3-2 engineering programs with CalTech, Columbia; 3-2 law with Columbia. 12-College Exchange with New England colleges; exchanges with Tougaloo and U of Dundee, Scotland. Many domestic and foreign off-campus study programs. Elementary and secondary education certification. Biological field station in New Brunswick. 4 research centers. Art museum, computing center. 650,000-volume library with microform resources.

Financial CEEB CSS. College scholarships and loans; PELL, SEOG, NDSL, CWS. Application deadline January 15.

Admissions High school graduation with 16 units required. SAT and ACH may be submitted but not required. Interview recommended. $25 application fee. Application deadline January 15. Notification in mid-April. Acceptance of offer of admission and $100 fee required by May 1. *Early Decision* and *Early Entrance* programs. Admission deferral possible. Some transfers accepted; freshmen may enter only in fall. Credit possible for CEEB AP and departmental exams.

Student Life Student government and admissions interviewing board. Newspapers, literary magazine, yearbook, radio station. Music, drama, dance groups. Religious and social service organizations. Franco-American, Afro-American societies. Women's Association. Gay-Straight Alliance. 10 coed fraternities. 45% of students join. Dorms, college-owned apartments and houses. 90% of students live on campus. Honor system. 16 intercollegiate sports for men, 9 for women; intramurals. Student body composition: 0.7% Asian, 3% Black, 0.3% Hispanic, 94.3% White, 1.7% Other. 85% from out of state.

COLBY COLLEGE $$$

Waterville 04901, (207) 873-1131
Dean of Admissions: Robert P. McArthur

- **Undergraduates:** 875m, 825w
- **Tuition (1984–1985):** $8,660
- **Room and Board (1984–1985):** $3,320;   **Fees:** $420
- **Degrees offered:** BA
- **Mean SAT:** 560v, 600m

- **Student-faculty ratio:** 11 to 1
- **Calendar system:** 4–1–4

A private college founded in 1813. 900-acre semi-rural campus on a hill 2 miles from downtown Waterville, about 75 miles north of Portland. Airport, bus station in Waterville.

Academic Character NEASC and professional accreditation. 4-1-4 system. Majors offered in administrative science, art, biology, chemistry, classics, economics, English, French, geology, German, government, history, math, music, philosophy, physics, psychology, religion, sociology, and Spanish. Several combined and interdisciplinary majors. Self-designed majors. Distributive requirements. Senior comprehensive exams in some majors. Accelerated study. Honors and Senior Scholars programs. Phi Beta Kappa. Independent study. Pass/fail credit possible for field experience. Preprofessional programs in administrative science, dentistry, engineering, government, law, medicine, theology, veterinary science. 3-2 engineering programs with U of Rochester, Case Western Reserve. Exchanges with Fisk, Pomona, Pitzer, Howard. Washington and Mystic Seaport Semesters, Sea Semester. Secondary education certification. Language lab, computer center. 365,000-volume library with microform resources.

Financial CEEB CSS. College scholarships and loans, payment plan; PELL, SEOG, GSL, NDSL, FISL, CWS. Application deadline for scholarships and grants March 15. Deadline for loans varies.

Admissions High school graduation with 16 units required. SAT or ACT, 3 ACH, and English teacher's recommendation required. $30 application fee. Application deadline February 1. Notification about April 15. Acceptance of offer and $200 tuition deposit required by May 1. *Early Decision* and *Early Entrance* programs. Admission deferral possible. Transfers accepted. Credit possible for CEEB AP and departmental exams.

Student Life Student government. Newspaper, literary magazine, yearbook, radio station. Music, drama, and public speaking groups. Student Arts Festival. Outing Club. Student Organization for Black Unity. Women's Group. Community service, religious, and special interest groups. 8 fraternities with houses, 2 sororities with chapter rooms. 35% of men and 8% of women join. Coed and single-sex dorms. No married-student housing. 92% of students live on campus. 3 semester hours of phys ed required. 12 intercollegiate sports for men, 11 for women; intramurals, club rugby for men and women. AIAW, ECAC, NCAA, NESCAC. Student body composition: 1% Asian, 2% Black, 1% Hispanic, 95% White, 1% Other. 86% from out of state.

## MAINE, UNIVERSITY OF, AT ORONO	$

Orono 04469, (207) 581-7568
Director of Admissions: William J. Munsey

- **Undergraduates:** 5,097m, 4,056w
- **Tuition (1984–1985):** $1,509 (in-state), $4,560 (out-of-state)
- **Room and Board (1984–1985):** $2,921   **Fees:** $82
- **Degrees offered:** BA, BS, BSEd, BMus, BET, AS
- **Mean SAT:** 466v, 520m
- **Student-faculty ratio:** 17 to 1
- **Calendar system:** Semester

A public university established in 1865. Suburban main campus in Orono. University also owns 900 acres of farmland, 2,000 acres of forest, 360 acres of bog, 33 acres of woodland preserve. 2-year branch campus, airport, and bus station 9 miles away in Bangor.

Academic Character NEASC and professional accreditation. Semester system, 4 3-week and 3 6-week summer terms. Over 70 majors offered by the Colleges of Arts & Sciences, Business Administration, Education, Engineering & Science, Forest Resources, Life Sciences & Agriculture. Double, self-designed, and interdisciplinary concentrations possible. Many minors offered. Distributive requirements. Graduate degrees granted. Independent and accelerated study. Honors program. Phi Beta Kappa. Cooperative work/study, internships. Pass/fail. Preprofessional programs in dentistry, medicine. Registration for courses at Bangor Theological Seminary possible. Living/Learning program. Study abroad. Elementary, secondary, and special education certification. ROTC, AFROTC. Several centers and institutes on campus. Northeast Archive of Folklore and Oral History, art collection, museum. Computer center, farm. 551,000-volume libraries.

Financial CEEB CSS. University scholarships, loans, payment plan; PELL, SEOG, NDSL, CWS. Application deadline March 1.

Admissions High school graduation with 16 units required; some programs have additional requirements. SAT and 2 ACH required. $10 application fee. Rolling admissions; application deadline March 1. $25 tuition and $50 room deposits required on acceptance of offer of admission. *Early Admission* Program. Transfers accepted. Credit possible for CEEB AP, CLEP, and departmental exams.

Student Life Student government. Newspaper, magazines, yearbook, radio & TV stations. Music, drama, dance, and speaking groups. Debate. Athletic, academic, religious, service, and special interest groups. 16 fraternities, 15 with houses, and 10 sororities. Coed and single-sex dorms. 70% of students live on campus. 16 intercollegiate sports for men and women; intramurals. AIAW. Student body composition: 1.6% Minorities, 98.4% White. 25% from out of state.

Maryland

GOUCHER COLLEGE $$$

Dulaney Valley Road, Towson 21204, (301) 337-6000
Director of Admissions: Janis Boster

- **Undergraduates:** 1,100w
- **Tuition (1984–1985):** $7,700
- **Room and Board (1984–1985):** $3,850; **Fees:** $105
- **Degrees offered:** BA
- **Mean SAT:** 518v, 522m, **Mean ACT:** 23
- **Student-faculty ratio:** 10 to 1
- **Calendar system:** Semester

A private college established in 1885. 330-acre suburban campus 8 miles north of Baltimore. Served by air and rail in Baltimore, which is 20 minutes away by bus.

Academic Character MSACS. Semester system. 33 majors offered by the Faculty of Languages, Literature, Philosophy, Religion & the Arts, the Faculty of History & the Social Sciences, and the Faculty of the Natural Sciences & Mathematics. Self-designed and combined majors. Interdepartmental programs in public affairs, and in Black and women's studies. Distributive requirements; one off-campus experience required. Senior thesis option. MA granted. Independent study. Phi Beta Kappa. Limited pass/fail for freshmen and sophomores, unlimited for upperclasses. 5-year BA/MHS with Johns Hopkins. Field Politics Center. Center for Sociological Study. Computer center. Language house. 197,149-volume library with microform resources.
Financial CEEB CSS. College scholarships, grants, loans, PELL, SEOG, NDSL, GSL, CWS. Application deadline March 1.
Admissions High school graduation with 16 units required. Interview required. SAT or ACT required. $25 application fee. Rolling admissions. $150 deposit required on acceptance of offer of admission. *Early Admission* and *Early Decision* programs. Admission deferral possible. Transfers accepted. Credit possible for CEEB AP exams.
Student Life Student government. Newspaper, literary magazine, yearbook. Dance group. Riding club. Newman Club. Jewish Student's Association. Black Student's Association. International Club. Christian Fellowship. Students must live at home or on campus. Special interest housing, language floors. 70% of students live on campus. 3 semesters of phys ed required. 10 intercollegiate sports; extensive intramurals. AIAW, EAIAW, MAIAW. Student body composition: 2.8% Asian, 6.8% Black, 2.1% Hispanic, 0.2% Native American, 86% White, 2.1% Other. 70% from out of state.

HOOD COLLEGE $$

Frederick 21701, (301) 663-3131
Director of Admissions & Financial Aid: Diane R. Wilson

- **Undergraduates:** 106m, 980w
- **Tuition (1984–1985):** $6,790
- **Room and Board (1984–1985):** $3,530; **Fees:** $100
- **Degrees offered:** BA, BS

- **Mean SAT:** 480v, 480m
- **Student-faculty ratio:** 12 to 1
- **Calendar system:** Semester

A private college established in 1893, male commuting students accepted since 1971. 100-acre suburban campus, 45 miles northwest of Washington, DC, 45 miles west of Baltimore. Served by bus.

Academic Character MSACS accreditation. Semester system. 33 majors offered in the areas of liberal arts & sciences, education, environmental studies, home economics, computer science, management, medical technology, music, radiologic technology, recreation, religion, and social work. Special and self-designed majors. Double majors. Courses in 7 additional areas. Distributive requirements. MA, MS granted. Independent study. Honors program. Pass/fail, students may schedule own exams. Internships, field projects. Preprofessional programs in the health professions and law. 3-1 programs in medical and radiological technology. 3-2 engineering program with George Washington U. Cross-registration with Frederick and Hagerstown. Study abroad. Elementary, secondary, and special education certification. Nursery school. Observatory. Language lab. Computer center. Art gallery. 140,000-volume library.

Financial CEEB CSS. College scholarships, grants, loans, academic and state scholarships, PELL, SEOG, NDSL, GSL, CWS, student employment program. Preferred application deadline March 31.

Admissions High school graduation with 16 units expected. Interview recommended. SAT or ACT required. $20 application fee. Rolling admissions. $150 deposit ($100 for commuters) required on acceptance of offer of admission. *Early Admission* and *Early Decision* programs. Admission deferral possible. Transfers accepted. Credit possible for CEEB AP and CLEP results; college has own advanced placement program. Some conditional admissions.

Student Life Student government. Newspaper, literary magazine, yearbook. Choral, dance, and drama groups. Black Student Union. Outing club. Big Sister Program. Honorary, political, professional, and religious groups. Students must live at home or on campus. Single-sex dorms. Language and home economics residences. 63% of students live on campus. 2 semesters of phys ed required. Honor system. 6 intercollegiate sports; intramurals. Student body composition: 1% Asian, 3% Black, 2% Hispanic, 94% White. 41% from out of state.

JOHNS HOPKINS UNIVERSITY $$$

Baltimore 21218, (301) 338-8171
Director of Admissions: Jerome D. Schnydman

- **Undergraduates:** 1,550m, 750w
- **Tuition (1984–1985):** $8,600
- **Room and Board (1984–1985):** $3,300
- **Degrees offered:** BA, BES
- **Mean SAT:** 616v, 670m
- **Student-faculty ratio:** 10 to 1
- **Calendar system:** 4–1–4

A private university established in 1876, became coed in 1970. 140-acre campus located in residential section of northern Baltimore. Served by air, rail, and bus.

Academic Character MSACS and professional accreditation. 4-1-4 system, 6- to 8-week summer term. 22 majors offered by the School of Arts & Sciences, 8 by the School of Engineering. Interdepartmental liberal arts major. 5 area majors. Self-designed majors. Courses in 3 additional areas. Distributive requirements. Graduate degrees granted. Individual study, research. Honors program in humanistic studies. Phi Beta Kappa. Limited pass/fail, internships. Preprofessional programs in engineering, foreign service, law. BA/MD Human Biology program. 7-year medical program with medical school. BA/PhD psychology program. 5-year BA/MA international studies program. Evening college. Cross-registration with Goucher, Maryland Institute of Art, Peabody Conservatory of Music, and other area schools. Study abroad. Elementary and secondary education certification. ROTC; AFROTC at Maryland. 4 major research centers. 2,000,000-volume library with microform resources; specialized libraries available to students.

Financial CEEB CSS. University scholarships, grants, loans, PELL SEOG, NDSL, FISL, GSL, PLUS, ALAS, CWS. Application deadline February 1.

Admissions High school graduation with 17 units strongly recommended. Interview highly recommended. SAT or ACT required; SAT preferred. 3 ACH required. $30 application fee. Application deadline January 15. $200 deposit required on acceptance of admissions offer. *Early Admission* and *Early Decision* programs. Admission deferral possible. Transfers accepted. Credit possible for CEEB AP exams.

Student Life Student Council. Student Activities Committee. Newspaper, literary magazines, departmental journals, handbook, yearbook, radio station. Music and theatre groups. Debating Council. International Student Association. Young Democrats, Young Republicans. Tutoring. Community service. Black Students' Union. Women's Center. Rathskeller. Honorary and special interest groups. 8 fraternities, 5 with houses; 3 sororities. 20% of students join. Freshmen must live at home or in dorms. Coed and single-sex housing. Married-student apartments. 25% of students live on campus. 12 intercollegiate sports for men, 8 for women; extensive intramurals. AIAW, NCAA, MAC. Student body composition: 6.3% Asian, 2.8% Black, 1.3% Hispanic, 0.2% Native American, 89.4% White. 50% from out of state.

MARYLAND, UNIVERSITY OF $

College Park 20742, (301) 454-5550
Director of Undergraduate Admissions: Dr. Linda Clement

- **Undergraduates:** 15,763m, 13,747w
- **Tuition (1984–1985):** $1,410 (in-state), $3,952 (out-of-state)
- **Room and Board (1984–1985):** $3,347
- **Degrees offered:** BA, BS, BMus, BArch, BGS
- **Mean SAT:** 464v, 525m
- **Student-faculty ratio:** 16 to 1
- **Calendar system:** Semester

A public university established in 1812. 300-acre suburban campus outside of Washington, DC. Served by air, rail, and bus.

Academic Character MSACS and professional accreditation. Semester system, 2 6-week summer terms. 93 majors offered by the Divisions of Agricultural & Life Science, Arts & Humanities, Behavioral & Social Sciences, Human & Community Resources, Mathematical & Physical Sciences, and Engineering. Distributive requirements. Individual Study Program. Freshman honors program. Some pass/fail, credit by exam. Preprofessional programs in numerous areas. Binary programs with University Schools of Dentistry, Law, and Medicine. Elementary, secondary, and special education certification. AFROTC. 2,000-acre University farms. Many scientific research facilities. 1,563,000-volume library with microform resources.

Financial CEEB CSS. University scholarships, grants, National Achievement program; PELL, SEOG, NDSL, GSL, CWS. Application deadline February 15.

Admissions High school graduation required. SAT required. $20 application fee. Rolling admissions. $100 deposit required with housing contract. *Early Decision* Program for Maryland residents only. *Early Admission* and *Concurrent Enrollment* programs. Transfers accepted. Credit possible for CEEB AP exams.

Student Life Student government. Newspaper, magazines, yearbook, radio station. Music and drama groups. Debate. Black Student Union. Academic, honorary, religious, service, and special interest groups. 29 fraternities, 22 with houses; 22 sororities, 18 with houses. 8,100 housing spaces available. Graduate married-student housing. 33% of students live on campus. Freshmen and sophomores may not have cars on campus. 12 intercollegiate sports for men, 9 for women; extensive intramurals. AIAW, NCAA, Atlantic Coast Conference. Student body composition: 4.1% Asian, 7.6% Black, 1.9% Hispanic, 0.3% Native American, 80.4% White. 24% from out of state.

ST. JOHN'S COLLEGE $$$

Annapolis 21404, (301) 263-2371
Director of Admissions: John Christensen

- **Undergraduates:** 226m, 177w
- **Tuition (1984–1985):** $8,250
- **Room and Board (1984–1985):** $2,900;   **Fees:** $100
- **Degrees offered:** BA
- **Mean SAT:** 630v, 600m
- **Student-faculty ratio:** 8 to 1
- **Calendar system:** Semester

A private college established in 1696, became coed in 1951. 36-acre campus in the historic district, 30 miles from Washington, DC. Served by bus; air service at Baltimore-Washington International Airport, 20 miles away.

Academic Character MSACS accreditation. Semester system, 10-week summer term. No·majors or electives. 4-year study sequence of great books from Homer to present in conjunction with programs in language, mathematics, laboratory science, and 1 year of music theory. Classes organized around discussion. Academic year has 6 divisions: seminars, language, mathematics, and music tutorials, laboratory, and formal lectures. Oral exams at end of each semester; comprehensive orals in fall of senior year. Senior thesis defended in oral examination. Students may spend one or more years at Santa Fe campus. Masters degrees granted. 80,000-volume library.

Financial CEEB CSS. College scholarships, grants, payment plan; PELL, SEOG, NDSL, FISL, CWS. Scholarship application deadline January 31.

Admissions High school graduation with college-prep courses advised. Interview encouraged, sometimes required. Rolling admissions. $200 deposit due on acceptance of admissions offer. *Early Decision* and *Early Admission* programs. Admission deferral possible. Students accepted only as freshmen.

Student Life Student Polity regulates dorms and activities. Newspaper, literary magazine. Music and drama groups. Chess club. Extracurricular classes. Arts, crafts, religious, and special interest groups. Single students not living at home usually live and board on campus. Coed and single-sex dorms. No married-student housing. 75% of students live on campus. Illegal drugs prohibited. Extensive intramural sports program. Student body composition: 1% Asian, 1% Black, 1% Hispanic, 1% Native American, 96% White. 85% from out of state.

UNITED STATES NAVAL ACADEMY $

Annapolis 21402, (301) 267-6100
Director of Admissions: Rear Adm. Robert W. McNitt, USN (Ret.)

- **Undergraduates:** 4,851m, 416w
- **Degrees offered:** BS
- **Mean SAT:** 574v, 665m,   **Mean ACT:** 25e, 31m
- **Student-faculty ratio:** 10 to 1
- **Calendar system:** Semester

A public service academy, established in 1845, became coed in 1976. On graduation, each midshipman is commissioned an ensign in the Navy or a 2nd Lieutenant in the Marine Corps and is required to serve 5 years active duty. 329-acre campus, 30 miles from Washington, DC, and Baltimore. Served by bus; air and rail in Baltimore.

Academic Character MSACS and professional accreditation. Semester system, mandatory 2-month summer term. Majors offered in aerospace engineering, electrical, general, marine, mechanical, ocean, and systems engineering, and in naval architecture, English, history, applied science, chemistry, mathematics, oceanography, physical science, physics, economics, and political science. Courses in 7 additional areas, including Chinese and Russian. Trident Scholars Program offers independent research and study for superior firstclassmen. Professional training program includes physical education, practical training, and drills. Distributive requirements. Plebe (1st-year) summer: instruction in seamanship, navigation, signaling, infantry drill, and physical conditioning. Third class summer: 6-8 weeks training at sea. Second class summer: training in warfare specialties. First class summer: training at sea as junior officers. Exchange programs with Air Force, Coast Guard, and military (West Point) academies. Educational Resource Center. Computer Center. Fleet of over 100 small craft. 515,000-volume library.

Financial Full 4-year government scholarships for all students. Midshipmen receive $461 basic pay per month to cover uniform and book costs, personal expenses, etc.

Admissions High school graduation with 15 units recommended. GED considered. Interview recommended. All applicants must be between 17 and 21 on July 1 of admission year, unmarried US citizens with no parental responsibilities. Nomination by a member of Congress, the Vice-President, or the President necessary. Rolling admissions; suggest applying by September. $500 deposit required on entrance. Transfers accepted as first-year students (Plebes) only. Credit possible for CEEB AP and ACH exams; Naval Academy Preparatory School Program has 1-year training to prepare unsuccessful nominees.

Student Life Magazine, yearbook, radio station. Music and drama groups.

Debate. Cultural Affairs Program. Yard Patrol Squadron. Aviation Training. Big Brothers. Academic, honorary, professional, religious, service, and special interest groups. All students live on campus. Some coed dorms. 8 semesters of phys ed required. Only seniors may have cars. Liquor permitted only at Officers Club or in private homes. Mandatory dismissal for drug involvement. Uniforms required. Class attendance required. Honor Code. Marriage not permitted. 18 intercollegiate sports for men, 7 for women; intramurals. Student body composition: 4% Asian, 4.4% Black, 3.7% Hispanic, 0.5% Native American, 87.3% White. 94% from out of state.

WASHINGTON COLLEGE $$

Chestertown 21620, (301) 778-2800
Director of Admissions: A. M. DiMaggio

- **Undergraduates:** 350m, 350w
- **Tuition (1984–1985):** $6,130
- **Room and Board (1984–1985):** $2,720
- **Degrees offered:** BA, BS
- **Mean SAT:** 500v, 520m
- **Student-faculty ratio:** 12 to 1
- **Calendar system:** Semester

A private college established in 1782. 100-acre small town campus, 71 miles east of Baltimore.

Academic Character MSACS accreditation. Semester system. Majors offered in art, biology, chemistry, drama, economics, English, French, German, history, mathematics, music, philosophy, physics, political science, psychology, sociology, Spanish, American studies, humanities, and international studies. Special majors. Minors. Distributives and senior exam required. Independent study. Honors program. Limited pass/fail, internships, apprenticeships, field-work programs. 3-2 programs arranged in dentistry, engineering, law, medical technology, medicine, nursing, veterinary medicine. Washington Semester. Study abroad. Secondary education certification. ROTC at U of Delaware. Computer center. Language labs. Over 135,000-volume library.

Financial CEEB CSS and ACT FAS. College scholarships, grants, loans, merit awards, payment plans; PELL, SEOG, NDSL, CWS. Application deadline February 15.

Admissions High school graduation with 16 units required. Interview recommended. SAT or ACT required; ACH optional. $15 application fee. Rolling admissions. $100 deposit due on acceptance of admissions offer. *Early Admission* and *Early Decision* programs. Admission deferral possible. Transfers accepted. Credit possible for CEEB AP and CLEP exams.

Student Life Student Council. Newspaper, literary magazine, yearbook. Music, dance, and drama groups. Film society. Debate, Writers Union. Academic, honorary, political, religious, and special interest groups. 4 fraternities with houses, 3 sororities without housing. 21% of men and women join. Permission required to live off campus. Coed and single-sex dorms. Language halls. No married-student housing. 95% of students live on campus. 8 intercollegiate sports for men, 4 for women; intramurals. NCAA, Middle Atlantic Conference, Mason-Dixon Conference. Student body composition: 2% Black, 98% White. 49% from out of state.

WESTERN MARYLAND COLLEGE $$

Westminster 21157, (301) 848-7000
Dean of Admissions & Financial Aid: L. Leslie Bennett

- **Undergraduates:** 650m, 700w
- **Tuition (1984–1985):** $6,175
- **Room and Board (1984–1985):** $2,460;   **Fees:** $50
- **Degrees offered:** BA
- **Mean SAT:** 500v, 530m
- **Student-faculty ratio:** 14 to 1
- **Calendar system:** 4–1–4

A private college established in 1867. 160-acre small town campus, 28 miles from Baltimore. Served by bus; air and rail facilities in Baltimore and Washington.

Academic Character MSACS and professional accreditation. 4-1-4 system, 2 5-week summer terms. Majors offered in American studies, art, biology, business, chemistry, comparative literature, drama, economics, English, French, German, history, mathematics, music, philosophy-religion, physics, political science, psychobiology, psychology, social work, sociology, and Spanish. Special majors. Distributive requirements. Graduate degrees granted. Honors program. Phi Beta Kappa. Limited pass/fail, internships. Preprofessional programs in dentistry, law, medicine, the ministry. 3-2 engineering program with U of Maryland and Washington U. 3-2 forestry program with Duke. 2-2 nursing program with Emory. Study abroad. Elementary, secondary, and deaf education certification. ROTC; AFROTC & NROTC at Maryland. Language labs. 130,000-volume library.

Financial CEEB CSS. College scholarships, grants, loans, payment plan; PELL, SEOG, NDSL, CWS. Application deadline March 15.

Admissions High school graduation with 16 units recommended. Interview desirable. SAT required; language ACH required for placement. $15 application fee. Rolling admissions. $150 deposit due on acceptance of admissions offer. *Early Admission* Program. Admission deferral possible. Transfers accepted. Credit possible for CEEB AP and CLEP exams.

Student Life Student government. Newspaper, literary magazine, yearbook. Black Student Union. Music and drama groups. Academic, honorary, political, religious, and service organizations. 4 fraternities and 4 sororities. 30% of men and women join. Students must live on campus or at home. Coed and single-sex dorms. 90% of students live on campus. 3 semester hours of phys ed required. Honor system. Class attendance expected. 8 intercollegiate sports for men, 5 for women; many intramurals. AIAW, NCAA, Penn-Mar and Middle Atlantic Athletic Conferences. Student body composition: 1% Asian, 7% Black, 90% White, 2% Other. 30% from out of state.

Massachusetts

AMHERST COLLEGE $$$

Amherst 01002, (413) 542-2328
Dean of Admissions: Henry F. Bedford

- **Undergraduates:** 895m, 627w
- **Tuition and Room/Board Combined(1984–1985):** $12,400
- **Degrees offered:** BA
- **Mean SAT:** 617v, 654m
- **Student-faculty ratio:** 10 to 1
- **Calendar system:** 4–0–4

A private college established in 1821, became coed in 1975. 1,000-acre small-town campus, 90 miles west of Boston and 150 miles north of New York. Served by bus; 5-college exchange bus.
Academic Character NEASC accreditation. 4-0-4 system. Majors offered in American studies, anthropology, Asian studies, astronomy, biology, Black studies, chemistry, classics, dramatic arts, economics, English, European studies, fine arts, French, geology, German, Greek, history, Latin, mathematics, music, neuroscience, philosophy, physics, political science, psychology, religion, Romance languages, Russian, sociology, and Spanish. Self-designed and interdisciplinary majors. Required freshman year program. Comprehensive exams required. Independent study and honors programs. Phi Beta Kappa, pass/fail, internships. Preprofessional program in medicine. 5-college cooperation with Hampshire, Mt. Holyoke, Smith, and UMass provides cross-registration, shared facilities & programs. 12-college exchange with other northeastern schools. Numerous study abroad programs. ROTC at UMass. Museums. 584,684-volume library.
Financial CEEB CSS. College scholarships, loans, payment plan; PELL SEOG, NDSL, FISL, CWS. Application deadline January 15 (November 15 for early decision).
Admissions Sound high school preparation required. Interview urged. SAT & 3 ACH, or ACT required. $30 application fee (waiver possible). Application deadline January 15. $200 deposit required on acceptance of admissions offer. *Early Decision* and *Early Entrance* programs. Admission deferral possible. Transfers accepted. Placement possible for CEEB AP exams.
Student Life Newspaper, literary magazine, yearbook, radio station. Music & drama groups. Debate. Academic, honorary, special interest groups. Numerous activities with 5-college exchange. 6 fraternities with houses. Upperclass students may live off campus with permission. Coed dorms, special interest & language houses. 95% of students live on campus. 15 intercollegiate sports for men, 11 for women; intramurals. AIAW, ECAC, NCAA, NESCAC. Student body composition: 4% Asian, 6% Black, 2% Foreign, 2% Hispanic, 86% White. 82% from out of state.

BABSON COLLEGE $$$

Babson Park 02157, (617) 235-1200
Director of Admission: Joseph B. Carver

- **Undergraduates:** 901m, 502w
- **Tuition (1984–1985):** $7,424
- **Room and Board (1984–1985):** $3,910;   **Fees:** $242
- **Degrees offered:** BS
- **Mean SAT:** 500v, 600m
- **Student-faculty ratio:** 20 to 1
- **Calendar system:** Semester

A private college of management founded in 1919, became coed in 1968. 450-acre suburban campus in Wellesley, 12 miles from Boston. Air, rail, and bus service.

Academic Character NEASC and professional accreditation. Semester system, 2 6-week summer terms. Majors offered in accounting/law, American studies, communication, economics, entrepreneurial studies, finance, investments, management & organizational behavior, marketing, quantitative methods (with economics, finance, investments, marketing), and society & technology. Self-designed majors. Courses in humanities and social sciences. Distributive requirements. MBA granted. Independent study, honors program, internships. Cross-registration with Pine Manor and Regis colleges, and Brandeis U. Study abroad. Computer center, management lab. 81,000-volume library with microform resources.

Financial CEEB CSS. College scholarships, grants, loans, state scholarships, payment plan; PELL, SEOG, NDSL, GSL, CWS, college work program. Suggest filing FAF in early January; application deadline February 15.

Admissions High school graduation with college prep program required. SAT or ACT required. ACHs and interview recommended. $25 application fee. Application deadline February 1. $100 deposit required on acceptance of admissions offer (May 1). *Early Decision* Program. Admission deferral possible. Transfers accepted. Credit possible for CEEB AP and CLEP exams, and for life/work experience.

Student Life Student government. Newspaper, yearbook. Drama, film, and music groups. Student businesses & Chamber of Commerce. Circle K. Black Society. Academic, athletic, honorary, outing, professional, and special interest clubs. 2 fraternities and 2 sororities. Coed and single-sex dorms. Married-student housing. 70% of students live on campus. 2 semesters of phys ed required. 12 intercollegiate sports for men, 9 for women; club and intramural sports. AIAW, ECAC, NCAA. Student body composition: 1% Black, 92% White, 7% Other. 39% from out of state.

BENTLEY COLLEGE $$

Waltham 02254, (617) 891-2244
Dean of Admissions & Financial Aid: Kent P. Ericson

- **Undergraduates:** 2,012m, 1,898w
- **Tuition (1984–1985):** $6,100
- **Room and Board (1984–1985):** $3,300
- **Degrees offered:** BA, BS
- **Mean SAT:** 465v, 544m
- **Student-faculty ratio:** 23 to 1
- **Calendar system:** Semester

A private college founded in 1917. 100-acre suburban campus 9 miles from Boston. Air, rail, and bus service nearby.

Academic Character NEASC and professional accreditation. Semester system, 2 summer terms. BS offered with majors in accountancy, business communication computer information systems, economics, economics/finance, finance, general business, management, marketing management, public administration, quantitative analysis. BA offered with self-designed and interdisciplinary majors in areas including behavioral sciences, communications, environmental studies, history & government, legal studies, literature, philosophy, and psychology. AS offered with majors in accountancy, management, and paralegal studies. Distributive requirements. Directed study, honors program, internships. Cross-registration with Regis College. AFROTC at U of Lowell. Computer center. 102,000-volume library.

Financial CEEB CSS and ACT FAS. College scholarships, grants, minority grants-in-aid, payment plan; PELL, SEOG, NDSL, GSL, PLUS, CWS. File FAF by February 1; application deadline March 1.

Admissions High school graduation with 16 units required. GED accepted. Interview recommended. SAT or ACT required. $25 application fee. Application deadline March 10. $100 tuition and $200 room deposits required on acceptance of admissions offer (May 1). *Early Decision, Early Entrance, Concurrent Enrollment* programs. Admission deferral possible. Transfers accepted. Credit possible for CEEB AP and CLEP exams; college has own advanced placement program.

Student Life Student government. Newspaper, yearbook. Music, debate, and drama groups. Academic, athletic, professional, religious, service, and special interest groups. 6 fraternities and 3 sororities. 6% of men and 4% of women join. Coed dorms, apartments. No married-student housing. 59% of students live on campus. 2 semesters of phys ed required. 9 intercollegiate sports for men, 5 for women; intramurals. AIAW, ECAC, NCAA. Student body composition: 1% Black, 97% White, 2% Other. 40% from out of state.

BOSTON COLLEGE $$

Chestnut Hill 02167, (617) 969-0100
Director of Admissions: Charles Nolan

- **Undergraduates:** 3,839m, 5,089w
- **Tuition (1984–1985):** $6,800
- **Room and Board (1984–1985):** $3,500;   **Fees:** Vary
- **Degrees offered:** AB, BS
- **Mean SAT:** 509v, 557m
- **Student-faculty ratio:** 15 to 1
- **Calendar system:** Semester

A private Catholic college conducted by Jesuits, founded in 1863, became coed in 1947. 200-acre suburban campus in Chestnut Hill area of Newton, 6 miles from Boston, plus 40-acre Newton College campus. Rapid transit to Boston, airport, rail and bus stations.

Academic Character NEASC and professional accreditation. Semester system, 6-week summer term. Majors offered in accounting, American studies, art (2), biology, chemistry, classical studies, computer science, economics, education (4), English, finance, geology & geophysics, Germanic studies, history, linguistics, management, marketing, mathematics, modern languages (5), nursing, organizational studies, philosophy, physics, political science, psychology, quantitative analysis, Slavic studies, speech communication, speech/theatre, and theology. Double majors. Interdepartmental programs in 7 areas. 2 theology courses required; other requirements vary with programs. Graduate and professional degrees granted. Independent study, honors programs, Phi Beta Kappa, pass/fail, internships. Preprofessional programs in dentistry, law, medicine. PULSE combines community work with study of philosophy & theology. Bachelors/Masters programs. Cross-registration at BU, Brandeis, Tufts, and Hebrew, Pine Manor, and Regis colleges. New England Consortium on Environmental Protection. Study abroad. Elementary, secondary, and special education certification. ROTC, AFROTC, & NROTC at Northeastern. Computer center. Over 1,000,000-volume library.

Financial CEEB CSS. College scholarships, grants; PELL, SEOG, NSS, NDSL, NSL, GSL, CWS. Application deadline February 1.

Admissions High school graduation with minimum of 11½ units (more for nursing) recommended. Interview urged. 5-8 slides of work for studio art majors. ACT or SAT, and 3 ACH required. $30 application fee. Application deadline January 15. $100 tuition and $100 room deposits required on acceptance of admissions offer (May 1). *Early Decision* and *Early Entrance* programs. Admission deferral possible. Transfers accepted. Credit possible for CEEB AP and CLEP exams. Options Through Education Program.

Student Life Campus Council. Radio station, magazines. Music, drama, debate groups. PIRG, Hillel, Black Forum. Academic, ethnic, honorary, political, professional, religious, service, and special interest clubs. Coed, single-sex, honors, and language dorms. Apartments. No married-student housing. 75% of students live on campus. No cars for resident freshmen & sophomores. 11 intercollegiate sports for men, 10 for women; many intramural & club sports. Student body composition: 3% Asian, 2% Black, 5% Hispanic, 1% Native American, 88% White, 1% Other. 52% from out of state.

BOSTON UNIVERSITY $$$

Commonwealth Avenue, Boston 02215, (617) 353-2000
Director of Admissions: Anthony T. G. Pallett

- **Undergraduates:** 6,245m, 6,525w
- **Tuition (1984–1985):** $8,996
- **Room and Board (1984–1985):** $4,000
- **Degrees offered:** BA, BAA, BA/DMD, BFA, BLS, BS, BSEd, BSBA, AAA, AS
- **Mean SAT:** 543v, 578m
- **Student-faculty ratio:** 15 to 1
- **Calendar system:** Semester

A private university established in 1869. 68-acre urban campus on the Charles River. Air, rail, and bus service.

Academic Character NEASC and professional accreditation. Semester system, 2 summer terms. 8 majors offered by the College of Engineering, 46 by the College of Liberal Arts, 5 by the Program in Artisanry, 6 by Sargent College of Allied Health Professions, 13 by the School for the Arts, 15 by the School of Education, 7 by the School of Management, 1 by the School of Nursing, and 6 by the School of Public Communication. The College of Basic Studies offers a 2-year, non-traditional liberal arts program for transfer within the University. University Professors Program offers independent study, tutorials, self-designed majors for exceptional students. Self-designed majors. Minors. Distributive requirements. Graduate and professional degrees granted. Independent study, honors program, Phi Beta Kappa, credit by exam, internships. Preprofessional programs in allied health fields, dentistry, medicine, veterinary medicine. 4-yr BA/MA, 5-yr MBA, 6-yr BA/MD & BA/DMD programs. 8-yr program for a BA/MD. Cross-registration with Boston College, Brandeis, Tufts. Study abroad. Elementary, secondary, and special education certification. ROTC, AFROTC, NROTC at Northeastern. Labs and research institutes. Computer center. 1,347,000-volume library with microform resources.

Financial CEEB CSS. University scholarships, grants; PELL, SEOG, NSS, NDSL, GSL, NSL, CWS. Application deadline March 1.

Admissions High school graduation with 16 units required. Audition required for music & theatre majors, portfolio for visual arts & program in artisanry. SAT or ACT required. ACH for some programs. $30 application fee. Application deadline February 15. $200 deposit required on acceptance of admissions offer. *Early Admission* and *Early Decision* programs. Admission deferral possible. Transfers accepted. Credit possible for CEEB AP, CLEP, & ACH exams. Minority Application Program.

Student Life Student government. Newspapers, magazines, radio & TV stations. Music, drama, debate, film groups. Honorary, ethnic, professional, religious, political, academic, and special interest clubs. 2 fraternities, 1 with house; 3 sororities without houses. 5% of students join. Single freshmen under 21 must live at home or on campus. Coed, single-sex, married-student housing. 60% of students live on campus. No cars for boarding freshmen & sophomores. Many intercollegiate and intramural sports. Student body composition: 2% Asian, 5% Black, 2% Hispanic, 83% White, 8% Other. 75% from out of state.

BRANDEIS UNIVERSITY $$$

Waltham 02154, (617) 647-2878
Dean of Admissions: David L. Gould

- **Undergraduates:** 1,357m, 1,321
- **Tuition (1984–1985):** $9,350
- **Room and Board (1984–1985):** $3,985;   **Fees:** $240
- **Degrees offered:** BA
- **Mean SAT:** 580v, 610m
- **Student-faculty ratio:** 10 to 1
- **Calendar system:** Semester

A private university founded under Jewish auspices in 1948. 250-acre suburban campus on the banks of the Charles River, 10 miles from Boston. Rail and bus to Boston.

Academic Character NEASC accreditation. Semester system, limited summer term. Majors offered in African & Afro-American studies, American studies, anthropology, biochemistry, biology, chemistry, Classical & Oriental studies, comparative literature, computer science, economics, English & American literature, English & Classics, fine arts, French, general science, German, history, history of western thought, Italian, Latin American studies, linguistics, mathematics, music, Near Eastern & Judaic studies, philosophy, physics, politics, psychology, Russian, sociology, Spanish, theatre arts. Independent majors. Distributive requirements. MA, MFA, PhD granted. Independent study, honors program, Phi Beta Kappa, pass/fail, internships. 4-year BA/MA programs. Cross-registration with Boston College, Boston and Tufts Universities. Washington Semester. Study abroad in Israel and other countries. International Coordinate Degree Program with up to 2 years of foreign study. Elementary and secondary education certification. Research institutes. Computer center, language lab. Over 816,270-volume library.

Financial CEEB CSS. University scholarships, grants, deferred payment; PELL, SEOG, NDSL, GSL, CWS. Application deadline February 1.

Admissions High school graduation with 15-16 units required. SAT and 3 ACH required. $25 application fee. Application deadline February 1. $150 deposit required on acceptance of admissions offer (May 1). *Early Decision* and *Early Entrance* programs. Admission deferral possible. Transfers accepted. Credit possible for CEEB AP exams. University has own advanced placement program. Transitional Year Program for students not normally admissable.

Student Life Student government. Newspaper, literary magazine, yearbook, radio station. Music, dance, drama, photography groups. Debate. Hillel, Amnesty International. African Circle, Gay Alliance, Women's Coalition. Academic, outing, political, professional, religious, service, and special interest groups. Dorms coed by floor. 83% of students live on campus. 1 year of phys ed required. 9 intercollegiate sports for men, 9 for women, and coed sailing; intramurals. AIAW, ECAC, NAIA, NCAA. Student body composition: 11% minority. 80% from out of state.

CLARK UNIVERSITY $$$

Worcester 01610, (617) 793-7431
Dean of Admissions: Richard W. Pierson

- **Undergraduates:** 905m, 1,057w
- **Tuition (1984–1985):** $8,400
- **Room and Board (1984–1985):** $2,820;   **Fees:** $206
- **Degrees offered:** BA
- **Mean SAT:** 530v, 560m
- **Student-faculty ratio:** 14 to 1
- **Calendar system:** Semester

A private university founded in 1887. 50-acre urban campus located 40 miles west of Boston. Air, rail, and bus service.

Academic Character NEASC and professional accreditation. Semester system, optional May/June term, summer term. Majors offered in art (fine, history, studio), biochemistry, biology, business-management, chemistry, comparative literature, computer science, economics, English, French, geography, German, government-international relations, history, international development-social change, mathematics, music, philosophy, physics, psychology, Romance languages, sociology-social anthropology, Spanish, theatre arts, and science, technology, & society. Self-designed majors. Interdisciplinary programs. Distributive requirements. MA, MBA, MAEd, EdD, PhD granted. Independent study, honors program, Phi Beta Kappa, pass/fail, internships. 4- or 5-year BA/MA programs in several areas. 5-year BA/MBA program. Cross-registration through Worcester Consortium for Higher Education. Washington Semester. Study abroad. Elementary, secondary, and special education certification. AFROTC & ROTC at Worcester Polytechnic; NROTC at Holy Cross. Language lab. 400,000-volume library with microform resources.

Financial CEEB CSS. University scholarships, payment plan; PELL, SEOG, NDSL, GSL, CWS. File FAF by February 15.

Admissions High school graduation with 16 units required. Interview urged. Portfolio required for art majors. SAT and 3 ACH required. $25 application fee. Application deadline February 15. $100 tuition and $100 room deposits required on acceptance of admissions offer (May 1). *Early Decision* and *Early Entrance* programs. Admission deferral possible. Transfers accepted. Credit possible for CEEB AP exams.

Student Life Student government. Newspaper, magazine, yearbook, radio station. Drama and several music groups. Debate. Third World Cultural Center. Academic, honorary, religious, service, and special interest groups. One fraternity with house. 7% of men join. Freshmen must live at home or on campus. Coed, single-sex, language dorms. 75% of students live on campus. 9 intercollegiate sports for men, 6 for women; many intramurals. ECAC, MAIAW, NCAA, NECAC. Student body composition: 94% White, 6% Other. 70% from out of state.

CURRY COLLEGE $$

1071 Blue Hill Avenue, Milton 02186, (617) 333-0500
Director of Admissions: Dana Denault

- **Undergraduates:** 475m, 420w
- **Tuition (1984–1985):** $6,850
- **Room and Board (1984–1985):** $3,700; **Fees:** $295
- **Degrees offered:** BA, BSN
- **Mean SAT:** 400v, 420m
- **Student-faculty ratio:** 15 to 1
- **Calendar system:** Semester

A private, preprofessional liberal arts college established in 1879. 120-acre suburban campus 7 miles from downtown Boston. Bus service to Boston, airport, and rail station.

Academic Character NEASC accreditation. Semester system, 6-week summer term. Majors offered in biology, chemistry, communication arts & sciences (radio & TV, speech), elementary education (learning disabilities), English, fine arts (art, music), management, moderate special needs education, nursing, philosophy, physics, political & historical studies, psychology, socio-cultural studies. Interdisciplinary and self-designed majors. Minors in most major fields and in computer science, dance, theatre, and visual arts. Courses in Spanish. Independent study, pass/fail. Exchange programs with Johnston College and U of Redlands in California. Credit for foreign study. Elementary and secondary education certification. Language lab. Over 100,000-volume library.

Financial CEEB CSS. College scholarships, payment plan; PELL, SEOG, NDSL, GSL, CWS. Priority application deadline March 1.

Admissions High school graduation with 16 units required. Interview urged. SAT or ACT required. $15 application fee. Rolling admissions; suggest applying by February 15. $50 tuition and $50 room deposits required on acceptance of admissions offer (May 1). *Early Decision* and *Early Entrance* programs. Admission deferral possible. Transfers accepted. Credit possible for CEEB AP and CLEP exams, and for life/work experience.

Student Life Student government. Newspaper, arts magazine, yearbook, radio station. Music, dance, drama groups. Athletic, professional, religious, and special interest clubs. Students must live at home or on campus. Coed dorms. No married-student housing. 70% of students live on campus. 6 intercollegiate sports for men, 4 for women; intramurals. NCAA, New England Football Conference. Student body composition: 2.9% Black, 94.1% White, 3% Other. 40% from out of state.

EMERSON COLLEGE $$$

Boston 02116, (617) 262-2010
Director of Admissions: Anne Heller

- **Undergraduates:** 662m, 888w
- **Tuition (1984–1985):** $6,990
- **Room and Board (1984–1985):** $4,440;   **Fees:** $225
- **Degrees offered:** BA, BS, BFA, BLI, BSSp
- **Mean SAT:** 470v, 450m
- **Student-faculty ratio:** 17 to 1
- **Calendar system:** Semester

A private college founded in 1880. Urban campus in Boston's Back Bay. Air, rail, bus, and subway service.

Academic Character NEASC accreditation. Semester system, 6-week summer term. Majors offered in acting, business & organizational communications, communication disorders, creative writing, directing, film, mass communications (broadcast, film, journalism, radio, TV), musical theatre, oral interpretation, orchestral instrumentation, piano/organ, public relations & advertising, speech/communications studies, technical theatre, theatre arts, theatre education, and voice. Interdisciplinary and self-designed majors. Courses in additional areas. Distributive requirements. MA, MS in Speech granted. Honors program, internships. Cross-registration with Boston Museum School, Longy School of Music, Suffolk U. Elementary, secondary, and special education certification. Radio/TV studios, speech/hearing clinic, pre-school deaf nursery. Member Fenway Library Consortium. 87,750-volume library.

Financial CEEB CSS. College scholarships, grants, state grants, payment plan; PELL, SEOG, NDSL, GSL, PLUS, CWS. Application deadline March 1.

Admissions High school graduation with 12 units required. Creative writing sample required of all applicants, plus audition for BFA in theatre majors, portfolio for BFA in technical theatre majors. SAT or ACT required. $25 application fee. Rolling admissions; suggest applying by March 1. $125 tuition and $125 room deposits required on acceptance of admissions offer, refundable to May 15. *Early Decision* and *Early Entrance* programs. Admission deferral possible. Transfers accepted. Credit possible for CEEB AP and CLEP exams. 6-week Communications Skills summer program for underprepared students.

Student Life Student government. Newspaper, magazines, yearbook, radio station, closed-circuit TV. Music, arts, drama, film, TV groups. Intercollegiate debate. Ethnic, honorary, professional, religious, service, and special interest groups. 3 fraternities and 2 sororities. Freshmen under 21 must live at home or on campus. Coed and single-sex dorms. 40% of students live on campus. 9 intercollegiate sports; intramurals. Student body composition: 1.5% Asian, 8% Black, 2% Hispanic, 1% Native American, 87.5% White. 60% from out of state.

HAMPSHIRE COLLEGE $$$

Amherst 01002, (413) 549-4600
Director of Admissions: Robert L. deVeer

- **Undergraduates:** 550m, 550w
- **Tuition (1984–1985):** $10,175
- **Room and Board (1984–1985):** $2,785
- **Degrees offered:** BA
- **Mean SAT:** 545v, 545m
- **Student-faculty ratio:** 13 to 1
- **Calendar system:** 4–1–4

A private college established in 1969. 550-acre rural campus 90 miles west of Boston. Bus to Springfield.

Academic Character NEASC accreditation. 4-1-4 system. 15 areas of concentration are offered by the School of Humanities & Arts, 12 by Language & Communications, 13 by Natural Science, and 8 by Social Science. All majors are self-designed; several interdisciplinary programs are possible. Students must pass one exam in each school at the Basic Studies level, one exam in the concentration, and one in advanced study. Students direct their own study, help fashion their own exams, and are graded by written personal evaluations. They learn through courses, independent reading & study, and field study. 5-College Consortium allows cross-registration with Amherst, Mount Holyoke, Smith, and UMass. Study abroad. Elementary and secondary education certification. ROTC & AFROTC at UMass (Amherst). Arts village, computer. 65,000-volume library plus access to 5-College libraries.

Financial CEEB CSS. College scholarships, grants, loans, payment plan; PELL, SEOG, NDSL, GSL, PLUS, CWS. Application deadline February 15.

Admissions High school graduation required; college prep program recommended. Interview strongly recommended. SAT or ACT accepted. $30 application fee. Application deadline February 15. $200 deposit required on acceptance of admissions offer (May 1). *Early Entrance, Early Decision, Early Action* programs. Admission deferral possible. Transfers accepted. Credit possible for CEEB AP and college exams.

Student Life Student government. Newspaper, arts magazine, radio. Third World group. Women's Center. Coed & single-sex dorms and houses. Student apartments. No married-student housing. 95% of students live on campus. Outdoor Program, several intramural sports. Student body composition: 2% Asian, 4% Black, 2% Hispanic, 92% White. 87% from out of state.

HARVARD AND RADCLIFFE COLLEGES $$$

Cambridge 02138, (617) 495-1551
Acting Director of Admissions: William R. Fitzsimmons

- **Undergraduates:** 3,860m, 2,677w
- **Tuition (1984–1985):** $9,800
- **Room and Board (1984–1985):** $4,300
- **Degrees offered:** BA, BS
- **Student-faculty ratio:** 10 to 1
- **Calendar system:** Semester

A private university established in 1636. Radcliffe, an affiliated, independent women's college, was founded in 1879. Classes became coed in 1943. Facilities, organizations, most athletics, and housing are coed. Urban campus across the Charles River from Boston. Air, rail, bus, and subway service.

Academic Character NEASC and professional accreditation. Semester system, 6- and 8-week summer terms. Majors offered in over 60 areas including Afro-American studies, anthropology, archaeology, astronomy, classics, East Asian studies, economics, engineering, environmental sciences, fine arts, folklore & mythology, languages & literatures, linguistics, math, philosophy & religion, Portuguese-Brazilian, Sanskrit & Indian Studies, sciences, Slavic languages & literatures, social sciences, statistics, and visual & environmental studies. Self-designed and interdepartmental majors. 10 graduate schools offer numerous graduate & professional degrees. Independent study, Phi Beta Kappa. Tutorial method of instruction. Study abroad. AFROTC, NROTC, ROTC at MIT. Many research centers, museums, and other facilities. Extension and summer schools. Language labs, computer. Over 10,260,571-volume library with microform resources.

Financial CEEB CSS. College scholarships, loans, payment plan; PELL, SEOG, NDSL, GSL, CWS. Application deadlines January 1 (scholarships), September 1 (loans).

Admissions Applicants chosen by a joint Harvard/Radcliffe Admissions Committee. High school graduation with 16 units recommended. Interview required; local alumni interviews possible. SAT and 3 ACH required. $30 application fee. Suggest applying by November 15 of 12th year. Deadline January 1. Notification in mid-April; candidate must accept offer by May 1. *Early Action* Program. Admission defferal possible. Transfers accepted. Credit possible for CEEB AP, CLEP, and university exams. Admission program for students without a high school diploma.

Student Life Newspapers, magazines, yearbook, radio station. Many music and drama groups. Debate. Special interest, social, athletic, academic, political, religious, and service clubs. Freshmen live at home or in coed dorms. Upperclass students live in Houses with their own libraries, dining, social, cultural, and athletic facilities. Cooperative and married-student housing. 92% of students live on campus. 19 intercollegiate sports for men, 15 for women; intramural & club sports. ECAC, Ivy League. Student body composition: 16% minority. 80% of students from out of state.

HOLY CROSS, COLLEGE OF THE $$$

Worcester 01610, (617) 793-2443
Director of Admissions: James R. Halpin

- **Undergraduates:** 1,272m, 1,264w
- **Tuition (1984–1985):** $7,700
- **Room and Board (1984–1985):** $3,300; **Fees:** $165
- **Degrees offered:** BA
- **Mean SAT:** 570v, 590m
- **Student-faculty ratio:** 14 to 1
- **Calendar system:** Semester

A private Jesuit college founded in 1843, became coed in 1972. 174-acre urban campus, 40 miles west of Boston. Air, rail, and bus service.

Academic Character NEASC accreditation. Semester system. Majors offered in biology, chemistry, classics, economics, economics-accounting, English, European literature studies, French, German, history, math, music, philosophy, physics, political science, psychology, religious studies, Russian,

Russian studies, sociology, Spanish, and visual arts. Self-designed and interdisciplinary majors. Courses in 4 additional areas. MS granted. Independent study, honors programs, Phi Beta Kappa, pass/fail, internships. Preprofessional programs in dentistry, law, medicine. 3-2 dual degree program in engineering with Worcester Polytechnic Institute. Worcester Consortium for Higher Education provides extensive cross-registration opportunities and cooperative gerontology studies program. Washington Semester. Study abroad. AFROTC & NROTC; ROTC at WPI. Institute of Industrial Relations. Computer. 390,000-volume library.

Financial CEEB CSS. College scholarships, grants, loans, payment plan; PELL, SEOG, NDSL, FISL, CWS. Application deadline February 1.

Admissions High school graduation with at least 14 units recommended. SAT and 3 ACH required. $25 application fee. Suggest applying by December 1. Deadline February 1. $200 deposit required on acceptance of admissions offer (May 1). *Early Decision* and *Early Entrance* programs. Admission deferral possible. Transfers accepted. Credit possible for CEEB AP exams.

Student Life Student government. Newspapers, literary magazine, yearbook, radio station. Several music, drama, debate groups. Black Student Union. Athletic, professional, religious, service, and special interest clubs. Coed dorms. No married-student housing. 80% of students live on campus. No cars for resident freshmen & sophomores. 17 intercollegiate sports for men, 7 for women; several intramurals. AIAW, ECAC, NCAA, NECAC. Student body composition: 95% White, 5% Other. 52% from out of state.

MASSACHUSETTS, UNIVERSITY OF, AMHERST $

Amherst 01003, (413) 545-0222
Director of Freshman Admissions: David Taggart

- **Undergraduates:** 10,000m, 9,000w
- **Tuition (1984–1985):** $1,656 (in-state), $4,212 (out-of-state)
- **Room and Board (1984–1985):** $3,344
- **Degrees offered:** BA, BS, BMus, BFA
- **Mean SAT:** 462v, 508m
- **Student-faculty ratio:** 18 to 1
- **Calendar system:** Semester

Academic Character NEASC and professional accreditation. Semester system, 2 5-week summer terms. Over 100 majors offered by the colleges of Arts & Sciences and of Foods & Natural Resources, and by the schools of Business Administration, Education, Engineering, Health Sciences, and Physical Education. Double and self-designed majors. Interdisciplinary programs. Distributive requirements. Graduate and professional degrees granted. Independent study, honors program, Phi Beta Kappa, pass/fail, cooperative work/study, internships. 5-college cooperation with Smith, Mount Holyoke, Amherst, and Hampshire provides cross-registration and shared programs & facilities. Regional exchange with other New England state schools allows special programs at in-state tuition. National Student Exchange. Elementary and secondary education certification. ROTC, AFROTC; NROTC in Worcester. Child Guidance Center, Population Research Institute. Computer center, language lab. Over 3,000,000-volume library.

Financial CEEB CSS. University scholarships, tuition waivers, state scholarships; PELL, SEOG, NDSL, GSL, CWS. Application deadline March 15.

Admissions High school graduation with 16 units required. Specific requirements for some programs. Audition required for music and dance majors; portfolio for art majors. SAT required; 3 ACH recommended. $18 (in-state), $25 (out-of-state) application fees. Rolling admissions; application deadline March 1. $62 deposit required on acceptance of admissions offer (May 1). Early entrance for exceptional high school juniors possible. Admission deferral possible. Transfers accepted. Credit possible for CEEB AP and CLEP exams; placement for ACH and departmental exams. University Without Walls, Upward Bound, special programs for minority and low-income applicants.

Student Life Student government. Newspaper, magazines, yearbook, radio station. Several music groups. Theatre, debate clubs. Mass PIRG. Over 500 student organizations. 15 fraternities and 9 sororities with houses. 1 coed fraternity. 8% of men and 14% of women join. Single freshmen and sophomores, except veterans, must live on campus or at home. Coed and single-sex dorms. Special interest and some married-student housing. 57% of students live on campus. 15 intercollegiate sports for men, 14 for women; intramurals. ECAC, NCAA, Yankee Conference. Student body composition: 10-12% minority. 15% from out of state.

MASSACHUSETTS INSTITUTE OF TECHNOLOGY $$$

Cambridge 02139, (617) 253-4791
Director of Admissions: Peter H. Richardson

- **Undergraduates:** 3,400m, 1,056w
- **Tuition (1984–1985):** $10,300
- **Room and Board (1984–1985):** $4,100
- **Degrees offered:** BS
- **Student-faculty ratio:** 5 to 1
- **Calendar system:** Quarter

A private institute founded in 1861. 130-acre urban campus across the Charles River from Boston. Subway and bus to Boston, airport, rail and bus stations.
Academic Character NEASC and professional accreditation. Quarter system, 10-week summer term. 4 majors offered by the School of Architecture & Planning, 10 by the School of Engineering, 18 by the School of Humanities & Social Sciences, 4 by the School of Management, and 7 by the School of Science. Self-designed and interdepartmental majors. Distributive requirements. Graduate and professional degrees granted. Independent study, Phi Beta Kappa, cooperative work/study, internships. Freshmen graded pass/fail only. Preprofessional programs in law and medicine. Undergraduate research opportunities program encourages student-faculty research. 5-year BS/MS programs in aeronautics & astronautics, electrical engineering, mechanical engineering. Cross-registration with Wellesley College and Harvard. Programs with Harvard and Woods Hole Oceanographic Institute. Study abroad. Elementary and secondary education certification. AFROTC, NROTC, ROTC. Numerous research labs, nuclear reactor, computer center. Over 1,750,000-volume library.
Financial CEEB CSS. Institute scholarships, grants, loans, payment plan; PELL, SEOG, NDSL, GSL, CWS, institutional work program. Application deadline January 1.
Admissions High school graduation with math & science background required. Interview required. SAT and 3 ACH required. $30 application fee.

Application deadline January 1. *Early Action* and *Early Entrance* programs. Admission deferral possible. Transfers accepted. Credit possible for CEEB AP exams. University has own advanced standing exams.

Student Life Student government. Newspapers, magazines, yearbook, radio stations. Music, drama, debate groups. Outing Club. Academic, athletic, political, professional, religious, service, social, and special interest clubs. 35 fraternities (4 coed). 40% of students join. Freshmen must live at home, on campus, or in fraternities. Coed, single-sex, language, cooperative, married-student, and special interest housing. 85% of students live on campus or in fraternities. 8 points of phys ed required. 20 intercollegiate sports for men, 12 for women; numerous intramurals. AIAW, ECAC, NCAA, NECAC. Student body composition: 3.1% Asian, 3.6% Black, 19.2% Foreign, 1.5% Hispanic, 0.2% Native American, 72.4% White. 89% from out of state.

MOUNT HOLYOKE COLLEGE $$$

South Hadley 01075, (617) 538-2000
Director of Admissions: Susan P. Staggers

- **Undergraduates:** 1,897w
- **Tuition (1984–1985):** $9,400
- **Room and Board (1984–1985):** $3,050; **Fees:** $85
- **Degrees offered:** AB
- **Student-faculty ratio:** 9 to 1
- **Calendar system:** 4–1–4

A private women's college founded in 1837. 800-acre campus in a rural residential area, 90 miles from Boston. Bus service, airport and rail station nearby.

Academic Character NEASC accreditation. 4-1-4 system. Majors offered in anthropology, art (2), astronomy, biological sciences, Black studies, chemistry, classics, dance, economics, English (3), French, geography, geology, German, Greek, history, Italian, Latin, mathematics, music (2), philosophy, physics, politics, psychology, religion, Russian, sociology, Spanish, and theatre arts. Interdisciplinary majors in biochemistry, international relations, psychobiology, psychology & education, Romance languages & literature, and American, Asian, Latin American, medieval, urban, and women's studies. Special majors. Courses include computer science, education. Distributives and 2 interims required. Graduate degrees granted. Independent study, honors program, Phi Beta Kappa, pass/fail, internships. 5-college cooperation provides cross-registration with Amherst, Hampshire, Smith, and U of Mass. 12-college exchange for a year at Amherst, Bowdoin, Connecticut, Dartmouth, Mount Holyoke, Trinity, Vassar, Wellesley, Wesleyan, Wheaton, Williams. Study abroad in Europe, India, Japan, the Philippines. Elementary and secondary education certification. AFROTC & ROTC at UMass. Child study, A-V centers. 471,734-volume library.

Financial CEEB CSS. College scholarships, grants, state grants, loans, payment plan; PELL, SEOG, NDSL, FISL, GSL, PLUS, CWS. Application deadline February 1 (November 15 for Early Decision).

Admissions High school graduation with solid college prep work recommended. Interview expected for those within 200 miles; urged for others. SAT and 3 ACH required. $25 application fee. Suggest applying early in 12th year. Deadline February 1. $300 deposit required on acceptance of admissions offer (May 1). *Early Decision, Early Evaluation, Early Entrance* programs. Admission deferral possible. Transfers accepted. Credit possible for CEEB AP exams; departments give placement exams.

Student Life Student government. Newspaper, literary magazine, yearbook, radio station. Several music groups. Academic, ethnic, political, religious, service, and special interest clubs. Students must live at home or on campus. Women's dorms, international residence hall. 95% live on campus. Honor code. 1½ years of phys ed required. 11 intercollegiate sports; intramurals. NCAA. Student body composition: 4% Asian, 4% Black, 4% Foreign, 2% Hispanic, 86% White. 79% from out of state.

NORTHEASTERN UNIVERSITY $$

Boston 02115, (617) 437-2200
Dean of Admissions: Philip R. McCabe

- **Undergraduates:** 10,274m, 6,027w
- **Tuition (1984–1985):** $5,850–$6,300 (depending on college)
- **Room and Board (1984–1985):** $3,840–$4,185
- **Degrees offered:** BA, BS, BSEd, BSBA, BSN, BSEngTech, BSE
- **Student-faculty ratio:** 20 to 1
- **Calendar system:** Trimester

A private university founded in 1898. 50-acre urban campus in the Back Bay section of Boston. Air, rail, bus, and subway service.

Academic Character NEASC and professional accreditation. Trimester system, summer term. 27 majors offered by the College of Arts & Sciences, 9 by the College of Business Administration, 1 by the College of Criminal Justice, 10 by the College of Engineering, 1 by the College of Nursing, 5 by the College of Pharmacy & Allied Health Professions, and 14 by the Boston-Bouve College of Human Development Professions. Lincoln College offers 5-day cooperative programs in engineering technology, and University College offers adult degree programs at Burlington branch campus and off-campus centers. Distributive requirements. Graduate and professional degrees granted. Certificate program. Honors programs, pass/fail. Beginning in 2nd year, 5-year cooperative education plan alternates classroom study and work in various fields, provides work experience, and defrays education costs. 3-2 programs with professional schools. 2-year AS/certificate program with Forsyth School for Dental Hygienists. Study abroad. Early childhood, elementary, and secondary education certification. AFROTC, ROTC. Computer center. 857,000-volume library.

Financial CEEB CSS. University scholarships, loans, state grants, payment plan; PELL, SEOG, NSS, NDSL, GSL, PLUS, NSL, CWS. University cooperative work/study plan. Application deadline February 15.

Admissions High school graduation required. Courses required vary with programs. SAT or ACT, and 3 ACH required. $25 application fee. Rolling admissions; suggest applying early in 12th year. $100 tuition and $100 room deposits required on acceptance of admissions offer (May 1). *Early Entrance* and *Concurrent Enrollment* programs. Admission deferral possible. Transfers accepted. Credit possible for CEEB AP and CLEP exams.

Student Life Student Council. Newspaper, literary magazine, yearbook, radio station. Music & arts groups. Debate. Academic, ethnic, honorary, political, professional, religious, and special interest clubs. 14 fraternities with houses and 5 sororities without houses. 5% of men and 2% of women join. Coed and single-sex dorms, student apartments. No married-student housing.

50% of freshmen live on campus. No cars on campus for boarding freshmen. 10 intercollegiate sports for men, 9 for women; several intramurals. AIAW, ECAC, NCAA. Student body composition: 4% Black, 1% Hispanic, 46% White, 49% Unknown. 35% from out of state.

SIMMONS COLLEGE $$$

300 The Fenway, Boston 02115, (617) 738-2000
Director of Admissions: Linda Cox Maguire

- **Undergraduates:** 1,723w
- **Tuition (1984–1985):** $7,680
- **Room and Board (1984–1985):** $3,698; **Fees:** $230
- **Degrees offered:** BA, BS
- **Mean SAT:** 450v, 460m
- **Student-faculty ratio:** 12 to 1
- **Calendar system:** Semester

A private women's college with coed graduate programs, founded in 1899. Urban campus in Boston. Air, rail, bus, and subway service.

Academic Character NEASC and professional accreditation. Semester system, 7-week summer term. Majors offered in applied computer science, art, biology, communications (4), chemistry, economics, education, English, French, government, history, human services, international relations, management (3), mathematics, music, nursing, nutrition (2), philosophy, physics, psychology, sociology, and women's studies. Prince Program in Retail Management. Self-designed, interdepartmental, and double majors. Distributive requirements. Graduate degrees granted. Independent study, honors programs, pass/fail, field work, internships. 4-year BA/MA in English. 4½-year BS in physical therapy with Children's Medical Center. 4-year BS in medical technology with Lynn Hospital. Graphic & publishing arts major with School of Museum of Fine Arts. 5½-year dual degree program in chemistry & pharmacy with Mass College of Pharmacy. 5-year dual degree engineering programs with Dartmouth and Boston U. Cross-registration with Emmanuel and Hebrew Colleges, New England Conservatory of Music, School of Museum of Fine Arts. Exchanges with Mills, Fisk, Johnston (U of Redlands), and Spelman Colleges. Washington Semester. Study abroad. Early childhood, elementary, secondary, and special education certification. ROTC at Northeastern. 200,000-volume library plus access to 10 area libraries.

Financial CEEB CSS. College scholarships, grants, loans, state grants; PELL, SEOG, NDSL, GSL, PLUS, CWS. Application deadline March 1.

Admissions High school graduation with strong college prep program recommended. Interview strongly encouraged. SAT or ACT, and 3 ACH required. $25 application fee. Rolling admissions; deadline March 15. $100 tuition and $150 room deposits required on acceptance of admissions offer (May 1). *Early Entrance* Program. Admission deferral possible. Transfers accepted. Credit possible for CEEB AP exams.

Student Life Student government. Newspaper, literary magazine, yearbook, radio station. Music, dance, drama groups. Outing Club. Academic, cultural, ethnic, religious, and special interest clubs. Women's dorms. 75% of students live on campus. Honor code. 1 year of phys ed required. 5 intercollegiate sports for women. AIAW. Student body composition: 2.3% Asian, 8.6% Black, 1.3% Hispanic, 84% White, 3.8% Other. 50% from out of state.

SIMONS'S ROCK OF BARD COLLEGE $$$

Great Barrington 01230, (413) 528-0771

- **Undergraduates:** 135m, 165w
- **Tuition (1984–1985):** $8,580
- **Room and Board (1984–1985):** $2,960;   **Fees:** $350
- **Degrees offered:** BA, AA
- **Mean SAT:** 579v, 551m
- **Student-faculty ratio:** 9 to 1
- **Calendar system:** Trimester

A private liberal arts institution designed to provide a collegiate program for students 15 to 20 years old. Founded in 1964, became a part of Bard College in 1979.
Academic Character NEASC accreditation. Trimester system. 7 interdisciplinary liberal arts majors offered leading to a BA. Other majors offered leading to an AA, students with these majors may transfer to Bard or another college to complete their bachelor's degree. Transitional Studies Program for students who have completed one year of high school.
Financial Financial aid available.
Admissions Students admitted after their 9th, 10th, 11th, and 12th years of high school. Admission is based on interview, questionnaires, recommendations, school records, and SAT, PSAT, or SSAT scores. A strong academic record and evidence of self-motivation and self-discipline are essential for admission. Rolling admissions. *Early Decision* Program.

SMITH COLLEGE $$$

Northampton 01063, (413) 584-2700
Director of Admissions: Lorna R. Blake

- **Undergraduates:** 2,550w
- **Tuition (1984–1985):** $9,170
- **Room and Board (1984–1985):** $3,570
- **Degrees offered:** BA
- **Mean SAT:** 600v, 600m
- **Student-faculty ratio:** 9 to 1
- **Calendar system:** 4–1–4

A private women's college established in 1875. 125-acre campus in a small city 18 miles from Springfield. Rail and bus service.
Academic Character NEASC and professional accreditation. 4-1-4 system. Majors offered in Afro-American studies, art, astronomy, biological sciences, chemistry, economics, education & child study, geology, government, Hispanic studies, history, languages & literatures (classical, English, French, German, Italian, & Russian), mathematics, music, philosophy, physics, psychology, religion/Biblical literature, sociology/anthropology, and theatre. Interdepartmental majors in biochemistry, comparative literature, computer science, and American, ancient, & medieval studies. Self-designed majors. Graduate degrees granted. Independent study, honors program, Phi Beta Kappa, pass/fail, internships. Preprofessional programs in law and medicine. 5-year AB/BS or MS in engineering program with U of Mass. 5-college cooperation provides cross-

registration with Amherst, Hampshire, Smith, and UMass. 12-college exchange allows for year exchange at Amherst, Bowdoin, Connecticut, Dartmouth, Mount Holyoke, Trinity, Vassar, Wellesley, Wesleyan, Wheaton, Williams. Semester in Washington. Numerous study abroad programs. Elementary, secondary, and special education certification. AFROTC & ROTC at UMass. Observatory, language lab, museum. 950,000-volume library.

Financial CEEB CSS. College grants, loans, state grants, payment plan; PELL, SEOG, GSL, CWS, college work program. Application deadline February 1 (November 15 for Early Decision).

Admissions High school graduation with 16 units required. Interview encouraged. SAT and 3 ACH required. $25 application fee. Suggest applying early in 12th year. Deadline February 1. $300 deposit required on acceptance of admissions offer (May 1). *Early Decision, Early Evaluation, Early Admission* programs. Admission deferral possible. Transfers accepted. Credit possible for CEEB AP exams. Ada Comstock Program for adults.

Student Life Student government. Newspaper, magazine, yearbook, radio station. Several music, drama, dance groups. Black Students Alliance. Academic, athletic, political, religious, service, and special interest clubs. Married students and Northampton residents may live off campus. Residential houses with dining facilities. 99% live on campus. No cars for 1st-year and financial aid students. 15 intercollegiate sports; intramurals. AIAW, NCAA. Student body composition: 5% Asian, 4% Black, 4% Foreign, 2% Hispanic, 85% White. 75% from out of state.

SPRINGFIELD COLLEGE $

Springfield 01109, (413) 787-2030

- **Undergraduates:** 894m, 1,006w
- **Tuition (1984–1985):** $5,376
- **Room and Board (1984–1985):** $2,574
- **Degrees offered:** BA, BS
- **Mean SAT:** 422v, 464m
- **Student-faculty ratio:** 18 to 1
- **Calendar system:** Semester

A private college established in 1885. 156-acre suburban residential campus on Lake Massasoit, 90 miles west of Boston and 150 miles north of New York City. Air, rail, and bus service.

Academic Character NEASC and professional accreditation. Semester system, 3- and 6-week summer terms. Over 40 majors offered in the areas of art in urban life, biology, business management, chemistry, community service, education, English, environmental studies, health education, history, mathematics, medical technology/lab science, physical education, political science, psychology, recreation & leisure services, rehabilitation services, social services, and sociology. Double majors. Minors. Programs in Afro-American, American, and international studies. Distributive requirements; 2 years of foreign language required for BA. Graduate degrees granted. Independent research, pass/fail, internships. Preprofessional programs in dentistry, law, medicine, theology. Courses at Morven Park Equestrian Institute in Virginia. Cross-registration through Cooperative Colleges of Greater Springfield. Cooperative programs with YMCA. Study abroad. Elementary and secondary education certification. ROTC at Western New

England College. International center, language lab, summer day camp. 115,000-volume library.

Financial CEEB CSS. College scholarships, state grants, payment plan; PELL, SEOG, NDSL, GSL, CWS, college work program. File FAF by February 15. Application deadline April 1

Admissions High school graduation with college prep program required. Portfolio required for art in urban life majors. Interview & SAT required. $25 application fee. Rolling admissions; suggest applying in fall of 12th year Deadline April 1. $100 deposit required on acceptance of admissions offer (May 1). *Early Entrance* and *Concurrent Enrollment* programs. Admission deferral possible. Transfers accepted. Credit possible for CEEB AP and CLEP exams.

Student Life Student government. Newspaper, magazine, yearbook, radio station. Drama & music groups. Performing dance & gymnastics groups. Academic, athletic, religious, service, and special interest clubs. Freshmen must live on campus. Coed and single-sex dorms. 75% of students live on campus. Juniors and seniors may have cars on campus. 4 semester hours of health/phys ed required. 13 intercollegiate sports for men, 12 for women; many intramurals. AIAW, ECAC, NCAA, New England Conference on Athletics. 66% of students from out of state.

TUFTS UNIVERSITY $$$

Medford 02155, (617) 628-0990
Dean of Undergraduate Admissions: Michael C. Behnke

- **Undergraduates:** 2,230m, 2,195w
- **Tuition (1984–1985):** $9,280
- **Room and Board (1984–1985):** $4,280;   **Fees:** $276
- **Degrees offered:** BA, BS, BSME, BSCE, BSCE, BSEE, BSE, BSOT
- **Mean SAT:** 575v, 632m
- **Student-faculty ratio:** 14 to 1
- **Calendar system:** Semester

A private university established in 1852. 150-acre suburban campus 6 miles from Boston. Bus to Boston.

Academic Character NEASC and professional accreditation. Semester system, 6-week summer term. Over 45 majors offered in the areas of area studies, archaeology, arts, child study, education, engineering, humanities, languages & literatures, mental health, occupational therapy, psychology, sciences, and social sciences. Self-designed majors. Experimental College for innovative & student-designed courses. Distributive requirements. Graduate and professional degrees granted. Independent study, honors program, Phi Beta Kappa, pass/fail, internships. BA/MA and BS/MS programs. 4-yr program for a BS in Occupational Therapy 5-yr BA/BS in liberal arts & engineering. 5-yr BA/MA in international affairs with Fletcher School of Law & Diplomacy. BFA, BSEd, BA/BFA, BS/BFA programs with School of Museum of Fine Arts; BA/BMus, BS/BMus with New England Conservatory of Music. Cross-registration with Boston College, Brandeis, Boston U. Washington and Maritime Studies programs. Exchange with Swarthmore College. Several study abroad options. Elementary and secondary education certification. AFROTC, NROTC, ROTC at MIT. Computer center, language lab, research labs. 584,000-volume library with microform resources

Financial CEEB CSS. University scholarships, payment plan; PELL, SEOG, NDSL, CWS. Application deadline February 1.

Admissions High school graduation with college prep program recommended. SAT or ACT, and 3 ACH required. $30 application fee. Application deadline January 15. $200 deposit required on acceptance of admissions offer (May 1). *Early Admission* and *Early Decision* programs. Admission deferral possible. Transfers accepted. Credit possible for CEEB AP exams.

Student Life Student government. Newspapers, magazines, yearbook, radio & TV stations. Several music, dance, drama, film groups. Debate. African American Center. Mountain Club. Numerous academic, athletic, ethnic, political, professional, religious, and special interest groups. 10 fraternities and 3 sororities with houses. 10% of students join. Freshmen and sophomores must live at home or on campus. Coed & single-sex dorms, special interest houses, coop apartments. 75% of stuents live on campus. No cars for freshmen. 14 intercollegiate sports for men, 12 for women; intramural & club sports. AIAW, ECAC, NESCAC. Student body composition: 4% Asian, 6% Black, 2% Hispanic, 88% White. 65% from out of state.

WELLESLEY COLLEGE $$$

Wellesley 02181, (617) 235-0320
Director of Admissions: Mary Ellen Ames

- **Undergraduates:** 2,016w
- **Tuition (1984–1985):** $9,260
- **Room and Board (1984–1985):** $3,570;   **Fees:** $90
- **Degrees offered:** BA
- **Mean SAT:** 610v, 620m
- **Student-faculty ratio:** 11 to 1
- **Calendar system:** 4–1–4

A private women's college established in 1875. 600-acre suburban campus 12 miles west of Boston. Bus to Boston.

Academic Character NEASC accreditation. 4-1-4 system. Over 35 majors offered in the areas of area studies, anthropology, arts, astronomy, biology, chemistry, classics, economics, geology, history, humanities, languages & literatures, mathematics, music, philosophy, political science, psychobiology, psychology, religion, social sciences, and theatre. Self-designed and interdisciplinary majors. Distributive requirements. Independent study, honors program, Phi Beta Kappa, pass/fail, internships. Cross-registration with MIT. 12-college exchange with Amherst, Bowdoin, Connecticut, Dartmouth, Mount Holyoke, Smith, Trinity, Vassar, Wesleyan, Wheaton, Williams. Exchange with Spelman College in Atlanta. Summer urban studies program. Study abroad in several countries. Secondary education certification. AFROTC, NROTC, ROTC at MIT. Computer center, observatory, language lab, child study center. Over 600,000-volume library.

Financial CEEB CSS. College scholarships, grants, payment plan; PELL, SEOG, NDSL, GSL, CWS. Application deadline February 1 (November 15 for early decision).

Admissions High school graduation with college prep program expected. Interview required. SAT and 3 ACH required. $25 application fee. Application deadline February 1. $300 deposit required on acceptance of admissions offer (May 1). *Early Entrance* and *Early Decision* programs. Admission deferral possible. Transfers accepted. Credit possible for CEEB AP exams. College has departmental exams.

Student Life Student government. Newspaper, magazines, yearbook, radio station. Music & theatre groups. Black and Jewish Community Centers. Academic, athletic, ethnic, honorary, professional, religious, and special interest clubs. Women's dorms, special interest & language housing. 96% live on campus. Honor system. 1 year of phys ed required. 11 intercollegiate sports; intramurals. AIAW, NIAC. Student body composition. 7% Asian, 6.3% Black, 3.2% Hispanic, 0.1% Native American, 78.1% White, 5.3% Other 75% from out of state.

WHEATON COLLEGE $$$

Norton 02766, (617) 285-7722
Director of Admissions: Andronike Janus

- **Undergraduates:** 1,165
- **Tuition (1984–1985):** $9,155
- **Room and Board (1984–1985):** $3,525;   **Fees:** $90
- **Degrees offered:** BA
- **Mean SAT:** 530v, 540m
- **Student-faculty ratio:** 11 to 1
- **Calendar system:** Semester

A private women's college established in 1834. 300-acre campus in a small town 35 miles southwest of Boston, and 15 miles from Providence, RI. Rail and bus service.

Academic Character NEASC accreditation. Semester system. Majors offered in American history & literature, anthropology, art, Asian studies, biochemistry, biology, chemistry, classical civilization, classics (Greek, Latin), economics, English, French, German, government, history, Italian studies, mathematics, music, philosophy, physics, psychobiology, psychology, religion, Russian, Russian studies, sociology, and Spanish. Interdepartmental and self-designed majors. Courses in 7 additional areas. Departmental proficiency exams. Independent study, Phi Beta Kappa, career exploration internships. Preprofessional programs in law, medicine. Dual-degree programs in computer science, engineering, health systems, management science with Georgia Tech. Programs in business & management with Tuck School of Dartmouth College, and with U of Rochester. Program in religion & theology with Andover-Newton Theological Seminary. Cross-registration with Stonehill College. Exchange program with Mills College (CA), and through 12-college exchange. Washington, Mystic Seaport, National Theatre Institute semester programs. Study abroad. Preschool and secondary education certification possible. ROTC at Stonehill. Language lab, observatory, computer. 220,000-volume library.

Financial CEEB CSS. College scholarships, grants, payment plan; PELL, SEOG, NDSL, GSL, CWS. Application deadline February 1.

Admissions High school graduation with 16 units required. Interview encouraged. SAT and 2 ACH required. $25 application fee. Application deadline February 1. $300 deposit required on acceptance of admissions offer (May 1). *Early Admission* and *Early Decision* programs. Transfers accepted. Admission deferral possible. Credit possible for CEEB AP exams.

Student Life Student government. Newspaper, literary magazine, yearbook, radio station. Music, theatre, dance groups. Crafts Center. Black Student Society. Academic, professional, religious, service, and special interest clubs. Women's dorms & houses. 98% of students live on campus. Honor code. 2 semesters of phys ed required. 9 intercollegiate sports for women;

intramurals. AIAW. Student body composition: 2% Asian, 3% Black, 2% Hispanic, 93% White. 66% from out of state.

WHEELOCK COLLEGE $$

200 Riverway, Boston 02215, (617) 734-5200
Dean of Admissions: Joan Wexler

- **Undergraduates:** 7m, 466w
- **Tuition (1984–1985):** $6,528
- **Room and Board (1984–1985):** $3,260;   **Fees:** $200
- **Degrees offered:** BS, BSW
- **Mean SAT:** 410v, 440m
- **Student-faculty ratio:** 12 to 1
- **Calendar system:** Semester

A private college established in 1888, became coed in 1972. 5-acre residential urban campus on the Riverway in Boston. Air, rail, and bus service.
Academic Character NEASC and professional accreditation. Semester system. Majors offered in teaching children, children in health care settings, and social services for children & families. Programs in infants & toddlers and their families; young children & their families; children in day care & their families; multicultural settings; primary classrooms; museum as a learning center; young children with special needs; moderate special needs; special needs in family & clinical settings. Liberal arts minors offered in art, English, history, music, philosophy, psychology, sociology, science, and theater arts. Courses in economics, math, political science, Spanish. Distributive requirements. MSEd and CAGS granted. ASEd offered on a part-time basis. Independent study, pass/fail, internships. Field work and student teaching stressed. Combined BS/MS program. Study abroad. Early childhood and special education certification. Member Fenway Library Consortium. 65,000-volume library with children's literature collection.
Financial CEEB CSS and ACT FAS. College scholarships, grants, loans, state grants, payment plan; PELL, SEOG, NDSL, GSL, PLUS, CWS. Application deadline March 1 (December 1 for Early Decision).
Admissions High school graduation required. 16 units and child care experience recommended. Interview required. SAT or ACT required. Application deadline February 15. $100 tuition and $100 room deposits required on acceptance of admissions offer (May 1). *Early Decision* Program. Transfers accepted. Admission deferral possible. Credit possible for CEEB AP and CLEP exams.
Student Life Student Board. Newspaper, yearbook. Music, drama, dance groups. Black Student Organization. Women's Center. Academic, professional, and special interest clubs. Freshmen must live at home or on campus. Coed and single-sex dorms. No married-student housing. 70% of students live on campus. Cars discouraged on campus. Regular class attendance expected. One health & phys ed course required. Intercollegiate field hockey and tennis. Recreational sports. Student body composition: 6% Black, 92% White, 2% Other. 48% from out of state.

WILLIAMS COLLEGE $$$

Williamstown 01267, (413) 597-2211
Director of Admissions: Philip F. Smith

- **Undergraduates:** 1,185m, 916w
- **Tuition (1984–1985):** $8,550
- **Room and Board (1984–1985):** $2,955;   **Fees:** $895
- **Degrees offered:** BA
- **Mean SAT:** 630v, 670m,   **Mean ACT:** 29
- **Student-faculty ratio:** 12 to 1
- **Calendar system:** 4–1–4

A private college established in 1793, became coed in 1970. 450-acre small-town campus in the Berkshire hills, 140 miles from Boston. Bus service to Pittsfield, Boston, and New York.

Academic Character NEASC accreditation. 4-1-4 system. Majors offered in American studies, art (2), astronomy & physics, biology, chemistry, classics (2), economics, English, French, geology, German, history, history of ideas, math/computer science, music, philosophy, physics, political economy, political science, psychology, religion, Russian, sociology, Spanish, theatre. Double, self-designed majors. Distributive requirements. Interdisciplinary programs. Independent study, honors program, Phi Beta Kappa, internships. Several research programs. 3-2 engineering program with Columbia U. Maritime studies term at Mystic Seaport (CT). Cross-registration at North Adams State and Bennington Colleges. 12-college and other exchange programs. Study abroad in Spain, Japan, and elsewhere. Center for Developmental Economics. Computer, museums, observatory & planetarium. 489,000-volume library.

Financial CEEB CSS. College and state scholarships, payment plan; PELL, SEOG, NDSL, PLUS, GSL, CWS. Application deadline January 15 (November 15 for early decision).

Admissions High school graduation with strong college prep program recommended. Interview encouraged. SAT or ACT, and 3 ACH required. $30 application fee. *Early Decision* and *Early Entrance* programs. Admission deferral possible. Transfers accepted. Credit possible for CEEB AP exams.

Student Life Student government. Newspapers, literary magazine, yearbook, radio station. Several music, drama, film, and dance groups. Intercollegiate debate. Black Student Union, women's and gay student groups. Academic, honorary, outing, service, and special interest organizations. Coed and single-sex dorms for freshmen and residential houses for upperclass students. 94% of students live on campus. No cars for 1st-semester freshmen. 2 years of phys ed required. Honor system. 14 intercollegiate sports for men, 10 for women; club and intramural sports. AIAW, NCAA, NESCAC. Student body composition: 2.5% Asian, 5.3% Black, 1.9% Hispanic, 0.5% Native American, 89.8% White. 87% from out of state.

WORCESTER POLYTECHNIC INSTITUTE   *$$$*

Worcester 01609, (617) 793-5286
Director of Admissions: Roy A. Seaberg, Jr.

- **Undergraduates:** 2,050m, 482w
- **Tuition (1984–1985):** $8,000
- **Room and Board (1984–1985):** $3,100;   **Fees:** $100
- **Degrees offered:** BS
- **Mean SAT:** 550v, 650m,   **Mean ACT:** 28
- **Student-faculty ratio:** 12 to 1
- **Calendar system:** 4 seven-week terms

A private institute established in 1865, became coed in 1968. 56-acre campus in a residential area of Worcester, 45 miles west of Boston. Additional 227-acre research & lab facilities in nearby Holden. Air and bus service.

Academic Character NEASC and professional accreditation. 4-term system, optional summer term. WPI Plan provides student-designed programs that stress projects, individualized study, and tutorials with self-paced learning that balances classroom and real-life experience. Degrees awarded on basis of demonstrated competence rather than specific course credits. Calendar permits flexibility for acceleration, employment, or internship experiences. Majors include applied mathematics, biology-biotechnology, chemistry, computer science, economics, humanities-technology, management, management-engineering, mathematics, physics, social science-technology, urban-environmental planning, and biomedical, chemical, civil, computer, electrical, environmental, materials, mechanical, & nuclear engineering. Minor, humanities sufficiency, and independent study requirements. MS and PhD granted. Internships. 5-year cooperative work/study option. 16 off-campus project centers. 3-2 dual degree programs with Holy Cross, St. Lawrence, 6 other schools. Study abroad in England and Switzerland. ROTC; AFROTC & NROTC at Holy Cross. Many research labs. Computer center, nuclear reactor. 165,000-volume library.

Financial CEEB CSS. Institute scholarships, grants, loans, state scholarships; PELL, SEOG, NDSL, GSL, CWS. Suggest filing FAF in early February. Application deadline March 1.

Admissions High school graduation with a college prep program required. Interview strongly recommended. SAT & 3 ACH, or ACT required. $25 application fee. Application deadline Feburary 15. $200 deposit required on acceptance of admissions offer (May 1). *Early Entrance* and *Early Decision* programs. Admission deferral possible Transfers accepted. Credit possible for CEEB AP exams.

Student Life Student government. Newspaper, yearbook, radio station. Music and drama groups. Professional, academic, honorary, religious, women's, and special interest groups. 12 fraternities with houses. 35% of men join. Freshmen encouraged to live on campus. Coed and men's dorms. 70% of students live on campus. Freshmen may not keep cars on campus. 2 years of phys ed required. 10 intercollegiate sports for men, 5 for women; many club & intramural sports. AIAW, NCAA, ECAC, NECAC. Student body composition: 3% Asian, 2% Black, 2% Hispanic, 1% Native American, 92% White. 50% from out of state.

Michigan

ALBION COLLEGE $$

Albion 49224, (517) 629-5511
Director of Admissions: Frank Bonta

- **Undergraduates:** 908m, 802w
- **Tuition (1984–1985):** $5,918
- **Room and Board (1984–1985):** $2,862;   **Fees:** $446
- **Degrees offered:** BA, BFA
- **Mean SAT:** 530v, 590m,   **Mean ACT:** 24
- **Student-faculty ratio:** 15 to 1
- **Calendar system:** Semester

A private college affiliated with the Methodist Church, established in 1835. 181-acre small-city campus, 15 miles from Jackson and 20 miles from Battle Creek. Served by rail; airport in Jackson.

Academic Character NCACS and professional accreditation. Semester system, 7-week summer term. Majors offered in anthropology & sociology, biology, chemistry, economics & management, English, French, geological sciences, German, history, home economics, mathematics, physics, music, philosophy, physical education, political science, psychology, religious studies, Spanish, speech communication & theatre, and visual arts. Distributive requirements. Honors program. Phi Beta Kappa. Some pass/fail. Internships. Preprofessional programs in dentistry, engineering, medical technology, law, medicine, nursing. Business management program. 3-2 programs in engineering, forestry, wildlife management. 3-1 program in medical technology. Member association with 11 area schools. Philadelphia, Oak Ridge, Washington Semesters. New York arts program. Study abroad. Elementary and secondary education certification. Language house, computer center, nature center. 220,000-volume library.

Financial CEEB CSS. College scholarships, grants, loans, state scholarships and grants, payment plan; PELL, SEOG, GSL, NDSL, CWS. Application deadline March 15.

Admissions High school graduation with 15 units required. Interview encouraged. SAT or ACT required. $15 application fee. Rolling admissions; application deadline April 1. $150 deposit required on acceptance of offer of admission. Admission deferral possible. Transfers accepted. Credit possible for CEEB AP and CLEP exams; college has own advanced placement program.

Student Life Student government. Newspaper, magazine, yearbook. Music, debate, speaking, drama groups. Tutorial association. Religious, academic, honorary, service, and special interest groups. 6 fraternities with houses and 6 sororities without houses. 60% of men and 40% of women join. Single students must live with relatives or on campus. Dorms for men & women, co-op women's dorm. Married-student housing. 96% of students live on campus. Freshmen may not have cars on campus. Liquor, drugs prohibited on campus. Class attendance required. 10 intercollegiate sports for men, 10 for women; intramurals. MIAA. Student body composition: 2% Black, 98% White. 12% from out of state.

ALMA COLLEGE $$

Alma 48801, (800) 292-9078 (in-state); (800) 248-9267 (out-of-state)
Director of Admissions: Ted C. Rowland

- **Undergraduates:** 473m, 536w
- **Tuition (1984–1985):** $6,440
- **Room and Board (1984–1985):** $2,640;   **Fees:** $102
- **Degrees offered:** BA, BS, BFA, BM
- **Mean ACT:** 24
- **Student-faculty ratio:** 15 to 1
- **Calendar system:** 4–4–1

A private college affiliated with the Presbyterian Church of USA, established in 1886. 80-acre campus in residential section of Alma, 120 miles from Detroit. Served by bus.

Academic Character NCACS and professional accreditation. 4-4-1 system. Majors offered in art, biology, business administration, chemistry, computer studies, economics, education, English, foreign service, French, German, history, international business, mathematics, music, philosophy, physical education, physics, political science, psychology, public service, religion, social work, sociology, Spanish, speech/theatre, and theatre/dance. Self-designed majors. Courses in 7 additional areas. Distributives, GRE, and senior exams required. Independent study. Honors program. Phi Beta Kappa. Pass/fail. Preprofessional programs in dentistry, engineering, foreign service, law, medicine, public service, social work, theology. 3-1 program in medical technology. 3-2 programs in engineering, natural studies with U Michigan. Cooperative programs with Merrill-Palmer Institute, Wayne State. Consortium with 7 area schools. Princeton Critical Language Program. Washington workshop. Elementary, secondary, and bilingual education certification. Study abroad. Teaching program in Nigeria. ROTC at Central Michigan. Language lab. 150,000-volume library.

Financial CEEB CSS and ACT FAS. College scholarships, grants, loans, state scholarships and grants, payment plan; PELL, SEOG, NDSL, CWS. Application deadlines March 1 (scholarships), June 1 (loans).

Admissions High school graduation with 16 units required. Interview encouraged. SAT or ACT required. $10 application fee. Rolling admissions; suggest applying soon after October 1. *Early Decision* and *Early Admission* programs. Admission deferral possible. Transfers accepted. Credit possible for CEEB AP and CLEP exams.

Student Life Student government. Newspaper, magazine, yearbook, radio & TV stations. Music, debate, oratory, drama groups. Afro-American society. College quiz bowl. Academic, honorary, religious, and special interest groups. 4 fraternities and 3 sororities with houses. 38% of men and 35% of women join. Students must live at home or on campus. Coed and single-sex dorms and cottages. 90% of students live on campus. Gambling and drugs prohibited on campus. Attendance required at 2 convocations per year. 10 intercollegiate sports for men, 9 for women; intramurals. AIAW, MIAC. Student body composition: 1% Black, 1% Hispanic, 97% White, 1% Other. 5% from out of state.

ANDREWS UNIVERSITY $$

Berrien Springs 49104, (616) 471-7771

Toll-free: (800) 632-2248 (in-state), (800) 253-2874 (out-of-state)
Director of Admissions & Records: Douglas K. Brown

- **Undergraduates:** 919m, 1,012w
- **Tuition (1984–1985):** $5,625
- **Room and Board (1984–1985):** $2,880; **Fees:** $15
- **Degrees offered:** BA, BS, BMus, BSW, BBA, BFA, BArch Tech, BET, BInd Tech, AA, AS, AArch Tech, AET, AInd Tech
- **Mean ACT:** 18.2
- **Student-faculty ratio:** 14 to 1
- **Calendar system:** Quarter

A private university affiliated with the Seventh-day Adventist Church, established in 1874. 1,000-acre rural campus in small town of Berrien Springs, 20 miles from South Bend, Indiana. Served by bus.

Academic Character NCACS and professional accreditation. Quarter system, 8-week summer term. 86 majors offered in the areas of arts & sciences, agriculture, engineering & technology, business & economics, education, health, home economics, communication, and physical education. Minor or interdisciplinary major required. Minors offered in most major fields and in 20 additional areas. Distributives, comprehensive exams, and 18 credits in religion required. Graduate and professional degrees granted. Independent study. Honors program. Cooperative work/study, pass/fail, internships. Preprofessional programs in 19 areas. 2-2 engineering program with Walla Walla. Cooperative programs with Loma Linda U in dental assistant, dental hygiene, medical record administration, occupational therapy, physical therapy, respiratory therapy. Study abroad. Elementary, secondary, and special education certification. A-V center, lab school. 777,847-volume library with microform resources.

Financial CEEB CSS and ACT FAS. University and state scholarships, grants, loans, grants-in-aid, tuition discounts for siblings; PELL, SEOG, NSS, NDSL, FISL, NSL, CWS; university has own work program. Recommended application deadline June 1.

Admissions High school graduation with 10 units required. GED accepted with restrictions. Interview recommended. ACT required. $15 application fee. Rolling admissions; suggest applying 9 months before intended date of entrance. $50 deposit required on acceptance of offer of admission. Admission deferral possible. Transfers accepted. Credit possible for CEEB AP and CLEP exams; university has own advanced placement program.

Student Life Student government. Newspaper, yearbook, radio station. Music groups. Academic, honorary, religious, service, and special interest groups. Single students under 25 must live at home or on campus. Single-sex dorms. Some married-student housing. 71% of students live on campus. First term freshmen may not have cars on campus. Liquor, tobacco, drugs, card playing, dancing, profanity, obscene materials, improper associations prohibited. Class, chapel, and convocation attendance required. 3 credits of phys ed required. Intramural and club sports. Student body composition: 3% Asian, 13% Black, 6% Hispanic, 1% Native American, 57% White, 20% Other. 58% from out of state.

FERRIS STATE COLLEGE $

Big Rapids 49307, (616) 796-9971
Director of Admissions: Karl S. Walker

- **Undergraduates:** 6,409m, 4,358w
- **Tuition (1984–1985):** $1,566
- **Room and Board (1984–1985):** $2,336; **Fees:** $105
- **Degrees offered:** BS, AA, AAS
- **Student-faculty ratio:** 18 to 1
- **Calendar system:** Quarter

A public college established in 1884. 650-acre campus located in small town of Big Rapids, 1 hour from Grand Rapids. Air, rail, and bus in Grand Rapids.

Academic Character NCACS and professional accreditation. Quarter system, 10-week summer term. 6 majors offered by the School of Allied Health, 26 by the School of Business, 11 by the School of Education & Learning Resources, 5 by the School of General Education, 1 by the School of Pharmacy, and 5 by the School of Technical & Applied Arts. Dual degrees possible. Independent study. Cooperative work/study. Internships. Secondary education certification. Art gallery, computer center. 210,000-volume library with microform resources.

Financial College scholarships, grants, loans, athletic scholarships, health professions loans, state loans; PELL, SEOG, NSS, NDSL, CWS. Application deadline 2 months before beginning of term.

Admissions High school graduation required. GED accepted. ACT required. Rolling admissions. $130 deposit required on acceptance of offer of admission. Transfers accepted. Credit possible for CEEB AP and CLEP exams; college has own advanced placement program.

Student Life Student government. Newspaper, magazine, yearbook, radio station. Music, drama, debate groups. Academic, religious, honorary, professional, service, and special interest organizations. 14 fraternities and 8 sororities. Coed and single-sex dorms. Married-student housing. 50% of students live on campus. Boarding freshmen may not have cars on campus. 3 hours of phys ed required. 10 intercollegiate sports for men, 6 for women; intramurals. NAIA, AIAW, NCAA. Student body composition: 3.8% Black, 0.2% Hispanic, 0.3% Native American, 95% White, 0.7% Other. 3.6% from out of state.

GMI ENGINEERING AND MANAGEMENT INSTITUTE $

Formerly General Motors Institute
1700 West 3rd Avenue, Flint 48502, (313) 762-7865
Toll-free: (800) 572-9908 (in-state), (800) 521-7436 (out-of-state)
Associate Dean of Admissions, Records, & Financial Aid: Dr. Fern Ramirez

- **Undergraduates:** 1,752m, 741w
- **Tuition (1984–1985):** $4,400
- **Room and Board (1984–1985):** $2,000; **Fees:** $64
- **Degrees offered:** BEE, BSME, BIE, BIA
- **Mean SAT:** 535v, 635m, **Mean ACT:** 27
- **Student-faculty ratio:** 14 to 1
- **Calendar system:** Semester

A private institute established in 1919, became coed in 1965. 45-acre campus located in residential section of Flint. Served by air, rail, and bus.

Academic Character NCACS and professional accreditation. Semester system. Majors offered in electrical engineering, industrial engineering, industrial administration, and mechanical engineering. All are 5-year, cooperative work/study programs. Courses in 10 additional areas. Thesis required. Independent study. Dual degree programs with several graduate schools. 6-week overseas work periods at General Motors units. Resources of over 140 cooperative units available. Extensive engineering labs. 90,000-volume library.

Financial All students are employees of a sponsoring GM unit and draw salaries. Institute loans; PELL, CWS.

Admissions High school graduation with 16 units required. SAT or ACT required; SAT preferred. 2 ACH required for placement. $10 application fee. Rolling admissions; application deadline January 18. $100 deposit required on acceptance of offer of admission. *Early Decision* Program. Transfers accepted. Credit possible for CEEB AP and CLEP exams; institute has own advanced placement program.

Student Life Student government. Newspaper, magazine, yearbook, radio station. Music, drama, photography groups. Black Unity Congress, International Club. Honor societies. Professional, religious, and special interest groups. 17 fraternities, 12 with houses, 5 sororities, 3 with houses. Single freshmen must live in dorms on campus. Limited upperclass housing. 40% of students live on campus. Class attendance required. Intramural and club sports. Student body composition: 6% Asian, 10% Black, 3% Hispanic, 1% Native American, 80% White. 56% from out of state.

HILLSDALE COLLEGE $$

Hillsdale 49242, (517) 437-7341
Director of Admissions: Russell L. Nichols

- **Undergraduates:** 495m, 505w
- **Tuition (1984–1985):** $5,800
- **Room and Board (1984–1985)** $2,800;   **Fees:** $170
- **Degrees offered:** BA, BS
- **Mean SAT:** 450v, 500m,   **Mean ACT:** 22
- **Student-faculty ratio:** 14 to 1
- **Calendar system:** Semester

A private college established in 1844. 200-acre campus located in small city of Hillsdale, 100 miles from Detroit, 70 miles from Toledo. Served by air and bus.

Academic Character NCACS accreditation. Semester system, 2 3-week and 1 6-week summer terms. Majors offered in accounting, American studies, art, biology, business administration, chemistry, communication arts, comparative literature, early childhood education, economics, education, English, environmental business, European studies, French, German, history, humanities, international business, math, music, philosophy-religion, physical education/health, physics, political economy, psychology, sociology, social work, Spanish, speech, and theatre arts. Minors offered in all major fields. Distributive requirements. Paralegal certification. Independent study. Honors program. Journalism internships. Preprofessional programs in forestry, nursing, osteopathy. 3-1 programs in allied health, dentistry, engineering, law, medicine, medical technology. 3-2 and 4-2 programs in engineering with Northwestern Tech. Study abroad. Early childhood, elementary, and secondary education certification. Preschool lab, psychology lab, language lab. 100,000-volume library.

Financial CEEB CSS. College scholarships, grants, loans; PELL, GSL, NDSL. Application deadline March 15.

Admissions High school graduation required. Interview encouraged. SAT or ACT required; ACH encouraged. $15 application fee. Rolling admissions; suggest applying at end of 11th year. $150 deposit required on acceptance of offer of admission. *Early Admission* Program. Admission deferral possible. Transfers accepted. Credit possible for CEEB AP and CLEP exams.

Student Life Student government. Newspaper, magazine, yearbook. Music, debate, film, theatre groups. Blacks United. Academic, honorary, political, religious, and special interest groups. 6 fraternities and 3 sororities with houses. 52% of men and 40% of women join. Freshmen must live at home or in dorms. Single-sex dorms. 80% of students live on campus. 1 year of phys ed required. 7 intercollegiate sports for men, 6 for women; intramurals. NAIA, Great Lakes Conference. Student body composition: 0.3% Asian, 3.1% Black, 0.2% Hispanic, 95.7% White. 51% from out of state.

KALAMAZOO COLLEGE $$

Kalamazoo 49007, (616) 383-8408
Toll-free: (800) 632-5757 (in-state), (800) 253-3602 (out-of-state)
Director of Admissions: David M. Borus

- **Undergraduates:** 548m, 582w
- **Tuition (1984–1985):** $7,275
- **Room and Board (1984–1985):** $2,721
- **Degrees offered:** BA
- **Mean SAT:** 540v, 580m, **Mean ACT:** 26
- **Student-faculty ratio:** 14 to 1
- **Calendar system:** Quarter

A private college affiliated with the American Baptist Churches, USA, established in 1833. 60-acre suburban campus within walking distance of downtown Kalamazoo, 140 miles from Chicago and Detroit. Served by air and bus.

Academic Character NCACS accreditation. Quarter system, 9½-week summer term. Majors offered in anthropology, anthropology-sociology, art, art history, biology, chemistry, computer science, economics-business administration, English, French, German, health sciences, history, mathematics, music, philosophy, physics, political science, psychology, religion, sociology, and theatre–communication arts. Self-designed majors. Special programs in 9 additional areas including African studies. Neglected language program in Japanese, Mandarin Chinese, Portuguese, Swahili. Distributive requirements. Senior exams. Independent study. Phi Beta Kappa. Internships. Pass/fail. 3-1 programs in dentistry, medicine, optometry, osteopathy, podiatry. 3-2 programs in engineering with Georgia Tech, U of Michigan, Washington U. Consortium with Western Michigan. Member Great Lakes College Association. Washington, New York, Philadelphia, Oak Ridge Semesters. Newberry Library term. Outward Bound. Study abroad. Secondary education certification. Computer center, language lab. 250,000-volume library with microform resources.

Financial CEEB CSS (preferred) and ACT FAS. College scholarships, grants, loans, state scholarships & grants, payment plans; PELL, SEOG, NDSL, CWS. Scholarship application deadline March 15.

Admissions High school graduation with 16 units preferred. Interview encouraged. ACT or SAT, and 3 ACH required. $20 application fee. Rolling admissions; suggest applying by March 15. $125 deposit required by May 1.

Early Admission Program. Admission deferral possible. Transfers accepted. Credit possible for CEEB AP exams; college has own advanced placement program.

Student Life Student government. Newspaper, magazine, yearbook, radio station. Music, speech, drama groups. Women's Interest Group, Black Student Organization, Jewish fellowship organization. Religious, service, academic, and special interest groups. Seniors may live off-campus; others must live on campus or with relatives. Coed and single-sex dorms, small houses, language houses. Married-student housing. 92% of students live on campus. Freshmen may not have cars on campus. 6 quarters of phys ed required. 9 intercollegiate sports for men, 8 for women; several intramural and club sports. NCAA, MIAA. Student body composition: 2% Asian, 2% Black, 1% Hispanic, 95% White. 25% from out of state.

MICHIGAN, THE UNIVERSITY OF $/$$

Ann Arbor 48109, (313) 764-7433
Director of Admissions: Cliff Sjogren

- **Undergraduates:** 11,096m, 9,433w
- **Tuition (1984–1985):** $2,172 (in-state), $6,732 (out-of-state)
- **Room and Board (1984–1985):** $2,780
- **Degrees offered:** BA, BS, BGS, BM, BBA, BSN, BSEng, BSMedChe, BFA, BSEd, BMA, BSForestry
- **Mean SAT:** 550v, 620m,   **Mean ACT:** 26.4
- **Student-faculty ratio:** varies by school
- **Calendar system:** Trimester

A public university established in 1817. 2,542-acre campus in small city of Ann Arbor, 35 miles from Detroit.

Academic Character NCACS and professional accreditation. Trimester system, summer half term. 12 majors offered by the College of Engineering, 2 by the College of Pharmacy, 8 by the School of Art, 1 by the School of Business Administration, 8 by the School of Education, 12 by the School of Music, 7 by the School of Natural Resources, 1 by the School of Nursing, and 70 by the College of Literature, Science, & the Arts. Self-designed majors. Distributives and GRE required. Graduate and professional degrees granted. Honors program, Phi Beta Kappa. Pass/fail. Internships. Preprofessional programs in business administration, dentistry, law, education, medical technology, medicine, physical therapy, social work. 3-2 program with College of Engineering, 2-2 program with School of Business Administration. Study abroad. Elementary, secondary, and special education certification. ROTC, AFROTC, NROTC. Biological station, Fresh Air Camp (education, psychology, sociology, social work), geology, music, speech correction camps. Museums, computer center, A-V center. 5,800,000-volume library with microform resources.

Financial CEEB CSS and ACT FAS. University scholarships, grants, loans, athletic grants; PELL, SEOG, NDSL, GSL, HPL, CWS.

Admissions High school graduation with 16 units required. Portfolio required for art majors, audition for music majors. ACT or SAT required. $20 application fee. Rolling admissions; equal consideration deadline March 1. $100 deposit required on acceptance of offer of admission. *Early Admission* Program. Admission deferral possible. Transfers accepted. Credit possible for CEEB AP and CLEP exams.

Student Life Student government. Radio and TV stations. Music and dance groups. Over 500 student organizations. 36 fraternities, most with houses, and 19 sororities with houses. 10% of men and 13% of women join. Freshmen expected to live with relatives or on campus. Coed and single-sex dorms, co-op dorms, special interest housing. Married-student housing. 65% of students live on campus. Several intercollegiate and intramural sports for men and women. Student body composition: 3% Asian, 6% Black, 2% Hispanic, 1% Native American, 88% White. 32% from out of state.

MICHIGAN STATE UNIVERSITY $

East Lansing 48824, (517) 355-8332
Director of Admissions: Charles Seeley

- **Undergraduates:** 14,625m, 14,476w
- **Tuition (1984–1985):** $1,884 (in-state), $4,494 (out-of-state)
- **Room and Board (1984–1985):** $2,412
- **Degrees offered:** BA, BS
- **Mean SAT:** 460v, 520m, **Mean ACT:** 22.2
- **Student-faculty ratio:** 15 to 1
- **Calendar system:** Quarter

A public university established in 1855. 5,320-acre suburban campus outside of Lansing, 82 miles from Detroit. Served by air and bus.

Academic Character NCACS and professional accreditation. Quarter system. Over 100 majors offered by the Colleges of Agriculture & Natural Resources, Arts & Letters, Business, Communication Arts & Sciences, Education, Engineering, Human Ecology, Natural Science, Nursing, Social Science, Veterinary Medicine, and the Colleges of James Madison and Lyman J. Briggs. Distributive requirements. Graduate and professional degrees granted. Independent study. Honors program, honors college, Phi Beta Kappa. Pass/fail, internships, credit by exam. Preprofessional programs in dentistry, law, medicine, optometry, osteopathy, theology, veterinary medicine. 5-year engineering programs for international service. 40 overseas programs. Elementary, secondary, and special education certification. ROTC, AFROTC. China Relations Center, Mathematics Teaching Center. Several research centers. Botanical garden, experimental farm. Planetarium, cyclotron, museum, language labs. Audio library, Broadcasting Service Division. 2,650,000-volume library.

Financial CEEB CSS and ACT FAS. University and state scholarships, grants, loans, payment plan; PELL, SEOG, NSS, NDSL, FISL, NSL, CWS. Suggest filing FAF or FFS by February.

Admissions High school graduation with 16 units required. ACT or SAT required. $20 application fee. Rolling admissions; suggest applying before January. Limited *Concurrent Enrollment* Program. Admission deferral possible. Transfers accepted. Credit possible for CEEB AP exams; university has own advanced placement program. Special admission programs.

Student Life Student government. Newspaper, magazine, yearbook, radio and TV stations. Music, debate, speaking, drama groups. 450 honorary, professional, religious, and special interest groups. 26 fraternities and 15 sororities; most have houses. 6% to 8% of men and women join. Freshmen and sophomores under 20 must live at home or on campus. Coed and single-sex dorms; honors, quiet houses. Co-op dorms. Married-student housing. 41% of students live on campus. Freshmen may not have cars on campus. Many intercollegiate, intramural, and club sports. NCAA, Big Ten. Student body composition: 0.9% Asian, 5.6% Black, 0.9% Hispanic, 0.2% Native American, 86.6% White, 6% Other. 14% from out of state.

MICHIGAN TECHNOLOGICAL UNIVERSITY $

Houghton 49931, (906) 487-1885
Director of Admissions: Ernest R. Griff

- **Undergraduates:** 5,359m, 1,725w
- **Tuition (1984–1985):** $1,764 (in-state), $3,816 (out-of-state)
- **Room and Board (1984–1985):** $2,438
- **Degrees offered:** BA, BS, AAS
- **Mean SAT:** 486v, 595m, **Mean ACT:** 24.6
- **Student-faculty ratio:** 19 to 1
- **Calendar system:** Quarter

A public university established in 1885. 240-acre campus in small city of Houghton on Michigan's Upper Peninsula, 325 miles from Milwaukee. Served by air and bus.

Academic Character NCACS and professional accreditation. Quarter system, 2 6-week summer terms. Majors offered in liberal arts and theater technology (BA), and in applied geophysics, applied physics, biological sciences, business administration, chemistry, computer science, engineering administration, forestry, geology, interdisciplinary engineering, land surveying, mathematics, medical technology, physics, social sciences, scientific & technical communication, wood & fiber utilization, and in chemical, civil, electrical, geological, mechanical, metallurgical, and mining engineering. Self-designed majors. Associate degrees in civil engineering technology, electrical engineering technology, electromechanical engineering technology, forest technology, general studies, mechanical design engineering technology. Distributive requirements. Graduate and professional degrees granted. Independent study. Internships, cooperative work/study. Preprofessional programs in dentistry, law, medicine. Cooperative programs in business administration, computer sciences, engineering, forestry. Dual degree programs in engineering and forestry with several colleges. Secondary school science education certification. ROTC, AFROTC. 4,000-acre forestry center, simulation lab. Computer center, language lab. 543,590-volume library with microform resources.

Financial CEEB CSS and ACT FAS. University scholarships, grants, loans, state scholarships, tuition waivers for children of deceased veterans, aid for physically handicapped; PELL, SEOG, GSL, NDSL, FISL, CWS. Application deadline March 1.

Admissions High school graduation with 15 units required. Interview encouraged. ACT required for counseling purposes. $20 application fee. Rolling admissions; suggest applying after October 1. $50 deposit required on acceptance of offer of admission. *Early Admission* Program. Admission deferral possible. Transfers accepted. Credit possible for CEEB AP and CLEP exams; university has own advanced placement program.

Student Life Student government. Newspaper, yearbook, radio stations. Music and drama groups. 125 academic, professional, religious, service, and special interest groups. 12 fraternities with houses and 3 sororities, 1 with house. 6% of men and 4% of women join. Single freshmen and sophomores must live at home or on campus. Coed and single-sex dorms and apartments, special interest houses. 43% of students live on campus. 6 quarters of phys ed required. 7 intercollegiate sports for men, 4 for women; intramurals. AIAW, NCAA, CCHA, Great Lakes Intercollegiate Athletic Conference. Student body composition: 0.6% Asian, 0.5% Black, 0.5% Hispanic, 0.3% Native American, 95.2% White, 2.9% Other. 12% from out of state.

WAYNE STATE UNIVERSITY $

5980 Cass Avenue, Detroit 48202, (313) 577-3577
Director of Admissions: Ronald C. Hughes

- **Undergraduates:** 9,896m, 10,626w
- **Tuition (1984–1985):** $1,456 (in-state), $3,276 (out-of-state)
- **Room and Board (1984–1985):** $3,440;   **Fees:** $80
- **Degrees offered:** BA, BS, BGS, BET, BSN, BSW, BPA, BFA, BMus
- **Mean SAT:** 431v, 491m,   **Mean ACT:** 21
- **Student-faculty ratio:** 20 to 1
- **Calendar system:** Semester

A public university established in 1933. 180-acre urban campus in Detroit. Served by air, rail, and bus.

Academic Character NCACS and professional accreditation. Semester system, spring and summer terms. 52 majors offered by the College of Liberal Arts, 5 by the School of Business Administration, 15 by the College of Education, 12 by the College of Engineering, 6 by the College of Pharmacy & Allied Health Professions; additional majors in nursing, social work. Distributive requirements. Graduate and professional degrees granted. Independent study. Honors program. Phi Beta Kappa. Cooperative work/study in engineering. Pass/fail. Preprofessional programs in business administration, dentistry, education, law, library science, medicine, medical technology, mortuary science, occupational therapy, optometry, osteopathy, pharmacy, physical therapy, radiation therapy, social work. Dual degree programs in allied health, business administration, distributive education, engineering technology. Study abroad. Elementary, secondary, and special education and library science certification. ROTC at U of Detroit; AFROTC at U Michigan-Ann Arbor. Language lab, computer center. Black studies, cognitive processes, engineering, gerontology, health, labor, peace, urban centers. 1,839,429-volume library with microform resources.

Financial University scholarships, grants, loans; PELL, SEOG, NDSL, GSL, CWS.

Admissions High school graduation required. SAT or ACT required for students not meeting minimum requirements and for Liberal Arts applicants. $15 application fee. Rolling admissions. *Early Decision* Program. Transfers accepted. Credit possible for CEEB AP and CLEP exams; university has own advanced placement program. PROJECT 350.

Student Life Student government. Publications. Music groups. Academic, religious, service, and special interest groups. 14 fraternities and 13 sororities; some have houses. Limited university housing. No married-student housing. 2% of students live on campus. Intercollegiate and intramural sports for men and women. NCAA, GLIAC. Student body composition: 2.5% Asian, 22.5% Black, 1.7% Hispanic, 0.9% Native American, 72.7% White. 30% from out of state.

WESTERN MICHIGAN UNIVERSITY $

Kalamazoo 49008, (616) 383-1950
Director of Admissions: Duncan A. Clarkson

- **Undergraduates:** 7,589m, 6,567w
- **Tuition (1984–1985):** $1,379 (in-state), $3,352.50 (out-of-state)
- **Room and Board (1984–1985):** $2,240;   **Fees:** $72
- **Degrees offered:** BA, BS, BBA, BFA, BMus, BSE, BSMed, BSW
- **Mean ACT:** 19.7
- **Student-faculty ratio:** 17 to 1
- **Calendar system:** Trimester

A public university established in 1903. 400-acre suburban campus in Kalamazoo, 145 miles from Chicago and Detroit. Served by air, rail, and bus.
Academic Character NCACS and professional accreditation. Trimester system, 7½-week spring and summer terms. 37 majors offered by the College of Applied Science, 36 by the College of Arts & Sciences, 15 by the College of Business Administration, 8 by the College of Education, 24 by the College of Fine Arts, and 7 by the College of Health & Human Services. Self-designed majors. Dual degrees in manufacturing, health studies, applied liberal studies. Minor required. Courses in area and cultural studies. Distributive requirements. Graduate and professional degrees granted. Independent study. Honors program. Pass/fail. Internships, cooperative work/study. Preprofessional programs in architecture, engineering, medical technology, social work, speech pathology. 3-1 program in medical technology, 3-2 program in occupational therapy with area hospitals. Member consortium with Kalamazoo, Kalamazoo Valley, Nazareth colleges. Study abroad. Elementary, secondary, and special education certification. ROTC. Language labs. 1,677,248-volume library with microform resources.
Financial CEEB CSS. University scholarships, grants, loans, payment plans; PELL, SEOG, NDSL, FISL, CWS; university has own work program. Application deadlines February 15 (scholarships), March 15 (loans).
Admissions High school graduation with 3 units in English required. ACT required; ACH recommended. Audition required for music. $15 application fee. Rolling admissions; suggest applying after October 1. $50 deposit required on acceptance of offer of admission. Transfers accepted. Credit possible for CEEB AP, CLEP, and ACT PEP exams. Martin Luther King Program for minority applicants.
Student Life Student government. Newspaper, magazine, radio station. Music, debate, drama groups. Several academic, honorary, political, professional, religious, and special interest organizations. 17 fraternities and 10 sororities. Coed and single-sex dorms. Married-student housing. 31% of students live on campus. Liquor prohibited. 2 hours of phys ed required (ROTC students excepted). 14 intercollegiate sports; intramurals. AIAW, CCAC, Mid-American Athletic Conference. Student body composition: 0.3% Asian, 5.3% Black, 0.5% Hispanic, 0.2% Native American, 89.1% White, 4.6% Other. 11% from out of state.

Minnesota

CARLETON COLLEGE $$

Northfield 55057, (507) 663-4190
Dean of Admissions: Richard E. Steele

- **Undergraduates:** 913m, 944w
- **Tuition (1984–1985):** $8,400
- **Room and Board (1984–1985):** $2,440;   **Fees:** $60
- **Degrees offered:** BA
- **Mean SAT:** 604v, 632m,   **Mean ACT:** 28.3
- **Student-faculty ratio:** 12 to 1
- **Calendar system:** 3–3 (3 10-week terms, 3 courses per term)

A private college established in 1866 in the small town of Northfield. 950-acre campus 40 miles south of Minneapolis/St. Paul. 450-acre arboretum on campus. Bus station in Northfield.

Academic Character NCACS accreditation. Trimester system. Majors offered in American studies, art, biology, Black studies, chemistry, classical languages, classical studies, economics, English, geology, history, Latin American studies, math, modern languages (French, German, Hebrew, Japanese, Russian, Spanish), music, philosophy, physics & astronomy, political science, psychology, religion, and sociology & anthropology. 13 interdepartmental programs include Asian, computer, environmental, film, Russian, theatre, urban, and women's studies. Self-designed majors. Distributive requirements. Independent study. Phi Beta Kappa. Credit by exam and for directed summer reading, satisfactory/unsatisfactory option. Internships, cooperative work/study. 3-2 engineering with Columbia and Washington U (St. Louis); 3-3 law with Columbia. Several off-campus study opportunities. Study abroad. Secondary education certification. Computer, language labs. 310,000-volume library.

Financial ACT FAS (for Minnesota residents) and CEEB CSS. College scholarships and grants, payment plan; PELL, SEOG, NDSL, FISL, GSL, CWS and college part-time employment. Application deadline February 15.

Admissions High school graduation with 15 units required. ACH and interview recommended. SAT or ACT required. $25 application fee. Application deadline February 1. Notification by April 15. $100 deposit required on acceptance of offer of admission. *Early Admission, Early Decision* programs. Admission deferral possible. Transfers accepted. Credit possible for CEEB AP exams. Applicants who do not meet academic admission standards, but who show unusual ability and interest, are considered.

Student Life Student government. Newspaper, magazines, photo journal, yearbook. Radio station. Music, dance, and drama groups. Coffeehouse. Many community service programs. Amnesty International. All students must live at least one year on campus. 11 dorms and 22 student houses; most are coed. Special interest housing. No married-student housing. 95% of students live on campus. Permission required to have a car or motorcycle in Northfield. Hazing and firearms forbidden. Intercollegiate, intramural, and recreational sports. MCAC, AIAW, NCAA. Student body composition: 3% Asian, 3% Black, 2% Hispanic, 0.5% Native American, 91.5% White. 70% from out of state.

GUSTAVUS ADOLPHUS COLLEGE $$

St. Peter 56082, (507) 931-7676
Director of Admissions: Owen Sammelson

- Undergraduates: 980m, 1,200w
- Tuition (1984–1985): $6,500
- Room and Board (1984–1985): $2,250
- Degrees offered: BA
- Mean SAT: 520v, 570m,   Mean ACT: 25
- Student-faculty ratio: 14 to 1
- Calendar system: 4–1–4

A private college established in 1862 and affiliated with the Lutheran Church in America. 246-acre campus overlooking the small city of St. Peter, 65 miles southwest of Minneapolis. Bus station in St. Peter. Airport in Mankato and Minneapolis, train in Minneapolis.
Academic Character NCACS and professional accreditation. 4-1-4 system, 4-week summer term. Majors offered in accounting, art, biology, business, chemistry, computer science, economics, education, English, French, geography, geology, German, Greek, health education, history, Latin, math, music, nursing, philosophy, physics, political science, psychology, religion, sociology/anthropology, Spanish, speech, theatre, and phys ed, health, & athletics. Interdisciplinary programs. Self-designed majors. Distributives, 1 religion course, and senior comprehensive exam required. Independent study, honors program. Internships, cooperative work/study. Preprofessional programs in accounting, architecture, arts administration, many health fields, church work, theology, engineering, communications, law, forestry, social work, and veterinary medicine. 3-2 engineering with Washington U and other schools. 3-1 medical technology program. Cross-registration with Mankato State. Many study abroad and off-campus programs. Elementary and secondary education certification. ROTC with Mankato State. Language lab. 289,000-volume library.
Financial Guaranteed tuition. CEEB CSS and ACT FAS. College scholarships & grants; state scholarships, grants, and loans; payment plans; PELL, SEOG, NDSL, GSL, NSL, CWS. Application deadline March 1.
Admissions High school graduation required with 13 units recommended. Interview recommended. SAT, ACT, or PSAT required. $15 application fee. Suggest applying by February 1; deadline April 1. Notification on Dec. 1, Feb. 15, Mar. 15, or Apr. 15. $100 deposit required on acceptance of offer of admission. *Early Decision, Early Entrance* programs. Admission deferral possible. Transfers accepted. Credit possible for CEEB AP and CLEP exams.
Student Life Student government. Newspaper, literary magazine, yearbook. Music, drama, and speaking clubs. International Students organization. Coffeehouse. Academic, honorary, special interest groups. 8 fraternities and 6 sororities; about 25% of students join. No married-student housing. Special interest housing, coed and single-sex dorms. 95% of students live on campus. Liquor allowed only in dorm rooms of students of legal age. 1 phys ed course required. 12 intercollegiate sports for men, 10 for women; intramurals. AIAW, MIAC. Student body composition: 1% Black, 98% White, 1% Other. 24% from out of state.

MACALESTER COLLEGE $$

St. Paul 55105, (612) 696-6357
Dean of Admissions: William M. Shain

- **Undergraduates:** 862m, 833w
- **Tuition (1984–1985):** $7,520
- **Room and Board (1984–1985):** $2,600; **Fees:** $75
- **Degrees offered:** BA
- **Mean SAT:** 561v, 579m, **Mean ACT:** 26.3
- **Student-faculty ratio:** 12 to 1
- **Calendar system:** 4–1–4

A private college established in 1874 and related to the United Presbyterian Church. 50-acre campus in a residential area of St. Paul. Airport, bus and train stations.

Academic Character NCACS and professional accreditation. 4-1-4 system, 8-week summer term. Majors offered in anthropology, art, biology chemistry, classics, computer studies, dramatic arts, East Asian studies, economics & business, English, environmental studies, French, general science, geography, geology, German, history, humanities, international studies, Japan studies, law & society, library science, linguistics, math, music, philosophy, phys ed, physics, political science, psychology, religious studies, Russian, Russian area studies, social science, sociology, Spanish, speech communications, and urban studies. Interdepartmental, self-designed majors, minors. Distributive requirements. Independent study, internships. Credit by exam. Satisfactory/D/No credit grading option. Honors program. Phi Beta Kappa. Preprofessional programs in several areas. Many exchange programs, urban studies programs. Study abroad. ROTC with St. Thomas. Elementary and secondary education certification. Observatory/planetarium, electron microscope, language lab, computer Natural history area, Arizona geology center. Over 290,000-volume library.

Financial CEEB CSS and ACT FAS. College and state scholarships, loans, and grants, Presbyterian scholarships, payment plan; PELL, SEOG, NDSL, GSL, PLUS, CWS. Application deadline March 1

Admissions High school graduation with 13 units expected. SAT or ACT required; state residents may substitute PSAT 3 ACH suggested. $20 application fee. Application deadline March 15. Notification on March 1 or April 1. $50 tuition and $50 room deposits required on acceptance of offer of admission. *Early Decision, Early Entrance, Concurrent Enrollment* programs. Admission deferral possible. Transfers accepted. Credit possible for CEEB AP exams. Minority admissions program.

Student Life Student government. Newspaper, literary quarterly, radio station. Music, dance, drama, and debate clubs. Community Involvement Program. Political, athletic, academic, and special interest groups. Scottish Country Fair in May Coed dorms, special interest and language housing. No married-student housing. 65% of students live on campus. Intercollegiate and intramural sports for men and women. AIAW, MIAC. Student body composition: 1% Asian, 3% Black, 3% Hispanic, 1% Native American, 92% White. 65% from out of state.

MINNESOTA, UNIVERSITY OF, TWIN CITIES $

Minneapolis 55455, (612) 373-2144
Director of Admissions: Leo D. Abbott

- **Undergraduates:** 18,966m, 15,748w
- **Tuition (1984–1985):** $1,659.15 (in-state), $4,562.55 (out-of-state)
- **Room and Board (1984–1985):** $2,352–$3,072

- **Degrees offered:** BA, BS
- **Mean SAT:** 488v, 538m,   **Mean ACT:** 22.4
- **Student-faculty ratio:** 14 to 1
- **Calendar system:** Quarter

A public university established in 1851. 280-acre campus in Minneapolis, with additional 70 acres in northern St. Paul. Airport, bus and train stations in Minneapolis/St. Paul.

Academic Character NCACS and professional accreditation. Quarter system, 2 summer terms. Over 140 majors offered by the Colleges of Agriculture, Biological Sciences, Business Administration, Education, Forestry Home Economics, Liberal Arts, and Pharmacy, and by the General College, the Institute of Technology, the School of Nursing, and the Department of Mortuary Science. Self-designed interdepartmental majors. Distributive requirements. Graduate and professional degrees granted. Independent study, honors programs. Phi Beta Kappa. Pass/fail, cooperative work/study. Preprofessional programs in architecture, dentistry, medicine, social work. 2-2, 3-1, and 1-3 transfer programs from College of Liberal Arts to other Colleges within the University. Study abroad. Elementary, secondary, and special education certification. ROTC, AFROTC, NROTC. Language lab. 4,030,654-volume library.

Financial ACT FAS. University scholarships, grants, and loans, Martin Luther King Fund; PELL, SEOG, NDSL, GSL, CWS. Application deadline March 1.

Admissions High school graduation required; unit requirements vary with Colleges. ACT, PSAT, or SAT required. General College admissions open to MN, WI, ND, and SD residents. $15 application fee. Rolling admissions; suggest applying before April of 12th year. Deadline July 15. *Early Entrance* Program. Transfers accepted to most colleges. Credit possible for CEEB AP and CLEP exams.

Student Life 400 student activities groups. 28 fraternities and 13 sororities with houses. 4% of students join. Coed and single-sex dorms. Married-student and special interest housing. 10% of students live on campus. Intercollegiate and intramural sports. AIAW, Big Ten. Student body composition: 2.4% Asian, 2% Black, 1% Hispanic, 0.5% Native American, 94.1% White. 10% of freshmen from out of state.

ST. OLAF COLLEGE $$

Northfield 55057, (507) 663-2222
Director of Admissions: Bruce K. Moe

- **Undergraduates:** 1,310m, 1,565w
- **Tuition (1984–1985):** $6,550
- **Room and Board (1984–1985):** $2,200
- **Degrees offered:** BA, BMus, BSN
- **Mean SAT:** 525v, 580m,   **Mean ACT:** 25
- **Student-faculty ratio:** 14 to 1
- **Calendar system:** 4–1–4

A private college established in 1874 and affiliated with the American Lutheran Church. Wooded 350-acre campus 1 mile west of the small town of Northfield, and 40 miles south of Minneapolis-St. Paul. Bus station in Northfield.

Academic Character NCACS and professional accreditation. 4-1-4 system, 2 5½-week summer terms. Majors in American minority studies, American studies, ancient & Medieval studies, art, art history, Asian studies, biology, chemistry, classics, dance, economics, English, fine arts, French, German, health studies, Hispanic studies, history, home economics, literature, math, music, Norwegian, nursing, philosophy, phys ed, physics, political science, psychology, religion, Russian, Russian studies, social studies education, sociology, Spanish, speech-theatre, urban studies. Self-designed majors. Concentrations in computer science, statistics, and in Afro-American, American Indian, Latin American, Western European, and women's studies. Distributives and 3 religion courses required. Independent study and research, Phi Beta Kappa. Pass/no credit, credit by exam, internships. Several alternate study selections for qualified students. Cross-registration with Carleton; exchange with Fisk. Art courses through Union of Independent Colleges of Art. 3-2 engineering programs. Several off-campus and study abroad programs. Summer natural sciences program at wilderness station. Secondary education certification; elementary certification possible through Augsburg. Computer center, language labs. 325,000-volume library

Financial CEEB CSS and ACT FAS. College scholarships, grants, and loans, PELL, SEOG, NDSL, GSL, NSL, CWS.

Admissions High school graduation required, with 15 units recommended. ACT, SAT, or PSAT required. $15 application fee. Rolling admissions; application deadline February 15. $100 deposit required on acceptance of offer of admission. *Early Decision* and *Early Entrance* programs. Transfers accepted. Credit possible for CEEB AP and CLEP exams, and for extracurricular academic work.

Student Life Student government. Newspaper, literary magazine, yearbook, radio station. Music, debate, and drama groups. Academic clubs and honorary fraternities. Political and volunteer groups. Coed, single-sex, and language dorms. No married-student housing. Off-campus students must eat one meal a day in the dining hall. 99% of students live on campus. Students may not have cars on campus. Honor system. Liquor prohibited on campus. 2 phys ed courses required. 12 intercollegiate sports for men, 9 for women; many intramurals. AIAW, NAIA, NCAA, MIAC. Student body composition: 97% White, 3% Other 35% from out of state.

Mississippi

MILLSAPS COLLEGE $

Jackson 39210, (601) 354-5201
Director of Admissions: John H. Christmas

- **Undergraduates:** 604m, 569w
- **Tuition (1984–1985):** $4,980
- **Room and Board (1984–1985):** $2,110;   **Fees:** $175
- **Degrees offered:** AB, BMus, BBA, BS, BSEd
- **Mean SAT:** 550v, 550m,   **Mean ACT:** 24
- **Student-faculty ratio:** 14 to 1
- **Calendar system:** Semester

A private college affiliated with the United Methodist Church, established in 1892. 100-acre urban campus in the center of Jackson, 180 miles from New Orleans, 190 miles from Memphis. Served by air and rail.

Academic Character SACS accreditation. Semester system, 2 5-week summer terms. Majors offered in accounting, administration, art, biology, chemistry, church music, economics, elementary education, English, French, geology, German, history, mathematics, music, music education, philosophy, physical education, physics, political science, psychology, psychology-sociology, religion, sociology-anthropology, Spanish, and theatre. Courses in 7 additional areas. Distributive requirements, senior exams, 6 credits in religion/philosophy required. Independent study, honors program. Internships. Preprofessional programs in medicine, law, ministry, education. 3-2 programs in engineering with Auburn, Columbia, Georgia Tech, Vanderbilt, Washington U. 3-1 medical technology and medical records librarianship programs. Member Southern College and University Union. Study abroad. UN, Washington, London, Oak Ridge semesters. Elementary and secondary education certification. ROTC at Jackson State. Computer center. 155,000-volume library.

Financial CEEB CSS. University scholarships, grants, loans, Methodist and ministerial grants and loans, payment plans; PELL, SEOG, NDSL, FISL, CWS. Application deadline April 1.

Admissions High school graduation with 12 units required. GED accepted. Interview encouraged. ACT or SAT required. $10 application fee. Rolling admissions. $25 tuition and $50 room deposits required on acceptance of offer of admission. *Early Admission* Program. Transfers accepted. Credit possible for CEEB AP and CLEP exams; college has own advanced placement program.

Student Life Student government. Newspaper, magazine, yearbook. Music, debate, drama groups. Black Students Association. Academic, honorary, religious, and special interest groups. 4 fraternities with houses, and 4 sororities without houses. 38% of men and 35% of women join. Freshmen and sophomores must live at home or on campus. Some married-student housing. 72% of students live on campus. Liquor, gambling prohibited. 1 hour of phys ed required. 5 intercollegiate sports for men, 2 for women; intramurals. AIAW, NCAA. Student body composition: 6% Black, 1% Hispanic, 93% White. 28% from out of state.

MISSISSIPPI, UNIVERSITY OF $

University 38677, (601) 232-7226, in MS: (800) 222-5102
Director of Admissions & Records: Kenneth L. Wooten

- **Undergraduates:** 3,928m, 3,650w
- **Tuition and Fees (1984–1985):** $1,321 (in-state), $2,297 (out-of-state)
- **Room and Board (1984–1985):** $2,000
- **Degrees offered:** BA, BS, BAE, BM, BFA
- **Mean ACT:** 20
- **Student-faculty ratio:** 17 to 1
- **Calendar system:** Semester

A public university established in 1848. Campus of 640 acres adjacent to Oxford, in the northern part of the state 75 miles from Memphis.
Academic Character SACS and professional accreditation. Semester system, 2 5½-week summer terms. 55 majors offered by the College of Liberal Arts, 1 by the School of Accountancy, 13 by the School of Business Administration, 22 by the School of Education, 9 by the School of Engineering, 1 by the School of Pharmacy, and 4 by the School of Health Related Professions. Minor required in some divisions. Distributive requirements. Graduate and professional degrees granted. Independent study Honors program. Limited pass/fail. Cooperative work/study, internships. 2-3 program in pharmacy. 3-1 programs in medicine, dentistry Study abroad. Elementary, secondary, and special education certification. ROTC, AFROTC, NROTC. Computer center, Engineering Experiment Station, center for women's studies, center for Southern culture. 6 libraries comprising 1,750,000 volumes; all have microform resources.
Financial CEEB CSS. University scholarships and loans; PELL, SEOG, NDSL, FISL. File FAF by March 1, application deadline April 1
Admissions High school graduation with 15 units required. ACT required; SAT may be substituted by out-of-state applicants. Rolling admissions; suggest applying soon after mid-year *Early Admission* Program. Transfers accepted. Credit possible for CEEB AP and CLEP exams.
Student Life Student government. Newspaper, magazine, yearbook, radio station. Music, debate, drama groups. Academic, honorary, and special interest organizations. 21 fraternities, 16 with houses, and 14 sororities, 11 with houses. 40% of men and 45% of women join. Freshmen must have permission to live off campus. Dorms for men and women. Cafeteria. Married-student housing. 60% of students live on campus. Cars discouraged. Activity courses for freshmen and sophomores required by some divisions. 7 intercollegiate sports; intramurals. Southeastern Conference. Student body composition: 8% Black, 90% White, 2% Other 28% from out of state.

MISSISSIPPI UNIVERSITY FOR WOMEN $

Columbus 39701, (601) 328-5891
Director of Admissions: James B. Alinder

- **Undergraduates:** 309m, 1,969w
- **Tuition (1984–1985):** $825 (in-state), $1,801 (out-of-state)
- **Room and Board (1984–1985):** $1,660
- **Degrees offered:** BA, BS, BSMedTech, BSN, BMus, BMus Ed, BFA, BSW
- **Mean ACT:** 20

- **Student-faculty ratio:** 10 to 1
- **Calendar system:** Semester

A public university for women established in 1884; men are admitted to the nursing program. 110-acre campus located in the small city of Columbus, 120 miles from Birmingham. Served by air and bus; rail nearby.

Academic Character SACS and professional accreditation. Semester system, 2 5-week summer terms. Majors offered in art, art history, biology, broadcast journalism, broadcasting, business administration, chemistry, education, English, French, history, 5 home economics areas, journalism, mathematics, microbiology, music, nursing, paralegal studies, physical sciences, political science, psychology, social sciences, social work, Spanish, speech communication, speech pathology, and theatre. Distributive requirements. MA, MS, MEd granted. Independent study. Honors program. Cooperative work/study, pass/fail, internships. Preprofessional programs in dentistry, law, medicine, pharmacy, physical therapy, veterinary medicine. 3-2 program in engineering with Auburn, Mississippi State. Elementary, secondary, and special education certification. AFROTC. Computer center, language lab, museum, TV studio. 200,000-volume library with microform resources.

Financial CEEB CSS. University scholarships, grants, and loans; athletic, ROTC scholarships, music scholarships, state loans, payment plan; PELL, SEOG, NDSL, FISL, CWS. Application deadline June 1.

Admissions High school graduation with 15 units and ACT score of 15 required. $10 application fee. Rolling admissions; suggest applying by July 15. $25 deposit required on acceptance of offer of admission. *Early Admission,* Pre-College Enrichment programs. Admission deferral possible. Transfers accepted. Credit possible for CEEB AP and CLEP exams; university has own advanced placement program.

Student Life Student government. Newspaper, magazine, yearbook, radio station. Music, mime, dance, comic groups. Black, Chinese culture organizations. Honorary, religious, academic, and special interest groups. 17 social clubs. 30% of women join. Students must live at home or on campus. Dormitories. Married-student and single-parent housing. 60% of students live on campus. Liquor prohibited. 2 semesters of phys ed required. 7 intercollegiate sports; intramurals. AIAW. Student body composition: 0.4% Asian, 19.7% Black, 0.1% Hispanic, 0.4% Native American, 77.9% White. 18% from out of state.

Missouri

MISSOURI, UNIVERSITY OF $

Columbia 65201, (314) 882-2121
Director of Admissions & Registrar: Gary L. Smith

- **Undergraduates:** 9,358m, 8,981w
- **Tuition (1984–1985):** $1,288 (in-state), $2,576 (out-of-state)
- **Room and Board (1984–1985):** $2,004–$2,327; **Fees:** $67
- **Degrees offered:** AB, BS, BES, BFA, BGS, BMus, BSBA, BSEd, BSN, BSW, BSE, BJournalism, BHealthSci
- **Mean SAT:** 479v, 520m, **Mean ACT:** 23
- **Student-faculty ratio:** 17 to 1
- **Calendar system:** Semester

A public university established in 1839. Urban campus. Served by air and bus.
Academic Character NCACS and professional accreditation. Semester system, 4-, 6-, and 8-week summer terms. 17 majors offered by the College of Agriculture, 36 by the College of Arts & Sciences, 13 by the College of Business & Public Administration, 35 by the College of Education, 13 by the College of Engineering, 3 by the School of Forestry, Fisheries, & Wildlife, 6 by the School of Health-Related Professions, 6 by the College of Home Economics, 6 by the School of Journalism, 1 by the School of Nursing, and 2 by the College of Public & Community Services. Self-designed majors. Distributive requirements. Graduate and professional degrees granted. Independent study Honors program. Phi Beta Kappa. Limited pass/fail, internships. Cross-registration with U Nebraska, U Kansas at Lawrence and at Manhattan, and Wichita State in certain programs. Study abroad. Elementary, secondary, and special education certification. ROTC, AFROTC, NROTC. Computer center Museums. Language lab. 1,000,000-volume library with microform resources.
Financial CEEB CSS. PELL, SEOG, NSS, NDSL, FISL, NSL, CWS. Application deadline April 1
Admissions High school graduation with 20 units required. GED accepted. SAT, ACT, or SCAT required. Rolling admissions. $20 deposit due on acceptance of admissions offer *Early Admission* Program. Admission deferral possible. Transfers accepted. Credit possible for CEEB AP, CLEP, and university exams.
Student Life Student government. Newspaper, yearbook, radio and TV stations. Music and theatre groups. Debate. Athletic, academic, honorary, religious, service, and special interest groups. 29 fraternities and 18 sororities, all with houses. Coed and single-sex dorms. Co-op women's dorms. Married-student housing. 25% of students live on campus. Many intercollegiate and intramural sports for men and women. Student body composition: 1% Asian, 4% Black, 1% Hispanic, 1% Native American, 88% White, 5% Other 16% from out of state.

STEPHENS COLLEGE $$

Columbia 65215, (314) 442-2211
Dean of Admissions: Martha G. Wade

- **Undergraduates:** 26m, 1,141w
- **Tuition and Fees (1984–1985):** $6,274
- **Room and Board (1984–1985):** $2,830
- **Degrees offered:** BA, BS, BFA, AA
- **Student-faculty ratio:** 10 to 1
- **Calendar system:** Semester

A private college established in 1833. 325-acre campus in a small city 125 miles from St. Louis. Airport, bus station.

Academic Character NCACS accreditation. Semester system, 7-week summer term. 27 majors offered in the areas of fine arts, business, communications, equestrian science, fashion, humanities, and physical education. Self-designed majors. Minors offered in most major fields. Distributive requirements. Independent study. Honors program. Pass/fail, internships. "House Plan" study course for freshmen. Preprofessional programs in law and medicine. 3-2 engineering programs with Georgia Tech, Washington U. Animal science and engineering programs with U Missouri at Columbia. Mid-Missouri Association of Colleges and Universities. Study abroad. Elementary and special education certification. ROTC, NROTC, AFROTC at Columbia. 125,000-volume library.

Financial CEEB CSS and ACT FAS. College scholarships, grants, loans, payment plan; PELL, SEOG, NDSL, FISL, CWS. Application deadline March 15 (scholarships), May 1 (loans).

Admissions High school graduation with 12 units in college prep program recommended. Interview recommended. ACT or SAT required. $25 application fee. Rolling admissions. $275 deposit due on acceptance of admissions offer. *Early Admission* Program. Admission deferral possible. Transfers accepted. Credit possible for CEEB AP and CLEP exams.

Student Life Student government. Students serve on faculty and administrative committees. Newspaper, literary magazine, yearbook, radio and TV stations. Music and theatre groups. Honorary, political, service, and special interest groups. 4 sororities without houses. 20% of women join. Except for a special group of seniors, students must live at home or on campus. 95% of students live in residence halls. Juniors and seniors may have cars on campus. 4 terms of phys ed required. 5 intercollegiate sports; intramurals. Student body composition: 0.8% Asian, 6% Black, 1% Hispanic, 0.2% Native American, 92% White. 80% from out of state.

WASHINGTON UNIVERSITY $$$

St. Louis 63130, (314) 889-6000
Director of Admissions: William H. Turner

- **Undergraduates:** 2,562m, 1,985w
- **Tuition (1984–1985):** $8,600
- **Room and Board (1984–1985):** $3,600
- **Degrees offered:** AB, BS, BFA
- **Mean SAT:** 560v, 620m,   **Mean ACT:** 27
- **Student-faculty ratio:** 14 to 1
- **Calendar system:** Semester

A private university established in 1853. 176-acre suburban campus. Served by air, rail, and bus.

Academic Character NCACS and professional accreditation. Semester system, 4 summer terms. 38 majors offered by the College of Arts & Sciences, 1 by the School of Architecture, 4 by the School of Business Administration, 8 by the School of Engineering & Applied Science, 9 by the School of Fine Arts, and 2 by the School of Medicine. Self-designed majors. Distributive requirements. Graduate and professional degrees granted. 4-year program combines 2 years of Common Studies and 2 years of Independent Studies. Honors programs. Phi Beta Kappa. Limited pass/fail. Internships. Preprofessional programs in architecture, business, dentistry, health administration, law, medicine, occupational therapy, physical therapy, social work, teaching the deaf. Study abroad. Elementary, secondary, and special education certification. ROTC, AFROTC. Language lab. 1,800,000-volume library with microform resources.

Financial Guaranteed tuition. CEEB CSS. University scholarships, grants, loans, payment plans; PELL, SEOG, NDSL, FISL, CWS.

Admissions High school graduation with high academic performance required. Interview encouraged. SAT or ACT required; ACH encouraged. $20 application fee. Rolling admissions. $200 deposit due on acceptance of admissions offer. *Early Decision* Program. Admission deferral possible. Transfers accepted. Credit possible for CEEB AP exams and for university placement exams.

Student Life Student Senate. Newspaper, literary magazine, journals, yearbook. Music and drama groups. Opera Workshop. Dance theatre. Honorary, religious, social, and special interest groups. 10 fraternities with houses. 6 sororities. 10% of students join. Freshmen must live at home or on campus. Coed and single-sex dorms. Special interest houses. 75% of students live on campus. 10 intercollegiate sports for men, 3 for women; intramurals. AIAW, NCAA. Student body composition: 3% Asian, 9% Black, 0.5% Hispanic, 0.5% Native American, 87% White. 77% from out of state.

WILLIAM WOODS COLLEGE $

Fulton 65251, (314) 642-2251
Acting Director of Admissions: Janet White

- **Undergraduates:** 750w
- **Tuition (1984–1985):** $5,550
- **Room and Board (1984–1985):** $2,240
- **Degrees offered:** BA, BS, BFA, BSW
- **Mean SAT:** 430v, 425m,   **Mean ACT:** 19
- **Student-faculty ratio:** 13 to 1
- **Calendar system:** 5–4–1

A private college established in 1870. 160-acre small-town campus, 20 miles east of Columbia, 80 miles west of St. Louis. Airport, bus station.

Academic Character NCACS and professional accreditation. 5-4-1 system plus 3-week post session. 64 majors offered by the Divisions of Fine Arts, Humanities, Natural & Applied Sciences, Social Sciences, and Administrative & Consumer Services. Minors offered in many fields. Distributive requirements. Independent study. Internships. Advanced projects. 3-3 program in law with Duke. 3-2 engineering program with USC, Washington U, Georgia Tech. 3-1 medical technology program. Cooperative programs with 5 area schools. Cooperative nursing program. Study abroad. Broadway semester. Early childhood, elementary, secondary, and special education certification. ROTC at Westminster. Computer center. Language lab. 152,000-volume joint library with Westminster; microform resources.

Financial CEEB CSS. College scholarships, grants, loans, 2nd-family-member discount (applicable at Woods or Westminster), athletic scholarships, state grants, payment plans; PELL, SEOG, GSL, PLUS, NDSL, FISL, CWS.

Admissions High school graduation with 16 units required. Interview recommended. SAT or ACT required. $25 application fee. Rolling admissions. $250 deposit required on acceptance of offer of admission. *Early Admission* and *Early Decision* programs. Admission deferral possible. Transfers accepted. Credit possible for CEEB AP and CLEP exams; college has own advanced placement program.

Student Life Student government. Newspaper, yearbook. Art, music, drama, and dance groups. Athletic, academic, honorary, political, professional, religious, and special interest groups. 4 sororities with houses. 40% of women join. Single students must live at home or in dorms. 95% of students live on campus. Attendance at 3 convocations a year required. Liquor and drugs prohibited. Academic honor code. Regular class attendance required. 6 intercollegiate sports; intramurals. NAIA. Student body composition: 0.2% Asian, 2% Black, 0.5% Hispanic, 96.8% White, 0.5% Other. 55% from out of state.

Montana

CARROLL COLLEGE $

Helena 59625, (406) 442-3450, ext. 286
Director of Admissions: Allen Kohler

- **Undergraduates:** 687m, 839w
- **Tuition (1984–1985):** $3,200
- **Room and Board (1984–1985):** $2,200; **Fees:** $190
- **Degrees offered:** BA, AA
- **Mean SAT:** 412v, 441m, **Mean ACT:** 20.3
- **Student-faculty ratio:** 15 to 1
- **Calendar system:** Semester

A private Roman Catholic college controlled by the Diocese of Helena, established in 1909. 55-acre urban campus in capital of Montana, located in the Rocky Mountains. Served by air, bus, and rail.

Academic Character NASC and professional accreditation. Semester system, 6-week summer term. Majors offered in American studies, biology, business administration (3 areas), classical languages, communication arts, dental hygiene, economics, elementary education, English, French, history, mathematics, medical records administration, medical technology, nursing, philosophy, physical education (K-12), political science, psychology, religious education, sciences, social sciences, social work, Spanish, and theology. Interdepartmental majors. Minors offered in most major fields and in art, chemistry, physics, secondary education. Courses in German, Greek, music. Comprehensive exam required. Independent study. Honors program. Limited pass/fail. Preprofessional programs in dentistry, engineering, law, medicine, pharmacy, seminary, veterinary medicine. 3-2 engineering programs with 6 schools including Notre Dame, Columbia, and USC. Affiliation with 3 area hospitals. Study in Mexico, France. Elementary and secondary education certification. Observatory, seismograph, language lab, computer center. 100,000-volume library.

Financial CEEB CSS. College scholarships, grants, loans, family discounts, payment plan; PELL, SEOG, SSIG, NDSL, FISL, NSL, CWS. Application deadlines March 1 (scholarships), April 1 (loans).

Admissions High school graduation with 15 units required. Interview encouraged. ACT or SAT required. $20 application fee. Rolling admissions; suggest applying at least 3 weeks before registration. $50 deposit required on acceptance of offer of admission. *Early Admission* Program. Admission deferral possible. Transfers accepted. Credit possible for CEEB AP exams.

Student Life Student government. Newspaper, magazine, yearbook. Music, debate, drama groups. Academic, religious, and special interest organizations. Students must live at home or on campus. Dormitories and dining hall. Married-student housing available near campus. 61% of students live on campus. 2 courses in phys ed required. 7 intercollegiate sports for men, 2 for women; intramurals. AIAW, NAIA, Frontier Conference. Student body composition: 1.4% Asian, 0.4% Black, 0.5% Hispanic, 1.5% Native American, 95.6% White, 0.6% Other. 34% from out of state.

MONTANA, UNIVERSITY OF $

Missoula 59812, (406) 243-6266
Director of Admissions: Michael Akin

- **Undergraduates:** 4,841m, 4,530w
- **Tuition and Fees (1984–1985):** $1,005 (in-state), $2,697 (out-of-state)
- **Room and Board (1984–1985):** $2,081
- **Degrees offered:** BA, BS
- **Mean ACT:** 19.8
- **Student-faculty ratio:** 20 to 1
- **Calendar system:** Quarter

A public university established in 1893. 201-acre campus in the Rocky Mountain town of Missoula. Served by air and bus.

Academic Character NASC and professional accreditation. Quarter system, 4- and 8-week summer terms. 39 majors offered by the College of Arts & Sciences, 4 by the School of Business Administration, 6 by the School of Education, 5 by the School of Fine Arts, 4 by the School of Forestry, 2 by the School of Journalism, and 4 by the School of Pharmacy & Allied Health Sciences. Courses in Chinese. Distributive requirements. Graduate and professional degrees granted. Independent study. Honors program. Cooperative work/study, pass/fail/internships. Preprofessional program in medical sciences. National Student Exchange Program. Study abroad in Europe, Russia, New Zealand, Taiwan. Elementary, secondary, and special education certification. ROTC. Biological station, experimental forestry lab. 675,000-volume library with microform resources.

Financial CEEB CSS. University scholarships and loans; PELL, SEOG, SSIG, GSL, NDSL, FISL, CWS. Application deadlines March 1 (scholarships), April 1 (NDSL).

Admissions High school graduation with 4 units required. GED accepted. ACT or SAT required. $20 application fee. Rolling admissions; application deadline September 1 $100 room deposit (for boarders) required on acceptance of offer of admission. *Early Admission* Program. Transfers accepted. Credit possible for CEEB AP and CLEP exams.

Student Life Student association. Newspaper, magazines. Music, drama groups. Religious, honorary, professional, service, and special interest organizations. 7 fraternities and 5 sororities, all with houses. 3% of men and 2% of women join. Coed and single-sex dorms. Coop dorm for women. Married-student apartments. 28% of students live on campus. 7 intercollegiate sports for men, 7 for women; intramurals. AIAW, NCAA, Big Sky, Mountain West. Student body composition: 1% Asian, 0.7% Black, 1% Hispanic, 3% Native American, 94.3% White. 28% from out of state.

MONTANA STATE UNIVERSITY AT BOZEMAN $

Bozeman 59717, (406) 994-2452
Director of Admissions: Jaynee Drange Groseth

- **Undergraduates:** 5,360m, 3,875w
- **Tuition (1984–1985):** $884 (in-state), $2,576 (out-of-state)
- **Room and Board (1984–1985):** $2,470
- **Degrees offered:** BA, BS
- **Mean ACT:** 22

- **Student-faculty ratio:** 19 to 1
- **Calendar system:** Quarter

A public university established in 1893. 1,170-acre campus in the small city of Bozeman, 90 miles north of Yellowstone Park. Served by air and bus.

Academic Character NASC and professional accreditation. Quarter system, one 9- and 2 4½-week summer terms. 6 majors offered by the College of Agriculture, 5 by the College of Arts & Architecture, 4 by the College of Education, 11 by the College of Engineering, 27 by the College of Letters and Science, 7 by the School of Business, and 1 by the School of Nursing. Self-designed majors. Distributive requirements. Graduate degrees granted. Independent study. Honors program. Internships. Pass/fail. Preprofessional programs in dentistry, medicine, optometry. Consortium with U of Washington Medical School. National Student Exchange, WICHE programs. Study abroad in England. Elementary, secondary, and special education certification. ROTC, AFROTC. Museum of the Rockies, Water Resources Center, nature area, computer center. 622,000-volume library with microform resources.

Financial CEEB CSS. University scholarships, grants, loans; PELL, SEOG, NDSL, GSL, CWS. Application deadline September 1.

Admissions High school graduation with 16 units recommended. GED accepted. SAT or ACT required. $20 application fee. Rolling admissions; suggest applying at least 30 days before registration. $100 deposit required on acceptance of offer of admission. *Early Admission* and *Concurrent Enrollment* programs. Transfers accepted. Credit possible for CEEB AP and CLEP exams; university has own advanced placement program.

Student Life Student government. Newspaper, magazines, yearbook, radio station. Music, debate, and drama groups. Honorary, professional, and special interest organizations. 11 fraternities and 7 sororities, all with houses. 11% of men and 22% of women join. Coed and single-sex dorms. Coop men's dorm. Family housing. 40% of students live on campus. Liquor prohibited except in private rooms. 7 intercollegiate sports for men, 6 for women; many intramurals. AIAW, Big Sky Conference. Student body composition: 2% Native American, 96% White, 2% Other. 18% from out of state.

Nebraska

CREIGHTON UNIVERSITY $

2500 California Street, Omaha 68178, (402) 280-2703
Director of Admissions: Howard Bachman

- **Undergraduates:** 1,594m, 1,620w
- **Tuition (1984–1985):** $4,800
- **Room and Board (1984–1985):** $2,402
- **Degrees offered:** BA, BS, BSN, BSBA, BFA, BSW
- **Mean ACT:** 23.2
- **Student-faculty ratio:** 12 to 1
- **Calendar system:** Semester

A private Roman Catholic university conducted by the Society of Jesus, established in 1878. 85-acre suburban campus, 10 minutes from downtown Omaha. Served by air, rail, and bus.

Academic Character NCACS and professional accreditation. Semester system; 11-week, 3-term summer semester 30 majors offered by the College of Arts & Sciences, 7 by the College of Business Administration, 1 by the School of Nursing, and concentrations in communication arts, natural science, social sciences, social work, and education. Minors offered in some fields. Distributives and 6 hours of theology required. Graduate & professional degrees granted. Independent study Greek honors program. Pass/fail, internships. Preprofessional programs in architecture, dentistry, engineering, law, librarianship, medicine, mortuary science, occupational therapy, optometry pharmacy, physical therapy, veterinary medicine. 3-1 medical technology program. 2-2 radiologic technology program. 2-3 engineering program with U of Detroit. Elementary and secondary education certification. ROTC, AFROTC. Educational television. Observatory Language lab. 457,911-volume library

Financial CEEB CSS and ACT FAS. University scholarships, grants, loans, 2nd-family-member discount; PELL, SEOG, NDSL, FISL, HELP, CWS. Application deadline March 1

Admissions High school graduation with 15 units required. ACT required. $20 application fee. Rolling admissions. $100 deposit due on acceptance of admissions offer *Early Decision* Program. Admission deferral possible. Transfers accepted. Credit possible for CEEB AP and CLEP exams, and for high ACT scores.

Student Life Student Union. Newspaper, literary magazine, yearbook, radio & TV stations. Music, drama, and literary groups. Honorary, service, and special interest clubs. 6 fraternities, one with house, and 5 sororities. 25% of men and 17% of women join. Juniors and seniors may live off campus. Coed and single-sex dorms. No married-student housing. 60% of students live on campus. 5 intercollegiate sports for men, 4 for women; club & intramural sports. AIAW Student body composition: 3% Asian, 3% Black, 2% Hispanic, 92% White. 60% from out of state.

NEBRASKA, UNIVERSITY OF $

Lincoln 68508, (402) 472-3601
Director of Admissions: Al Papik

- **Undergraduates:** 14,166m, 10,623w
- **Tuition (1984–1985):** $1,100 (in-state), $3,090 (out-of-state)
- **Room and Board (1984-1985):** $2,150; **Fees:** $186
- **Degrees offered:** BA, BS, BFA, BMus, BMus Ed, BSAS
- **Mean ACT:** 21.7
- **Student-faculty ratio:** 18 to 1
- **Calendar system:** Semester

A public university established in 1869. 556-acre urban campus. Airport, bus station.

Academic Character NCACS and professional accreditation. Semester system, 2 5-week summer terms. 15 majors offered by the College of Agriculture, 1 by the College of Architecture, 42 by the College of Arts & Sciences, 8 by the College of Business Administration, 9 by the College of Engineering & Technology, 1 by the College of Nursing, 37 by the Teachers College, and 6 by the College of Home Economics. Self-designed majors. Graduate and professional degrees granted. Independent study. Honors program. Phi Beta Kappa. Cooperative work/study, pass/fail, internships. Preprofessional programs in chemistry, geology, microbiology, social work, government. Cooperative engineering program. Several study abroad programs. Elementary, secondary, and special education certification. ROTC, AFROTC, NROTC. Art galleries. State museum. Recital hall, theatres. 1,160,000-volume library with microform resources.

Financial CEEB CSS. University scholarships, loans, athletic grants, state grants; PELL, SEOG, NDSL, GSL, CWS. Application deadlines February 1(scholarships), March 1 (loans).

Admissions High school graduation with 16 units required. Interview required for nursing students. Audition for music majors. ACT required; SAT may be substituted. $10 (in-state), $25 (out-of-state) application fees. Rolling admissions. *Early Admissions* Program. Transfers accepted. Credit possible for CEEB AP and CLEP exams; departmental advanced placement program.

Student Life Student government. Associated Women Students. Newspaper, literary magazine, yearbook, educational TV station. Academic, ethnic, honorary, and special interest groups. 26 fraternities, 24 with houses; 15 sororities with houses. 25% of men and 33% of women join. Freshmen under 20 must live at home or on campus. Coed, single-sex, coop dorms. Special-interest houses. Limited married-student housing. 45% of students live on campus. Liquor prohibited. 1 year of phys ed required. Extensive intercollegiate and intramural sports program. AIAW, NCAA, Big Eight Conference. Student body composition: 0.7% Asian, 1.6% Black, 0.9% Hispanic, 96.8% White. 9% from out of state.

UNION COLLEGE $

3800 South 48th Street, Lincoln 68506, (402) 488-2331
Director of Admissions: Leona Murray

- **Undergraduates:** 496m, 544w
- **Tuition (1984–1985):** $5,800
- **Room and Board (1984–1985):** $2,090
- **Degrees offered:** BA, BTh, BMus, BS, BSW, AS
- **Mean ACT:** 17.8
- **Student-faculty ratio:** 14 to 1
- **Calendar system:** Semester

A private college conducted by the Seventh-day Adventist Church, established in 1891 Suburban campus. Served by air rail, and bus.

Academic Character NCACS and professional accreditation. Semester system, 4 summer terms. 36 majors offered in the areas of business, education & psychology, fine arts, history & social work, home economics, language arts, mathematics, nursing, physical education, religion, and sciences. Self-designed majors. Associate degrees offered in art, business, business computer programming, early childhood education, engineering, foods & nutrition, health science, home economics, secretarial science, social services. Distributive requirements. Honors program. Credit for missionary work. Limited credit/no credit. Preprofessional programs in allied health, dentistry, medicine. Cross-registration with Nebraska Wesleyan and U Nebraska-Lincoln. Study abroad. Elementary, secondary, and special education certification. 116,014-volume library

Financial Guaranteed tuition. College scholarships, grants, loans, payment plan; PELL, SEOG, NSS, NDSL, FISL, GSL, NSL, CWS. Scholarship application deadline June 15.

Admissions High school graduation with 18 units required. GED accepted. ACT required. $10 application fee. Rolling admissions. $100 deposit due on acceptance of admissions offer Transfers accepted. Credit possible for CEEB CLEP exams; college has own advanced placement program. Freshman Development Program for students not normally admissable.

Student Life Student government. Newspaper Music groups. Union for Christ. Campus ministry Academic, social, religious, recreational, and special interest groups. Students under 24 must live at home or on campus. Single-sex dorms. Married-student housing. 74% of students live on campus. Attendance at 12 religious services and 3 convocations required in each 2-week period. Dress code. Curfew 2 phys ed courses required. Intramural sports. Student body composition: 5% Black, 11% Foreign, 2% Hispanic, 0.3% Native American, 81.7% White. 78% from out of state.

Nevada

NEVADA, UNIVERSITY OF, LAS VEGAS $

4505 South Maryland Parkway, Las Vegas 89154, (702) 739-3443
Director of Admissions: Joeanne Adler

- **Undergraduates:** 4,229m, 4,132w
- **Tuition (1984–1985):** $1,080 (in-state), $3,280 (out-of-state)
- **Room and Board (1984–1985):** $2,515
- **Degrees offered:** BA, BS, BFA, AA, AS
- **Mean SAT:** 412v, 464m, **Mean ACT:** 17.1
- **Student-faculty ratio:** 22 to 1
- **Calendar system:** Semester

A public university established in 1955. 355-acre suburban campus. Airport, bus station.

Academic Character NASC accreditation. Semester system, 2 5-week summer terms, January mini-term. 3 majors offered by the College of Allied Health Professions, 19 by the College of Arts & Letters, 6 by the College of Business & Economics, 4 by the College of Education, 1 by the College of Hotel Administration, and 8 by the College of Science, Mathematics, & Engineering. Self-designed majors. Minors in 6 areas. Masters degrees granted. Limited pass/fail, internships, credit by exam. Preprofessional programs in dentistry, medicine, veterinary medicine. Study abroad. Elementary, secondary, and special education certification. ROTC. Computer center. Environmental Protection Agency Monitoring and Support Lab. Desert Research Institute. 750,000-volume library.

Financial ACT FAS. University scholarships, loans; PELL, SEOG, BIA, NDSL, GSL, NSL, CWS. Application deadline April 1.

Admissions High school graduation with 2.3 GPA required. ACT or SAT required. $5 application fee. Rolling admissions; application deadline one week before start of classes. *Early Decision* and *Concurrent Enrollment* programs. Transfers accepted. Credit possible for CEEB AP and CLEP exams. Acceptance on probation possible for students not normally admissible.

Student Life Student government. Newspaper, radio station. Music, film, and drama groups. Academic, ethnic, political, service, and special interest groups. 7 fraternities and 2 sororities. Single-sex dorms & one coed dorm; some have air-conditioning. No married-student housing. 2% of students live on campus. Liquor restrictions. 10 intercollegiate sports for men, 5 for women; intramurals. NCAA, PCAA. Student body composition: 2% Asian, 5.6% Black, 3% Hispanic, 0.4% Native American, 87.1% White. 14% from out of state.

NEVADA, UNIVERSITY OF, RENO $

Reno 89557, (702) 784-6865
Director of Admissions: Jack H. Shirley

- **Undergraduates:** 3,732m, 3,443w
- **Tuition (1984–1985):** $1,080 (in-state), $3,280 (out-of-state)
- **Room and Board (1984–1985):** $2,064–$2,624

- **Degrees offered:** BA, BS, BACriminal Justice, BAEcon, BAJournalism, BSBA, BSEng, AS English
- **Mean SAT:** 437v, 485m,   **Mean ACT:** 19.7
- **Student-faculty ratio:** 22 to 1
- **Calendar system:** Semester

A public university established in 1874. 195-acre hillside campus overlooking the cities of Reno and Sparks. Served by air, rail, and bus.

Academic Character NASC and professional accreditation. Semester system, 2 5-week summer terms, 3-week minisession. 16 majors offered by the College of Agriculture, 32 by the College of Arts & Sciences, 9 by the College of Business Administration, 25 by the College of Education, 4 by the College of Engineering, 6 by the College of Home Economics, 2 by the College of Medical Sciences, 7 by the College of Mines, and 1 by the School of Nursing. Special majors. Minors offered in many fields. Distributive requirements. Independent study. Honors program. Pass/fail, internships, credit by exam. Preprofessional programs in dentistry, law, medicine, pharmacy, physical therapy. National Student Exchange program. Study abroad. Congressional Intern Program. Elementary, secondary, and special education certification. ROTC. Planetarium. Desert Research Institute. Seismological lab. 705,533-volume libraries with microform resources.

Financial ACT FAS. University scholarships, grants, loans, agricultural & home economics loans, payment plan; PELL, SEOG, NDSL, FISL, NSL, CWS.

Admissions High school graduation with 2.3 GPA required; Nevada residents with 2.0 admitted on probation. ACT required; SAT may be substituted. $5 application fee. Rolling admissions. *Early Decision, Early Admission, Concurrent Enrollment* programs. Transfers accepted. Credit possible for CEEB AP, CLEP, ACT PEP, and departmental exams.

Student Life Associated Students. Newspaper, literary magazine, yearbook, radio station. Music and drama groups. Debate. Academic, honorary, and special interest groups. 7 fraternities and 5 sororities with houses. 10% of men and 13% of women join. Coed and single-sex dorms. Special interest wings. Married-student housing. 11% of students live on campus. Liquor prohibited for students under 21. 9 intercollegiate sports for men, 7 for women; many intramurals. NCAA, Big Sky Conference. Student body composition: 2% Asian, 2% Black, 2% Hispanic, 1% Native American, 90% White, 3% Other. 12% from out of state.

New Hampshire

COLBY-SAWYER COLLEGE $$

New London 03257, (603) 526-2010
Dean of Admissions & Financial Aid: Peter R. Dietrich

- **Undergraduates:** 550w
- **Tuition, Room and Board (1984–1985):** $10,740
- **Degrees offered:** BA, BFA, BS, BSN, AA, AS
- **Mean SAT:** 450v, 450m
- **Student-faculty ratio:** 11 to 1
- **Calendar system:** 4–1–4

A private women's liberal arts college established in 1837 in rural New London. 40-acre campus 100 miles from Boston. Bus service; airport 30 minutes away in Lebanon.
Academic Character NEASC and professional accreditation. 4-1-4 system. Majors offered in American studies, art, biology, business administration, child study, health records administration, medical technology, nursing, orthoptics, and theatre (acting, dancing, design). Self-designed majors. Courses offered in 13 additional areas. Associate degrees in liberal arts, recreation leadership, administrative services, and science-medical fields. Distributive requirements. Independent study. Phi Beta Kappa. Pass/fail, internships. Consortium with other New Hampshire colleges. Study abroad. Pre-school and kindergarten education certification. 60,000-volume library with microform resources.
Financial CEEB CSS. College scholarships, loans, grants, payment plan; PELL, SEOG, NDSL, GSL, CWS. Preferred application deadline February 15.
Admissions High school graduation with 15 units required. GED accepted. Interview recommended. SAT or ACT required. $25 application fee. Rolling admissions; suggest applying by January 1. *Early Decision, Early Admission* programs. Admission deferral possible. Transfers accepted. Credit possible for CEEB AP and CLEP exams, and for professional experience. College has own placement program.
Student Life Student government. Newspaper, magazine, yearbook. Music, drama, dance, art, athletic, outing, religious, academic, special interest groups. 98% of students live on campus. Women's dorms. 4 semesters of phys ed required. 8 intercollegiate sports, 13 intramural sports. AIAW, EIAW. Student body composition: 93% White, 7% Other. 84% from out of state.

DARTMOUTH COLLEGE $$$

Hanover 03755, (603) 646-1110
Director of Admissions: Alfred T. Quirk

- **Undergraduates:** 2,400m, 1,700w
- **Tuition (1984–1985):** $9,810
- **Room and Board (1984–1985):** $3,837
- **Degrees offered:** AB, BSE
- **Mean SAT:** 610v, 660m

- **Student-faculty ratio:** 12 to 1
- **Calendar system:** Quarter

A private college established in 1769, became coed in 1972. 175-acre small-town campus on the Connecticut River. Bus service; airport and rail station nearby.

Academic Character NEASC and professional accreditation. Year-round system of four 10-week terms. Freshmen attend fall/winter/spring. Students plan their own enrollment patterns, usually including 11 study terms, with 1 summer & 6 on-campus terms required. Majors offered in anthropology, art, Asian studies, biochemistry, biology, chemistry, classics, comparative literature, drama, earth sciences, economics, education, engineering sciences, English, French, geography, German, government, history, Italian, mathematics, math & social sciences, music, philosophy, physics/astronomy, policy studies, psychology, religion, Russian, sociology, and Spanish. Special majors. Interdisciplinary programs. Distributive requirements. Graduate and professional degrees granted. Independent study, honors programs, Phi Beta Kappa, pass/fail and non-recording option. Extensive internship program. Combined programs with graduate schools of business, engineering, and medicine. 12-college exchange, exchange with UCalifornia San Diego and other schools. Numerous language and other study abroad programs. Elementary and secondary education certification. ROTC at Norwich U. Public Affairs Center. Computer center, observatory. Over 1,500,000-volume library with microform resources.

Financial CEEB CSS. College scholarships, grants, loans, payment plans; PELL, SEOG, NDSL, GSL, CWS. Application deadline January 15.

Admissions High school graduation with strong college prep program recommended. SAT and 3 ACH required. Alumni interview in applicant's home area required. $30 application fee. Application deadline January 1. *Early Decision* Program. Transfers not accepted. Credit possible for CEEB AP, ACH, and college exams. Intensive Academic Support/Equal Opportunity Programs.

Student Life Student government. Newspapers, magazines, yearbook, radio station. Several music and drama groups, film society, intercollegiate debate. Outing club. Academic, ethnic, honorary, political, professional, religious, service, women's, and special interest groups. 22 fraternities (4 coed) with houses, and 4 sororities, 1 with house. 50% of students join. Freshmen must live on campus. Coed and single-sex dorms. Apartment, language, and married-student housing. 92% of students live on campus. No cars for 1st- and 2nd-term freshmen. Honor code. 3 terms of phys ed required. 15 intercollegiate sports for men, 14 for women, and 3 coed; several intramural and club sports. EAIAW, NCAA, ECAC, Ivy League. Student body composition: 1.1% Asian, 7.5% Black, 0.5% Hispanic, 0.9% Native American, 87.2% White, 2.8% Other. 95% from out of state.

NEW HAMPSHIRE, UNIVERSITY OF $/$$

Durham 03824, (603) 862-1360
Director of Admissions: Stanwood C. Fish

- **Undergraduates:** 4,233m, 5,198w
- **Tuition (1984–1985):** $2,080 (in-state), $5,650 (out-of-state)
- **Room and Board (1984–1985):** $2,246–$2,602; **Fees:** $276
- **Degrees offered:** BA, BS, BFA, BMus, AA, AAS

- **Mean SAT:** 487v, 547m
- **Student-faculty ratio:** 16 to 1
- **Calendar system:** Semester

A public university established in 1866. 188-acre rural campus in Durham, 15 miles from the seacoast and 50 miles north of Boston.

Academic Character NEASC and professional accreditation. Semester system, summer terms. 29 majors offered by the College of Liberal Arts, 18 by the College of Life Sciences & Agriculture, 20 by the College of Engineering & Physical Sciences, 3 by the Whittemore School of Business & Economics, and 7 by the School of Health Studies. University also contains Thompson School of Applied Science and Graduate School. Self-designed and interdepartmental majors. Minors offered. Associate degrees available in 17 areas. Distributive requirements. Graduate degrees granted. Independent study. Honors program. Phi Beta Kappa. Pass/fail, internships. Preprofessional programs in law, medicine, dentistry, optometry, osteopathy, podiatry, pharmacy, physician assistant. 4-year program leads to BS/MT; 5-year programs lead to BA/MBA, BS/MBA, BA/ME, BS/ME. New Hampshire College and University Council exchange program. New England Regional Student Program. California Exchange Program. Study abroad. Elementary and secondary education certification. AFROTC, ROTC. Computer center, language lab. 813,785-volume library with microform resources.

Financial CEEB CSS. University scholarships, grants, loans; PELL, SEOG, NDSL, CWS. Application deadline February 1.

Admissions High school graduation with 16 units required. SAT required. Application fees $10 (in-state), $25 (out-of-state). Application deadline February 1 (March 1 for transfers). $100 (in-state), $300 (out-of-state) tuition deposit required on acceptance of offer of admission; $50 room deposit required with housing application. *Early Decision* Program. Admission deferral possible. Transfers accepted. Credit possible for CEEB AP exams.

Student Life Student government. Newspaper, yearbook, TV and radio stations. Music, drama, cultural, political, academic, honorary, international, women's, religious, service, and special interest groups. 12 fraternities and 5 sororities, all with houses. 8% of men and 4% of women join. Dorms and dining halls. Limited married-student housing. 43% of students live on campus. Freshmen and sophomores may not have cars on campus without permission. 16 intercollegiate sports for men, 10 for women; many intramural sports. NCAA, Yankee Athletic Conference, ECAC. Student body composition: 0.3% Asian, 0.3% Black, 0.3% Hispanic, 0.2% Native American, 98.1% White, 0.7% Other. 30% from out of state.

NEW HAMPSHIRE COLLEGE $$

2500 North River Road, Manchester 03104, (603) 668-2211
Director of Admissions: Michael L. DeBlasi

- **Undergraduates:** 936m, 778w
- **Tuition (1984–1985):** $6,237
- **Room and Board (1984–1985):** $3,447;   **Fees:** $60
- **Degrees offered:** BS, AS
- **Mean SAT:** 410v, 470m
- **Student-faculty ratio:** 20 to 1
- **Calendar system:** Semester

A private college established in 1932. 700-acre dual-site campus located on the outskirts of Manchester, 50 miles north of Boston. Air and bus service.

Academic Character NEASC accreditation. Semester system, 2 5-week summer terms. Majors offered in accounting, business communications, business/distributive teacher education, economics/finance, hotel/restaurant management, human services, management, management advisory systems, management information systems, marketing, office administration, and retailing. Techni-business major for transfers with non-business associate degrees to earn a BBus. Associate degrees offered in accounting, administrative assistant/word processing specialist, electronic data processing, executive secretarial, fashion merchandising, general studies, legal secretarial, and management. Courses in English, fine art, government, history, math, philosophy, psychology, science. Masters degrees granted; evening MBA program. Independent study. Cooperative work/study, pass/fail, internships. New Hampshire College and University Council exchange program. Secondary education certification. AFROTC at U of Lowell; ROTC at U of New Hampshire. Continuing education program at 10 locations in NH, Maine, and Puerto Rico, with enrollment over 4,000. Computer center. Language lab. Over 67,000-volume library with microform resources.

Financial CEEB. CSS. College scholarships, state grants; PELL, SEOG, NDSL, GSL, CWS. Application deadline March 15.

Admissions High school graduation required. GED accepted. Interview recommended. SAT required. Rolling admissions; suggest applying by March 1. $100 room and $100 tuition deposits required on acceptance of offer of admission. *Early Entrance* Program. Admission deferral possible. Transfers accepted. Credit possible for CEEB AP, CLEP and ACT PEP exams; departmental testing for placement. Freshman Entrance Program for underprepared students; students complete a 3-course summer program before admission to regular degree program.

Student Life Student government. Newspaper, yearbook, radio station. Religious, outing, honorary, academic, and special interest groups. 3 fraternities and 3 sororities, without houses. Students must live on campus or at home. Coed and single-sex dorms; apartments and townhouses. No married-student housing. 80% of students live on campus. Class attendance required. 6 intercollegiate sports for men, 5 for women; 17 intramural sports for men & women. AIAW, ECAC, NAIA, NCAA, NECAC. Student body composition: 1% Asian, 5% Black, 90% White, 4% Other. 75% from out of state.

ST. ANSELM COLLEGE $$

Manchester 03102, (603) 669-1030
Director of Admissions: Donald E. Healy

- **Undergraduates:** 800m, 800w
- **Tuition (1984–1985):** $5,600
- **Room and Board (1984–1985):** $2,900
- **Degrees offered:** BA, BSN
- **Mean SAT:** 480v, 520m
- **Student-faculty ratio:** 13 to 1
- **Calendar system:** Semester

A private Roman Catholic college founded in 1889 by the Benedictines of St. Mary's Abbey. 300-acre suburban campus in Manchester, 50 miles north of Boston. Airport, bus station.

Academic Character NEASC and professional accreditation. Semester system, 2-, 3- and 2 4-week summer terms. Majors offered in biology, business, chemistry, classical languages, computer science, criminal justice, economics, English, French, history, math, natural science, nursing, philosophy, politics, psychology, sociology, Spanish, and theology. Combined and interdisciplinary studies. Soviet Studies Program. AS in criminal justice. Distributive requirements. 3 theology courses required of Catholic students. Independent study, internships. Preprofessional programs in dentistry, engineering, law, medicine, theology. Member of New Hampshire College and University Council. Study abroad. Secondary education certification. ROTC & AFROTC at U of New Hampshire and U of Lowell. 145,000-volume library with microform resources.

Financial CEEB CSS. College scholarships, grants, loan;. PELL, SEOG, NSS, NDSL, GSL, NSL, CWS. Application deadline April 15.

Admissions High school graduation with 16 units required. Interview recommended. SAT required. $15 application fee. Application deadline February 15 for nursing program. Rolling admissions. $100 tuition deposit required on acceptance of offer of admission. *Early Decision* and *Early Entrance* programs. Admission deferral possible. Transfers accepted. Credit possible for CEEB AP and CLEP exams.

Student Life Student government. Newspaper, periodical. Debate, drama, political, academic, honorary, religious, service, and special interest groups. Freshmen and sophomores must live on campus or at home. 11 single-sex dorms. No married-student housing. 65% of students live on campus. Class attendance expected. 8 intercollegiate sports for men, 6 for women; 3 club sports and several intramurals. NCAA, ECAC, AIAW. Student body composition: 1% Black, 1% Hispanic, 97% White, 1% Other. 83% from out of state.

New Jersey

DREW UNIVERSITY $$$

Madison 07940, (201) 377-3000
Director of Admissions: Daniel R. Boyer

- **Undergraduates:** 592m, 887w
- **Tuition (1984–1985):** $8,200
- **Room and Board (1984–1985):** $2,804;   **Fees:** $685
- **Degrees offered:** BA
- **Mean SAT:** 535v, 553m
- **Student-faculty ratio:** 15 to 1
- **Calendar system:** 4–1–4

A private university established in 1866. 186-acre suburban-rural campus located in Madison, 27 miles from New York City. Served by train. Airport and bus station in New York City.

Academic Character MSACS accreditation. 4-1-4 system, 6-week summer term. Majors offered in anthropology, art, behavioral science, biology, botany, chemistry, classics, economics, English, French, German, history, mathematics, music, philosophy, physics, political science, psychobiology, psychology, religion, Russian, Russian studies, sociology, Spanish, theatre arts, zoology. Special, double, self-designed majors. Distributives and senior comprehensive project required. Graduate and professional degrees granted. Independent study. Honors program. Phi Beta Kappa. Cooperative work/study, pass/fail, internships. 3-2 program in engineering and technology with Georgia Tech, Washington U. 5-year forestry, environmental management program with Duke. Study abroad. Marine biology semester. Washington, London, Brussels, UN semesters. New York art semester. Elementary and secondary education certification with College of St. Elizabeth. Computer center, language lab, instructional services center. 440,000-volume library.

Financial CEEB CSS. University scholarships, loans, Methodist scholarships and loans, payment plans; PELL, SEOG, NDSL, CWS. Application deadline March 1.

Admissions High school graduation with 16 units required. Interview encouraged. SAT or ACT required. $20 application fee. Application deadline March 1. $300 deposit required on acceptance of offer of admission. *Early Decision, Early Admission* programs. Admission deferral possible. Transfers accepted. Credit possible for CEEB AP and CLEP exams. EOF Program.

Student Life Student government. Newspaper, magazine, yearbook, radio station. Music, debate, drama groups. Women's Resource Center. Minority, international students' organizations. Religious, honorary, special interest groups. Students must live at home or on campus. Coed and single-sex dorms. No married-student housing. 90% of students live on campus. Only seniors and commuters may have cars. 7 intercollegiate sports for men, 6 for women; intramural and club sports. AIAW, ECAC, NCAA, Mid-Atlantic Conference. Student body composition: 1.4% Asian, 4.5% Black, 1.5% Foreign, 2.7% Hispanic, 89.8% White, 1.9% Other. 50% from out of state.

MONMOUTH COLLEGE $$

West Long Branch 07764, (201) 222-6600
Director of Admissions: Robert N. Cristadoro

- **Undergraduates:** 882m, 919w
- **Tuition (1984–1985):** $5,660
- **Room and Board (1984–1985):** $2,508–$3,248 **Fees:** $220
- **Degrees offered:** BA, BS, BSN, BFA, BSW
- **Mean SAT:** 443v, 482m
- **Student-faculty ratio:** 14 to 1
- **Calendar system:** Semester

A private college established in 1933. 125-acre campus in West Long Branch, 50 miles from New York City. Served by rail and bus.
Academic Character MSACS and professional accreditation. Semester system, 7 summer terms. 51 majors offered in the areas of business, humanities, art, education, sciences, communication, media studies, and music. Interdisciplinary study. Distributive requirements. Masters degrees granted. Independent study. Honors program. Internships, cooperative work/study. Preprofessional programs in dentistry, law, medicine, veterinary science. Study abroad. Elementary and secondary education certification. ROTC, AFROTC. Language and computer labs. 229,000-volume library.
Financial CEEB CSS. College scholarships, grants, and loans, payment plans; PELL, SEOG, NDSL, GSL, CWS. Application deadline March 1.
Admissions High school graduation with 16 units required. Interview encouraged. SAT required. $20 application fee. Rolling admissions; suggest applying early in 12th year. $100 tuition and $150 room deposits required on acceptance of offer of admission. *Early Admission, Credit in Escrow* programs. Admission deferral possible. Transfers accepted. Credit possible for CEEB AP and CLEP exams; college has own advanced placement program. Educational Opportunity Program.
Student Life Student government. Newspaper, magazine, yearbook, radio station. Music groups. Black Student Union. Academic, honorary, religious, service, and special interest groups. 6 fraternities, 3 with houses, and 4 sororities, some with houses. 15% of men and 5% of women join. Single freshmen under 21 must live at home or on campus. Coed and single-sex dorms. No married-student housing. 35% of students live on campus. 2 hours of phys ed required. 10 intercollegiate sports for men, 9 for women; intramurals. AIAW, NAIA, NCAA. Student body composition: 2% Asian, 3% Black, 2% Hispanic, 92% White, 1% Other. 11% from out of state.

NEW JERSEY INSTITUTE OF TECHNOLOGY $

Newark 07102, (201) 645-5321
Director of Admissions: Neil Holtzman

- **Undergraduates:** 4,518m, 664w
- **Tuition (1984–1985):** $1,596 (in-state), $2,720 (out-of-state)
- **Room and Board (1984–1985):** $2,900; **Fees:** $340
- **Degrees offered:** BS, BArch
- **Mean SAT:** 456v, 591m
- **Student-faculty ratio:** 17 to 1
- **Calendar system:** Semester

A public institute established in 1881. 25-acre urban campus in Newark, less than an hour from New York City. Airport, rail and bus stations.

Academic Character MSACS and professional accreditation. Semester system, 10- to 15-week summer term. Majors offered in architecture, computer science, engineering science, engineering technology, industrial administration, man & technology, surveying, and chemical, civil, electrical, industrial, and mechanical engineering. MS, DEngSci granted. Independent study. Honors program. Cooperative work/study. Cross-registration with Rutgers-Newark, Essex County College, New Jersey College of Medicine and Dentistry. ROTC, AFROTC. Computer center. 127,000-volume library.

Financial CEEB CSS. Institute scholarships, grants, and loans, payment plan; PELL, SEOG, NDSL, CWS. Scholarship application deadline March 1.

Admissions High school graduation with 16 units required. GED accepted. Interview may be required. SAT required; ACH required for some majors. $10 application fee. Rolling admissions; suggest applying by March 1. $50 deposit ($100 for out-of-state students) required on acceptance of offer of admission. *Early Admission* Program. Admission deferral possible. Transfers accepted. Credit possible for CEEB AP and CLEP exams; institute has own advanced placement program. Educational Opportunity Program.

Student Life Student government. Newspaper, magazine, yearbook. Debate, drama groups. Society of Women Engineers. Honorary, professional, and special interest groups. 13 fraternities. Coed dorms house 210 students. Cafeteria. 9% of students live on campus. Freshmen must attend class. 2 semesters of phys ed required. 19 intercollegiate sports; intramurals. NCAA. Student body composition: 7% Black, 5% Hispanic, 83% White, 5% Other. 3% from out of state.

PRINCETON UNIVERSITY $$$

Princeton 08544, (609) 452-3060
Dean of Admissions: James W. Wickenden

- **Undergraduates:** 2,868m, 1,656w
- **Tuition (1984–1985):** $10,200
- **Room and Board (1984–1985):** $3,730
- **Degrees offered:** AB, BSE
- **Mean SAT:** 649v, 695m
- **Student-faculty ratio:** 7 to 1
- **Calendar system:** Semester

A private university established in 1746, became coed in 1969. 2,200-acre campus in the small city of Princeton, 50 miles from New York City, 45 miles from Philadelphia. Served by rail and bus.

Academic Character MSACS and professional accreditation. Semester system. 42 majors offered in the areas of science, social science, arts & letters, and in history, philosophy, religion; 11 engineering majors. Self-designed majors. Senior comprehensive exam and thesis required. Graduate and professional degrees granted. Woodrow Wilson School of Public and International Affairs admits students in junior year. Independent study. Honors program. Phi Beta Kappa. Limited pass/fail. Study abroad. ROTC; AFROTC. Secondary education certification. Computer center, language lab. 3,000,000-volume library with microform resources.

Financial CEEB CSS. Scholarships, grants, and loans, payment plan; PELL, SEOG, NDSL, FISL, PLUS, CWS. Application deadline January 10.

Admissions High school graduation with 16 units required. SAT and 3 ACH required. $35 application fee. Application deadline January 1. *Early Decision* Program. Admission deferral possible. Transfers accepted for September admission. Credit possible for CEEB AP exams; university has own advanced placement program.

Student Life Student government. Newspaper, magazines, yearbook. Music, drama groups. Religious, service, and special interest groups. Upperclass eating clubs. Residential colleges. Freshmen and sophomores must live on campus. Coed and single-sex dorms. 98% of students live on campus. Games required for freshmen. 17 intercollegiate sports for men, 13 for women; intramurals. Student body composition: 3.2% Asian, 7.5% Black, 4.4% Hispanic, 0.3% Native American, 84.6% White. 87% from out of state.

RUTGERS UNIVERSITY/DOUGLASS COLLEGE $

New Brunswick 08903, (201) 932-3770
University Director of Undergraduate Admissions: Natalie Aharonian

- **Undergraduates:** 3,428w
- **Tuition (1984–1985):** $1,520 (in-state), $3,040 (out-of-state), $1,602 (in-state pharmacy and engineering), $3,204 (out-of-state pharmacy and engineering)
- **Room and Board (1984–1985):** $2,498
- **Degrees offered:** BA, BS
- **Mean SAT:** 490v, 520m
- **Student-faculty ratio:** 17 to 1
- **Calendar system:** Semester

An undergraduate women's college of a public university, established in 1918. Suburban campus on the edge of New Brunswick, 33 miles from New York City. Served by rail and bus.

Academic Character MSACS and professional accreditation. Semester system, 3 4-week summer terms. 60 majors offered in the areas of cultural & area studies, political & social sciences, arts, archaeology, sciences, business, languages & literature, ecology, humanities, communication, physical education, and mathematics. Special programs in education. Distributive requirements. Independent study. Honors program, Phi Beta Kappa. Pass/fail, internships. Preprofessional programs in dentistry, law, medicine. 2-3 program with College of Engineering. 3-1 program in medical technology. Students may take courses at other New Brunswick colleges. Study abroad. ROTC, AFROTC. Several education certification programs. 2,580,000-volume university library.

Financial CEEB CSS. College and state scholarships, grants, loans; PELL, SEOG, NDSL, GSL, CWS. FAF deadline March 1.

Admissions High school graduation with 16 units required. SAT required. $15 application fee ($20 for 2 Rutgers colleges, $25 for 3). Rolling admissions; application deadline February 1. *Early Decision* and *Early Admission* programs. Admission deferral possible. Transfers accepted. Credit possible for CEEB AP and CLEP exams; college has own advanced placement program. Educational Opportunity Program.

Student Life Student government. Newspaper, magazine, yearbook, radio station. Music and drama groups. Black Students Congress. United Puerto Rican Students. Sophia group for women out of school 4 or more years. Several academic, religious, service, political, and special interest groups. Sororities at other university colleges. Freshmen must live at home or on campus. Language houses. Afro-American, Puerto Rican houses. 62% of students live on campus. Only commuters and seniors may have cars on campus. 13 intercollegiate sports; intramurals. AIAW, NCAA. Student body composition: 2% Asian, 10% Black, 3% Hispanic, 83% White, 1% Other. 6% from out of state.

RUTGERS UNIVERSITY/RUTGERS COLLEGE $

New Brunswick 08903, (201) 932-3770
University Director of Undergraduate Admissions: Natalie Aharonian

- **Undergraduates:** 4,260m, 3,797w
- **Tuition (1984–1985):** $1,520 (in-state), $3,040 (out-of-state), $1,602 (in-state pharmacy and engineering), $3,204 (out-of-state pharmacy and engineering)
- **Room and Board (1984–1985):** $2,498
- **Degrees offered:** BA, BS
- **Mean SAT:** 510v, 570m
- **Student-faculty ratio:** 17 to 1
- **Calendar system:** Semester

An undergraduate college of a public university, established in 1766, became coed in 1972. Campus in and around New Brunswick, 33 miles from New York City. Served by rail and bus.

Academic Character MSACS and professional accreditation. Semester system, 3 4-week summer terms. 56 majors offered in the areas of cultural & area studies, social & political sciences, arts, natural sciences, business, languages & literatures, humanities, and communication. Self-designed majors. Minor required; double major and additional minors encouraged. Distributive requirements. Independent study. Honors programs, Phi Beta Kappa. Pass/fail. Preprofessional programs in dentistry, law, library & information studies, medicine, social work. 2-3 engineering program with College of Engineering. National Student Exchange. Study abroad. Elementary, secondary, and special education certification. ROTC, AFROTC. Language lab. 2,580,000-volume university library.

Financial CEEB CSS. College and state scholarships, grants, loans; PELL, SEOG, NDSL, GSL, CWS. FAF deadline March 1.

Admissions High school graduation with 16 units required. SAT required. $15 application fee ($20 for 2 Rutgers colleges, $25 for 3). Rolling admissions; application deadline February 1. *Early Decision* and *Early Admission* programs. Admission deferral possible. Transfers accepted. Credit possible for CEEB AP and CLEP exams; college has own advanced placement program. Educational Opportunity Program.

Student Life Student government. Newspaper, magazine, yearbook, radio station. Music, drama, debate groups. Honorary, academic, professional, religious, and special interest groups. 27 fraternities and 10 sororities. 10% of students join. Coed and single-sex dorms. Special interest housing. Married-student housing. 54% of students live on campus. 14 intercollegiate sports for men, 13 for women; intramural and club sports. NCAA, AIAW, Eastern Eight. Student body composition: 3% Asian, 8% Black, 4% Hispanic, 83% White, 1% Other. 8% from out of state.

SETON HALL UNIVERSITY $

South Orange 07079, (201) 761-9332
Director of Admissions: Lee W. Cooke

- **Undergraduates:** 2,848m, 3,161w
- **Tuition (1984–1985):** $4,570
- **Room and Board (1984–1985):** $2,792; **Fees:** $200
- **Degrees offered:** BA, BS, BSN, BSMed Tech
- **Mean SAT:** 438v, 466m
- **Student-faculty ratio:** 17 to 1
- **Calendar system:** Semester

A private Roman Catholic university controlled by the Archdiocese of Newark, established in 1856, became coed in 1968. 56-acre campus in the village of South Orange, 14 miles from New York City. Served by bus and rail.

Academic Character MSACS and professional accreditation. Semester system, 2 4-week summer terms, 3-week May term. 39 majors offered in the areas of business, cultural studies, social & political sciences, arts, natural sciences, communication, education, health, and humanities. Distributive requirements. Religious studies required for Catholic students. Graduate and professional degrees granted. Independent study. Honors program in College of Arts and Sciences. Internships. Study abroad. Elementary, secondary, and special education certification. ROTC; AFROTC at NJ Tech. Computer center, art gallery, language lab. 325,000-volume library with microform resources.

Financial CEEB CSS. University scholarships, grants, loans, athletic & debate scholarships, state scholarships, payment plan; PELL, SEOG, NSS, NDSL, NSL, CWS. Scholarship application deadline April 15.

Admissions High school graduation with 16 units required. SAT or ACT required. $25 application fee. Rolling admissions; preferred application deadline March 1. $100 deposit required on acceptance of offer of admission. *Early Admission* Program. Admission deferral possible. Transfers accepted. Credit possible for CEEB AP and CLEP exams. Educational Opportunity Program.

Student Life Student government. Newspaper, magazine, yearbook, radio station, TV studios. Music, debate, drama groups. Black Studies Center. Puerto Rican Institute. Honorary, professional, religious, academic, and special interest organizations. 10 fraternities and 5 sororities. Coed dorms. No married-student housing. 22% of students live on campus. 11 intercollegiate sports for men, 6 for women; intramural and club sports. AIAW, ECAC, NCAA. Student body composition: 1% Asian, 13% Black, 3% Hispanic, 82% White, 1% Other. 10% from out of state.

STEVENS INSTITUTE OF TECHNOLOGY $$$

Hoboken 07030, (201) 420-5194
Director of Admissions: Robert H. Seavy

- **Undergraduates:** 1,355m, 250w
- **Tuition (1984–1985):** $8,000
- **Room and Board (1984–1985):** $3,350; **Fees:** $100
- **Degrees offered:** BS, BSE
- **Mean SAT:** 520v, 630m
- **Student-faculty ratio:** 10 to 1
- **Calendar system:** Semester

A private institute established in 1870. 55-acre suburban campus in Hoboken, across the Hudson River from New York City. Airport, bus and rail stations in New York City.

Academic Character MSACS and professional accreditation. Semester system, 6-week summer term. Majors offered in applied psychology, biology, chemical engineering, chemistry, civil engineering, computer science, electrical engineering, engineering, engineering physics, industrial engineering, management science, materials/metallurgical engineering, materials science, mathematics, mechanical engineering, ocean engineering, and physics. Distributive requirements. MS, MEng, PhD granted. Independent study. Honors program. Pass/fail, internships, credit by exam. Dual degree programs. Mini-graduate program. ROTC at St. Peter's; AFROTC at NJ Tech. Computer center, hydrodynamics lab, psychology lab, energy center. 190,000-volume library.

Financial CEEB CSS. Institute scholarships and loans, payment plan; PELL, SEOG, NDSL, GSL, CWS. Application deadline February 1.

Admissions High school graduation with 12 units required. Interview encouraged. SAT and 3 ACH required. $25 application fee. Rolling admissions; suggest applying late in 11th year or early in 12th. $100 tuition and $100 room deposits required on acceptance of offer of admission. *Early Decision* Program. Admission deferral possible. Transfers accepted. Credit possible for CEEB AP and CLEP exams; institute has own advanced placement program.

Student Life Student government. Newspaper, yearbook, radio station. Music and drama groups. Black Student Union, Latin American Club, Chinese Association, India Student Association. Honorary, political, religious, and special interest organizations. 10 fraternities with houses, and 1 sorority with rooms. 35% of students join. Freshmen must live at home or on campus. Single-sex dorms. Married-student housing. 80% of students live on campus. 3 hours of phys ed a week for 3 years required. 12 intercollegiate sports for men, 3 for women; intramurals. AIAW, ECAC, NCAA. Student body composition: 3.8% Asian, 2.8% Black, 5.2% Hispanic, 84% White. 40% from out of state.

New Mexico

NEW MEXICO INSTITUTE OF MINING AND TECHNOLOGY $

Socorro 87801, (506) 835-5424
Director of Admissions: Louise E. Chamberlin

- **Undergraduates:** 698m, 257w
- **Tuition (1984–1985):** $421.20 (In-state), $2,210.40 (out-of-state)
- **Room and Board (1984–1985):** $2,470;   **Fees:** $257
- **Degrees offered:** BA, BS, BGS, AGS
- **Mean ACT:** 25.4
- **Student-faculty ratio:** 15 to 1
- **Calendar system:** Semester

A public institute established in 1889. 320-acre campus (with 7,000 additional acres for research) in a small city in the Rio Grande Valley, 75 miles south of Albuquerque. Served by bus.

Academic Character NCACS and professional accreditation. Semester system, 8-week summer term. Majors offered in basic sciences, biology, chemistry, computer science, general studies, geology, geophysics, history, mathematics, medical technology, physics, psychology, social science, and in environmental, geological, material, metallurgical, mining, and petroleum engineering. Distributive requirements. Independent study. On-site mining experience possible. Cooperative work/study, limited pass/fail. Preprofessional programs in dentistry, law, medical technology, medicine, nursing, optometry, physical therapy, pharmacy, veterinary science. 3-2 programs with Reed and SUNY College at New Paltz. WICHE Program. Secondary education certification. Computer center. Observatory. Mineral museum. Scanning electron microscope facility. 90,000-volume library with microform resources.

Financial CEEB CSS and ACT FAS. Institute scholarships, grants, loans, state loans; PELL, SEOG, SSIG, NDSL, FISL, GSL, CWS, honors work program, industrial work/study program.

Admissions High school graduation with 15 units required. Open admission to students with appropriate secondary school background, 2.0 GPA, and ACT 19 composite. GED accepted. Interview recommended. ACT required. $10 application fee. Rolling admissions. $50 tuition and $55 room deposits due on acceptance of admissions offer. *Early Admission* Program. Transfers accepted. Credit possible for CEEB AP exams; institute has own advanced placement program.

Student Life Student government. Newspaper. Music and drama groups. Professional, community, and special interest groups. Coed and single-sex dorms. Married-student housing. 47% of students live on campus. Liquor prohibited. Informal club sports with area schools; intramurals. Student body composition: 2% Asian, 1% Black, 8% Hispanic, 1% Native American, 83% White, 5% Other. 27% from out of state.

NEW MEXICO, UNIVERSITY OF $

Albuquerque 87131, (505) 277-0111
Dean of Admissions & Records: Robert M. Weaver

- **Undergraduates:** 9,424m, 10,173w
- **Tuition** (1984–1985): $818 (in-state), $2,786 (out-of-state)
- **Room and Board** (1984–1985): $2,175
- **Degrees offered:** BA, BS, BBA, BAS, BFA
- **Mean ACT:** 19.7
- **Student-faculty ratio:** 21 to 1
- **Calendar system:** Semester

A public university established in 1889. 600-acre campus overlooking the Rio Grande River. Served by air, rail, and bus.

Academic Character NCACS and professional accreditation. Semester system, 8-week summer term. 36 majors offered by the College of Arts & Sciences, 22 by the College of Education, 6 by the College of Engineering, 7 by the College of Fine Arts, 1 by the College of Nursing, 3 by the College of Pharmacy, 2 by the School of Architecture & Planning, and 8 by the School of Management. All freshmen enroll in University College. Sophomores enroll in other Colleges. Juniors select major/minor, 2 majors, or a special curriculum. Graduate degrees granted. Independent study. Honors programs. Phi Beta Kappa. Cooperative work/study, limited pass/fail, credit by exam. Preprofessional programs in dentistry, forestry, medicine. Programs in physical therapy and medical technology with area hospitals. 3-2 business-economics program. Elementary, secondary, and special education certification. ROTC, NROTC. Anthropological, art, biological, geological museums. Computer center. 1,043,936-volume library with microform resources.

Financial CEEB CSS. University scholarships, grants, loans; PELL, SEOG, NSS, NDSL, FISL, NSL, CWS. Application deadline March 1.

Admissions High school graduation with 13 units required. ACT required. $15 application fee. Rolling admissions. $25 room deposit due on acceptance of admissions offer. *Early Admission* and *Early Decision* programs. Transfers accepted. Credit possible for CEEB AP and CLEP exams.

Student Life Student government. Newspaper, literary magazine. Music and theatre groups. Women's Center. Academic, ethnic, honorary, religious, service, and special interest groups. 9 fraternities and 8 sororities, all with houses. 5% of men and 4% of women join. Coed and single-sex dorms. Limited married-student housing. 9% of students live on campus. Liquor prohibited. 13 intercollegiate sports; extensive intramurals. AIAW, IAC, NCAA, WAC. Student body composition: 1% Asian, 2% Black, 2.5% Foreign, 22% Hispanic, 3.5% Native American, 69% White. 8% from out of state.

ST. JOHN'S COLLEGE $$$

Santa Fe 87501, (505) 982-3691
Director of Admissions: Mary McCormick Freitas

- **Undergraduates:** 180m, 130w
- **Tuition** (1984–1985): $8,250
- **Room and Board** (1984–1985): $2,900
- **Degrees offered:** BA
- **Mean SAT:** 600v, 580m
- **Student-faculty ratio:** 8 to 1
- **Calendar system:** Semester

A private college established in 1964, as a sister campus of St. John's College of Annapolis, MD. 330-acre suburban campus, 60 miles from Albuquerque. Served by bus. Rail service 20 miles away in Lamy; airport in Albuquerque.

Academic Character NCACS accreditation. Semester system, 10-week summer term for students who entered in January 4-year sequential study of great books from Homer to present combined with language, mathematics, laboratory science, and 1 year of music theory Discussion classes. Academic year consists of 6 divisions: seminars, language, mathematics, and music tutorials, laboratory, and formal lecture. Oral exam at the end of each semester; comprehensive exam in fall of senior year Senior thesis defended in oral examination. Students may spend one or more years at Annapolis campus. MLA granted. Art gallery 52,600-volume library

Financial CEEB CSS. College scholarships, grants, payment plans; PELL, SEOG, NDSL, FISL, CWS, student aid program. Scholarship application deadline in early February.

Admissions High school graduation with college prep program expected. Interview encouraged; may be required. SAT or ACT recommended. Rolling admissions. $200 deposit due on acceptance of admissions offer. *Early Decision* and *Early Admission* programs. Admission deferral possible. Transfers accepted, but enter as freshmen.

Student Life Literary magazine. Music, film, and drama groups. Search-and-rescue team. Art, athletic, crafts, service, and special interest groups. Single students not living at home live on campus. Seniors may live off campus. Coed dorms. Limited married-student housing. 80% of students live on campus. Intercollegiate fencing and soccer; individual and intramural sports programs. Student body composition: 2% Asian, 2% Hispanic, 96% White. Freshmen range in age from 16 to 30 years old. 90% from out of state.

New York

ADELPHI UNIVERSITY $$

Garden City 11530, (516) 294-8700
Director of Admissions: Susan Reardon

- **Undergraduates:** 2,073m, 4,382w
- **Tuition (1984–1985):** $5,600
- **Room and Board (1984–1985):** $3,280;   **Fees:** $380
- **Degrees offered:** BA, BS, BBA, BFA
- **Mean SAT:** 490v, 520m
- **Student-faculty ratio:** 15 to 1
- **Calendar system:** 4-1-4

A private university established in 1896. 75-acre campus in suburban Garden City, Long Island, 20 miles from Manhattan. Air, bus, rail service.
Academic Character MSACS and professional accreditation. 4-1-4 system, 2 4-week summer terms. 30 majors offered by the College of Arts & Sciences, 5 by the School of Business, and one each by the schools of Nursing and Social Work. Associate degrees granted. Minors offered in most areas. Courses in 10 additional areas. Distributive requirements. Graduate and professional degrees granted. Independent study. Honors program. Pass/fail, internships. Preprofessional programs in dentistry, engineering, law, medicine, physical therapy, veterinary medicine. 3-2 programs in social welfare and business. 5-year BA/BS engineering (through other universities). Study abroad. "Adelphi-On-Wheels" commuter classroom School of Business. PRIDE program for underqualified students. Member of Long Island Regional Advisory Council on Higher Education. ROTC at Hofstra. Computing Center, language lab. 377,941-volume library with microform resources; departmental libraries and research facilities.
Financial CEEB CSS. University scholarships, grants. PELL, SEOG, NSS, NDSL, NSL, CWS, state programs. Application deadline April 15. HEOP.
Admissions High school graduation with 16 units required. SAT or ACT required. $20 application fee. Rolling admissions; application deadline for financial aid applicants February 1. $200 tuition and $100 room deposits required on acceptance of offer of admission. *Early Admission* and *Concurrent Enrollment* programs. Admission deferral possible. Transfers accepted. Credit possible for CEEB AP and CLEP exams.
Student Life Student government. Newspaper, magazine, yearbook, radio station. Music, drama, dance groups. Academic, honorary, religious, language, special interest clubs. 6 fraternities, 5 sororities without houses. 7% of students join. Community housing available on request. Coed and women's dorms. Special interest housing. 20% of students live on campus. 12 intercollegiate sports for men, 5 for women; 11 intramurals. AIAW, ECAC, ICYA, NAIA, NCAA. Student body composition: 1% Asian, 13% Black, 4% Hispanic, 0.2% Native American, 75% White, 6.8% Other. 13% from out of state.

ALFRED UNIVERSITY $$

Alfred 14802, (607) 871-2115
Director of Admissions: Paul P. Piggon

- **Undergraduates:** 1,050m, 1,000w
- **Tuition (1984–1985):** $7,910
- **Room and Board (1984–1985):** $2,860
- **Degrees offered:** BA, BS, BFA
- **Mean SAT:** 500v, 540m, **Mean ACT:** 24
- **Student-faculty ratio:** 13 to 1
- **Calendar system:** Semester

A private university, including public New York State College of Ceramics, established in 1836. 232-acre rural campus in Alfred, 70 miles south of Rochester Air, bus, rail service.

Academic Character MSACS and professional accreditation. Semester system, 2 summer terms. 11 majors offered by the College of Ceramics, 25 by the College of Liberal Arts & Sciences, 2 by the College of Nursing & Health Care, 7 by the College of Business & Administration, and a Division of Industrial Engineering major Self-designed major. Distributive requirements. Graduate and professional degrees granted. Independent study. Honors program. Cooperative work study, pass/fail, internships. Preprofessional programs in dentistry, law, medical laboratory technology, medicine, veterinary medicine. 3-2 program in forestry and environmental studies with Duke. 4-1 MBA with Clarkson College. 5-year program in engineering with Columbia. Member consortium with Rochester Area Colleges. United Nations Semester Washington Semester World Campus Afloat. Study abroad. Elementary and secondary education certification. ROTC at St. Bonaventure. Computer Center, language lab. 210,000-volume library.

Financial CEEB CSS. University scholarships, grants, state programs; PELL, SEOG, NDSL, NSL, CWS. Priority application deadline February 15.

Admissions High school graduation with 16 units required. Portfolio required of Ceramic Art and Design applicants. Interview recommended. SAT or ACT required. $20 application fee. Rolling admissions; application deadline February 1 $200 tuition deposit required on acceptance of offer of admission. *Early Decision* and *Early Admission* programs. Admission deferral possible. Transfers accepted. Credit possible for CEEB AP and CLEP exams.

Student Life Student government. Student assembly. Newspaper, literary review, yearbook, radio station. Music, drama, religious, and special interest groups. 5 fraternities and 3 sororities with houses. 25% of men and 20% of women join. Freshmen and sophomores live in dormitories. Coed and single-sex dorms. 85% of students live on campus. 2 phys ed courses required. 10 intercollegiate sports for men, 7 for women. Extensive intramural program. ECAC, NCAA, ICAC. Student body composition: 2% Black, 0.5% Hispanic, 0.5% Native American, 97% White. 30% from out of state.

BARD COLLEGE $$$

Annandale-on-Hudson 12504, (914) 758-6822
Director of Admissions: Karen G. Wilcox

- **Undergraduates:** 300m, 380w
- **Tuition (1984–1985):** $9,800
- **Room and Board (1984–1985):** $3,200;   **Fees:** $350
- **Degrees offered:** BA
- **Mean SAT:** 570v, 540m
- **Student-faculty ratio:** 10 to 1
- **Calendar system:** 4–1–4

A private college established in 1860, became coed in 1944. 1,000-acre rural campus in Annandale-on-Hudson, 100 miles north of New York City.

Academic Character MSACC accreditation. 4-1-4 system. 31 majors offered in the areas of arts, sciences, math, music, humanities, social sciences, religion, women's studies, and economics through four college divisions: the Arts, Languages & Literature, Natural Sciences & Mathematics, Social Sciences. Distributive requirements. MFA degree program. Independent study. Honors program. Internships, honors/pass/fail. Preprofessional programs in medicine, law. 3-2 engineering program with Columbia; BA/MS in forestry and environmental studies at Duke. "Professional Option" allows entrance to approved graduate school after 3 years at Bard. Bard/Hudson Valley Studies. Individual study. Winter field Period. Study abroad. Workshop in Language and Thinking. Senior Project. Ecology field station. Language lab. Performing arts complex, art institute. 155,000-volume library with microform resources.

Financial CEEB CSS. College scholarships, awards, prizes; PELL, SEOG, NDSL, GSL, CWS. Application deadline March 15.

Admissions High school graduation with 16 units required. SAT or ACT recommended. GED accepted. Interview recommended. $20 application fee. Regular application deadline March 15. $250 tuition deposit required on acceptance of offer of admission. *Immediate Decision Plan;* one-day program on campus where applicant is told whether or not he or she is accepted. *Early Admission* and *Concurrent Enrollment* programs. Admission deferral possible. Transfers accepted. Credit possible for CEEB AP exams. HEOP.

Student Life Student government. Newspapers, literary magazines, journals. Music, drama, religious, academic, special interest groups. Coed and women's dorms. 85% of students live on campus. Firearms and pets prohibited. Intercollegiate soccer, cross-country, basketball, tennis for men; basketball, cross-country, volleyball, softball, tennis for women. Club sports and intramural program. NEAC, NAIA. Student body composition: 0.3% Asian, 7.5% Black, 3% Hispanic, 0.1% Native American, 88.6% White, 2.5% Other. 57% from out of state.

BARNARD COLLEGE $$$

606 West 120th Street, New York 10027, (212) 280-2014
Director of Admissions: R. Christine Royer

- **Undergreaduates:** 2,240w
- **Tuition (1984–1985):** $9,320
- **Room and Board (1984–1985):** $4,070–$4,668; **Fees:** $378
- **Degrees offered:** BA
- **Mean SAT:** 600v, 510m
- **Student-faculty ratio:** 10 to 1
- **Calendar system:** Semester

A private women's college coordinate with undergraduate coed Columbia College. Established in 1889, joined Columbia University in 1900. 4-acre urban campus in Morningside Heights area of New York City. Air, rail, bus, and subway service.

Academic Character MSACS accreditation. Semester system, 2 6-week summer terms. Over 50 majors offered in the areas of American studies, ancient studies, anthropology, architecture, art history, biopsychology, computer, education, English, foreign area studies, French translation &

literature, geography, geology, history, languages & literatures, linguistics, maths, Medieval & Renaissance studies, music, Oriental studies, philosophy, psychology, religion, sciences, social sciences, urban studies, and women's studies. Program in the arts for students gifted in dance, music, theatre, visual arts, writing. Self-designed majors. Programs in health & society, humanities, experimental studies. Distributive requirements; GRE required in some majors. Independent study, Phi Beta Kappa, pass/fail, internships. Senior Scholar Program. Cross-registration with Columbia College and other University divisions. 5-year programs with University graduate schools including schools of Engineering and International Affairs. 3-3 program with Law School. Study possible at Jewish Theological Seminary, Manhattan School of Music. Study abroad. Elementary and secondary education certification. Language lab, theatre. 150,000-volume library plus access to University library of over 5,000,000 volumes.

Financial CEEB CSS. College scholarships, grants, loans, payment plans; PELL, SEOG, NDSL, GSL, CWS, institutional work program. Application deadline February 1 (scholarships & grants).

Admissions High school graduation with college prep program recommended. Interview strongly recommended. SAT and 3 ACH required. $25 application fee. Application deadline January 15; notification in mid-April. *Early Decision* and *Early Admission* programs. Admission deferral possible. Transfers accepted. Credit possible for CEEB AP exams. HEOP for New York State residents.

Student Life Student Council. Newspaper, literary magazine, yearbook, radio station. Several music groups. Drama groups, Gilbert and Sullivan Society. Debate. Women's Center. Service, academic, religious, pre-professional, special interest, and political clubs. Women's, coed, and apartment-style dorms. 58% of students live on campus. Honor system. Regular class attendance expected. 2 years of phys ed required. 9 intercollegiate sports, intramural & club sports. Student body composition: 10% Asian, 5% Black, 5% Hispanic, 80% White. 65% from out of state.

CITY COLLEGE, THE (CUNY) $

Convent Avenue & West 138 Street, New York 10031, (212) 690-6977
Director of Admissions: Dr. Saul Friedman

- **Undergraduates:** 6,925m, 3,842w
- **Tuition (1984–1985):** $1,225 (in-state), $2,025 (out-of-state)
- **Fees:** $66
- **Degrees offered:** BA, BS, BFA, BSE, BSN, BArch, BSEd
- **Student-faculty ratio:** 15 to 1
- **Calendar system:** Semester

A public college founded in 1847. Urban campus in Manhattan. Air, rail, bus, and subway service.

Academic Character MSACS and professional accreditation. Semester system, 7½-week summer term. Over 55 majors offered in the areas of architecture, area studies, arts, computer, education, engineering, English, Hebrew, languages & literatures, linguistics, mathematics, meteorology, nursing, oceanography, psychology, sciences, social sciences, and speech/pathology. Programs in dance, film, music, and theatre. Masters degrees granted. Phi Beta Kappa. Preprofessional programs in dentistry, journalism, medicine. 6-year BS/JD program. 7-year BS/MD program. Elementary, secondary, and special education certification. Center for the Performing Arts. 937,000-volume library.

Financial Application procedures vary with programs. College grants, loans, state scholarships, grants, loans, aid to Native Americans, payment plan; PELL, SEOG, GSL, NDSL, NSL, PLUS, CWS. Application deadline January 15 for scholarships & grants.

Admissions High school graduation or equivalent required. GED accepted. SAT or ACT recommended. $20 application fee. Rolling admissions; suggest applying by January 15. *Early Entrance* Program. Transfers accepted. Credit possible for CEEB AP and CLEP exams.

Student Life Student government. Newspaper, yearbook. Academic, service, social, and special interest groups. Fraternities. No college housing. 2 semesters of phys ed required. Class attendance required. 19 intercollegiate and several intramural sports for men & women. CUNY Conference. Student body composition: 13% Asian, 34% Black, 21% Hispanic, 1% Native American, 31% White.

CLARKSON COLLEGE OF TECHNOLOGY $$$

Potsdam 13676, (315) 268-6400
Director of Freshman Admissions: Robert A. Croot

- **Undergraduates:** 2,750m, 850w
- **Tuition (1984–1985):** $7,690
- **Room and Board (1984–1985):** $3,400;   **Fees:** $100
- **Degrees offered:** BS
- **Mean SAT:** 540v, 640m
- **Student-faculty ratio:** 19 to 1
- **Calendar system:** Semester

A private college established in 1896. 650-acre small-city campus in Potsdam, 140 miles north of Syracuse. Bus service.

Academic Character MSACS and professional accreditation. Semester system, 2 5-week summer terms. Majors offered in accounting, biology, chemistry, computer science, economics & finance, engineering, history, humanities, industrial distribution, industrial hygiene/environmental toxicology, management & marketing, mathematics, physics, psychology, social sciences, sociology, technical communications. Self-designed & interdisciplinary studies. Distributive requirements. Graduate and professional degrees granted. Independent study. Pass/fail. Preprofessional programs in law, dentistry, medicine. 3-2 programs in engineering with several New York state colleges. Cross-registration with SUNY College at Potsdam and St. Lawrence U. Member of Associated Colleges of St. Lawrence Valley consortium. STRETCH Program. Study abroad. ROTC, AFROTC. Institute of Colloid and Surface Science. Division of Research. Educational Resources Center, incorporating computer center, technologically-assisted education, and library with microform resources.

Financial CEEB CSS. College scholarships, grants, loans, state aid; PELL, SEOG, NDSL, GSL, CWS. Application deadline February 1.

Admissions High school graduation with 16 units required. Interview and 3 ACH recommended. SAT or ACT required. $25 application fee. Rolling admissions; application deadline April 1. $50 tuition and $100 room deposits required on acceptance of offer of admission. *Early Decision, Early*

Admission, Concurrent Enrollment programs. Admission deferral possible. Transfers accepted. Credit possible for CEEB AP and CLEP exams; college has own placement exams.

Student Life Student government. Newspaper, magazine, yearbook, radio and TV stations. Music, drama, athletic, academic, honorary, professional, religious, special interest groups. 13 fraternities with houses. 20% of men join. Students live on campus unless living at home. 84% of students live on campus. 11 intercollegiate sports for men, 9 for women. Intramural sports program. ECAC, ICAC, NCAA, AIAW. Student body composition: 0.2% Black, 0.3% Hispanic, 0.2% Native American, 96% White, 3.3% Other.

COLGATE UNIVERSITY $$$

Hamilton 13346, (315) 824-1000
Director of Admissions: David S. Perham

- **Undergraduates:** 1,450m, 1,150w
- **Tuition (1984–1985):** $9,075
- **Room and Board (1984–1985):** $3,265;   **Fees:** $80
- **Degrees offered:** BA
- **Mean SAT:** 605v, 640m,   **Mean ACT:** 28.5
- **Student-faculty ratio:** 14 to 1
- **Calendar system:** 4–1–4

A private university established in 1819. University became coed in 1970. 1,400-acre rural campus, 40 miles southeast of Syracuse. Bus service.
Academic Character MSACS accreditation. 4-1-4 system. 36 majors offered in the areas of fine arts, music, humanities, math, sciences, social sciences, economics, religion, peace studies, international relations, political science. Minors offered in all fields. Distributive requirements. MA, MAT granted. Independent study. Honors program. Phi Beta Kappa. Pass/fail, internships. Preprofessional programs in engineering, theology, law, medicine, government service, business and management. 3-2, 3-3 programs in engineering, management engineering with Carnegie-Mellon, Columbia, Dartmouth, RPI, U of Rochester. Colgate Visiting Student Program. Off-Campus, Study Group Programs. Sea Semester. Washington Semester. January Special Studies Period. Study abroad. Secondary education certification. Observatory, Computer Center, Dana Arts Center. Eric Ryan Studio. 360,000-volume library with microform resources; departmental libraries.
Financial CEEB CSS. University scholarships, grants, loans, state aid; PELL, SEOG, NDSL, CWS. Application deadline February 1.
Admissions High school graduation with 16 units required. SAT and ACH, or ACT required. Campus visit recommended. $35 application fee. Application deadline January 15. $300 deposit required on acceptance of offer of admission. *Early Decision* and *Early Admission* programs. Admission deferral possible. Transfers accepted. Credit possible for CEEB AP, CLEP, state, departmental exams. University has own placement program. HEOP; University Scholars Program.
Student Life Student government. Newspapers, magazines, yearbook, radio and TV stations. Music, debate, drama, outing, service, academic, religious, athletic, honorary, special interest groups. 10 fraternities, 2 sororities, 1 coed fraternity. Students live on campus. Coed, single-sex, language, and special interest housing. 87% of students live on campus. 8 units of phys ed and

survival swim test required. 11 intercollegiate sports for men, 8 for women; many intramural and club sports. AIAW, ECAC, NCAA. Student body composition: 3% Asian, 6% Black, 2% Hispanic, 89% White. 50% from out of state.

COLUMBIA UNIVERSITY $$

Broadway & West 116th Street, New York 10027, (212) 280-2521

- **Undergraduates:** 703m, 792w (Columbia College)
- **Tuition (1984–1985):** $8,550
- **Degrees offered:** BA, BS
- **Mean SAT:** 630v, 650m
- **Student-faculty ratio:** 5 to 1
- **Calendar system:** Semester

A private university including the undergraduate coed Columbia College, which is coordinate with Barnard College for women. Established in 1754. Urban campus in Morningside Heights area of New York City. Air, rail, bus, and subway service.

Academic Character MSACS and professional accreditation. Semester system, 2 6-week summer terms. Over 45 majors offered in the areas of ancient studies, anthropology, architecture, art history, computer, East Asian studies, geography, geology, geophysics, history, 10 languages & literatures, linguistics, math, Medieval-Renaissance studies, Middle East studies, music, philosophy, psychology, religion, sciences, social sciences, statistics, and urban studies. Interdepartmental and self-designed majors. Special programs in chemistry. Courses in other areas including film, Korean, Portuguese. Distributive requirements. Graduate and professional degrees granted. Independent study, Phi Beta Kappa, pass/fail, internships. Seminar institute for some junior and seniors, who take one intensive course per semester. Preprofessional programs in medicine and dentistry. Cross-registration with Barnard and other University divisions. 5-year programs with University graduate schools including Arts, Engineering, International Affairs, and Teachers College. Study abroad. Numerous research institutes and centers. Computer Center. Language lab. Over 5,000,000-volume library.

Financial CEEB CSS. University scholarships, grants, loans, payment plans; PELL, SEOG, NDSL, GSL, part-time employment. Application deadlines February 16 (scholarships & grants), August 1 (loans).

Admissions High school graduation with college prep program recommended. SAT and 3 ACH required. $30 application fee. Application deadline January 1; notification in mid-April. *Early Admission* and *Early Decision* programs. Transfers accepted. Credit possible for CEEB AP exams.

Student Life Student government. Newspaper, magazines, yearbook, radio & TV stations. Several music groups. Drama groups, Gilbert and Sullivan Society. Debate. Asian Student Union, Black Student Union, Chicano Caucus. Service, academic, athletic, religious, special interest, and political clubs. 18 fraternities, most with houses. 16% of men join. Freshmen must live at home or on campus. Men's and coed dorms. 85% of students live on campus. Class attendance required for freshmen. 2 terms of phys ed required. Many intercollegiate and intramural sports. Ivy League. Student body composition: 10% Asian, 8% Black, 6% Hispanic, 75% White, 1% Other. 62% from out of state.

COOPER UNION $

New York 10003, (212) 254-6300
Director of Admissions: Herbert Liebeskind

- **Undergraduates:** 700m, 300w
- **Tuition (1984–1985):** None
- **Fees:** $300
- **Degrees offered:** BFA, BArch, BSE
- **Mean SAT:** 490–580v, 510–720m
- **Student-faculty ratio:** 10 to 1
- **Calendar system:** Semester

A private college established in New York City in 1859. City campus of 3 buildings in Cooper Square. Air, bus, rail service.
Academic Character MSACS and professional accreditation. Semester system. Majors offered in architecture, drawing, graphic design, painting, photography, sculpture, chemical engineering, civil engineering, electrical engineering, mechanical engineering. Certificates offered in art. Courses in liberal arts. Distributive requirements. Graduate degrees granted. Independent study. Honors program. Pass/fail, internships. Exchange program with 6 East Coast schools, 1 West Coast school, 4 European schools for art majors. Joint BS/BE, BS/ME programs with New York U. Cross-registration with Parsons School of Design. Interim Year offered at School of Architecture. 95,000-volume library; access to other area libraries.
Financial No tuition charges; admission to Cooper Union constitutes a full tuition scholarship. CEEB CSS. College grants, awards, state aid; PELL, SEOG, NDSL, GSL, CWS. FAF application deadline March 30.
Admissions High school graduation with 16 units required. Home project required of applicant to schools of art or architecture. SAT required; also 2 ACH for engineering applicants. $10 application fee. Application deadlines January 1 for art and architecture, February 1 for engineering. $300 deposit required on acceptance of offer of admission. *Early Admission* program. Admission deferral possible. Transfers accepted. Credit possible for CEEB AP and CLEP exams.
Student Life Student councils. Newspaper, literary and graphics magazine, yearbook. Music, drama, honorary, academic, professional, special interest groups. No student housing; 80% of students live at home. Class attendance required. Intercollegiate bowling; intramural programs. Student body composition: 7.4% Asian, 1.5% Black, 3.4% Hispanic, 86.4% White, 1.3% Other. 20% from out of state.

CORNELL UNIVERSITY $/$$/$$$

Ithaca 48103, (607) 256-1000
Dean of Admissions: James Scannell

- **Undergraduates:** 6,766m, 5,707w
- **Public School Tuition (1984–1985):** $4,060 (in-state), $6,600 (out-of-state)
- **Private School Tuition (1984–85):** $9,600
- **Room and Board (1984–1985):** $2,197–$3,448
- **Degrees offered:** BA, BS, BArch, BFA
- **Mean SAT:** 587v, 652m
- **Student-faculty ratio:** 6 to 1
- **Calendar system:** Semester

A private university established in 1865. 3 divisions are New York State colleges. 734-acre campus in Ithaca, 45 miles from Syracuse. Air and bus service.

Academic Character MSACS and professional accreditation. Semester system, 3-, 6-, and 8-week summer terms. 38 majors offered by the College of Arts & Sciences, 40 by the College of Agriculture & Life Sciences, 8 by the College of Architecture, Art, & Planning, 11 by the College of Engineering, 9 by the College of Human Ecology, and majors in the schools of Hotel Administration and Industrial & Labor Relations. Self-designed majors. Interdisciplinary programs and courses. Distributive requirements. Graduate and professional degrees granted. Independent study. Honors programs. Phi Beta Kappa. Cooperative work/study, pass/fail, internships. Preprofessional programs in business, law, dentistry, medicine, veterinary medicine. 5-year BA/MA programs in business administration, public administration, hospital and health services administration. 6-year BS/MBA/ME. Study abroad. Cornell-in-Washington Program. Program on Science, Technology, and Society. Secondary education certification. AFROTC, NROTC, ROTC. Computer Services. Language labs. Remedial education programs. Observatory. Research facilities. Herbert F. Johnson Museum of Art. 16 libraries with 4,500,000 volumes and microform resources.

Financial CEEB CSS. University scholarships, grants, loans, state aid; PELL, SEOG, NDSL, GSL, CWS. Application deadline January 15.

Admissions High school graduation with 16 units required. College of Architecture, Art, and Planning, School of Industrial & Labor Relations, and School of Hotel Management require interviews. SAT or ACT required; some colleges require ACH exams. $30 application fee. Application deadline January 1. $200 deposit required on acceptance of offer of admission. *Early Decision* and *Early Admission* programs. Admission deferral possible. Transfers accepted. Credit possible for CEEB AP programs and CLEP exams; some departmental advanced placement exams. COSEP, HEOP, EOP.

Student Life Student government. Newspapers, magazines, yearbook, radio station. Music, debate, drama, service, religious, academic, honorary, political, special interest groups. 48 fraternities, 12 sororities all with houses; 37% of men and 22% of women join. Coed and non-coed dorms, cooperative, special interest, married-student housing; 50% of students live on campus. 2 semesters of phys ed required. 20 intercollegiate sports for men, 16 for women; 19 intramurals. Ivy League. Student body composition: 4% Asian, 7% Black, 2% Hispanic, 85% White. 46% from out of state.

ELMIRA COLLEGE $$

Elmira 14901, (607) 734-3911
Director of Admissions: Robert French

- **Undergraduates:** 349m, 665w
- **Tuition (1984–1985):** $6,350
- **Room and Board (1984–1985):** $2,500;   **Fees:** $90
- **Degrees offered:** BA, BS, AA, AAS
- **Mean SAT:** 426v, 460m
- **Student-faculty ratio:** 14 to 1
- **Calendar system:** 4–4–1

A private college established in 1855. College became coed in 1969. 38-acre campus in residential area of Elmira. Airport, bus service.

Academic Character MSACS accreditation. 4-4-1 system, 6-week summer term. 41 majors offered in the areas of arts, sciences, math, business, social sciences, humanities, music, nursing, medical technology, speech & hearing, dance, theatre, education, computer science. Self-designed majors. Associate degrees granted in liberal arts, business, computer systems and programming, human services, mechanical technology. Minors in 21 areas. Distributive requirements. MSEd granted. Independent study. Honors program. Phi Beta Kappa. Cooperative work/study, pass/fail, internships. Preprofessional programs in law, medicine, dentistry, osteopathy. 3-2 engineering programs with Georgia Tech and Worcester Polytech. 3-1 medical technology program with approved hospital. Spring Term Consortium. 13-13-6 system. Washington Semester. United Nations Semester. Junior Year Study in the United States. Washington Center for Learning Alternatives. Critical Languages study. Study abroad. San Salvador campus. Elementary and secondary education certification. ROTC at Cornell. 135,000-volume library with microform resources.

Financial CEEB CSS. College scholarships, awards, loans, prizes, state aid; PELL, SEOG, NSS, NDSL, GSL, CWS. Application deadlines March 1 (scholarships), February 1 (loans). $100 tuition discount for each enrolled sibling.

Admissions High school graduation with 17 units required. Interview recommended. SAT or ACT recommended. $20 application fee. Rolling admissions. $100 deposit required on acceptance of offer of admission. *Early Decision* and *Early Admission* programs. Admission deferral possible. Transfers accepted. Credit possible for CEEB AP, CLEP, and ACT PEP exams; some departmental exams. HEOP.

Student Life Student government. Newspaper, magazine, yearbook, radio station. Music, drama, dance, outing, ski, international relations clubs. Academic, political, religious, special interest groups. Freshmen and sophomores are required to live on campus or at home. Coed dorms. Single-sex dorms with overnight visitation restrictions. 80% of students live on campus. Class attendance expected. Two phys ed activities required. 5 intercollegiate sports for men, 5 for women; intramural and club sports. AIAW, ECAC, NAIA, NCAA, Private College Athletic Conference. 42% of students from out of state.

HAMILTON COLLEGE $$$

Clinton 13323, (315) 859-4421
Dean of Admissions: Douglas C. Thompson

- **Undergraduates:** 900m, 700w
- **Tuition (1984–1985):** $9,300
- **Room and Board (1984-1985):** $3,050
- **Degrees offered:** BA
- **Mean SAT:** 580v, 610m
- **Student-faculty ratio:** 12 to 1
- **Calendar system:** 4–1–4

A private college established in 1812. College became coed in 1978. 15-acre campus in Clinton, 11 miles from Utica. Air, bus, rail service to Utica; bus to Clinton.

Academic Character MSACS accreditation. 4-1-4 system. 28 majors offered in areas of arts, sciences, math, social sciences, humanities, religion, economics, theatre, music, writing, government. Self-designed majors.

Interdisciplinary studies. Distributive requirements. Independent study. Honors programs. Phi Beta Kappa. Pass/fail, internships. Preprofessional programs in law, veterinary medicine, dentistry, medicine. 3-2 engineering program with Columbia, U of Rochester, Washington U; 3-3 program with RPI. 3-3 law program with Columbia. Cross-registration with Colgate, Syracuse, Utica. Winter Term. Hamilton College Term in Washington. Williams College Mystic Seaport program. Study abroad. Afro-Latin Cultural Center. Computer Center. List Art Center. Observatory. 360,000-volume library with microform resources.

Financial CEEB CSS and ACT FAS. College scholarships, loans, state aid; PELL, SEOG, NDSL, GSL, FISL, CWS. Application deadline February 1.

Admissions High school graduation with 16 units required. Interview recommended. SAT or ACT required. Application fee $30. Application deadline January 15. $100 deposit required on acceptance of offer of admission. *Early Decision, Early Admission* programs. Admission deferral possible. Transfers accepted. Credit possible for CEEB AP exams. HEOP.

Student Life Student government. Newspaper, magazine, yearbook, radio station. Music, debate, drama clubs. Outing, academic, honorary, service, special interest groups. 8 fraternities with houses. 40% of men and some women join. Coed dorms. Language and special interest housing. Some married-student housing. 98% of students live on campus. Class attendance expected. Swimming and physical fitness test, 2 seasonal sports required. 12 intercollegiate sports for men, 9 for women; intramurals. AIAW, ECAC, NCAA, NESCAC. Student body composition: 1% Asian, 3% Black, 1% Hispanic, 95% White. 45% from out of state.

HOBART AND WILLIAM SMITH COLLEGES $$$

Geneva 14456, (315) 789-5500
Hobart Director of Admissions: Leonard A. Wood, Jr.
William Smith Director of Admissions: Mara O'Laughlin

- **Undergraduates:** 1,100m, 700w
- **Tuition (1984–1985):** $8,835
- **Room and Board (1984–1985):** $3,303; **Fees:** $200
- **Degrees offered:** BA, BS
- **Mean SAT:** 550v, 560m, **Mean ACT:** 26
- **Student-faculty ratio:** 14 to 1
- **Calendar system:** Trimester

Private coordinate colleges located in Geneva. Hobart College for men established in 1822, William Smith College for women established in 1908. 17-acre campus on shore of Seneca Lake, 40 miles southeast of Rochester and 50 miles west of Syracuse.

Academic Character MSACS accreditation. Trimester system. 27 majors offered in areas of art, humanities, science, math, social sciences, religion, music, economics. Student-designed majors. General education and interdisciplinary courses. 3-part program: First Year (general education), the Middle Years (Baccalaureate Essay), the Baccalaureate year (Baccalaureate Colloquium). Distributive requirements. Independent study. Honors programs. Phi Beta Kappa. Internships. Preprofessional programs in law, dentistry, medicine. 3-2 engineering programs with Columbia, U of Rochester, RPI. 4-1 BA/MBA with Clarkson. Member of 15-college Rochester Area College Consortium. Washington Semester. Philadelphia Urban Semester.

United Nations Semester. Art term in New York City. Visiting Student Program. Study abroad. Elementary and secondary education certification. Developmental Learning Center. Computing system. 225,000-volume library with microform resources.

Financial CEEB CSS. College scholarships, state aid; PELL, SEOG, NDSL, FISL, CWS. Application deadline March 1.

Admissions High school graduation with 16 units required. Interview recommended. SAT and English ACH, or ACT required. $20 application fee. Application deadline February 15. $250 tuition and $100 room deposits required on acceptance of offer of admission. *Early Decision* and *Early Acceptance* programs. Admission deferral possible. Transfers accepted. Credit possible for CEEB AP, CLEP, and departmental exams. HEOP.

Student Life Student government. Newspaper, yearbook, magazines, radio station. Music, drama, community service, honorary, special interest groups. 9 fraternities with houses; 35% of men join. Single-sex, coed, and co-op housing. Class attendance required. Swimming test required. 12 intercollegiate sports for men, 6 for women. Intramural programs and club sports. NCAA, USILA, AIAW, ICAC. Student body composition: 0.2% Asian, 3.3% Black, 2.5% Hispanic, 94% White. 52% from out of state.

HOFSTRA UNIVERSITY $/$$

Hempstead 11550, (516) 560-6600
Director of Admissions: Joan E. Isaac

- **Undergraduates:** 3,228m, 2,872w
- **Tuition (1984–1985):** $5,550
- **Room and Board (1984–1985):** $2,050-$3,290; **Fees:** $350
- **Degrees offered:** BA, BS, BBA, BSE, BFA, BSEd, B/JD, BBA/JD
- **Mean SAT:** 500v, 520m, **Mean ACT:** 23
- **Student-faculty ratio:** 18 to 1
- **Calendar system:** 4–1–4

A private university established in 1935. 238-acre campus in Hempstead, Long Island, 25 miles east of New York City. Bus and rail service.

Academic Character MSACS and professional accreditation. 4-1-4 system, 2 5-week summer terms. 47 majors offered by the College of Liberal Arts & Sciences, 5 by the School of Business, 17 by the School of Education. New College liberal arts programs. Interdisciplinary studies. Self-designed majors. Minors in most fields. AAS specialization in elementary education. Distributive requirements. Graduate and professional degrees granted. Independent study. Honors programs. Phi Beta Kappa. Pass/fail, internships. Preprofessional programs in dentistry, forestry, law, medicine, veterinary medicine. Cooperative program with Jewish Theological Seminary. 3-2 BA/BS and 4-1 BS/MS engineering programs with Columbia. Visiting Student program. Study abroad. Elementary, secondary, and special education certification. Computer center, language lab. Center for cultural and Intercultural Studies, Emily Lowe Gallery. ROTC. 930,000-volume library with microform resources.

Financial CEEB CSS. University scholarships, grants, loans, state aid; PELL, SEOG, NDSL, CWS. Application deadline February 15.

Admissions High school graduation with 16 units required. Interview recommended. SAT or ACT required; ACH recommended. $20 application fee. Rolling admissions; preferred application deadline February 15. $100 tuition and $100 room deposits required on acceptance of offer of admission. *Early Decision* and *Early Admission* programs. Admission deferral possible. Transfers accepted. Credit possible for CEEB AP, CLEP, and state exams; university has own advanced placement program. Army Cooperative Education Program.

Student Life Student government. Newspaper, magazine, yearbook, radio station. Music, debate, drama clubs. Service, athletic, dance, academic, honorary, special interest organizations. 11 fraternities and 4 sororities. 15% of men and women join. Coed and single-sex dorms. Special interest housing. 45% of students live on campus. 8 intercollegiate sports for men, 8 for women; intramurals. Student body composition: 0.2% Asian, 6.2% Black, 2.1% Hispanic, 0.2% Native American, 89.6% White, 1.7% Other. 20% from out of state.

IONA COLLEGE $$

New Rochelle 10801, (914) 636-3100
Director of Admissions: Francis I. Offer, C.F.C.

- **Undergraduates:** 2,005m, 1,457w
- **Tuition (1984–1985):** $4,880
- **Room and Board (1984–1985):** $3,150
- **Degrees offered:** BA, BS, BBA
- **Student-faculty ratio:** 20 to 1
- **Calendar system:** 4–1–4

A private college founded in 1940 by the Congregation of the Christian Brothers of Ireland. Suburban campus in New Rochelle. Rail and bus stations in New Rochelle; airport in nearby New York City.

Academic Character MSACS accreditation. 4-1-4 system, 2 5-week summer terms. 37 majors offered in the areas of humanities, communications, business, science, math, social sciences, gerontology, speech & dramatic arts, computer & information sciences, education, religious studies. Interdisciplinary studies. Minors in most fields. Distributives and 6 credits in religion required. Masters degrees granted. Independent study. Honors program. Pass/fail, internships. Preprofessional programs in law, dentistry, medicine, veterinary medicine, engineering. Coop work/study BE in engineering program at U of Detroit. Cross-registration with area colleges. Elementary, secondary, special, and bilingual education certification. ROTC at Fordham. Language lab, computer center. 191,000-volume library; access to other area libraries.

Financial CEEB CSS. College scholarships, grants, state aid; PELL, SEOG, NDSL, GSL, CWS. Application deadline April 15.

Admissions High school graduation with 16 units required. Interview recommended. SAT or ACT required. $15 application fee. $100 deposit required on acceptance of offer of admission. Rolling admissions. *Early Decision* and *Early Admission* programs. Transfers accepted. Credit possible for CEEB AP and CLEP exams. HEOP.

Student Life Student government. Academic, honorary, religious, service, athletic, journalism, special interest groups. Social fraternities and sororities. 1 coed dorm. 5% of students live on campus. Intercollegiate and intramural sports programs. Student body composition: 0.5% Asian, 3.7% Black, 3.4% Hispanic, 91% White, 1.4% Other. 80% from out of state.

ITHACA COLLEGE $$

Ithaca 14850, (607) 274-3124
Director of Admissions: Peter A. Stace

- **Undergraduates:** 2,147m, 2,694w
- **Tuition (1984–1985):** $6,026
- **Room and Board (1984–1985):** $2,880
- **Degrees offered:** BA, BS, BFA, BMus
- **Mean SAT:** 490v, 530m
- **Student-faculty ratio:** 15 to 1
- **Calendar system:** Semester

A private college established in 1892. 250-acre campus on Cayuga Lake in Ithaca, 50 miles south of Syracuse. Air and bus service.
Academic Character MSACS and professional accreditation. Semester system, 3 4-week summer terms. 5 majors offered by the School of Allied Health Professions, 4 by the School of Business, 5 by the School of Communications, 3 by the School of Health, Physical Education, & Recreation, 25 by the School of Humanities & Science, and 7 by the School of Music. Self-designed majors. Interdisciplinary majors. Minors offered in most major areas. Distributive requirements. Independent study. Internships, pass/fail. Preprofessional programs in law, medicine, veterinary medicine, dentistry. 3-2 engineering programs and cross-registration with Cornell. Study abroad. Elementary and secondary education certification. ROTC, NROTC, AFROTC at Cornell. Instructional Resources Center. Reading and Writing labs. Computer services. 207,000-volume library with microform resources.
Financial CEEB CSS. University scholarships, awards, state aid; PELL, SEOG, NDSL, GSL, CWS. Application deadline March 1.
Admissions High school graduation with 16 units required. Auditions required of music and theatre arts applicants. SAT required; English ACH recommended. $20 application fee. Rolling admissions; preferred application deadline March 1. $100 deposit required on acceptance of offer of admission. *Early Decision* and *Early Admission* programs. Admission deferral possible. Transfers accepted. Credit possible for CEEB AP and state exams. HEOP/EOP.
Student Life Student government. Newspaper, magazine, yearbook, TV and radio stations. Music, drama, academic, religious, special interest groups. 6 fraternities, 2 sororities housed in dorms. Students under 21 required to live on campus or at home. Coed and single-sex dorms. Some married-student housing. 80% of students live on campus. 13 intercollegiate sports for men, 12 for women; club and intramural sports. AIAW, ECAC, NCAA. Student body composition: 0.4% Asian, 2% Black, 1% Hispanic, 0.3% Native American, 96.3% White. 50% from out of state.

MANHATTANVILLE COLLEGE $$$

Purchase 10577, (914) 694-2200
Dean of Admissions: Marshall Raucci

- **Undergraduates:** 330m, 620w
- **Tuition (1984–1985):** $7,700
- **Room and Board (1984–1985):** $3,800
- **Degrees offered:** BA, BFA, BMus

- **Mean SAT:** 530v, 530m
- **Student-faculty ratio:** 11 to 1
- **Calendar system:** Semester

A private college established in 1841, became coed in 1971. 220-acre campus in suburban Purchase, 24 miles from New York City. Bus service.

Academic Character MSACS and professional accreditation. Semester system, 2 summer terms. Majors offered in art, art history, biochemistry, biology, business management, chemistry, classics, computer science, economics, English, environmental studies, French, history, math, music, philosophy, physics, political science, psychobiology, psychology, religion, Romance languages, Russian, sociology, Spanish. Interdisciplinary and self-designed majors. Certificate programs. Courses in several areas. Distributive requirements. Masters degrees granted. Independent study. Honors programs. Cooperative work/study, internships, pass/fail. Pre-law program. Portfolio evaluation required of seniors. Exchanges with SUNY College at Purchase, Mills College (CA). Visiting Student Program. 6-year BA/JD with New York Law School. 5-year BA/MBA and 5-year BA/MS computer science with New York U. Washington Semester. Study abroad. Elementary and secondary education certification. College Skills Center. Learning Center. Language Resource Center. English Language Institute. 250,000-volume library.

Financial CEEB CSS and ACT FAS. College scholarships, grants, state aid; PELL, SEOG, NDSL, FISL, GSL, CWS. Priority application deadline March 1.

Admissions High school graduation required. Two admission plans: 1) submit letters of recommendation, transcripts, SAT or ACT scores or 2) submit letters of recommendation, transcripts, examples of academic work. Interview recommended, required in some cases. Audition required for music candidates, portfolio for art candidates. $20 application fee. Rolling admissions; preferred deadline March 1. $100 tuition and $100 room deposits required on acceptance of offer of admission. *Early Decision* and *Early Acceptance* programs. Admission deferral possible. Transfers accepted. Credit possible for CEEB AP exams. HEOP.

Student Life Student government. Newspaper, magazine, yearbook. Music, drama, academic, special interest groups. Weekly socials. 88% of students live on campus. 9 intercollegiate sports; intramurals. Student body composition: 0.4% Asian, 11.2% Black, 3.7% Hispanic, 0.1% Native American, 84.6% White. 54% from out of state.

NEW YORK, POLYTECHNIC INSTITUTE OF $$

333 Jay Street, Brooklyn 11201, (212) 643-2150
Director of Admissions: Elizabeth Sharp Ross

- **Undergraduates:** 2,356m, 303w
- **Tuition (1984–1985):** $7,800
- **Room and Board (1984–1985):** $2,650;   **Fees:** $10
- **Degrees offered:** BS
- **Mean SAT:** 467v, 604m
- **Student-faculty ratio:** 14 to 1
- **Calendar system:** Semester

A private institute founded in 1854. Merged with New York University School of Engineering & Science in 1973. Main campus in Brooklyn. Long Island campus in Farmingdale (Rt. 110, Farmingdale 11735). Graduate center in White Plains. Air, rail, and bus service.

Academic Character MSACS and professional accreditation. Semester system, 2 6-week summer terms. Majors offered in engineering (areospace. chemical, electrical, industrial, mechanical, metallurgical, nuclear), humanities, social sciences, computer science, operations research, information management, chemistry, life sciences, math, physics, and science, technical, and financial writing. Distributive requirements. Graduate degrees granted. Independent study. Honors program. Cooperative work/study, pass/fail, credit by exam. Preprofessional program in medicine. 5-year BS/MS in engineering with bioengineering or life sciences. Research institutes and labs. Center for Urban Environmental Studies. Computer center. 265,000-volume library with microform resources.

Financial CEEB CSS. Institute scholarships, grants, state aid; PELL, SEOG, NDSL, GSL, CWS.

Admissions High school graduation with 16 units preferred. Interview recommended. SAT or ACT, and 3 ACH required. $20 application fee. Rolling admissions. $50 deposit required on acceptance of admissions offer. *Early Decision, Early Admission, Concurrent Enrollment* programs. Transfers accepted. Credit possible for CEEB AP exams.

Student Life Student government. Newspaper, magazines, yearbook, radio station. Debate. Academic, honorary, professional, and special interest groups. 6 fraternities with houses. 15-20% of men join. Coed and single-sex dorms. 2% of students live on campus. Phys ed required of freshmen & sophomores. 9 intercollegiate sports; intramurals. Metropolitan Conference. Student body composition: 19% Asian, 8% Black, 5% Hispanic, 68% White. 11% from out of state.

NEW YORK UNIVERSITY $$$

25 West 4th Street, New York 10012, (212) 598-3591
Director of Admissions: Harold R. Doughty

- **Undergraduates:** 5,000m, 5,000w
- **Tuition (1984–1985):** $7,850
- **Room and Board (1984–1985):** $3,800
- **Degrees offered:** BA, BS, AA, AAS
- **Mean SAT:** 550v, 595m
- **Student-faculty ratio:** 13 to 1
- **Calendar system:** Semester

A private university established in 1831. Urban campus surrounds Washington Square in New York City. Additional centers: Institute of Fine Arts (1 E. 78th St.), Medical Center (550 First Ave.), Brookdale Dental Center (421 First Ave.), Graduate Business Center (100 Trinity Place). Air, bus, rail, subway service.

Academic Character MSACS and professional accreditation. Semester system, 2 6-week summer terms. 52 majors offered by the College of Arts & Sciences, 13 by the College of Business & Public Administration, 10 by the School of Arts, 35 by the School of Education, Health, Nursing, and Arts Professions, and one by the School of Social Work. Self-designed majors. Joint degree programs. Distributive requirements. Graduate and professional degrees granted. AA and AS granted by School of Continuing Education. Independent study, honors programs, Phi Beta Kappa. Cooperative work/study, internships, pass/fail. Preprofessional programs in law, dentistry, medicine, optometry, podiatry. Joint bachelor's/master's degree programs.

BS/BEng, BS/MEng programs with Cooper Union. Elementary, secondary, and special education certification. Visiting Students. Study abroad. Computer center, language lab. Several libraries with over 3,000,000 volumes and microform resources.

Financial CEEB CSS. University scholarships, grants, state aid; PELL, SEOG, NDSL, CWS. Application deadline February 15.

Admissions High school graduation with 16 units required. Interview recommended; audition, interview, portfolio required in some cases. SAT or ACT required; ACH sometimes required. $25 application fee. Rolling admissions; application deadline February 1. $200 tuition and $200 room deposits required on acceptance of admissions offer. *Early Decision. Early Admission, Concurrent Enrollment* programs. Admission deferral possible. Transfers accepted. Credit possible for CEEB AP and CLEP exams. Special programs for disadvantaged students.

Student Life Student government. 4 newspapers. 2 radio stations. Over 160 student clubs. 9 fraternities. 3 sororities. 11% of men and 4% of women join. Single-sex dorms, French House, German House house 2,000 students. 30% of students live on or near campus. 10 intercollegiate sports for men, 4 for women. Intramurals. Student body composition. 8% Asian, 8% Black, 6% Hispanic, 75% White, 3% Other. 35% from out of state.

PACE UNIVERSITY $

Pace College Plaza, New York 10038, (212) 285-3323
Director of Admissions: Stuart L. Medow

- **Undergraduates:** 4,535m, 6,347 w
- **Tuition (1984–1985):** $4,500
- **Room and Board (1984–1985):** $3,130;   **Fees:** $200
- **Degrees offered:** BA, BS, BBA, BPS, BBA/MBA, AA, AAS, AS
- **Mean SAT:** 429v, 471m
- **Student-faculty ratio:** 22 to 1
- **Calendar system:** 4–4–1

A private university established in 1906. 3-acre urban main campus in New York City; branch campuses in Pleasantville/Briarcliffe and the College of White Plains. Air, bus, rail service.

Academic Character MSACS and professional accreditation. 4-4-1 system, 2 6-week summer terms. 52 majors offered in the areas of arts, sciences, math, humanities, social sciences, communications, education, computer science, medical fields, accounting, business, professional studies. Associate degrees in arts & sciences, theatre, general science, early childhood education, industrial relations, and business fields. Certificate programs. Distributive requirements. Graduate degrees granted. Independent study. Honors program. Cooperative work/study, internships, pass/fail. BBA/MBA, BA/BS-MBA programs. Cross-registration at White Plains and Pleasantville/Briarcliff campuses. Visiting Student Program. Open Curriculum Program. Study abroad. Elementary and secondary education certification. InterFuture. Institute for Sub/Urban Governance. Math lab, language lab, computer center. 293,000-volume library with microform resources.

Financial CEEB CSS. University scholarships, grants, state aid; PELL, SEOG, NSS, NDSL, FISL, NSL, CWS. Application deadline March 15.

Admissions High school graduation with 16 units required. GED accepted. Interview recommended. SAT or ACT required; ACH recommended. $15 application fee. Rolling admissions; deadline August 15. $100 deposit required on acceptance of admissions offer. *Early Decision* and *Early Admission* programs. Admission deferral possible. Transfers accepted. Credit possible for CEEB AP, CLEP, and ACT PEP exams, and for life experience. University has own advanced placement program. CAP program for underprepared students.

Student Life Student government. Newspapers, magazine, yearbook, radio station. Music, drama, political, religious, service, special interest groups. Coed dorms. 7% of students live on campus. 3 fraternities, 3 sororities. 10 intercollegiate sports for men, 9 for women. Intramurals. NCAA, ECAC, NAIAW. Student body composition: 6% Asian, 19% Black, 1% Foreign, 13% Hispanic, 1% Native American, 60% White. 11% from out of state.

PRATT INSTITUTE $$

Brooklyn 11205, (212) 636-3669
Director of Admissions: Daniel S. Kimball

- **Undergraduates:** 1,985m, 1,145w
- **Tuition (1984–1985):** $6,500
- **Room and Board (1984–1985):** $1,695–$2,080; **Fees:** $268
- **Degrees offered:** BS, BFA, BPS, BSE, AOS, AAS
- **Student-faculty ratio:** 13 to 1
- **Calendar system:** Semester

A private institute established in 1887. 25-acre urban campus in Brooklyn. Air, rail, bus service.

Academic Character MSACS and professional accreditation. Semester system, 2 summer terms. Majors offered in architecture, art & design, construction, drawing, engineering, environmental design, fashion design, fashion merchandising, film, food service/management, industrial design, interior design, nutrition/dietetics, painting, photography, printmaking, science, sculpture. Self-designed majors. Interdisciplinary studies. Distributive requirements. Graduate degrees granted. Independent study. Cooperative work/study, pass/fail, internships. 6-year program leads to BArch/MS (planning) or BArch/MS (urban design). 5-year engineering/science program. Member consortium with East Coast Schools of Art. Study abroad. Elementary and secondary art education certification. ROTC at St. John's U. Computer center. 220,000-volume library with microform resources.

Financial CEEB CSS. Institute scholarships, grants, awards, loans, state aid; PELL, SEOG, NDSL, CWS. Application deadline February 1.

Admissions High school graduation with 16 units required. Interview & portfolio may be required; home exam required of art & design applicants. SAT or ACT required; ACH required in some cases. $25 application fee. Rolling admissions; deadline April 1. $100 deposit required on acceptance of offer of admission. *Early Decision* and *Early Admission* programs. Admission deferral possible. Transfers accepted. Credit possible for CEEB AP and CLEP exams. HEOP.

Student Life Student government. Newspaper, yearbook, radio station. Student gallery. Honorary, professional, religious, and special interest groups. 1 fraternity with house, 1 sorority. 22% of students live on campus in coed and single-sex dorms. Married-student housing. 7 intercollegiate sports for men, 5 for women. ECAC, NCAA. Student body composition: 5.7% Asian, 15% Black, 6% Hispanic, 63.7% White, 9.6% Other. 31% from out of state.

RENSSELAER POLYTECHNIC INSTITUTE $$$

Troy 12181, (518) 270-6216
Dean of Admissions & Financial Aid: Christopher Small

- **Undergraduates:** 3,774m, 927w
- **Tuition (1984–1985):** $9,050
- **Room and Board (1984–1985):** $3,210;   **Fees:** $340
- **Degrees offered:** BS
- **Mean SAT:** 571v, 691m,   **Mean ACT:** 29
- **Student-faculty ratio:** 10 to 1
- **Calendar system:** Semester

A private institute established in 1824. 260-acre urban campus overlooking the Hudson River, 15 miles from Schenectady and Albany. Served by air, bus, and rail.

Academic Character MSACS and professional accreditation. Semester system, 8-week summer term. Majors offered in aeronautical engineering, architecture, biology, biomedical engineering, building science, chemical engineering, chemistry, civil engineering, communication, computer & systems engineering, computer science, economics, electrical engineering, electrical power engineering, engineering science, environmental engineering, geology, German, interdisciplinary science, management, management engineering, materials engineering, mathematics, mechanical engineering, nuclear engineering, philosophy, physics, and psychology. Distributive requirements. MS, MArch, PhD granted. Independent study. Honors program. Cooperative work/study, pass/fail, internships. Pre-medical program. 3-2 programs with 15 liberal arts colleges. 6-year biology-medicine program with Albany Medical College; biology-dentistry program with U of Penn; management-law with Albany Law. Member Hudson-Mohawk Consortium. Study abroad. ROTC, NROTC, AFROTC. Fresh Water Institute, computer center.

Financial CEEB CSS. Institute scholarships and grants, payment plan; PELL, SEOG, NDSL, campus employment. Scholarship application deadline January 31.

Admissions High school graduation with 10 units required. Interview encouraged. ACT or SAT, and 3 ACH required. $25 application fee. Application deadline January 1. $100 deposit required on acceptance of offer of admission. *Early Decision* and *Early Admission* programs. Admission deferral possible. Transfers accepted. Credit possible for CEEB AP exams. HEOP.

Student Life Student government. Newspaper, magazines, yearbook, radio station. Music and drama groups. Several academic and special interest groups. 24 fraternities (some coed) and 2 sororities; some have houses. 35% of students join. Freshmen must live at home or on campus. Coed and single-sex dorms. Married-student apartments. 80% of students live on campus. 1 ½ years of phys ed required. 15 intercollegiate sports for men, 4 for women; intramurals. AIAW, ECAC, NCAA. Student body composition: 5% Asian, 3% Black, 4% Hispanic, 87% White, 1% Other. 60% from out of state.

ROCHESTER, UNIVERSITY OF $$$

Rochester 14627, (716) 275-3221
Dean of Admissions & Student Aid: Timothy Scholl

- **Undergraduates:** 2,665m, 1,789w
- **Tuition (1984–1985):** $8,240
- **Room and Board (1984–1985):** $3,585;   **Fees:** $238
- **Degrees offered:** BA, BS, BMus
- **Mean SAT:** 539v, 614m,   **Mean ACT:** 27
- **Student-faculty ratio:** 13 to 1
- **Calendar system:** 4–4–X (X is optional period of varying length)

A private university established in 1850. Campus in residential section of Rochester. Served by air, bus, and rail.

Academic Character MSACS and professional accreditation. Semester system, optional May term, summer term. Divisions include College of Arts & Science, Graduate School of Education & Human Development, College of Engineering & Architecture, School of Medicine & Dentistry, School of Nursing, Eastman School of Music, Graduate School of Management. 30 majors offered for the BA degree, 14 for the BS, 5 for the BMus, and part-time general studies major. Offers only undergraduate degree in optics in U.S. Self-designed majors. Distributive requirements. Graduate and professional degrees granted. Independent study. Honors program. Phi Beta Kappa. Pass/fail. Internships in some majors. 3-2 bachelor's-master's programs in human development, management, optics, political science, biology-geology, community health. Dual-degree program in liberal arts and engineering. 8-year medical school program. Cross-registration with Rochester Area Colleges Consortium. Washington Semester. Study abroad. Politics, fine arts semesters in Britain. Internships in London, St. Croix. NROTC. Centers for Brain Research, Visual Science. Laser lab. Observatory. Space Science Center. Computer Center. Over 1,956,000-volume library with microform resources.

Financial CEEB CSS. University scholarships, grants, loans, payment plans; PELL, SEOG, NDSL, NSL, FISL, CWS. Application deadline January 31.

Admissions High school graduation with 16 units required. Interview encouraged. Audition required for BA in Music applicants. SAT or ACT required; 3 ACH recommended. $25 application fee. Preferred application deadline January 15. $200 deposit required on acceptance of offer of admission. *Early Decision* and *Early Admission* programs. Admission deferral possible. Transfers accepted. Credit possible for CEEB AP exams; unversity has own advanced placement program.

Student Life Student government. Newspaper, magazine, yearbook, radio station. Music, drama, dance, film groups. Black Student Union. Spanish and Latin American Student Association. 90 religious, academic, service, and special interest groups. 11 fraternities, 7 with houses, and 5 sororities. Coed and single-sex dorms. Special interest housing. Married-student housing. 85% of students live on campus. 10 intercollegiate sports for men, 7 for women, 1 coed; intramurals. AIAW, ECAC, NCAA. Student body composition: 3% Black, 1% Hispanic, 89% White, 7% Other. 44% from out of state.

ROCHESTER INSTITUTE OF TECHNOLOGY $$

Rochester 14623, (716) 475-6631
Director of Admissions: E. Louis Guard

- **Undergraduates:** 8,928m, 4,705w
- **Tuition (1984–1985):** $6,255
- **Room and Board (1984–1985):** $3,321;   **Fees:** $135

- **Degrees offered:** BS, BFA, BT, AA, AS, AAS
- **Mean SAT:** 497v, 587m,   **Mean ACT:** 25
- **Student-faculty ratio:** 17 to 1
- **Calendar system:** Quarter

A private institute established in 1829. 1,300-acre suburban campus in Henrietta, 5 miles from Rochester. Air, bus, and rail in Rochester.

Academic Character MSACS and professional accreditation. Quarter system, 2 5-week summer terms. 20 majors offered by the College of Applied Science & Technology, 4 by the College of Business, 5 by the College of Engineering, 10 by the College of Fine & Applied Arts, 2 by the College of General Studies, 11 by the College of Graphic Arts & Photography, 11 by the College of Science, and 4 by the National Technical Institute for the Deaf. Distributive requirements. ME, MS, MST, MBA, MFA granted. Cooperative work/study, internships. Member Rochester Area Colleges Consortium. Dual-degree program with Mass. College of Pharmacy. Study abroad in Scandinavia. ROTC; NROTC at U of Rochester. Media Resource Center, TV Center, Graphic Arts Center. 194-000-volume library.

Financial CEEB CSS. Institute scholarships, grants, loans, state grants, payment plans; PELL, SEOG, NDSL, FISL, CWS, institute has own work program. Priority application deadline for scholarships March 1.

Admissions High school graduation with 16 units required. Interview encouraged. Portfolio required for College of Fine & Applied Arts. SAT or ACT required; ACH recommended. $25 application fee. Rolling admissions; suggest applying early in fall. $200 deposit required on acceptance of offer of admission. *Early Decision* and *Early Admission* programs. Admission deferral possible. Transfers accepted. Credit possible for CEEB AP, CLEP, and state exams; university has own advanced placement program. HEOP.

Student Life Student government. Newspaper, magazine, yearbook. Drama, debate groups. Black Awareness Coordinating Committee. Academic, religious, honorary, service, and special interest organizations. 10 fraternities and 3 sororities, all with houses. 10% of men and 1% of women join. Freshmen must live at home or on campus. Coed and single-sex dorms. Special interest housing. Married-student housing. Coop dorms. 50% of students live on campus. 6 quarters of phys ed required. 9 intercollegiate sports for men, 4 for women; intramurals. AIAW, ECAC, NCAA, ICAC. Student body composition: 12% minority. 45% from out of state.

ST. BONAVENTURE UNIVERSITY $

St. Bonaventure 14778, (716) 375-2400
Director of Admissions: Donald C. Burkard

- **Undergraduates:** 1,222m, 1,117w
  Tuition (1984–1985): $4,990
  Room and Board (1984–1985): $2,650
- **Degrees offered:** BA, BS, BBA
- **Mean SAT:** 481v, 522m,   **Mean ACT:** 24
- **Student-faculty ratio:** 15 to 1
- **Calendar system:** Semester

A private university established in 1856 by the Franciscan Fathers. 500-acre campus in small city of Saint Bonaventure, 65 miles from Buffalo. Served by bus; air nearby.

Academic Character MSACS accreditation. Semester system, 4- and 5-week summer terms. Majors offered in classical languages, English, history, mass communications, modern languages, philosophy, psychology, social science, sociology, theology, biology, chemistry, computer science, economics, elementary education, mathematics, medical technology, physical education, physics, psychology, accounting, finance, management sciences, and marketing. Interdisciplinary majors. Graduate degrees granted. Senior exams, 9 hours of theology, 9 of philosophy required. Honors program. Pass/fail, internships. Preprofessional programs in dentistry, engineering, law, medicine, osteopathy, pharmacy, veterinary medicine. 2-3 engineering program with U of Detroit. Member Western NY Consortium, Visiting Student Program. Study abroad. Elementary and secondary education certification. ROTC. Computer center, language lab. 253,000 volume library.

Financial CEEB CSS. University scholarships, grants, loans, state grants, loans, scholarships, payment plan; PELL, SEOG, GSL, NDSL, FISL, CWS. Application deadlines March 1 (scholarships), April 30 (loans).

Admissions High school graduation with 16 units required. GED accepted. Interview encouraged. SAT or ACT required. $20 application fee. Rolling admissions. $125 deposit required on acceptance of offer of admission. *Early Decision, Concurrent Enrollment, Early Admission* programs. Admission deferral possible. Transfers accepted. Credit possible for CEEB AP, CLEP, and ACT PEP exams. HEOP.

Student Life Student government. Newspaper, magazine, yearbook, radio station. Music, drama groups. Women's Council. Academic, honorary, religious, service, and special interest groups. Single students under 21 must live at home or on campus. Single-sex dorms. No married-student housing. 84% of students live on campus. 10 intercollegiate sports for men, 6 for women; intramurals. AIAW, ECAC, NCAA, Little 3. Student body composition: 1% Black, 99% White. 20% from out of state.

ST. LAWRENCE UNIVERSITY $$$

Canton 13617, (315) 379-5261
Director of Admissions: Conrad J. Sharrow

- **Undergraduates:** 1,100m, 1,100 w
- **Tuition (1984–1985):** $8,460
- **Room and Board (1984–1985):** $2,865; **Fees:** $65
- **Degrees offered:** BA, BS
- **Mean SAT:** 525v, 570m
- **Student-faculty ratio:** 13 to 1
- **Calendar system:** 4–1–4

A private university established in 1856. 1,000-acre campus located in small town of Canton in St. Lawrence River Valley, 80 miles from Syracuse and Montreal. Served by bus.

Academic Character MSACS and professional accreditation. 4-1-4 system, 2 5-week summer terms. Majors offered in Canadian studies, economics, English, fine arts, French, German, government, history, modern languages, music, philosophy, religious studies, sociology, Spanish, theatre arts, biology, biochemistry, biophysics, chemistry, environmental studies, geology, geophysics, mathematics, physical education, physics, psychology. Self-designed majors. Distributive requirements. Masters degrees granted. Independent study. Honors programs. Phi Beta Kappa. Pass/fail, internships.

3-2 engineering programs with Clarkson, Columbia, Rensselaer, U of Rochester, others. 4-1 MBA program with Clarkson. 3-1 programs in dentistry, law, medicine. Cross-registration with area colleges. Study abroad in Canada, Europe, Kenya. Secondary education certification. ROTC; AFROTC at Clarkson. Computer lab, language lab. 310,000-volume library with microform resources.

Financial CEEB CSS. University scholarships and loans, state scholarships, payment plan; PELL, SEOG, NDSL, GSL, CWS. Scholarship application deadline February 15.

Admissions High school graduation required. Interview encouraged. SAT and 3 ACH, or ACT required. $30 application fee. Application deadline February 1. $500 deposit required on acceptance of offer of admission (May 1). *Early Decision* Program. Admission deferral possible. Transfers accepted. Credit possible for CEEB AP, CLEP, and state exams.

Student Life Student government. Newspaper, magazine, yearbook, radio stations. Music, speaking, drama groups. Black Student Union. Native American, Jewish organizations. Honorary, tutoring groups. 7 fraternities and 5 sororities; all have houses. 40% of men and 35% of women join. Students must live on campus. Coed and single-sex dorms. Special interest housing. 99% of students live on campus. Cars discouraged. 1 year of phys ed required. 12 intercollegiate sports for men, 9 for women, 1 coed; intramurals. AIAW, ICAC. Student body composition: 1% Black, 1% Native American, 98% White. 50% from out of state.

SARAH LAWRENCE COLLEGE $$$

Bronxville 10708 (914) 793-4242
Director of Admissions: Dudley F. Blodget

- **Undergraduates:** 170m, 670w
- **Tuition (1984–1985):** $9,980
- **Room and Board (1984–1985):** $4,200; **Fees:** $100
- **Degrees offered:** BA
- **Mean SAT:** 530v, 500m
- **Student-faculty ratio:** 10 to 1
- **Calendar system:** Semester

A private college established in 1928, became coed in 1968. 35-acre suburban campus in Bronxville, 15 miles north of New York City. Served by bus and rail.
Academic Character MSACS accreditation. Semester system. Self-designed majors. Courses in anthropology, architecture, art, Asian studies, biology, chemistry, classical languages, dance, economics, film, French, German, history, international studies, Italian, Latin, literature, mathematics, music, philosophy, physics, political science, psychology, religion, Russian, sociology, Spanish, theatre, women's studies, and writing. MA, MFA, MS, MPS granted. Independent study. Pass/fail, internships. Preprofessional programs in medicine, human genetics. Study abroad in cooperation with U of Michigan. Early Childhood Center. 166,000-volume library with microform resources.
Financial CEEB CSS. College scholarships and loans, state grants, Native American aid, payment plan; PELL, SEOG, NDSL, GSL, CWS; college has own work program. Application deadline February 1.
Admissions High school graduation with 16 units required. Interview encouraged. SAT, ACT, or 3 ACH required. $25 application fee. Application deadline February 15. $250 deposit required on acceptance of offer of

admission. *Early Admission* and *Early Decision* programs. Admission deferral possible. Transfers accepted in January. Credit possible for CEEB AP exams.
Student Life Student government. Newspaper, magazine. Music, dance groups. Political, academic, environmental, and special interest clubs. Coed and single-sex dorms. 80% of students live on campus. 1 year of phys ed required. 4 intercollegiate sports; intramurals. Student body composition: 3% Asian, 5% Black, 1% Hispanic, 91% White. 65-70% from out of state.

SKIDMORE COLLEGE $$$

Saratoga Springs 12866, (518) 584-5000
Director of Admissions: Louise B. Wise

- **Undergraduates:** 735m, 1,380w
- **Tuition (1984–1985):** $8,050
- **Room and Board (1984–1985):** $3,450
- **Degrees offered:** BA, BS
- **Mean SAT:** 530v, 540m,   **Mean ACT:** 26
- **Student-faculty ratio:** 12 to 1
- **Calendar system:** 4–1–4

A private college established in 1922, became coed in 1971. 650-acre wooded campus in Saratoga Springs, 2 hours from Lake Placid, 34 miles from Albany. Served by bus and rail; airport in Albany.
Academic Character MSACS and professional accreditation. 4-1-4 system, 6-week summer term. 21 majors offered for the BA, 8 for the BS, 20 interdepartmental. Self-designed programs. Courses in Asian or Russian studies, computer applications. Senior exam or project required. Independent study. Honors program. Phi Beta Kappa. Pass/fail, internships. Preprofessional programs in art, business, law, medicine, physical education, theatre. 3-2 engineering program with Dartmouth. 4-1 MBA program with Clarkson. BS-RN program. Exchange with Colgate, 6 others. Washington Semester, New York City year. Hudson-Mohawk Association. Study abroad. Early childhood, elementary, and secondary education certification. Computer center, language lab, art gallery. 290,000-volume library.
Financial CEEB CSS. College scholarships, grants, loans, payment plan; PELL, SEOG, NSS, NDSL, NSL, CWS. Scholarship application deadline February 1.
Admissions High school graduation required with 16 units recommended. Interview encouraged. SAT required; ACT accepted. 3 ACH recommended. $30 application fee. Application deadline February 1. $300 deposit required on acceptance of offer of admission. *Early Admission* and *Early Decision* programs. Admission deferral possible. Transfers accepted. Credit possible for CEEB AP and CLEP exams. HEOP.
Student Life Student government. Newspaper, magazines, yearbooks, radio station. Music, dance, film, drama groups. Black, Latin, International Student organizations. Academic, religious, service, and special interest groups. Freshmen must live on campus. Coed and single-sex dorms. Special interest housing. No married-student housing. 85% of students live on campus. 8 intercollegiate sports for men, 12 for women, 1 coed; intramurals. AIAW, NAIA, NAC, NIAC, Mayflower Conference. Student body composition: 1% Asian, 2.6% Black, 1.3% Hispanic, 0.1% Native American, 90% White, 5% Other. 64% from out of state.

STATE UNIVERSITY OF NEW YORK ALBANY $

Western & Washington Avenues, Albany 12222, (518) 457-3300
Director of Admissions & Records: Rodney A. Hart

- **Undergraduates:** 5,543m, 5,849w
- **Tuition (1984–1985):** $1,467 (in-state), $2,767 (out-of-state)
- **Room and Board (1984–1985):** $2,363;   **Fees:** $117
- **Degrees offered:** BA, BS
- **Mean SAT:** 515v, 582m
- **Student-faculty ratio:** 15 to 1
- **Calendar system:** Semester

A public university founded in 1844, joined SUNY in 1948. 350-acre urban main campus with 284-acre Mohawk River campus 15 miles away and 800-acre recreational Adirondack campus 75 miles north. Air, rail, and bus service.
Academic Character MSACS and professional accreditation. Semester system, 3- & 6-week summer terms. Over 50 majors offered by the Schools & Colleges of Business, Education, Humanities & Fine Arts, Science & Mathematics, Social & Behavioral Science, Social Welfare, Criminal Justice, and Public Affairs. Self-designed majors. Distributive requirements. Graduate and professional degrees granted. Independent study, honors program, Phi Beta Kappa, pass/fail, credit by exam, internships. Preprofessional programs include dentistry, law, medicine. BA/MA, BS/MS programs in 6 fields. Exchange with 60 schools in NY state through Visting Student Program. Cross-registration with 8 area schools. Over 80 study abroad programs. Secondary education certification. ROTC. AFROTC & NROTC nearby. Computer center, meteorological lab. Art gallery. 1,000,000-volume library.
Financial CEEB CSS. College scholarships, loans, state scholarships, grants, loans, aid to Native Americans; PELL, SEOG, NSS, NDSL, NSL, GSL, CWS, work incentive program. Application deadline April 25.
Admissions High school graduation with 18 units required. Portfolio required for art majors; audition for music majors. Interview for some programs. SAT or ACT required. $10 application fee. Rolling admissions; suggest applying by January 5. $50 tuition deposit required on acceptance of admissions offer (May 1). *Early Entrance* and *Concurrent Enrollment* programs. Admission deferral possible. Transfers accepted. Credit possible for CEEB AP, CLEP, and state exams. Talented Student Admission Program. Educational Opportunity Program.
Student Life Student government. Newspaper, arts magazine, yearbook, radio station. Music & drama groups. Many academic, honorary, political, religious, service, and special interest groups. 7 fraternities and 4 sororities. 12% of men and 5% of women join. Coed and single-sex dorms. No married-student housing. 59% of students live on campus. 11 intercollegiate sports for men, 9 for women; many intramurals. AIAW, ECAC, SUNY Conference. Student body composition: 1.4% Asian, 2.9% Black, 2.7% Foreign, 1.7% Hispanic, 0.3% Native American, 91% White. 1% from out of state.

STATE UNIVERSITY OF NEW YORK AT BINGHAMTON $

Binghamton 13901, (607) 798-2171
Asst. Vice President for Admissions & Financial Aid: Geoffrey Gould

- **Undergraduates:** 4,065m, 4,585w
- **Tuition (1984–1985):** $1,496 (in-state), $2,796 (out-of-state)

- **Room and Board (1984–1985):** $2,754
- **Degrees offered:** BA, BS
- **Mean SAT:** 532v, 590m
- **Student-faculty ratio:** 20 to 1
- **Calendar system:** Semester

A public university established in 1946. 606-acre suburban campus 185 miles northwest of New York City, and one hour from 225-acre recreation & field study area. Air and bus service.

Academic Character MSACS and professional accreditation. Semester system, 4- & 6-week summer terms. Over 45 majors offered by the Harpur College (of Arts & Sciences), schools of Management, Nursing, and General Studies & Professional Education (for adult/evening programs). Many area studies programs. Self-designed majors. Distributive requirements. Graduate degrees granted. Independent, group, field study. Honors program, Phi Beta Kappa, internships. Preprofessional programs in dentistry, engineering, health sciences, law, medicine. 3-2 program in management. 3-2 engineering programs with 5 schools. Exchanges with 60 schools in NY state through Visting Student Program. Cross-registration with Broome Community College. Many study abroad programs. AFROTC, NROTC, ROTC at Cornell. Center for Medieval & Renaissance Studies. Computer, language lab. 1,017,000-volume library with microform resources.

Financial CEEB CSS. College scholarships, grants, loans; state scholarships, grants, loans, aid to Native Americans; PELL, SEOG, NDSL, NSL, GSL, CWS. Application deadlines February 1 (scholarships & grants), April 1 (loans).

Admissions High school graduation required. Course requirements vary with program. SAT or ACT required. $10 application fee. Rolling admissions; suggest applying in October or November. Deadline February 15. $50 tuition deposit required on acceptance of admissions offer (May 1); $125 room deposit by July 1. *Early Entrance* and *Concurrent Enrollment* programs. Admission deferral possible. Transfers accepted. Credit possible for CEEB AP, CLEP, and university exams. Talented Student Admission Program Educational Opportunity Program.

Student Life Student government. Newspaper, journals, yearbook, radio station. Several music groups. Drama club. Many ethnic, academic, honorary, religious, service, women's, and special interest groups. Single freshmen must live at home or on campus. University composed of 1 commuter's & 5 residential colleges. Coed dorms. No married-student housing. 52% of students live on campus. Class attendance required. 2 semesters of phys ed required. 8 intercollegiate sports for men, 7 for women; many intramurals. AIAW, ECAC, NCAA, SUNY Conference. 4% of students from out of state.

STATE UNIVERSITY OF NEW YORK COLLEGE AT FREDONIA $

Fredonia 14063, (716) 673-3251
Director of Admissions: William S. Clark

- **Undergraduates:** 2,358m, 2,539w
- **Tuition (1984–1985):** $1,459 (in-state), $2,759 (out-of-state)
- **Room and Board (1984–1985):** $2,636;   **Fees:** $134
- **Degrees offered:** BA, BS, BSEd, BFA, BMus, BASS, BSSS
- **Mean SAT:** 460v, 520m,   **Mean ACT:** 23
- **Student-faculty ratio:** 18 to 1
- **Calendar system:** Semester

A public college established in 1826. 230-acre campus in a residential community near Lake Erie, 45 miles from Buffalo. Bus service.

Academic Character MSACS and professional accreditation. Semester system, 2 5-week summer terms. Over 35 majors offered in the areas of accounting, arts, business administration, communications, education, engineering, English, geology, geophysics, history, languages, math & computer science, medical technology, music, music education, music therapy, musical theatre, philosophy, physics, psychology, sciences, social sciences, sound recording, speech pathology & audiology, theatre. Special & self-designed majors. Distributive requirements. Masters degrees granted. Independent study, Phi Beta Kappa, pass/fail, internships. Preprofessional programs in dentistry, law, medicine, theology. Cooperative programs in agriculture with Cornell; in special education with SUNY Buffalo & D'Youville; in engineering with 11 schools including Cornell, Columbia, RPI, Ohio State, Clarkson. Consortium with other western NY schools. Study abroad, exchange programs in Europe. Early childhood, elementary, secondary, and special education certification. ROTC. Education research centers. Computer. 300,000-volume library.

Financial CEEB CSS. College scholarships, grants, loans, state aid; PELL, SEOG, NDSL, GSL, CWS. File FAF by April 1.

Admissions High school graduation with 16 units recommended. Specific requirements for some programs. Music majors must audition. SAT or ACT required. $10 application fee. Rolling admissions; suggest applying by May 1. $100 deposit required on acceptance of admissions offer (May 1). *Early Entrance, Early Decision, Concurrent Enrollment* programs. Admission deferral possible. Transfers accepted. Credit possible for CEEB AP, CLEP, and college exams. Nontraditional applicants accepted. Educational Development Program.

Student Life Student government. Newspaper, literary magazine, yearbook, radio station. Many music groups. Drama & dance groups. Honorary, academic, religious, special interest, and service groups. 2 fraternities and 2 sororities. Freshmen must live on campus. Single-sex and coed dorms. No married-student housing. 60% of students live on campus. 8 intercollegiate sports for men, 5 for women; intramurals. ECAC, NAIA, AIAW, NCAA, SUNY Conference. Student body composition: 3% minority. 5% of students from out of state.

STATE UNIVERSITY OF NEW YORK COLLEGE AT GENESEO $

Geneseo 14454, (716) 245-5571
Dean of Admissions: William L. Caren

- **Undergraduates:** 4,492 combined
- **Tuition (1984–1985):** $1,475 (in-state), $2,775 (out-of-state)
- **Room and Board (1984–1985):** $2,300;   **Fees:** $125
- **Degrees offered:** BA, BS, BSEd
- **Mean SAT:** 520v, 562m,   **Mean ACT:** 25
- **Student-faculty ratio:** 20 to 1
- **Calendar system:** Semester

A public college established in 1867. Campus in a small town 30 miles south of Rochester. Bus to Rochester.

Academic Character MSACS and professional accreditation. Semester system, 2 3- and one 5-week summer terms. Over 35 majors offered in the areas of American civilization, arts, Black studies, comparative literature, computer, drama, education, English, geography, geology, languages, management, math, medical technology, music, philosophy, psychology, sciences, social sciences, and speech. Double majors. Minors in 13 additional areas. Distributive requirements. Masters degrees granted. Independent study, honors program, pass/fail, internships. Preprofessional programs in dentistry, law, medicine, medical technology, nursing, planning, public service, theology, veterinary medicine. 3-2 MBA program. 3-2 program in engineering with 8 schools; in environmental science & forestry with SUNY-Syracuse. Visting Student Program. Washington Semester. Cross-registration with area colleges. Many study abroad programs. Elementary, secondary, and special education certification. ROTC at Rochester Institute of Technology. Computer center. 342,000-volume library with microform resources.

Financial CEEB CSS and ACT FAS. College scholarships, grants, loans, state aid; PELL, SEOG, NDSL, GSL, CWS. File FAF by February 1.

Admissions High school graduation with 18 units recommended. Interview urged. SAT or ACT required. $10 application fee. Rolling admissions; suggest applying in November of 12th year. Priority application deadline March 15. $50 tuition and $50 room deposits required on acceptance of admissions offer (May 1). *Early Entrance* Program. Admission deferral possible. Transfers accepted. Credit possible for CEEB AP, CLEP, and college exams, and for military learning experience. Talented Student Admission Program. Educational Opportunity Program.

Student Life Student Association. Newspaper, literary magazine, yearbook, radio station. Music, debate, and drama groups. Special interest clubs. 6 fraternities and 7 sororities. Freshmen must live at home or on campus. Coed, single-sex, special interest, language dorms. 65% of students live on campus. 4 semesters of phys ed required. 7 intercollegiate sports for men, 6 for women; many intramurals. ECAC, AIAW, NCAA, SUNY Conference. Student body composition: 0.3% Asian, 2.1% Black, 0.8% Hispanic, 0.2% Native American, 96.6% White. 2% from out of state.

SYRACUSE UNIVERSITY $$

Syracuse 13210, (315) 423-3611
Dean of Admissions & Financial Aid: Thomas F. Cummings, Jr.

- **Undergraduates:** 6,305m, 5,734w
- **Tuition (1984–1985):** $7,140
- **Room and Board (1984–1985):** $3,600;   **Fees:** $205
- **Degrees offered:** BA, BS, BFA, BID, BMus
- **Mean SAT:** 495v, 530m
- **Student-faculty ratio:** 15 to 1
- **Calendar system:** Semester

A private university established in 1870. 200-acre main campus in residential section of Syracuse. Served by air, bus, and rail.

Academic Character MSACS and professional accreditation. Semester system, 2 6-week summer terms. 39 majors offered by the College of Arts & Sciences, 8 by the School of Education, 12 by the L.C. Smith College of Engineering, 7 by the SUNY College of Environmental Science & Forestry, 6 by the College for Human Development, 12 by the School of Management, 8 by the School of Public Communications, 33 by the College of Visual & Performing Arts, and majors in architecture, computer science, nursing, and social work. Graduate and professional degrees granted. Honors program. Phi Beta Kappa. Dual degree programs in most colleges. 3-year degree programs. 3-2 engineering program. 3-1 medicine, dentistry programs. 6-year AB-MArch program. Study abroad. ROTC, AFROTC. Special Education Center, nursery school, audio-visual center. Language labs, computer center. 2,000,000-volume library with microform resources.

Financial CEEB CSS. University scholarships, grants, loans, payment plan; PELL, SEOG, NDSL, CWS. Scholarship application deadline February 1.

Admissions High school graduation with 16 units required. Interview encouraged. Audition or portfolio required for arts majors. SAT or ACT required. $25 application fee. Suggested application deadline February 1. $150 tuition and $100 room (for boarders) deposits required on acceptance of offer of admission. *Early Decision* and *Early Admission* programs. Admission deferral possible. Transfers accepted. Credit possible for CEEB AP, CLEP, and state exams. HEOP.

Student Life Student government. Newspaper, magazine, yearbook, radio & TV stations. Music, drama, debate groups. Political, religious, and special interest organizations. 30 fraternities and 25 sororities; all have houses. 12% of men and 8% of women join. Freshmen must live on campus. Married-student housing. Coop dorms. 82% of students live on campus. Freshmen and sophomores may not have cars or motorcycles. Intercollegiate and intramural sports. Student body composition: 1% Asian, 10% Black, 2% Hispanic, 0.2% Native American, 86.8% White. 55% from out of state.

UNION COLLEGE AND UNIVERSITY $$$

Schenectady 12308, (518) 370-6112
Dean of Admissions: Kenneth A. Nourse

- **Undergraduates:** 1,250m, 750w
- **Tuition (1984–1985):** $8,710
- **Room and Board (1984–1985)**$3,070   **Fees:** $126
- **Degrees Offered:** AB, BS, BSCE, BSEE, BSME
- **Mean SAT:** 560v, 630m,   **Mean ACT:** 25
- **Student-faculty ratio:** 13 to 1
- **Calendar system:** Trimester

A private college established in 1795, became coed in 1970. 100-acre urban campus, 15 miles from Albany. Served by air, bus, and rail.

Academic Character MSACS and professional accreditation. Trimester system, summer term. Majors offered in art, biology, chemistry, classics, computer science, drama, economics, engineering (5 areas), English, general science, general social science, history, mathematics, medical education, modern languages, music, philosophy, physics, political science, psychology, and sociology. Self-designed majors. Distributive requirements. MA, MS, PhD granted. Independent study. Honors program. Phi Beta Kappa. Pass/fail, internships. 3-2 BA-MA programs. 2-4 medical and 3-3 law programs with Albany Medical and Law schools. Cross-registration with 16 area schools. Study abroad. International exchange programs. Secondary education certification. ROTC at Siena, RPI; AFROTC, NROTC at RPI. Horticultural garden, language lab, computer center. 400,000-volume library with microform resources.

Financial CEEB CSS. University scholarships, grants, loans, payment plan;

NDSL, GSL, CWS; university has own work program. Scholarship application deadline February 1.

Admissions High school graduation with 16 units required. Interview encouraged. SAT and 3 ACH, or ACT required. $30 application fee. Application deadline February 1. $200 deposit required on acceptance of offer of admission. *Early Decision* and *Early Admission* programs. Admission deferral possible. Transfers accepted. Credit possible for CEEB AP, CLEP, and state exams. EOP.

Student Life Student government. Newspaper, magazine, yearbook, radio stations. Music, speaking, drama, film groups. Political, religious, academic, professional, service, and special interest organizations. 16 fraternities and 3 sororities. 36% of men and 19% of women join. Freshmen must live on campus. Coed and single-sex dorms. 75% of students live on campus. 12 intercollegiate sports for men, 10 for women; intramural & club sports. AIAW, ECAC, NCAA. Student body composition: 1.8% Black, 94.4% White, 3.8% Other. 40% from out of state.

UNITED STATES MERCHANT MARINE ACADEMY $

Kings Point, Great Neck 11024, (516) 482-8200
Director of Admissions: Emmanuel L. Jenkins

- **Undergraduates:** 970m, 89w
- **Fees:** $700
- **Degrees offered:** BS
- **Mean SAT:** 510v, 620m
- **Student-faculty ratio:** 13 to 1
- **Calendar system:** Quarter

A federal academy controlled by the Department of Commerce, established in 1943, became coed in 1974. 68-acre suburban campus in Kings Point, 20 miles from New York City.

Academic Character MSACS accreditation. Quarter system. Majors offered in marine engineering, nautical science, and a dual license. Minors offered in 15 areas. Courses in humanities, management, science. 4-year program leading to license as merchant marine deck or engineering officer and commission as Ensign in Naval Reserve. Distributive requirements. Independent study. Junior year spent on merchant vessels. Maritime Research Center, Operations Research Facility. Over 80 vessels, small craft. 100,000-volume library.

Financial 4-year government scholarship covers expenses. $461 monthly salary.

Admissions High school graduation with 15 units required. Candidates must be US citizens between 17 and 25 years of age. Congressional nomination required. SAT or ACT required. Application deadline March 1.

Student Life Regiment organization under senior class. Newspaper, yearbook. Music, debate groups. Professional, honorary, and special interest societies and clubs. Students must live on campus. Upperclassmen may have cars. Class attendance required. Military rules. Midshipmen may not marry. Weekend liberty and holiday leaves granted. Phys ed required each semester. 15 intercollegiate sports for men and women; intramurals. Students from each state; quota system.

UNITED STATES MILITARY ACADEMY $

West Point 10996, (914) 938-4041
Director of Admissions: Col. Manley E. Rogers

- **Undergraduates:** 3,920m, 480w
- **Degrees Offered:** BS
- **Mean SAT:** 560v, 640m,   **Mean ACT:** 27
- **Student-faculty ratio:** 7 to 1
- **Calendar system:** Semester

A public service academy established in 1802, became coed in 1976. On graduation cadets are commissioned as 2nd Lieutenants and must serve five years in the army. 16,000-acre campus on Hudson River near small town of Highland Falls, 50 miles from New York City. Rail station nearby; airport and bus station in New York City.

Academic Character MSACS accreditation. Semester system, 2-month summer term. 9 concentrations offered in applied sciences & engineering, 4 in basic sciences, 10 in humanities, 9 in national security & public affairs, and 2 interdisciplinary. Double majors. Distributive requirements. Independent study. Honors program. Summer military training programs in US and abroad. Exchange programs with Air Force, Coast Guard, Naval Academies. Science Research Lab, computer center, TV system, military museum. 400,000-volume library.

Financial No tuition, room & board, or fees. Cadets receive $5,536 salary per year for expenses. Free medical and dental care.

Admissions High school graduation with 13 units required. GED accepted. Applicants must be unmarried US citizens between 17 and 22 years of age, and without parental responsibilities. Nomination from approved source required. SAT or ACT required. Rolling admissions; suggest applying by September of 12th year. $500 deposit required on entrance. *Early Decision* Program. Admission deferral possible. Transfers accepted as first-semester freshmen. Credit possible for CEEB AP and CLEP exams.

Student Life Military structure. Newspaper, magazine, yearbook, radio station. Music, debate, art, film, drama groups. Academic, religious, and special interest organizations. Students must live on campus. Seniors may keep cars on campus. Class attendance required. Honor code. Leaves granted. 8 semesters of phys ed and intercollegiate or intramural sports required. 22 intercollegiate sports for men, 9 for women; several intramural and club sports. AIAW, NCAA. Student body composition: 2.9% Asian, 6.3% Black, 3.8% Hispanic, 0.3% Native American, 86.7% White. 88% from out of state.

VASSAR COLLEGE $$$

Poughkeepsie 12601, (914) 452-7000
Director of Admissions: Fred R. Brooks, Jr.

- **Undergraduates:** 947m, 1,411w
- **Tuition (1984–1985):** $8,800
- **Room and Board (1984–1985):** $3,720;   **Fees:** $180
- **Degrees offered:** AB
- **Mean SAT:** 600v, 600m
- **Student-faculty ratio:** 11 to 1
- **Calendar system:** Semester

A private college established in 1861, became coed in 1969. 1,000-acre rural campus outside the small city of Poughkeepsie, 75 miles north of New York City. Served by air, bus, and rail.

Academic Character MSACS accreditation. Semester system. Concentrations offered in Africana studies, American culture, anthropology, art, astronomy, biochemistry, biology, biopsychology, chemistry, classics, computer science, drama, East Asian studies, economics, English, environmental science, French, geography-anthropology, geology, German, Greek, Hispanic studies, history, Italian, Latin, mathematics, music, philosophy, physics, political science, psychology, religion, Russian, sociology, and science, technology & society. Self-designed majors. MA, MS granted. Independent study. Honors programs. Phi Beta Kappa. Pass/fail, internships. 4-year AB-MA programs in chemistry, French, Hispanic studies. 12-College Exchange. College Venture program. Washington Semester, theatre semester, Mystic Seaport semester. Study abroad. Elementary and secondary education certification. 543,125-volume library.

Financial CEEB CSS. College scholarships, state grants, payment plan; PELL, SEOG, NDSL, FISL, GSL, CWS; college has own work program. File FAF by February 1.

Admissions High school graduation required. Interview encouraged. SAT and 3 ACH required. $20 application fee. Application deadline February 1. $200 deposit required on acceptance of offer of admission. *Early Decision* and *Early Admission* programs. Admission deferral possible. Transfers accepted. Credit possible for CEEB AP, CLEP, and state exams.

Student Life Student government. Newspaper, magazines, yearbook, radio station. Music, dance, drama, film groups. 33 academic, honorary, political, religious, service, and special interest organizations. Coed and women's dorms. Married-student housing. Coop and apartment housing. 97% of students live on campus. Attendance at Fall Convocation required. 6 intercollegiate sports for men, 7 for women, 1 coed; intramural and club sports, ECAC, AIAW. Student body composition: 3% Asian, 5% Black, 6% Hispanic, 86% White. 60% from out of state.

YESHIVA UNIVERSITY $$

500 West 185 Street, New York 10033, (212) 960-5400
Director of Admissions: Paul S. Glasser

- **Undergraduates:** 855m, 651 w
- **Tuition (1984–1985):** $6,230
- **Room and Board (1984–1985):** $3,300;   **Fees:** $185
- **Degrees offered:** BA, BS, AA
- **Mean SAT:** 560v, 590m
- **Student-faculty ratio:** 8 to 1
- **Calendar system:** Semester

A private university under Jewish auspices with coordinate undergraduate colleges and coed graduate schools. Established in 1886. Urban campus with Stern College for Women at 245 Lexington Avenue and branch campus in the Bronx. Air, bus, and rail service.

Academic Character MSACS accreditation. Semester system. Majors offered in accounting, biology, chemistry, computer sciences, economics, English, history, mathematics, political science, pre-health, psychology, sociology, and speech-drama. Yeshiva College also offers classics, French,

Hebrew, music, philosophy, physics, pre-engineering, and pre-law. Stern College also offers education, Hebraic studies, and nursing. Minors offered. Distributives, comprehensive major exam, and Jewish studies required. Graduate and professional degrees granted. Independent study. Honors program. Men's college has 3-2 engineering program with NY Polytechnic and Columbia; 3-4 program with NY College of Podiatry. Women's college has cooperative programs in art, design, and fashion with Fashion Institute; Shanah program of intensive Jewish studies. Year in Israel. Language labs. Museum. 850,000-volume library with microform resources.

Financial CEEB CSS. University scholarships, grants, loans, state aid; PELL, SEOG, NDSL, FISL, work/study contracts.

Admissions High school graduation with 16 units required. GED accepted. Interview required. SAT required; Hebrew ACH required. $25 application fee. Rolling admissions. *Early Admission* and *Concurrent Enrollment* programs. Admission deferral possible. Transfers accepted. Credit possible for CEEB AP, CLEP, ACT PEP, and state exams. Conditional admission may be arranged.

Student Life College Senates. Newspapers, yearbooks, publications. Drama groups. Academic, service, and special interest groups. Students not living with relatives live in residence halls. 85% of men and 90% of women live on campus. 2 hours of phys ed required. 5 intercollegiate sports for men, 1 for women; intramurals. NCAA, ECAA. Yeshiva College student body composition: 0.3% Asian, 0.1% Black, 95.7% White. 46% of Yeshiva students from out of state; 66% of Stern students from out of state.

North Carolina

APPALACHIAN STATE UNIVERSITY $

Boone 28608, (704) 262-2000
Director of Admissions: T. Joe Watts

- **Undergraduates:** 4,561m, 4,495w
- **Tuition and fees (1984–1985):** 770.50 (in-state), $3,082 (out-of-state)
- **Room and Board (1984–1985):** $1,520
- **Degrees offered:** BA, BS, BMus, BSBA, BT
- **Mean SAT:** 425v, 467m, **Mean ACT:** 18
- **Student-faculty ratio:** 16 to 1
- **Calendar system:** Semester

A public university established in 1889. 75-acre small-town campus, 95 miles from Asheville. Served by bus; air service in Asheville.

Academic Character SACS and professional accreditation. Semester system, 4- and 6-week summer terms, summer semester. 23 majors offered by the College of Arts & Sciences, 14 by the College of Business, 17 by the College of Fine & Applied Arts, and 13 by the College of Learning & Human Development. Minors required in some programs. Minors offered in most major fields and in 10 others. Distributive requirements. Graduate degrees granted. Independent study. Honors program. Cooperative work/study, limited pass/fail, internships, credit by exam. Preprofessional programs in dentistry, law, medicine, theology. 3-2 engineering program with Auburn. 2-year transfer programs in engineering, forestry, nursing, pharmacy. Appalachian Consortium. Study abroad. Elementary, secondary, library science, and special education certification. ROTC. Computer center. Language lab. 412,000-volume library with microform resources.

Financial CEEB CSS and ACT FAS. University scholarships, grants, loans, payment plan; PELL, SEOG, NDSL, CWS, self-help program. Application deadline March 15.

Admissions High school graduation with 16 units required. GED accepted. Audition required for music majors. SAT or ACT required. $15 application fee. Rolling admissions. $200 deposit due on acceptance of admissions offer. *Early Admission* Program. Admission deferral possible. Transfers accepted. Credit possible for CEEB AP, CLEP, and departmental exams.

Student Life Student government. Newspaper, literary magazine, yearbook. Music groups. Debate. Student Research Union. Academic, honorary, religious, service, and special interest groups. Fraternities and sororities. Single freshmen live at home or on campus. Married-student housing. 49% of students live on campus. Freshmen may not have cars on campus. Class attendance expected. 2 semesters of phys ed required. 12 intercollegiate sports for men, 8 for women, and one coed; intramurals. AIAW, NCAA, SC. Student body composition: 0.1% Asian, 2.4% Black, 0.2% Hispanic, 0.1% Native American, 96.9% White. 7% from out of state.

BELMONT ABBEY COLLEGE $

Belmont 28012, (704) 825-3711
Director of Admissions: Robin R. Roberts

- **Undergraduates:** 490m, 360w
- **Tuition (1984–1985):** $3,100 (in-state), $3,710 (out-of-state)
- **Room and Board (1984–1985):** $1,995;   **Fees:** $130
- **Degrees offered:** BA, BS
- **Mean SAT:** 407v, 423m
- **Student-faculty ratio:** 17 to 1
- **Calendar system:** Semester

A private college founded by Benedictine Monks, established in 1876, became coed in 1972. 650-acre campus, 10 miles west of Charlotte. Served by air, rail, and bus.

Academic Character SACS accreditation. Semester system. Majors offered in accounting, art education, biology, business, chemistry, distribution management, economics, English, environmental science, history, medical technology, natural science, political science, recreation, religion, and sociology. Majors in art, education, psychology, and special education offered with Sacred Heart. Distributives, 6 hours of theology, and senior comprehensive exam required. Independent study. Honors program. Pass/fail, internships. Preprofessional programs in dentistry, law, medicine, pharmacy, veterinary medicine. Cross-registration with Sacred Heart, 10 area schools, and 20 state schools. Study in France. Elementary and special education certification. ROTC, AFROTC at UNC Charlotte. Language lab. 100,000-volume library with microform resources.

Financial CEEB CSS. College scholarships, grants, loans, payment plan; PELL, SEOG, NDSL, CWS. Application deadlines April 1 (scholarships), March 15 (loans).

Admissions High school graduation with 16 units required. Interview recommended. SAT or ACT required. $15 application fee. Rolling admissions. $150 deposit due on acceptance of admissions offer. *Early Admission* and *Early Decision* programs. Admission deferral possible. Transfers accepted. Credit possible for CEEB AP and CLEP exams.

Student Life Student government. Newspaper, literary magazine, yearbook, radio station. Drama group. Campus ministry. Honorary, political, professional, religious, and special interest groups. 3 fraternities with houses. 70% of men join. Students must live at home or on campus. 77% of students live on campus. Beer permitted in dorms. Class attendance required of freshmen. 4 intercollegiate sports for men, 2 for women; intramurals. Student body composition: 2% Asian, 7% Black, 3% Foreign, 1% Hispanic, 87% White. 67% from out of state.

CAMPBELL UNIVERSITY $

Buies Creek 27506, (919) 893-4111
Director of Admissions: Winslow Carter

- **Undergraduates:** 1,100m, 900w
- **Tuition (1984–1985):** $5,150 (in-state), $5,202 (out-of-state)
- **Room and Board (1984–1985):** $2,125
- **Degrees offered:** BA, BS, BBA, BSME, BHS, BSS, AA
- **Mean SAT:** 380v, 400m   **Mean ACT:** 20
- **Student-faculty ratio:** 18 to 1
- **Calendar system:** Semester

A private university affiliated with the North Carolina Baptist Convention, established in 1887. 850-acre rural campus, 30 miles from Raleigh. Served by air, rail, and bus.

Academic Character SACS and professional accreditation. Semester system, 2 5-week summer terms. 33 majors offered in the areas of business, church ministries, communications, data processing, education, home economics, humanities, modern languages, mathematics, music, natural sciences, physical education, physical sciences, religion, social sciences, and trust management. Distributives and 6 hours of religion required. Graduate degrees granted. Independent study. Honors program. Internships. 3-1 medical technology program. Exchange program with Baptist College in Wales. Pre-school, elementary, and secondary education certification. ROTC. 160,000-volume library.

Financial CEEB CSS and ACT FAS. University scholarships, loans, payment plans; PELL, SEOG, NDSL, GSL, CWS. Scholarship application deadline April 15.

Admissions High school graduation with 18 units required. Interview recommended. SAT or ACT required. $15 application fee. Rolling admissions. $100 deposit due on acceptance of admissions offer. *Early Decision, Early Admission, Concurrent Enrollment* programs. Admission deferral possible. Transfers accepted. Credit possible for CEEB AP and CLEP exams.

Student Life Student government. Newspaper, literary magazine, yearbook, radio station. Music and drama groups. Academic, honorary, religious, and special interest groups. Students must live at home or on campus. Single-sex dorms. Married-student housing. 70% of students live on campus. Liquor prohibited. Class attendance expected. Attendance at biweekly convocations required. 2 hours of phys ed required. 8 intercollegiate sports for men, 4 for women; intramurals. AIAW, NCAA. Student body composition: 10% Black, 87% White, 3% Other. 20% from out of state.

DAVIDSON COLLEGE $$

Davidson 28036, (704) 892-2000
Director of Admissions & Financial Aid: John V. Griffith

- **Undergraduates:** 835m, 536 w
- **Tuition (1984–1985):** $6,390
- **Room and Board (1984–1985):** $2,500
- **Degrees offered:** BA, BS
- **Mean SAT:** 603v, 627m
- **Student-faculty ratio:** 13 to 1
- **Calendar system:** Trimester

A private college affiliated with the Presbyterian Church, established in 1837, became coed in 1972. 450-acre small-town campus, 20 miles north of Charlotte. Served by bus; air and rail service in Charlotte.

Academic Character SACS accreditation. Trimester system. Majors offered in art, biology, chemistry, classics, economics, English, French, German, history, mathematics, music, philosophy, physics, political science, medicine, psychology, religion, sociology, Spanish, and theatre. Preprofessional pre-medicine major offered. Distributives, 3 religion and philosophy courses, and GRE, comprehensive exam, or research project required. Independent study. Honors program. Phi Beta Kappa. Pass/fail. 3-2 engineering program with Columbia, NC State, Georgia Tech, Washington U. Several study abroad programs. Washington Semester. Foreign Policy

Semester. Secondary education certification. ROTC. Computer facilities. Language lab. Center for Special Studies. 270,000-volume library with microform resources.

Financial CEEB CSS. College scholarships, grants, loans, payment plan; PELL, SEOG, NDSL, GSL, CWS. Application deadline February 15.

Admissions High school graduation with 16 units required. Interview encouraged. SAT required; 3 ACH recommended. $25 application fee. Application deadline February 15. $200 deposit due on acceptance of admissions offer. *Early Decision* and *Early Admission* programs. Transfers accepted. Credit possible for CEEB AP exams.

Student Life Student government. Newspaper, literary magazine, yearbook, radio station. Music and drama groups. Debate. Black Student Coalition. Academic, honorary, political, religious, service, and special interest groups. 4 fraternities and 6 social-eating clubs; all without housing. 70% of students join. Coed and single-sex dorms. Limited married-student housing. 87% of students live on campus. Honor code. 2 team sports and 3 individual sports required. 12 intercollegiate sports for men, 5 for women; many intramurals. AIAW, NCAA, SC. Student body composition: 5% Black, 93% White, 2% Other. 64% from out of state.

DUKE UNIVERSITY $$

Durham 27706, (919) 684-8111
Director of Undergraduate Admissions: Jean A. Scott

- **Undergraduates:** 3,132m, 2,792w
- **Tuition (1984–1985):** $7,380
- **Room and Board (1984–1985):** $3,245;   **Fees:** $270
- **Degrees offered:** BA, BS, BSE
- **Mean SAT:** 606v, 657m,   **Mean ACT:** 30
- **Student-faculty ratio:** 14 to 1
- **Calendar system:** Semester

A private university established in 1838. 800-acre suburban campus, 25 miles northwest of Raleigh.

Academic Character SACS and professional accreditation. Semester system, 3 5-week summer terms. 36 majors offered by the College of Arts & Sciences, and 4 by the School of Engineering. Courses include African and Asian languages. Distributive requirements in Program I; seminars, tutorials, or independent study required during first two years; two small group courses required during junior and senior years. Program II allows self-designed majors with possible credit for off-campus work. Graduate and professional degrees granted. Honors program. Phi Beta Kappa. Pass/fail, internships. 3-1 programs in business, forestry/environmental studies, law, medicine with graduate school. Reciprocal enrollment with UNC, NC State, and NC Central. Several study abroad programs. Education certification. ROTC, AFROTC, NROTC. Computer center. Language lab. Record library. Duke Forest. 2,800,000-volume library with microform resources.

Financial CEEB CSS. University scholarships, grants, loans, payment plans; PELL, SEOG, NDSL, FISL, CWS, university work program. Recommended application deadline February 1.

Admissions High school graduation with at least 12 units in college prep program. SAT required; ACT accepted. 3 ACH required. $30 application fee.

Application deadline January 15. $130 deposit due on acceptance of admissions offer. *Early Decision* and *Early Admission* programs. Admission deferral possible. Transfers accepted. Credit possible for CEEB AP and departmental exams; university has own advanced placement program.
Student Life Student government. Newspaper, 3 magazines, yearbook, radio and television stations. Music and drama groups. Black Students Alliance. Elcirculo Hispano. Jewish Forum. Circle K. Academic, honorary, professional, political, religious, service, and special interest groups. 16 fraternities and 8 sororities without houses. 45% of men and 42% of women join. Freshmen must live on campus. 70% of students live on campus. 12 intercollegiate sports for men, 8 for women; many club and intramural sports. AIAW, ACC. Student body composition: 1.2% Asian, 4.8% Black, 0.6% Hispanic, 0.1% Native American, 91.1% White. 85% from out of state.

EAST CAROLINA UNIVERSITY $

East Fifth Street, Greenville 27834, (919) 757-6131
Director of Admissions: Walter M. Bortz, II

- **Undergraduates:** 5,015m, 6,266w
- **Tuition (1984–1985):** $820 (in-state), $2,968 (out-of-state)
- **Room and Board (1984–1985):** $2,010;   **Fees:** $336
- **Degrees offered:** BA, BS
- **Mean SAT:** 406v, 444m
- **Student-faculty ratio:** 15 to 1
- **Calendar system:** Semester

A private university established in 1907. 600-acre small-city campus, 85 miles east of Raleigh. Airport 30 miles away in Kinston.
Academic Character SACS and professional accreditation. Semester system, 2 5½-week summer terms. 112 majors offered by the College of Arts & Sciences and by the schools of Allied Health & Social Professions, Art, Business, Education, Home Economics, Medicine, Music, Nursing, and Technology. Minors required in some areas and recommended in others. Distributive requirements. Graduate degrees granted. Independent study. Honors seminars. Cooperative work/study, internships, credit by exam. Preprofessional programs in dentistry, law, medicine, optometry, pharmacy, veterinary medicine. 2-2 engineering program with NCSU Raleigh. Cooperative programs in agriculture, forestry, pulp and paper technology, wood science with NCSU. Study in Costa Rica. Elementary, secondary, special, and library science education certification. AFROTC. Estuarine lab. Health Sciences Library. Computer center. Language labs. 655,205-volume library with microform resources.
Financial CEEB CSS. University scholarships, grants, loans, PELL, SEOG, MPGP, NDSL, FISL, NSL, CWS. Application deadline March 1.
Admissions High school graduation with 16 units required. Audition required for music majors. SAT or ACT required. $10 application fee. Rolling admissions. $25 deposit due on acceptance of admissions offer. *Early Decision* Program. Transfers accepted. Credit possible for CEEB AP and CLEP exams.
Student Life Student government. Newspaper, minority newspaper, literary magazine, yearbook, radio and television stations. Music, opera, and drama groups. Crafts center. Athletic, academic, honorary, political, professional, religious, and special interest groups. 6 fraternities and 8 sororities, most with

houses. 11% of men and 8% of women join. International House. Coed and single-sex dorms. 41% of students live on campus. Freshmen may use cars only on weekends. Liquor use limited on campus. 3 hours of phys ed required. 8 intercollegiate sports for men, 6 for women; club and intramural sports. AIAW, ECAC, NCAA. Student body composition: 0.5% Asian, 10.1% Black, 0.3% Hispanic, 0.5% Native American, 88.2% White, 0.4% Other. 11% from out of state.

GUILFORD COLLEGE $

5800 Friendly Avenue, Guilford College 27410, (919) 292-5511
Director of Admissions: Herbert Poole

- **Undergraduates:** 567m, 483w
- **Tuition (1984–1985):** $5,114
- **Room and Board (1984–1985):** $2,404;   **Fees:** $122
- **Degrees offered:** BA, BS, BAS, BFA, AA
- **Mean SAT:** 500v, 500m
- **Student-faculty ratio:** 16 to 1
- **Calendar system:** Semester

A private college affiliated with the Society of Friends, established in 1837. 290-acre suburban campus in Greensboro. Served by air, rail, and bus.
Academic Character SACS accreditation. Semester system, 2 5-week summer terms. Majors offered in accounting, administration of justice, biology, chemistry, drama/speech, economics, education, English, French, geology, history, humanistic studies, management, mathematics, philosophy, physical education, physics, political science, psychology, religion, sociology, Spanish, sports management, and sports medicine. Majors in art, art education, German, music, music education, and special education offered through cooperative consortium program. Distributive requirements. Independent study. Honors program. Limited pass/fail, internships. Preprofessional programs in dentistry, law, medicine, ministry, veterinary medicine. 3-2 engineering program with Georgia Tech. BS/MS forestry and environmental science program with Duke. 3-1 medical technology and physician's assistant programs with Bowman Gray. Cross-registration with A&T State, Bennett, Greensboro, High Point, UNC Greensboro. Study abroad. New York, Philadelphia, Washington, Florida seminars. Geology field trips. Elementary, secondary, and special education certification. ROTC, AFROTC, NROTC at A&T State. Computer center. Language lab. 190,000-volume library with microform resources.
Financial ACT FAS. College scholarships, grants, loans, grants for Quaker students, payment plan; PELL, SEOG, NDSL, employment opportunities. Application deadline April 15.
Admissions High school graduation with 16-18 units recommended. Interview encouraged. SAT or ACT required. $15 application fee. Rolling admissions; preferred application deadline April 1. $100 deposit due on acceptance of admissions offer. *Early Decision* and *Early Admission* programs. Admission deferral possible. Transfers accepted. Credit possible for CEEB AP and CLEP exams; college has own advanced placement program.
Student Life Student government. Newspaper, literary magazine, journals, yearbook, radio station. Music and drama groups. Debate. Academic, ethnic, religious, service, and special interest groups. Single students under 21 live on

campus. Married-student housing. 85% of students live on campus. Gambling and firearms prohibited. Honor code. 9 intercollegiate sports for men, 5 for women; several intramurals. AIAW, NAIA, CC. Student body composition: 0.2% Asian, 6% Black, 0.7% Hispanic, 0.1% Native American, 93% White. 60% from out of state.

NORTH CAROLINA, UNIVERSITY OF, AT CHAPEL HILL $

Chapel Hill 27514, (919) 966-3621
Director of Undergraduate Admissions: Richard Cashwell

- **Undergraduates:** 5,068m, 8,589w
- **Tuition (1984–1985):** $765.50 (in-state), $3,127.50 (out-of-state)
- **Room and board (1984–1985):** $2,375
- **Degrees offered:** BA, BS, BFA
- **Mean SAT:** 512v, 574m
- **Student-faculty ratio:** 14 to 1
- **Calendar system:** Semester

A public university established in 1789. 622-acre small-city campus, 30 miles from Raleigh. Served by air, rail, and bus.

Academic Character SACS and professional accreditation. Semester system, 2 6-week summer terms. 61 majors offered by the College of Arts & Sciences, 1 by the School of Business Administration, 4 by the School of Education, 3 by the School of Journalism, 3 by the School of Medicine, 1 by the School of Nursing, 1 by the School of Pharmacy, 5 by the School of Public Health, and 1 by the Division of Health Affairs. Courses in 9 additional areas, including Arabic, Celtic, Chinese, Hebrew, and Sanskrit. Self-designed majors. Freshmen and sophomores enroll in General College. Graduate degrees granted. Independent study. Honors programs. Phi Beta Kappa. Pass/fail, internships. Many study abroad programs. Elementary and secondary education certification. AFROTC, NROTC. Institutes of Latin American Studies, Fisheries Research, Natural Science, Anthropology, Folk Music. Communications center. Language lab. 3,000,000-volume library with microform resources.

Financial CEEB CSS and ACT FAS. University scholarships, grants, loans, state grants; PELL, SEOG, NDSL, GSL, CWS, departmental work. Application deadline March 1.

Admissions High school graduation with 16 units required. Auditions required for performance majors in drama and music. SAT required; ACH or AP exams recommended for placement. $15 application fee. Rolling admissions. Room deposit due with housing application. Transfers accepted. Credit possible for CEEB AP and challenge exams. Special admissions possible for disadvantaged.

Student Life Student government. Newspaper, magazines, radio station. Music, dance, drama, and film groups. Debate. Numerous academic, honorary, political, religious, social, service, and special interest groups. 24 fraternities and 4 sororities, all with houses. 22% of men and 17% of women join. Freshmen must live at home or on campus. Coed and single-sex dorms. Academic floors. Limited married-student housing. 45% of students live on campus. Freshmen may not have cars on campus; upperclassmen with C average may have cars. Honor Code. Campus Code. 1 year of phys ed required. Intercollegiate sports; several intramurals. AIAW. Student body composition: 8.4% Black, 90% White, 1.6% Other. 15% from out of state.

NORTH CAROLINA STATE UNIVERSITY $

Raleigh 27650, (919) 737-2434
Director of Admissions: Anna P. Keller

- **Undergraduates:** 14,515m, 8,117w
- **Tuition (1984–1985):** $726 (in-state), $3,088 (out-of-state)
- **Room and Board (1984–1985):** $2,250
- **Degrees offered:** BA, BS
- **Mean SAT:** 476v, 552 m
- **Student-faculty ratio:** 15 to 1
- **Calendar system:** Semester

A public university established in 1889. Urban campus. Served by air, rail, and bus.

Academic Character SACS and professional accreditation. Semester system, 2 5-week summer terms. 16 majors offered by the School of Agricultural & Life Sciences, 3 by the School of Design, 9 by the School of Education, 11 by the School of Engineering, 5 by the School of Forest Resources, 13 by the School of Humanities & Social Sciences, 7 by the School of Physical & Mathematical Sciences, and 4 by the School of Textiles. Self-designed majors. Distributive requirements. Graduate degrees granted. Independent study. Honors programs. Cooperative work/study, limited pass/fail, internships. 2-2 engineering program with UNC Asheville; dual degree engineering program with Shaw. Cross-registration with 4 area schools. National and international student exchange program. International program for agriculture students. Secondary and middle grades education certification. ROTC, AFROTC; NROTC at UNC Chapel Hill. 2-year Agricultural Institute. Computer center. Language labs. Biological Field Lab. Water Resources Research Institute. Electron microscope center. 1,000,000-volume library with microform resources.

Financial CEEB CSS. University scholarships, loans, state grants; PELL, SEOG, MIG, NDSL, GSL, CWS, university employment. Scholarship application deadline February 1.

Admissions High school graduation with 11 units required. Interview required for School of Design. SAT or ACT required. $15 application fee. Rolling admissions. Room deposit required. *Early Admission* and *Early Decision* programs. Admission deferral possible. Transfers accepted. Credit possible for CEEB AP and CLEP exams. Special admissions for disadvantaged.

Student Life Student government. Newspaper, magazines, yearbook, radio and TV stations. Music and drama groups. Academic, honorary, professional, and technical groups. 22 fraternities, 9 with houses; 5 sororities, 2 with houses. 12% of men and 5% of women join. Coed and single-sex dorms. Special interest housing. Married-student housing. Living-learning program for freshmen. Transition residence for 60 freshmen. 30% of students live on campus. Boarding freshmen may not have cars. Phys ed required of freshmen and sophomores. 14 intercollegiate sports for men, 8 for women; intramurals. AIAW, NCAA, ACC. Student body composition: 1.6% Asian, 7.4% Black, 3.7% Foreign, 0.7% Hispanic, 0.3% Native American, 86.3% White. 14% from out of state.

WAKE FOREST UNIVERSITY $

Winston-Salem 27109, (919) 761-5201
Director of Admissions: William G. Starling

- **Undergraduates:** 1,870m, 1,188w
- **Tuition (1984–1985):** $5,050
- **Room and Board (1984–1985):** $1,740–$2,130
- **Degrees offered:** BA, BS
- **Mean SAT:** 536v, 590m
- **Student-faculty ratio:** 14 to 1
- **Calendar system:** Semester

A private university affiliated with the North Carolina Baptist Convention, established in 1834. 470-acre urban campus. Served by bus.

Academic Character SACS and professional accreditation. Semester system, 2 5-week summer terms. 36 majors offered in the areas of anthropology, art, biology, business, chemistry, classics, economics, education, English, history, mathematics, medical sciences, modern languages, music, philosophy, physical education, physics, politics, psychology, religion, sociology, and speech. Courses in 8 additional areas, including Hindi and Norwegian. Distributives, senior exams, 1 course in religion, and English competency exam required. Graduate degrees granted. Honors programs. Phi Beta Kappa. Limited pass/fail. Cooperative programs in law, medical science, medical technology, microbiology, and physician's assistant with Wake Forest. 3-2 engineering program with NCSU. 3-2 forestry program with Duke. Study abroad. Elementary and secondary education certification. ROTC. Computer center. Fine Arts Center. 818,711-volume library with microform resources.

Financial CEEB CSS. University scholarships, grants, loans, ministerial grants, payment plans; PELL, SEOG, NDSL, FISL, CWS, university work program. Preferred application deadline February 1.

Admissions High school graduation with 16 units required. Interview recommended. SAT required. $20 application fee. Preferred application deadline January 15. $200 deposit due on acceptance of admissions offer. *Early Decision* and *Early Admission* programs. Admission deferral possible. Transfers accepted. Credit possible for CEEB AP and CLEP exams.

Student Life Student government. Newspaper, literary magazine, yearbook, radio station. Music and drama groups. Extensive debate program. Afro-American Society. Academic, honorary, and special interest groups. 10 fraternities with chapter rooms; 6 sororities. 40% of men and 60% of women join. Freshmen not living at home live on campus. Coed and single-sex dorms. Married-student housing. Language dorms. 85% of students live on campus. Honor system. Class attendance expected. 1 year of phys ed required. 8 intercollegiate sports for men, 6 for women; many club and intramural sports. AIAW, NCAA, ACC. Student body composition: 0.3% Asian, 3.7% Black, 0.5% Hispanic, 0.2% Native American, 94.5% White, 0.8% Other. 55% from out of state.

North Dakota

NORTH DAKOTA, UNIVERSITY OF $

Box 8135, University Station, Grand Forks 58202, (701) 777-2011
Director of Admissions & Records: D. J. Wermers

- **Undergraduates:** 4,849m, 4,408w
- **Tuition (1984–1985):** $1,082 (in-state), $1,988 (out-of-state)
- **Room and board (1984–1985):** $1,750
- **Degrees offered:** BA, BFA, BSN, BBA, BPA, BS in 14 areas
- **Mean ACT:** 21
- **Student-faculty ratio:** 24 to 1
- **Calendar system:** Semester

A public university established in 1883. 472-acre campus in the small city of Grand Forks. Served by air, bus, and rail.

Academic Character NCACS and professional accreditation. Semester system, mini-semester in May & June, 8-week summer term. 41 majors offered by the College of Arts & Sciences, 11 by the College of Business & Public Administration, 7 by the College of Engineering, 4 by the College of Fine Arts, 9 by the College for Human Resources Development, 3 by the School of Medicine, 24 by the Center for Teaching & Learning, and 1 in nursing. Composite majors. Minors offered in most major subjects and in 4 additional areas. Distributive requirements. Graduate and professional degrees granted. Honors program. Phi Beta Kappa. Pass/fail. Preprofessional programs in dentistry, law, medicine, optometry. Study abroad. Elementary and secondary education certification. ROTC. Language lab. 592,923-volume library with microform resources.

Financial ACT FAS. University scholarships, loans; PELL, SEOG, NDSL, FISL, CWS. Application deadline March 15.

Admissions High school graduation with 14 units required. GED accepted. Interview encouraged. ACT, SAT, or PSAT required. $20 application fee. Application deadline July 1. *Early Decision* and *Early Admission* programs. Admission deferral possible. Transfers accepted. Credit possible for CEEB AP and CLEP exams.

Student Life Student government. Newspaper, yearbook, radio and TV stations. Music, debate, drama groups. Women's organizations. Academic, professional, religious, honorary, and special interest groups. 13 fraternities and 8 sororities; all have houses. 22% of men and 24% of women join. Dorms for men and women. Married-student housing. 60% of students live on campus. Liquor prohibited on campus. 11 intercollegiate sports for men, 10 for women, wheelchair basketball; intramurals. Student body composition: 0.4% Asian, 0.5% Black, 0.2% Hispanic, 1.9% Native American, 96.2% White. 25% from out of state.

NORTH DAKOTA STATE UNIVERSITY $

Fargo 58105, (701) 237-8643
Director of Admissions: George H. Wallman

- **Undergraduates:** 4,936m, 3,169w
- **Tuition (1984–1985):** $1,008 (in-state), $1,146 (Minnesota residents), $1,854 (out-of-state)
- **Room and Board (1984–1985):** $1,764
- **Degrees offered:** BA, BS, BFA, BArch
- **Mean ACT:** 20.9
- **Student-faculty ratio:** 20 to 1
- **Calendar system:** Quarter

A public university established in 1890. 2,300-acre urban campus in Fargo, at the eastern edge of the state. Served by air, bus, and rail.

Academic Character NCACS and professional accreditation. Quarter system, 2 5-week summer terms. 13 majors offered by the College of Agriculture, 20 by the College of Humanities & Social Sciences, 14 by the College of Science & Mathematics, 10 by the College of Engineering & Architecture, 8 by the College of Home Economics, and 3 by the College of Pharmacy. Self-designed majors. Distributive requirements. Graduate degrees granted. Independent study. Honors program. Cooperative work/study, pass/fail, internships. Preprofessional programs in law, medicine, dentistry. Pre-engineering program with area schools. 3-1 medical technology program, 2-2 physical therapy program. Cross-registration with Concordia, Moorhead State. Elementary and secondary education certification. ROTC, AFROTC. Genetics institute. Language lab. 358,960-volume library.

Financial CEEB CSS and ACT FAS. University scholarships, grants, loans; PELL, SEOG, NDSL, FISL, NSL, HPL, CWS. Application deadline April 15.

Admissions High school graduation with 15 units required. GED accepted. ACT, SAT, or PSAT required; ACT preferred. $20 application fee. Rolling admissions. *Early Admission* Program. Transfers accepted. Credit possible for CEEB AP, CLEP, and ACT PEP exams; university has own advanced placement program.

Student Life Student government. Newspaper, radio station. Music and drama groups. Academic, service, and special interest groups. 11 fraternities and 6 sororities; all have houses. Freshmen under 19 must live on campus or at home. Coed and single-sex dorms. Married-student housing. 35% of students live on campus. Liquor prohibited on campus. 3 terms of phys ed required for non-ROTC students. 9 intercollegiate sports for men, 6 for women; intramurals. NCIAC, NCAA. Student body composition: 1.1% Asian, 0.6% Black, 0.1% Native American, 96% White, 2.2% Other. 29% from out of state.

Ohio

ANTIOCH COLLEGE $$

Yellow Springs 45387 (513) 767-7331
Director of Admissions: Benjamin F. Thompson

- **Undergraduates:** 300m, 280w
- **Tuition (1984–1985):** $6,800
- **Room and Board (1984–1985):** $2,900;   **Fees:** $180
- **Degrees offered:** BA, BS, BFA
- **Student-faculty ratio:** 10 to 1
- **Calendar system:** Quarter

A private college established in 1852. 100-acre small-town campus with 1,000-acre adjacent nature preserve, 18 miles east of Dayton. Programs also in Los Angeles, San Francisco, Venice, Honolulu, Seattle, Denver, Philadelphia, Chicago, Keene (NH), and Fairbault (MN).

Academic Character NCACS accreditation. Quarter system. Majors offered in arts, humanities, social sciences, and environmental studies & urban studies, with concentrations in 22 areas and interdisciplinary programs in 5 additional disciplines. Major plus concentration required. Distributive requirements. 6 quarters of co-op jobs and community participation required; approximately 50% of students are on co-op jobs each term. University emphasizes rigorous scholarship, practical work experience, and leadership development. Undergraduate, graduate, and professional degrees offered at other University centers. Written evaluations of course work; letter grades upon request. Preprofessional programs in dentistry, law, medicine, veterinary science. Joint programs with over 20 colleges. 3-2 engineering with Boston U, Washington U (St. Louis), Georgia Inst. of Technology. 3-2 nursing with Case Western Reserve (Cleveland). Study in Asia, Europe, South America. Elementary and secondary education certification. Computer Activities Center. Environmental Studies Center. Language lab. 250,000-volume library.

Financial CEEB CSS. College scholarships, grants, loans; PELL, SEOG, NDSL, CWS, co-op job program required. Application deadline March 1.

Admissions High school graduation required; college prep program recommended. Interview recommended. ACT or SAT recommended. $20 application fee for out-of-state students. Rolling admissions. $150 deposit due on acceptance of admissions offer. *Early Admission, Early Decision, Concurrent Enrollment* programs. Admission deferral possible. Transfers accepted. Credit possible for CEEB AP, CLEP, and college's proficiency exams.

Student Life Community Council. Newspaper, radio station. Music, dance, drama, and film groups. Gay Center. Women's Center. Third World Alliance. Academic, political, professional, social, service, and special interest groups. Single students expected to live on campus. Coed dorms. Married-student housing. 90% of students live on campus. 4 hours of phys ed required. Extensive intramural, individual, and recreational sports programs. Student body composition: 1% Asian, 12% Black, 1% Hispanic, 1% Native American, 83% White, 2% Other. 89% from out of state.

BOWLING GREEN STATE UNIVERSITY $

Bowling Green 43403, (419) 372-2086
Director of Admissions: John W. Martin

- **Undergraduates:** 6,446m, 8,419w
- **Tuition (1984–1985):** $1,878 (in-state), $4,098 (out-of-state)
- **Room and Board (1984–1985):** $1,888
- **Degrees offered:** BA, BS
- **Mean SAT:** 439v, 482m,   **Mean ACT:** 20.8
- **Student-faculty ratio:** 16 to 1
- **Calendar system:** Semester

A public university established in 1910. 1,250-acre suburban campus, 25 miles south of Toledo. Served by air and bus.

Academic Character NCACS and professional accreditation. Semester system, 2 summer terms. 122 majors offered by the Colleges of Arts & Sciences, Business Administration, Education, Musical Arts, Health & Community Services; the Schools of Journalism, Technology, Nursing, and Health, Physical Education & Recreation; and the Department of Home Economics. Self-designed majors. Minors offered in some major fields. Distributive requirements. Graduate degrees granted. Independent study. Honors program. Cooperative work/study, pass/fail, internships. Preprofessional programs in dentistry, engineering, home economics, law, library science, mathematics, medicine, mortuary science, occupational therapy, optometry, osteopathy, pharmacy, religion, veterinary medicine. National Student Exchange. Washington Semester. Study abroad. Elementary, secondary, and special education certification. ROTC, AFROTC. Computer center. Language lab. 694,000-volume library with microform resources.

Financial CEEB CSS and ACT FAS. University scholarships, grants, loans, special talent grants, payment plans; PELL, SEOG, NSS, NDSL, NSL, CWS. Scholarship application deadline February 1.

Admissions High school graduation with 16 units required. GED accepted. Audition required for music majors. ACT or SAT required. $25 application fee. Rolling admissions. $100 room deposit due on acceptance of offer of admission. *Early Admission* and *Concurrent Enrollment* programs. Transfers accepted. Credit possible for CEEB AP and CLEP exams. Project Search minority recruitment.

Student Life Student government. Newspaper, yearbook, radio and TV stations. Music and theatre groups. Debate. Black Student Union. Spanish Student Union. 17 fraternities and 12 sororities; all have houses. 20% of students join. Juniors and seniors may live off campus. Coed and single-sex dorms. Special interest housing. 56% of students live on campus. 3 quarters of phys ed required. Several intercollegiate and intramural sports. AIAW, NCAA, MAC. Student body composition: 0.6% Asian, 4.1% Black, 0.6% Hispanic, 93.9% White, 0.8% Other. 8% from out of state.

CASE WESTERN RESERVE UNIVERSITY $$$

University Circle, Cleveland 44106, (216) 368-4450
Assoc. Dean of Student Affairs & Undergraduate Admissions: Donald W. Chenelle

- **Undergraduates:** 2,476m, 1,076w
- **Tuition (1984–1985):** $7,650
- **Room and Board (1984–1985):** $3,390; **Fees:** $320
- **Degrees offered:** BA, BS, BFA
- **Mean SAT:** 548v, 636m, **Mean ACT:** 28
- **Student-faculty ratio:** 10 to 1
- **Calendar system:** Semester

A private university established in 1967 by the federation of Case Institute of Technology (est.1880) and Western Reserve University (est.1826). 125-acre and 500-acre campuses, 20 minutes from downtown Cleveland. Served by air and bus.

Academic Character NCACS and professional accreditation. Semester system, 6-week summer term. Case offers 22 majors in mathematics & sciences. Western Reserve offers 43 majors in liberal arts & sciences, accounting, gerontology, legal studies, music & art education, nutrition, and theatre. Minors in most major fields. Special majors. Distributive requirements. Graduate degrees granted. Independent study. Undergraduate Scholars Program. Phi Beta Kappa. Cooperative work/study at Case, pass/fail, credit by exam. Preprofessional programs in dentistry, law, library science, management, medicine, nursing, social work. Case offers 3-2 engineering program with 32 colleges. 6-year dental program. Cross-registration with 6 area schools. Washington Semester. Study abroad. Art and music education certification. NROTC; ROTC at John Carroll, AFROTC at Akron. Computer center, observatories, biological research station. 1,613,000-volume library with microform resources.

Financial CEEB CSS. University scholarships, grants, loans, payment plans; PELL, SEOG, NDSL, FISL, GSL, CWS. Application deadline February 1.

Admissions High school graduation with 16 units required. Interview recommended. Audition required for music applicants; portfolio for art students. ACT or SAT required; 3 ACH recommended. $20 application fee. Rolling admissions. $150 deposit due on acceptance of offer of admission. Admission deferral possible. Transfers accepted. Credit possible for CEEB AP and departmental exams.

Student Life Student government. Newspaper, magazines, yearbook, radio station. Music, film, and drama groups. Afro-American Society. Women's Center. Commuter Club. Academic, honorary, professional, religious, and special interest groups. 16 fraternities, all with houses; 3 sororities with limited housing. 20% of students join. Single students live at home or on campus. Coed and single-sex dorms. Married-student apartments. 85% of students live on campus. 1 year of phys ed required for freshmen. 6 intercollegiate sports for men, 6 for women; many club and intramural sports. PAC, AIAW. Student body composition: 3.2% Asian, 3.9% Black, 0.8% Hispanic, 0.3% Native American, 91.8% White. 48% from out of state.

CINCINNATI, UNIVERSITY OF $

Cincinnati 45221, (513) 475-3427
Director of Admissions: Robert W. Neel

- **Undergraduates:** 15,473m, 14,963w
- **Tuition (1984–1985):** $1,803 (in-state), $4,329 (out-of-state)
- **Room and Board (1984–1985):** $2,816; **Fees:** $75
- **Degrees offered:** BA, BS, BBA, BFA, BGS, BMus, BSEd, BS in Man, AA, AS

- **Mean SAT:** 468v, 528m, **Mean ACT:** 22.5
- **Student-faculty ratio:** 17 to 1
- **Calendar system:** Quarter

A public university established in 1819. 200-acre urban campus, 2 miles from downtown Cincinnati. Served by air, rail, and bus.

Academic Character NCACS and professional accreditation. Quarter system, 3 summer terms totaling 10 weeks. 36 majors offered in the arts & sciences, 4 in applied sciences, 9 in business, 4 in community service, 20 in music, 9 in design, architecture, & art, 10 in education, 8 in engineering, and majors in nursing and pharmacy. Self-designed majors. Distributive requirements. Senior comprehensive exams required in some departments. Graduate degrees granted. Independent study. Honors program. Phi Beta Kappa. Cooperative work/study, pass/fail, internships. Exchange programs with Art Academy and Hebrew Union. Cincinnati Consortium of Colleges. Washington Semester. Study abroad. Elementary, secondary, and special education certification. ROTC, AFROTC. Language lab. 1,600,000-volume library with microform resources.

Financial CEEB CSS. University scholarships, grants, loans, state grants & loans, payment plan; PELL, SEOG, NSS, NDSL, NSL, CWS, college has own work program. Application deadline February 1.

Admissions High school graduation with 12 units required for Arts & Sciences. Specific course requirements for professional colleges. Audition required for music and dance majors. 2 letters of professional recommendation necessary for broadcasting majors. SAT or ACT required. $25 application fee. Rolling admissions. $75 deposit required on acceptance of offer of admission. Transfers accepted. Credit possible for CEEB AP and CLEP exams.

Student Life Student government. Newspaper, literary magazine. Music and drama groups. Debate. Student Community Involvement Program. Athletic, academic, honorary, political, special interest, and vocational groups. 21 fraternities and 15 sororities, all with houses. 7% of men and 9% of women join. Freshmen & sophomores under 21 must live at home or on campus as long as space is available. Coed, single-sex, and special interest dorms. Married-student housing. 7% of students live on campus. 11 intercollegiate sports; intramural & club sports. AIAW, NCAA, MCAC. Student body composition: 1% Asian, 10% Black, 80% White, 9% Other. 14% from out of state.

DENISON UNIVERSITY $$

Granville 43023, (614) 587-0810
Director of Admissions: Richard F. Boyden

- **Undergraduates:** 1,064m, 1,047w
- **Tuition (1984–1985):** $7,640
- **Room and Board (1984–1985):** $2,710; **Fees:** $410
- **Degrees offered:** BA, BS, BMus, BFA
- **Mean SAT:** 500v, 535m, **Mean ACT:** 23
- **Student-faculty ratio:** 13 to 1
- **Calendar system:** 4–1–4

A private university established in 1831. 1,000-acre small-town campus, 27 miles east of Columbus. Airport in Columbus.

Academic Character NCACS and professional accreditation. 4-1-4 system. 33 majors offered in the areas of art, dance, English, history, mathematics, modern languages, music, philosophy, physical education, political science, psychology, religion, science, sociology, speech, and several area studies. Self-designed majors. Minors offered in most major fields. Distributives, 2 January terms, and 1 credit in philosophy or religion required. Senior comprehensive exams required in some areas. Independent study. Honors program. Phi Beta Kappa. Pass/fail, internships. Preprofessional programs in business, dentistry, law, medicine. 3-1 medical technology program. 3-2 engineering program with Case Western Reserve, Columbia, Rensselaer, U Rochester. 3-2 programs in forestry and natural resources with Duke and U Michigan. Cross-registration with 12 midwestern liberal arts colleges. Black College Student Exchange Program. New York City Arts Program. Human development semester at Merrill-Palmer. Management semester at Keller. Urban semester in Philadelphia. Oak Ridge Semester. Washington Semester. Newberry Library Semester. Study abroad. Secondary education certification. Computer center. Language lab. 248,000-volume library.

Financial CEEB CSS. University scholarships, grants, loans, state grants, payment plan; PELL, SEOG, NDSL, GSL, CWS. Scholarship application deadline February 15.

Admissions High school graduation with 16 units expected. Interview recommended. ACT or SAT required; ACH recommended. $20 application fee. Application deadline February 1. $200 deposit due on acceptance of offer of admission. *Early Decision* and *Early Admission* programs. Admission deferral possible. Transfers accepted. Credit possible for CEEB AP, CLEP, and university exams. Special attention to minority groups.

Student Life Student government. Newspaper, literary magazine, yearbook, radio station. Music, dance, and drama groups. Black Student Union. Academic, political, religious, service, and special interest groups. 10 fraternities with houses, 5 sororities with non-residential chapter houses. 60% of men and 46% of women join. All freshmen live on campus. Coed and single-sex dorms. Some married-student housing. 91% of students live on campus. Upperclassmen may have cars. 10 intercollegiate sports for men, 10 for women; several intramurals. AIAW, NCAA, OAC. Student body composition: 4% Black, 95% White, 1% Other. 74% from out of state.

HIRAM COLLEGE $$

Hiram 44234, (216) 569-3211
Dean of Admissions: John P. Pirozzi

- **Undergraduates:** 600m, 550w
- **Tuition (1984–1985):** $7,231
- **Room and Board (1984–1985):** $2,260;   **Fees:** $250
- **Degrees offered:** BA
- **Mean SAT:** 480v, 500m
- **Student-faculty ratio:** 14 to 1
- **Calendar system:** Quarter

A private college affiliated with the Disciples of Christ, established in 1850. 145-acre rural campus, 35 miles southeast of Cleveland.
Academic Character NCACS and professional accreditation. Quarter

system, November interterm, 3- and 6-week summer terms. 32 majors offered in the areas of liberal arts & sciences, computer science, education, management, physical education, and religion. Special and self-designed majors. Minors offered in most major fields and in 12 other areas. Courses in Arabic, Greek, Latin. Distributives and 1 religion or philosophy course required. Some independent study. Honors program. Phi Beta Kappa. Limited pass/fail, internships. Preprofessional programs in dentistry, medicine, optometry, podiatry, veterinary medicine. 3-1 medical technology program. 3-2 nursing program with Case Western Reserve. 3-2 engineering with Case Western, Washington U. 3-2 agriculture and home economics programs with Ohio State. Many study abroad programs. United Nations Semester. Washington Semester. Elementary, secondary, and special education certification. AFROTC; ROTC at Kent State. Computer center. Art and music centers. Observatory. Language lab. 150,000-volume library.

Financial CEEB CSS. College scholarships, grants, loans, chemistry and music scholarships, payment plan; PELL, SEOG, NDSL, GSL, CWS.

Admissions High school graduation with 16 units recommended. Interview recommended. SAT or ACT required. $15 application fee. Rolling admissions. $100 deposit due on acceptance of offer of admission. *Early Admission* Program. Admission deferral possible. Transfers accepted. Credit possible for CEEB AP and CLEP exams; college has own advanced placement program.

Student Life Student government. Newspaper, literary magazine, yearbook, radio station. Music and drama groups. Alliance for Black Consciousness. Academic, honorary, tutoring, and special interest groups. 3 social clubs for men, 3 for women. 20% of students join. Freshmen must live at home or on campus. Coed and single-sex dorms. Special interest houses. Married-student housing. 90% of students live on campus. 6 activity units, including 3 in phys ed, required. 8 intercollegiate sports for men, 5 for women, 3 coed; club & intramural sports. AIAW, NCAA, PAC, WRAC. Student body composition: 0.6% Asian, 9.1% Black, 0.4% Hispanic, 89.8% White. 35% from out of state.

KENT STATE UNIVERSITY $

Kent 44242, (216) 672-2444
Director of Admissions: Bruce L. Riddle

- **Undergraduates:** 7,318m, 8,673w
- **Tuition (1984–1985):** $1,872 (in-state), $3,072 (out-of-state)
- **Room and Board (1984–1985):** $2,206
- **Degrees offered:** BA, BS, BGS, BSBA, BFA, BMus, BArch, BMus Ed, BSN
- **Mean SAT:** 450v, 450m, **Mean ACT:** 19
- **Student-faculty ratio:** 20 to 1
- **Calendar system:** Semester

A public university established in 1910. 1,200-acre small-city campus with a 232-acre airport, 12 miles east of Akron. Served by bus.

Academic Character NCACS and professional accreditation. Semester system, 2 5-week and one 8-week summer terms. 37 majors offered by the College of Arts & Sciences, 13 by the College of Business Administration, 27 by the College of Education, 3 by the College of Fine & Professional Arts, 6 by the School of Art, 7 by the School of Home Economics, 6 by the School of Journalism, 8 by the School of Music, 5 by the School of Speech, 8 by the School of Technology, 3 by the School of Physical Education, Recreation, &

Dance, and 1 by the School of Nursing. Self-designed majors. Minors required in some departments. Minors offered in most major fields. Distributive requirements. Graduate degrees granted. Independent study. Honors program. Phi Beta Kappa. Cooperative work/study, pass/fail, internships, credit by exam. Preprofessional programs in dentistry, legal professions, medicine, pharmacy, osteopathy, veterinary medicine. 3-1 programs in medical technology and in natural resources areas. Many international study programs. Honors and Experimental Colleges. Elementary, secondary, and special education certification. ROTC, AFROTC. Computer center. Center for Peaceful Change. World Music Center. Liquid Crystal Institute. Arboretum. 1,500,000-volume library with microform resources.

Financial CEEB CSS and ACT FAS. University scholarships, grants, loans, state grants, payment plans; PELL, SEOG, NSS, NDSL, GSL, NSL, CWS. Application deadline June 1.

Admissions Ohio residents admitted unconditionally with either a 16-unit college preparatory program or a 2.5 GPA and ACT 19 composite. Out-of-state students must have a college preparatory curriculum, satisfactory GPA, and ACT 19 or SAT 900. Audition required for music applicants. ACT or SAT accepted; ACT preferred. $25 application fee. Rolling admissions. $50 room deposit due on acceptance of admissions offer. *Early Admission* and *Concurrent Enrollment* programs. Transfers accepted. Credit possible for CEEB AP, CLEP, and departmental exams.

Student Life Student government. Newspaper, literary magazine, yearbook, radio and TV studios. Numerous student organizations. 15 fraternities and 10 sororities, most with houses. 5% of students join. Juniors and seniors may live off campus. Coed and single-sex dorms. Special interest housing. Married-student housing. 40% of students live on campus. 10 intercollegiate sports for men, 9 for women; several intramurals. NCAA, MAC. Student body composition: 1% Asian, 9% Black, 1% Hispanic, 0.1% Native American, 85.9% White, 3% Other. 8% from out of state.

KENYON COLLEGE $$$

Gambier 43022, (614) 427-2244
Director of Admissions: John D. Kushan

- **Undergraduates:** 750m, 700w
- **Tuition (1984–1985):** $8,250
- **Room and board (1984–1985):** $2,717;   **Fees:** $333
- **Degrees offered:** BA
- **Mean SAT:** 560v, 570m,   **Mean ACT:** 27
- **Student-faculty ratio:** 12 to 1
- **Calendar system:** Semester

A private college affiliated with the Episcopal Church, established in 1824, became coed in 1969. 600-acre rural campus, 50 miles north of Columbus.

Academic Character NCACS accreditation. Semester system. Majors offered in anthropology, art, biology, chemistry, classics, drama, economics, English, French studies, German studies, history, mathematics, modern foreign languages & literature, music, philosophy, physics, political science, psychology, religion, Russian studies, sociology, and Spanish studies. Self-designed majors. Distributive requirements. Independent study. Honors program. Phi Beta Kappa. Pass/fail. Preprofessional programs in law and

medicine. 3-2 engineering program with Case Western Reserve and
Washington U. Urban semester in Philadelphia. Newberry Library Semester.
Oak Ridge Lab Semester. Study in Africa, Colombia, Hong Kong, India, Japan,
Europe. Computer center. 286,000-volume library with microform resources.
Financial CEEB CSS. College scholarships, grants, loans, honor
scholarships, payment plan; PELL, SEOG, NDSL, CWS. Scholarship
application deadline March 1.
Admissions High school graduation with 15 units required. Interview urged.
SAT or ACT required. $20 application fee. Rolling admissions. $200 deposit
due on acceptance of admissions offer. *Early Decision* Program. Admission
deferral possible. Transfers accepted. Credit possible for CEEB AP exams.
Student Life Student Council. Student-faculty Senate. Newspaper, journal,
photographic publications, yearbook, radio station. Music and drama groups.
Debate. Poetry Society. Kenyon Wilderness Experience. Women's Center.
Athletic, academic, religious, service, and special interest groups. 10
fraternities housed in dorms. 40% of men join. All students live on campus.
Coed and single-sex dorms. Language houses. 10 intercollegiate sports for
men, 8 for women; many intramural & club sports. AIAW, NCAA, OAC. Student
body composition: 0.7% Asian, 0.9% Black, 0.3% Hispanic, 97.1% White. 71%
from out of state.

MIAMI UNIVERSITY $

Oxford 45056, (513) 529-2531
Director of Admissions: Charles R. Schuler

- **Undergraduates:** 6,834m, 8,036w
- **Tuition (1984–1985):** $2,350
- **Room and Board (1984–1985):** $2,225
- **Degrees offered:** BA, BS, BFA
- **Mean SAT:** 500v, 560m, **Mean ACT:** 24
- **Student-faculty ratio:** 21 to 1
- **Calendar system:** Semester

A public university established in 1809. 1,100-acre rural campus, 35 miles
north of Cincinnati. Served by bus.
Academic Character NCACS and professional accreditation. Semester
system, summer term. 47 majors offered by the College of Arts & Sciences, 5
by the School of Applied Science, 9 by the School of Business Administration,
16 by the School of Education & Allied Professions, 6 by the School of Fine
Arts, and several by the School of Interdisciplinary Studies. Self-designed
majors. Minors offered in many major fields. Courses in Chinese, Hebrew,
Japanese. Distributive requirements; senior comprehensive exam required.
Graduate degrees granted. Independent study. Honors program. Phi Beta
Kappa. Pass/fail, internships. Preprofessional programs in dentistry, law,
medicine, physical therapy, veterinary medicine. 3-2 engineering programs
with Case Western Reserve, Columbia. 3-2 forestry program with Duke. 3-1
medical technology program with area hospitals. Cross-registration with
many area colleges. Study abroad. Elementary, secondary, and special
education certification. AFROTC, NROTC. Computer center. Art Museum.
1,100,000-volume library with microform resources.
Financial CEEB CSS. University scholarships, grants, loans, athletic
scholarships, payment plan; PELL, SEOG, NSS, NDSL, GSL, CWS
Application deadlines February 1 (scholarships), March 1 (grants & loans)

Admissions High school graduation with 16 units required. ACT or SAT required. $15 application fee. Rolling admissions. $110 deposit ($60 for commuters) due on acceptance of offer of admission. Admission deferral possible. Transfers accepted. Credit possible for CEEB AP and CLEP exams; university has own advanced placement program. EOP for disadvantaged students.

Student Life Student government. Newspaper, literary magazine, yearbook, radio station. Music and drama groups. Debate. Professional, academic, honorary, political, religious, service, and special interest groups. 24 fraternities with houses; 22 sororities with suites. 35% of men and 30% of women join. Juniors and seniors may live off campus. Coed and single-sex dorms. Language residences. Married-student housing. 58% of students live on campus. Cars prohibited. Many intercollegiate, club, and intramural sports. AIAW, NCAA, MAC. Student body composition: 3% Black, 96% White, 1% Other. 20% from out of state.

MUSKINGUM COLLEGE $$

New Concord 43762, (614) 826-8137
Director of Admissions: Jay R. Leiendecker, Jr.

- **Undergraduates:** 528m, 512w
- **Tuition (1984–1985):** $6,450
- **Room and Board (1984–1985):** $2,420; **Fees:** $100
- **Degrees offered:** BA, BS
- **Mean SAT:** 450v, 480m, **Mean ACT:** 21
- **Student-faculty ratio:** 16 to 1
- **Calendar system:** Semester

A private college affiliated with the United Presbyterian Church, established in 1837. 215-acre small-town campus, 70 miles east of Columbus. Served by air and bus.

Academic Character NCACS and professional accreditation. Semester system, 8-week summer term. 31 majors offered in the areas of business, communication, education, humanities, music, physical education, psychology, public affairs, science, religion, sociology, and theatre. Self-designed majors. Minors offered; required for elementary education majors. Distributives and 1 religion course required. Independent study. Honors program. Cooperative work/study, limited pass/fail, internships, credit by exam. Preprofessional programs in dentistry, law, medicine, ministry, physical therapy, veterinary science. 3-1 medical technology program. 3-3 nursing program with Case. East Central College Consortium. Washington Semester. Merrill-Palmer terms for psychology and sociology students. Critical Languages Program at Princeton. Study abroad. Elementary, secondary, and special education certification. ROTC at Ohio U. Language lab. 172,000-volume library.

Financial CEEB CSS. College scholarships, grants, loans, Presbyterian tuition allowances, 2nd-family-member discounts, payment plans; PELL, SEOG, NDSL, CWS. Recommended scholarship application deadline April 15.

Admissions High school graduation with 15 units required. Interview recommended. SAT or ACT required. $15 application fee. Rolling admissions. $100 deposit due on acceptance of offer of admission. *Early Admission* Program. Admission deferral possible. Transfers accepted. Credit possible for CEEB AP, CLEP, and college proficiency exams.

Student Life Student Senate. Newspaper, literary magazine, yearbook, radio and TV stations. Music and drama groups. Debate. Academic, honorary, political, religious, and special interest groups. 2 fraternities and 3 social clubs for men; limited housing. 4 social clubs, with houses, for women. 65% of men and 70% of women join. Students live at home or on campus. Single-sex dorms. Special interest houses. 95% of students live on campus. Liquor restricted. Smoking prohibited in some areas. Students must notify Personnel Office of marriage plans. 3 hours of phys ed required. 10 intercollegiate sports for men, 9 for women; intramurals. AIAW, OAISW, NCAA, OAC. Student body composition: 2% Black, 1% Hispanic, 95% White, 2% Other. 25% from out of state.

OBERLIN COLLEGE $$$

Oberlin 44074, (216) 775-8411
Director of Admissions: Carl W. Bewig

- **Undergraduates:** 1,279m, 1,510w
- **Tuition (1984—1985):** $9,175
- **Room and Board (1984—1985):** $3,340;   **Fees:** $265
- **Degrees offered:** BA, BMus, BFA
- **Mean SAT:** 600v, 616m,   **Mean ACT:** 27
- **Student-faculty ratio:** 12 to 1
- **Calendar system:** 4—1—4

A private college established in 1833. 440-acre small-town campus, 34 miles southwest of Cleveland. Air, rail, and bus service nearby.
Academic Character NCACS and professional accreditation. 4-1-4 system. 41 majors offered by the College of Arts & Sciences and 9 by the Conservatory of Music. Special majors. Minors offered. Distributive guidelines, no requirements. Independent study. Honors Program. Phi Beta Kappa. Senior Scholars Program. Experimental College. Choice of letter grades or credit/no credit. Some internships. 3-2 engineering programs with Case, U Penn, Washington U. Exchange programs with Tougaloo, Fisk, Gallaudet, and 11 colleges of the Great Lakes Association. Philadelphia Urban Semester. New York Arts Semester. Oak Ridge Science Semester. Wharton Business Semester. Newberry Library Program. Music education certification. Computer center. Isotope lab. Language labs. 800,000-volume library.
Financial CEEB CSS. College scholarships, grants, loans, state grants, payment plan; PELL, SEOG, NDSL, GSL, CWS. Application deadline February 15.
Admissions High school graduation with 15-18 units recommended. Interview strongly encouraged. Audition required for Conservatory applicants. SAT or ACT required; ACH recommended for foreign languages. $25 application fee. Application deadline February 15 (Feb. 1 for *Early Decision*); urge applying early in 12th year. $200 deposit due on acceptance of offer of admission. *Early Decision* and *Early Admission* programs. Admission deferral possible. Transfers accepted. Credit possible for CEEB AP exams.
Student Life Student Senate. Student representation on most faculty committees. Newspaper, magazines, yearbook, radio station. Several music groups. Dance and drama groups. Debate. Honorary, language, political, religious, and special interest organizations. Freshmen and sophomores must live on campus. Coed and single-sex dorms. Co-op dorms. Special interest and language houses. Married-student housing. 80% of students live on

campus. Freshmen may not have cars; upperclassmen must have Dean's permission. Illegal possession of drugs, liquor, firearms, firecrackers prohibited. Honor system. 9 intercollegiate sports for men, 9 for women; intramurals. AIAW, OAC, Centennial Conference. Student body composition: 3.7% Asian, 8.6% Black, 1.3% Hispanic, 0.1% Native American, 86.3% White. 87% from out of state.

OHIO STATE UNIVERSITY, THE $

Columbus 43210, (614) 422-3980
Director of Admissions: James J. Mager

- **Undergraduates:** 22,652m, 18,595w
- **Tuition (1984–1985):** $1,641 (in-state), $4,251 (out-of-state)
- **Room and Board (1984–1985):** $2,709   **Fees:** $45
- **Degrees offered:** BS, BFA, BA,
- **Mean SAT:** 460v, 520m,   **Mean ACT:** 21
- **Student-faculty ratio:** 20 to 1
- **Calendar system:** Quarter

A public university established in 1870. 3,251-acre suburban campus. Served by air, rail, and bus.
Academic Character NCACS and professional accreditation. Quarter system, summer term. 201 programs and 6,700 courses offered by 211 divisions. Self-designed majors. Distributive requirements. Graduate degrees granted. Independent study. Honors program. Phi Beta Kappa. Cooperative work/study, limited pass/fail, internships. Professional schools of dentistry, law, medicine, optometry, veterinary medicine. Study abroad. Elementary, secondary, and special education certification. ROTC, AFROTC, NROTC. Planetarium. Art gallery. 3,615,108-volume library with microform resources.
Financial CEEB CSS. University scholarships, grants, loans; PELL, SEOG, NDSL, CWS. Scholarship application deadline March 1.
Admissions High school graduation with 15 units recommended. SAT or ACT required. $10 application fee. Rolling admissions. $40 deposit due on acceptance of admissions offer. *Early Admission* Program. Admission deferral possible. Transfers accepted. Credit possible for CEEB AP, CLEP, and departmental exams. Freshman Foundation Program offered by Minority Affairs Office.
Student Life Student government. Newspaper, radio and TV stations. Music, dance, and drama groups. Over 500 athletic, academic, honorary, political, service, and special interest groups. 39 fraternities, 36 with houses; 21 sororities, 18 with houses. 9% of students join. Single freshmen must live on campus or at home. Special-interest houses. Coed and single-sex dorms. Married-student housing. 25% of students live on campus. 18 intercollegiate sports for men, 15 for women; intramurals. AIAW, NCAA, NAIA, Big Ten Conference. Student body composition: 1% Asian, 4% Black, 1% Hispanic, 1% Native American, 93% White. 11% from out of state.

OHIO UNIVERSITY $

Athens 45701, (614) 594-5174
Director of Admissions: James C. Walters

- **Undergraduates:** 6,101m, 4,942w
- **Tuition (1984–1985):** $1,782 (in-state), $3,633 (out-of-state)
- **Room and Board (1984–1985):** $2,529
- **Degrees Offered:** BS, BSJ, BSC, BBA, BSE, BSEd, AB
- **Mean SAT:** 436v, 465m, **Mean ACT:** 19.4
- **Student-faculty ratio:** 19 to 1
- **Calendar system:** Quarter

A public university established in 1804. 600-acre campus in a small city 76 miles southeast of Columbus. Served by rail and bus.

Academic Character NCACS and professional accreditation. Quarter system, 2 5-week summer terms. 28 majors offered by the College of Arts & Sciences, 12 by the College of Business Administration, 14 by the College of Communication, 28 by the College of Education, 6 by the College of Engineering & Technology, 12 by the College of Fine Arts, 28 by the College of Health & Human Services, and 1 by the College of Osteopathic Medicine. Honors Tutorial College: selective program with 1-to-1 student-faculty relationship; 20 majors offered. University College offers an AA in general studies for students with undeclared majors. Minors required in some majors; offered in most major fields. Distributive requirements. Graduate degrees granted. Phi Beta Kappa. Limited pass/fail, credit by exam. Senior *in absentia* possible. Preprofessional programs include agri-business, criminology, dentistry, environmental studies, foreign service, law, medicine, optometry, pharmacy, physical therapy, public administration, theology, urban planning, veterinary medicine. Cooperative forestry programs with U Michigan, North Carolina, Duke. 3-1 medical technology program. Study abroad. Elementary, secondary, and special education certification. ROTC, AFROTC. Computer center. Center for International Studies. Language labs. 1,107,000-volume library with microform resources.

Financial CEEB CSS. University scholarships, grants, loans, special talent & corporate scholarships, state grants, payment plans; PELL, SEOG, NSS, NDSL, FISL, CWS. Application deadlines February 15 (scholarships), April 1 (loans).

Admissions High school graduation required. GED accepted. ACT or SAT required; ACT preferred. $25 application fee. Rolling admissions. $100 room deposit due on acceptance of admissions offer. *Early Admission* Program. Admission deferral possible. Transfers accepted. Credit possible for CEEB AP and CLEP exams.

Student Life Student Senate. Newspaper, magazines, yearbook, radio & TV stations. Music, dance, and drama groups. International houses. Academic, honorary, professional, recreational, volunteer, and special interest groups. 18 fraternities and 12 sororities; most with houses. Students with less than 90 quarter hours must live on campus. Coed and single-sex dorms. Married-student housing. 50% of students live on campus. Hazing prohibited. 9 intercollegiate sports for men, 8 for women; many club and intramural programs. NCAA, AIAW, MAC. Student body composition: 0.3% Asian, 4.9% Black, 0.3% Hispanic, 0.3% Native American, 84.2% White, 10% Other. 19% from out of state.

OHIO WESLEYAN UNIVERSITY $$

Delaware 43015, (614) 369-4431, ext. 550
Dean of Admissions: Fred E. Weed

- **Undergraduates:** 828m, 800w
- **Tuition (1984–1985):** $7,130
- **Room and Board (1984–1985):** $2,845
- **Degrees offered:** BA, BM, BFA, BSN
- **Mean SAT:** 449v, 484m, **Mean ACT:** 22
- **Student-faculty ratio:** 11 to 1
- **Calendar system:** Semester

A private university controlled by the United Methodist Church, established in 1842. 200-acre campus in a small city 20 miles north of Columbus. Served by bus; airport in Columbus.

Academic Character NCACS and professional accreditation. Semester system, 6-week summer term. 41 majors offered in the areas of the arts, Black studies, business, education, humanities, journalism, music, nursing, physical education, religion, sciences, social sciences, and urban studies. Self-designed majors. Minors offered. Distributive requirements. Independent study. Honors program. Phi Beta Kappa. Limited pass/fail, internships, credit by exam. Preprofessional programs in art therapy, dentistry, law, medicine, music therapy, occupational therapy, optometry, pharmacy, public administration, theology, veterinary medicine. 3-2 engineering program with Case, Rensselaer, Washington U, California Tech, Georgia Tech, NY Polytechnic. 3-1 medical technology program. 3-2 physical therapy program. Exchange programs with Hampton, Spelman, Fisk. United Nations, Washington, Oak Ridge, Newberry Library semesters. New York art program. Philadelphia urban studies program. Human development at Merrill-Palmer. Study abroad. Elementary and secondary education certification. AFROTC at Ohio State. Computer center. Drama center. Observatory. 450,000-volume library with microform resources.

Financial CEEB CSS. University scholarships, grants, loans, Methodist scholarships, payment plans; PELL, SEOG, NDSL, GSL, CWS. Suggested scholarship application deadline February 1.

Admissions High school graduation with 16 units recommended. Interview strongly recommended. Audition required for music majors. SAT or ACT required; ACH recommended. $20 application fee. Application deadline March 1. $200 deposit due on acceptance of admissions offer. *Early Decision* and *Early Admission* programs. Admission deferral possible. Transfers accepted. Credit possible for CEEB AP exams; university offers credit for own exams and for off-campus experience.

Student Life Student government. Newspaper, literary magazine, yearbook, radio station. Music and drama groups. Orchesis. Academic, professional, religious, tutorial, social action, and special interest groups. 11 fraternities with houses; 8 sororities with non-residential houses. 45% of men and 40% of women join. Seniors may live off campus. Special interest houses. One single-sex and 6 coed dorms. No married-student housing. 95% of students live on campus. Financial aid recipients may not have cars. 12 intercollegiate sports for men, 11 for women. AIAW, NCAA, OAC. Student body composition: 1% Asian, 6% Black, 1% Hispanic, 92% White. 64% from out of state.

WITTENBERG UNIVERSITY $$

Springfield 45501, (800) 762-5911 (in Ohio), (800) 543-5977 (elsewhere)
Director of Admissions: Kenneth G. Benne

- **Undergraduates:** 1,027m, 1,180w
- **Tuition (1984–1985):** $6,774
- **Room and Board (1984–1985):** $2,385; **Fees:** $357
- **Degrees offered:** BA, BFA
- **Mean SAT:** 498v, 532m, **Mean ACT:** 23.6
- **Student-faculty ratio:** 15 to 1
- **Calendar system:** Trimester

A private university supported by the Ohio and Indiana-Kentucky Synods of the Lutheran Church in America, established in 1845. 70-acre suburban campus, 45 miles west of Columbus. Served by bus; airport 25 miles away in Dayton.

Academic Character NCACS and professional accreditation. Trimester system, 6-week summer term. 48 majors offered in the areas of business administration, education, fine & applied arts, foreign languages, humanities, mathematics & sciences, music, physical education, radiation & laboratory medicine, sociology; American, East Asian, future, and urban studies. Special majors. Minors offered. Courses in 6 additional areas, including Chinese. Distributives and one religion course required. MSacred Music granted. Independent study. Honors program. Cooperative work/study, limited pass/fail, internships. Preprofessional programs in dentistry, law, medicine, pharmacy, veterinary medicine. 3-2 engineering programs with Case, Columbia, Georgia Tech, Washington U. 3-2 nursing program with Case. 3-2 forestry and environmental programs with Duke. Cross-registration with 15 area schools. Exchange programs in Great Britain. Study abroad. Elementary, secondary, and special education certification. ROTC, AFROTC, NROTC nearby. Language lab. 500,000-volume library.

Financial CEEB CSS. University scholarships, grants, loans, tuition reduction for children of Lutheran pastors; PELL, SEOG, NDSL, CWS. Application deadline March 1.

Admissions High school graduation with 12 units required. Interview recommended. Audition required for music students. SAT or ACT required; ACH used for placement. $20 application fee. Rolling admissions. $100 deposit due on acceptance of admissions offer. *Early Admission* Program. Admission deferral possible. Transfers accepted. Credit possible for CEEB AP, CLEP, and university's proficiency exams.

Student Life Student government. Newspaper, literary magazines, yearbook, radio station. Music and drama groups. Debate. Concerned Black Students. Academic, honorary, religious, service, and special interest groups. 8 fraternities and 9 sororities, all with houses. 42% of men and 46% of women join. Freshmen live at home or on campus. Coed and single-sex dorms. Language houses. Married-student housing. 61% of students live on campus. Freshmen may not have cars. 3 phys ed courses required. 10 intercollegiate sports for men, 10 for women; intramurals. NCAA. OAC. Student body composition: 0.2% Asian, 5% Black, 0.1% Hispanic, 0.1% Native American, 94.1% White, 0.5% Other. 47% from out of state.

WOOSTER, THE COLLEGE OF $$

Wooster 44691, (800)362-7386 (in Ohio)
Dean of Admissions: Samuel Barnett

- **Undergraduates:** 877m, 787w
- **Tuition, Room, Board and Fees:** $10,430
- **Degrees offered:** BA, BMus, BMus Ed
- **Mean SAT:** 490v, 530m,   **Mean ACT:** 24
- **Student-faculty ratio:** 12 to 1
- **Calendar system:** Semester

A private college affiliated with the Presbyterian Church, established in 1866. 320-acre small-city campus, 60 miles from Cleveland. Airports, bus stations in Cleveland and Akron.

Academic Character NCACS and professional accreditation. Semester system, 6-week summer term. 43 majors offered in the areas of art, Black studies, computer science, cultural area studies, foreign languages, the humanities, international relations, music, physical education, science, social science, religion, theatre, and urban studies. Special and self-designed majors. Courses include archaeology, Hebrew, Russian. Distributives and one religion course required. Independent study. Phi Beta Kappa. Limited pass/fail, internships. Preprofessional programs in law, medicine, religion, and business. 3-2 engineering programs with Case, U Michigan, Washington U. 3-year special law program with Columbia. 3-2 social work program with Case. 3-year graduate school programs in economics, math, physics with U Michigan. 3-2 nursing program with Case. 3-2 forestry and environmental studies program with Duke. Washington, UN, Oak Ridge, Newberry Library semesters. Many study abroad programs. Elementary and secondary education certification. Computer center. Language lab. Art center. 525,000-volume library.

Financial CEEB CSS. College scholarships, grants, loans, Presbyterian Church grants, payment plans; PELL, SEOG, NDSL, FISL, CWS. Application deadline April 15.

Admissions High school graduation with 15 units required. Interview recommended. SAT or ACT required. $15 application fee. Rolling admissions. $100 deposit due on acceptance of admissions offer. *Early Admission* and *Early Decision* programs. Admission deferral possible. Transfers accepted. Credit possible for CEEB AP and CLEP exams.

Student Life Student government. Newspaper, magazine, yearbook, radio station. Music, dance, and drama groups. Debate. Japan Association. Black Student Association. International Student Association. Academic, religious, and special interest groups. 7 social clubs for men and 4 for women; housed as units in dorms. 30% of men and 24% of women join. Freshmen live on campus. Coed and single-sex dorms. Special interest housing. 90% of students live on campus. Cars permitted after 1st quarter of 1st year. 11 intercollegiate sports for men, 9 for women; many intramurals. AIAW, NCAA, OAC. Student body composition: 1% Asian, 5% Black, 1% Hispanic, 86% White, 7% Other. 55% from out of state.

Oklahoma

OKLAHOMA, UNIVERSITY OF $

Norman 73019, (405) 325-2251
Director of Admissions: Barbara Cousins

- **Undergraduates:** 9,537m, 6,927w
- **Tuition (1984–1985):** $820 (in-state), $2,225 (out-of-state)
- **Room and Board (1984–1985):** $2,490; **Fees:** $120
- **Degrees offered:** BA, BS, BBA, BFA, BMus, BLS, BMus Ed, BArch, BSE
- **Mean Act:** 21
- **Student-faculty ratio:** 20 to 1
- **Calendar system:** Semester

A public university established in 1890. 2,695-acre suburban campus, 15 miles south of Oklahoma City. Served by bus; airport in Oklahoma City.

Academic Character NCACS and professional accreditation. Semester system, 8-week summer term. 65 majors offered by the College of Arts & Sciences, 8 by the College of Business Administration, 19 by the College of Education, 18 by the College of Engineering, 3 by the College of Environmental Design, 26 by the College of Fine Arts, and 1 each in the colleges of Liberal Studies, Nursing, and Pharmacy. Special majors. Distributive requirements; freshmen take at least 2 semesters in University College. Graduate degrees granted. Honors program. Phi Beta Kappa. Some cooperative work/study, pass/fail, credit by exam. Preprofessional programs. Study abroad. Elementary, secondary, and special education certification. ROTC, AFROTC, NROTC. Computer center. Hacienda El Cobano. Art museum. Science and history museum. Language lab. 1,800,000-volume library with microform resources.

Financial CEEB CSS. University scholarships, grants, loans; PELL, SEOG, NSS, NDSL, FISL, NSL, GSL, CWS. Application deadlines March 1 (scholarships), May 1 (loans).

Admissions High school graduation required. ACT required for in-state students. $10 application fee for out-of-state students. Rolling admissions. Transfers accepted. Credit possible for CEEB AP, CLEP, ACT PEP, and departmental exams. Special admissions program.

Student Life Student government. Newspaper, yearbook, radio and TV stations. Music and drama groups. Debate. Model UN. Academic, political, and volunteer groups. 22 fraternities and 15 sororities; most have houses. 11% of men and 15% of women join. Single students under 21 live at home or on campus. Coed and single-sex dorms. Special-interest housing. Married-student housing. 27% of students live on campus. Liquor prohibited. Several intercollegiate and intramural sports. AIAW, Big Eight Conference. Student body composition: 4% Black, 1% Hispanic, 3% Native American, 80% White, 12% Other. 19% from out of state.

OKLAHOMA STATE UNIVERSITY $

Stillwater 74078, (405) 624-6348
Director of Admissions: Raymond Girod

- **Undergraduates:** 10,869m, 7,885w
- **Tuition (1984–1985):** $775 (in-state), $2,195 (out-of-state)
- **Room and Board (1984–1985):** $2,026;   **Fees:** $129
- **Degrees offered:** BA, BS, BMus, BMus Ed, BFA, BAEd, BUniversity Studies
- **Mean ACT:** 17
- **Student-faculty ratio:** 20 to 1
- **Calendar system:** Semester

A public university established in 1890. 150-acre campus in a small city 70 miles from Oklahoma City. Airport nearby.

Academic Character NCACS and professional accreditation. Semester system, 8-week summer term. 12 majors offered by the College of Agriculture, 47 by the College of Arts & Sciences, 10 by the College of Business Administration, 6 by the College of Education, 18 by the College of Engineering, and 6 by the College of Home Economics. Distributive requirements. Graduate degrees granted. Honors program. Pass/fail. Several preprofessional programs. Early childhood, elementary, secondary, and special education certification. ROTC, AFROTC. Performing arts center. 1,250,000-volume library with microform resources.

Financial University scholarships, grants, loans; PELL, SEOG, NDSL, GSL, CWS. Scholarship application deadline March 1.

Admissions High school graduation required. ACT required; SAT accepted from out-of-state students. $10 application fee for out-of-state applicants. Rolling admissions; suggest applying by March 1. *Concurrent Enrollment* Program. Transfers accepted. Credit possible for CEEB AP exams; university has own advanced placement program. Probationary admission possible.

Student Life Student government. Newspaper, literary magazine, yearbook. Music and drama groups. Debate. Academic, ethnic, honorary, religious, and special interest groups. 25 fraternities, 22 with houses; 14 sororities, 10 with houses. 20% of men and 25% of women join. Freshmen live on campus. Single-sex dorms. Co-op dorms. Married-student housing. 32% of students live on campus. Liquor prohibited. 12 intercollegiate sports; many intramurals. Big Eight Conference. Student body composition: 7% Asian, 3% Black, 1% Hispanic, 2% Native American, 87% White. 14% from out of state.

ORAL ROBERTS UNIVERSITY $

7777 South Lewis Avenue, Tulsa 74171, (918) 495-6518
Director of Admissions: Tim Cameron

- **Undergraduates:** 1,772m, 1,831w
- **Tuition (1984–1985):** $3,800
- **Room and Board (1984–1985):** $2,350–$2,592;   **Fees:** $80
- **Degrees offered:** BA, BS, BMus, BMus Ed
- **Mean SAT:** 460v, 498m,   **Mean ACT:** 20.6
- **Student-faculty ratio:** 12 to 1
- **Calendar system:** Semester

A private university established in 1963. 500-acre suburban campus. Served by air and bus.

Academic Character NCACS and professional accreditation. Semester system, 3 summer terms. 44 majors offered in the areas of the arts, business administration, education, engineering, humanities, music, nursing, physical education, science, and theology. Self-designed majors. Minor required. Distributives and religion courses required; senior paper required in most disciplines. Graduate degrees granted. Independent study. Pass/fail, internships. Preprofessional programs in business, dentistry, law, medicine. 3-2 business program. Study in France and Germany. Elementary, secondary, and special education certification. Closed circuit TV. Programmed learning facilities. 1,000,000-volume library with microform resources.

Financial CEEB CSS. University scholarships, grants, loans, payment plans; PELL, SEOG, GSL, NDSL, FISL, CWS, university work program.

Admissions High school graduation with 16 units required. Interview recommended. Minister's recommendation required. ACT or SAT required. $15 application fee. Rolling admissions; suggest applying by end of 11th year. *Early Decision, Early Admission, Concurrent Enrollment* programs. Credit possible for CEEB AP and CLEP exams; university has own advanced placement program.

Student Life Student government. Academic, religious, and special interest groups. Students live at home or on campus. Single-sex dorms. Married-student housing. 82% of students live on campus. Liquor prohibited. Dress code. Attendance in class, at church, and at twice-weekly chapel required. Physical Activity and Aerobics program required. 6 intercollegiate sports for men, 4 for women; many intramurals. AIAW, NCAA, MCC. Student body composition: 1.5% Asian, 4.5% Black, 1.5% Hispanic, 0.5% Native American, 88% White, 4% Other. 90% from out of state.

TULSA, UNIVERSITY OF $

Tulsa 74104, (918) 592-6000
Dean of Records & Admissions: Charles Malone

- **Undergraduates:** 2,202m, 2,014w
- **Tuition (1984–1985):** $4,200
- **Room and Board (1984–1985):** $2,400; **Fees:** $70
- **Degrees offered:** BA, BS, BFA, BMus, BMus Ed, BSBA, BSN
- **Mean SAT:** 500v, 540m, **Mean ACT:** 24
- **Student-faculty ratio:** 16 to 1
- **Calendar system:** Semester

A private university founded in 1894. 115-acre urban campus, 2 miles from downtown Tulsa. Served by air and bus.

Academic Character NCACS and professional accreditation. Semester system, 12-week summer flexterm. 28 majors offered by the College of Arts & Sciences, 5 by the College of Business Administration, 11 by the College of Education, 11 by the College of Engineering, and 1 by the College of Nursing. Self-designed majors. Distributive requirements. Graduate degrees granted. Independent study. Honors program. Pass/fail, internships. Preprofessional programs in dentistry, law, medicine, optometry, osteopathy, pharmacy, physical therapy, social service, veterinary medicine. Study abroad. Elementary, secondary, and special education certification. Computer center. Language labs. 1,000,000-volume library with microform resources.

Financial ACT FAS. University scholarships, grants, loans, athletic and performance scholarships, state grants and loans; PELL, SEOG, NDSL, NSL, FISL, GSL, CWS. Priority application deadline March 1.

Admissions High school graduation with 15 units required. Interview encouraged. Audition required for music majors. SAT or ACT required. $10 application fee. Rolling admissions. $25 tuition deposit and $100 room deposit (for boarders) due on acceptance of admissions offer. *Early Admission* Program. Admission deferral possible. Transfers accepted. Credit possible for CEEB AP, CLEP, and university exams.

Student Life Student government. Newspaper, literary magazine, yearbook, radio and TV stations. Music and drama groups. Art competition. Academic, ethnic, honorary, professional, religious, and special interest groups. 6 fraternities and 8 sororities, all with houses. 15% of men and 20% of women join. Coed and single-sex dorms. Athletic and honors houses. 36% of students live on campus. Firearms and hazing prohibited. 7 intercollegiate sports for men, 7 for women; intramurals. AIAW, MVC. Student body composition: 0.4% Asian, 3% Black, 1% Hispanic, 1.8% Native American, 85% White, 8.8% Other. 41% from out of state.

Oregon

LEWIS AND CLARK COLLEGE $$

0615 SW Palatine Hill Road, Portland 97219, (503) 244-6161
Director of Admissions: Robert H. Loeb, III

- **Undergraduates:** 775m, 879w
- **Tuition and Fees (1984–1985):** $7,008
- **Room and Board (1984–1985):** $2,811
- **Degrees offered:** BA, BS, BM
- **Mean SAT:** 520v, 545m, **Mean ACT:** 25
- **Student-faculty ratio:** 14 to 1
- **Calendar system:** Trimester

A private college affiliated with the United Presbyterian Church, established in 1867. 130-acre suburban campus, 6 miles from downtown Portland. Served by air, rail, and bus.

Academic Character NASC and professional accreditation. Trimester system, 2 4½-week summer terms. 26 majors offered in the areas of liberal arts & sciences, business, education, fine arts, physical education, and religion. Self-designed majors. Distributive requirements. Graduate degrees granted. Independent study. Honors program. Pass/fail, internships. Preprofessional programs in dentistry, law, medicine. 3-2 engineering program with Columbia and Washington U. Washington term. Theatre term in New York City. Study abroad. Elementary and secondary education certification. Computer center. Language labs. Concert hall and theatre. 200,000-volume library with microform resources.

Financial CEEB CSS. College scholarships, grants, loans, family plan; PELL, SEOG, NDSL, GSL, CWS. Application deadline February 15.

Admissions High school graduation with 15 units recommended. Interview encouraged. SAT or ACT required. $25 application fee. Application deadline March 1. $100 deposit ($50 for commuters) due on acceptance of admissions offer. *Early Decision* and *Early Admission* programs. Admission deferral possible. Transfers accepted. Credit possible for CEEB AP exams.

Student Life Student government. Newspaper, literary magazine, radio station. Music and drama groups. Debate. Model UN. Black Student Union. Athletic, academic, ethnic, professional, service, and special interest groups. 3 fraternities without houses. Freshmen under 21 live at home or on campus. Coed and single-sex dorms. Co-op dorms. 65% of students live on campus. 1 term of phys ed required. 9 intercollegiate sports for men, 8 for women; intramurals. AIAW, PNIAC. Student body composition: 1% Black, 2% Hispanic, 1% Native American, 83% White, 13% Other. 65% from out of state.

LINFIELD COLLEGE $$

McMinnville 97128, (503) 472-4121
Dean of Admissions: Thomas Meicho

- **Undergraduates:** 585m, 606w
- **Tuition (1984–1985):** $5,980
- **Room and Board (1984–1985):** $2,274; **Fees:** $100

- **Degrees offered:** BA, BS
- **Mean SAT:** 449v, 488m
- **Student-faculty ratio:** 13 to 1
- **Calendar system:** 4—1—4

A private college affiliated with the Baptist Church, established in 1849. 90-acre small-town campus, 38 miles southwest of Portland. Served by air and bus.

Academic Character NASC and professional accreditation. 4-1-4 system, 2 5-week summer terms. 48 majors offered in the areas of art, business, education, home economics, humanities, music, physical education, religion, science, and social science. Self-designed and special majors. Minors offered. Distributives and GRE required. Independent study. Honors program. Cooperative work/study, pass/fail, internships. Preprofessional programs in dentistry, law, medicine, veterinary medicine. 3-1 medical technology program. 3-2 engineering programs with USC, Oregon State, Washington State. Study abroad. Elementary and secondary education certification. Linfield Research Institute. Computer center. Language lab. Environmental field station. 120,000-volume library with microform resources.

Financial CEEB CSS. College scholarships, grants, loans, family plan, payment plans; PELL, SEOG, NDSL, GSL, CWS. Preferred FAF deadline March 15.

Admissions High school graduation with 17 units recommended. Interview recommended. SAT or ACT required; WPCT accepted. $15 application fee. Rolling admissions; suggest applying by March 1. $100 deposit due on acceptance of admissions offer. *Early Decision, Early Admission, Concurrent Enrollment* programs. Admission deferral possible. Transfers accepted. Credit possible for CEEB AP and CLEP exams.

Student Life Student government. Newspaper, yearbook, radio station. Music and drama groups. Debate. Black Student Union. Academic, honorary, service, religious, and special interest groups. 3 fraternities and 3 sororities with rooms. 30% of men and 40% of women join. Seniors may live off campus. Coed and single-sex dorms. Special interest housing. Married-student housing. 78% of students live on campus. 2 hours of phys ed required. 9 intercollegiate sports for men, 7 for women; several intramurals. AIAW, NC. Student body composition: 4% Asian, 2% Black, 1% Hispanic, 1% Native American, 88% White, 4% Other. 54% from out of state.

OREGON, UNIVERSITY OF $

Eugene 97403, (503) 686-3201
Director of Admissions: James R. Buch

- **Undergraduates:** 7,891m, 7,579w
- **Tuition (1984—1985):** $1,450 (in-state), $4,140 (out-of-state)
- **Room and Board (1984—1985):** $2,150; **Fees:** $50
- **Degrees offered:** BA, BS, BArch, BInt Arch, BLand Arch, BFA, BBA, BEd, BPhysEd, BMus
- **Mean SAT:** 470v, 496m, **Mean ACT:** 21.2
- **Student-faculty ratio:** 19 to 1
- **Calendar system:** Quarter

A public university established in 1872. 187-acre urban campus. Served by air, bus, and rail.

Academic Character NASC and professional accreditation. Quarter system, 8- and 11-week summer terms. 6 majors offered by the School of Architecture & Allied Arts, 9 by the College of Business Administration, 2 by the School of Community Service & Public Affairs, 3 by the College of Education, 4 by the College of Health, Physical Education & Recreation, 1 by the School of Journalism, 34 by the College of Liberal Arts, and 5 by the School of Music. Special majors. Distributive requirements. Graduate degrees granted. Independent study. Honors College. Phi Beta Kappa. Pass/fail, internships. Preprofessional programs in 13 areas. 3-2 medical technology program. 2-2 dental hygiene program. Member National Student Exchange. Study in Europe, Japan, Mexico. Elementary, secondary, and special education certification. ROTC. Computer center. Art and natural history museums. Language lab. 2,100,000-volume library with microform resources.
Financial CEEB CSS. University scholarships, grants, loans; PELL, SEOG, NDSL, GSL, CWS. Scholarship application deadline March 1.
Admissions High school graduation with 12-14 units recommended. Music majors must audition. SAT or ACT required. $25 application fee. Rolling admissions. $50 room deposit due on acceptance of admissions offer. Transfers accepted. Credit possible for CEEB AP, CLEP, and challenge exams. EOP.
Student Life Student government. Newspaper, literary magazine, yearbook, radio station. Music, dance, and drama groups. Debate. PIRG. PLUS. Women's Resource Service. Academic, ethnic, honorary, religious, service, and special interest groups. 14 fraternities and 12 sororities, all with houses. 15% of undergraduates join. Coed and single-sex dorms. Special interest and co-op dorms. Married-student housing. 20% of students live on campus. Liquor prohibited in dorms. 1 course in health education required. 8 intercollegiate sports for men, 8 for women; intramurals. AIAW, NCAA, NCWSA, Pac-10. Student body composition: 2% Asian, 2% Black, 1% Hispanic, 1% Native American, 93% White, 1% Other. 25% from out of state.

OREGON STATE UNIVERSITY $

Corvallis 97331, (503) 754-4411
Director of Admissions: Wallace E. Gibbs

- **Undergraduates:** 7,756m, 5,636w
- **Tuition (1984–1985):** $1,410 (in-state), $4,035 (out-of-state)
- **Room and Board (1984–1985):** $2,100; **Fees:** $25
- **Degrees offered:** BA, BS, BFA, BAgE
- **Mean SAT:** 446–457v, 480–537m, **Mean ACT:** 17.31–20.91
- **Student-faculty ratio:** 17 to 1
- **Calendar system:** Quarter

A public university established in 1868. 397-acre campus in a small city 85 miles south of Portland. Served by bus; airport 40 miles away in Eugene.
Academic Character NASC and professional accreditation. Quarter system, 8- and 11-week summer terms. 13 majors offered by the School of Agriculture, 9 by the School of Business, 3 by the School of Education, 14 by the School of Engineering, 4 by the School of Forestry, 2 by the School of Health & Physical Education, 13 by the School of Home Economics, 20 by the College of Liberal Arts, 3 by the School of Pharmacy, and 19 by the College of Science. Self-designed majors. Minors offered in many major fields. Distributive requirements. Graduate degrees granted. Independent study.

Honors program. Phi Beta Kappa. Cooperative work/study, limited pass/fail, internships. Preprofessional programs in dentistry, dental hygiene, medicine, medical technology, nursing, optometry, physical therapy, podiatry, veterinary medicine. Cooperative mining engineering program with Idaho. WICHE exchange program with schools in the 13 Western states. National Student Exchange Program with 53 state schools. Several study abroad programs. Elementary and secondary education certification. ROTC, AFROTC, NROTC. Language lab. Marine Science Center. Natural History Museum. Art gallery. 919,789-volume library with microform resources.

Financial CEEB CSS. University scholarships, grants, loans; PELL, SEOG, GSL, NDSL, CWS. Preferred application deadline February 1.

Admissions High school graduation required. SAT or ACT required. $25 application fee. Rolling admissions. $50 room deposit due on acceptance of admissions offer. *Early Admission* and *Early Decision* programs. Transfers accepted. Credit possible for CEEB AP and CLEP exams. EOP.

Student Life Student government. Newspaper, yearbook. Music and drama groups. Debate. Academic, political, service, tutorial, and special interest groups. 28 fraternities and 15 sororities, all with houses. Single freshmen live on campus. Coed and single-sex dorms. Co-op houses. Married-student housing. 40% of students live on campus. Liquor prohibited. 3 hours of phys ed required. 8 intercollegiate sports for men, 9 for women; club and intramural sports. AIAW, NCAA, AAWU, PTC. Student body composition: 4% Asian, 1.4% Native American, 87.5% White, 7.1% Other. 18% from out of state.

PACIFIC UNIVERSITY $$

Forest Grove 97116, (503) 357-6151
Director of Admissions: Marie B. Williams

- **Undergraduates:** 482m, 397w
- **Tuition (1984–1985):** $5,990
- **Room and Board (1984–1985):** $2,420;   **Fees:** $115
- **Degrees offered:** BA, BS, BM
- **Mean SAT:** 424v, 462m
- **Student-faculty ratio:** 12 to 1
- **Calendar system:** Semester

A private university affiliated with the United Church of Christ, established in 1849. Rural campus, 25 miles from Portland. Served by bus; airport and rail station in Portland.

Academic Character NASC and professional accreditation. Semester system, 3 3-week summer terms. 48 majors offered in the areas of communications, education, fine arts, humanities, legal services, mathematics, medical technology, music, physical education, physical therapy, religion, science, social science, and speech. Special majors. Distributive requirements. Graduate degrees granted. Independent study. Honors program. Limited pass/fail, internships, credit by exam. Preprofessional programs in dentistry, law, medicine, nursing, optometry, pharmacy, physical therapy, theology, veterinary medicine. 3-1 medical technology program. 3-2 engineering programs with Georgia Tech, Oregon State, Washington State, Washington U. Study abroad. Elementary, secondary, and special education certification. Media center. Language lab. 128,000-volume library with microform resources.

Financial CEEB CSS. University scholarships, grants, loans; PELL, SEOG, NDSL, GSL, FISL, CWS. Preferred application deadline April 15.

Admissions High school graduation with 18 units recommended. Interview recommended. SAT or ACT required. $15 application fee. Rolling admissions; suggest applying by February 1. $100 deposit due on acceptance of admissions offer. *Early Admission* Program. Admission deferral possible. Transfers accepted. Credit possible for CEEB AP and CLEP exams.

Student Life Student government. Newspaper, literary magazine, yearbook, radio and TV studios. Music and drama groups. Debate. 1 fraternity and 2 sororities without houses. Juniors and seniors may live off campus. Dorms for men and women. Married-student housing. 40% of students live on campus. 10 intercollegiate sports for men, 9 for women; intramurals. WCIC, NC. Student body composition: 14.5% Asian, 4.3% Black, 1.5% Hispanic, 2.4% Native American, 76.5% White. 65% from out of state.

REED COLLEGE $$$

3203 Southeast Woodstock Blvd., Portland 97202, (503) 777-7511
Dean of Admissions: Robin Cody

- **Undergraduates:** 643m, 485w
- **Tuition (1984–1985):** $8,190
- **Room and Board (1984–1985):** $2,830;   **Fees:** $100
- **Degrees offered:** BA
- **Mean SAT:** 611v, 622m
- **Student-faculty ratio:** 11 to 1
- **Calendar system:** Semester

A private college established in 1909. 100-acre suburban campus, 5 miles from downtown Portland. Served by air, rail, and bus.

Academic Character NASC accreditation. Semester system, January interim. 21 majors offered by the divisions of Humanities; Arts; History & Social Sciences; Literature & Languages; Mathematics & Natural Sciences; Philosophy , Education, Religion, & Psychology; and in 13 interdisciplinary fields. Self-designed majors. Distributive requirements. Junior Qualifying Exam. Independent research, oral exam, original work, and thesis required of seniors. Independent study. Phi Beta Kappa. Limited pass/fail. Internships. Preprofessional program in medicine. 3-2 engineering programs with Cal Tech, Columbia, Rensselaer. 3-2 forestry program with Duke. 3-2 computer science program with U Washington. 3-2 applied physics program with Oregon Graduate Center. Exchange program with Howard U. Study abroad. Computer center. Nuclear reactor. Language lab. Studio arts center. 300,000-volume library.

Financial CEEB CSS. College scholarships, grants, loans, payment plans; PELL, SEOG, NDSL, GSL, CWS. Application deadlines February 1 (FAF), March 1 (scholarships).

Admissions High school graduation with 14 units recommended. SAT required; ACT accepted. 3 ACH recommended. $20 application fee. Rolling admissions; application deadline February 15. $100 deposit due on acceptance of admissions offer. *Early Decision* and *Early Admission* programs. Admission deferral possible. Transfers accepted. Credit possible for CEEB AP exams; college has own advanced placement program.

Student Life Community government. Newspaper, literary magazine, yearbook, radio station. Music, dance, and drama groups. Educational Policy Committee. Ethnic, religious, and special interest groups. Coed and single-sex dorms. Language houses. No married-student housing. 49% of students live on campus. 3 semesters of phys ed required. Several personal sports programs, club sports. Student body composition: 8% Asian, 1% Black, 3% Hispanic, 1% Native American, 87% White. 85% from out of state.

WILLAMETTE UNIVERSITY $$

Salem 97301, (503) 370-6300
Director of Admissions: Franklin D. Meyer

- **Undergraduates:** 625m, 580w
- **Tuition (1984–1985):** $6,400
- **Room and Board (1984–1985):** $2,700;   **Fees:** $50
- **Degrees offered:** BA, BS, BMus, BTheatre, BMus Ed
- **Mean SAT:** 500v, 540m,   **Mean ACT:** 24
- **Student-faculty ratio:** 13 to 1
- **Calendar system:** Semester

A private university affiliated with the United Methodist Church, established in 1842. 60-acre urban campus, 45 miles south of Portland. Served by air, rail, and bus.

Academic Character NASC and professional accreditation. Semester system. 31 majors offered in the areas of American studies, art, computer science, environmental science, humanities, international studies, languages, mathematics, music, physical education, religion, science, social science, and theatre. Distributive requirements. Graduate degrees granted. Independent study. Limited pass/fail, internships. Preprofessional programs in business, dentistry, government, law, medical technology, medicine, religion, nursing, social service. 3-2 management program with Atkinson Graduate School. 3-2 engineering programs with Columbia and Stanford. 3-2 forestry program with Duke. Combined education program with Western Oregon. UN and Washington Semesters. Study in Europe, Japan, Mexico. Secondary education certification. AFROTC at U Portland. Art gallery. Playhouse. Language lab. 236,035-volume library with microform resources.

Financial CEEB CSS. University scholarships, grants, loans, state grants, payment plan; PELL, SEOG, NDSL, FISL, GSL, CWS. Recommended application deadline February 1.

Admissions High school graduation with 16 units required. GED accepted. Interview recommended. Audition required for music majors. SAT, ACT, or WPCT required. $20 application fee. Recommended application deadline March 1. $100 deposit due on acceptance of admissions offer. *Early Decision* and *Early Admission* programs. Admission deferral possible. Transfers accepted. Credit possible for CEEB AP and departmental exams.

Student Life Student government. Newspaper, literary magazine, yearbook. Music, dance, drama groups. Debate. Minority Student Union. Professional, religious, service, and special interest groups. 6 fraternities and 3 sororities, all with houses. Juniors and seniors may live off campus. Coed and single-sex dorms. Special interest houses. No married-student housing. 75% of students live on campus. Some phys ed recommended. 12 intercollegiate sports for men, 10 for women; several inframurals. AIAW, WCIC, NC. Student body composition: 4% Asian, 1% Black, 2% Hispanic, 88% White, 5% Other. 47% from out of state.

Pennsylvania

ALBRIGHT COLLEGE $$

PO Box 516, Reading 19604, (215) 921-2381
Director of Admissions: Dale H. Reinhart

- **Undergraduates:** 617m, 796w
- **Tuition (1984–1985):** $6,720
- **Room and Board (1984–1985):** $2,525;   **Fees:** $65
- **Degrees offered:** BA, BS
- **Mean SAT:** 524v, 574m
- **Student-faculty ratio:** 14 to 1
- **Calendar system:** 4–1–5

A private college affiliated with the United Methodist Church, established in 1856. 80-acre suburban campus at base of Mount Penn in Reading, one hour from Philadelphia. Served by air, bus, and rail.

Academic Character MSACS accreditation. 4-1-5 system, summer terms. Majors offered in American studies, art, economics, English, French, German, government service, history, home economics, philosophy, political science, psychology, religion, social welfare, sociology, Spanish, accounting, biochemistry, biology, business administration, chemistry, computer science, home economics, math, medical technology, nursing, physics, and psychobiology. Self-designed and interdisciplinary majors. Distributives and 9 hours of philosophy/religion required. Independent study in languages. Pass/fail. Internships. Preprofessional programs in dentistry, dietetics, medicine, veterinary medicine, Christian education, law, social welfare, theology. 3-2 engineering programs with Penn State, U Penn. 4-1 engineering program with U Penn. 3-2 program in forestry and environmental management with Duke. Washington, NY semesters. Study abroad. Secondary education certification. Computer center, language lab. 155,000-volume library with microform resources.

Financial CEEB CSS. College scholarships, grants, loans, state grants, payment plan; PELL, SEOG, NSS, NDSL, GSL, FISL, PLUS, CWS. Application deadlines April 1 (scholarships), May 1 (loans).

Admissions High school graduation with 15 units required. Interview encouraged. SAT or ACT, and 3 ACH required. $15 application fee. Rolling admissions; suggest applying by March 15. $100 deposit required on acceptance of offer of admission. *Early Decision* and *Early Admission* programs. Admission deferral possible. Transfers accepted. Credit possible for CEEB AP and CLEP exams.

Student Life Student government. Newspaper, magazine, yearbook, radio station. Music, drama, oratory activities. Women's Resource Committee. Service, religious, academic, honorary, and special interest groups. 5 fraternities with houses, and 5 sororities without houses. 20% of students join. Freshmen must live on campus. Coed and single-sex dorms, senior houses. 80% of students live on campus. Freshmen may not have cars on campus. Liquor prohibited; gambling, drinking, immorality, narcotics cause for suspension or expulsion. 4 semesters of phys ed required. 9 intercollegiate sports for men, 8 for women; intramurals. AIAW, ECAC, NCAA, WAA, MASCAC. Student body composition: 1% Black, 97% White, 2% Other. 52% out of state.

ALLEGHENY COLLEGE $$

Meadville 16335, (814) 724-4351
Dean of Admissions: Richard A. Stewart

- **Undergraduates:** 995m, 905w
- **Tuition (1984–1985):** $7,050
- **Room and Board (1984–1985):** $2,385
- **Degrees offered:** BA, BS
- **Mean SAT:** 533v, 580m,   **Mean ACT:** 26
- **Student-faculty ratio:** 14 to 1
- **Calendar system:** 3 ten-week terms

A private college established in 1815. 165-acre campus in small city of Meadville, 90 miles from Pittsburgh and Cleveland. Served by air and bus.
Academic Character MSACS accreditation. Trimester system, 2 5-week summer terms. Majors offered in aquatic environments, art, biology, chemistry, comparative literature, computer science, dramatic art, economics, English, French, geology, German, history, international studies, mathematics, music, philosophy, physics, political science, psychology, religious studies, Russian, sociology, Spanish, speech communication. Special majors. Distributive requirements. MA granted. Independent study. Phi Beta Kappa. Pass/fail. Preprofessional programs in 16 areas. 3-2 engineering programs with Case Western Reserve, Columbia. Cooperative programs in forestry, resource management, environmental protection with Duke, U of Michigan; in medical technology with Case Western Reserve; in nursing with U of Rochester, Case Western Reserve. Exchange programs. Washington, Appalachian semesters. Study abroad. Elementary and secondary education certification. Observatory, language lab, planetarium. 300,000-volume library.
Financial College scholarships, awards, loans, state aid, payment plans; PELL, SEOG, NDSL, FISL, CWS. Application deadline March 1.
Admissions High school graduation with 12 units required. Interview encouraged. SAT or ACT required; 3 ACH recommended. $20 application fee. Rolling admissions; suggest applying in fall. $150 deposit required on acceptance of offer of admission. *Early Decision* and *Early Admission* programs. Admission deferral possible. Transfers accepted. Credit possible for CEEB AP and CLEP exams. Project 101.
Student Life Student government. Newspaper, magazine, yearbook, radio station. Music, debate, drama groups. Association of Black Collegians. Honorary, academic, political, religious, and special interest groups. 8 fraternities with houses, and 4 sororities without houses. 40% of upperclass men and 35% of upperclass women join. Freshmen must live on campus. Coed and single-sex dorms; language and special interest housing. Freshmen, students receiving financial aid may not have cars on campus. Phys ed required for freshmen, sophomores; swimming test required. 11 intercollegiate sports for men, 7 for women; intramural and club sports. AIAW, NCAA, PAC, KAC. Student body composition: 1% Asian, 4% Black, 1% Hispanic, 92% White, 2% Other. 50% from out of state.

BRYN MAWR COLLEGE $$$

Bryn Mawr 19010, (215) 645-5152
Director of Admissions: Elizabeth G. Vermey

- **Undergraduates:** 1,130w
- **Tuition (1984–1985):** $9,000
- **Room and Board (1984–1985):** $3,900;   **Fees:** $140
- **Degrees offered:** AB
- **Mean SAT:** mid 600's v, mid 600's m
- **Student-faculty ratio:** 10 to 1
- **Calendar system:** Semester

A private women's college with coed graduate programs, established in 1885. 125-acre suburban campus in residential Bryn Mawr, 11 miles west of Philadelphia. Served by rail. Airport and bus station in Philadelphia.
Academic Character MSACS accreditation. Semester system. Majors offered in anthropology, astronomy, biology, chemistry, classical & Near Eastern archaeology, classical languages, economics, English, fine art, French, geology, German, Greek, growth & structure of cities, Hispanic & Hispanic/American studies, history, history of art, history of religion, Italian, Latin, mathematics, music, philosophy, physics, political science, psychology, religion, Romance languages, Russian, Russian studies, sociology, Spanish. Special majors. Courses in performing arts, education. Senior Conference in major required. MA, MSS, PhD granted. Independent study, honors program. Pass/fail, internships. Self-scheduled examinations. Premedical program. 3-2 engineering program with Caltech. BA/MD program for PA residents with Medical College of Pennsylvania. 4-college program with Haverford, Swarthmore, U of Pennsylvania. Study abroad. Secondary education certification. ROTC at U Penn. Computer center, language lab. 750,000-volume library with microform resources.
Financial CEEB CSS. College scholarships, grants, loans, state grants; PELL, SEOG, NDSL. Scholarship application deadline January 15.
Admissions High school graduation with 16 units required. Interview encouraged. SAT and 3 ACH required. $25 application fee. Application deadline February 1. $100 deposit required on acceptance of offer of admission. *Early Decision* and *Early Admission* programs. Admission deferral possible. A few transfers accepted. Credit possible for CEEB AP exams; college has own advanced placement program.
Student Life Student government. Newspaper, literary review. Music, drama, debate groups. Religious and special interest groups. Activities with Haverford students. Upperclass students may live off campus with permission. Single-sex dorms; coed and co-op dorms with Haverford. 96% of students live on campus. 2 years of phys ed required. Intercollegiate and intramural sports. AIAW, NCAA. Student body composition: 4.6% Asian, 3% Black, 2.1% Hispanic, 0.1% Native American, 90.2% White. 87% from out of state.

BUCKNELL UNIVERSITY $$$

Lewisburg 17837, (717) 524-1101
Director of Admissions: Richard C. Skelton

- **Undergraduates:** 1,600m, 1,550w
- **Tuition (1984–1985):** $9,000
- **Room and Board (1984–1985):** $2,200;   **Fees:** $150
- **Degrees offered:** BS, BA, BMus, BSBA, BSEd, BSE
- **Mean SAT:** 555v, 620m
- **Student-faculty ratio:** 14 to 1
- **Calendar system:** 4–1–4

A private university established in 1846. 300-acre rural campus in the small town of Lewisburg, 60 miles from Harrisburg and 160 miles from Philadelphia. Served by bus and air.

Academic Character MSACS and professional accreditation. 4-1-4 system, 6-week summer term. 27 majors offered for a BA degree, 8 for a BS, 7 for a BMusic, 7 for a BS Business Administration, 4 for a BS in Education, and 6 for a BS in Engineering. Self-designed majors. Distributive requirements. MA, MS granted. Independent study. Honors program. Phi Beta Kappa. Internships. Dual degree program in engineering. BS-MS programs in biology, chemistry, engineering. Exchange program with Penn State. Washington Semester. Study abroad in Europe, Japan; students may study abroad at any accredited university. Elementary, secondary, and early childhood education certification. ROTC; AFROTC at Penn State. Computer center, observatory, language lab, environmental science center, greenhouse. 450,000-volume library.

Financial CEEB CSS. University scholarships, grants, loans, payment plan; PELL, SEOG, NDSL, CWS. Application deadline January 15.

Admissions High school graduation required. Interview encouraged. Audition required for BMus candidates, recommended for BA music majors. SAT and 3 ACH required. $20 application fee. Application deadline January 1. $200 deposit required on acceptance of offer of admission. *Early Decision* and *Early Admission* programs. Admission deferral possible. Transfers accepted. Credit possible for CEEB AP and CLEP exams; university has own advanced placement program.

Student Life Student government. Newspaper, magazines, yearbook, radio station. Music, debate, dance, drama groups. Honorary, religious, service, professional, and special interest organizations. 14 fraternities with houses and 8 sororities with suites. 60% of men and 50% of women join. Freshmen must live at home or on campus. Coed and single-sex dorms, language houses. 90% of students live on campus. First-semester freshmen may not have cars on campus. Liquor prohibited on campus. 2 years of phys ed required. Several intercollegiate and intramural sports for men and women. AIAW, ECAC, MAC. Student body composition: 5% Asian, 4% Black, 1% Hispanic, 1% Native American, 89% White. 70% from out of state.

CARNEGIE—MELLON UNIVERSITY $$$

5000 Forbes Avenue, Pittsburgh 15213, (412) 578-2000
Vice President for Enrollment: William F. Elliott

- **Undergraduates:** 2,782m, 1,348w
- **Tuition (1984–1985):** $8,400
- **Room and Board (1984–1985):** $3,400; **Fees:** $50
- **Degrees offered:** BA, BS, BFA, BArch
- **Mean SAT:** Over 1200 combined
- **Student-faculty ratio:** 9 to 1
- **Calendar system:** Semester

A private university established in 1900. 100-acre campus 4 miles from downtown Pittsburgh. Served by air, bus, and rail.

Academic Character MSACS and professional accreditation. Semester system, 6- and 8-week summer terms. 8 majors offered by the Carnegie Institute of Technology, 17 by the College of Fine Arts, 16 by the College of

Humanities & Social Sciences, 21 by the Mellon College of Science, and 2 by the School of Industrial Administration. Self-designed and double majors. Distributive requirements in some colleges. MA, MFA, MS, ME, PhD granted. Independent study. Honors program. Cooperative work/study. Internships. Cross-registration with 5 Pittsburgh schools. 6-year BS-JD program with Duquesne. 5 year bachelor's-master's in social science/public policy & engineering/urban-public affairs. Washington Semester. Study abroad. Early childhood education certification at Chatham College. ROTC, AFROTC. Computer center. 604,128-volume library.

Financial CEEB CSS. University scholarships, grants, loans, state grants, music scholarships, payment plans; PELL, SEOG, NDSL, GSL, FISL, CWS, Rent-a-Tech Program. Scholarship application deadline March 1.

Admissions High school graduation with 16 units required. Interview encouraged. Audition required for music and drama; portfolio for arts; other requirements for specific programs. SAT and 3 ACH required. $25 application fee. Application deadline March 1. $200 tuition and $100 room (for boarders) deposits required on acceptance of offer of admission. *Early Decision* and *Early Admission* programs. Transfers accepted. Credit possible for CEEB AP exams. Academic preview programs for high school students. Carnegie-Mellon Action Program.

Student Life Student government. Newspaper, magazines, yearbook, radio station. Music groups. Several professional, service, and special interest groups. 12 fraternities and 5 sororities with houses. 11% of men and 6% of women join. Freshmen must live at home or on campus. Coed and single-sex dorms. No married-student housing. 80% of students live on campus. Several intercollegiate and intramural sports. NCAA, PAC. Student body composition: 1% Asian, 9% Black, 1% Hispanic, 1% Native American, 81% White, 7% Other. 62% from out of state.

DICKINSON COLLEGE   *$$$*

Carlisle 17013, (717) 245-1231
Director of Admissions: J. Larry Mench

- **Undergraduates:** 821m, 955w
- **Tuition (1984–1985):** $8,240
- **Room and Board (1984–1985):** $2,800;   **Fees:** $83
- **Degrees offered:** BA, BS
- **Mean SAT:** 531v, 561m
- **Student-faculty ratio:** 12 to 1
- **Calendar system:** Semester

A private college established in 1773. 48-acre campus in small city of Carlisle, 18 miles from Harrisburg.

Academic Character MSACS accreditation. Semester system, summer terms. Majors offered in American studies, anthropology, biology, chemistry, computer science, economics, English, fine arts, French & Italian, geology, German, Greek, history, international studies, Judaic studies, Latin, mathematics, music, philosophy, physics, policy & management studies, political science, psychology, religion, Russian & Soviet area studies, sociology, Spanish, theatre & dramatic literature, and Western social & political thought. Self-designed majors. Independent study. Honors program. Phi Beta Kappa. Pass/fail. Credit by exam. Internships. Preprofessional programs in dentistry, law, medicine, optometry, osteopathy, podiatry, social work, theology. Central PA Consortium. 3-1 Asian studies program with U Penn. 3-2 engineering programs with Case Western Reserve, Rensselaer, and U Penn. Harrisburg, India, Washington, Appalachian semesters. Several programs for study abroad. ROTC. Plantarium, observatory. 3,800-acre wildlife sanctuary. Language lab. 328,303-volume library.

Financial CEEB CSS. College scholarships, grants, loans, state aid, payment plans; PELL, SEOG, NDSL, GSL, PLUS, CWS. Application deadline February 15.

Admissions High school graduation with 16 units required. SAT or ACT required; ACH recommended. $20 application fee. Preferred application deadline March 1. $200 deposit required on acceptance of offer of admission. *Early Decision* and *Early Admission* programs. Admission deferral possible. Transfers accepted. Credit possible for CEEB AP exams.

Student Life Student government. Newspaper, magazine, yearbook, radio station. Music, debate, literary, drama groups. Afro-American Society. Service, professional, academic, honorary, and special interest groups. 10 fraternities with houses and 4 sororities without houses. 50% of men and 45% of women join. Freshmen must live at home or on campus. Coed and single-sex dorms; language and special interest houses. No married-student housing. 3 units of phys ed required. 10 intercollegiate sports for men, 8 for women; intramural and club sports. AIAW, ECAC, NCAA, MACAC. Student body composition: 1% Asian, 1% Black, 1% Hispanic, 96% White, 1% Other. 53% from out of state.

DREXEL UNIVERSITY $$

Philadelphia 19104, (215) 895-2400
Director of Admissions: John R. McCullough

- **Undergraduates:** 5,191m, 2,283w
- **Tuition (1984–1985):** $5,268
- **Room and Board (1984–1985):** $2,756–$3,326; **Fees:** $362
- **Degrees offered:** BS
- **Mean SAT:** 500v, 570m
- **Student-faculty ratio:** 20 to 1
- **Calendar system:** Quarter

A private university established in 1891. 40-acre urban campus in University City, west of Philadelphia. Served by air, bus, and rail.

Academic Character MSACS and professional accreditation. Quarter system, 11-week summer term. 10 majors offered by the College of Business & Administration, 6 by the College of Engineering, 17 by the Nesbitt College of Design, Nutrition, Human Behavior, Home Economics, 3 by the College of Humanities & Social Sciences, and 7 by the College of Science. Distributive requirements. MS, MBA, PhD granted. Independent study in some departments. Honors programs. Extensive cooperative work/study program. Elementary education certification. ROTC; AFROTC, NROTC nearby. Evening College. Computer center, audio-visual center, TV studio. 409,000-volume library.

Financial CEEB CSS. University scholarships and loans, payment plan; PELL, SEOG, NDSL, FISL, GSL, CWS. Application deadlines March 1 (scholarships), April 1 (loans).

Admissions High school graduation with 16 units recommended. Interview encouraged. SAT or ACT required; 3 ACH required by some colleges. $10 application fee. Rolling admissions; application deadline April 1. $50 tuition deposit and $50 room deposit (for boarders) required on acceptance of offer of admission. *Early Admission* Program. Transfers accepted. Credit possible for CEEP AP and CLEP exams; university has own advanced placement program.
Student Life Student government. Newspaper, magazine, yearbook, radio station. Music, drama groups. Over 50 honorary and professional societies; religious, service, and special interest clubs. 12 fraternities with houses and 4 sororities with apartments. 20% of men and 25% of women join. Freshmen must live at home or on campus. No married-student housing. 45% of students live on campus. 2 quarters of phys ed required. Several intercollegiate and intramural sports for men and women. AIAW, NCAA, ECAA, MASCAA. Student body composition: 13% minority. 31% from out of state.

DUQUESNE UNIVERSITY $$

Pittsburgh 15282, (412) 434-6220
Director of Admissions: Frederick H. Lorensen

- **Undergraduates:** 1,938m, 2,349w
- **Tuition (1984–1985):** $5,100
- **Room and Board (1984–1985):** $2,610; **Fees:** $330
- **Degrees offered:** BA, BS, BM, BSEd, BSN, BSBA, BSPh
- **Mean SAT:** 453v, 484m
- **Student-faculty ratio:** 13 to 1
- **Calendar system:** Semester

A private, Roman Catholic university operated by the Holy Ghost Fathers, established in 1878. 38-acre urban campus overlooking downtown Pittsburgh. Served by air, rail, and bus.
Academic Character MSACS and professional accreditation. Semester system, summer terms. 40 majors offered by the College of Liberal Arts & Sciences, 7 by the School of Business Adminstration, 4 by the School of Education, 5 by the School of Music, and 3 by the School of Pharmacy. Minor required in most fields. Distributives and 3 religion/philosophy credits required. Graduate and professional degrees granted. Independent study. Honors program. Cooperative work/study, pass/fail, internships. Preprofessional programs in dentistry, engineering, law, medicine, speech pathology/audiology, theology, veterinary medicine. 3-2 engineering program with Case Western Reserve. Cross-registration with 9 Pittsburgh institutions. Study abroad. Elementary, secondary, special, and music education certification. ROTC; AFROTC at U of Pittsburgh. Language labs. 402,000-volume library.
Financial CEEB CSS. University scholarships, grants, loans, PELL, SEOG, NSS, NDSL, GSL, NSL, HPL, CWS. Application deadline May 1.
Admissions High school graduation with 16 units required. Interview encouraged. Audition and music theory test required by School of Music. SAT or ACT required. $20 application fee. Rolling admissions; application deadline July 1. Deposit required by May 1. *Early Decision* and *Early Admission* programs. Admission deferral possible. Transfers accepted. Credit possible for CEEB AP and CLEP exams.
Student Life Student government. Newspaper, magazine, yearbook, radio

station, TV studio. Music, dance, drama, debate groups. Professional, honorary, service, religious, and academic organizations. 19 fraternities and 12 sororities without houses. 15% of men and women join. Freshmen and sophomores must live at home or on campus. Coed and single-sex dorms; special interest housing. 55% of students live on campus. 8 intercollegiate sports for men, 5 for women; intramurals. AIAW, NCAA, EAA. Student body composition: 10% minority. 20% from out of state.

FRANKLIN AND MARSHALL COLLEGE $$$

Lancaster 17604, (717) 291-3951
Director of Admissions: Ronald D. Potier

- **Undergraduates:** 1,094m, 916w
- **Tuition (1984–1985):** $8,160
- **Room and Board (1984–1985):** $2,890
- **Degrees offered:** BA
- **Mean SAT:** 565v, 593m,   **Mean ACT:** 27
- **Student-faculty ratio:** 14 to 1
- **Calendar system:** Semester

A private college established in 1787, became coed in 1969. 102-acre campus in a residential section of Lancaster, 60 miles from Philadelphia. Served by air, bus, and rail.

Academic Character MSACS accreditation. Semester system, 10-week summer term. Majors offered in American studies, anthropology, art, biology, business administration, chemistry, classics, drama, economics, English, European studies, French, geology, German, government, history, mathematics, philosophy, physics, psychology, religious studies, sociology, and Spanish. Self-designed majors. Distributive requirements. Independent study. Honors program. Phi Beta Kappa. Pass/fail. Internships. Credit by exam. Member Central Penn. Consortium. 3-2 engineering programs with Case Western, Columbia, Georgia Tech, Rensselaer. 3-2 forestry program with Duke. Washington, Harrisburg semesters. Archaeological field work. Study abroad. Secondary education certification. ROTC at Millersville State. Psychology lab, language lab, museum, observatory/planetarium, computer center. 188,000-volume library.

Financial CEEB CSS. College scholarships, grants, loans; PELL, SEOG, CWS. FAF deadline March 1.

Admissions High school graduation with 16 units recommended. Interview encouraged. SAT or ACT required; SAT preferred. English composition ACH required. $25 application fee. Application deadline February 10. $200 tuition deposit required on acceptance of offer of admission. *Early Decision* and *Early Admission* programs. Admission deferral possible. Transfers accepted. Credit possible for CEEB AP and CLEP exams. College has own advanced placement program.

Student Life Student-faculty government. Newspaper, magazine, yearbook, radio stations. Music, literary, film, drama groups. Black Student Union. Honorary, academic, political, and special interest organizations. 10 fraternities with houses and 2 sororities. 35% of men and 1% of women join. Freshmen must live at home or on campus. Coed dorms, language houses. 72% of students live on campus. Students receiving financial aid may not have cars on campus. 12 intercollegiate sports for men, 11 for women; intramural and club sports. AIAW, EIWA, NCAA, MAC. Student body composition: 1% Asian, 4% Black, 1% Hispanic, 92% White, 2% Other. 68% from out of state.

GETTYSBURG COLLEGE $$

Gettysburg 17325, (717) 334-3131
Director of Admissions: Delwin K. Gustafson

- **Undergraduates:** 950m, 950w
- **Tuition (1984—1985):** $7,740
- **Room and Board (1984—1985):** $2,520
- **Degrees offered:** BA, BSMus Ed
- **Mean SAT:** 515v, 550m
- **Student-faculty ratio:** 13 to 1
- **Calendar system:** 4—1—4

A private college affiliated with the Lutheran Church in America, established in 1832. 200-acre campus in Gettysburg, 36 miles from Harrisburg. Served by bus. Harrisburg airport 45 miles away.

Academic Character MSACS accreditation. 4-1-4 system, summer term. Majors offered in art, biology, business administration, chemistry, classical studies, economics, English, French, German, Greek, health & physical education, history, Latin, mathematics, music, philosophy, physics, political science, psychology, religion, sociology & anthropology, Spanish, and theatre arts. Self-designed majors. Distributives and one religion course required. Independent study. Honors program. Phi Beta Kappa. Pass/fail. Member Central Penn. Consortium. Asian studies program in cooperation with U Penn. 5-year forestry program with Duke, 5-year engineering programs with Penn State, RPI, Washington U. CPA program. Washington, Colombia, India, UN, Harrisburg semesters. Study abroad. Elementary and secondary education certification. ROTC. Computer center, planetarium/observatory, language lab, electron microscopy lab. 250,000-volume library.

Financial CEEB CSS. College scholarships, grants, loans; PELL, SEOG, NDSL, CWS. FAF deadline February 1.

Admissions High school graduation required. Interview encouraged; required for music, art, physical education majors. SAT or ACT required; SAT preferred. $20 application fee. Application deadline February 15. $200 deposit required by May 1. *Early Decision* and *Early Admission* programs. Admission deferral possible. Transfers accepted. Credit possible for CEEB AP exams.

Student Life Student government. Newspaper, magazine, yearbook, radio station. Music, dance, drama groups. Service, political, academic, religious, and special interest groups. 11 fraternities with houses, and 7 sororities without houses. 75% of men and 50% of women join. Freshmen must live on campus. Coed and single-sex dorms, special interest houses. 85% of students live on campus. Quiet hours, parietals enforced. Liquor restricted. 2 years of phys ed required. 8 intercollegiate sports for men, 7 for women; intramurals. ECAC, NCAA, MASC. Student body composition: 0.5% Black, 0.5% Hispanic, 99% White. 70% from out of state.

HAVERFORD COLLEGE $$$

Haverford 19041, (215) 896-1000
Director of Admissions: William W. Ambler

- **Undergraduates:** 600m, 400w
- **Tuition and Fees (1984–1985):** $9,245
- **Room and Board (1984–1985):** $3,427
- **Degrees offered:** BA,BS
- **Mean SAT:** 68% have above 600v, 87% have above 600m
- **Student-faculty ratio:** 12 to 1
- **Calendar system:** Semester

A private college established in 1833, became coed in 1977. 226-acre suburban campus in village of Haverford, 15 minutes from Philadelphia by train.
Academic Character MSACS accreditation. Semester system. Majors offered in astronomy, biology, chemistry, classics, economics, English, fine arts, French, German, history, mathematics, music, philosophy, physics, political science, psychology, religion, Russian, sociology & anthropology, and Spanish. Self-designed and double majors. 5 additional majors offered at Bryn Mawr. Distributive requirements. Independent study. Phi Beta Kappa. 4-year bachelor's-master's programs. 3-2 engineering with U Penn. Cross-registration with Bryn Mawr, Swarthmore, U Penn. Off-campus study in the U.S. and abroad. Computer center, observatory, art gallery, language lab. 425,000-volume library with microform resources, interlibrary loan facilities.
Financial CEEB CSS. College scholarships, grants, loans, payment plan; PELL, SEOG, NDSL, CWS. Application deadlines January 31 (scholarships), January 15 (loans).
Admissions High school graduation with 12 units required. Interview advised. SAT and 3 ACH required. $25 application fee. Application deadline January 31. *Early Decision* and *Early Admission* programs. Admission deferral possible. Transfers accepted. Credit possible for CEEB AP exams.
Student Life Student government. All activities are with Bryn Mawr. Newspaper, magazine, yearbook, radio station. Music, drama, debate groups. Academic, honorary, service, and special interest organizations. Students must live at home or on campus. Dorm exchange with Bryn Mawr. Coed dorms, single-sex floors, campus apartments. Language houses at Bryn Mawr. 95% of students live on campus. Gambling prohibited. Honor code. 6 quarters of phys ed required. 11 intercollegiate sports for men, 5 for women; intramural and club sports. AIAW, NCAA, MAAC. Student body composition: 9.7% minority. 80% from out of state.

LAFAYETTE COLLEGE $$$

Easton 18042, (215) 250-5000
Director of Admissions: Richard W. Haines

- **Undergraduates:** 1,150m, 850w
- **Tuition (1984–1985):** $8,350
- **Room and Board (1984–1985):** $3,025
- **Degrees offered:** BA, BS
- **Mean SAT:** 560v, 630m
- **Student-faculty ratio:** 13 to 1
- **Calendar system:** Semester

A private college affiliated with United Presbyterian Church, established in 1826, became coed in 1970. 100-acre urban campus overlooking city of Easton, 80 miles from New York City. Served by bus; airport 20 minutes away.

Academic Character MSACS and professional accreditation. Semester system, 6-week summer term. Majors offered in American civilization, anthropology & sociology, art, biology, chemistry, classics, comparative literature, economics & business, engineering (5 areas), English, French, German, geology, government & law, history, international affairs, mathematics, music, philosophy, physics, psychology, religion, Russian, Spanish. Self-designed majors. Minor required in some departments. Distributive requirements. Honors program. Phi Beta Kappa. Pass/fail. Internships. 5-year AB?BS programs. Cross-registration with area colleges. Consortium with 5 area schools. Washington Semester. Study abroad in several countries. Elementary and secondary education certification. ROTC; AFROTC at Lehigh. 370,000-volume library with microform resources.

Financial CEEB CSS. College scholarships, grants, loans, payment plans; PELL, SEOG, NDSL, GSL, FISL, PLUS, CWS. FAF deadline February 1.

Admissions High school graduation with 16 units required. Interview encouraged. SAT and 3 ACH required. $25 application fee. Application deadline February 15. $100 deposit required on acceptance of offer of admission. *Early Decision* and *Early Admission* programs. Admission deferral possible. Transfers accepted. Credit possible for CEEB AP exams.

Student Life Student government. Newspaper, magazine, yearbook, radio station. Music, drama groups. Association of Black Collegians. Women's Caucus. Academic, professional, religious, service, and special interest groups. 17 fraternities, 5 sororities, 2 coed social dorms. 60% of men and 30% of women join. Freshmen must live on campus. Coed and single-sex dorms. Honors and international housing. No married-student housing. 95% of students live on campus. Freshmen and sophomores may not have cars on campus. Liquor prohibited in dorms. Gambling, hazing prohibited. 12 intercollegiate sports for men, 8 for women; intramural and club sports. AIAW, ECAC, NCAA, NC, ECC. Student body composition: 0.7% Asian, 3.4% Black, 1.9% Foreign, 0.6% Hispanic, 93.4% White. 74% from out of state.

LEHIGH UNIVERSITY $$$

Bethlehem 18015, (215) 691-7000
Director of Admissions: Samuel H. Missimer

- **Undergraduates:** 3,047m, 1,301w
- **Tuition (1984–1985):** $8,750
- **Room and Board (1984–1985):** $3,120
- **Degrees offered:** BA, BS, BSEng
- **Mean SAT:** 554v, 645m
- **Student-faculty ratio:** 15 to 1
- **Calendar system:** Semester

A private university established in 1865, became coed in 1971. 700-acre urban campus in Bethlehem, 50 miles from Philadelphia. Served by air, bus, and rail.

Academic Character MSACS and professional accreditation. Semester system. 34 majors offered by the College of Arts & Sciences, 5 by the College of Business & Economics, and 11 by the College of Engineering & Physical Sciences. Minors in education, law, Russian studies, technology & human values. Distributive requirements; senior exams. Graduate degrees granted. Independent study, honors program. Phi Beta Kappa. Pass/fail. Internships. Cooperative work/study. 5-year, dual-degree programs. Cross-registration with 5 area schools. 6-year BA-MD program with Medical College of PA. 7-year program with U of Penn. Dental School. 5-year teaching program. Harrisburg, Washington Semesters. Marine science program. Study abroad. ROTC, AFROTC. Center for Information Sciences. 730,000-volume library with microform resources.

Financial CEEB CSS. University scholarships, grants, loans; PELL, SEOG, NDSL, CWS. Application deadline January 31.

Admissions High school graduation with 16 units required. Interview encouraged. SAT and 3 ACH required. $25 application fee. Application deadline March 1. $50 deposit required on acceptance of offer of admission. *Early Admission* and *Early Decision* Program. Admission deferral possible. Transfers accepted. Credit possible for CEEB AP exams; university has own advanced placement program.

Student Life Student government. Newspaper, yearbook. Music and drama groups Academic, honorary, professional, and special interest groups. 32 fraternities, 27 with houses. 50% of upperclass men join. Students must live at home or on campus. Coed and single-sex dorms, special interest housing. No married-student housing. 90% of students live on campus. Only upperclass students may have cars. Intercollegiate and intramural sports. AIAW, NCAA. Student body composition: 4% Asian, 3% Black, 1% Hispanic, 92% White. 64% from out of state.

MUHLENBERG COLLEGE $$

Allentown 18104, (215) 433-3191
Dean of Admissions & Freshmen: George W. Gibbs

- **Undergraduates:** 750m, 700w
- **Tuition (1984–1985):** $7,385
- **Room and Board (1984–1985):** $2,315
- **Degrees offered:** BA, BS
- **Mean SAT:** 540v, 590m
- **Student-faculty ratio:** 13 to 1
- **Calendar system:** Semester

A private college affiliated with the Lutheran Church, established in 1848, became coed in 1957. 75-acre campus in residential section of Allentown, 55 miles from Philadelphia.

Academic Character MSACS and professional accreditation. Semester system, 2 summer terms. Majors offered in accounting, American studies, art, biology, business administration, chemistry, classics, communications studies, drama, economics, English, French, German, Greek, history, humanity, Latin, mathematics, music, natural sciences/mathematics, philosophy, physics, political science, psychology, Russian studies, social science, social work, sociology, and Spanish. Self-designed majors. Minors in some major fields and in computer science, religion. Distributives and 2 semesters of religion required. Independent study. Honors program. Phi Beta Kappa. Pass/fail, internships. 3-2 and 4-2 engineering programs with Columbia and Washington U. 3-2 forestry program with Duke. Cross-registration with 5 area schools. Study abroad. Elementary and secondary education certification. AFROTC, ROTC at Lehigh. 180,000-volume library.

Financial CEEB CSS. College scholarships and loans, state aid, payment plans; PELL, SEOG, NDSL, FISL, CWS. Application deadlines February 15 (scholarships), February 1 (loans).

Admissions High school graduation with 16 units required. Interview encouraged. SAT and 3 ACH required. $25 application fee. Application deadline February 15. $100 tuition deposit and $200 room deposit (for boarders) required on acceptance of offer of admission. *Early Decision* and *Early Admission* programs. Admission deferral possible. Transfers accepted. Credit possible for CEEB AP and CLEP exams and ACH test scores.

Student Life Student government. Newspaper, magazine, yearbook, radio stations. Music, debate, drama groups. International Students. Environmental Action. Religious, academic, service, professional, honorary, and special interest groups. 5 fraternities with houses. 40% of men join. Coed and single-sex dorms, college-owned houses, special interest houses. 90% of full-time single students (not in fraternities) live on campus. Freshman boarders may not have cars on campus. 4 semesters of phys ed required. 9 intercollegiate sports for men, 5 for women; intramural and club sports. NCAA, ECAC, MAC. 66% of students from out of state.

PENNSYLVANIA, UNIVERSITY OF $$$

Philadelphia 19104, (215) 243-7507
Director of Admissions: Willis J. Stetson, Jr.

- **Undergraduates:** 5,229m, 3,796w
- **Tuition (1984–1085):** $9,600
- **Room and Board (1984–1985):** $4,276
- **Degrees offered:** BA, BS
- **Mean SAT:** 600v, 650m
- **Student-faculty ratio:** 8 to 1
- **Calendar system:** Semester

A private university established in 1740. 147-acre urban campus in West Philadelphia, on Schuylkill River. Served by air, bus, and rail.

Academic Character MSACS and professional accreditation. Semester system, 2 6-week summer terms. 44 majors offered by the College of Arts & Sciences, 9 by the College of Engineering & Applied Sciences, 1 by the School of Nursing, and 14 by the Wharton School of Business. Self-designed and double majors. Distributive requirements. Graduate and professional degrees granted. Independent study. Honors programs. Phi Beta Kappa. Pass/fail. Preprofessional programs in city regional planning, dentistry, foreign service, government, law, medicine, theology, veterinary medicine. AB-AM program in museum curatorship. 3-2 liberal arts/engineering and business/engineering programs. 3-4 dual degree program with School of Veterinary Medicine. Dual degree architecture and landscape architecture programs. Consortium with Bryn Mawr, Haverford, Swarthmore. Study abroad; exchange with U of Edinburgh, French language exchange. Teacher certification. NROTC, ROTC; AFROTC at St. Joseph's. Several research institutes. Computer center, language lab, observatory. 3,000,000-volume library with microform resources.

Financial CEEB CSS. University scholarships and loans; PELL, SEOG, NDSL, GSL, FISL, CWS. Application deadline January 1.

Admissions High school graduation with 16 units required. Interview required by the School of Nursing. SAT and 3 ACH required. $30 application fee; fee waiver possible. Application deadline January 1. $50 deposit, refundable at graduation, required on acceptance of offer of admission. *Early Decision* and *Early Admission* programs. Admission deferral possible.

Transfers accepted. Credit possible for CEEB AP exams.
Student Life Student government. Newspaper, magazine, yearbook, radio and TV stations. Music, debate, and drama groups. Women's Liberation. Ethnic associations. Academic, religious, and special interest groups. 30 fraternities with houses and 2 sororities, 1 with house. 30% of students join. Coed dorms, special interest houses. Married-student housing. 80% of students live on campus. 21 intercollegiate sports for men, 13 for women. Ivy League. Student body composition: 3.9% Asian, 5.3% Black, 2% Hispanic, 0.?% Native American, 87% White. 75% from out of state.

PENNSYLVANIA STATE UNIVERSITY $

University Park 16802, (814) 865-4700
Dean of Admissions: Donald G. Dickason

- **Undergraduates:** 33,064m, 23,267w
- **Tuition (1984–1985):** $2,562 (in-state), $5,146 (out-of-state)
- **Room and Board (1984–1985):** $2,620
- **Degrees offered:** BA, BS, BArch, BArch Eng, BFA, BLA, BMus, PhB
- **Mean SAT:** 510v, 565m
- **Student-faculty ratio:** 18 to 1
- **Calendar system:** Semester

A public university established in 1855. 5,005-acre campus in small city of University Park, 70 miles from Harrisburg.
Academic Character MSACS and professional accreditation. Semester system, 10-week summer terms. 18 majors offered by the College of Agriculture, 10 by the College of Arts & Architecture, 8 by the College of Business Administration, 10 by the College of Earth & Mineral Sciences, 8 by the College of Education, 11 by the College of Engineering, 3 by the College of Health, Physical Education, Recreation, 7 by the College of Human Development, 35 by the College of Liberal Arts, and 12 by the College of Science. Graduate and professional degrees granted. Independent study. Honors program. Phi Beta Kappa. Cooperative work/study, internships. 3-2 liberal arts programs with engineering or earth/mineral sciences. Medical program with Thomas Jefferson U. Study abroad. Elementary, secondary, and special education certification. ROTC, AFROTC, NROTC. Computer center, language lab. 2,380,215-volume library with microform resources.
Financial CEEB CSS. University scholarships, grants, and loans; PELL, SEOG, NDSL, GSL, CWS. Application deadlines February 15 (scholarships), April 1 (loans).
Admissions High school graduation with 15 units required. SAT required. $20 application fee. Rolling admissions; suggest applying by November 30. $102 tuition deposit and $45 deposit (for boarders) required on acceptance of offer of admission. Transfers accepted. Credit possible for CEEB AP and CLEP exams; university has own advanced placement program. EOP.
Student Life Student government. Newspaper, magazine, yearbook. Music, debate, drama groups. Many religious, academic, honorary, professional, service, and special interest groups. 50 fraternities with houses and 19 sororities without houses. 13% of men and 8% of women join. Freshmen under 21 must live at home or on campus. Freshmen may not have cars on campus. 4 hours of phys ed required. 16 intercollegiate sports for men, 14 for women; several intramural sports. Student body composition: 0.9% Asian, 2.4% Black,

0.6% Hispanic, 0.1% Native American, 94.2% White 1.8% Other. 10% from out of state.

PITTSBURGH, UNIVERSITY OF $/$$

4200 Fifth Avenue, Pittsburgh 15260, (412) 624-4141
Director of Admissions & Student Aid: Joseph A. Merante

- **Undergraduates:** 10,142m, 9,159w
- **Tuition (1984–1985):** $2,650 (in-state), $5,300 (out-of-state)
- **Room and Board (1984–1985):** $2,732 **Fees:** $115
- **Degrees offered:** BA, BS, BSW, BSE, BSHRP, BSPh, BSN
- **Mean SAT:** 470v, 520m
- **Student-faculty ratio:** 11 to 1
- **Calendar system:** 3-term

A private, state-related university established in 1787. 125-acre urban campus in Pittsburgh. Served by air, bus, and rail.
Academic Character MSACS and professional accreditation. 3-term system. Freshmen may enter the College of Arts & Sciences, College of General Studies, School of Engineering, and School of Nursing; upon earning required distribution credits they may then make application to other schools of the University. 45 majors offered by the College of Arts & Sciences, 35 by the College of General Studies, 6 by the School of Education, 7 by the School of Engineering, 7 by the School of Health-Related Professions; also majors offered by the schools of Library & Information Science, Nursing, Pharmacy, and Social Work. Self-designed and interschool majors. Minor required. Courses in astronomy, several languages. Distributive requirements. Graduate and professional degrees granted. Independent study. Honors program. Phi Beta Kappa. 5-year liberal arts/engineering dual degree program. Member consortium with other Pittsburgh schools. Study abroad. AFROTC, ROTC. Language labs. 3,721,596-volume library with microform resources.
Financial CEEB CSS. University scholarships, grants, loans, pharmacy student loans, payment plan; PELL, SEOG, NSS, NDSL, NSL, CWS. Application deadline March 1.
Admissions High school graduation with 15 units required. Interview encouraged. SAT or ACT required. $15 application fee. Rolling admissions; suggest applying in fall. $50 deposit required on acceptance of offer of admission. *Early Admission, Concurrent Enrollment* programs. Admission deferral possible. Transfers accepted. Credit possible for CEEB AP exams; university has own advanced placement program. UCEP.
Student Life Student government. Newspaper, magazine, yearbook, radio station. Music and drama groups. Many academic, service, and special interest groups. 22 fraternities, 15 with houses, and 15 sororities, 10 with suites, 2 with houses. 10% of students join. Coed and single-sex dorms. 22% of students live on campus. Many intercollegiate and intramural sports. AIAW, ECAC, ICAAAA, NCAA, CCIEE, ISL. Student body composition: 1% Asian, 9% Black, 90% White. 13% from out of state.

SAINT JOSEPH'S UNIVERSITY $$

City Avenue and 54th Street, Philadelphia 19131, (215) 879-7400
Director of Admissions: Randy H. Miller

- **Undergraduates:** 1,487m, 1,231w
- **Tuition (1984–1985):** $4,940
- **Room and Board (1984–1985):** $3,230
- **Degrees offered:** BA, BS
- **Mean SAT:** 1050 Combined
- **Student-faculty ratio:** 15 to 1
- **Calendar system:** Semester

A private university controlled by the Society of Jesus, established in 1851, became coed in 1970. 47-acre suburban campus in residential section of Philadelphia. Served by air, bus, and rail.

Academic Character MSACS accreditation. Semester system, 2 6-week summer terms. Majors offered in economics, English, French, German, history, international relations, philosophy, politics, psychology, sociology, Spanish, theology, accounting, biology, chemistry, computer science, engineering physics, finance, food marketing, industrial relations, information systems, management, marketing, mathematics, physics, and public administration. Special majors. Distributives and 9 credits in theology required. Masters degrees granted. Independent study. Honors program. Pass/fail, cooperative work/study, internships. Preprofessional programs in dentistry, law, medicine. Institute of Latin American Studies. Jesuit Student Exchange. Washington, Appalachian, Mexico City semesters. Study abroad. Brazilian Institute. Elementary and secondary education certification. AFROTC; NROTC at Villanova and U.Penn; ROTC at Drexel. Computer center, language lab. 190,412-volume library with microform resources.

Financial CEEB CSS. University scholarships, grants, loans, payment plan; PELL, SEOG, NDSL, GSL, CWS. Application deadline March 1; FAF deadline February 1.

Admissions High school graduation with 15 units required. Interview encouraged. SAT required. $20 application fee. Rolling admissions beginning March 15; suggest applying by March 1. $100 tuition deposit and $150 room deposit required on acceptance of offer of admission. *Early Decision* and *Early Admission* programs. Admission deferral possible. Transfers accepted. Credit possible for CEEB AP exams.

Student Life Student association. Newspaper, quarterly, yearbook, radio station. Music, drama, debate groups. Black Awareness Society. International Student Association. Religious, service, academic, honorary, and special interest groups. Fraternities. Students must live with relatives or on campus. Coed and single-sex dorms, special interest houses. No married-student housing. 41% of students live on campus. 7 intercollegiate sports for men, 5 for women; intramural and club sports. AIAW, ECAC, NCAA, ECCC. Student body composition: 5% Black, 2% Hispanic, 92% White, 1% Other. 30% from out of state.

SUSQUEHANNA UNIVERSITY $$

Selinsgrove 17870, (717) 374-0101
Director of Admissions: Paul W. Beardslee

- **Undergraduates:** 767m, 678w
- **Tuition (1984–1985):** $6,200
- **Room and Board (1984–1985):** $2,685;   **Fees:** $195
- **Degrees offered:** BA, BSBA, BMus
- **Mean SAT:** 470v, 520m

- **Student-faculty ratio:** 15 to 1
- **Calendar system:** Trimester

A private university affiliated with the Lutheran Church in America, established in 1858. 185-acre campus located in small town of Selinsgrove, 50 miles from Harrisburg. Airport in Harrisburg.

Academic Character MSACS and professional accreditation.Trimester system, 6-week summer term. Majors offered in biology, chemistry, classics, communications & theatre arts, computer & information science, economics, elementary education, English, French, geology, German, Greek, history, Latin, mathematics, philosophy, physics, political science, psychology, religion, sociology, Spanish, and 5 business majors and 4 music majors. Self-designed and double majors. Many minors offered. Courses in art, secondary education. Anesthesia major for RNs. Distributive requirements. 1 course in religion/philosophy required. Independent study. Honors program. Pass/fail, internships. Preprofessional programs in dentistry, engineering, law, medicine, ministry, music, optometry, teaching, veterinary medicine. 3-2 and 4-2 engineering programs with U Penn. 3-2 forestry program with Duke. Washington, UN, Appalachian, Baltimore semesters. Study abroad. Elementary and secondary education certification. ROTC at Bucknell. Language lab. 125,000-volume library with microform resources.

Financial CEEB CSS. University scholarships, grants, loans, Lutheran grants, payment plans; PELL, SEOG, NDSL, FISL, CWS. Application deadline May 1.

Admissions High school graduation with 17 units required. Interview encouraged, required for *Early Decision* and transfer applicants. Audition required for music majors. SAT or ACT required. $20 application fee. Rolling admissions; application deadline March 15. $200 deposit required on acceptance of offer of admission. *Early Decision* and *Early Admission* programs. Admission deferral possible. Transfers accepted. Credit possible for CEEB AP and CLEP exams; university has own advanced placement program.

Student Life Student government. Newspaper, magazine, yearbook, radio station. Music, drama groups. Religious, honorary, and special interest organizations. 5 fraternities with houses and 4 sororities without houses. 32% of students join. Freshmen must live at home or on campus. Coed and single-sex dorms, language houses. 82% of students live on campus. 4 terms of phys ed required. 10 intercollegiate sports for men, 7 for women; intramurals. NCAA, ECAC, MAC. 55% of students from out of state.

SWARTHMORE COLLEGE $$$

Swarthmore 19081, (215) 447-7300
Dean of Admissions: Robert A. Barr, Jr.

- **Undergraduates:** 695m, 601w
- **Tuition (1984–1985):** $9,050
- **Room and Board (1984–1985):** $3,525
- **Degrees offered:** BA, BS
- **Mean SAT:** 645v, 652m
- **Student-faculty ratio:** 9 to 1
- **Calendar system:** Semester

A private college established in 1864. 300-acre suburban campus in small town of Swarthmore, 30 minutes from Philadelphia. Air, bus, and rail service in Philadelphia.

Academic Character MSACS and professional accreditation. Semester system. Majors offered in art, art history, astronomy, biology, chemistry, economics, engineering (5 areas), English literature, French, German, Greek, history, Latin, linguistics, literature, mathematics, medieval studies, music, philosophy, physics, political science, psychology, religion, Russian, sociology/anthropology, Spanish, and theatre/dramatics. Self-designed majors. Minor required. Distributive requirements. MA granted (rarely). Independent study. Honors program. Phi Beta Kappa. First semester is pass/fail. Cooperative program with Bryn Mawr, Haverford, U Penn. Exchanges with Middlebury, Mills, Pomona, Rice, Tufts. Study abroad in France, Spain, Taiwan. Employment exchange program abroad for engineering/science majors. Secondary education certification. Observatory, computer center, language lab. 750,000-volume library.

Financial CEEB CSS. College scholarships, grants, loans, payment plan; PELL, SEOG, NDSL, CWS. Scholarship application deadline January 15.

Admissions High school graduation required. SAT and 3 ACH required. $25 application fee. Application deadline February 1. $100 deposit required on acceptance of offer of admission. Fall and Winter *Early Decision* Programs. Admission deferral possible. Transfers accepted. Credit possible for CEEB AP exams.

Student Life Extracurricular activities are an integral part of a sound Swarthmore education; they include: Student government. Newspaper, magazine, yearbook, radio station. Music, debate, drama, folk dance groups. Academic, honorary, religious, service, political, senior, and special interest groups. 3 fraternities with nonresidential houses. 15% of men join. Special permission needed to live off campus. Coed and single-sex dorms, special interest housing. 90% of students live on campus. Cars on campus limited. 2 semesters of phys ed required. 12 intercollegiate sports for men, 9 for women; intramurals. AIAW, NCAA, MACC. Student body composition: 15% minority. 80% of students from out of state.

TEMPLE UNIVERSITY $

Philadelphia 19122, (215) 787-7000
Director of Admissions: R. Kenneth Haldeman

- **Undergraduates:** 9,493m, 8,826w
- **Tuition (1984–1985):** $2,752(in-state), $4,936(out-of-state)
- **Room and Board (1984–1985):** $2,998; **Fees:** $50
- **Degrees offered:** BA, BArch, BBA, BFA, BFAw/TC, BM, BS, BSArch, BSE, BSW, AS, AT
- **Mean SAT:** 478v, 504m
- **Student-faculty ratio:** 13 to 1
- **Calendar system:** Semester

A public university established in 1888. 233-acre urban campus in Philadelphia. Served by air, bus, and rail.

Academic Character MSACS and professional accreditation. Semester system, 3 summer terms. 5 majors offered by the College of Allied Health Professions, 14 by the College of Education, 9 by the College of Engineering Technology, 4 by the College of Health, Physical Education, Recreation, & Leisure Studies, 36 by the College of Liberal Arts, 7 by the College of Music, 1 by the Department of Criminal Justice, 13 by the School of Business Administration, 3 by the School of Communications & Theater, 1 by the School of Pharmacy, 2 by the School of Social Administration, and 8 by the Tyler School of Art. Graduate and professional degrees granted. Honors program. Cooperative work/study. Study abroad. ROTC; AFROTC at St. Joseph's. Computer center, several special facilities. 1,800,000-volume library with microform resources.

Financial CEEB CSS. University scholarships, grants, loans, state aid, payment plan; PELL, SEOG, NDSL, GSL. Application deadline May 1.

Admissions High school graduation with 16 units required. GED accepted. SAT or ACT required. $15 application fee. Rolling admissions; suggest applying in September. $50 deposit required on acceptance of offer of admission. *Early Admission* and *Early Decision* programs. Admission deferral possible. Transfers accepted. Credit possible for CEEB AP and CLEP exams. Special Recruitment and Admissions Program.

Student Life Student government. Newspaper, magazine, yearbook, radio station. Music and drama groups. Business, professional, and special interest groups. 12 fraternities with houses and 7 sororities with nonresidential houses. 10% of men and women join. 18% of students live on campus. Liquor, gambling, firearms prohibited on campus. 14 intercollegiate sports for men, 14 for women; intramurals. AIAW, NCAA, ECAC. Student body composition: 22% minority.

VILLANOVA UNIVERSITY $$

Villanova 19085, (215) 645-4000
Director of Admissions: Rev. Harry J. Erdlen, OSA

- **Undergraduates:** 3,656m, 2,476w
- **Tuition (1984–1985):** $5,700
- **Room and Board (1984–1985):** $3,700; **Fees:** $175
- **Degrees offered:** BA, BS, BSCE, BSEE, BSME, BSChE, BSN
- **Mean SAT:** 505v, 560m
- **Student-faculty ratio:** 14 to 1
- **Calendar system:** Semester

A private, Roman Catholic university started by the Augustinian Fathers, established in 1842, became coed in 1965. 240-acre suburban campus in Villanova, 6 miles from Philadelphia. Served by bus and rail; airport in Philadelphia.

Academic Character MSACS and professional accreditation. Semester system, 2 5-week summer terms. 8 majors offered by the College of Commerce & Finance, 4 by the College of Engineering, 23 by the College of Liberal Arts & Sciences, and 1 by the College of Nursing. 6 additional concentrations offered. Distributives and 9 credits in religious studies required. Graduate degrees granted. Honors program. Pass/fail, internships. Study abroad. Elementary, secondary, and special education certification. NROTC; AFROTC at St. Joseph's. Computer center, language lab, Augustinian Historical Institute. 453,750-volume library with microform resources.

Financial CEEB CSS. University scholarships, and loans; PELL, SEOG, NSS, NDSL, CWS. Application deadlines March 1 (FAF), March 15 (loans).

Admissions High school graduation with 16 units required. Interview encouraged. SAT or ACT required; foreign language ACH required for Arts &

Sciences. $20 application fee. Application deadline February 15. $200 deposit required on acceptance of offer of admission. *Early Decision* Program. Transfers accepted. Credit possible for CEEB AP and CLEP exams; university has own advanced placement program.

Student Life Student government. Newspaper, magazines, yearbook. Music, debate, and drama groups. Political, service, academic, professional, and special interest organizations. 16 fraternities and sororities without houses. 20% of students join. Limited university housing. Single-sex dorms. 43% of students live on campus. Junior and senior residents may have cars on campus. 11 intercollegiate sports for men, 11 for women; intramurals. NCAA. 65% of students from out of state.

WASHINGTON AND JEFFERSON COLLEGE $$

Washington 15301, (412) 222-4400
Director of Admissions: Thomas P. O'Connor

- **Undergraduates:** 634m, 404w
- **Tuition (1984–1985):** $7,000
- **Room and Board (1984–1985):** $2,390; **Fees:** $220
- **Degrees offered:** BA
- **Mean SAT:** 500v, 550m,   **Mean ACT:** 23
- **Student-faculty ratio:** 10 to 1
- **Calendar system:** 4–1–4

A private college established in 1781, became coed in 1970. 30-acre campus located in small city of Washington, 30 miles from Pittsburgh. Served by bus; airport and rail station in Pittsburgh.

Academic Character MSACS accreditation. 4-1-4 system, 8-week summer term. Majors offered in art, biology, chemistry, economics & business, English, French, German, history, industrial chemistry/management, mathematics, philosophy, physics, political science, psychology, sociology, and Spanish. Self-designed majors. Distributive requirements. Independent study. Honors program. Phi Beta Kappa. Pass/fail, internships. 3-2 engineering programs with Case Western Reserve, Washington U. 3-1 medical technology program. Cooperative 3-4 podiatry and optometry programs. Washington Semester. Study abroad. Secondary education certification. ROTC. 185,000-volume library.

Financial CEEB CSS. College scholarships, grants, loans, state aid, payment plan; PELL, SEOG, NDSL, GSL, CWS. FAF deadline March 15.

Admissions High school graduation with 15 units required. Interview encouraged. SAT and 3 ACH, or ACT required. $15 application fee. Application deadline March 1. $100 deposit required on acceptance of offer of admission. *Early Decision* and *Early Admission* programs. Admission deferral possible. Transfers accepted. Credit possible for CEEB AP and CLEP exams.

Student Life Student government. Newspaper, magazine, yearbook, radio station. Music, literary, debate, drama groups. Academic, religious, honorary, and special interest organizations. 11 fraternities with houses and 2 sororities. 55% of men join fraternities. Students must live at home or on campus. Coed dorms. 90% of students live on campus. Limited class absences allowed. 1 year of phys ed (except for ROTC students) required. 12 intercollegiate sports for men, 5 for women; intramurals. AIAW, ECAC, NCAA, PAC, Penn Wood West. 35% of students from out of state.

Rhode Island

BROWN UNIVERSITY $$$

79 Waterman Street, Providence 02912, (401) 863-2378
Director of Admissions: James H. Rogers

- **Undergraduates:** 2,745m, 2,567w
- **Tuition (1984–1985):** $9,290
- **Room and Board (1984–1985):** $3,345
- **Degrees offered:** BA, BS
- **Mean SAT:** 640v, 670m
- **Student-faculty ratio:** 11 to 1
- **Calendar system:** Semester

A private university established in 1764, became coed in 1971 by merging with coordinate Pembroke College. 150-acre main campus on the East Side of Providence. Airport in Warwick, bus and train stations in Providence.

Academic Character NEASC and professional accreditation. Semester system. Majors offered in American civilization, ancient & Medieval cultures, anthropology, applied math, aquatic biology, art, biochemistry, biological & medical sciences, biology, biomedical ethics, biophysics, chemistry, classics, comparative literature, computer science, economics, engineering, English, French studies, geological sciences, German, Hispanic studies, history, human biology, international relations, Italian studies, Latin American studies, linguistics, math, modernization, music, operations reserach, organizational behavior, philosophy, physics, political science, Portuguese & Brazilian studies, psychology, religious studies, Renaissance studies, Russian studies, science education for the inner city, semiotics, Slavic languages, sociology, urban society. Combined and self-designed majors. Graduate and professional degrees granted. Flexible grading system. Independent study. Honors program. Phi Beta Kappa. Undergraduate research. Medical Education Program leads to BA in 4 years and MD in 7. Exchange program with Dartmouth Medical School. Member of Ivy League consortium. Study abroad. Secondary education certification. Language lab, computer. 2,600,000-volume library.

Financial CEEB CSS. University scholarships, grants, loans, payment plan; PELL, SEOG, FISL, CWS. Application deadline January 1.

Admissions High school graduation with at least 10 units required. Other course requirements for ScB candidates. SAT and 3 ACH required. Interview recommended. $35 application fee. Application deadline January 1; notification in mid-April. $50 committment deposit required on acceptance of offer of admission (May 1). *Early Action* and *Early Admission* programs. Admission deferral possible. Transfers accepted. Credit possible for CEEB AP, CLEP, ACH, and university placement exams.

Student Life Student government. Newspaper, literary magazines, yearbook, radio station. Music, debate, and drama groups. Over 100 students organizations and groups. 6 fraternities with houses, 1 sorority. 15% of men join fraternities. Permission required to live off campus. Coed and single-sex dorms. Special interest housing. Many intercollegiate and intramural sports for men and women. ECAC, NCAA, AIAW, Ivy League. Student body composition: 6% Asian, 9% Black, 1% Hispanic, 82.5% White, 1.5% Other. 90% from out of state.

BRYANT COLLEGE $

Smithfield 02917, (401) 231-1200
Dean of Admissions: Roy A. Nelson

- **Undergraduates:** 1,715m, 1,413w
- **Tuition (1984–1985):** $4,525
- **Room and Board (1984–1985):** $3,320
- **Degrees offered:** BS, BSBA
- **Mean SAT:** 460v, 533m
- **Student-faculty ratio:** 25 to 1
- **Calendar system:** Semester

A private college established in 1863. 295-acre suburban campus 12 miles
from Providence. Bus and train stations in Providence, airport in Warwick.
Academic Character NEASC accreditation. Semester system, 3- and 5-
week summer terms. Majors offered in business administration (accounting,
applied actuarial math, business communications, computer information
systems, economics, finance, management marketing, and hotel, restaurant,
& institutional management) and in criminal justice. Distributive
requirements. MBA, MS granted. Courses offered in the liberal arts. Political
science internships. Study abroad. ROTC. Evening division. Center for
Management Development. Computer center. Over 100,000-volume library.
Financial CEEB CSS. College scholarships and loans, sibling tuition
discounts, payment plan; PELL, SEOG, NDSL, GSL, CWS. Application
deadlines February 15 (scholarships & grants), February 1 (loans).
Admissions High school graduation with 16 units required. GED accepted.
SAT or ACT required. Interview recommended. $20 application fee. Rolling
admissions; no deadline. $100 tuition and $100 room deposits required on
acceptance of offer of admission. *Early Decision* and *Early Entrance*
programs. Admission deferral possible. Transfers accepted. Credit possible
for CEEB AP, CLEP, and college proficiency exams.
Student Life Student government. Newspaper, yearbook, radio station.
Music and drama groups. Student Services Foundation. Big Brothers.
Religious, special interest, and professional groups. 8 fraternities and 6
sororities. 34% of men, 31% of women join. Single students under 20 live on
campus. Coed and single-sex dorms. Townhouse apartments on campus. 61%
of students live on campus. 8 intercollegiate sports for men, 7 for women;
intramurals. AIAW, ECAC, Northeast 7, and 8 other associations. Student
body composition: 0.5% Asian, 0.5% Black, 99% White. 75% from out of state.

RHODE ISLAND, UNIVERSITY OF $/$$

Kingston 02881, (401) 792-2164
Director of Admissions: Richard A. Edwards

- **Undergraduates:** 4,690m, 4,292w
- **Tuition (1984–1985):** $1,694(in-state), $5,076.50(out-of-state)
- **Room and Board (1984–1985):** $3,045; **Fees:** $430
- **Degrees offered:** BA, BS, BFA, BMus, BGS, AS
- **Mean SAT:** 441v, 497m
- **Student-faculty ratio:** 12 to 1
- **Calendar system:** Semester

A public university established in 1892. 1,200-acre main campus 5 miles from ocean, 30 miles from Providence. 165-acre Graduate School of Oceanography campus at Narragansett Bay and 2,300-acre W. Alton Jones Campus Research & Conference Center at West Greenwich. Bus and train stations available.

Academic Character NEASC and professional accreditation. Semester system, 2 5-week summer terms. 70 majors offered by the colleges of Arts & Sciences, Business Administration, Engineering, Human Science & Services, Nursing, Pharmacy, and Resource Development. Interdepartmental and interdisciplinary programs. Distributive requirements. MA, MS, PhD granted. Independent study. Honors program. Phi Beta Kappa. Pass/fail. Internships, Year for Action. Regional Cooperative Program with other New England land grant colleges. Preprofessional programs in dentistry, law, medicine, social work, veterinary medicine. Study abroad. Sea semester. Living/learning project. Elementary and secondary education certification. ROTC. Several research labs and centers for research and development. Over 1,300,000 volumes and microform items in several libraries.

Financial CEEB CSS. University scholarships, grants and loans, payment plan; PELL, SEOG, NSS, NDSL, GSL, NSL, HPL, CWS. File FAF by February 15.

Admissions High school graduation with 16 units required. Audition required of music applicants, DHAT of dental hygiene applicants. SAT required. $15 application fee. Rolling admissions; application deadline March 1. $50 deposit and $100 housing deposit required on acceptance of offer of admission. *Early Decision, Early Entrance, Concurrent Enrollment* programs. Admission deferral possible. Transfers accepted. Credit possible for CEEB AP and CLEP exams. Special Program for Talent Development for minority and disadvantaged applicants.

Student Life Student government. Newspaper, gazette, magazine, yearbook, radio and shortwave stations. Music, drama, and debate groups. Over 120 other student organizations. 17 fraternities, 9 sororities. About 1,300 students join. Coed, women's, and married-student housing. 60% of students live on campus. Limited parking space. Intercollegiate and intramural sports for men and women. AIAW, ECAC, NCAA, New England Conference of State Universities.

RHODE ISLAND SCHOOL OF DESIGN   *$$$*

2 College Street, Providence 02903, (401) 331-3511
Director of Admissions: Edward Newhall

- **Undergraduates:** 757m, 1,018w
- **Tuition (1984–1985):** $8,150
- **Room and Board (1984–1985):** $3,500;   **Fees:** $70
- **Degrees offered:** BFA, BArch, BIArch, BIDesign, BLandArch
- **Mean SAT:** 494v, 527m
- **Student-faculty ratio:** 14 to 1
- **Calendar system:** 4–1–4

A private college established in 1877. Campus covers 2 city blocks in Providence. Bus and train stations in Providence, airport in Warwick.

Academic Character NEASC and professional accreditation. 4-1-4 system, 4 6-week summer terms. Majors offered in apparel design, architecture, ceramics, film/video, glass, graphic design, industrial design, illustration, interior architecture, painting, photography, printmaking, sculpture, textile design. Fifth-year architectural program leads to professional degree. Courses offered in liberal arts. Freshmen must take foundation courses. Senior project required. Master's degrees granted. Letter grades are accompanied by written evaluations. Cross-registration with Brown. European Honors Program. Summer workshops. Museum of Art with 50 galleries. 33-acre farm on Narragansett Bay. 60,500-volume library with 87,000 slides and 30,000 mounted photographs.

Financial CEEB CSS. School scholarships and loans, payment plan; PELL, SEOG, FISL, GSL, NDSL, CWS. Application deadline February 15.

Admissions High school graduation with courses in art and art history required. GED accepted. Portfolio required. Interview recommended. SAT required. Application deadline January 21. $300 matriculation fee required on acceptance of offer of admission. *Early Entrance* program. Admission deferral possible. Transfers accepted. Placement possible for CEEB AP exams.

Student Life Student government. Newspaper, literary magazine (with Brown), yearbook. 42 artistic student clubs on campus. Third World Coalition. International Club. Freshmen under 21 must live at home or on campus. Coed and single-sex dorms. No married-student housing. 30% of students live on campus. Liquor prohibited in dorms. 2 intercollegiate sports, intramurals. Student body composition: 2% Asian; 2% Black, 2% Hispanic, 1% Native American, 93% White. 89% from out of state.

South Carolina

CITADEL, THE $

Charleston 29409, (803) 792-5230
Director of Admissions: Capt. Wallace I. West

- **Undergraduates:** 1,984m
- **Tuition, Room and Board (1984–1985):** $4,380 (in-state), $6,328 (out-of-state)
- **Degrees offered:** BA, BS, BSBA, BSE
- **Mean SAT:** 480v, 530m,   **Mean ACT:** 23
- **Student-faculty ratio:** 13 to 1
- **Calendar system:** Semester

A public college established in 1842. 110-acre urban campus. Served by air, rail, and bus.

Academic Character SACS and professional accreditation. Semester system, 2 5-week summer terms. Majors offered in biology, business administration, chemistry, civil engineering, computer science, education, electrical engineering, English, history, mathematics, modern languages, physical education, physics, political science, and psychology. Masters degrees granted. Phi Beta Kappa. Elementary, secondary, and special education certification. ROTC, AFROTC, NROTC required. Computer center. Language lab. 250,000-volume library with microform resources.

Financial CEEB CSS. College scholarships, grants, loans, payment plans; PELL, SEOG, NDSL, GSL, FISL. Application deadlines February 1 (scholarships), March 15 (loans).

Admissions High school graduation with 15 units required. Interview recommended. SAT or ACT required; English and math ACH recommended. $15 application fee. Rolling admissions. $100 deposit due on acceptance of admissions offer. Transfers accepted. Credit possible for CEEB AP and CLEP exams.

Student Life Newspaper, literary magazine, yearbook. Music and drama groups. Yacht Club. Literary, military, professional, and recreational clubs. All cadets live on campus. Freshmen may not have cars. Liquor prohibited. Daily room inspection. Uniforms must be worn at all times. Honor code. Cadets may not marry while in school. Class attendance mandatory. 4 semesters of phys ed required. 11 intercollegiate sports; many intramurals. NCAA. Student body composition: 4.5% Black, 94% White, 1.5% Other. 59% from out of state.

CLEMSON UNIVERSITY $

Clemson 29631, (803) 656-2287
Director of Admissions: W. Richard Mattox

- **Undergraduates:** 5,957m, 4,373w
- **Tuition (1984–1985):** $1,652 (in-state), $3,580 (out-of-state)
- **Room and Board (1984–1985):** $1,850
- **Degrees offered:** BA, BS, BArch, BTT
- **Mean SAT:** 471v, 543m
- **Student-faculty ratio:** 16 to 1
- **Calendar system:** Semester

A public university established in 1889. 600-acre small-town campus. Served by rail and bus.

Academic Character SACS and professional accreditation. Semester system, one 9-week summer term. 12 majors offered by the College of Agricultural Sciences, 6 by the College of Education, 9 by the College of Engineering, 3 by the College of Forest & Recreation Resources, 8 by the College of Industrial Management/Textile Science, 6 by the College of Liberal Arts, 1 by the College of Nursing, 11 by the College of Sciences, and 2 by the School of Architecture. Minor required in liberal arts. Distributive requirements. Graduate degrees granted. Independent study, honors program. Cooperative work/study, pass/fail, internships. Study abroad. Elementary, secondary, and special education certification. ROTC, AFROTC. 801,023-volume library with microform resources.

Financial CEEB CSS. University scholarships, grants, loans; PELL, SEOG, NDSL, CWS. Application deadlines February 15 (scholarships), April 1 (loans).

Admissions High school graduation required. SAT required; math ACH required. $15 application fee. Rolling admissions. $80 deposit due on acceptance of admissions offer. *Early Entrance* program. Transfers accepted. Credit possible for CEEB AP exams.

Student Life Student government. Newspaper, literary journal, yearbook, radio station. Music and drama groups. Debate. Honorary, religious, and special interest groups. 15 fraternities and 8 sororities, most with dorm floors. 12% of men and 20% of women join. Coed and single-sex dorms. Married-student housing. 60% of students live on campus. 8 intercollegiate sports; many intramurals. AIAW, NCAA, ACC. Student body composition: 0.4% Asian, 3.5% Black, 0.2% Hispanic, 0.1% Native American, 96% White. 25% from out of state.

FURMAN UNIVERSITY $$

Greenville 29613, (803) 294-2034
Director of Admissions: Charles E. Brock

- **Undergraduates:** 1,271m, 1,230w
- **Tuition (1984–1985):** $5,300
- **Room and Board (1984–1985):** $2,900
- **Degrees offered:** BA, BS, BMus
- **Mean SAT:** 550v, 560m
- **Student-faculty ratio:** 13 to 1
- **Calendar system:** Three-term

A private university affiliated with the South Carolina Baptist Convention, established in 1826. 750-acre suburban campus. Served by air, rail, and bus.

Academic Character SACS and professional accreditation. Trimester system, 6- and 4-week summer terms. 30 majors offered in the areas of classical languages, computer science, economics, education, fine arts, humanities, modern languages, physical education, sciences, and social sciences. Self-designed majors. Distributive requirements. Graduate degrees granted. Independent study. Phi Beta Kappa. Limited pass/fail, credit by exam, internships. 3-2 engineering program with Georgia Tech. 3-2 forestry programs with Duke and Clemson. 3-1 programs arranged in dentistry, law, medical technology, medicine, physical therapy, religion, social service.

Study abroad. Pre-school, elementary, and secondary education certification. ROTC. Language labs. 450,000-volume library.

Financial CEEB CSS. University scholarships, grants, loans, discount for children of missionaries and Baptist ministers, payment plan; PELL, SEOG, NDSL, GSL, CWS. Application deadline February 1.

Admissions High school graduation with college prep program and B average expected. Interview recommended. Music students should audition. SAT required. $20 application fee. Rolling admissions. $100 deposit due on acceptance of admissions offer. *Early Decision* and *Early Admission* programs. Transfers accepted. Credit possible for CEEB AP exams.

Student Life Student government. Newspaper, literary magazine, yearbook, radio station. Music and drama groups. Academic, honorary, professional, religious, service, and special interest groups. 4 fraternities without houses. 10% of men join. Single freshmen and sophomores live at home or on campus. Single-sex dorms. 68% of students live on campus. Liquor prohibited. One phys ed course required. 11 intercollegiate sports for men, 7 for women; several intramurals. AIAW, NCAA, SAC. Student body composition: 1% Asian, 3% Black, 1% Hispanic, 95% White. 59% from out of state.

SOUTH CAROLINA, UNIVERSITY OF $

Columbia 29208, (803) 777-7700
Director of Admissions: John Bolin

- **Undergraduates:** 8,063m, 8,060w
- **Tuition (1984–1985):** $1,440 (in-state), $2,970 (out-of-state)
- **Room and Board (1984–1985):** $2,130
- **Degrees offered:** BA, BS, BFA, BMus, BArtium et Scientiae (Honors College)
- **Mean SAT:** 453v, 492m,   **Mean ACT:** 22
- **Student-faculty ratio:** 17 to 1
- **Calendar system:** Semester

A public university established in 1801. 262-acre urban campus. Served by air and rail.

Academic Character SACS and professional accreditation. Semester system, 2 5-week summer terms. 8 majors offered in Business Administration, 1 in Criminal Justice, 5 in Education, 4 in Engineering, 2 in Health, 21 in Humanities & Social Science, 3 in Journalism, 1 in Nursing, 1 in Pharmacy, and 7 in Science & Mathematics. Self-designed majors in College of General Studies. Minors offered in some fields and in 4 others. Many foreign language courses. Distributive requirements in some disciplines. Graduates and professional degrees granted. Honors College, honors programs. Phi Beta Kappa. Independent study. Limited pass/fail, internships. 3-1 medical technology program. Exchange programs with over 50 state-supported institutions. International Student Exchange. Exchange programs with Warwick and Kent in England. Elementary and secondary education certification. ROTC, AFROTC, NROTC. Computer facilities. Language labs. Museums. 3,681,701-volume library with microform resources.

Financial CEEB CSS and ACT FAS. University scholarships, grants, loans; PELL, SEOG, NDSL, FISL, NSL, CWS. Priority application deadline February 15.

Admissions High school graduation with college prep program recommended. GED accepted. SAT or ACT required. $25 application fee.

Rolling admissions. $115 room deposit due on acceptance of admissions offer. *Early Admission* and *Concurrent Enrollment* programs. Transfers accepted. Credit possible for CEEB AP, CLEP, and university exams. Opportunity Scholars Program for disadvantaged students.

Student Life Student government. Newspaper, literary magazine, yearbook, radio station. Music and drama groups. Debate. Academic, honorary, professional, religious, service, and special interest groups. 20 fraternities and 14 sororities. Freshmen must live on campus. Coed and single-sex dorms. Honors houses. Married-student housing. 30% of all students live on campus. Liquor limited to living quarters and other designated areas. Drugs, firearms, gambling prohibited. Limited class cuts. 9 intercollegiate sports for men, 6 for women; many intramurals. AIAW, NCAA. Student body composition: 0.8% Asian, 13% Black, 0.5% Hispanic, 0.1% Native American, 83% White, 2.6% Other. 18% from out of state.

WOFFORD COLLEGE $

Spartanburg 29301, (803) 585-4821
Director of Admissions: Charles H. Gray

- **Undergraduates:** 774m, 268w
- **Tuition (1984–1985):** $4,595
- **Room and Board (1984–1985):** $2,455
- **Degrees offered:** BA, BS
- **Mean SAT:** 490v, 520m
- **Student-faculty ratio:** 15 to 1
- **Calendar system:** 4–1–4

A private college affiliated with the United Methodist Church, established in 1854, became coed in 1971. 90-acre urban campus. Served by air, rail, and bus.

Academic Character SACS accreditation. 4-1-4 system, 2 5-week summer terms. Majors offered in accounting, biology, chemistry, economics, English, foreign languages, government, history, humanities, intercultural studies, mathematics, philosophy, physics, psychology, religion, and sociology. Self-designed and interdepartmental majors. Distributives and 3 hours of religion required. Independent study. Honors program. Phi Beta Kappa. Cooperative work/study, limited pass/fail, internships. Preprofessional programs in dentistry, law, medicine, ministry, veterinary medicine. 3-2 liberal arts and engineering program with Columbia U and Georgia Tech. Cooperative nursing program with Emory. Cross-registration with Converse offers 11 additional majors. Study abroad. Secondary education certification. ROTC. Language lab. Planetarium. 189,428-volume library with microform resources.

Financial CEEB CSS. College scholarships, grants, loans, ministerial scholarships, state grants, payment plan; PELL, SEOG, NDSL, GSL, CWS. Application deadline March 1.

Admissions High school graduation with 16 units recommended. GED accepted. Interview recommended. SAT or ACT required. $15 application fee. Rolling admissions. $100 ($50 for commuters) deposit due on acceptance of admissions offer. *Early Admission* and *Concurrent Enrollment* programs. Admission deferral possible. Transfers accepted. Credit possible for CEEB AP, CLEP, and college proficiency exams.

Student Life Student Union. Newspaper, literary magazine, yearbook.

Music and drama groups. Afro-American Association. Association of Women. Honorary, professional, religious, and special interest groups. 10 fraternities and sororities without houses. 40% of students join. Single students live at home or on campus. Coed and single-sex dorms. No married-student housing. 77% of students live on campus. Class attendance expected. 2 hours of sophomore phys ed required. 9 intercollegiate sports; many club and intramural sports. AIAW, NAIA. Student body composition: 0.8% Asian, 8% Black, 0.5% Hispanic, 90.7% White. 27% from out of state.

South Dakota

AUGUSTANA COLLEGE $

Sioux Falls 57197, (800) 952-3527 or (800) 843-3370
Director of Admissions: Dean A Schueler

- **Undergraduates:** 732m, 1219w
- **Tuition (1984–1985):** $5,795
- **Room and Board (1984–1985):** $2,191
- **Degrees offered:** BA, AA
- **Mean ACT:** 23
- **Student-faculty ratio:** 15 to 1
- **Calendar system:** 4–1–4

A private college affiliated with the American Lutheran Church, established in 1860. 100-acre campus in southeastern South Dakota, 15 miles from Minnesota and Iowa. Airport, bus station.

Academic Character NCACS and professional accreditation. 4-1-4 system, May/June miniterm, 8-week summer term. BA offered in accounting, art, biology, business administration, business education, chemistry, comparative literature, computer science, criminal justice, economics, education, engineering physics, English, French, geography, German, government/international affairs, Greek, health/hospital services administration, history, journalism, liberal arts, math, music, nursing, philosophy, physical education, physics, planning, psychology, religion, social studies teaching, social work & community development, sociology, Spanish, theology, and speech, drama, & communications. Self-designed majors. 3-1 major in medical technology. AA offered in aviation, computer science, criminal justice, liberal studies, mortuary science, professional pilot, secretarial science. Distributives and 2 religion courses required. MAT granted. Honors program. Independent study. Pass/fail, cooperative work/study, credit by exam, internships. Several preprofessional programs. 2-2, 3-2, 4-2 engineering programs. Cross-registration with Sioux Falls College, North American Baptist Seminary. YMCA directors program. Living-learning semester in Minneapolis area; several other urban studies programs. Study abroad. Elementary, secondary, and special education certification. 225,000-volume library with microform resources.

Financial ACT FAS. College scholarships, grants, loans, payment plan; PELL, SEOG, NSS, NDSL, GSL, NSL, CWS. Priority application deadline February 15.

Admissions High school graduation with a college prep program required. GED accepted. Interview recommended. ACT or SAT recommended. ACH recommended for placement. $15 application fee. Rolling admissions. Application deadlines September 1 (February 1 for nursing). $100 enrollment and $30 housing deposits required on acceptance of offer of admission. Admission deferral possible. Transfers accepted. Credit possible for summer school credits, CEEB AP and CLEP exams.

Student Life Student government. Newspaper, literary magazine, yearbook. Radio station. Music, drama, and debate clubs. Volunteer groups. Native American Council. Circle K. Honorary, professional, religious, and special interest groups. 6 fraternities and 6 sororities without houses. 23% of men, 21%

of women join. 1st- and 2nd-year students from out of town may live off campus only with Dean's permission. Coed, single-sex, special interest, and married-student housing. 60% of students live on campus. Liquor and gambling prohibited. Class attendance required in lower division courses. 2 phys ed credits required. 10 intercollegiate sports for men, 6 for women; intramurals. NCAA, NCIAC. Student body composition: 0.2% Asian, 0.4% Black, 0.7% Native American, 98% White, 0.7% Other. 45% from out of state.

SOUTH DAKOTA, UNIVERSITY OF $

Vermillion 57069, (605) 677-5434
Director of Admissions: Gary Gullickson

- **Undergraduates:** 2,212m, 2,467w
- **Tuition (1984–1985):** $978(in-state), $2,080(out-of-state)
- **Room and Board (1984–1985):** $1,634; **Fees:** $337.60
- **Degrees offered:** BA, BFA, BS, AA
- **Mean ACT:** 21.1
- **Student-faculty ratio:** 17 to 1
- **Calendar system:** Semester

A public university established in 1862. 216-acre small-town campus, 35 miles northwest of Sioux City. Served by bus.
Academic Character NCACS and professional accreditation. Semester system, 8-week summer term. 29 majors offered by the College of Arts & Sciences, 5 by the College of Fine Arts, 4 by the Division of Allied Health, 4 by the School of Business, 9 by the School of Education, 2 by the School of Medicine, and 1 by the School of Nursing. Self-designed majors. Distributive requirements. Graduate and professional degrees granted. Independent study. Honors program. Phi Beta Kappa. Pass/fail, internships. Preprofessional programs in dentistry, law, medicine, mortuary science, optometry, osteopathy, pharmacy, physical therapy, veterinary medicine. 3-1 medical technology program. 2- and 4-year dental hygiene programs. Exchange program with Westfield State College (Mass). Member of University of Mid-America Consortium. Elementary, secondary, and special education certification. ROTC. Business Research Bureau. Child Study Center Institute of Indian Studies. Museum. Natural sciences field station. History of musical instruments center. 425,000-volume library with microform resources.
Financial CEEB CSS and ACT FAS. University scholarships, loans; PELL, SEOG, NDSL, GSL, CWS. Recommended application deadline March 1.
Admissions High school graduation with 16 units required. ACT required, $15 application fee. Rolling admissions. $35 room deposit due on acceptance of admissions offer. *Early Decision* and *Concurrent Enrollment* programs. Transfers accepted. Credit possible for CEEB CLEP and university placement exams. Upward Bound Program.
Student Life Student government. Newspaper, humor magazine, yearbook, radio and television stations. Music and drama groups. Debate. Athletic, academic, honorary, political, professional, religious, service, and social groups. 9 fraternities and 5 sororities, all with houses. 30% of students join. Freshmen and sophomores under 21 must live at home or on campus. Coed and single-sex dorms. Married-student housing. 38% of students live on campus. 8 intercollegiate sports for men, 7 for women; intramurals. AIAW, NCAA, NCIAC. Student body composition: 1% Black, 3% Native American, 95% White, 1% Other. 21% from out of state.

Tennessee

CARSON-NEWMAN COLLEGE $

Jefferson City 37760, (615) 475-9061
Director of Admissions: Jack Shannon

- **Undergraduates:** 861m, 857w
- **Tuition (1984–1985):** $3,400
- **Room and Board (1984–1985):** $1,800;   **Fees:** $25
- **Degrees offered:** BA, BS, BMus, BSN
- **Mean SAT:** 400v, 425m,   **Mean ACT:** 17.5
- **Student-faculty ratio:** 16 to 1
- **Calendar system:** Semester

A private college affiliated with the Tennessee Baptist Convention, established in 1851. Rural campus located in small town of Jefferson City, 30 miles from Knoxville. Served by bus; airport in Knoxville.
Academic Character SACS and professional accreditation. Semester system, 3-week miniterm in May, 3 3-week summer terms. 42 majors offered in the areas of humanities, social sciences, natural sciences & mathematics, fine arts, applied arts & sciences, business & economics, and nursing. Self-designed majors. Distributive requirements. 2 religion courses required. Independent and accelerated study. Honors program. Pass/fail, internships. Credit by exam and for experience. Preprofessional programs in law, medicine. 3-2 programs in engineering with Georgia Tech, U of Tenn; in forestry with Duke. 3-1 medical technology program. Study abroad. Elementary, secondary, and special education certification. ROTC. Language lab, media center, Home Management House. 150,000-volume library.
Financial College scholarships, grants, and loans; PELL, SEOG, NDSL, FISL, Tuition Plan, deferred payment, CWS. Preferred application deadline for scholarships soon after January 1.
Admissions High school graduation with 16 units required. ACT required. $15 application fee. Rolling admissions; suggest applying early in 12th year. $50 deposit required on acceptance of offer of admission. *Early Decision, Early Admission, ACT-Application* programs. Transfers accepted. Credit possible for CEEB AP and CLEP exams.
Student Life Student government. Newspaper, yearbook. Music, film, debate groups. Black Students Cultural Society. Honorary, academic, professional, religious, and special interest groups. Seniors and students over 21 may live off campus. Married-student housing. 85% of students live on campus. Liquor, hazing, drugs, fireworks, firearms prohibited on campus. Attendance in class and at weekly chapel required. 8 intercollegiate sports for men, 3 for women; intramurals. AIAW, NCAA, Volunteer State Athletic Conference. Student body composition: 5% Black, 94% White, 1% Other. 50% from out of state.

FISK UNIVERSITY $

17th Avenue, North, Nashville 37203, (615) 329-8500
Director of Admissions: Aline Rivers

- **Undergraduates:** 217m, 457w
- **Tuition (1984–1985):** $3,850
- **Room and Board (1984–1985):** $2,085; **Fees:** $350
- **Degrees offered:** BA, BS
- **Student-faculty ratio:** 12 to 1
- **Calendar system:** Semester

A private university established in 1866. 40-acre urban campus overlooking Nashville. Served by air, bus and rail.

Academic Character SACS and professional accreditation. Semester system. Majors offered in art, biology, chemistry, dramatics & speech, economics, English, French, health care administration & planning, history, management, mathematics, music, music education, physics, political science, psychology, religious & philosophical studies, sociology, and Spanish. Self-designed majors. Distributive requirements. MA granted. Independent study. Honors program. Phi Beta Kappa. Cooperative work/study, pass/fail, internships. Credit by exam. Preprofessional programs in dentistry, law, medicine, mass communication media, theological studies. 5-year MBA program and dual-degree programs in science and engineering with Vanderbilt. 2-2 medical technology, nursing programs. Several exchange programs. Study abroad. ROTC, NROTC at Vanderbilt; AFROTC at Tenn. State. Computer center, language lab. 188,400-volume library with microform resources.

Financial CEEB CSS. University scholarships, grants, loans; PELL, SEOG, NDSL, GSL, CWS. Member United Negro College Fund. Application deadline April 1.

Admissions High school graduation with 15 units required. Health examination required. SAT or ACT recommended. $10 application fee. Rolling admissions; application deadline June 15. *Early Admission* Program. Transfers accepted. Credit possible for CEEB AP exams.

Student Life Student government. Newspaper, magazine, yearbook, radio station. Music, drama, dance groups. Foreign, international student organizations. Academic, religious, and special interest groups. 5 fraternities and 4 sororities. 29% of students join. Students must live at home or on campus. No coed dorms. No married-student housing. 85% of students live on campus. 7 intercollegiate sports for men, 5 for women; intramurals. AIAW, NCAA, SIAC. Student body composition: 99% Black, 1% White. 88% from out of state.

MARYVILLE COLLEGE $

Maryville 37801, (615) 982-6412
Director of Admissions: Larry M. West

- **Undergraduates:** 277m, 360w
- **Tuition (1984–1985):** $4,300
- **Room and Board (1984–1985):** $2,360; **Fees:** $85
- **Degrees offered:** BA, BMus
- **Mean SAT:** 457v, 492m, **Mean ACT:** 22
- **Student-faculty ratio:** 13 to 1
- **Calendar system:** 4–1–4

A private college affiliated with the United Presbyterian Church, established in

1819. 350-acre campus in Maryville, 16 miles from Knoxville. Served by bus. Airport 4 miles away.

Academic Character SACS and professional accreditation. 4-1-4 system, 6-week summer term. Majors offered in art, biology, business administration, chemistry, economics, elementary education, English, history, interdisciplinary majors, interpreter training for deaf, mathematics, medical technology, music, physical education, physics, political science, psychology, recreation, religion, Spanish. Self-designed majors. Distributives and 1 religion course required. Senior comprehensive exams. Independent study. Honors program. Pass/fail, internships. Field work. Preprofessional programs in engineering, law, medicine. Cooperative program with 12 area schools. 3-2 engineering programs with Georgia Tech, U of Tenn. Study abroad. Washington semester. Elementary and secondary education certification. ROTC at U of Tenn-Knoxville. Environmental Education Center in Great Smoky Mountains, Washington Center for Learning Alternatives. Language lab, art gallery. 115,000-volume library.

Financial CEEB CSS. College scholarships, grants, loans; PELL, SEOG, NDSL, GSL, Insured Tuition Plan, Tuition Plan, Education Funds, CWS.

Admissions High school graduation with 15 units required. Interview encouraged. SAT or ACT required. $10 application fee. Rolling admissions; suggest applying in fall. $100 deposit required on acceptance of offer of admission. *Early Admission* Program. Transfers accepted. Admission deferral possible. Credit possible for CEEB AP and CLEP exams.

Student Life Student government. Newspaper, yearbook. Music, debate, drama groups. Academic, religious, service, and special interest groups. 2 societies for men, 2 for women, 1 for married students; all have rooms. Single students must live with relatives or on campus. Coed and single-sex dorms. No married-student housing. 90% of students live on campus. Freshmen may not have cars on campus. 6 intercollegiate sports for men, 5 for women; intramurals. Student body composition: 4.3% Black, 93.4% White, 2.3% Other. 65% from out of state.

SOUTH, UNIVERSITY OF THE   **$$**

Sewanee 37375, (615) 598-5931
Director of Admissions: Albert S. Gooch, Jr.

- **Undergraduates:** 621m, 435w
- **Tuition (1984–1985):** $7,700
- **Room and Board (1984–1985):** $2,060;   **Fees:** $75
- **Degrees offered:** BA, BS
- **Mean SAT:** 540v, 560m,   **Mean ACT:** 25
- **Student-faculty ratio:** 11 to 1
- **Calendar system:** Semester

A private university controlled by the Episcopal Church, established in 1858, became coed in 1969. 10,000-acre campus including rural village of Sewanee, 50 miles from Chattanooga. Served by air and bus.

Academic Character SACS accreditation. Semester system, 6-week summer term. Majors offered in American studies, Asian studies, biology, chemistry, comparative literature, economics, English, fine arts, French, German, Greek, history, Latin, mathematics, Medieval studies, music, natural resources, philosophy, physics, political science, psychology, religion, Russian, Russian/Soviet studies, and Spanish. Distributives and 2 religion/philosophy courses required. MDiv, DMin granted. Independent study. Phi Beta Kappa. Pass/fail. Preprofessional programs in dentistry, law, medicine, veterinary medicine. 3-2 programs in engineering with Columbia, Duke, Georgia Tech, Rensselaer, Vanderbilt, Washington U. 3-2 forestry program with Duke. Oak Ridge Semester. Study abroad. Secondary education certification. Language labs. 8,500-acre university forest. 435,000-volume library.

Financial CEEB CSS. University scholarships, grants, loans; PELL, SEOG, NDSL, Tuition Plan, CWS. Application deadline March 1.

Admissions High school graduation with 15 units required. Interview encouraged. SAT required. $15 application fee. Application deadline March 1. $150 deposit required on acceptance of offer of admission. *Early Decision, Early Admission* programs. Transfers accepted. Admission deferral possible. Credit possible for CEEB AP exams.

Student Life Student government. Newspaper, magazine, yearbook, radio station. Music, drama, literary groups. Fire department. Honorary, outing, service, and special interest groups. 11 fraternities with houses and 5 sororities. 65% of men and 35% of women join. Students must live at home or on campus. Married-student housing. 95% of students live on campus. Dress code. 2 semesters of phys ed required. 10 intercollegiate sports for men, 8 for women; intramurals. Student body composition: 1% Black, 99% White. 80% from out of state.

TENNESSEE, UNIVERSITY OF $

Knoxville 37996, (615) 974-2591
Dean of Admissions and Records: John J. McDow

- **Undergraduates:** 10,542m, 9,077w
- **Tuition (1984–1985):** $960 (in-state), $1,956 (out-of-state)
- **Room and Board (1984–1985):** $2,560;   **Fees:** $140
- **Degrees offered:** BA, BS, BMus
- **Mean ACT:** 21.4
- **Student-faculty ratio:** 17 to 1
- **Calendar system:** Quarter

A public university established in 1794. Urban campus in Knoxville. Served by air and bus.

Academic Character SACS and professional accreditation. Quarter system, 1 10-week, 2 5-week summer terms. 11 majors offered by the College of Agriculture, 14 by the College of Business Administration, 3 by the College of Communications, 16 by the College of Education, 10 by the College of Engineering, 7 by the College of Home Economics, 39 by the College of Liberal Arts, 1 by the College of Nursing, and 1 by the School of Architecture. Self-designed majors. Minors offered. Independent study. Honors program. Phi Beta Kappa. Cooperative work/study in some colleges. Pass/fail. Credit by exam. Preprofessional programs in several fields. 3-1 programs in dentistry, medicine, pharmacy. Member National, International Student Exchange programs. Elementary, secondary, and special education certification. ROTC, AFROTC. Research organizations, computer center. 1,587,009-volume library with microform resources.

Financial CEEB CSS. University scholarships, grants, loans; PELL, SEOG, NSS, NDSL, FISL, NSL, deferred payment, CWS, university has own work program. Priority application deadline for scholarships March 1.

Admissions High school graduation with 16 units required. GED accepted. ACT required. $10 application fee. Rolling admissions; suggest filing in 11th year or early 12th. $25 room deposit (for boarders) required on acceptance of offer of admission. *Early Admission* Program. Transfers accepted. Admission deferral possible. Credit possible for CEEB AP and CLEP exams.

Student Life Student government. Newspaper, magazine, yearbook, radio station. Music, debate, drama groups. Over 300 academic, honorary, political, professional, religious, and special interest groups. 27 fraternities, 24 with houses, and 20 sororities without houses. 14% of men and 15% of women join. Single freshmen must live with relatives or on campus. Liquor prohibited on campus. 9 intercollegiate sports for men, 6 for women; intramurals. AIAW, NCAC, Southeastern Conference, Tennessee Collegiate Women's Sports Federation. Student body composition: 0.4% Asian, 5.3% Black, 0.3% Hispanic, 0.2% Native American, 90.2% White, 3.6% Other. 14% from out of state.

VANDERBILT UNIVERSITY $$

Nashville 37212, (615) 322-2561
Director of Undergraduate Admissions: Kathlynn Ciompi

- **Undergraduates:** 2,644m, 2,763w
- **Tuition (1984–1985):** $6,800
- **Room and Board (1984–1985):** $3,100; **Fees:** $545
- **Degrees offered:** BA, BS, BSN, BSE
- **Mean SAT:** 548v, 594m, **Mean ACT:** 26
- **Student-faculty ratio:** 9 to 1
- **Calendar system:** Semester

A private university established in 1873. 320-acre campus in University Center section of Nashville. Served by air and bus.

Academic Character SACS and professional accreditation. Semester system, 11-week summer term. 36 majors offered by the College of Arts & Sciences, 7 by the School of Engineering, 1 by the School of Nursing, and 5 by the George Peabody College for Teachers. Special majors. Students at College of Arts & Sciences may take courses at schools of Divinity, Engineering, Law, Medicine, Nursing. Distributive requirements. Graduate and professional degrees granted. Independent study for seniors. Honors program. Phi Beta Kappa. Limited pass/fail. Preprofessional programs in health professions, law, social work, speech and hearing. 5-year BA/MBA program. 3-2 engineering programs with several schools. Consortium with 7 Southern Colleges. Oak Ridge Semester. University has off-campus centers in Europe and Ghana. Experiment in International Living. Elementary, secondary, and special education certification. NROTC, ROTC; AFROTC at Tennessee State. Language lab, observatory. 1,400,000-volume library.

Financial CEEB CSS. Scholarships, grants, loans; PELL, SEOG, NDSL, CWS. Preferred application deadline February 15.

Admissions High school graduation with 15 units required. Interview encouraged. SAT required; ACT accepted. English comp ACH required. $15 application fee. Application deadline February 15. $100 deposit required on acceptance of offer of admission. *Early Decision, Early Admission* programs.

Transfers accepted. Admission deferral possible. Credit possible for CEEB AP exams.

Student Life Student association. Newspaper, magazine, yearbook, radio station. Music, debate, drama groups. Religious, academic, honorary, service, literary, and special interest groups. 15 fraternities and 10 sororities; all have houses. 45% of men and 40% of women join. Freshmen must live on campus. Married-student, special interest housing. 85% of students live on campus. 13 intercollegiate sports for men, 6 for women; intramurals. SEC. Student body composition: 4% Black, 94% White, 2% Other. 80% from out of state.

Texas

BAYLOR UNIVERSITY $

Waco 76706, (817) 755-1011
Director of Admissions: Herman D. Thomas

- **Undergraduates:** 4,396m, 5,100w
- **Tuition (1984–1985):** $3,210
- **Room and Board (1984–1985):** $2,569;   **Fees:** $186
- **Degrees offered:** BA, BS, BBA, BSN, BM
- **Mean SAT:** 490v, 537m,   **Mean ACT:** 24
- **Student-faculty ratio:** 21 to 1
- **Calendar system:** Semester

A private university controlled by the Baptist General Convention of Texas, established in 1845. 350-acre suburban campus. Served by air and bus.
Academic Character SACS and professional accreditation. Semester system, 2 6-week summer terms. 44 majors offered by the College of Arts & Sciences, 18 by the School of Business, 7 by the School of Education, 13 by the School of Music, and 1 by the School of Nursing. Self-designed majors. Distributives, 6 hours of religion, and 2 semesters of University Forum required. Graduate degrees granted. Independent study. Honors program. Phi Beta Kappa. Pass/fail, internships. Credit by exam. 3-2 engineering programs with Case, Texas A&M, Texas Tech, Columbia, Washington U, U Texas. 3-1 forestry program with Duke, 3-1 medical technology program. Cooperative preprofessional programs in accounting, dental hygiene, law, medicine, nursing, pharmacy, physical therapy, with several colleges. Study abroad. Early childhood, elementary, secondary, and special education certification; bilingual, counseling, learning resource specialist preparation. AFROTC. 961,567-volume library with microform resources.
Financial CEEB CSS. University scholarships, grants, loans, music scholarships, payment plans, PELL, SEOG, GSL, NDSL, FISL, CWS. Scholarship application deadline March 1.
Admissions High school graduation with 16 units required. Interview encouraged. SAT or ACT required. $30 application fee. Rolling admissions; suggest applying 1 year before desired enrollment. $100 deposit due on acceptance of admissions offer. *Early Admission* Program. Admission deferral possible. Transfers accepted. Credit possible for CEEB AP and CLEP exams.
Student Life Newspaper, yearbook. Music and fine arts groups. Theatre. Numerous special interest groups. Fraternities and sororities. Single-sex dorms. Married-student apartments. 40% of students live on campus. Academic honor code. Liquor prohibited. 75% class attendance required. Freshmen may not use cars on campus. 4 semesters of phys ed required. Many intercollegiate and intramural sports. NCAA, SAC. Student body composition: 1% Asian, 1.5% Black, 2% Hispanic, 0.3% Native American, 95.2% White. 22% from out of state.

DALLAS, UNIVERSITY OF $

Irving 75061, (214) 579-5119
Director of Admissions: Daniel J. Davis

- **Undergraduates:** 528m, 542w
- **Tuition (1984–1985):** $4,030
- **Room and Board (1984–1985):** $2,520;   **Fees:** $400
- **Degrees offered:** BA, BS
- **Mean SAT:** 603v, 630m,   **Mean ACT:** 26
- **Student-faculty ratio:** 14 to 1
- **Calendar system:** Semester

A private university controlled by the Roman Catholic Church, established in 1955. 1,000-acre suburban campus, northwest of Dallas. Served by air, rail, and bus.

Academic Character SACS accreditation. Semester system, 2 5-week summer terms. Majors offered in art, biochemistry, biology, chemistry, classics, drama, economics, education, English, foreign languages, history, mathematics, philosophy, physics, politics, psychology, and theology. Self-designed majors. Distributives, 6 credits in theology, and comprehensive exams required. Graduate degrees granted. Limited pass/fail, credit for activities. Preprofessional programs in architecture, business management, dentistry, engineering, law, medicine. 3-2 engineering program. 3-1 medical technology and physical therapy programs. 5-year MBA program. Sophomore year in Rome. Elementary and secondary education certification. ROTC at U Texas, Arlington; AFROTC at North Texas. Art center. Theater. Language lab. 218,800-volume library with microform resources.

Financial CEEB CSS and ACT FAS. University scholarships, grants, loans, state scholarships, family discounts, payment plans; PELL, SEOG, NCSP, NDSL, GSL, CWS. Application deadline April 1.

Admissions High school graduation with 16 units required. Interview recommended. SAT or ACT required. $15 application fee. Rolling admissions; suggest applying by January 1. $100 deposit due on acceptance of admissions offer. *Early Admission* and *Early Decision* programs. Admission deferral possible. Transfers accepted. Credit possible for CEEB AP and CLEP exams.

Student Life Student government. Literary journal, yearbook. Music, film, and drama groups. Spring Olympics. Academic, social, and special interest groups. Single students live at home or on campus. Single-sex dorms. No married-student housing. 70% of students live on campus. Class attendance expected. 5 intercollegiate sports for men, 4 for women; several intramurals. AIAW, NAIA. Student body composition: 1.7% Asian, 1.6% Black, 5.3% Hispanic, 0.3% Native American, 86.2% White, 4.9% Other. 53% from out of state.

HOUSTON, UNIVERSITY OF $

Houston 77004, (713) 749-2236
Director of Admissions: Lee Elliott Brown

- **Undergraduates:** 7,199m, 5,494w
- **Tuition and fees (1984–1985):** $420 (in-state), $1,500 (out-of-state)
- **Room and Board (1984–1985):** $2,400
- **Degrees offered:** BA, BS
- **Mean SAT:** 451v, 503m,   **Mean ACT:** 21.5
- **Student-faculty ratio:** 14 to 1
- **Calendar system:** Semester

A public university established in 1927. 384-acre suburban campus, 3 miles from downtown Houston. Served by air, rail, and bus.

Academic Character SACS and professional accreditation. Semester system, 12-week summer term. One major offered by the College of Architecture, 9 by the College of Business Administration, 6 by the College of Education, 5 by the College of Engineering, 1 by the College of Hotel & Restaurant Management, 16 by the College of Humanities & Fine Arts, 8 by the College of Natural Sciences & Mathematics, 1 by the College of Optometry, 1 by the College of Pharmacy, 11 by the College of Social Science, and 8 by the College of Technology. Graduate and professional degrees granted. Honors program. Preprofessional programs in dentistry, medical technology, medicine, physical therapy. Cooperative African studies program with Rice, Saint Thomas, and Texas Southern. Elementary and secondary education certification. ROTC; NROTC at Rice. Language lab. 1,000,000-volume library with microform resources.

Financial ACT FAS. University scholarships, grants, loans, PELL, NDSL, GSL, FISL, CWS. File FFS by March 1.

Admissions High school graduation with 16 units required. SAT or ACT required; 3 ACH recommended. Rolling admissions; suggest applying by April 15. *Early Admission* and *Early Decision* programs. Transfers accepted. Credit possible for CEEB AP and CLEP exams.

Student Life Student government. Newspaper, literary magazine, yearbook, TV station. Music and drama groups. Debate. Academic, honorary, and religious groups. 14 fraternities, 10 with houses; 10 sororities, 3 with houses. 4% of men and 3% of women join. 8% of students live on campus. Class attendance required. 2 hours of phys ed required. 8 intercollegiate sports for men, 3 for women; intramurals. AIAW, NCAA, SC. Student body composition: 1.3% Asian, 10.3% Black, 7% Hispanic, 0.4% Native American, 76.4% White. 13% from out of state.

RICE UNIVERSITY $

6100 South Main, Houston 77251, (713) 527-4036
Director of Admissions: Ron W. Moss

- **Undergraduates:** 1,600m, 1,000w
- **Tuition (1984–1985):** $3,900
- **Room and Board (1984–1985):** $3,550;   **Fees:** $225
- **Degrees offered:** BA, BS, BArch, BMus, BFA
- **Mean SAT:** 620v, 680m
- **Student-faculty ratio:** 9 to 1
- **Calendar system:** Semester

A private university established in 1912. 300-acre urban campus. Served by air, rail, and bus.

Academic Character SACS and professional accreditation. Semester system, limited summer term. 39 majors offered in the areas of architecture, art, computer science, engineering, humanities, physical education, mathematics, music, science, and social sciences. Self-designed and special majors. Distributive requirements. Graduate degrees granted. Independent study. Phi Beta Kappa. Pass/fail, internships. Preprofessional programs in dentistry, law, medicine. 5-year programs in accounting, architecture, engineering. Exchange program with Trinity College, Cambridge. Swarthmore semester. Secondary education certification. ROTC, NROTC. Language labs. 1,100,000-volume library with microform resources.

Financial CEEB CSS. University scholarships, grants, loans, state grants, payment plans; PELL, SEOG, NDSL, FISL, part-time employment. FAF deadline February 1.

Admissions High school graduation with 16 units required. Interview required. Audition required for music majors. Architecture applicants should submit portfolio. SAT and 3 ACH required. Application deadline February 1. $100 tuition and $50 room deposits due on acceptance of admissions offer. *Early Decision, Early Admission, Concurrent Enrollment* programs. Admission deferral possible. Transfers accepted. Credit possible for CEEB AP exams.

Student Life Eight residential colleges, each with its own programs and student government. Student Senate. Newspaper, magazine, yearbook, radio station. Music and drama groups. Debate. Black Students Union. Mexican American Students. Chinese Students Association. Academic, honorary, professional, religious, special interest groups. Limited housing for upperclassmen. Coed and single-sex dorms. No married-student housing. 60% of students live on campus. Phys ed required of freshmen. 11 intercollegiate sports for men, 5 for women; several intramural and club sports. AIAW, SAC. Student body composition: 1.2% Asian, 4% Black, 3% Hispanic, 0.2% Native American, 90.8% White, 0.8% Other. 40% from out of state.

SOUTHERN METHODIST UNIVERSITY $$$

PO Box 296, Dallas 75275, (214) 692-2058
Director of Admissions: Scott F. Healy

- **Undergraduates:** 3,109m, 3,039w
- **Tuition (1984–1985):** $6,880
- **Room and Board (1984–1985):** $3,668;   **Fees:** $716
- **Degrees offered:** BA, BS, BBA, BFA, BMus
- **Mean SAT:** 500v, 554m,   **Mean ACT:** 24
- **Student-faculty ratio:** 15 to 1
- **Calendar system:** Semester

A private university affiliated with the United Methodist Church, established in 1911. 164-acre suburban campus, 5 miles from downtown Dallas. Served by air, rail, and bus.

Academic Character SACS and professional accreditation. Semester system, 2 5-week summer terms, January and May inter-terms. 60 majors offered by the schools of Arts, Business Administration, Dedman College (humanities & sciences), and Engineering & Applied Science. Self-designed majors. Minors in many major fields and in 7 others. Distributive requirements. Graduate degrees granted. Independent study. Honors program. Phi Beta Kappa. Limited pass/fail, internships. Preprofessional programs in dentistry, law, medicine. Cooperative program in engineering. Study abroad. Elementary and secondary education certification. AFROTC at North Texas. Computer center. Herbarium. Electron microscopy lab. Seismological observatory. Museums. 1,800,000-volume library with microform resources.

Financial CEEB CSS. University scholarships, grants, loans, ministerial scholarships, scholarships for Methodist ministers' children, federal and state grants and loans, payment plan, student employment. Priority application deadline for scholarships March 1.

Admissions High school graduation with 13 units required. Interview recommended; urged for broadcast/film and journalism majors. Audition required for dance, music, and theatre applicants. SAT or ACT required. $20 application fee. Rolling admissions; application deadline April 1. $200 deposit due on acceptance of admissions offer. Admission deferral possible. Transfers accepted. Credit possible for CEEB AP and CLEP exams.

Student Life Student government. Newspaper, literary magazine, yearbook, radio station. Music, dance, and drama groups. Debate. Athletic, academic, honorary, professional, religious, service, and special interest groups. 15 fraternities and 12 sororities, all with houses. 50% of men and women join. Freshmen live at home or on campus. Coed and single-sex dorms. Co-op dorms. Married-student housing. 51% of students live on campus. 2 hours of phys ed required. 7 intercollegiate sports for men, 4 for women; many intramurals. AIAW, NCAA, SC. Student body composition: 3% Black, 2% Hispanic, 90% White, 5% Other. 55% from out of state.

TEXAS, THE UNIVERSITY OF $

Austin 78712, (512) 471-1711
Director of Admissions: Shirley Binder

- **Undergraduates:** 19,481m, 17,206w
- **Tuition (1984–1985):** $120 (in-state), $1,200 (out-of-state)
- **Room and Board (1984–1985):** $3,600
- **Degrees offered:** BA, BArch, BBA, BES, BFA, BJ, BMus, BSW, BS
- **Mean SAT:** 490v, 551m,   **Mean ACT:** 23
- **Student-faculty ratio:** 23 to 1
- **Calendar system:** Semester

A public university established in 1881. 445-acre urban campus. Served by air, rail, and bus.

Academic Character SACS and professional accreditation. Semester system, 2 6-week summer terms. 14 majors offered by the College of Business Administration, 8 by the College of Communication, 7 by the College of Education, 10 by the College of Engineering, 13 by the College of Fine Arts, 33 by the College of Liberal Arts, and 22 by the College of Natural Sciences. 5-year programs in pharmacy and architecture. Distributive requirements. Graduate degrees granted. Honors program. Phi Beta Kappa. Cooperative work/study, pass/fail, credit by exam. Preprofessional programs in many areas. Elementary, secondary, and special education certification. ROTC, AFROTC, NROTC. Computer center. Marine science institute. Observatory. Museum. 4,500,000-volume library with microform resources.

Financial CEEB CSS and ACT FAS. University scholarships, grants, loans, state scholarships; PELL, SEOG, NDSL, GSL, NSL, CWS, assistantships. Application deadline March 1.

Admissions High school graduation with 16 units required. Audition required for music majors. SAT required; ACT accepted. Rolling admissions; application deadline June 1. Transfers accepted. Credit possible for CEEB AP, CLEP, and university exams. Provisional admission possible.

Student Life Student government. Newspaper, magazine, yearbook, radio-television guild. Music and drama groups. Many athletic, debate, academic, professional, religious, service, and special interest groups. 33 fraternities and 21 sororities, all with houses. Freshmen encouraged to live on campus. Coed and single-sex dorms. Co-op housing. Special interest houses. Married-student apartments. 12% of students live on campus. Gambling, drinking, immoral conduct, dishonesty, hazing prohibited. 9 intercollegiate sports; intramurals. AIAW, SC. Student body composition: 1.4% Asian, 2.5% Black, 7.8% Hispanic, 0.2% Native American, 83.3% White, 4.8% Other. 14% from out of state.

TEXAS A&M UNIVERSITY $

College Station 77843, (713) 845-1031
Director of Admissions: Billy G. Lay

- **Undergraduates:** 18,133m, 11,765w
- **Tuition (1984–1985):** $120 (in-state), $1,200 (out-of-state)
- **Room and Board (1984–1985):** $3,220;   **Fees:** $360
- **Degrees offered:** BA, BS, BBA, BAEd
- **Mean SAT:** 491v, 527m
- **Student-faculty ratio::** 21 to 1
- **Calendar system:** Semester

A public university established in 1876. 5,200-acre small-city campus, 100 miles north of Houston. Served by air and bus.
Academic Character SACS and professional accreditation. Semester system, 2 5½-week summer terms. 20 majors offered by the College of Agriculture, 3 by the College of Architecture & Environmental Design, 4 by the College of Business Administration, 6 by the College of Education, 17 by the College of Engineering, 4 by the College of Geosciences, 11 by the College of Liberal Arts, 1 by College of Medicine, 8 by the College of Science, 2 by the College of Veterinary Medicine, and 7 by the Galveston marine division. GRE required. Honors program. Cooperative work/study, limited pass/fail, internships. Elementary and secondary education certification. RTOC, AFROTC, NROTC. Language Lab. 1,300,000-volume library with microform resources.
Financial CEEB CSS. University scholarships, grants, loans, state grants and loans; PELL, SEOG, NDSL, GSL, CWS. Application deadline April 1
Admissions High school graduation with 16 units required. SAT and 2 ACH required. Rolling admissions; suggest applying after September 12. *Early Decision* and *Early Admission* programs. Transfers accepted. Credit possible for CEEB AP and university placement exams.
Student Life Student government. Newspaper, literary magazine, yearbook. Music groups. Discussion and Debate Club. Numerous academic, honorary, technical, and special interest groups. Limited housing; students may apply 10 months in advance. Single-sex dorms. Married-student apartments. 33% of students live on campus. Hazing prohibited. 2 years of phys ed required. 10 intercollegiate sports for men, 10 for women; many intramurals. AIAW, NCAA, SC. Student body composition: 1% Asian, 1% Black, 3% Hispanic, 1% Native American, 94% White. 9% from out of state.

TEXAS CHRISTIAN UNIVERSITY $

2800 University Drive, Fort Worth 76129, (817) 921-7490
Dean of Admissions: Edward G. Boehm, Jr.

- **Undergraduates:** 4,800 combined
- **Tuition (1984–1985):** $4,500
- **Room and Board (1984–1985):** $1,856;   **Fees:** $510

- **Degrees offered:** BA, BS, BBA BFA, BGS, BMus, BMusEd, BSEd, BSN
- **Mean SAT:** 550v, 550m, **Mean ACT:** 22
- **Student-faculty ratio:** 17 to 1
- **Calendar system:** Semester

A private university controlled by the Disciples of Christ, established in 1873. 243-acre suburban campus. Served by air, rail, and bus.

Academic Character SACS and professional accreditation. Semester system, 3-week and 2 5-week summer terms. 72 majors offered by the College of Arts & Sciences, the School of Business, the School of Education, the School of Fine Arts, and the College of Nursing. Self-designed and special majors. Minors offered in most major fields and in 3 other areas. Distributives and one religion course required. Graduate degrees granted. Independent study. Honors program. Phi Beta Kappa. Pass/fail, internships. 3-2 engineering program with Washington U. 3-1 medical technology program. 9-month range management program. Washington Semester. Study abroad. Elementary, secondary, and special education certification. ROTC. AFROTC. Computer center. Observatory. Radio and TV studios. 1,000,000-volume library with microform resources.

Financial CEEB CSS. University scholarships, grants, loans, tuition discounts for dependents of ministers and missionaries of the Christian Church, ministerial student grants, state grants and loans, payment plan; PELL, SEOG, NDSL, GSL, CWS. Application deadline June 1.

Admissions High school graduation with 13 units recommended. GED accepted. Interview recommended. Audition required of music majors. SAT or ACT required. $15 application fee. Rolling admissions. $100 room deposit due on acceptance of offer of admission. *Early Admission* Program. Admission deferral possible. Transfers accepted. Credit possible for CEEB AP and CLEP exams; university has own advanced placement program.

Student Life Student government. Newspaper, literary magazine, radio and TV studios. Music and drama groups. Debate. International Student Association. Academic, honorary, political, professional, religious, service, and special interest groups. 10 fraternities and 12 sororities without houses. 30% of men and 38% of women join. Freshmen and sophomores live at home or at school. Single-sex dorms. Special interest housing. 66% of students live on campus. Liquor permitted in dorm rooms only. Gambling and hazing prohibited. Class attendance expected. 1 year of phys ed required. 11 intercollegiate sports for men, 8 for women; several intramurals. AIAW, NCAA, SAC. Student body composition: 5% Black, 92% White, 3% Other. 42% from out of state.

TEXAS WOMAN'S UNIVERSITY $

Denton 76204, (817) 566-1451
Director of Admissions & Registrar: J.E. Tompkins, Jr.

- **Undergraduates:** 161m, 4,090w
- **Tuition (1984–1985):** $474 (in-state), $1,609 (out-of-state)
- **Room and Board (1984–1985):** $2,100; **Fees:** $344
- **Degrees offered:** BA, BBA, BFA, BS, BSW
- **Student-faculty ratio:** 13 to 1
- **Calendar system:** Semester

A public university established in 1901. 270-acre urban campus, 35 miles from Dallas. Served by bus; airport in Dallas.

Academic Character SACS and professional accreditation. Semester system, 2 6-week summer terms. 8 majors offered by the College of Education, 4 by the College of Health, Physical Education, & Recreation, 21 by the College of Humanities & Fine Arts, 18 by the College of Natural & Social Sciences, 19 by the College of Nutrition, Textiles, & Human Development, 1 by the College of Nursing, 4 by the College of Health Care Services, and 1 each by the Colleges of Library Science, Occupational Therapy, and Physical Therapy. Major/minor required. Minors offered in all major fields and in 3 other areas. Graduate degrees granted. Honors program. Preprofessional programs in dentistry and medicine. Elementary and secondary education certification. ROTC; AFRTOC at North Texas. Language lab. 550,497-volume library.
Financial CEEB CSS and ACT FAS. University scholarships, grants, loans, state aid; PELL, SEOG, NSS, NDSL, FISL, GSL, CWS.
Admissions High school graduation with 15 units required. ACT or SAT required. Rolling admissions. $25 room deposit due on acceptance of admissions offer. *Early Decision, Early Admission, Concurrent Enrollment* programs. Admission deferral possible. Transfers accepted. Credit possible for CEEB AP exams; university has own advanced placement program.
Student Life Campus government. Newspaper, literary magazine, yearbook. Music and drama groups. Academic, honorary, literary, political, religious, and special interest groups. Students under 21 live at home or on campus. 35% of students live on campus. Class attendance required. 4 hours of phys ed required. 8 intercollegiate sports. AIAW, NCAA. Student body composition: 11.2% Black, 6.5% Hispanic, 0.2% Native American, 76.6% White, 5.5% Other. 10% from out of state.

TRINITY UNIVERSITY $$

715 Stadium Drive, San Antonio 78284, (512) 736-7207
Director of Admissions: Russell Gossage

- **Undergraduates:** 1,121m, 1,320w
- **Tuition (1984–1985):** $5,400
- **Room and Board (1984–1985):** $2,875
- **Degrees offered:** BA, BS, BM
- **Mean SAT:** 557v, 583m, **Mean ACT:** 26
- **Student-faculty ratio:** 12 to 1
- **Calendar system:** Semester

A private university affiliated with the Presbyterian Church, established in 1869. 107-acre suburban campus, 4 miles north of downtown San Antonio. Served by air, rail, and bus.
Academic Character SACS and professional accreditation. Semester system, 2 5-week summer terms. 39 majors offered in the areas of art, business, education, engineering, environmental studies, foreign languages, physical education, media, music, science, social science, speech, and cultural studies. Self-designed majors. Courses in Sanskrit, Swedish. Distributive requirements. Masters degrees granted. Independent study. Honors program. Phi Beta Kappa. Pass/fail, internships, credit by exam. Preprofessional programs in dentistry, law, medical technology, medicine, ministry. Study abroad. Administration, counseling, teaching the deaf, elementary, and secondary education certification. ROTC. Communications center. Computer center. Theater. 536,000-volume library with microform resources.

Financial CEEB CSS. University scholarships, grants, loans, tuition exchange plan, discount for ministers' children, ministerial scholarships, payment plans; PELL, SEOG, NDSL, FISL, CWS. Scholarship application deadline February 1.

Admissions High school graduation with 16 units required. Interview recommended. SAT or ACT required. Rolling admissions. $400 deposit due on acceptance of admissions offer. *Early Decision* Program. Admission deferral possible. Credit possible for CEEB AP and CLEP exams.

Student Life Student government. Newspaper, arts review, yearbook, radio station. Music, film, drama groups. Chicano Students Association. Community Service Program. Academic, political, religious, service, and special interest groups. 6 fraternities and 6 sororities without housing. 10% of men and 15% of women join. Single students live at home or on campus. Coed and single-sex dorms. No married-student housing. 58% of students live on campus. 2 semesters of phys ed required. 11 intercollegiate sports for men, 8 for women; many intramurals. AIAW, NCAA, TIAA. Student body composition: 1.5% Asian, 2.5% Black, 14.5% Hispanic, 80% White, 2% Other. 29% from out of state.

Utah

BRIGHAM YOUNG UNIVERSITY $

Provo 84602, (801) 378-2507
Dean of Admissions and Records: Robert W. Spencer

- **Undergraduates:** 14,001m, 11,209w
- **Tuition (1984–1985):** $1,400 (for Mormons), $2,100 (others)
- **Room and Board (1984–1985):** $2,184
- **Degrees offered:** BA, BS, BFA, BMus, Blnd St
- **Mean ACT:** 23
- **Student-faculty ratio:** 22 to 1
- **Calendar system:** Modified Trimester

A private university controlled by the Church of Jesus Christ of Latter-Day Saints (Mormons), established in 1875. 500-acre campus in small city of Provo, 45 miles from Salt Lake City. Served by air, bus, and rail.

Academic · Character NASC and professional accreditation. 4-4-2-2 system. 91 majors offered by the colleges of Biological & Agricultural Sciences, Business, Education, Engineering Sciences and Technology, Fine Arts & Communications, Humanities, Nursing, Physical & Mathematical Sciences, Physical Education, and Family, Home, & Social Sciences, and by the schools of Library & Information Sciences and Management. Distributives and 14 hours of religion (including 4 on Book of Mormon) required. Graduate degrees granted. Independent study. Honors program. Cooperative work/study. Preprofessional programs in architecture, biomedical engineering, chiropractic medicine, dental hygiene, dentistry, forestry, health administration, law, management, medicine, occupational therapy, optometry, pharmacy, physician's assistant, podiatry, public health, veterinary medicine. Home Study Program. Washington Semester. Study in New York City, Detroit. Study abroad. Elementary, secondary, special education and guidance certification. AFROTC, ROTC. Lab nursery school. Mineralogical museum. School farms. Language lab, computer center. 1,250,000-volume library with microform resources.

Financial CEEB CSS and ACT FAS University scholarships, grants, church loans, athletic scholarships, PELL, GSL, FISL, deferred payment. Application deadline for scholarships April 30.

Admissions High school graduation required. GED accepted. Interview required. ACT required. $15 application fee. Rolling admissions; application deadline April 30 *Early Decision, Early Admission* programs. Transfers accepted. Credit possible for CEEB AP and CLEP exams.

Student Life Student government Newspaper, magazine, yearbook, radio and TV stations. Music, dance, debate groups. Honorary, service, and special interest groups. Students must live on campus or in approved housing. No coed dorms. Special interest housing Married-student housing. 24% of students live on campus Dress code. Abstinence from liquor, coffee, tea, drugs, tobacco required Class attendance required. 1 hour of physical fitness and 1 of phys ed required Several intercollegiate and intramural sports for men and women. AIAW, NCAA, Western Athletic Conference. Student body composition. 0.5% Asian, 0.2% Hispanic, 1.4% Native American, 94.2% White, 3.7% Other 75% from out of state.

UTAH, UNIVERSITY OF $

Salt Lake City 84112, (801) 581-7200
Director of Admissions: Robert Finley

- **Undergraduates:** 12,325m, 8,565w
- **Tuition and Fees (1984–1985):** $1,050 (in-state), $3,000 (out-of-state)
- **Room and Board (1984–1985):** $2,570
- **Degrees offered:** BA, BFA, BMus, BS, BUS
- **Mean SAT:** 425v, 425m,   **Mean ACT:** 20.1
- **Student-faculty ratio:** 19 to 1
- **Calendar system:** Quarter

A public university established in 1850. 1,500-acre urban campus in Salt Lake City. Served by air, rail, and bus.

Academic Character NASC and professional accreditation. Quarter system, 8-week summer term. 5 majors offered by the College of Business, 3 by the College of Education, 8 by the College of Engineering, 5 by the College of Fine Arts, 5 by the College of Health, Physical Education, & Recreation, 13 by the College of Humanities, 1 by the College of Nursing, 2 by the College of Pharmacy, 4 by the College of Science, 7 by the College of Social and Behavioral Sciences, 1 by the School of Architecture, and 8 by the State College of Mines and Mineral Institutes. Self-designed majors. Distributive requirements. Independent study. Honors program. Phi Beta Kappa. Pass/fail, internships. Preprofessional programs in dentistry, law, medicine. Exchange programs with 35 US universities. Study abroad. Elementary, secondary, and special education certification. AFROTC, NROTC, ROTC. Institute of Government. Genetics lab, environment research lab. 1,900,000-volume library with microform resources.

Financial CEEB CSS. University scholarships, grants, PELL, SEOG, NSS, NDSL, FISL, Education Funds, CWS. Scholarship application deadline February 1.

Admissions High school graduation required with 16 units recommended. Audition required for ballet majors. ACT required, SAT accepted out-of-state. $25 application fee. Rolling admissions. *Early Admission, Concurrent Enrollment* programs. Transfers accepted. Credit possible for CEEB AP and CLEP exams; university has own advanced placement program.

Student Life Student government. Newspaper, magazine, radio and TV stations. Music, debate, dance, drama groups. Academic, honorary, professional, religious, service, and special interest organizations. 11 fraternities and 10 sororities; all have houses. Married-student housing. 10% of students live on campus. Liquor prohibited on campus. 7 intercollegiate sports for men, 7 for women; intramurals. AIAW, Western Athletic Conference. Student body composition: 1.8% Asian, 0.5% Black, 1.7% Hispanic, 0.7% Native American, 92% White, 3% Other. 16% from out of state.

UTAH STATE UNIVERSITY OF AGRICULTURE AND APPLIED SCIENCE $

Logan 84322, (801) 750-1000
Assistant Vice-President, Student Affairs: Bill Sampson

- **Undergraduates:** 5,672m, 4,045w
- **Tuition (1984–1985):** $1,002 (in-state), $2,820 (out-of-state)
- **Room and Board (1984–1985):** $2,205;   **Fees:** $196

- **Degrees offered:** BA, BS, BLA, BMus, BFA
- **Mean SAT:** 900 combined
- **Student-faculty ratio:** 19 to 1
- **Calendar system:** Quarter

A public university established in 1888. 130-acre campus in small city of Logan, 80 miles from Salt Lake City. Served by air, bus, and rail.

Academic Character NASC accreditation. Quarter system. 9 majors offered by the College of Agriculture, 11 by the College of Business, 17 by the College of Education, 10 by the College of Engineering, 7 by the College of Family Life, 18 by the College of Humanities, Arts & Sciences, 14 by the College of Natural Resources, and 15 by the College of Science. Minor required. Distributive requirements. MA, EdD, PhD granted. Independent study. Honors program. Phi Beta Kappa. Pass/fail. Cooperative work/study, internships in some programs. Preprofessional programs in foreign service, dentistry, law, medicine. Study in Mexico, Europe, Hawaii. Elementary, secondary, and special education certification. AFROTC, ROTC. Agriculture and engineering experiment stations. Water Research Lab. Wildlife and Fishery Research Unit. Computer center. 1,000,000-volume library with microform resources.

Financial CEEB CSS. University scholarships and grants, state grants; PELL, SEOG, NDSL, FISL, deferred payment, CWS. Application deadlines March 15 (scholarships), August 1 (loans).

Admissions High school graduation required. ACT required. $15 application fee. Rolling admissions; suggest applying after 11th year. *Early Decision, Early Admission* programs. Transfers accepted. Credit possible for CEEB AP and CLEP exams. "Special Services" program.

Student Life Student government. Newspaper, magazine, yearbook, radio and TV stations. Music, debate, drama groups. Academic, professional, honorary, religious, and special interest organizations. 6 fraternities and 3 sororities; all have houses. 5% of men and 6% of women join. Freshmen women expected to live on campus. No coed dorms. Special interest housing. Married-student housing. 25% of students live on campus. Liquor prohibited on campus; smoking restricted. 7 intercollegiate sports for men, 5 for women; intramurals. AIAW, NCAA, PCAA. Student body composition: 0.7% Asian, 0.6% Black, 0.8% Hispanic, 0.4% Native American, 86.3% White, 11.2% Other. 29% from out of state.

Vermont

BENNINGTON COLLEGE $$$

Bennington 05201, (802) 422-5401
Director of Admissions and Financial Aid: John Nissen

- **Undergraduates:** 409m, 205w
- **Tuition (1984–1985):** $11,720
- **Room and Board (1984–1985):** $2,870;   **Fees:** $50
- **Degrees offered:** BA
- **Student-faculty ratio:** 9 to 1
- **Calendar system:** Semester

A private college established in 1932, became coed 1969. 550-acre campus 4 miles from Bennington, 175 miles north of New York City, 45 miles east of Albany. Air, rail service to Albany; bus to Bennington.

Academic Character NEASC accreditation. Semester system with Non-Resident Term from January to March, summer terms. 8 divisions; 3 disciplines in Black music, 4 in dance, 3 in drama, 3 in literature and languages, 5 in music, 3 in natural sciences and mathematics, 7 in social science, 8 in visual arts. Students encouraged to pursue work in 4 of the divisions during first 2 years. Tentative plan must be submitted by student before end of second year indicating major during final 2 years. Concentration may be divisional or interdisciplinary. Regular faculty-student meetings regarding program of study. Independent study during latter 2 years (confirmation of Plan) results in senior thesis. Internships (job experience) during Non-Resident Term required. Graduate degrees granted. Pass/fail. Visiting students. Study abroad, terms at other institutions. Post-baccalaureate pre-med and allied health sciences program. Computer center. 100,000-volume library with microform resources.

Financial CEEB CSS. College scholarships and funds; PELL, SEOG, FISL, GSL, CWS. Application deadline February 1.

Admissions High school graduation required. Interview required. SAT or ACT recommended. $25 application fee. Application deadline March 1. $250 deposit required on acceptance of admissions offer. *Early Decision, Early Admission* programs. Transfers accepted. Admission deferral possible.

Student Life Student government. News bulletin, college calendar. Music, drama, dance groups. Tutoring program. Political, academic, special interest groups. Coed and single-sex dorms. 15 self-governing student houses. Freshmen must live on campus. 80% of students live on campus. Men's and women's soccer and tennis teams. Intramurals. Student body composition: 1% Asian, 3% Black, 1% Hispanic, 10% Foreign, 85% White. 95% of students from out of state.

MIDDLEBURY COLLEGE $$$

Middlebury 05753, (802) 388-3711
Director of Admissions: Fred F. Neuberger

- **Undergraduates:** 950m, 950w
- **Tuition, Room and Board (1984–1985):** $12,600;   **Fees:** $60

- **Degrees offered:** BA
- **Mean SAT:** 580v, 610m
- **Student-faculty ratio:** 13 to 1
- **Calendar system:** 4-1-4

A private college established in 1800. 500-acre campus in the village of Middlebury, 30 miles south of Burlington. Bus in Middlebury, airport in Burlington.

Academic Character NEASC accreditation. 4-1-4 system. Majors offered in American literature, American studies, art, biology, chemistry, classical studies, classics, East Asian studies, economics, English, environmental studies, French, geography, geology, German, history, Italian, literary studies, math, music, northern studies, philosophy, physics, political science, psychology, religion, Russian, sociology/anthropology, Spanish, theater. Joint majors. Programs in writing, computer science, teacher education. Summer Breadloaf School of English, Breadloaf Writer's Conference, and summer foreign language schools are held on campus. Distributive requirements. MA, MS, DML granted. Independent study. Phi Beta Kappa. Honors program. Honors/pass/fail, internships. Preprofessional programs in medicine, dentistry, veterinary medicine. 3-2 engineering programs with Case Western Reserve, Columbia, Georgia Tech, RPI, University of Rochester. 3-2 business programs with Boston U, Columbia, Dartmouth (Amos Tuck School), NYU, Rutgers, U of Chicago, U of Rochester. 3-2 law program with Syracuse. Exchange with Swarthmore. Junior year at Institute for Architecture and Urban Studies in New York. Washington Semester. Mystic Seaport Program .Study abroad. Elementary and secondary education certification. Computer center. Observatory. 450,000-volume library with microform resources.

Financial CEEB CSS. College scholarships, grants, loans, state aid; PELL, SEOG, NDSL, GSL, CWS. Application deadline January 31.

Admissions High school graduation with 16 units recommended. Interview recommended. SAT and 3 ACH required. $30 application fee. Application deadline January 15. $100 deposit required on acceptance of admissions offer *Early Decision* Program. Some transfers accepted. Admission deferral possible. Credit possible for CEEB AP exams. Minority recruiting program.

Student Life Student government. Newspaper, magazines, yearbook, radio station. Music, visual arts groups. Language, religious, outing, special interest groups. 6 fraternities with houses; 15% of men and some women join. Coed and single-sex dorms; language houses. 98% of students live on campus. 1 year of phys ed required. 11 intercollegiate sports for men, 11 for women; club and intramural sports. AIAW, ECAC, NCAA, NECAC, NESCAC. Student body composition: 1% Asian, 3% Black, 1% Hispanic, 95% White. 95% of students from out of state.

NORWICH UNIVERSITY $$

Northfield 05663, (802) 485-5011
Dean of Admissions: William S. Neal

- **Undergraduates:** 1,400m, 400w
- **Tuition, Room and Board (1984–1985):** $10,100 (4-year program) $9,100 (2-year program)
- **Degrees offered:** BA, BS, AA, AS
- **Mean SAT:** 450v, 500m

- **Student-faculty ratio:** 14 to 1
- **Calendar system:** Semester

A private 2-campus university, which became coed when Norwich University (all-male military school established 1819) merged with Vermont College (women's college established 1834) in 1972. 1,000-acre Norwich U campus is in Northfield; Vermont College campus is in nearby Montpelier. Air, bus, and rail service.

Academic Character NEASC and professional accreditation. Semester system with 2 5-week summer terms. 34 majors offered in areas of accounting, biology, business administration, chemistry, communications, computer science, criminal justice, earth science, economics, education, engineering, English, government, history, humanities, international studies, math, medical technology, military studies, modern languages, philosophy, phys ed, physics, recreation, religion. Associate degrees in 10 areas. Minors in some fields. 5-year 2-degree program. Interdisciplinary majors. Distributive requirements, ROTC required for men. Independent study. Honors program. Internships. Marine Corps Commissioning Program. Russian School on campus. Study abroad. 4- and 2-year ROTC, AFROTC programs. Mountain and Cold Weather Training. Computer services. Learning Skills Center. 150,000-volume library with microform resources.

Financial CEEB CSS. University scholarships; PELL, SEOG, NSS, NDSL, FISL, NSL, CWS. Application deadline March 1.

Admissions High school graduation with 18 units required. Interview recommended. SAT or ACT, ACH recommended. $20 application fee. Rolling admissions. $150 deposit required on acceptance of admissions offer. *Early Admission, Early Decision* programs. Transfers accepted. Admission deferral possible. Credit possible for CEEB AP and CLEP exams. University has own placement exams.

Student Life Student government. Newspaper, magazine, yearbook, radio station. Music groups. Parachute club. Mountain Rescue Team. Service, academic, athletic, honorary, religious, and special interest organizations. No coed dorms. No married-student housing. 90% of students live on campus. Freshmen may not have cars. ROTC cadets at Norwich must wear uniforms. 2 semesters of phys ed required. 12 intercollegiate sports for men, 8 for women; intramural and club sports. ECAC, NCAA, NEIAA. Student body composition: 1% Asian, 3% Black, 1% Hispanic, 1% Native American, 92% White, 2% Other. 80% of students from out of state.

SAINT MICHAEL'S COLLEGE $$

Winooski 05404, (802) 655-2000
Dean of Admissions: Jerry E. Flanagan

- **Undergraduates:** 802m, 800w
- **Tuition (1984–1985):** $6,300
- **Room and Board (1984–1985):** $2,630;   **Fees:** $70
- **Degrees offered:** BA
- **Mean SAT:** 478v, 521m
- **Student-faculty ratio:** 16 to 1
- **Calendar system:** Semester

A private college affiliated with the Roman Catholic Church. Established 1889, college became coed in 1970. 430-acre campus in Winooski, suburb of Burlington, 90 miles from Montreal. Air, bus, and rail service.

Academic Character NEASC accreditation. Semester system, 6-week summer term. Majors offered in art, accounting, American studies, biology, business administration, chemistry, classics, computer science, economics, elementary education, English literature, environmental science, fine arts, French, history, journalism, math, philosophy, physics, political science, psychology, religion, sociology, Spanish. Self-designed majors. Distributives and 2 courses in religion required. Masters degrees granted; certificate programs offered. Independent study, honors program. Credit by exam. Pass/fail, internships. Preprofessional programs in dentistry, law, medicine. 3-2 engineering program with Clarkson. Exchange programs. Study abroad. Elementary and secondary education certification. Computer center. Observatory. North Campus. AFROTC; ROTC at UVM. 130,000-volume library with microform resources.

Financial CEEB CSS and ACT FAS. College scholarships and grants, state aid; PELL, SEOG, NDSL, FISL, HELP, GSL, CWS. Application deadline March 15.

Admissions High school graduation with 16 units required. Interview encouraged. SAT or ACT required. $20 application fee. Rolling admissions. $150 deposit required on acceptance of admissions offer. *Early Admission* Program. Transfers accepted. Admission deferral possible. Credit possible for CEEB AP and CLEP exams.

Student Life Student government. Newspaper, magazine, yearbook, radio station. Music, drama groups. Service, honorary, religious, and special interest groups. Students must live on campus unless living at home. Special interest and single-sex dorms. 85% of students live on campus. Residence halls have visitation restrictions. 11 intercollegiate sports for men, 11 for women; intramurals. 83% of students from out of state.

VERMONT, UNIVERSITY OF $/$$

Burlington 05405, (802) 656-3370
Director of Admissions: Jeff M.S. Kaplan

- **Undergraduates:** 3,143m, 4,206w
- **Tuition (1984–1985):** $2,529 (in-state), $6,640 (out-of-state)
- **Room and Board (1984–1985):** $2,926;   **Fees:** $299
- **Degrees offered:** BA, BS, BEd
- **Mean SAT:** 502v, 560m
- **Student-faculty ratio:** 10 to 1
- **Calendar system:** Semester

A public university established 1791. 715-acre campus in Burlington, 100 miles south of Montreal. Air, bus, and rail service.

Academic Character NEASC and professional accreditation. Semester system, one 4- to 8-week summer term. 17 majors offered by the College of Agriculture, 29 by the College of Arts and Sciences, 10 by the College of Education and Social Sciences, 7 by College of Engineering and Mathematics, 5 by the School of Business Administration, 4 by the School of Allied Health Sciences, 5 by the School of Natural Resources, 1 by the School of Nursing. Self-designed majors. Associate degrees in some allied health services. Distributive requirements. Graduate and professional degrees granted. Independent study. Honors programs. Phi Beta Kappa. Cooperative work/study, internships, pass/fail. Preprofessional programs in law, veterinary medicine, medicine, dentistry. Member of Vermont Colleges Consortium. NERSP. Exchange programs. Study abroad.. Elementary, secondary, and special education certification. Government Research and World Affairs Centers. Agricultural Experiment Station. Morgan Horse Farm in Weybridge. Living/Learning Center. Language lab. Computer center. 1,000,000-volume library with microform resources.

Financial ACT FAS. University scholarships; PELL, SEOG, NDSL, health professions loans and grants, CWS. Application deadline March 1.

Admissions High school graduation with 16 units required. Interview recommended. SAT required. $25 application fee. Application deadline February 1. $125 deposit required on acceptance of admissions offer. *Early Decision* Program. Transfers accepted. Admission deferral possible. Credit possible for CEEB AP, CLEP, and university placement exams. Minority student program.

Student Life Student government. Newspaper, magazine, yearbook, radio and TV station. Music, drama, debate, dance groups. Gay Union. Outing, athletic, language, honorary, service, special interest organizations. 15 fraternities and 6 sororities; all with houses. 15% of men and 10% of women join. Freshmen must live on campus or at home. Coed and single-sex dorms. Special interest and married-student housing. 55% of students live on campus. 1 year of phys ed required. Class attendance expected. Extensive intercollegiate and intramural programs. AIAW, ECAC, NCAA, NEIAA, EAIAW, NECAC, Yankee Conference, Olde New England Conference. 53% of students from out of state.

Virginia

HOLLINS COLLEGE $$

Hollins College 24020, (703) 362-6000
Director of Admissions: Sandra J. Lovinguth

- **Undergraduates:** 870w
- **Tuition (1984–1985):** $7,100
- **Room and Board (1984–1985):** $3,300;   **Fees:** $90
- **Degrees offered:** BA
- **Mean SAT:** 510v, 510m
- **Student-faculty ratio:** 10 to 1
- **Calendar system:** 4–1–4

A private women's college with coed graduate programs, established in 1842. 450-acre suburban campus, 6 miles north of downtown Roanoke. Served by air and bus.
Academic Character SACS and professional accreditation. 4-1-4 system. 34 majors offered in the areas of American studies, classical studies, computer science, economics/business, fine arts, liberal arts, modern languages, music, religion, science, social sciences, statistics, and theatre. Self-designed majors. Distributive requirements. MA, MALS granted. 4-week January special project. Independent study. Honors program. Phi Beta Kappa. Limited pass/fail, internships. Preprofessional programs in law and medicine. 3-2 engineering programs with Washington U, VPI. 3-2 nursing program with UVA. 4-2 architecture program with VPI. Cross-registration with 6 area schools. UN Semester. Washington Semester. Study abroad. Elementary and secondary education certification. ROTC at Washington and Lee. Language labs. 205,000-volume library.
Financial CEEB CSS. College scholarships, grants, loans, payment plans; PELL, SEOG, NDSL, FISL, USAF, GSL, CWS, on-campus employment. Application deadline March 1.
Admissions High school graduation with 16 units required. Interview recommended. SAT required. $20 application fee. Rolling admissions. $400 deposit due on acceptance of admissions offer. *Early Decision* and *Early Admission* programs. Admission deferral possible. Transfers accepted. Credit possible for CEEB AP exams.
Student Life Student government. Newspaper, literary magazine, yearbook. Music, dance, drama, and opera groups. Debate. Community Security Council. Athletic, academic, religious, and special interest groups. Women's dorms. French House. 95% of students live on campus. Honor system. Liquor restricted. Class attendance expected. 8 intercollegiate sports; intramurals. Student body composition: 2% Black, 96% White, 2% Other. 63% from out of state.

JAMES MADISON UNIVERSITY $

Harrisonburg 22807, (703) 433-6147
Director of Admissions: Francis E. Turner

- **Undergraduates:** 3,714m, 4,468w
- **Tuition (1984–1985):** $2,006 (in-state), $3,326 (out-of-state)

- **Room and Board (1984–1985):** $2,496
- **Degrees offered:** BA, BS, BSN, BGS, BSW, BFA, BMus, BBA BMusEd
- **Mean SAT:** 491v, 537m
- **Student-faculty ratio:** 17 to 1
- **Calendar system:** Semester

A public university established in 1908, became coed in 1966. 365-acre small-city campus, 125 miles from Richmond and Washington, DC. Served by bus; airport 20 minutes away.

Academic Character SACS and professional accreditation. Semester system, 3-, 4-, 6-, and 8-week summer terms. 22 majors offered by the College of Letters & Sciences, 11 by the School of Business, 15 by the School of Education & Human Services, 5 by the School of Fine Arts & Communication, and 1 by the School of Nursing. Minors offered in most major fields and in interdisciplinary studies and secondary education. Distributive requirements. Masters degrees granted. Independent study. Honors program. Limited pass/fail, credit by exam, internships. Preprofessional programs in dentistry, law, medicine, theology. 2-year transfer programs in engineering, physical therapy. Cross-registration with 7 area schools. Study abroad. Elementary, secondary, library science, and special education certification. ROTC. Computer center. Child Development Center. Language lab. TV/film center. Farm. 380,000-volume library with microform resources.

Financial CEEB CSS. University scholarships, grants, loans; PELL, SEOG, NDSL, FISL, CWS. Application deadline March 1.

Admissions High school graduation with 16 units required. GED accepted. Audition required for music majors. SAT required; ACT not accepted. $15 application fee. Rolling admissions. $100 room deposit due on acceptance of admissions offer. *Early Decision* and *Concurrent Enrollment* programs. Transfers accepted. Credit possible for CEEB AP and CLEP exams.

Student Life Student government. Newspaper, literary magazine, yearbook, radio station. Music, dance, and drama groups. Debate. Black Student Alliance. Saturday Adoption Program. Academic, honorary, political, religious, and special interest groups. 9 fraternities and 8 sororities. 10% of students join. Freshmen must live at home or on campus. Coed and single-sex dorms. Language and music houses. No married-student housing. 65% of students live on campus. Seniors and commuters may have cars. Honor system. 2 hours of phys ed required. 12 intercollegiate sports for men, 12 for women; intramurals. AIAW, NCAA. Student body composition: 4% Black, 95% White, 1% Other. 20% from out of state.

LYNCHBURG COLLEGE $$

Lynchburg 24501, (804) 522-8100, ext. 300
Dean of Admissions: E.R. Chadderton

- **Undergraduates:** 650m, 847w
- **Tuition (1984–1985):** $5,950
- **Room and Board (1984–1985):** $3,045
- **Degrees offered:** BA, BS
- **Mean SAT:** 440v, 470m
- **Student-faculty ratio:** 11 to 1
- **Calendar system:** Semester

A private college affiliated with the Christian Church (Disciples of Christ), established in 1903. 214-acre wooded, suburban campus, 100 miles west of Richmond. Served by air, rail, and bus.

Academic Character SACS accreditation. Semester system, 4 3-week summer terms. 42 majors offered in the areas of American studies, art, business, education, health, journalism, liberal arts, mathematics, medical technology, modern languages, music, nuclear medical technology, nursing, physical education, recreation, religion, science, social sciences, and theatre. Joint BA/BS majors in 8 areas. Minor required. Distributive requirements; varied degree requirement options. Masters degrees granted. Independent study. Honors program. Phi Beta Kappa. Limited pass/fail, internships. Preprofessional programs in dentistry, forestry/wildlife management, journalism, law, library science, medicine, ministry, nursing, optometry, pharmacy, physical therapy, social work, veterinary medicine. 3-2 engineering programs with Old Dominion and Georgia Tech. 3-2 MBA program. 3-2 professional programs possible. Cross-registration with Randolph-Macon Women's College, Sweet Briar. Study abroad. Elementary, secondary, and special education certification. ROTC. Computer center. Language labs. 178,000-volume library with microform resources.

Financial Guaranteed tuition and comprehensive fees. CEEB CSS. College scholarships, grants, loans, ministers' dependent grants, church-vocation grants, payment plan; PELL, SEOG, NDSL, CWS, college work programs. Application deadlines March 15 (scholarships), April 1 (loans).

Admissions High school graduation with 15 units required. GED may be accepted. Interview recommended. SAT or ACT required; 3 ACH required. $15 application fee. Rolling admissions. $100 deposit due on acceptance of admissions offer. *Early Admission* and *Early Decision* programs. Admission deferral possible. Transfers accepted. Credit possible for CEEB AP, CLEP, and college proficiency exams.

Student Life Student government. Newspaper, literary magazine, yearbook, radio station. Music and drama groups. Athletic, academic, honorary, religious, service, and special interest groups. Fraternities and sororities. Seniors may live off campus. Single-sex dorms. Apartments. 90% of students live on campus. Dormitory students may not have cars. 10 intercollegiate sports for men, 8 for women; many club and intramural programs. AIAW, NCAA, ODAC, VIC. Student body composition: 2.5% Black, 0.5% Hispanic, 95.1% White, 1.9% Other. 45% from out of state.

MARY BALDWIN COLLEGE $$

Staunton 24401, (703) 885-0811
Director of Admissions: Clair Carter Bell

- **Undergraduates:** 750w
- **Tuition (1984–1985):** $5,600
- **Room and Board (1984–1985):** $4,100;   **Fees:** $50
- **Degrees offered:** BA
- **Mean SAT:** 450v, 450m
- **Student-faculty ratio:** 12 to 1
- **Calendar system:** 4–4–1

A private women's college affiliated with the Presbyterian Church of the United States, established in 1842. 50-acre small-city campus, 100 miles west of Richmond. Served by air, rail, and bus.

Academic Character SACS accreditation. Semester system, 4-week May term. 25 majors offered in the areas of art, biology, business, chemistry, economics, English, French, history, mass communications, mathematics, medical technology, music, political science, psychology, religion-philosophy, sociology, Spanish, speech, and theatre. Distributives and senior exams or projects required. Independent study. Phi Beta Kappa. Limited pass/fail, externships. Preprofessional programs in Christian ministry, law, medicine, veterinary medicine. Cross-registration with 6 area schools. Summer marine biology program. Study abroad. Elementary, secondary, and special education certification. ROTC at James Madison. Communications lab. 150,000-volume library.

Financial CEEB CSS. College scholarships, grants, loans, state aid, payment plan; PELL, SEOG, NDSL, FISL, GSL, CWS, college work program. Application deadline March 1.

Admissions High school graduation with 16 units required. Interview welcomed. SAT and 3 ACH required. $20 application fee. Rolling admissions. $200 deposit due on acceptance of admissions offer. *Early Decision* and *Early Admission* programs. Admission deferral possible. Transfers accepted. Credit possible for CEEB AP and college proficiency exams.

Student Life Student government. Newspaper, literary magazine, yearbook. Music, dance, and drama groups. Honorary, service, and special interest groups. Students must live with families or on campus. Women's dorms. 90% of students live on campus. Honor system. 7 intercollegiate sports; intramurals, horse shows. NCAA, ODAC. Student body composition: 1% Asian, 2% Black, 0.5% Hispanic, 96.5% White. 60% from out of state.

RANDOLPH-MACON WOMAN'S COLLEGE $$

Lynchburg 24508, (804) 846-7392
Director of Admissions: Robert T. Merritt

- **Undergraduates:** 750w
- **Tuition (1984–1985):** $7,000
- **Room and Board (1984–1985):** $3,300;   **Fees:** $80
- **Degrees offered:** BA
- **Mean SAT:** 550v, 550m
- **Student-faculty ratio:** 15 to 1
- **Calendar system:** Semester

A private college affiliated with the Methodist Church, established in 1891. 100-acre suburban campus, 50 miles northeast of Roanoke. Served by air, bus, and rail.

Academic Character SACS accreditation. Semester system. 34 majors offered in the areas of American studies, Asian civilization, classics, communication, education, fine arts, international studies, Latin American studies, liberal arts, mathematics, medical technology, religion, Russian studies, science, social sciences, theatre, and urban studies. Distributive requirements. Independent study. Juniors and seniors may read for honors. Phi Beta Kappa. 3-2 engineering programs with Vanderbilt and Duke. 5-year special education program with UVA. Cross-registration with 8 area colleges. UN and Washington semesters. Study in England, Athens, Rome. Near East Archaeological seminar. Language lab. 150,000-volume library with microform resources.

Financial CEEB CSS. College scholarships, grants, ministerial grants, loans; PELL, SEOG, NDSL, GSL, CWS. Scholarship application deadline March 1.

Admissions High school graduation with 16 units recommended. Interview recommended. SAT or ACT, and 3 ACH required. $20 application fee. Rolling admissions. $300 deposit due on acceptance of admissions offer. *Early Decision* and *Early Admission* programs. Admission deferral possible. Transfers accepted. Credit possible for CEEB AP and CLEP exams.

Student Life Student government. Newspaper, literary magazine, yearbook, radio station. Music, dance, and drama groups. Minority Affairs Club. Women's Coalition. Academic, religious, service, and special interest groups. Single students live at home or on campus. 98% of students live on campus. Class attendance expected. 2 years of phys ed required. 6 intercollegiate sports; intramurals. AIAW. Student body composition: 2.6% Black, 0.4% Hispanic, 94.4% White, 2.6% Other. 70% from out of state.

RICHMOND, UNIVERSITY OF $$

Richmond 23173, (804) 285-6262
Dean of Admissions: Thomas N. Pollard, Jr.

- **Undergraduates:** 1,368m, 1,245w
- **Tuition (1984–1985):** $6,750
- **Room and Board (1984–1985):** $2,310
- **Degrees offered:** BA, BM, BS, BSBA, BAST, AAST
- **Mean SAT:** 520v, 560m
- **Student-faculty ratio:** 13 to 1
- **Calendar system:** Semester

A private university affiliated with the Baptist Church, established in 1830. 350-acre suburban campus. Served by air, rail, and bus.

Academic Character SACS and professional accreditation. Semester system, summer terms. 43 majors offered in the areas of American studies, business, classics, criminal justice, education, humanities, journalism, mathematics, modern languages, music, physical education, religion, Russian studies, science, social science, speech, theatre, urban and women's studies. Distributive requirements. Graduate and professional degrees granted. Independent studies. Honors program. Phi Beta Kappa. Limited pass/fail. Preprofessional programs in dentistry, forestry, law, medicine. Cooperative forestry program with Duke. New York and Washington programs. Study abroad. Early childhood, elementary, and secondary education certification. ROTC. Undergraduate research program. Computer center. Fine arts center. 410,000-volume libraries with microform resources.

Financial CEEB CSS. University scholarships, grants, loans, ministerial scholarships, state aid, payment plan; PELL, SEOG, NDSL, GSL, CWS, university employment. Scholarship application deadline March 15.

Admissions High school graduation with 16 units required. SAT or ACT, and 3 ACH required. $25 application fee. Application deadline February 1. $250 tuition and $250 room deposits due on acceptance of admissions offer. *Early Decision* and *Early Admission* programs. Admission deferral possible. Few transfers accepted. Credit possible for CEEB AP and CLEP exams.

Student Life Student government. Newspaper, literary magazine, yearbook, radio station. Music and drama groups. Debate. Honorary, religious, service, and special interest groups. 11 fraternities with houses. 45% of men join. Single-sex dorms. No married-student housing. 85% of students live on campus. Honor code. Class attendance expected. 4 semesters of phys ed required. 12 intercollegiate sports for men, 9 for women; many intramurals. AIAW, ECAC, NCAA. Student body composition: 0.8% Asian, 6% Black, 0.2% Hispanic, 0.4% Native American, 92.6% White. 70% from out of state.

SWEET BRIAR COLLEGE $$

Sweet Briar 24595, (804) 381-5548
Director of Admissions: Terry Scarborough

- **Undergraduates:** 780w
- **Tuition (1984–1985):** $7,850
- **Room and Board (1984–1985):** $2,650; **Fees:** $60
- **Degrees offered:** AB
- **Mean SAT:** 500v, 500m, **Mean ACT:** 24
- **Student-faculty ratio:** 9 to 1
- **Calendar system:** 4–1–4

A private women's college established in 1901. 3,300-acre rural campus, 12 miles north of Lynchburg. Served by air, rail, and bus.
Academic Character SACS and professional accreditation. 4-1-4 system. 37 majors offered in the areas of American, French, German, and Italian studies, anthropology, classics, dance, economics, English, government, history, international affairs, mathematics, modern languages, music, philosophy, physics, political economy, psychology, religion, sociology, studio art, and theatre. Self-designed majors. Distributive requirements; senior exam, thesis, or project required. Independent study emphasized. Honors program. Phi Beta Kappa. Limited pass/fail, internships. Preprofessional programs in engineering, law, medicine. 3-2 engineering programs with Columbia, Georgia Tech, Washington U. 3-2 business program with UVA. Junior year environmental studies program. Cross-registration with 7 area colleges. Washington Semester. Exchange with St. Andrew's in Scotland. Study in Europe. Elementary and secondary education certification. Fine arts center. Laboratory nursery school. Museum. Computer facilities. 180,000-volume library with microform resources.
Financial CEEB CSS. College scholarships, grants, loans; PELL, SEOG, NDSL, CWS. Scholarship application deadline March 1.
Admissions High school graduation with 16 units required. Interview recommended. SAT and 3 ACH required. $20 application fee. Application deadline March 1. $300 deposit due on acceptance of admissions offer. *Early Decision* and *Early Admission* programs. Admission deferral possible. Transfers accepted. Credit possible for CEEB AP and college placement exams.
Student Life Student government. Newspaper, literary magazine, yearbook, radio station. Music, dance, and drama groups. Academic, political, service, social, and special interest groups. Students live at home or on campus. 8 women's dorms and 2 houses. 99% of students live on campus. Honors system. 2 semesters of phys ed required. 8 intercollegiate sports; intramurals. Student body composition: 3% Asian, 1% Black, 96% White. 80% from out of state.

VIRGINIA, UNIVERSITY OF $

Box 3728, University Station, Charlottesville 22903, (804) 924-7751
Dean of Undergraduate Admissions: Jean L. Rayburn

- **Undergraduates:** 5,378m, 5,589w
- **Tuition (1984–1985):** $1,803 (in-state), $4,340 (out-of-state)
- **Room and Board (1984–1985):** $2,570; **Fees:** $16
- **Degrees offered:** BA, BS
- **Mean SAT:** 577–596v (varies), 614–677m (varies)
- **Student-faculty ratio:** 11 to 1
- **Calendar system:** Semester

A public university established in 1819, became coed in 1970. 2,000-acre small-city campus. Served by air, rail, and bus.

Academic Character SACS and professional accreditation. Semester system, summer terms. 33 majors offered by the College of Arts & Sciences, 3 by the School of Architecture, 5 by the School of Commerce, 5 by the School of Education, 10 by the School of Engineering & Applied Science, and 1 by the School of Nursing. Self-designed majors. Distributive requirements. Graduate and professional degrees granted. Independent study. Honors program. Phi Beta Kappa. Pass/fail, internships. Preprofessional programs in architecture, business, commerce, education, law, medicine, nursing. Study abroad. Elementary, secondary, and special education certification. ROTC, AFROTC, NROTC. Atomic reactor. Biological station. Computer facilities. Farm. Language labs. Political economy center. Observatories. 2,500,000-volume library with microform resources.

Financial CEEB CSS. University scholarships, grants, loans, payment plans; PELL, SEOG, NDSL, CWS. Application deadline March 1.

Admissions High school graduation with 16 units required. SAT and 3 ACH required. $20 application fee. Application deadline February 1. $250 deposit due on acceptance of admissions offer. *Early Decision* Program. Limited number of transfers accepted. Credit possible for CEEB AP exams.

Student Life Student government. Newspapers, magazines, yearbook, 2 radio stations. Music and drama groups. Debate. Political, professional, religious, service, and special interest groups. 33 fraternities with houses, 13 sororities. 38% of men join fraternities. Unless living at home, freshmen live in dorms for 2 semesters. Coed and single-sex dorms. Married-student apartments. 43% of students live on campus. First-semester students may not have cars. Honor system. 13 intercollegiate sports for men, 10 for women; many intramurals. AIAW, ACC. Student body composition: 10% Black, 88% White, 2% Other. 35% from out of state.

VIRGINIA INTERMONT COLLEGE $

Bristol 24201, (703) 669-6101
Dean of Admissions & Financial Aid: Thomas M. Hughes

- **Undergraduates:** 150m, 450w
- **Tuition (1984–1985):** $3,850
- **Room and Board (1984–1985):** $2,400
- **Degrees offered:** BA, AA
- **Student-faculty ratio:** 14 to 1
- **Calendar system:** Semester

A private college affiliated with the Baptist Church, established in 1884, became coed in 1973. 16-acre urban campus. Airport, bus station nearby.

Academic Character SACS and professional accreditation. Semester system. 31 majors offered by the divisions of Applied & Professional Studies,

Behavioral & Social Sciences, Humanities, Natural Sciences & Mathematics, Performing Arts, Physical Education, and Visual Arts, including ballet, creative writing, horsemanship, photography. AA in the areas of allied health, applied & fine arts, drama-speech, general studies, liberal arts, preprofessional, general secretarial, medical lab technology. Distributive requirements. Independent study. Internships. Preprofessional programs in cytotechnology, dental hygiene, laboratory technology, medical record administration, nursing, occupational therapy, pharmacy, physical therapy. Cross-registration with King. Elementary and secondary education certification. Computer center. Language lab. Museum. Riding center. 55,979-volume library with microform resources.

Financial CEEB CSS. College scholarships, grants, loans, payment plans; PELL, SEOG, NDSL, GSL, FISL, CWS, college work program.

Admissions High school graduation with 15 units required. GED accepted. Interview recommended. SAT or ACT recommended. $15 application fee. Rolling admissions. $100 deposit due on acceptance of admissions offer. *Early Admission* and *Concurrent Enrollment* programs. Admission deferral possible. Transfers accepted. Credit possible for CEEB AP and CLEP exams.

Student Life Student government. Newspaper, literary magazine, yearbook, radio station. Music and drama groups. Academic, political, religious, service, and special interest groups. Students must live on campus or at home. No married-student housing. Single-sex dorms. 70% of students live on campus. Liquor prohibited. 4 hours of phys ed required. 1 intercollegiate sport for men, 4 for women; intramurals. Student body composition: 1% Asian, 5% Black, 4% Hispanic, 89% White, 1% Other. 59% from out of state.

VIRGINIA POLYTECHNIC INSTITUTE AND STATE UNIVERSITY $

Blacksburg 24061, (703) 961-6267
Director of Admissions: Archie G. Phlegar

- **Undergraduates:** 10,507m, 7,435w
- **Tuition (1984–1985):** $1,812 (in-state), $3,642 (out-of-state)
- **Room and Board (1984–1985):** $1,683
- **Degrees offered:** BS, BA, BArch, BLArch
- **Mean SAT:** 506v, 581m
- **Student-faculty ratio:** 10 to 1
- **Calendar system:** Quarter

A public university established in 1872. 2,300-acre small-city campus, 40 miles west of Roanoke. Served by bus; airport in Roanoke.

Academic Character SACS and professional accreditation. Quarter system, 2 6-week summer terms. 10 majors offered by the College of Agriculture & Life Sciences, 3 by the College of Architecture & Urban Studies, 30 by the College of Arts & Sciences, 7 by the College of Business, 14 by the College of Education, 10 by the College of Engineering, and 4 by the College of Human Resources. Minors offered in most major areas. Distributive requirements in some disciplines. Graduate degrees granted. Independent study. Honors program. Phi Beta Kappa. 5-year cooperative work/study in several areas. Limited pass/fail. Preprofessional programs in dentistry, law, medicine, pharmacy, veterinary medicine. Study abroad. Elementary, secondary, and industrial arts education certification. 2- and 4-year ROTC, AFROTC, NROTC; all cadets wear uniforms and live under military discipline. Agricultural Experimental Station. Energy, industrial, water, and environmental research divisions. Computer center. 1,515,169-volume library with microform resources.

Financial CEEB CSS. Institute scholarships, grants, loans, state aid; PELL, SEOG, NDSL, GSL, CWS. Application deadline March 1.

Admissions High school graduation with 18 units required. Audition or portfolio required for art, music, and theatre majors. SAT and 2 ACH required. $10 application fee. Application deadline January 1. $50 room deposit due on acceptance of admissions offer. *Early Decision* and *Early Admission* programs. Transfers accepted. Credit possible for CEEB AP and departmental exams.

Student Life Student government, including civilian and cadet students. Newspaper, literary magazine, yearbook, radio station. Music and drama groups. Debate. Academic, honorary, religious, service, and special interest groups. Single freshmen live at home or on campus. All cadets must live in dorms. Coed and single-sex dorms. 39% of students live on campus. Cars may not be used during class hours. Honor code. 10 intercollegiate sports for men, 5 for women; many intramurals. AIAW, NCAA, MAC. Student body composition: 4% Black, 95% White, 1% Other. 25% from out of state.

WASHINGTON AND LEE UNIVERSITY $$

Lexington 24450, (703) 463-9111, ext. 203
Director of Admissions: William M. Hartog

- **Undergraduates:** 1,356m
- **Tuition (1984–1985):** $6,515
- **Room and Board (1984–1985):** $2,805; **Fees:** $100
- **Degrees offered:** BA, BS
- **Mean SAT:** 555v, 595m
- **Student-faculty ratio:** 10 to 1
- **Calendar system:** 12–12–6

A private men's university with a coed School of Law. Established in 1749. 95-acre small-town campus, 50 miles from Roanoke. Served by bus.

Academic Character SACS and professional accreditation. 12-12-6 system. 41 majors offered in the areas of art, business, classics, drama, East Asian studies, humanities, journalism, languages, mathematics, natural & physical sciences, religion, and social sciences. Courses in 12 additional areas, including Chinese and Japanese. Self-designed majors. African, Latin American, Russian, and urban studies. Distributive requirements. Senior comprehensive exams required in some majors. JD granted. Independent study. Honors programs. Phi Beta Kappa. Limited pass/fail, internships. Preprofessional programs in dentistry, law, medicine, theology, veterinary science. 3-3 law programs. 3-2 engineering programs with Rensselaer, Washington U, Columbia. 3-2 forestry and environmental management programs with Duke. Cross-registration with 6 area schools. Interuniversity Consortium for Political and Social Research. Faculty exchange with Oxford. Exchange programs with Chinese University, Hong Kong, and Rikkyo University, Japan. Extensive study abroad programs. Luce Scholarships for year in East Asia. Secondary education certification. ROTC. Robert E. Lee Research Program. George C. Marshall Research Foundation. Art collection. Computer center. Nuclear science lab. Communications lab. Observatory. TV studio. Language labs. 568,000-volume library with microform resources.

Financial CEEB CSS. University scholarships, grants, loans, payment plans;

PELL, SEOG, NDSL, CWS. Application deadlines February 15 (scholarships), February 29 (loans).

Admissions High school graduation with 16 units required. Interview recommended. SAT and 3 ACH required. $20 application fee. Rolling admissions; application deadline February 15. $250 deposit due on acceptance of admissions offer. *Early Decision* Program. Admission deferral possible. Transfers accepted. Credit possible for CEEB AP and university placement exams.

Student Life Student government. Newspaper, literary magazines, yearbook, radio and TV stations. Music and drama groups. Debate. Religious, professional, and special interest groups. 17 fraternities with houses. 60% of men join. Freshmen not living at home live in dorms. Married-student housing. 40% of students live on campus. Liquor permitted in dorm rooms. Class attendance expected. Honor system. 2 years of phys ed required. 13 intercollegiate sports; many intramurals. NCAA, ODAC. Student body composition: 1% Black, 99% White. 75% from out of state.

WILLIAM AND MARY, COLLEGE OF $/$$

Williamsburg 23185, (804) 253-4000
Dean of Admissions: G. Gary Ripple

- **Undergraduates:** 2,225m, 2,507w
- **Tuition (1984–1985):** $2,000 (in-state), $5,420 (out-of-state)
- **Room and Board (1984–1985):** $2,340-$3,042
- **Degrees offered:** BA, BS
- **Mean SAT:** 577v, 615m
- **Student-faculty ratio:** 15 to 1
- **Calendar system:** Semester

A public college established in 1693. 1,200-acre campus, 40 miles west of Norfolk. Served by air, rail, and bus.

Academic Character SACS and professional accreditation. Semester system, 2 5-week summer terms. 36 majors offered in the areas of anthropology, business administration, classics, computer science, education, fine arts, humanities, mathematics, music, physical education, religion, science, social science, and theatre. Self-designed majors. Minors offered. Courses in Chinese, Portuguese. Distributive requirements. Graduate and professional degrees granted. Independent study. Honors programs. Phi Beta Kappa. Limited pass/fail, internships. Preprofessional programs in dentistry, engineering, medical technology, medicine, public health service, veterinary medicine. 3-2 and 4-2 engineering programs with RPI, Washington, Case Western, and Columbia. 3-2 forestry program with Duke. Study in Europe, the Phillipines. Elementary and secondary education certification. ROTC. Marine Science Institute. Learning Resources Center. Language lab. 717,449-volume library with 1,192,760 manuscripts and documents.

Financial CEEB CSS. College scholarships, grants, loans, state aid, payment plans; PELL, SEOG, NDSL, GSL, CWS. Recommended application deadline between January 1 and February 15.

Admissions High school graduation with strong academic program recommended. Campus visit recommended. SAT required; 3 ACH strongly recommended. $20 application fee. Application deadline January 15. $50 room deposit due on acceptance of admissions offer. *Early Decision, Early Admission, Concurrent Enrollment* programs. Admission deferral possible.

Transfers accepted. Credit possible for CEEB AP and college challenge exams.

Student Life Student assembly organizations. Newspaper, literary magazine, yearbook, radio station. Music, dance, drama, and film groups. Debate. Women's Forum. Academic, political, recreational, religious, service, and special interest groups. 10 fraternities and 10 sororities, all with houses. 33% of men and 36% of women join. Freshmen not living at home live on campus. Coed and single-sex dorms. Language houses. 80% of students live on campus. Upperclassmen may have cars. Hazing prohibited. Honor system. 2 years of phys ed required. 14 intercollegiate sports for men, 14 for women; many intramurals. AIAW, ECAC, NCAA, VFISW. Student body composition: 93% White, 7% Other. 30% from out of state.

Washington

Olympia 98505, (206) 866-6000
Director of Admissions: Arnaldo Rodriguez

- **Undergraduates:** 1,275m, 1,380w
- **Tuition (1984–1985):** $1,017 (in-state), $3,051 (out-of-state)
- **Room and Board (1984–1985):** $2,500
- **Degrees offered:** BA, BS
- **Student-faculty ratio:** 20 to 1
- **Calendar system:** Quarter

A public college established in 1967. 1,000-acre suburban campus on Puget Sound in Olympia, 60 miles from Seattle. Served by air, bus, and rail.
Academic Character NASC accreditation. Quarter system, 2 5-week summer terms. Interdisciplinary specialty areas offered in environmental studies, European & American studies, expressive arts, human development & health, management & the public interest, marine sciences & crafts, northwest Native American studies, political economy, and scientific knowledge & inquiry. Annual programs, basic programs offered. MPA granted. Coordinated studies (large group), group contracts (small group), and individual study. Cooperative work/study, pass/fail, internships. Consortium with U of Puget Sound. Exchange programs with St. Mary's College, Kobe U (Japan). Study abroad in Greece. Elementary and secondary education certification. Computer center, media center, self-paced learning lab. Sailing ship for marine studies. 185,000-volume library with microform resources.
Financial CEEB CSS. College scholarships, grants, loans, state grants, tuition waivers, emergency loans; PELL, SEOG, NDSL, FISL, CWS. Priority application deadline April 15.
Admissions High school graduation required. GED accepted. SAT or ACT recommended. $15 application fee. Rolling admissions; application deadline September 1. $50 tuition deposit and $60 room deposit (for boarders) required on acceptance of offer of admission. *Early Admission* Program. Transfers accepted. Admission deferral possible. Credit possible for CEEB AP and CLEP exams.
Student Life Student government. Newspaper, magazine, radio station. Third World Coalition. Native American Students Association. Women's Center. Special interest centers. Limited college housing. Coed and co-op dorms. Married-student housing. 37% of students live on campus. 5 intercollegiate sports; intramurals. AIAW, NAIA, Club Northwest, Northwest Collegiate Women's Soccer Association, US Swimming Congress, US Wrestling Federation. Student body composition: 1.4% Asian, 3.3% Black, 1% Hispanic, 1.5% Native American, 92.8% White. 20% from out of state.

GONZAGA UNIVERSITY $$

East 502 Boone Avenue, Spokane 99258, (509) 328-4220
Director of Admissions: James T. Mansfield

- **Undergraduates:** 1,184m, 1,123w
- **Tuition (1984–1985):** $5,800
- **Room and Board (1984–1985):** $2,700;   **Fees:** $114
- **Degrees offered:** BS, BA, BSN, BBA, BAEd
- **Mean SAT:** 462v, 486m,   **Mean ACT:** 22
- **Student-faculty ratio:** 14 to 1
- **Calendar system:** Semester

A private university controlled by the Society of Jesus (Jesuits), established in 1887. 75-acre urban campus in residential section of Spokane, 10 minutes from downtown. Served by air, bus, and rail.

Academic Character NASC and professional accreditation. Semester system, 6-week summer term. 33 majors offered by the College of Arts & Sciences, 10 by the School of Business Administration, 4 by the School of Education, and 6 by the School of Engineering. Minors offered in most major fields. Distributives, senior thesis or exam, and 3 religion courses required. Graduate and professional degrees granted. Independent study. Honors program. Limited pass/fail. Internships. Credit by exam. 5-year BS-MBA program in engineering. 3-1 programs in medicine possible. Study abroad. International Student Exchange. Elementary, secondary, and special education certification. ROTC; AFROTC, NROTC at Washington State. Computer center, TV center, language labs. Film library. 300,000-volume library with microform resources.

Financial CEEB CSS. University scholarships, grants, loans, state grants, family plan; PELL, SEOG, NDSL, FISL, payment plans, CWS. Application deadline March 1; FAF deadline March 15.

Admissions High school graduation with 16 units required. SAT or ACT required; Washington Pre-College Test accepted in-state. $15 application fee. Rolling admissions; application deadline August 15. $50 tuition deposit and $50 room deposit (for boarders) required on acceptance of offer of admission. *Concurrent Enrollment* Program. Transfers accepted. Admission deferral possible. Credit possible for CEEB AP and CLEP exams and ACT PEP. New Start Program.

Student Life Student government. Newspaper, magazine, yearbook. Music, debate, drama groups. Honorary, service, academic, and special interest groups. Seniors may live off campus. Coed and single-sex dorms. 75% of students live on campus. Attendance in class required. 7 intercollegiate sports for men, 4 for women; intramural and club sports. AIAW, NCAA, WCAC. Student body composition: 2% Asian, 1% Black, 1% Hispanic, 1% Native American, 84% White, 11% Other. 76% from out of state.

PACIFIC LUTHERAN UNIVERSITY $$

PO Box 2068, Tacoma 98447, (206) 531-6900
Dean of Admissions and Financial Aid: James Van Beek

- **Undergraduates:** 1,228m, 1,657w
- **Tuition (1984–1985):** $5,950
- **Room and Board (1984–1985):** $2,815
- **Degrees offered:** BA, BS, BAEd, BBA, BFA, BMus, BSN
- **Mean SAT:** 501v, 527m
- **Student-faculty ratio:** 14 to 1
- **Calendar system:** 4–1–4

A private university affiliated with the American Lutheran Church, established in 1890. 130-acre suburban campus in Parkland, 7 miles from Tacoma center. Served by air, bus, and rail.

Academic Character NASC and professional accreditation. 4-1-4 system, 2 4½-week summer terms. 29 majors offered by the College of Arts & Sciences, 3 by the School of the Arts, 5 by the School of Business Administration, 22 by the School of Education, 1 by the School of Nursing, and 3 by the School of Physical Education. Self-designed majors. Minors in several major fields and in 7 additional areas. Distributives and 8 hours of religious studies required. MA, MBA granted. Independent study. Honors program. Cooperative work/study, limited pass/fail, internships. Credit by exam. Preprofessional programs in allied health, dentistry, engineering, law, medicine, pharmacy, theology. 3-1 medical technology program. 3-2 engineering programs with Columbia, Stanford. 3-1, 3-2 programs in applied math, computer science, software. Study abroad. Elementary, secondary, and special education certification. AFROTC at U of Puget Sound. Language labs. 265,000-volume library with microform resources.

Financial CEEB CSS. University scholarships, grants, loans, ministers' dependent grants; PELL, SEOG, NSS, NDSL, GSL, NSL, monthly payment plan, CWS, state work program. Application deadlines March 1 (scholarships), February 1 (FAF, loans).

Admissions High school graduation required with 15 units recommended. Interview encouraged. Washington Pre-College Test (in-state), SAT, or ACT required. $25 application fee. Rolling admissions after December 1; suggest applying after October 1. $100 deposit required on acceptance of offer of admission. *Early Decision, Early Admission, Concurrent Enrollment* programs. Transfers accepted. Admission deferral possible. Credit possible for CEEB AP and CLEP exams; university has own advanced placement program.

Student Life Student government. Newspaper, yearbook, radio and TV stations. Music, debate, drama groups. Political, service, academic, honorary, religious, and special interest groups. Single underclassmen under 22 must live at home or on campus. Coed and single-sex dorms. Married-student housing. 65% of students live on campus. Liquor, gambling prohibited. Attendance in class required. Freshmen and sophomores must take 4 semesters of phys ed. 12 intercollegiate sports for men, 4 for women; intramurals. AIAW, PNIAC, WCIC. Student body composition: 2% Asian, 2% Black, 1% Hispanic, 1% Native American, 94% White. 38% from out of state.

WASHINGTON, UNIVERSITY OF $

1400 Northeast Campus Way, Seattle 98195, (206) 543-9686
Director of Admissions and Records: Wilbur Washburn

- **Undergraduates:** 12,257m, 11,272w
- **Tuition (1984–1985):** $1,302 (in-state), $3,618 (out-of-state)
- **Room and Board (1984–1985):** $2,600
- **Degrees offered:** BA, BS, BFA, BBA, BLandArch, BSA&A, BSBC, BSCerE, BSChE, BSEE, BSCE, BSE, BSFish, BSIE, BSME, BSMedTech, BSF, BSMetE, BMus, BSN, BSPharm, BSOcc Therapy, BSPhys Therapy
- **Mean SAT:** 497v, 566m, **Mean ACT:** 24.4
- **Student-faculty ratio:** 14 to 1
- **Calendar system:** Quarter

A public university established in 1861. 680-acre urban campus in residential area of Seattle. Served by air, bus, and rail.

Academic Character NASC and professional accreditation. Quarter system, 2 part summer term of 9 weeks. 4 majors offered by the College of Architecture & Urban Planning, 69 by the College of Arts & Sciences, 7 by the College of Education, 11 by the College of Engineering, 14 by the College of Fisheries, 8 by the Collge of Forest Resources, 4 by the School of Business Administration, 1 by the School of Dentistry, 4 by the School of Medicine, 3 by the School of Nursing, 2 by the School of Pharmacy, 5 by School of Public Health & Community Medicine, and 1 by the School of Social Work. Self-designed majors. Distributive requirements. Graduate and professional degrees granted. Independent study. Honors program. Phi Beta Kappa. Cooperative work/study, pass/fail, internships. Several preprofessional programs. Study abroad. Elementary, secondary, and special education certification. ROTC, AFROTC, NROTC. Center for Tibetan Studies, Asian Arts. Marine science labs. Computer center, language lab, arboretum. 3,877,238-volume library with microform resources.

Financial CEEB CSS. University scholarships, loans; PELL, SEOG, NDSL, FISL, CWS, state work program. Application deadline March 1.

Admissions High school graduation with 16 units required. Audition required for dance, music majors. SAT, ACT, or WPCT required. $15 application fee. Rolling admissions beginning in January; application deadline May 1. $50 deposit required on acceptance of offer of admission. *Early Admission, Early Decision* programs. Transfers accepted. Credit possible for CEEB AP exams. Educational Opportunity Program.

Student Life Student government. Newspaper, magazine, yearbook, radio and TV stations. Music, debate, drama groups. Special interest organizations. 26 fraternities and 19 sororities; all have houses. Coed dorms. Ethnic and religious housing. Limited married-student housing. 12% of students live on campus. Cars on campus discouraged. Several intercollegiate and intramural sports for men and women. AIAW, NCAA, Athletic Association of Western Universities. Student body composition: 16% Asian, 5% Black, 2% Hispanic, 2% Native American, 75% White. 12% of students from out of state.

WASHINGTON STATE UNIVERSITY $

Pullman 99164, (509) 335-5586
Director of Admissions: Stan Berry

- **Undergraduates:** 8,418m, 6,132w
- **Tuition (1984–1985):** $1,308 (in-state), $3,624 (out-of-state)
- **Room and Board (1984–1985):** $2,425
- **Degrees offered:** BA, BS, BAcc, BArch, BLA, BMus, BPha, BSAgr
- **Student-faculty ratio:** 15 to 1
- **Calendar system:** Semester

A public university established in 1890. 339-acre campus located in small town of Pullman, 80 miles south of Spokane. Served by plane.

Academic Character NASC and professional accreditation. Semester system, 6- and 8-week summer terms. 17 majors offered by the College of Agriculture, 3 by the College of Business & Economics, 6 by the College of Education, 11 by the College of Engineering, 6 by the College of Home Economics, 1 by the College of Pharmacy, 53 by the College of Sciences &

Arts, and 1 by the Center for Nursing. Distributive requirements. Graduate and professional degrees granted. Independent study. Honors program. Phi Beta Kappa. Cooperative work/study, pass/fail, internships. Preprofessional programs in dentistry, law, medicine. Transfer program in veterinary medicine. 3-1 programs possible. Cross-registration with U of Idaho (agriculture), Eastern Washington U and Whitworth (nursing). Study abroad in several countries. Elementary, secondary, and special education certification. AFROTC, ROTC; NROTC at WSU and U Idaho. Audio-visual center, nuclear reactor, observatory, computer center, language lab, electron microscope center. 1,265,979-volume library with microform resources.

Financial CEEB CSS. University scholarships, grants, loans, health profession loans; PELL, SEOG, NSS, NDSL, FISL, CWS. Application deadlines April 1 (scholarships), June 1 (NDSL).

Admissions High school graduation with 16 units required. WPCT and SAT or ACT required. $15 application fee. Rolling admissions; preferred application deadline May 1. $50 deposit required on acceptance of offer of admission. Transfers accepted. Credit possible for CEEB AP and CLEP exams.

Student Life Student government. Newspaper, magazine, yearbook, radio and TV stations. Music, debate, and drama groups. Academic, honorary, religious, service, and special interest groups. 24 fraternities and 15 sororities; all have houses. 28% of men and 20% of women join. Single freshmen must live at home or on campus. Coed and single-sex dorms. Special interest housing. Married-student housing. 70% of students live on campus. Several intercollegiate and intramural sports for men and women. AAWU, AIAW, PCC (PAC-10). Student body composition: 3% Asian, 2% Black, 1% Hispanic, 1% Native American, 93% White. 16% of students from out of state.

WHITMAN COLLEGE $$

Walla Walla 99362, (509) 527-5176
Director of Admissions: William D. Tingley

- **Undergraduates:** 639m, 582w
- **Tuition (1984–1985):** $6,830
- **Room and Board (1984–1985):** $2,920
- **Degrees offered:** BA
- **Mean SAT:** 550v, 600m
- **Student-faculty ratio:** 13 to 1
- **Calendar system:** Semester

A private college established in 1859. 45-acre campus located in small city of Walla Walla in the southeastern corner of the state, 235 miles from Portland, Oregon. Served by air and bus.

Academic Character NASC and professional accreditation. Semester system. Majors offered in art, biology, chemistry, dramatic arts, economics, English, foreign languages/literatures, geology, history, mathematics/computer science, music, philosophy, physics, political science, psychology, and sociology. Self-designed majors, interdepartmental majors. Minors offered in most major fields. Distributives and comprehensive exams required. Independent study. Honors program. Phi Beta Kappa. Pass/D/Fail. Internships. Credit by exam. Preprofessional programs in business management, dentistry, engineering, journalism, law, medical technology, medicine, ministry, public service, social work, and others. 3-2 programs in engineering with Caltech and Columbia, in forestry with Duke. 3-3 law program with Columbia. Cooperative science program with Battelle Northwest Labs. Washington, urban semesters. Study abroad. Elementary and secondary education certification. Computer center, language labs. 300,000-volume library.

Financial CEEB CSS and ACT FAS. College scholarships, grants, loans, state grants; PELL, SEOG, NDSL, GSL, Education Funds, Insured Tuition Payment Plan, CWS, state work program. FAF deadline February 15.

Admissions High school graduation with 16 units required. Interview encouraged. SAT, ACT, or WPCT required. $20 application fee. Application deadline March 1. $100 deposit required on acceptance of offer of admission. *Early Decision, Early Admission* programs. Transfers accepted. Admission deferral possible. Credit possible for CEEB AP exams.

Student Life Student government. Newspaper, magazine, yearbook, radio station. Music, drama, debate groups. Cultural activities. Honorary, academic, and special interest groups. 5 fraternities with houses and 5 sororities with section of dorms. 50% of students join. Freshmen and sophomores under 21 must live on campus. Coed and single-sex dorms. Foreign language, ethnic, and other special interest houses. No married-student housing. 80% of students live on campus. Liquor and drugs prohibited. 10 intercollegiate sports for men, 9 for women; intramural and club sports. AIAW, NAIA, NCWSA, Northwest Conference. Student body composition: 5% Asian, 2% Black, 1% Hispanic, 1% Native American, 91% White. 50% from out of state.

West Virginia

BETHANY COLLEGE $$

Bethany 26032, (304) 829-7000
Director of Admissions: David Wottle

- **Undergraduates:** 425m, 350w
- **Tuition (1984–1985):** $6,570
- **Room and Board (1984–1985):** $2,330;   **Fees:** $300
- **Degrees offered:** BA, BS
- **Mean SAT:** 470v, 500m;   **Mean ACT:** 20.8
- **Student-faculty ratio:** 11 to 1
- **Calendar system:** 4–1–4

A private college affiliated with the Christian Church (Disciples of Christ), established in 1840. 300-acre campus in the village of Bethany, 25 minutes from Wheeling. Airport 55 minutes away in Pittsburgh.

Academic Character NCACS and professional accreditation. Modified semester system, 2 5-week summer terms. Majors offered in art, biology, chemistry, communications, computer science, economics-business, elementary education, English, fine arts, foreign languages, health science, history-political science, mathematics, music, philosophy, physical education, physics, psychology, religious studies, secondary education, social work, sociology, and theatre. Distributives, one religion course, 4 practicums, senior project, UGRE required. Independent study. Honors program. Preprofessional programs in dentistry, engineering, law, medicine, ministry, professional chemistry. Cooperative engineering programs with Columbia, Georgia Tech, Case Western, Washington U (MO). Consortium with Heidelberg, Westminster, Hiram, Muskingham. Washington, UN, Merrill-Palmer semesters. Several programs for study abroad. Elementary and secondary education certification. Language lab, media center. 143,000-volume library with microform resources.

Financial CEEB CSS. College scholarships, grants, loans, payment plan; PELL, SEOG, NDSL, CWS. Application deadline March 15.

Admissions High school graduation with 15 units required. Interview encouraged. SAT or ACT required. $15 application fee. Rolling admissions November through May; suggest applying early in fall. $100 deposit required on acceptance of offer of admission. *Early Admission* Program. Admission deferral possible. Transfers accepted. Credit possible for CEEB AP and CLEP exams; college has own advanced placement program. Programs for learning disabled students.

Student Life Student government. Newspaper, magazines, yearbook, radio and cable TV stations. Music, debate, drama groups. International Relations Club. Academic, religious, honorary, and special interest organizations. 7 fraternities with houses and 4 sororities with suites or houses. 56% of men and 58% of women join. Students must live at home or on campus. Single-sex dorms. Married-student housing. 99% of students live on campus. Freshmen may not have cars on campus. 10 intercollegiate sports for men, 6 for women; intramurals. NCAA, AIAW, PAC. Student body composition: 2% Black, 0.5% Hispanic, 0.5% Native American, 97% White. 84% from out of state.

SALEM COLLEGE $

Salem 26426, (304) 782-5011
Director of Admissions: Stephen Ornstein

- **Undergraduates:** 400m, 350w
- **Tuition (1984-1985):** $4,023
- **Room and Board (1984-1985):** $2,400; **Fees:** $200
- **Degrees offered:** BA, BS, AA, AS
- **Mean SAT:** 400v, 450m, **Mean ACT:** 18
- **Student-faculty ratio:** 12 to 1
- **Calendar system:** Semester

A private college established in 1888. 150-acre small-town campus, 12 miles from Clarksburg. Air, bus, and rail in Clarksburg.
Academic Character NCACS accreditation. Semester system, 2 5-week summer terms. 36 majors offered in the areas of business, art, therapy, sciences, communications, aviation, criminal justice, education, engineering, equestrian studies, humanities, medicine, mining technology, physical education, and political & social sciences. Minors offered in most major fields and in arts with handicapped, music, real estate. Distributive requirements. Internships. Clergy Development Program. Career aviation with Aero-Mech, Inc. Mining technology with National Mine Health and Safety Academy. Elementary, secondary, and special education certification. ROTC. Museum of West Virginia culture. 140,000-volume library.
Financial CEEB CSS. College scholarships, grants, and loans, state grants, payment plans; PELL, SEOG, NSS, NDSL, GSL, NSL, CWS, college has own work program. Preferred application deadline April 15; deadline for state grants March 1.
Admissions High school graduation with 16 units required. GED accepted. Campus visit encouraged. ACT or SAT required. $10 application fee. Rolling admissions; suggest applying 1st semester of 12th year. $100 deposit required on acceptance of offer of admission. *Early Decision, Early Admission, Concurrent Enrollment* programs. Admission deferral possible. Transfers accepted. Credit possible for CEEB AP and CLEP exams. Special acceptance and development program.
Student Life Newspaper, yearbook. Music, debate, drama groups. Foster grandparent program. Political, academic, and special interest groups. 6 fraternities and 2 sororities. 35% of men and 20% of women join. Seniors, veterans, and married students may live off campus. Coed and single-sex dorms. No married-student housing. 80% of students live on campus. 7 intercollegiate sports for men, 5 for women; intramurals. MAIAW, NAIA, WVIAC. Student body composition: 9% Black, 1% Hispanic, 90% White. 75% from out of state.

WEST VIRGINIA UNIVERSITY $

Morgantown 26506, (304) 293-0111
Dean of Admissions & Records: John D. Brisbane

- **Undergraduates:** 7,928m, 6,013w
- **Tuition (1984–1985):** $1,160 (in-state), $3,140 (out-of-state)
- **Room and Board (1984–1985):** $2,873

- **Degrees offered:** BA, BS, BSF, BS/BSAgr, BSAgr, BSLA, BSR, BSBA, BMus, BFA, BSEnr in 6 areas, BSEEd, BSFamRes, BSSEd, BSJ, BSEM, BSPetE, BSN, BSPharm, BSPEd, BSW
- **Mean ACT:** 19.5
- **Student-faculty ratio:** 12 to 1
- **Calendar system:** Semester

A public university established in 1867. 74-acre main campus and 725-acre Evansdale campus in Morgantown, 72 miles from Pittsburgh. Served by air and bus.

Academic Character NCACS and professional accreditation. Semester system, 2 6-week summer terms. 9 majors offered by the College of Agriculture & Forestry, 19 by the College of Arts & Sciences, 5 by the College of Business & Economics, 4 by the Creative Arts Center, 1 by the School of Dentistry, 6 by the College of Engineering, 4 by the College of Human Resources & Education, 1 each by the schools of Journalism, Nursing, Pharmacy, Social Work, 3 by the College of Mineral & Energy Resources, 2 by the School of Medicine, and 2 by the School of Physical Education. Graduate and professional degrees granted. Honors program. Credit by exam. Elementary and secondary education certification. ROTC, AFROTC. Experimental farms. 961,828-volume library with microform resources.

Financial CEEB CSS. University scholarships and loans, athletic scholarships; PELL, SEOG, NDSL. Application deadlines January 15 (freshman scholarships), April 1 (loans).

Admissions High school graduation with 10 units required. GED accepted. ACT required. Rolling admissions. *Early Decision* and *Early Admission* programs. Admission deferral possible. Transfers accepted. Credit possible for CEEB AP and CLEP exams; university has own advanced placement program.

Student Life Student government. Newspaper, yearbook, TV station. Music, speaking, drama groups. Several honorary, academic, service, and special interest organizations. 20 fraternities and 11 sororities, all with houses. Freshmen must live at home or on campus. 3 dorms for men, 6 for women. Privately-owned dorms also available. Married-student housing. 24% of students live on campus. Liquor prohibited on campus. 1 year of phys ed required. 12 intercollegiate sports for men, 6 for women; intramurals. AIAW. Student body composition: 0.1% Asian, 2% Black, 0.1% Hispanic, 96.4% White, 1.4% Other. 35% from out of state.

WEST VIRGINIA WESLEYAN COLLEGE $

Buckhannon 26201, (304) 473-7011
Director of Admissions: Wenrich H. Green

- **Undergraduates:** 639m, 858w
- **Tuition (1984–1985):** $4,380
- **Room and Board (1984–1985):** $2,682;   **Fees:** $470
- **Degrees offered:** BA, BS, BSME, AA
- **Mean SAT:** 450v, 450m,   **Mean ACT:** 21
- **Student-faculty ratio:** 15 to 1
- **Calendar system:** 4–1–4

A private college affiliated with the United Methodist Church, established in 1890. 80-acre small-town campus, 25 miles from Clarksburg. Airport and rail station in Clarksburg.

Academic Character NCACS and professional accreditation. 4-1-4 system, 3 4-week and 2 6-week summer terms. 43 majors offered in the areas of arts, sciences, education, religion & philosophy, business & economics, humanities, political science, health, social science, communication, library science, and fashion merchandising. Major/minor or double major required. Distributives and one religion course required. MAT granted. Independent study. Honors program. Cooperative work/study, pass/fail, internships. Credit by exam. Preprofessional programs in business administration, chemistry, church assistance, dentistry, dietetics, law, medical technology, medicine, ministry, occupational therapy, optometry, pharmacy, physical therapy, religious education, social work. 3-2 and 4-1 engineering programs with U of Pennsylvania. 3-2 engineering program with U of Pittsburgh. 3-2½ forestry program with Duke. 4-college consortium. Cross-registration at College of Boca Raton. Merrill-Palmer semester. Study abroad. Early childhood, elementary, secondary, and special education certification. Language lab. 157,500-volume library.

Financial CEEB CSS and ACT FAS. College scholarships, grants, and loans, Methodist scholarships, ministers' dependents aid, payment plans; PELL, SEOG, NDSL, GSL, NSL, CWS. Application deadlines March 1 (scholarships), April 15 (loans).

Admissions High school graduation with 16 units required. Interview encouraged. ACT or SAT required. $25 application fee. Rolling admissions; suggest applying before May 1. $50 deposit required on acceptance of offer of admission. *Early Decision* and *Early Admission* programs. Admission deferral possible. Transfers accepted in January. Credit possible for CEEB AP and CLEP exams.

Student Life Student government. Newspaper, magazine, yearbook, radio station. Music, drama, debate groups. Academic, honorary, political, religious, service, and special interest organizations. 5 fraternities with houses and 4 sororities without houses. 32% of men and 35% of women join. Juniors and seniors may live off campus. Single-sex dorms. 94% of students live on campus. Class attendance required. 4 semester hours of phys ed required. 9 intercollegiate sports for men, 5 for women; intramural and club sports. AIAW, NAIA, NCAA, WVIAC. Student body composition: 2% Black, 98% White. 70% from out of state.

Wisconsin

ALVERNO COLLEGE $

3401 South 39 Street, Milwaukee 53215, (414) 647-5400
Director of Admissions: Stephanie Chapko

- **Undergraduates:** 1,425w
- **Tuition (1984–1985):** $2,362
- **Room and Board (1984–1985):** $1,900
- **Degrees offered:** BA, BS, BMus, BSEd, BSMed Tech, BSN, AA
- **Mean SAT:** 400v, **Mean ACT:** 18+
- **Student-faculty ratio:** 16 to 1
- **Calendar system:** Semester

A private women's college affiliated with the School Sisters of St. Francis, organized in 1887. 50-acre wooded campus in residential environment 15 minutes from downtown Milwaukee. Served by air, bus, and rail.
Academic Character NCACS and professional accreditation. Semester system, 2 4-week summer terms. Majors offered in art, art therapy, biology, chemistry, communications, education, English, history, management, mathematics, medical technology, music, nuclear medical technology, nursing, psychology, and religious studies. Support areas required; offered in most major fields and in 8 additional areas. Weekend College grants baccalaureate degrees in management, professional communications, and nursing (for RNs), and associate degree in liberal studies. Independent study. No grades; competence to be shown. Internships. Preprofessional programs in dentistry, law, medicine, veterinary medicine. 3-2 program in engineering with Milwaukee School of Engineering. Early childhood, elementary, secondary education certification. Campus elementary school, Child Development Center, Language lab. 192,089-volume library.
Financial CEEB CSS. College scholarships and grants, music scholarships; PELL, SEOG, NSS, NDSL, NSL, deferred payment, CWS; college has own work program. Suggested application deadline for scholarships March 1.
Admissions High school graduation with 10-12 units required. Audition and exam required for music majors and minors. ACT or SAT required. $10 application. Rolling admissions; suggest applying in 1st semester. $50 tuition deposit and $50 room deposit required on acceptance of offer of admission. *Early Decision* Program. Transfers accepted. Admission deferral possible. Credit possible for CLEP exams.
Student Life Student government. Newspaper. Music and drama groups. Research Center on Women. Academic, honorary, and special interest groups. 27% of full-time students live on campus. Individual sports. Student body composition: 4% Black, 1% Hispanic, 93% White, 2% Other.

BELOIT COLLEGE $$

Beloit 53511, (608) 365-3391
Director of Admissions: John W. Lind

- **Undergraduates:** 572m, 514w
- **Tuition (1984–1985):** $7,300

- **Room and Board (1984–1985): $2,344; Fees: $142**
- **Degrees offered:** BA, BS
- **Mean SAT:** 540v, 550m, **Mean ACT:** 25
- **Student-faculty ratio:** 12 to 1
- **Calendar system:** Semester

A private college established in 1846. 65-acre campus located in small city of Beloit, 50 miles from Madison and 100 miles northwest of Chicago. Served by air and bus.

Academic Character NCACS accreditation. Semester system. Majors offered in anthropology, art, biochemistry, biology, biology-medical technology, business administration, chemistry, classical civilization, classical philology, comparative literature, economics, economics/management, English composition, English literature, French, geology, German, government, history, international relations, mathematics, mathematics/computer science, modern languages, music, performing arts, philosophy, physics, psychology, religious studies, science for elementary teaching, sociology, Spanish, and theatre arts. Self-designed and interdepartmental majors. Distributive requirements. Independent and accelerated study. Honors program. Phi Beta Kappa. Pass/fail, internships. 3-2 programs in social work with U of Chicago, in engineering with Columbia and Georgia Tech, in forestry with Duke. 4-2 engineering program with Duke. 2-2 medical technology, nursing programs with Rush U. Study abroad. Washington, urban, Argonne semesters. Wilderness field program. Elementary and secondary education certification. Computer center, language lab, observatory. Limnology lab, social science lab. 250,000-volume library with microform resources.

Financial CEEB CSS. College scholarships, grants, loans, PELL, SEOG, NDSL, GSL, CWS. Application deadline March 1.

Admissions High school graduation with 16 units required. Interview encouraged. SAT or ACT required. $20 application fee. Rolling admissions in February–March. $100 deposit required on acceptance of offer of admission. *Early Admission* Program. Transfers accepted. Admission deferral possible. Credit possible for CEEB AP and CLEP exams.

Student Life Student government. Newspaper, magazine, yearbook, radio station. Music and drama organizations. Religious, political, and special interest groups. 4 fraternities and 2 sororities; most have houses. Seniors may live off campus. Coed and single-sex dorms. Language, special interest housing. Co-op dorms. 89% of students live on campus. 8 intercollegiate sports for men, 8 for women; intramural and club sports. NCAA, AIAW, MCAC. Student body composition: 1% Asian, 2% Black, 1% Hispanic, 93% White, 3% Other. 82% from out of state.

CARTHAGE COLLEGE $

Kenosha 53140, (414) 551-8531
Director of Admissions and Financial Aid: Kent Duesing

- **Undergraduates:** 607m, 751w
- **Tuition (1984–1985): $5,425**
- **Room and Board (1984–1985): $2,260; Fees: $120**
- **Degrees offered:** BA
- **Mean Act:** 23

- **Student-faculty ratio:** 14 to 1
- **Calender system:** 4-1-4

A private college affiliated with the Lutheran Church in America, established in 1847. 85-acre campus in city of Kenosha, 35 miles from Milwaukee. Served by air, bus, and rail.

Academic Character NCACS and professional accreditation. 4-1-4 system, summer terms. 42 majors offered by the divisions of Business & Economics, Teacher Education, Fine Arts, Humanities, Science & Mathematics, and Social Sciences. Self-designed majors. Distributives and 2 courses in religion required. Independent study. Honors program. Pass/fail, internships. Credit by exam. Preprofessional programs in dentistry, engineering, government, law, library science, medical technology, medicine, nursing, social service, theology, others. 3-2 engineering programs with Washington U, Case Western Reserve. 3-1, 4-1 medical technology programs. Study abroad. January studies in Mexico. Milwaukee Urban Semester. Elementary, secondary, and special education certification. Language lab. 208,539-volume library.

Financial CEEB CSS. College scholarships, grants, loans, state grants, Lutheran loans; PELL, SEOG, NDSL, GSL, Tuition Plan, CWS. Application deadlines February 15 (FAF), May 1 (loans).

Admissions High school graduation with 14 units required. GED accepted. ACT or SAT required; ACT preferred. $15 application fee. Rolling admissions; suggest applying early in 12th year. $200 deposit required on acceptance of offer of admission. *Early Admission, Early Decision* programs. Transfers accepted. Admission deferral possible. Credit possible for CEEB AP and CLEP exams.

Student Life Student government. Newspaper, magazine, yearbook. Music, debate, drama groups. Service, honorary, academic, professional, and special interest groups. 5 fraternities and 4 sororities; none have houses. 30% of men and 35% of women join. Single students must live at home or on campus. Coed and single-sex dorms. 93% of students live on campus. Liquor allowed only in dorms. Attendance required at half of chapel services and convocations. 2 phys ed courses required. 9 intercollegiate sports for men, 6 for women; intramurals. NCAA, CCIW, Chicago Metro Conference for Women. Student body composition: 4% Black, 1% Hispanic, 95% White. 55% from out of state.

LAWRENCE UNIVERSITY $$

Appleton 54912, (414) 735-6500
Director of Admissions: David E. Busse

- **Undergraduates:** 524m, 542w
- **Tuition (1984–1985):** $7,716
- **Room and Board (1984–1985):** $2,334
- **Degrees offered:** BA, BMus
- **Mean SAT:** 524v, 560m, **Mean ACT:** 25
- **Student-faculty ratio:** 10 to 1
- **Calendar system:** 3–3

A private university established in 1847. 72-acre campus on Fox River in small city of Appleton, 100 miles from Milwaukee. Served by air and bus.

Academic Character NCACS and professional accreditation. Trimester system. Majors offered in anthropology, art, biology, chemistry, classics, economics, English, French, geology, German, government, history, mathematics, music, philosophy, physics, psychology, religion, Slavic, sociology/anthropology, Spanish, and theatre-drama. Interdisciplinary majors. Distributive requirements. Independent study. Phi Beta Kappa. Pass/fail. Preprofessional programs in dentistry, law, medicine, business. 3-2 programs in engineering with Columbia, Washington U, Rensselaer, others, in health sciences with Rush Medical Center, in social services administration with U of Chicago, in forestry with Duke. 2-2 health science program. Associated Colleges of the Midwest consortium. Study abroad. Washington, Oak Ridge, urban semesters. Marine biology seminar. Elementary and secondary education certification. Wilderness field station. 325-acre estate in Door County. 230,000-volume library with microform resources.

Financial CEEB CSS. University scholarships, grants, loans, state grants; PELL, SEOG, NDSL, GSL, deferred payment, CWS. Suggested scholarship application deadline March 15.

Admissions High school graduation with 16 units recommended. Interview encouraged. Audition required for music majors. SAT or ACT required. $15 application fee. Rolling admissions after mid-January; suggest applying by March 15. Early Admission Program. Transfers accepted. Admission deferral possible. Credit possible for CEEB AP exams; university has own advanced placement program.

Student Life Student-faculty government. Newspaper, magazine, radio station. Music, drama groups. Honorary, service, and city-based organizations. 6 fraternities with houses and 4 sororities with rooms. 32% of students join. Students must live at home or on campus. Coed dorms. Some married-student housing. 98% of students live on campus. 3 terms of phys ed required. 11 intercollegiate sports for men, 10 for women; intramural and club sports. Midwest Conference. Student body composition: 1% Asian, 1.5% Black, 0.5% Hispanic, 0.2% Native American, 96% White. 54% from out of state.

MARQUETTE UNIVERSITY $$

1217 West Wisconsin Avenue, Milwaukee 53233, (414) 224-7302
Director of Admissions: Leo B. Flynn

- **Undergraduates:** 4,913m, 4,208w
- **Tuition (1984–1985):** $5,200
- **Room and Board (1984–1985):** $3,465; **Fees:** $26
- **Degrees offered:** BA, BS
- **Mean SAT:** 479v, 538m, **Mean ACT:** 23.9
- **Student-faculty ratio:** 15 to 1
- **Calendar system:** Semester

A private university conducted by the Society of Jesus (Jesuits), established in 1881. 64-acre urban campus in Milwaukee. Served by air and rail.
Academic Character NCACS and professional accreditation. Semester system, 2 6-week summer terms. Majors offered in accounting, anthropology, biology, biomedical engineering, business administration, business economics, chemistry, civil engineering, computer science, dental hygiene, economics, electrical engineering, English, foreign languages & literature, history, journalism, law enforcement, mathematics, mechanical engineering, medical technology, nursing, philosophy, physical therapy, physics, political science, psychology, social studies, social work, sociology, speech, and theology. Self-designed majors. Minors offered in all major fields and in 9

additiona⌐ ⌐eas Distributives and theology courses required. Graduate and professional degrees granted. Independent study. Honors program. Phi Beta Kappa Cooperative work/study, internships. Preprofessional programs in dentistry, law, medicine. Study abroad. Elementary and secondary education certification. ROTC. NROTC. Computer center. 700,000-volume library with microform resources.

Financial CEEB CSS. University scholarships, family discounts, state and nursing grants; PELL, SEOG, NSL, NDSL, FISL, HELP, ALAS, deferred payment, CWS. Preferred application deadline (loans) March 1.

Admissions High school graduation with 16 units recommended. Interview encouraged. SAT or ACT required. $15 application fee. Rolling admissions; suggest applying between October 1 and March 15. $50 deposit required on acceptance of offer of admission. Transfers accepted. Credit possible for CEEB AP and CLEP exams. Educational Opportunity Program.

Student Life Student government. Newspaper, magazine, yearbook. Music and drama groups. Over 200 religious, honorary, academic, and special interest groups. 8 fraternities and 5 sororities. Freshmen and sophomores must live on campus. Coed and single-sex dorms. Some married-student housing. 65% of students live on campus. 8 intercollegiate sports for men, 5 for women; intramurals. AIAW, NCA, WWIAC. Student body composition: 2% Asian, 5% Black, 2% Hispanic, 0.4% Native American, 90.6% White. 50% from out of state.

RIPON COLLEGE $$

Ripon 54971, (414) 748-8102, (800) 558-0248 (from out-of-state)
Dean of Admissions: John Corso

- **Undergraduates:** 510m, 390w
- **Tuition (1984–1985):** $7,294
- **Room and Board (1984–1985):** $2,100; **Fees:** $100
- **Degrees offered:** BA
- **Mean SAT:** 510v, 540m, **Mean ACT:** 24
- **Student-faculty ratio:** 12 to 1
- **Calendar system:** Semester

A private college established in 1851. 250-acre campus in small town of Ripon, 80 miles from Milwaukee. Served by bus; airport 19 miles away in Oshkosh.

Academic Character NCACS accreditation. Semester system. Majors offered in anthropology, art, biology, business, chemistry, chemistry/biology, drama, economics, English, German, history, Latin American studies, mathematics, music, philosophy, physical education, physics, political science, psychobiology, psychology, religion, Romance languages, sociology/anthropology, and speech. Self-designed majors. Distributive requirements. Independent study. Phi Beta Kappa. Pass/fail, internships. 3-1 programs with professional schools. 3-2 engineering programs with Rensselaer, USC, Washington U. 3-2 forestry and environmental science program with Duke. 3-2 social welfare program with U of Chicago. Member Associated Colleges of the Midwest. Study abroad. Washington, urban semesters. Newberry Library seminars. Elementary, secondary and special education certification. ROTC. Computer center, language labs. 118,000-volume library with microform resources.

Financial CEEB CSS. College scholarships, state scholarships, grants, and loans; PELL, SEOG, NDSL, deferred payment, CWS. Scholarship application deadline March 1.

Admissions High school graduation with 15 units required. Interview encouraged. SAT or ACT recommended. $15 application fee. Rolling admissions. $100 deposit required on acceptance of offer of admission. *Early Admission* Program. Transfers accepted. Admission deferral possible. Credit possible for CEEB AP and ACH scores.

Student Life Student government. Newspaper, magazine, yearbook, journal, radio station. Music, debate groups. Theatre. Academic, honorary, professional, religious, service, and special interest groups. 8 fraternities and 3 sororities; none have houses. 30% of men and 20% of women join. Students must live at home or on campus. Coed and single-sex dorms. 95% of students live on campus. 2 semesters of phys ed required. 10 intercollegiate sports for men, 5 for women; intramurals. AIAW, Midwest Conference. Student body composition: 1% Asian, 2% Black, 1% Hispanic, 96% White. 51% of students from out of state.

WISCONSIN, UNIVERSITY OF, MADISON $

140 Peterson Building, 750 University Avenue, Madison 54408, (608) 262-3961
Director of Admissions: David E. Vinson

- **Undergraduates:** 15,536m, 13,732w
- **Tuition (1984–1985):** $1,279 (in-state), $4,191 (out-of-state)
- **Room and Board (1984–1985):** $2,230
- **Degrees offered:** BA, BS, BBA, BMus, BSN
- **Mean SAT:** 504v, 579m,   **Mean ACT:** 24.1
- **Student-faculty ratio:** 18 to 1
- **Calendar system:** Semester

A public university established in 1848. 906-acre urban campus in Madison. Served by air and bus.

Academic Character NCACS and professional accreditation. Semester system, several summer terms. 30 majors offered by the College of Agricultural and Life Sciences, 9 by the College of Engineering, 69 by the College of Letters and Sciences, 4 by the School of Allied Health Professions, 11 by the School of Business, 9 by the School of Education, 16 by the School of Family Resources/Consumer Sciences, and 1 each by the Schools of Nursing and Pharmacy. Self-designed majors. Distributive requirements. Graduate and professional degrees granted. Independent study. Honors program. Phi Beta Kappa. Cooperative work/study, pass/fail, internships. Preprofessional programs in allied health fields, behavioral disabilities, elementary education, engineering, journalism, landscape architecture, secondary education, veterinary medicine, business, pharmacy. Transfer programs with Schools of Business, Pharmacy, Medicine, Law. Study abroad. Elementary, secondary, and special education certification. ROTC, AFROTC, NROTC. 3,600,000-volume library with microform resources.

Financial University grants, loans, scholarships, state grants and loans, pharmacy and nursing loans; PELL, SEOG, NDSL, GSL, PLUS, CWS. Priority application deadline March 1.

Admissions High school graduation with 16 units required. Audition required for music majors. $10 application fee. Rolling admissions; apply between October 1 and March 1. *Early Admission* Program. Transfers accepted. Credit possible for CEEB AP and CLEP exams; university has own advanced placement program. Academic Advancement Program.

Student Life Student government. Newspaper, journal, radio and TV stations. Music and drama groups. 28 fraternities, 25 with houses, and 9 sororities, 8 with houses. 8% of men and 7% of women join. Limited on-campus housing; preference given to in-state students. Coed and single-sex dorms, language housing. 23% of students live on campus. Several intercollegiate and intramural sports. AIAW, Big Ten, Western Conference. Student body composition: 1.4% Asian, 2% Black, 0.8% Hispanic, 0.2% Native American, 95.6% White. 26% of students from out of state.

Wyoming

WYOMING, UNIVERSITY OF $

Laramie 82070, (307) 766-5160
Director of Admissions & Registrar: Arland L. Grover

- **Undergraduates:** 5,791m, 4,457w
- **Tuition and Fees (1984–1985):** $716 (in-state), $2,226 (out-of-state)
- **Room and Board (1984–1985):** $2,470
- **Degrees offered:** BA, BS, BFA, BMus
- **Mean ACT:** 21.2
- **Student-faculty ratio:** 11 to 1
- **Calendar system:** Semester

A public university established in 1886. 791-acre campus in a small city in the mountains 2 hours from Denver, Colorado. Air, rail, and bus service.
Academic Character NCACS and professional accreditation. Semester system, 8-week summer term, additional short courses, workshops, and institutes. 10 majors offered by the College of Agriculture, 35 by the College of Arts & Sciences, 4 by the College of Commerce & Industry, 14 by the College of Education, 8 by the College of Engineering, and 3 by the College of Health Sciences. Special and double majors. Degree candidates enroll under 1 of 6 programs: traditional major, self-designed major, professional curriculum, preprofessional curriculum, Honors Program, or non-degree. Distributive requirements. Graduate and professional degrees granted. Independent and accelerated study. Honors program. Phi Beta Kappa. Pass/fail. Cooperative work/study, internships. Preprofessional programs in dentistry, forestry, law, library science, medicine, occupational therapy, optometry, pharmacy, and physical therapy. 2-2 forestry program with approved forestry school and 3-1 programs with other professional schools possible. Exchange program with Universities of AK, HI, ID, MT, NM. Study abroad. Elementary, secondary, and special education certification. ROTC, AFROTC. National Park Service Research Center, Water Resources Research Institute. Museums, art gallery. Language lab. 900,000-volume library.
Financial University scholarships and loans; PELL, SEOG, NSS, NDSL, GSL, NSL, CWS. Application deadline for scholarships and NDSL February 15.
Admissions Open admission to all graduates of accredited WY high schools. Out-of-state graduates eligible if GPA is 2.5 or better. ACT required. Rolling admissions. *Early Admission* Program. Transfers accepted. Credit possible for CEEB AP and CLEP exams, and for university placement exams.
Student Life Student government. Newspaper. Several music, drama, and speaking groups. Religious, academic, honorary, and special interest groups. 9 fraternities, 8 with houses, and 6 sororities with houses. 9% of men, 12% of women join. Single freshmen under 19 must live at home, on campus, or in fraternity or sorority. Married-student housing. 35% of students live on campus. Liquor permitted in some dorms and in Union. 2 semesters phys ed required. 10 intercollegiate sports for men, 8 for women; intramurals. AIAW, NCAA, Western Athletic Conference. Student body composition: 1% Black, 1% Hispanic, 1% Native American, 93% White, 4% Other. 32% from out of state.

Section Three

THE INDEXES

Alphabetical Index by Name of Institution

Colby-Sawyer College	NH	Georgia Institute of Technology	GA
Colgate University	NY	Gettysburg College	PA
Colorado, University of (Boulder)	CO	GMI Engineering and Management	
Colorado College	CO	Institute	MI
Colorado School of Mines	CO	Gonzaga University	WA
Colorado State University	CO	Goshen College	IN
Columbia University	NY	Goucher College	MD
Connecticut, University of	CT	Grambling State University	LA
Connecticut College	CT	Grinnell College	IA
Cooper Union College	NY	Guilford College	NC
Cornell College	IA	Gustavus Adolphus College	MN
Cornell University	NY		
Creighton University	NE	Hamilton College	NY
Curry College	MA	Hampshire College	MA
		Harding University	AR
Dallas, University of	TX	Hartford, University of	CT
Dartmouth College	NH	Harvard University	MA
Davidson College	NC	Harvey Mudd College	CA
Delaware, University of	DE	Haverford College	PA
Denison University	OH	Hawaii, University of (Hilo)	HI
Denver, University of	CO	Hillsdale College	MI
DePaul University	IL	Hiram College	OH
De Pauw University	IN	Hobart and William Smith College	NY
Dickinson College	PA	Hofstra University	NY
Drake University	IA	Hollins College	VA
Drew University	NJ	Holy Cross, College of the	MA
Drexel University	PA	Hood College	MD
Dubuque, University of	IA	Houston, University of	TX
Duke University	NC	Howard University	DC
Duquesne University	PA	Humboldt State University	CA
Earlham College	IN	Idaho, College of	ID
East Carolina University	NC	Idaho, University of (Moscow)	ID
Eckerd College	FL	Idaho State University	ID
Elmira College	NY	Illinois, University of	
Embry-Riddle Aeronautical		(Urbana/Champaign)	IL
University	FL	Illinois State University (Normal)	IL
Emerson College	MA	Indiana University (Bloomington)	IN
Emory University	GA	Iona College	NY
Evergreen State College	WA	Iowa, University of (Iowa City)	IA
		Iowa State University of Science	
Fairfield University	CT	and Technology	IA
Ferris State College	MI	Ithaca College	NY
Fisk University	TN		
Flagler College	FL	James Madison University	VA
Florida, University of	FL	Johns Hopkins University	MD
Florida Institute of Technology	FL		
Florida State University	FL	Kalamazoo College	MI
Franklin and Marshall College	PA	Kansas, University of (Lawrence)	KS
Furman University	SC	Kansas State University	
		(Manhattan)	KS
Gallaudet College	DC	Kent State University (Kent)	OH
George Washington University	DC	Kentucky, University of	KY
Georgetown University	DC	Kenyon College	OH
Georgia, University of (Athens)	GA	Knox College	IL

Principia College	IL
Purdue University (West Lafayette)	IN
Randolph-Macon Woman's College	VA
Reed College	OR
Regis College	CO
Rensselaer Polytechnic Institute	NY
Rhode Island, University of	RI
Rhode Island School of Design	RI
Rice University	TX
Richmond, University of	VA
Ripon College	WI
Rochester, University of	NY
Rochester Institute of Technology	NY
Rollins College	FL
Rutgers University (Douglass College)	NJ
Rutgers University (Rutgers College)	NJ
St. Anselm College	NH
St. Bonaventure University	NY
St. John's College	MD
St. John's College	NM
St. Joseph's University	PA
St. Lawrence University	NY
Saint Leo College	FL
St. Mary's College	IN
Saint Michael's College	VT
St. Olaf College	MN
Salem College	WV
Santa Clara, University of	CA
Sarah Lawrence College	NY
Seton Hall University	NJ
Simmons College	MA
Simon's Rock of Bard College	MA
Skidmore College	NY
Smith College	MA
South, University of the	TN
South Carolina, University of (Columbia)	SC
South Dakota, University of (Vermillion)	SD
Southern California, University of	CA
Southern Methodist University	TX
Spelman College	GA
Springfield College	MA
Stanford University	CA
Stephens College	MO
Stetson University	FL
Stevens Institute of Technology	NJ
Susquehanna University	PA
Swarthmore College	PA

Sweet Briar College	VA
Syracuse University	NY
Tampa, University of	FL
Taylor University	IN
Temple University	PA
Tennessee, University of (Knoxville)	TN
Texas, The University of (Austin)	TX
Texas A & M University	TX
Texas Christian University	TX
Texas Woman's University	TX
Transylvania University	KY
Trinity College	CT
Trinity University	TX
Tri-State University	IN
Tufts University	MA
Tulane University	LA
Tulsa, University of	OK
Tuskegee Institute	AL
Union College	NE
Union College and University	NY
United States Air Force Academy	CO
United States Coast Guard Academy	CT
United States Merchant Marine Academy	NY
United States Military Academy	NY
United States Naval Academy	MD
Utah, University of	UT
Utah State University of Agriculture and Applied Science	UT
Valparaiso University	IN
Vanderbilt University	TN
Vassar College	NY
Vermont, University of	VT
Villanova University	PA
Virginia, University of	VA
Virginia Intermont College	VA
Virginia Polytechnic Institute and State University	VA
Wabash College	IN
Wake Forest University	NC
Washington, University of	WA
Washington College	MD
Washington and Jefferson College	PA
Washington and Lee University	VA
Washington State University	WA
Washington University (St. Louis)	MO
Wayne State University	MI
Wellesley College	MA

Alphabetical Index
of Institutions Accepting
Learning Disabled Students

Flagler College	FL	Macalester College (rarely)	MN
Florida, University of	FL	Manhattanville College	NY
Florida Institute of Technology	FL	Marquette University	WI
Florida State University	FL	Mary Baldwin College	VA
Franklin and Marshall College	PA	Maryland, University of	
Furman University (possibly)	SC	(College Park)	MD
		Maryville College	TN
George Washington University	DC	Massachusetts, University of	
Georgetown University	DC	(Amherst)	MA
Georgia, University of (Athens)	GA	Massachusetts Institute of	
Georgia Institute of Technology	GA	Technology	MA
Goshen College	IN	Miami University	OH
Grinnell College (rarely)	IA	Michigan State University	MI
Guilford College	NC	Mills College	CA
		Missouri, University of	
Hamilton College (rarely)	NY	(Columbia)	MO
Hampshire College (occasionally)	MA	Monmouth College	NJ
Harding University	AR	Montana State University	
Harvard University	MA	(Bozeman)	MT
Hiram College	OH	Morehouse College	GA
Hofstra University	NY	Mount Holyoke College	MA
Holy Cross, College of the	MA	Muhlenberg College	PA
Hood College	MD	Muskingum College	OH
Howard University	DC		
Humboldt State University	CA	Nebraska, University of (Lincoln)	NE
		Nevada, University of (Las Vegas)	NV
Idaho, College of	ID	Nevada, University of (Reno)	NV
Idaho, University of (Moscow)	ID	New College of the University of	
Illinois State University (Normal)	IL	South Florida	FL
Indiana University (Bloomington)	IN	New Hampshire, University of	NH
Iowa, University of (Iowa City)	IA	New Hampshire College	NH
Iowa State University of Science		New Jersey Institute of	
and Technology	IA	Technology	NJ
Ithaca College	NY	New Mexico, University of	
		(Albuquerque)	NM
James Madison University	VA	New Mexico Institute of Mining	
Johns Hopkins University	MD	and Technology	NM
		New York, State University of	
Kalamazoo College	MI	(Albany)	NY
Kansas, University of (Lawrence)	KS	New York, State University of	
Kansas State University		(Binghamton)	NY
(Manhattan)	KS	New York University	NY
Kent State University (Kent)	OH	North Carolina, University of	
Knox College	IL	(Chapel Hill)	NC
		North Carolina State University	NC
Lafayette College	PA	North Dakota State University	
Lake Forest College	IL	(Fargo)	ND
Lawrence University	WI	Northwestern University	IL
Lewis and Clark College	OR	Norwich University	VT
Louisiana State University		Notre Dame, University of	IN
(Baton Rouge)	LA		
Louisville, University of	KY	Oberlin College	OH
Loyola University	IL	Ohio University	OH
Loyola University	LA	Ohio State University, The	OH
Luther College	IA	Oklahoma, University of	OK

About the Authors

Charles and Barbarasue Lovejoy Straughn have developed the most effective and comprehensive college guide today. For years they have visited colleges and universities and attended national education conferences to gather firsthand information on American schools.

Barbarasue Lovejoy Straughn is the president of Lovejoy's College Guide, Inc., and associate editor of *Lovejoy's Guidance Digest*. Charles Straughn is a professional career and educational counselor, and editor of *Lovejoy's Guidance Digest*.

The Straughns live in Middletown, New Jersey, with their two children, Amy-Beth and Jeffrey.